Readings in Adult Psychology:
Contemporary Perspectives

Harper & Row's
CONTEMPORARY PERSPECTIVES READER SERIES
Phillip Whitten, Series Editor

Readings in Adult Psychology: Contemporary Perspectives

1977-1978 edition

edited by
Lawrence R. Allman
and Dennis T. Jaffe

University of Southern California

Harper & Row, Publishers

New York   Hagerstown   San Francisco   London

Sponsoring Editor: George A. Middendorf
Project Editor: Robert Ginsberg
Production Supervisor: Kewal K. Sharma
Printer & Binder: The Murray Printing Company
Cover by Josefina Robirosa, Buenos Aires, Courtesy of I.T.T.
Drawings of section openers by Carol H. Eldridge, Marblehead, Mass.

Readings in Adult Psychology: Contemporary Perspectives

Library of Congress Cataloging in Publication Data
Main entry under title:

Readings in adult psychology.

    (Harper & Row's contemporary perspectives
reader series)
    1. Adulthood—Addresses, essays, lectures.
I. Allman, Lawrence R.   II. Jaffe, Dennis T.
BF724.5.R4   155.6   77–1486
ISBN 0–06–047054–2

The editors of this book, Lawrence R. Allman and Dennis T. Jaffe,
contributed equally to its creation. Their names are listed in
alphabetical order.

ACKNOWLEDGMENTS

I. THE ADULT LIFE PROGRESS: AN OVERVIEW

ERIK ERIKSON'S EIGHT AGES OF MAN by David Elkind.
Copyright © 1970 The New York Times Company.
Reprinted by permission.
Photograph of Erik Erikson by Clemens Kalischer.
Photographs of Eight Stages of Man by Ted Croner.

THE PHASES OF ADULT LIFE: A STUDY IN DEVELOPMENTAL
PSYCHOLOGY by Roger L. Gould. Copyright © 1972 by
the American Psychiatric Association. Reprinted by permission from the AMERICAN JOURNAL OF PSYCHIATRY,
vol. 127, pp. 521–531.

MEANINGFULNESS OF THE BIOGRAPHICAL APPROACH by
Charlotte Bühler, is reprinted with permission.

STRATEGIES OF ADAPTATION by Robert W. White from
COPING AND ADAPTATION edited by George V. Coelho,
David A. Hamburg, and John E. Adams, copyright © 1974
by Basic Books, Inc., Publishers, New York.
Photograph by George Gardner.

ADULT PERSONALITY: TOWARD A PSYCHOLOGY OF THE
LIFE CYCLE by Bernice L. Neugarten. An adapted version
of this paper appeared in a book of readings edited by E.
Vinacke (American Book Co., 1968). From MIDDLE AGE
AND AGING, Bernice L. Neugarten (ed.), Chicago: Univer-
sity of Chicago Press, 1968.
Photograph by Jean Claude LeJeune.

II. THE BIO-PHYSIOLOGY OF AGING

MEDICAL PERSPECTIVES ON ADULTHOOD by Herant A.
Katchadourian is reprinted by permission of DAEDALUS,
Journal of the American Academy of Arts and Sciences.
Boston, Massachusetts, Spring 1976.

A NEW AGE FOR AGING by Bernard L. Strehler is reprinted
with permission from NATURAL HISTORY Magazine,
February 1973. Copyright © The American Museum of
Natural History, 1973.

IN SEARCH OF THE ANTIAGING COCKTAIL by Arthur W.
Galston is reprinted with permission from NATURAL
HISTORY Magazine, March 1975. Copyright © The Ameri-
can Museum of Natural History, 1975.

III. YOUNG ADULTHOOD

THE YOUNG ADULT by Theodore Lidz. Chapter 11, from THE
PERSON by Theodore Lidz, © 1976 by Theodore Lidz, Basic
Books, Inc., Publishers, New York.

AN AMERICAN ISHMAEL by Kenneth Keniston is reprinted
by permission from the author.

THE GENERATION GAP by Vern L. Bengtson is reprinted from
YOUTH AND SOCIETY, Vol. 2, No. 1 (September 1970) pp.
7–32 by permission of the Publisher, Sage Publications,
Inc, and the author who is Laboratory Chief and Associate
Professor of Sociology, Andrus Gerontology Center, Uni-
versity of Southern California.
Photograph by Virginia Hamilton.

YOUTH: A 'NEW' STAGE OF LIFE by Kenneth Keniston is
reprinted with permission from the author.

CATCH-30 by Gail Sheehy is from PASSAGES by Gail Sheehy
(New York: E. P. Dutton & Co., Inc., 1976) Copyright ©
1974, 1976 by Gail Sheehy. Reprinted by permission of the
Author.
Photograph by Charles Gatewood.

32 THOUGHTS ON BEING 32 by Mopsy Strange Kennedy.
Copyright © 1975 by BOSTON Magazine. Reprinted with
permission.
Photograph by Jean Claude LeJeune.

IV. RELATIONSHIPS AND FAMILIES

SEXUALITY AND THE LIFE CYCLE: A BROAD CONCEPT OF
SEXUALITY is reprinted by permission. SIECUS Study
Guide No. 8, copyright © Sex Information Council of the
U.S., Inc., New York, 1969 and 1974.

CHANGE, CONFLICT, AND COUPLE STYLES by Lawrence R.
Allman and Dennis T. Jaffe is reprinted with permission
from the authors.
Photograph by Charles Gatewood.

MAN + WOMAN: A CONSUMER'S GUIDE TO CONTEM-
PORARY PAIRING PATTERNS INCLUDING MARRIAGE by
Carlfred B. Broderick. Copyright © 1972 HUMAN
BEHAVIOR Magazine. Reprinted by Permission.

THREE MARRIAGES—AND ONE GROWING PERSON by Carl
Rogers excerpted from BECOMING PARTNERS by Carl R.
Rogers. Copyright © 1972 by Carl R. Rogers. Reprinted
with the permission of Delacorte Press.

A MIDDLE AMERICAN MARRIAGE by Thomas J. Cottle is
reprinted by permission from the author from the Children's Defense Fund of the Washington Research Project.

DECISION MAKING AND THE FAMILY LIFE CYCLE by Reuben
Hill in SOCIAL STRUCTURE AND THE FAMILY, Ethel
Shanas and Gordon Streib, eds. © 1965. Reprinted by
permission of Prentice-Hall, Inc., Englewood Cliffs, New
Jersey.

THE FIRST FOUR LONG YEARS OF A FAMILY COMMUNE:
A CASE STUDY by Dennis T. Jaffe is reprinted by permission of the author. From Couples in Communes,
doctoral dissertation, Yale University, 1975.

DIVORCE FEVER by Erica Abeel. Copyright © 1974 by the
NYM Corp. Reprinted with the permission of NEW YORK
Magazine.
Artwork by Anita Siegel.

TRANSITION TO PARENTHOOD by Alice S. Rossi. Copyright
© 1968, JOURNAL OF MARRIAGE AND THE FAMILY,
National Council on Family Relations. Reprinted by
permission.

WHATEVER HAPPENED TO FATHER? by C. Christian Beels.
Copyright © 1974 by The New York Times Company.
Reprinted by permission.
Photograph by permission of Barbara Bengen, New York
City.

CONTENTS

ing his family situation, psychological resources, and the environment in which he grew up. This article reveals how childhood traumas can cause severe emotional difficulties in adult life.

How are we to define and prove the existence of what we experience so clearly as a "generation gap"? Some of the sociological theories that could explain generational and social change are presented here.

There is growing evidence that the period between adolescence and the attainment of adulthood ought to be considered as a newly emerging, separable stage of growth—youth. Keniston suggests some qualities of this period in our society.

In studying middle life and adolescence, social scientists have largely ignored the period in between—the thirties. Sheehy's comparison of social science and personal experience illustrates the dilemma of the young adult.

Far from being a dull, dreary period, the early thirties are becoming a period of great achievement, personal growth, and challenge for people like Kennedy, who shares her experience of the thirties as a time of expansion and growth.

A review of the wisdom, largely psychoanalytic, about adult sexuality and its development throughout life.

A married couple is a unit that is expected to accomplish certain tasks and live under certain pressures. This account suggests some of the major styles couples use to relate to each other, and the ways that marital difficulty can arise.

Contemporary families are not limited to one or two class-related patterns, but offer numerous styles of life and values about sexuality, children, leisure, and intimacy. This is a survey of these family patterns and their consequences.

The way in which the same person can experience different relationships and grow as a result of them is explored in this interview with a thrice-married woman, who has profited from her experiences.

The modern family is besieged by economic, social, and cultural pressures, as well as changing concepts of male and female sex roles. This account of the life space of one family illustrates how such pressures can burden a couple.

Families develop as individuals do, over time. Research can lead us to formulate a series of developmental stages that hold for families, and some of the major decisions and tasks that accompany each stage.

One family form which has been publicized recently is the collective family. This is the story of one such communal family, which breaks down many of the stereotypes of the counter-culture.

Divorce has changed in the past few years from a stigmatized and relatively rare event, to a likely event among certain upper middle-class families. The factors contributing to the rash of divorce among this social stratum, and the nature of the search that leads people to divorce are explored in this article.

recognized in older people. This essay explores the role of sexuality in later life, and its potential for fulfillment.

We live in a society in which a great number of families have old people living with them. What stresses and difficulties do older people present for a family, and what do they add to it?

As La Rochefoucauld said, "One cannot look directly at either the sun or death." Lifton and Olson explore the way old people confront their own immortality, and suggest that serenity in the face of death depends upon a sense that,

in some symbolic way, one's life will endure.

Although people today have the same kind of unconscious thoughts and fantasies about death that others had years ago, our society has changed and increasingly become a death-denying society. Most patients, Kübler-Ross writes, pass through five stages between their awareness of serious illness and death, when faced with a potentially fatal illness.

Rage, terror, sadness, helplessness, loneliness, and despondency are among the feelings people find most difficult to deal with; all are associated with grief. In his article, Paul explains the role of empathy in the resolution of grief.

PREFACE

Until recently, developmental psychology was almost completely concerned with the child. Theory and research reduced all human development to childhood stages, leaving the student with the feeling that development was over, for all practical purposes, at the close of childhood. Interestingly, that was also the period when one's schooling ended as well. At that point maturity, a sort of steady state where one accepted and met one's adult responsibilities, set in.

Since it is probably easier to study and theorize about people different from ourselves, psychologists, as adults, found it easier to study children and emotionally disturbed adults rather than to look at themselves. In recent years, for several reasons, this tendency has changed. In fact, during the past decade, psychologists have "discovered" several new life stages, including youth (young adulthood), middle life, the aged, and even death, as topics in need of serious study. These newly delineated life stages have been shown to possess characteristics which are different from childhood, and from one another. Instead of maturity meaning stasis, life is currently depicted as an ongoing process with a crisis occurring roughly once every decade, signaling a major transition and reorientation in life. What seems to have been discovered is *adult development,* the fact that adults can, and commonly do, change as much and as drastically as children. This reader presents some of the exciting. work going on in this new and vital area of adult psychology.

As students in the 1960s, we and our peers were drawn to courses in adolescent psychology because we were struggling with the issues of our own adolescence and inner turmoil (which was then mirrored in society). Now in our thirties, struggling with the issues of adulthood, we have become aware of the need to organize a book of readings which conveys the sense of immediate relevance, of opportunity to correlate social science research with personal experience, that we feel offers the most important learning experiences. We note with interest the trend toward lifelong education—toward adult continuing education, toward mid-career shifts, and toward an older population attending school—as signaling that education is no longer perceived as a province of childhood, but as a lifelong, ongoing process of renewed curiosity and reflection. It is no coincidence that along with this trend comes the demand for courses in adult developmental psychology, and for research in the area. Adult students would like an opportunity to look at their own life crises, and the crises of those around them, with the breadth and perspective that psychological, sociological, and biological theories and research can provide. It is our intention in this reader to provide that opportunity.

The articles provide a systematic overview of this new field of adult psychology as it is today. The book is organized to show the adult moving through several general stages of a *life cycle,* and living his or her life in a series of environmental *contexts,* each of which has particular effects on the person. The first section presents articles which discuss basic theoretical perspectives and an overview of the various stages and processes that represent adulthood, followed by sections representing major stages of adulthood—young adulthood, middle life, and aging and death, and sections in-between dealing with the major contexts of adult life—biological issues, intimate relationships, sex roles, the family, work, and leisure.

While this is primarily a reader in psychology—a person's experience of adulthood, how the person relates to his or her environment, and the major interpersonal relationships that create the life space—we feel that it is important to focus on two additional levels of information. The second major section presents some of the important biological developmental processes which are at the core of the psychological developmental processes. The other aspect of life is the social and historical processes that make up the themes of contemporary adult life, which is the subject matter of several selections. It is hard to separate the fields of biology, psychology, and sociology in a comprehensive treatment of adulthood.

The readings thus focus not only on the experience of adulthood, but also leading theories and research. The articles were selected for their clarity and writing style, as well as the quality of their information. The articles are presented as they appeared in their original sources, providing a variety of formats. The reader will be revised regularly, in response to suggestions from students and instructors, and will reflect changes in the field (see the response card at the end of the book to make input into this process).

We are especially indebted to Phil Whitten, the series editor, who made this reader a reality, and to Leslie Palmer, his very able administrative assistant.

LAWRENCE R. ALLMAN
DENNIS T. JAFFE

Readings in Adult Psychology:
Contemporary Perspectives

I. The Adult Life Process: An Overview

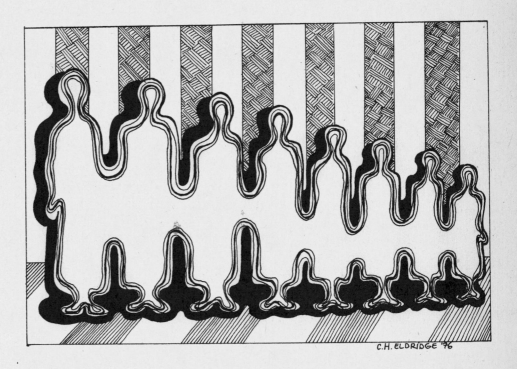

C.H. ELDRIDGE '76

Adulthood can be conceptualized as a continual process of coping with new demands and opportunities in ever-changing environmental contexts. Life is an unfolding process, as we respond to the issues of our own particular lives and develop our personal styles and systems of meaning in light of our experience. The articles in this section offer an overview of adulthood as a process of psychological development. By *process* we mean a systematic series of actions directed toward some end. Each stage of life can be seen as having a series of explicit or implicit goals—both behavioral and symbolic— that give meaning and direction to that life.

Psychoanalyst Erik Erikson, who studied with Freud and then emigrated to America where he lives today, made a great contribution to psychology by conceptualizing the life cycle from birth to death as a series of uniquely different internal struggles, which in turn create individualized styles and attitudes toward life and ways of handling life issues. Elkind's article presents an overview of his pioneering work. Erikson's work created a theoretical overview which needed to be filled in by systematic, empirical research into the way the phases of adulthood were actually experienced today, which Roger Gould, among others has begun to do. Each person, through life experiences, develops a unique sense of self, and style of life. Charlotte Bühler, a contemporary of Erikson and one of the first humanistic psychologists, studied the biographies of exceptional people in order to determine the way

1

they structured and made meaning out of their lives, and she writes here about the uniqueness and creativity that each individual brings to the process of living. Robert White next looks at the way in which individuals cope with each new psychological stage of life and the strategies each individual develops for responding to novelty and the unexpected. Adaptation is a part of everyday life. It presents both novelty and repetition, to which we have to respond. Bernice Neugarten, who has been one of the first and most active researchers to look at the second half of life, views the adult personality as a continual interaction of biological and sociological variables.

One man in his time
plays many psychosocial parts

Erik Erikson's Eight Ages of Man

By DAVID ELKIND

AT a recent faculty reception I happened to join a small group in which a young mother was talking about her "identity crisis." She and her husband, she said, had decided not to have any more children and she was depressed at the thought of being past the child-bearing stage. It was as if, she continued, she had been robbed of some part of herself and now needed to find a new function to replace the old one.

When I remarked that her story sounded like a case history from a book by Erik Erikson, she replied, "Who's Erikson?" It is a reflection on the intellectual modesty and literary decorum of Erik H. Erikson, psychoanalyst and professor of developmental psychology at Harvard, that so few of the many people who today talk about the "identity crisis" know anything of the man who pointed out its pervasiveness as a problem in contemporary society two decades ago.

Erikson has, however, contributed more to social science than his delineation of identity problems in modern man. His descriptions of the stages of the life cycle, for example, have advanced psychoanalytic theory to the point where it can now describe the development of the healthy personality on its own terms and not merely as the opposite of a sick one. Likewise, Erikson's emphasis upon the problems unique to adolescents and adults living in today's society has helped to rectify the one-sided emphasis on childhood as the beginning and end of personality development.

Finally, in his biographical studies, such as "Young Man Luther" and "Gandhi's Truth" (which has just won a National Book Award in philosophy and religion), Erikson emphasizes the inherent strengths of the human personality by showing how individuals can use their neurotic symptoms and conflicts for creative and constructive social purposes while healing themselves in the process.

It is important to emphasize that Erikson's contributions are genuine advances in psychoanalysis in the sense that Erikson accepts and builds upon many of the basic tenets of Freudian theory. In this regard, Erikson differs from Freud's early co-workers such as Jung and Adler who, when they broke with Freud, rejected his theories and substituted their own.

Likewise, Erikson also differs from the so-called neo-Freudians such as Horney, Kardiner and Sullivan who (mistakenly, as it turned out) assumed that Freudian

Erikson in a seminar at his Stockbridge, Mass., home.

"Young analysts are today proclaiming a 'new freedom' to see Freud in historical perspective, which reflects the Eriksonian view that one can recognize Freud's greatness without bowing to conceptual precedent."

theory had nothing to say about man's relation to reality and to his culture. While it is true that Freud emphasized, even mythologized, sexuality, he did so to counteract the rigid sexual taboos of his time, which at that point in history, were frequently the cause of neuroses. In his later writings, however, Freud began to concern himself with the executive agency of the personality, namely, the ego, which is also the repository of the individual's attitudes and concepts about himself and his world.

It is with the psychosocial development of the ego that Erikson's observations and theoretical constructions are primarily concerned. Erikson has thus been able to introduce innovations into psychoanalytic theory without either rejecting or ignoring Freud's monumental contribution.

The man who has accomplished this notable feat is a handsome Dane, whose white hair, mustache, resonant accent and gentle manner are reminiscent of actors like Jean Hersholt and Paul Muni. Although he is warm and outgoing with friends, Erikson is a rather shy man who is uncomfortable in the spotlight of public recognition. This trait, together with his ethical reservations about making public even disguised case material, may help to account for Erikson's reluctance to publish his observations and conceptions (his first book appeared in 1950, when he was 48).

In recent years this reluctance to publish has diminished and he has been appearing in print at an increasing pace. Since 1960 he has published three books, "Insight and Responsibility," "Identity: Youth and Crisis" and "Gandhi's Truth," as well as editing a fourth, "Youth: Change and Challenge." Despite the accolades and recognition these books have won for him, both in America and abroad, Erikson is still surprised at the popular interest they have generated and is a little troubled about the possibility of being misunderstood and misinterpreted. While he would prefer that his books spoke for themselves and that he was left out of the picture, he has had to accede to popular demand for more information about himself and his work.

The course of Erikson's professional career has been as diverse as it has been unconventional. He was born in Frankfurt, Germany, in 1902 of Danish parents. Not long after his birth his father died, and his mother later married the pediatrician who had cured her son of a childhood illness. Erikson's stepfather urged him to become a physician, but the boy declined and became an artist instead— an artist who did portraits of children. Erikson says of his post-adolescent years, "I was an artist then, which in Europe is a euphemism for a young man with some talent and nowhere to go." During this period he settled in Vienna and worked as a tutor in a family friendly with Freud's. He met Freud on informal occasions when the families went on outings together.

These encounters may have been the impetus to accept a teaching appointment at an American school in Vienna founded by Dorothy Burlingham and directed by Peter Blos (both now well known on the American psychiatric scene). During these years (the late nineteen-twenties) he also undertook and completed psychoanalytic training with Anna Freud and August Aichhorn. Even at the outset of his career, Erikson gave evidence of the breadth of his interests and activities by being trained and certified as a Montessori teacher. Not surprisingly, in view of that training. Eriksin's first articles dealth with psychoanalysis and education.

It was while in Vienna that Erikson met and married Joan Mowat Serson, an American artist of Canadian descent. They came to America in 1933, when Erikson was invited to practice and teach in Boston. Erikson was, in fact, one of the first if not the first child-analyst in the Boston area. During the next two decades he held clinical and academic appointments at Harvard, Yale and Berkeley. In 1951 he joined a group of psychiatrists and psychologists who moved to Stockbridge, Mass., to start a new program at the Austen Riggs Center, a private residential treatment center for disturbed young people. Erikson remained at Riggs until 1961, when he was appointed professor of human development and lecturer on psychiatry at Harvard. Throughout his career he has always held two or three appointments simultaneously and has traveled extensively.

PERHAPS because he had been an artist first, Erikson has never been a conventional psychoanalyst. When he was treating children, for example, he always insisted on visiting his young patients' homes and on having dinner with the families. Likewise, in the nineteen-thirties, when anthropological investigation was described to him by his friends Scudder McKeel, Alfred Kroeber and Margaret Mead, he decided to do field work on an Indian reservation. "When I realized that Sioux is the name which we [in Europe] pronounced "See ux" and which for us was *the* American Indian, I could not resist." Erikson thus antedated the anthropologists who swept over the Indian reservations in the post-Depression years. (So numerous were the field workers at that time that the stock joke was that an Indian family could be defined as a mother, a father, children and an anthropologist.)

Erikson did field work not only with the Oglala Sioux of Pine Ridge, S. D. (the tribe that slew Custer and was in turn slaughtered at the Battle of Wounded Knee), but also with the salmon-fishing Yurok of Northern California. His reports on these experiences revealed his special gift for sensing and entering into the world views and modes of thinking of cultures other than his own.

It was while he was working with the Indians that Erikson began to note syndromes which he could not explain within the confines of traditional psychoanalytic theory. Central to many an adult Indian's emotional problems seemed to be his sense of uprootedness and lack of continuity between his present life-style and that portrayed in tribal history. Not only did the Indian sense a break with the past, but he could not identify with a future requiring assimilation of the white culture's values. The problems faced by such men, Erikson recognized, had to do with the ego and with culture and only incidentally with sexual drives.

The impressions Erikson gained on the reservations were reinforced during World War II when he worked at a veterans' rehabilitation center at Mount Zion Hospital in San Francisco. Many of the soldiers he and his colleagues saw seemed not to fit the traditional "shell shock" or "malingerer" cases of World War I. Rather, it seemed to Erikson that many of these men had lost the sense of who and what they were. They were having trouble reconciling their activities, attitudes and feelings as soldiers with the activities, attitudes and feelings they had known before the war. Accordingly, while these men may well have had difficulties with repressed or conflicted drives, their main problem seemed to be, as Erikson came to speak of it all the time, "identity confusion."

It was almost a decade before Erikson set forth the implications of his clinical observations in "Childhood and Society." In that book, the summation and integration of 15 years of research, he made three major contributions to the study of the human ego. He posited (**1**) that, side by side with the stages of psychosexual development described by Freud (the oral, anal, phallic, genital, Oedipal and pubertal), were psychosocial stages of ego development, in which the individual had to establish new basic orientations to himself and his social world; (2) that personality development continued throughout the whole life cycle; and (3) that each stage had a positive *as well as* a negative component.

Much about these contributions—and about Erikson's way of thinking—can be understood by looking at his scheme of life stages. Erikson identifies eight stages in the human life cycle, in each of which a new dimension of "social interaction" becomes possible—that is, a new dimension in a person's interaction with himself, and with his social environment.

Trust vs. Mistrust

THE first stage corresponds to the oral stage in classical psychoanalytic theory and usually extends through the first year of life. In Erikson's view, the new dimension of social interaction that emerges during this period involves basic *trust* at the one extreme, and *mistrust* at the other. The degree to which the child comes to trust the world, other people and himself depends to a considerable extent upon the quality of the care that he receives. The infant whose needs are met when they arise, whose discomforts are quickly removed, who is cuddled, fondled, played with and talked to, develops a sense of the world as a safe place to be and of people as helpful and dependable. When, however, the care is inconsistent, inadequate and rejecting, it fosters a basic mistrust, an attitude of fear and suspicion on the part of the infant toward the world in general and people in particular that will carry through to later stages of development.

It should be said at this point that the problem of basic trust-versus-mistrust (as is true for all the later dimensions) is not resolved once and for all during the first year of life; it arises again at each successive stage of development. There is both hope and danger in this. The child who enters school with a sense of mistrust may come to trust a particular teacher who has taken the trouble to make herself trustworthy; with this second chance, he overcomes his early mistrust. On the other hand, the child who comes through infancy with a vital sense of trust can still have his sense of mistrust activated at a later stage if, say, his parents are divorced and separated under acrimonious circumstances.

This point was brought home to me in a very direct way by a 4-year-old patient I saw in a court clinic. He was being seen at the court clinic because his adoptive parents, who had had him for six months, now wanted to give him back to the agency. They claimed that he was cold and unloving, took things and could not be trusted. He was indeed a cold and apathetic boy, but with good reason. About a year after his illegitimate birth, he was taken away from his mother, who had a drinking problem, and was shunted back and forth among several foster homes. Initially he had tried to relate to the persons in the foster homes, but the relationships never had a chance to develop because he was moved at just the wrong times. In the end he gave up trying to reach out to others, because the inevitable separations hurt too much.

Like the burned child who dreads the flame, this emotionally burned child shunned the pain of emotional involvement. He had trusted his mother, but now he trusted no one. Only years of devoted care and patience could now undo the damage that had been done to this child's sense of trust.

Autonomy vs. Doubt

STAGE Two spans the second and third years of life, the period which Freudian theory calls the anal stage. Erikson sees here the emergence of *autonomy*. This autonomy dimension builds upon the child's new motor and mental abilities. At this stage the child can not only walk but also climb, open and close, drop, push and pull, hold and let go. The child takes pride in these new accomplishments and wants to do everything himself, whether it be pulling the wrapper off a piece of candy, selecting the vitamin out of the bottle or flushing the toilet. If parents recognize the young child's need to do what he is capable of doing at his own pace and in his own time, then he develops a sense that he is able to control his muscles, his impulses, himself and, not insignificantly, his environment—the sense of autonomy.

When, however, his caretakers are impatient and do for him what he is capable of doing himself, they reinforce a sense of shame and doubt. To be sure, every parent has rushed a child at times and children are hardy enough to endure such lapses. It is only when caretaking is consistently overprotective and criticism of "accidents" (whether these be wetting, soiling, spilling or breaking things) is harsh and unthinking that the child develops an excessive sense of shame with respect to other people and an excessive sense of doubt about own abilities to control his world and himself.

If the child leaves this stage with less autonomy than shame or doubt, he will be handicapped in his attempts to achieve autonomy in adolescence and adulthood. Contrariwise, the child who moves through this stage with his sense of autonomy buoyantly outbalancing his feelings of shame and doubt is well prepared to be autonomous at later phases in the life cycle. Again, however, the balance of autonomy to shame and doubt set up during this period can be changed in either positive or negative directions by later events.

It might be well to note, in addition, that too much autonomy can be as harmful as too little. I have in mind a patient of 7 who had a heart condition. He had learned very quickly how terrified his parents were of any signs in him of cardiac difficulty. With the psychological acuity given to children, he soon ruled the household. The family could not go shopping, or for a drive, or on a holiday if he did not approve. On those rare occasions when the parents had had enough and defied him, he would get angry and his purple hue and gagging would frighten them into submission.

Actually, this boy was frightened of this power (as all children would be) and was really eager to give it up. When the parents and the boy came to realize this, and to recognize that a little shame and doubt were a healthy counterpoise to an inflated sense of autonomy, the three of them could once again assume their normal roles.

Initiative vs. Guilt

IN this stage (the genital stage of classical psychoanaysis) the child, age 4 to 5, is pretty much master of his body and can ride a tricycle, run, cut and hit. He can thus initiate motor acivities of various sorts on his own and no longer merely responds to or imitates the actions of other children. The same holds true for his language and fantasy activities. Accordingly, Erikson argues that the social dimension that appears at this stage has *initiative* at one of its poles and *guilt* at the other.

Whether the child will leave this stage with his sense of initiative far outbalancing his sense of guilt depends to a considerable extent upon how parents respond to his self-initiated activities. Children who are given much freedom and opportunity to initiate motor play such as running, bike riding, sliding, skating, tussling and wrestling have their sense of initiative reinforced. Initiative is also reinforced when parents answer their children's questions (intellectual initiative) and do not deride or inhibit fantasy or play activity. On the other hand, if the child is made to feel that his motor activity is bad, that his questions are a nuisance and that his play is silly and stupid, then he may develop a sense of guilt over self-initiated activities in general that will persist through later life stages.

Industry vs. Inferiority

STAGE Four is the age period from 6 to 11, the elementary school years (described by classical psychoanalysis as the *latency phase*). It is a time during which the child's love for the parent of the opposite sex and rivalry with the same sexed parent (elements in the so-called family romance) are quiescent. It is also a period during which the child becomes capable of deductive reasoning, and of playing and learning by rules. It is not until this period, for example, that children can really play marbles, checkers and other "take turn" games that require obedience to rules. Erikson argues that the psychosocial dimension that emerges during this period has a sense of *industry* at one extreme and a sense of *inferiority* at the other.

The term industry nicely captures a dominant theme of this period during which the concern with how things are made, how they work and what they do predominates. It is the Robinson Crusoe age in the sense that the enthusiasm and minute detail with which Crusoe describes his activities appeals to the child's own budding sense of industry. When children are encouraged in their efforts to make, do, or build practical things (whether it be to construct creepy crawlers, tree houses, or airplane models—or to cook, bake or sew), are allowed to finish their products, and are praised and rewarded for the results, then the sense of industry is enhanced. But parents who see their children's efforts at making and doing as "mischief," and as simply "making a mess," help to encourage in children a sense of inferiority.

During these elementary-school years, however, the child's world includes more than the home. Now social institutions other than the family come to play a central role in the developmental crisis of the individual. (Here Erikson introduced still another advance in psychoanalytic theory, which heretofore concerned itself only with the effects of the parents' behavior upon the child's development.)

A child's school experiences affect his industry-inferiority balance. The child, for example, with an IQ of 80 to 90 has a particularly traumatic school experience, even when his sense of industry is rewarded and encouraged at home. He is "too bright" to be in special classes, but "too slow" to compete with children of average ability. Consequently he experiences constant failures in his academic efforts that reinforce a sense of inferiority.

On the other hand, the child who had his sense of industry derogated at home can have it revitalized at school through the offices of a sensitive and committed teacher. Whether the child develops a sense of industry or inferiority, therefore, no longer depends solely on the caretaking efforts of the parents but on the actions and offices of other adults as well.

Identity vs. Role confusion

WHEN the child moves into adolescence (Stage Five—roughly the ages 12-18), he encounters, according to traditional psychoanalytic theory, a reawakening of the family-romance problem of early childhood. His means of resolving the problem is to seek and find a romantic partner of his own generation. While Erikson does not deny this aspect of adolescence, he points out that there are other problems as well. The adolescent matures mentally as well as physiologically and, in addition to the new feelings, sensations and desires he experiences as a result of changes in his body, he develops a multitude of new ways of looking at and thinking about the world. Among other things, those in adolescence can now think about other people's thinking and wonder about what other people think of them. They can also conceive of ideal families, religions and societies which they can then compare with the imperfect families, religions and societies of their own experience. Finally, adolescents become capable of constructing theories and philosophies designed to bring all the varied and conflicting aspects of society into a working, harmonious and peaceful whole. The adolescent, in a word, is an impatient idealist who believes that it is as easy to realize an ideal as it is to imagine it.

Erikson believes that the new interpersonal dimension which emerges during this period has to do with a sense of *ego identity* at the positive end and a sense of *role confusion* at the negative end. That is to say, given the adolescent's newfound integrative abilities, his task is to bring together all of the things he has learned about himself as a son, student, athlete, friend, Scout, newspaper boy, and so on, and integrate these different images of himself into a whole that makes sense and that shows continuity with the past while preparing for the future. To the extent that the young person succeeds in this endeavor, he arrives at a sense of psychological identity, a sense of who he is, where he has been and where he is going.

In contrast to the earlier stages, where parents play a more or less direct role in the determination of the result of the developmental crises, the influence of parents during this stage is much more indirect. If the young person reaches adolescence with, thanks to his parents, a vital sense of trust, autonomy, initiative and industry, then his chances of arriving at a meaningful sense of ego identity are much enhanced. The reverse, of course, holds true for the young person who enters adolescence with considerable mistrust, shame, doubt, guilt and inferiority. Preparation for a successful adolescence, and the attainment of an integrated psychosocial identity must, therefore, begin in the cradle.

OVER and above what the individual brings with him from his childhood, the attainment of a sense of personal identity dpends upon the social milieu in which he or she grows up. For example, in a society where women are to some extent second-class citizens, it may be harder for females to arrive at a sense of psychosocial identity. Likewise at times, such as the present, when rapid social and technological change breaks down many traditional values, it may be more difficult for young people to find continuity between what they learned and experienced as children and what they learn and experience as adolescents. At such times young people often seek causes that give their lives meaning and direction. The activism of the current generation of young people may well stem, in part at least, from this search.

When the young person cannot attain a sense of personal identity, either because of an unfortunate childhood or difficult social circumstances, he shows a certain amount of *role confusion*—a sense of not knowing what he is, where he belongs or whom he belongs to. Such confusion is a frequent symptom in delinquent young people. Promiscuous adolescent girls, for example, often seem to have a fragmented sense of ego identity. Some young people seek a "negative identity," an identity opposite to the one prescribed for them by their family and friends. Having an identity as a "delinquent," or as a "hippie," or even as an "acid head," may sometimes be preferable to having no identity at all.

In some cases young people do not seek a negative identity so much as they have it thrust upon them. I remember another court case in which the defendant was an attractive 16-year-old girl who had been found "tricking it" in a trailer located just outside the grounds of an Air Force base. From about the age of 12, her mother had encouraged her to dress seductively and to go out with boys. When she returned from dates, her sexually frustrated mother demanded a kiss-by-kiss, caress-by-caress description of the evening's activities. After the mother had vicariously satisfied her sexual needs, she proceeded to call her daughter a "whore" and a "dirty tramp." As the girl told me, "Hell, I have the name, so I might as well play the role."

Failure to establish a clear sense of personal identity at adolescence does not guarantee perpetual failure. And the person who attains a working sense of ego identity in adolescence will of necessity encounter challenges and threats to that identity as he moves through life. Erikson, perhaps more than any other personality theorist, has emphasized that life is constant change and that confronting problems at one stage in life is not a guarantee against the reappearance of these problems at later stages, or against the finding of new solutions to them.

Intimacy vs. Isolation

STAGE Six in the life cycle is young adulthood; roughly the period of courtship and early family life that extends from late adolescence till early middle age. For this stage, and the stages described hereafter, classical psychoanalysis has nothing new or major to say. For Erikson, however, the previous attainment of a sense of personal identity and the engagement in productive work that marks this period gives rise to a new interpersonal dimension of *intimacy* at the one extreme and *isolation* at the other.

When Erikson speaks of intimacy he means much more than love-making alone; he means the ability to share with and care about another person without fear of losing oneself in the process. In the case of intimacy, as in the case of identity, success or failure no longer depends directly upon the parents but only indirectly as they have contributed to the individual's success or failure at the earlier stages. Here, too, as in the case of identity, social conditions may help or hinder the establishment of a sense of intimacy. Likewise, intimacy need not involve sexuality; it includes the relationship between friends. Soldiers who have served together under the most dangerous circumstances often develop a sense of commitment to one another that exemplifies intimacy in its broadest sense. If a sense of intimacy is not established with friends or a marriage partner, the result, in Erikson's view, is a sense of isolation—of being alone without anyone to share with or care for.

Generativity vs. Self-absorption

THIS stage—middle age—brings with it what Erikson speaks of as either *generativity* or *self-absorption*, and stagnation. What Erikson means by generativity is that the person begins to be concerned with others beyond his immediate family, with future generations and the nature of the society and world in which those generations will live. Generativity does not reside only in parents; it can be found in any individual who actively concerns himself with the welfare of young people and with making the world a better place for them to live and to work.

Those who fail to establish a sense of generativity fall into a state of self-absorption in which their personal needs and comforts are of predominant concern. A fictional case of self-absorption is Dickens's Scrooge in "A Christmas Carol." In his one-sided concern with money and in his disregard for the interests and welfare of his young employe, Bob Cratchit, Scrooge exemplifies the self-absorbed, embittered (the two often go together) old man. Dickens also illustrated, however, what Erikson points out: namely, that unhappy solutions to life's crises are not irreversible. Scrooge, at the end of the tale, manifested both a sense of generativity and of intimacy which he had not experienced before.

Integrity vs. Despair

STAGE Eight in the Eriksonian scheme corresponds roughly to the period when the individual's major efforts are nearing completion and when there is time for reflection—and for the enjoyment of grandchildren, if any. The psychosocial dimension that comes into prominence now has *integrity* on one hand and *despair* on the other.

The sense of integrity arises from the individual's ability to look back on his life with satisfaction. At the other extreme is the individual who looks back upon his life as a series of missed opportunities and missed directions; now in the twilight years he realizes that it is too late to start again. For such a person the inevitable result is a sense of despair at what might have been.

THESE, then, are the major stages in the life cycle as described by Erikson. Their presentation, for one thing, frees the clinician to treat adult emotional problems as failures (in part at least) to solve genuinely adult personality crises and not, as heretofore, as mere residuals of infantile frustrations and conflicts. This view of personality growth, moreover, takes some of the onus off parents and takes account of the role which society and the person himself play in the formation of an individual personality. Finally, Erikson has offered hope for us all by demonstrating that each phase of growth has its strengths as well as its weaknesses and that failures at one stage of development can be rectified by successes at later stages.

The reason that these ideas, which sound so agreeable to "common sense," are in fact so revolutionary has a lot to do with the state of psychoanalysis in America. As formulated by Freud, psychoanalysis encompassed a theory of personality development, a method of studying the human mind and, finally, procedures for treating troubled and unhappy people. Freud viewed this system as a scientific one, open to revision as new facts and observations accumulated.

The system was, however, so vehemently attacked that Freud's followers were constantly in the position of having to defend Freud's views. Perhaps because of this situation, Freud's system became, in the hands of some of his followers and defenders, a dogma upon which all theoretical innovation, clinical observation and therapeutic practice had to be grounded. That this attitude persists is evidenced in the recent remark by a psychoanalyst that he believed psychotic patients could not be treated by psychoanalysis because "Freud said so." Such attitudes, in which Freud's authority rather than observation and data is the basis of deciding what is true and what is false, has contributed to the disrepute in which psychoanalysis is widely held today.

Erik Erikson has broken out of this scholasticism and has had the courage to say that Freud's discoveries and practices were the start and not the end of the study and treatment of the human personality. In addition to advocating the modifications of psychoanalytic theory outlined above, Erikson has also suggested modifications in therapeutic practice, particularly in the treatment of young patients. "Young people in severe trouble are not fit for the couch," he writes. "They want to face you, and they want you to face them, not as a facsimile of a parent, or wearing the mask of a professional helper, but as a kind of over-all individual a young person can live with or despair of."

Erikson has had the boldness to remark on some of the negative effects that distorted notions of psychoanalysis have had on society at large. Psychoanalysis, he says, has contributed to a widespread fatalism—"even as we were trying to devise, with scientific determinism, a therapy for the few, we were led to promote an ethical disease among the many."

PERHAPS Erikson's innovations in psychoanalytic theory are best exemplified in his psycho-historical writings, in which he combines psychoanalytic insight with a true historical imagination. After the publication of "Childhood and Society," Erikson undertook the application of his scheme of the human life cycle to the study of historical persons. He wrote a series of brilliant essays on men as varied as Maxim Gorky, George Bernard Shaw and Freud himself. These studies were not narrow case histories but rather reflected Erikson's remarkable grasp of Europe's social and political history, as well as of its literature. (His mastery of American folklore, history and literature is equally remarkable.)

While Erikson's major biographical studies were yet to come, these early essays already revealed his unique psycho-history method. For one thing, Erikson always chose men whose lives fascinated him in one way or another, perhaps because of some conscious or unconscious affinity with them. Erikson thus had a sense of community with his subjects which he adroitly used (he calls it *disciplined subjectivity*) to take his subject's point of view and to experience the world as that person might.

Secondly, Erikson chose to elaborate a particular crisis or episode in the individual's life which seemed to crystallize a life-theme that united the activities of his past and gave direction to his activities for the future. Then, much as an artist might, Erikson proceeded to fill in the background of the episode and add social and historical perspective. In a very real sense Erikson's biographical sketches are like paintings which direct the viewer's gaze from a focal point of attention to background and back again, so that one's appreciation of the focal area is enriched by having pursued the picture in its entirety.

THIS method was given its first major test in Erikson's study of "Young Man Luther." Originally, Erikson planned only a brief study of Luther, but "Luther proved too bulky a man to be merely a chapter in a book." Erikson's involvement with Luther dated from his youth, when, as a wandering artist, he happened to hear the Lord's Prayer in Luther's German. "Never knowingly having heard it, I had the experience, as seldom before or after, of a wholeness captured in a few simple words, of poetry fusing the esthetic and the moral; those who have suddenly 'heard' the Gettysburg Address will know what I mean."

Erikson's interest in Luther may have had other roots as well. In some ways, Luther's unhappiness with the papal intermediaries of Christianity resembled on a grand scale Erikson's own dissatisfaction with the intermediaries of Freud's system. In both cases some of the intermediaries had so distorted the original teachings that what was being preached in the name of the master came close to being the opposite of what he had himself proclaimed. While it is not possible to describe Erikson's treatment of Luther here, one can get some feeling for Erikson's brand of historical analysis from his sketch of Luther:

"Luther was a very troubled and a very gifted young man who had to create his own cause on which to focus

The study of growth
is growing up, too

Professional models illustrate four of Erikson's eight stages in the life of man—about each of which the individual himself has a lot to say. In other words, childhood is not the end-all of development that it is often thought to be.

Freud's "Ages of Man"

Erik Erikson's definition of the "eight ages of man" is a work of synthesis and insight by a psychoanalytically trained and worldly mind. Sigmund Freud's description of human phases stems from his epic psychological discoveries and centers almost exclusively on the early years of life. A brief summary of the phases posited by Freud:

Oral stage—roughly the first year of life, the period during which the mouth region provides the greatest sensual satisfaction. Some derivative behavioral traits which may be seen at this time are *incorporativeness* (first six months of life) and *aggressiveness* (second six months of life).

Anal stage—roughly the second and third years of life. During this period the site of greatest sensual pleasure shifts to the anal and urethral areas. Derivative behavioral traits are *retentiveness* and *expulsiveness.*

Oedipal stage—roughly the fourth and fifth years of life. At this stage the young person takes the parent of the opposite sex as the object or provider of sensual satisfaction and regards the same-sexed parent as a rival. (The "family romance.") Behavior traits originating in this period are *seductiveness* and *competitiveness.*

Phallic stage—roughly the third and fourth years of life. The site of greatest sensual pleasure during this stage is the genital region. Behavior traits derived from this period include *intrusiveness* (male) and *receptiveness* (female).

Latency stage—roughly the years from age 6 to 11. The child resolves the Oedipus conflict by identifying with the parent of the opposite sex and by so doing satisfies sensual needs vicariously. Behavior traits developed during this period include *conscience* (or the internalization of parental moral and ethical demands).

Puberty stage—roughly 11 to 14. During this period there is an integration and subordination of oral, anal and phallic sensuality to an overriding and unitary genital *sexuality.* The genital sexuality of puberty has another young person of the opposite sex as its object, and discharge (at least for boys) as its aim. Derivative behavior traits (associated with the control and regulation of genital sexuality) are *intellectualization* and *estheticism.*

—D.E.

his fidelity in the Roman Catholic world as it was then. . . . He first became a monk and tried to solve his scruples by being an exceptionally good monk. But even his superiors thought that he tried much too hard. He felt himself to be such a sinner that he began to lose faith in the charity of God and his superiors told him, 'Look, God doesn't hate you, you hate God or else you would trust Him to accept your prayers.' But I would like to make it clear that someone like Luther becomes a historical person only because he also has an acute understanding of historical actuality and knows how to 'speak to the condition' of his times. Only then do inner struggles become representative of those of a large number of vigorous and sincere young people—and begin to interest some troublemakers and hangers-on."

After Erikson's study of "Young Man Luther" (1958), he turned his attention to "middle-aged" Gandhi. As did Luther, Gandhi evoked for Erikson childhood memories. Gandhi led his first nonviolent protest in India in 1918 on behalf of some mill workers, and Erikson, then a young man of 16, had read glowing accounts of the event. Almost a half a century later Erikson was invited to Ahmedabad, an industrial city in western India, to give a seminar on the human life cycle. Erikson discovered that Ahmedabad was the city in which Gandhi had led the demonstration about which Erikson had read as a youth. Indeed, Erikson's host was none other than Ambalal Sarabahai, the benevolent industrialist who had been Gandhi's host—as well as antagonist—in the 1918 wage dispute. Throughout his stay in Ahmedabad, Erikson continued to encounter people and places that were related to Gandhi's initial experiments with nonviolent techniques.

The more Erikson learned about the event at Ahmedabad, the more intrigued he became with its pivotal importance in Gandhi's career. It seemed to be the historical moment upon which all the earlier events of Gandhi's life converged and from which diverged all of his later endeavors. So captured was Erikson by the event at Ahmedabad, that he returned the following year to research a book on Gandhi in which the event would serve as a fulcrum.

AT least part of Erikson's interest in Gandhi may have stemmed from certain parallels in their lives. The 1918 event marked Gandhi's emergence as a national political leader. He was 48 at the time, and had become involved reluctantly, not so much out of a need for power or fame as out of a genuine conviction that something had to be done about the disintegration of Indian culture. Coincidentally, Erikson's book, "Childhood and Society," appeared in 1950 when Erikson was 48, and it is that book which brought him national prominence in the mental health field. Like Gandhi, too, Erikson reluctantly did what he felt he had to do (namely, publish his observations and conclusions) for the benefit of his ailing profession and for the patients treated by its practitioners. So while Erikson's affinity with Luther seemed to derive from comparable professional identity crises, his affinity for Gandhi appears to derive from a parallel crisis of generativity. A passage from "Gandhi's Truth" (from a chapter wherein Erikson addresses himself directly to his subject) helps to convey Erikson's feeling for his subject.

"So far, I have followed you through the loneliness of your childhood and through the experiments and the scruples of your youth. I have affirmed my belief in your ceaseless endeavor to perfect yourself as a man who came to feel that he was the only one available to reverse India's fate. You experimented with what to you were debilitating temptations and you did gain vigor and agility from your victories over yourself. Your identity could be no less than that of universal man, although you had to become an Indian—and one close to the masses—first."

The following passage speaks to Erikson's belief in the general significance of Gandhi's efforts:

"We have seen in Gandhi's development the strong attraction of one of those more inclusive identities: that of an enlightened citizen of the British Empire. In proving himself willing neither to abandon vital ties to his native tradition nor to sacrifice lightly a Western education which eventually contributed to his ability to help defeat British hegemony—in all of these seeming contradictions Gandhi showed himself on intimate terms with the actualities of his era. For in all parts of the world, the struggle now is for the *anticipatory development of more inclusive identities* . . . I submit then, that Gandhi, in his immense intuition for historical actuality and his capacity to assume leadership in 'truth in action,' may have created a ritualization through which men, equipped with both realism and strength, can face each other with mutual confidence."

THERE is now more and more teaching of Erikson's concepts in psychiatry, psychology, education and social work in America and in other parts of the world. His description of the stages of the life cycle are summarized in major textbooks in all of these fields and clinicians are increasingly looking at their cases in Eriksonian terms.

Research investigators have, however, found Erikson's formulations somewhat difficult to test. This is not surprising, inasmuch as Erikson's conceptions, like Freud's, take into account the infinite complexity of the human personality. Current research methodologies are, by and large, still not able to deal with these complexities at their own level, and distortions are inevitable when such concepts as "identity" come to be defined in terms of responses to a questionnaire.

Likewise, although Erikson's life-stages have an intuitive "rightness" about them, not everyone agrees with his formulations. Douvan and Adelson in their book, "The Adolescent Experience," argue that while his identity theory may hold true for boys, it doesn't for girls. This argument is based on findings which suggest that girls postpone identity consolidation until after marriage (and intimacy) have been established. Such postponement occurs, says Douvan and Adelson, because a woman's identity is partially defined by the identity of the man whom she marries. This view does not really contradict Erikson's, since he recognizes that later events, such as marriage, can help to resolve both current and past developmental crises. For the woman, but not for the man, the problems of identity and intimacy may be solved concurrently.

Objections to Erikson's formulations have come from other directions as well. Robert W. White, Erikson's good friend and colleague at Harvard, has a long-standing (and warm-hearted) debate with Erikson over his life-stages.

White believes that his own theory of "competence motivation," a theory which has received wide recognition, can account for the phenomena of ego development much more economically than can Erikson's stages. Erikson has, however, little interest in debating the validity of the stages he has described. As an artist he recognizes that there are many different ways to view one and the same phenomenon and that a perspective that is congenial to one person will be repugnant to another. He offers his stage-wise description of the life cycle for those who find such perspectives congenial and not as a world view that everyone should adopt.

It is this lack of dogmatism and sensitivity to the diversity and complexity of the human personality which help to account for the growing recognition of Erikson's contribution within as well as without the helping professions. Indeed, his psycho-historical investigations have originated a whole new field of study which has caught the interest of historians and political scientists alike. (It has also intrigued his wife, Joan, who has published pieces on Eleanor Roosevelt and who has a book on Saint Francis in press.) A recent issue of Daedalus, the journal for the American Academy of Arts and Sciences, was entirely devoted to psycho-historical and psycho-political investigations of creative leaders by authors from diverse disciplines who have been stimulated by Erikson's work.

NOW in his 68th year, Erikson maintains the pattern of multiple activities and appointments which has characterized his entire career. He spends the fall in Cambridge, Mass., where he teaches a large course on "the human life cycle" for Harvard seniors. The spring semester is spent at his home in Stockbridge, Mass., where he participates in case conferences and staff seminars at the Austen Riggs Center. His summers are spent on Cape Cod. Although Erikson's major commitment these days is to his psycho-historical investigation, he is embarking on a study of preschool children's play constructions in different settings and countries, a follow-up of some research he conducted with preadolescents more than a quarter-century ago. He is also planning to review other early observations in the light of contemporary change. In his approach to his work, Erikson appears neither drawn nor driven, but rather to be following an inner schedule as natural as the life cycle itself.

Although Erikson, during his decade of college teaching, has not seen any patients or taught at psychoanalytic institutions, he maintains his dedication to psychoanalysis and views his psycho-historical investigations as an applied branch of that discipline. While some older analysts continue to ignore Erikson's work, there is increasing evidence (including a recent poll of psychiatrists and psychoanalysts) that he is having a rejuvenating influence upon a discipline which many regard as dead or dying. Young analysts are today proclaiming a "new freedom" to see Freud in historical perspective—which reflects the Eriksonian view that one can recognize Freud's greatness without bowing to conceptual precedent.

Accordingly, the reports of the demise of psychoanalysis may have been somewhat premature. In the work of Erik Erikson, at any rate, psychoanalysis lives and continues to beget life.

2

The Phases of Adult Life: A Study in Developmental Psychology

by Roger L. Gould

The author believes that adulthood as a developmental period has been conceptually and empirically ignored in the psychiatric literature with but few exceptions. Two studies on the subject are reported: an observational study of psychiatric outpatients seen in age-homogeneous groups and a questionnaire study of 524 nonpatients. The author found discriminations between age groupings that center largely on the subjects' sense of time and on their attitudes toward self and others in relation to that variable.

IN THE WORK that is to be reported in this paper, the assumptions have been made that people continue to change over the period of time considered to be adulthood and that developmental phases may be found during the adult span of life if they are looked for properly. The focus of this work is on the sequential change that takes place with time rather than on a full description of any one stage. The work is intended to be descriptive and the hypotheses to be generating. The results of direct observations of patients and a questionnaire given to nonpatients will be presented.

When Freud began his exploration of the depths of the mind, he first found the submerged child in the supposed-to-be adult (1). He later carried out, against the resistance of the civilized world, the bold rescue of the sentient child from the sterile and static adultomorphism preferred by his culture (2). This two-fold discovery forced the world to abandon in part the preferred view that adults populate the world and act rationally as adults should. It is interesting to note that the preferred view that adults are rational is a strongly held prejudice of mankind and has fit well the needs of a Christian theology and a structure of civilization built on the law. It is against this ingrained view of man as a fully formed, static, rational adult that the observations and insights of dynamic psychiatry and psychoanalysis struggle.

Though adolescence has been shown, since the time of Freud, to be a period of dynamic and vital growth, we have not made any significant changes in our conceptualization of the periods of adulthood following the identity struggle of youth. We have not proposed any coherent view of the procession through time of the adult or of psycho-

logical growth and change as a function of time in the adult years. Adults are conceived of as being in dynamic conflict, but without direction. The resolution of conflict is thought to lead to higher levels of integration and adaptiveness, but not into a new personality era. Adulthood is still seen as a period of marking time and is not seen as a progression of stages much like the phases of rapid and slow growth of childhood and adolescence.

We have learned to understand the intrapsychic struggles of individuation in childhood and adolescence as struggles keyed by the imposed role task of progressive separation from objects and pushed from within by a complemental evolution of internally programmed biological changes. Both separation from objects and changes in our biological equipment are mediated by time. Why, in our conceptualizations, do we seem to assume that time no longer functions systematically after 21 years of age and to rely henceforth on thematic and adventitious factors to anchor our understanding of change? After all, both object and biological changes continue throughout life. In fact, object changes are even more dramatic in the period after 21 than before 21.

If we would take ego autonomy as our ideal state of individuation, we would have to consider under what conditions ego autonomy prevails. To be autonomous while living alone is entirely different from that in daily living with a spouse. To maintain autonomy while sorting out the pressing demands of spouse and children and employer is a task of greater magnitude than previous tasks and requires a more highly developed psychic apparatus if an optimal level of individuation is to be maintained. There is a difference between living in the world with live, healthy, and powerful parents in the background ready to support you and living with enfeebled, dependent parents in the background. If anything, the changes that take place in one's parents and in one's children would suggest that time-mediated object changes are of the utmost importance during the adult years and that the necessity for change is as imperative as in the period before age 21. From a commonsense point of view, then, there would be no justification for our conceptualizations to imply that time no longer functions systematically after 21 years of age and no justification for our theories of change to rely on thematic and adventitious factors as the essential elements.

Survey of the Literature

Although adulthood as a topic for developmental psychology has largely been ignored, several contributions have been made to the topic. Erikson's work on the seven stages of man (3) is probably the best known of these efforts. He considers his last three stages to be the stages of adulthood: the first adult stage is Intimacy and Distantiation versus Self-Absorption. It represents the success or failure in one's ability to be truly open and capable of a "trusting fellowship" rather than formal separateness or pseudo-intimacy. This is the task of young adults before they work on the next task, Generativity versus Stagnation. In this phase of adulthood, roughly spanning the mid-20s on, the individual must create for himself a continuing giving of himself to his world in a creative, caretaking, participatory way that is progressive, in order to avoid the pit of stagnation. The final stage, Integrity versus Despair, includes the span from later adulthood to death; in this stage the individual comes to grips with his own life as "one's one and only life cycle." Erikson's description of these life phases is very brief. He encourages others to flesh them out with detailed investigations and descriptions. When we compare these skeletal sections on adulthood with his fuller previous sections on childhood, we find vivid evidence that adulthood as a topic has been neglected. Erikson has broadly stroked the thematic dilemmas of being an adult while directing our attention to adulthood as a part of the series of phases extending throughout the life span.

T. Benedek (4) has added an in-depth view of the psychology of being a parent in her work "Parenthood as a Developmental Phase." She notes that there is an emotional normative symbiosis between parent and child that is based on the parent's prior experience of childhood and that operates through the mental principle that "the introjected object is merged with the introjected self in the drive experience and thereby object representations and self-representations are established in inseparable connection with each other." That is, the parent is capable of structural change because in the deep part of his mind the experiences he has with his child are opportunities to rework intimately tied, structure-determining memories of his own childhood. This is all made possible by a kind of limited regression and emotional symbiosis on the part of the adult parent to the level of the developing child. This normative regression and blurring of self-definition is a detailed look at what Erikson called mutuality during the stage of generativity.

Rangell (5), in his paper "The Role of the Parent in the Oedipus Complex," pointed out that the oedipus complex is a structure that continues into later life and organizes much of adult emotional behavior. His case examples illustrate particularly well the reversal of themes after the adult has passed his prime. The parent finds himself envious of his child, who is seen as being at the acme of instinctual potency.

Jacques (6) has offered a penetrating appraisal of the mid-life crisis occurring in the mid-30s and resolving itself in the early and mid-40s. He adds to his clinical observation and case example the weight of the words and lives of famous artists and writers. He discusses this crisis period as a painful confrontation with the inevitability of death and the finitude of time. He sees it as a period requiring that the depressive position be worked through again. The outcome depends on the balance of life-and-death forces that were structuralized in the style of living before the crisis, and its success or failure is judged in terms identical with those of Erikson's stage of Integrity versus Despair.

All these analytic contributions bring important clinical insights to bear on the subject of adult changes over time and suggest areas for more rigorous investigations. They lack, however, the base of detailed comprehensive data on the entire adult life span for a large number of people who can be compared on the same axis of measurement.

Other investigators have attempted to gather this base of data through three fundamentally different approaches. Bühler has spent a lifetime collecting individual biographies of creative and everyday people and has conceptualized her material predominantly from the view of value changes over the life span. This is the longitudinal approach. She finds that the phasic phenomena of the life cycle, as reflected in her biographical studies (7), can best be described as a three-phasic process: "1) a growth period from birth until the organism is fully developed; 2) a stationary growth period during which the organism's power to maintain itself and develop is equal to the forces of decline; and 3) a last period of decline" (p. 13). Each phase can be broken into subphases and given rough time zones that prescribe the orientation of the self and organize the goals of living for that time period.

Neugarten and associates (8), in a large field study in Kansas City, studied 710 people in the mid-1950s both by interview and by projective test schedules. They concentrated on middle life and their sample was from 40 to 90 years old:

> When all of the studies in this book are considered together, it appears that they form two groups. Those in which chronological age provides order in the data are those when the focus was on the intrapsychic, the processes of the personality that are not readily available to awareness or conscious control and which do not have direct expression in overt patterns of social behavior. The second group, those in which individual differences are relatively independent of age, are those where the focus was on more purposive processes in the personality, processes in which attempted control of the self and of the life situation are conspicuous elements (p. 192).

Another conclusion from these studies is that there is an increase of interiority as aging advances that is clearly demonstrable by the mid-40s and that there is a decrease in personality complexity with "an increasing dedication to a central core of values and to a set of habit patterns and a sloughing off of earlier cathexes which lose saliency for the individual . . ." (p. 198).

In a study concerning the changing time perspective in middle age, Dr. Neugarten (9) reported:

> Both sexes, although men more than women, talked of the new difference in the way time is perceived. Life is restructured in terms of time-left-to-live rather than

time-since-birth. Not only the reversal in directionality but the awareness that time in finite is a particularly conspicuous feature of middle age. Thus, "you hear so much about deaths that seem premature. That's one of the changes that comes over you over the years. Young fellows never give it a thought. . . ." The recognition that there is "only so much time left" was a frequent theme in the interviews. In referring to the death of a contemporary, one man said, "there is now the realization that death is very real. Those things don't quite penetrate when you're in your twenties and you think that life is all ahead of you. Now you know that death will come to you, too" (9, p. 97).

Another interviewee added: "It is as if there are two mirrors before me, each held at a partial angle. I see part of myself in my mother who is growing old, and part of her in me. In the other mirror, I see part of myself in my daughter. I have had some dramatic insights, just from looking in those mirrors. . . . It is a set of revelations that I suppose can only come when you are in the middle of three generations" (9, p. 98).

Dr. Neugarten noted that her studies have relevance for a theory of the life cycle in two ways:

> First, in indicating that the age structure of a society, the internalization of age-norms, and age-group identifications are important dimensions of the social and cultural *context* in which the course of the individual life line must be viewed; Second, because these concepts point to at least one additional way of structuring the passage of time in the life span of the individual, *providing a time clock* that can be superimposed over the biological clock, together they help us to comprehend the life cycle. The major punctuation marks in the adult life line tend (those, that is, which are orderly and sequential) to be more often social than biological— or, if biologically based, they are often biological events that occur to significant others rather than to oneself, like grandparenthood or widowhood (9, p. 146).

The third method adopted by psychologists has been to study specific questions over time—the ages of greatest happiness, most mental problems, most hospitalizations, greatest change in specific functions, most divorces, greatest contentment with age, etc. The composite of all of these studies could shed light on the life cycle as a whole. The number of such studies is great and they comprise a large percentage of the psychological and sociological literature. Several authors (10–16) have contributed studies that are pertinent to the issues in this paper.

Study I

Only Bühler and Erikson have looked at the whole life span, but neither of them supplies us with exactly the kind of information we are looking for. Erikson becomes quite sweeping and thematic in his approach to adulthood after the identity crisis and Bühler applies a rational overview of the life span in terms of physiological stages, but neither bears down on the chronological change in the subjective "sense of the world." By "subjective sense of the world" I mean the out-of-focus, interior, gut-level organizing percepts of self and nonself, safety, time, size, etc., that make up the background tone of daily living and shape the attitudes and value base from which decisions and action

emanate. Such a vague but central phenomenon requires a careful and thorough investigation (as well as a more precise definition) of individuals, with some optimal combination of the methods of psychonalytic investigation and Neugarten's methods. Before considering such an effort, we decided to inspect the terrain of the whole adult life span to see whether we could catalog the obvious and construct a platform from which to begin. This section of the paper presents the results of this attempt.

Method

We started with a simple descriptive effort. During 1968, all of the patients who were in group therapy at the UCLA Psychiatric Outpatient Clinic were assigned to homogeneous groups. There were seven groups, composed of the following age ranges: 16–18, 18–22, 22–28, 29–34, 35–43, 43–50, and 50–60 or more. At the end of six months a second set of seven groups was constituted and observed. These 14 groups were treated by 14 third-year residents as part of their psychiatric training. Each of the 14 groups was observed continuously by one of the study group staff, either as cotherapists or as supervisors via tape-recordings. The ten study group members (psychiatrists, psychologists, and an anthropologist) met every two weeks to report their observations and to make simple first-order comparisons.

Although many detailed observations were made, in order to begin our study on solid and safe ground we asked each member to characterize the age group he was studying on the simplest, most self-evident level. We asked for a level of psychological sophistication so low that any naïve, honest observer watching the group would have to agree with the description. We were apparently successful in achieving this goal of simplicity and replicability by two simply measures. With the composition of a second set of groups after six months, the staff rotated age groups and were able to confirm the observations of their colleagues on new groups. The following summer eight first-year medical students, psychologically naïve but bright, listened to the tapes of the group sessions and picked out the same central and salient characteristics.

Results

The observations made about each phase of life are familiar, often anticipated by common sense; many can easily be corroborated by everyday experience and anecdotal accounts. It is the interrelationship of each age phase with the others that is unique and that gives us an empirically based portrayal of the changes in the subjective "sense of the world" or "posturing of the self" over time.

In the group aged 16 to 18, we are unavoidably struck with the theme that was like a motto: "We have to get away from our parents." The theme is loud and repetitively verbalized but not connected with any implementary action. They are all safely part of their families and consider themselves more as family members than as true individuals. They see the future as some vague time "out there" when they will be liberated and mainly have a fantasy conception of what their own adulthood will be like. Their autonomy is precarious, often fortified by negativism, and subject to erosion from moment to moment. Although they long for deep close relationships with peers, the closeness most often found is instantaneous and unstable and is followed by a temporary rebound back to parents.

In the next age group, 18–22, we find a continuation of the theme "We have to get away from our parents" but from a different position. They feel themselves to be halfway out of the family and are worried that they will be reclaimed by the family pull and not make it out completely. They are involved in many kinds of implementing actions—living away from home at school, working, paying rent, owning their own cars—but are not quite totally committed to their current time base since it is not quite adult yet. The real living is just around the corner. They are especially supportive of each other in the group and talk of recreating with their peers the family they are leaving. The peer group becomes the ally that will help them out of the family, but in itself it becomes a new threat that endangers the pureness of their own authentic emerging beliefs by imposing the group belief as an essential for membership and alliance. They see their intimates as betrayers if the intimate person's way of thinking is not identical to their own or if the intimate cannot perform all of the soothing functions that the family had performed. Their own autonomy is felt to be established, but in jeopardy. They perceive a vague feeling that they have to keep a lid on themselves lest anger, fear, or depression escape.

There is a considerable shift in the next group, 22–28. They feel quite established and autonomous and separate from their families and feel they are engaged in the work of being adults. They particularly feel that what they are doing is the true course in life and there is very little energy wasted in considering whether their general commitments are the right ones or not. Most of their energy is spent mastering what they are supposed to be. They feel their "self" to be well-defined, even if they are not fully satisfied with it. They see their parents as people with whom they want to establish a modus vivendi, but to whom they still have to prove their competence as adults. The peers are still important but not to be relied on as much as self-reliance and, although they can still be hurt by a peer's response to them, it is not seen as potentially devastating. The spouse is seen as a person who may not be mature enough now, but with whom there is a commitment to make a marriage work. There is a definite feeling that "now" is the time for living as well as growing and building for the future. Extreme emotions are still guarded against, but now not so much to prevent a leak as to prevent disappointment. It is not sensible to get too high and excited because it may be followed by a low. The emphasis is on modulating the emotional tone in an experimental effort to learn the proper tone for adult life.

The following group, 29–34, seems to have quite a different experience of their world. Whereas those aged 22 to 28 felt they were on the relatively unquestioned true course of life and could devote themselves to the mastery af what they were supposed to be, the 29–34 age group was beginning to question: "What is this life all about now that I am doing what I am supposed to?" and "Is what I am the only way for me to be?" Marriage and career lines have been established and young children are growing, but some inner aspect is striving to be accounted for. They feel weary

of devoting themselves to the task of being what they are supposed to (although they continue on), and just want to be what they are. In particular, there is a dawning awareness that their will alone is not all of them, and that inner forces reproduce patterns of behavior and relationships that they don't particularly want to exist but can no longer ignore or will away. They no longer see the necessity to prove themselves to their parents or highlight their differences, and in such a situation feel free to acknowledge and accept parts of themselves as being like and coming from their parents. They often see their spouses as preventing this new emergence by acting as witness to their supposed-to-be former self and not being willing enough to see the new self. A most poignant desire is to be accepted by the spouse "for what I am." Their children are becoming companions and love objects.

Just as they want to be accepted for "what I am," they want to accept their own children for "what they are becoming" and not impose roles on them. This conscious attempt to let their children grow freely is interfered with by a series of confusing temporary identifications with their growing children. Often the anecdotes of their children's behavior described in the group sessions were so commingled with similar memories from their own pasts that it was unclear who felt what.

In the subsequent age group, 35–43, there is a continued look within and an existential questioning of self, values, and life itself, but with a change of tone toward quiet desperation and an increasing awareness of a time squeeze. This tone applies to themselves, their parents, and their children. Instead of "I just want to be" with a sense of timelessness, there is "Have I done the right thing?"; "Is there time to change?" The children are seen as emerging end products of their parenting and reflections of their worth. There is a sense that not only is there little time left to shape the behavior of their adolescent children but there is uncertainty about which value lines to follow in the shaping and how fast their control over the children is waning. Their own parents at this stage turn more toward them and there is a muffled renewal of old conflict lines that is kept suppressed by the thought that, since the parents are getting older and time is running out for them, direct criticism would be guilt-provoking. The sense of time during this stage emphasizes the finitude of time and there is an eye toward the past, present, and future equally. Under this time pressure of conflict and questioning, the person looks to the spouse, who is often in a similar life position and is looking for the same support. Work is often looked to as offering the hope of compensation for all of this, but in a fantasy way—"one last chance to make it big."

In the 43- to 50-year-old group, we see some definite changes from the 35- to 43-year-old group and in some ways it is as though the issues anticipated are now being lived with. That is, in the earlier group the emerging sense that time is finite is hedged by the compensating feeling that there is still time if you hurry to make some dreams come true but in the 40s it is not hedged. Finite time is resigned to as reality and as not so malleable by self-illusions. The "die is cast" feeling is present and is seen as a relief from the internal tearing apart of the immediately previous years even though it is a bitter pill to swallow. They feel as if their personalities are pretty well set and on occasion are vocally critical of their parents and tend to blame them for their life problems. They are eager to have social activities and friends, but more on a superficial basis and more tinged with negative competitive casts. They are still actively involved with their young adult children, but now not as ones emerging but as ones who have emerged and are separate. They tend to be watchful of their children's adult progress in a specific style, i.e., with a readiness to find the error in their ways. They very actively look for sympathy and affection from their spouses, who in many ways they seem to be dependent on in a mode similar to that of their former dependency on parents.

In the 50s there is a mellowing and warming up. The negative cast of the 40s diminishes in their relationships to themselves, their parents, their children, and their friends. Their parents are no longer the cause of their problems, but are affectionately called "Mom" and "Dad." The children's lives are now seen as potential sources of warm comfort and satisfaction and they are concerned not so much with their children's achievements as with their happiness in personal terms. They value their own spouses more and look within themselves at their own feelings and emotions, although not with the critical "time pressure" eye of the late 30s or with the infinite omnipotentiality of the early 30s but with a more self-accepting attitude of continued learning from a position of general stability. The spouse is seen now as a valuable source of companionship in life and less like a parent or source of supplies. Criticisms of the previous years are realigned to take into account this central change. However, all is not as comfortable as it might appear from the description of the 50s so far. There is a narrow time span, with little concern for the past or future, which seems to be related to the unmentioned but imminent presence of mortality. With this there is a renewed questioning about the meaningfulness of life as well as a review of one's own work contributions to the world. In addition, there is a hunger for personal relationships from a position of indelible uniqueness but a necessity to stay away from emotionally laden topics and a concentration on petty annoyances, health topics, and an unexpected guilty shadow about personal sexual views.

Study II

The results of Study I are given descriptively and stand for themselves. We were impressed by the facts that differences among age groups could be found by the use of simple observation and that the differences seemed quite substantial. We were not at all confident about the specificity of our age groupings nor about the generalizability of our observations to a non-help-seeking population. We had no socioeconomic data for disaggregating our sample into subgroups. This second study adds more information on age specificity and generalizability but does not contribute to our knowledge of possible sugroup variability based on such factors as sex, income, race, religion, or occupation.

Method

We constructed a questionnaire that could be administered simply to a nonpatient population. The items that composed the questionnaire were salient statements heard in the "phase of life" groups. To avoid overweighting the questionnaire with the clinical bias we developed during the group observations, we enlisted the aid of eight first-year medical students. These students were presented with all of the tape-recordings of the two sets of "phase of life" groups. The students broke up into small groups and listened to the tapes after receiving one simple instruction from me: "List the statements describing personal feelings that stood out during the tape-recorded sessions." A compilation of these statements from all the age groups was then organized into topical sections. The topical section titles were inductively arrived at from the content of the statements. We decided to include only 16 statements in each topical section since we had decided on a forced-choice ranking format.

The titles were not printed on the questionnaire but the eight titled sections were: 1) sense of time; relationships to 2) parents, 3) friends, 4) children, 5) spouses; and feelings about 6) own personality, 7) job, and 8) sex. We added two additional sections that were not empirically determined, sections 9 and 10. In section 9 we asked the subjects to rank order a list of major concerns in life. In section 10 we asked them to rank order the importance of the major people in their everyday life—children, parents, spouse, self, and boss—in regard to each of the following: companionship, approval, decision-making, and general influence. Section 1 of the questionnaire is included here as an example of the wording and type of statements in the questionnaire:

1. I feel that some exciting things are going to happen to me.
2. I never plan on what tomorrow may bring.
3. It hurts me to realize that I will not get some things in life I want.
4. I live for today; forget the past.
5. I think things aren't as good as they used to be.
6. I believe I will some day have everything I want in life.
7. My life doesn't change much from year to year.
8. There is little hope for the future.
9. I try to be satisfied with what I have and not to think so much about the things I probably won't be able to get.
10. I wish I could change the past.
11. I dream about life ten years from now.
12. I spend more time now thinking about the past than about the future.
13. There's still plenty of time to do most of the things I want to do.
14. I would be quite content to remain as old as I am now.
15. I find myself daydreaming about good experiences in the past.
16. I will have to settle for less than I expected, but I still think I will get most things I want.

The questionnaire was then given to a white middle-class educated population of 524 who were selected by two criteria; they were not psychiatric patients and they were available through a network of acquaintances emanating from a core of eight medical students and several hospital volunteers. Monitoring of the age of the respondent as the questionnaires were returned allowed us to purposively sample ages not represented in the early returns. Our final sample included approximately 20 subjects for each year between 16 and 33 and 20 subjects for each three-year span between 33 and 60. The male-female ratio was approximately 1:1 for the total sample but was unevenly distributed, with women being disproportionately represented over age 45.

Results

Each subject supplied each of the 16 statements in each section with a rank order from one to 16. Curves for each statement were plotted on the basis of the average rank ordering for the 20 subjects at each age. Since there were 142 separate statements composing the questionnaire, there were 142 scores for each age between 16 and 60 and 142 curves were developed from these scores. Each age-point on each curve therefore represents the *average* rank order of 20 same-aged subjects for that statement relative to the other 15 statements in its section.

By putting all of the curves on a single type of graph (using ages 16–60 as the abscissa), we were able to clearly see the unstable periods when response scores changed, i.e., when the greatest number of statements changed rank order (see figure 1). These change periods were interpreted as transitional periods or time zone boundaries. The bulk of the responses stabilized in the period between ages 22 and 29 and remained stable throughout the life span. The stable response curves of this period provide us with a well-established baseline. The responses of the 16- to 17-year-olds were almost identical, except in age-inappropriate areas (children, job security, etc.), to the stable patterns of those aged 22 to 29. In contrast, the 18- to 22-year-olds responded discontinuously. After 29, the rank order of selected statements began to change from the age baseline at two ages, 30 and 37. Most of these late-changing curves stabilized at around age 43. A less impressive but definite series of response fluctuations occurred at the end of the fourth decade. Thus there are suggestions of seven distinct age periods: 16–17, 18–21, 22–28, 29–36, 37–43, 44–50, and 51–60.

In the previous step, we were not interested in which statements changed rank order, only the number of changes in rank order at a certain time. To begin to look at the content of the statements with changing scores between 16 and 60, we graphed each topical section individually. Since the statements were empirically determined, there was no correct answer and no logical connection that could be applied in rank ordering the section. Therefore, the change in rank for each statement from one year to the next becomes the measure of a type of collective subjective accounting, representing the average "hunches" of 20 subjects at each age. A statement that rings a bell or connects with a feeling of immediacy will rise in rank for that age group and will have to compete with other such statements or consistently popular stereotyped statements.

For the purposes of establishing the time boundaries of the adult life span, those curves with the most rapid and stable changes (and face validity when compared with the bulk of unchanging curves) interest us the most and are presented in figure 1. Several of the curves lend weight to our clinical observation of the groups and add a knowledge of age specificity that we did not have. As can be seen in graph 1, the ranking of the statement "My personality is pretty well set" takes a dramatic jump to a new level between 41 and 43.

In another group observation, we noted that the strong desire to be "accepted for what I am by my spouse" is present in the 28- to 34-year-old group. That statement was present in two forms in the questionnaire under two separate sections: "I wish that people would accept me for what I am as a person" under the friend section, and the more specific "I want to be accepted for what I am by my spouse" under the marital section. The two curves are shown in graphs 2 and 3 and it can be seen that the excursion from the baseline is quite specifically related to spouse and takes place between ages 28 and 32.

In the statement "I am content to remain as old as I am," there is a gradual continuous rise during the 20s starting from a low at 18–19 until a peak is reached at 29 with a sharp descent in the 30s. This adds weight to our observation that there is a marked subjective experience in the early 30s that life is much more difficult and painful than it appeared in the 20s.

By comparing them with the 20s, we can use these three curves (graphs 2–4) to bracket the 30s with some evidence that a change or opening-up process begins in the 30s and a stabilization and closing-off process begins in the early 40s—around 43 as experienced and reported by our sample. Now let us look more closely at our curves for the 30s, which add weight to the observation that this age period is a time of active psychological change.

We can categorize the curves of the 30s as demonstrative of two major shifts. There is a gradual peeling away of the magical illusions of omnipotence and omnipotentiality and there is the identification of the self with the family.

Under the first category are the curves of graphs 5–11. As can be seen, there are significant changes beginning in the 30s as the sense of time becomes finite while a reconciliation with the limitations of being merely mortal involves work choice, the sense of well-being, money resources, and the deterioration of some general abilities. It is well to note that most of these processes start in the mid-30s and leave the early 30s free of the constricting sense of time that characterizes the late 30s and early 40s in our group observation.

The curves interpreted as part of the process of turning inward toward the family and a blurring of self-definition with the family are as shown in graphs 12–17. There is direct evidence in this series of curves that the preference schedule for involvement switches in the early 30s from the stable patterns of the 20s. There is a turning away from an active social life outside the family to a focus on their own children and a reconsideration of their parents' mistakes with them while they are considering their mistakes with their own children. In addition, there is a drifting downward in the sense of satisfaction in the marriage as compared with the highly valued marriage of the 20s. There is also increased difficulty in making the marriage work and complaints of not being able to communicate with the spouse (graph not shown). Parent, child, self, and spouse are all intimately interrelated and interchangeable by the substitution processes that seem to appear in these graphs.

In the 40s, two things happen to the curves of the questionnaire answers. Between 40 and 43 there is a series of temporary excursions from well-established lifelong baselines on statements dealing with personal comfort, indicating an acutely unstable period with a great deal of personal discomfort. In addition to the return to baseline on these statements at 43, there is a general stabilization and leveling off of the changes started in the early and mid-30s. This coincides with the dramatic affirmation of the feelings that one's personality is pretty well set (graph 1) and that life does not change from year to year (graph 7).

Marital happiness and contentment with the spouse continue to increase, along with a renewed interest in friends and social activities, as seen in graph 18. Friends and social activities are not substitutes for concern with one's own children, which continues at a very high level.

In the 50s the curves indicate that one begins to feel less responsible for one's children and begins to look for the children's approval as a meaningful concern to be ranked as coequal with self-approval and the spouse's approval. The concern with health increases during the 50s. The certainty that time is running out is reflected in several curves, especially graphs 5 and 6.

Discussion and Conclusions

There is a great danger in trying to use cross-sectional data as an aid to our understanding of a continuous process. The difference in responses by age may reflect the sequence of cultural values learned during formative years by different groups rather than a response determined primarily by the age of the responder. The questions with moral implications are most likely to fall in the former category. Most of the changing curves presented in this paper do not fall into the moral, learned response category but are questions related to time sense that are most likely to be age-determined. With these limitations in mind, I think we are on safe ground in considering that the longitudinal process is represented in this sequential series of cross-sectional samples.

Some of the results of our questionnaire study are happily supported by the few independent studies already in the psychological literature that deal with this subject. In particular, our curves on marital happiness (16), contentment to remain the same age (14, p. 373), anxiety in the 40s in relation to performance (17), a sense of the finiteness of time in the mid-30s (11), reconciliation in the 40s (12), health concerns (13), decreased interest in social activities in the 30s, and increased interest in friends and organizations in the 40s (15) all conform to the results of previous studies using different methodologies and different populations. The correlation of the questionnaire results with these independent studies, and the similarity of the findings of our direct observation of patients to those of the questionnaire study of nonpatients, certainly provide evidence that the adult period is a time of active and systematic change. In addition, there is strong evidence that a series of distinct stages can be demarcated.

The studies reported in this paper have been designed to cancel out individual differences in order to highlight whatever sameness inheres in a group of age-peers. Patients and nonpatients are not discriminable in these studies, but this in no way implies there is no difference between the groups. We looked only at the contents of the subjective experience relative to age, not the intensity of the degree to which this reality of time interacts with other powerful factors in people's lives. Although the results may be considered factual inasmuch as they can be confirmed or negated by other observers, they are not observations pertinent to any one individual but constructs derived from specific groups that may be applicable to other groups.

The results are best thought of as a description of a sequence of process fluctuations that define the posturing of the self to its inner and outer world over time. The fluctuations are time-dominated, but not necessarily age specific for any one individual. In addition, the fluctuations take place within the context of a total personality, lifestyle, and subculture and each man can be compared only with his own self at a former time. How these shifts are expressed and coped with is a matter of individual psychology beyond the scope of this paper. The subject of this paper has been the manner in which the passage of time influences the actuality of experiences during the adult life span.

Acknowledgments

This work was conducted with the generous support of the UCLA Department of Psychiatry outpatient staff. Special efforts and consultation were contributed by Peter Gelker, M.S., Allan Warner, M.D., and William Beckwith, Ph.D. Other contributing members of the "phase of life" study group were: Herbert Eveloff, M.D., Jerome Karasic, M.D., Louise Epps, Ph.D., Andrew Comrey, Ph.D., John Kennedy, Ph.D., Roberta Crutcher, M.D., and Craig MacAndrews, Ph.D.; and medical students: Alan Arnold, Richard Cicinelli, Bruce Merl, Edward Rose, William Schleiter, Peter Tamulevich, and Mikel Weinberg.

References

1. Freud S: Case studies (1893–1895), in Complete Psychological Works, standard ed, vol 2. Translated and edited by Strachey J. London, Hogarth Press, 1955, pp 135–183
2. Ferud S: Three essays on sexuality (1901–1905), in Complete Psychological Works, standard ed, vol 7, Translated and edited by Strachey J. London, Hogarth Press, 1955, pp 173–206
3. Erikson E: Growth and crises of the healthy personality. Psychol Issues 1:50–100, 1959
4. Benedek T: Parenthood as a developmental phase. J. Amer Psychoanal Ass 7:389–417, 1959
5. Rangell L: The role of the parent in the oedipus complex. Bull Menninger Clin 19:9–15, 1955
6. Jacques E: Death and the mid-life crisis. Int J Psychoanal 46:502–514, 1965
7. Bühler C, Massanik F (eds): The Course of Human Life. New York, Springer, 1968
8. Neugarten B, et al: Personality in Middle and Late Life. New York, Atherton Press, 1964
9. Neugarten B (ed): Middle Age and Aging. Chicago. University of Chicago Press, 1968

10. Lehman H: Age and Achievement. Princeton: Princeton University Press, 1953
11. Lewin K: Field theory and experiment in social psychology. Amer J Sociol 44:868–896, 1939
12. Slotkin JS: Life course in middle life. Social Forces 33:171–177, 1952
13. Dykman R, Heimann E, Ken W: Lifetime worry patterns of three diverse adult and cultural groups. J Soc Psychol 45:91–100, 1952
14. Pressey S, Kuhlen R: Psychological Development Through the Life Span. New York, Harper & Row, 1957
15. Strong E: Change of Interests with Age. Stanford, Stanford University Press, 1931
16. Terman L: Psychological Factors in Marriage Happiness. New York, McGraw-Hill, 1938
17. Welford AT: Age and skill: motor, intellectual and social, in Decision Making and Age, Interdisciplinary Topics in Gerontology, vol 4. Edited by Welford AT, Birren JE. New York, Karger, 1969, pp 1–22

3

Meaningfulness
of the
Biographical Approach

by Charlotte Bühler

What do we mean by the biographical approach and why is it meaningful in the context of our existentially and humanistically oriented psychology?

By the *biographical approach* we mean the study of life histories, whether they be written up in published biographies or whether they be written up by people in autobiographies or in diaries or memoirs; or whether they be put together on the basis of interviews either in case studies or psychotherapy work. They also might result from developmental longitudinal studies, if these are geared toward any evaluation of the person as a whole.

It is this that matters to us, the understanding of the *person as a whole*. Why?

The main psychological reason that I see is that only if we know more about the person as a whole, shall we know more about the way human beings live their lives.

Is that so new, you may ask. Did the social sciences not always try exactly that, namely study human lives, in history, literature, sociology, anthropology, social work, and before all, in psychology.

Yes, of course they did. But it seems that with all their studies we still don't have as yet a clear enough, a penetrating enough picture of the most adequate ways of living. What exactly are the main characteristics of the healthy, the appropriate, the convincing ways of living of the average person, with everyday gifts and deficiencies, everyday problems and conflicts, everyday goals and satisfactions? Is there such a thing as an appropriate whole of a course of life of a person? How can we establish it? In what kind of a *model* can we grasp this kind of a life history and describe it so that we really see the whole, understand its procedures, its goals, its meanings, and what it is all about?

Of course, there are, as you know, thousands of biographies as well as case histories in which lives are described and interpreted. We also have a number of models according to which the data can be grouped and categorized.

And I think some of us who in one capacity or another, have been working with people for years, often have an immediate or else a gradual grasp of what a person is about.

What a person is about—what do I mean by that? I mean something which I think you all understand immediately, the strange fact that for each person certain things seem to *matter*; matter more than other things. Matter, meaning what? Meaning that there are certain things which they seem to pursue more than other things; that either with persistence or else off and on, they behave in a certain manner which indicates they are after something or they are up to something, as the saying goes, or hung up on something. All this seems to amount to *goals*, be they immediate, be they short or long-range, sensible, suitable, constructive, or else lacking in all these, seeming futile, far out, or even destructive. In between we find people for whom nothing seems to matter. They seem to wander about, to do this and that. They themselves may feel, even say, they are floundering, because they feel they ought to be doing something that has some direction, something with a goal. Ought to—in what sense? Who is to say? Ought to is what some feel in themselves. Some feel it is a "waste" not to have some goal. Some also feel they used to have a goal and that was a waste, because it was the "wrong" goal for them. Wrong in what sense? This is another thing we shall have to explore.

But let us ask first, how things hang together for those who feel they know what they are doing and who know what they want.

How does it all hang together and what does it all amount to? Or is there such a thing as *ultimate total pursuits* and do they apply to everyone or only to some, and is there a formula that may help us to conceive of this whole?

Freud was the first to provide a formula, which he conceived in his psychiatric work. His formula was that all human beings want first of all their drives satisfied, and then afterwards, if they are hindered in that and if they are able to resign themselves to frustrations, they will accept the denials of reality and the demands of society as imposed on them by their parents. And all this they would do, because indirectly it would get them back to satisfaction. It would get them back because their environment would accept and love them for their conformity, and that would give them indirectly again that pleasure of love which they were seeking to obtain in the first instance.

Of course, pleasure and love mean all sorts of different things in all these instances, starting with the sucking pleasure and end with, say, fulfilling obligations to please and being pleased by doing so.

For this lack of discrimination and other reasons this original psychoanalytic theory, after being criticized by many of Freud's successors and students, was modified and reformulated in a more scientific version in which it says: All human striving has one basic tendency and this is toward restoring equilibrium, which is continuously lost in the process of living. This is the presently widely accepted *homeostasis* theory, homeostasis being the Greek word for equilibrium. The assumption is that whether by means of drive satisfaction pursued by what Freud called the *id* of a person, or by beans of adapting to reality by what Freud called the *ego*, or else by means of accepting society's demands by means of what Freud called the *superego*, alias conscience, individuals always operate so as to restore or keep their inner balance. The basic assumption here is that what a human being—perhaps generally speaking a living being—needs more than anything else, is equilibrium. And this equilibrium, or homeostasis, is attained only after a release of all tensions has taken place. Therefore tension release is the ultimate goal of all processes and actions in which an individual becomes engaged. This is considered by these thinkers the main goal, whether conscious or unconscious.

The theory, while still valid for a great many workers in the field, was rejected by a number of psychologists and psychiatrists as not giving an appropriate picture of what human beings are *ultimately* concerned with.

I think the scientifically most cogent criticism came from the neurophysiologist *Kurt Goldstein* (1939) who discussed in detail the fact that only the sick organism is constantly seeking *release from strain* or tension, whereas the healthy organism is able and apt to sustain certain amounts of strain or tension in the interest of other completely different goals that are important to the healthy person. Goldstein called these other goals the person's interest in *self-actualization*.

This concept was taken up by *A. Maslow*. He demonstrated in studies of healthy persons that their main interest was to become *creatively active* in the world, and that their creative self-actualization was what mattered to them most as their goal (1954). In the same period of the 1940s and 1950s *Karen Horney* and *Erich Fromm* had brought psychological and social arguments against the homeostasis theory and named as the basic human goal *self-realization*, which is a slight variation from the self-actualization concept.

I myself expressed the opinion that homeostasis is no goal at all, only a comfortable basis of functioning, and that human beings' real goal of life is what I called a *fulfillment*, which they hoped to attain by various things they accomplished in themselves and in the world outside. Several years earlier (1933) I had tried to demonstrate this trend toward fulfillment by means of biographies.

In the meantime, some excellent research with creative persons (*F. Barron, B. Eiduson*, and others) showed that creative people do not only not *avoid* difficulties, but *like* problems which require effort for their solution. That

means a certain amount of tension is interesting to them. This *creative tension* is different from the tension of pure frustration, but it is a tension just the same.

It also was found—as recently summarized in a survey by B. Eiduson (1968), that many young infants are observed to actively seek stimuli and that they explore their environment with a tension-increasing curiosity, with disregard for what may be a more confortable position.

These then are the insights that form the basic convictions of the humanistic psychologists, namely that humans' basic tendency is toward a fulfillment brought about by means of self-actualization or self-realization in doing certain things. We shall further discuss this *"doing"* later on. In the meantime it was explained by Horney as meaning to bring out what she called a person's *best potentials*. Optimistically she declared that these best potentials would be best not only for the person, but also for the environment.

Here of course, we have a problem. Can we really assume that what is best for the person is also always best for the environment, and what exactly is *"best"*?

And then comes the other question: What do we know now about the person? What can we do with what we know now?

I do not think we can do enough with what we know now. An example:

> Here comes *Joe* to me, a 24-year-old social worker. He says he was always insecure regarding himself, always watched himself and others, to see whether people liked him. He never could act spontaneously, was always guarded.
>
> He thinks he got this from his parents, who *also* are always concerned with what people think of them. He went along with what they said and believed they were right.
>
> But in the last months he suddenly became aware of his own behavior in comparison with that of some friends. And he did not like any more his lack of spontaneity and the values he had believed in. He felt this was all wrong, yet he did not know how to change it or how to find other values to believe in.

Now this is quite a typical case of our time. If we analyze what this young man says about his previous goals, it is that all he used to want was to be liked by people; not really because their liking as such was important to him, but because it made him feel more *secure* when he was accepted.

This need for *security* is what *Alfred Adler* first criticized about Freud, that he led back to people's *inferiority* feelings. He introduced the idea of inferiority complexes.

I do not intend to concern myself with the debate between Adler and the Freudians, who claimed that ultimately security needs also were needs for love. Also I do not believe that security needs have to be considered based necessarily on inferiority feelings. Personally I think that inferiority feelings are a sign of a neurotic incapacity to cope with life, while the need for security seems to me a natural outgrowth out of our *human existence* as such. It belongs to our human condition that we not only *feel*, but actually are living in insecure circumstances all our life. Even the medieval hymn said: "In the middle of life we are surrounded by death," and not only are we surrounded by death, but at all times we live in precarious circumstances, so that we could meet with accidents, failures, and debacles of all sorts. Of course, it is true, the healthy person does not dwell on these things. In fact, as has been stated, healthy people often go through life with the feeling they were immortal and immune to any disaster or even illness.

But all this does not mean that there is not in everyone a basic need for security, which seems to me to have to do more with survival than with love.

However, in the case of Joe we encounter something different from this basic existential security need. He does something of which he does not approve himself. He is guarded, he lost all spontaneity; he constantly watches people, whether they approve of him. He also says he does not know *anything* about himself, he has no values of his own, he just adopted his parents' values; he has no direction of his own, and does not know what to believe in any more.

Looking at this situation from the aspect of self-realization, we can see that this man is not realizing himself at all. But in order to understand what he is doing, we have to make some further considerations.

This man is obviously doing the direct opposite of self-realization, in curtailing his spontaneity so as to pursue values in which he cannot believe any longer. He lives with what we will call an excessively *self-limiting adaptation*, so as to *uphold an inner order*, which means to do what seems right to him according to what he had learned. But to his dismay, he no longer felt right about this excessive conformity which he accomplished by *repressing* all his own impulses. This latter interpretation, as you know, psychiatry has learned from psychoanalysis, and the concepts, study, and treatment of repression belong to this school's most lasting contributions. In repressing his own impulses and feelings from early in life, Joe conformed with his environment's demands, but in this way was never himself.

How then does a person who actually pursues his self-realization successfully behave? Does he just simply let go and follow all his impulses?

That is what some people seem to believe and to recommend these days. They go to the opposite extreme of repression and do what they like to do. But does self-realization lie in doing all that one *likes* to do?

First, there is the question of *what* a person likes to do. As you all know from your wishes and daydreams, there are innumerable things a person may like to do, beginning with the comparatively harmless desire to eat and drink anything one has an appetite for, over the now highly debated desire to practice sex whenever and however one likes it, to the fulfillment of desires for exercising violence or power to obtain certain forbidden or inaccessible need-satisfactions.

People's desires for need-satisfaction seem to be extremely different in type and degree. I wish we had some truly clarifying study of how people who live or lived their lives to their own satisfaction, discover the degree and type of desires that they had to have fulfilled to feel happy. One thing is sure—the extremes of doing what they want, never seem to work out well. Neither the Casa-

novas and Don Juan's of old, nor the sex interchanging *Couples* of John Updike are faring too well, and how the members of the Sexual Liberty Society are faring is—in terms of deeper analysis—not known to me.

As far as crime is concerned, I found it truly pathetic that Dick, the hero of Capote's well-documented story *In Cold Blood*, always assured his friend that he was a completely normal guy, while actually he was obviously miserable from the beginning to the end.

And as far as eating and drinking is concerned, the times of gluttonous feasts seem more or less to be a thing of the historical past, since most people are aware of health, if not waistlines. As the saying goes, all the good things are either immoral, illegal, or fattening.

On the other hand, even in our affluent society, not to speak of extremely poor nations, there are millions of people for whom satisfaction of basic needs remains a drive that overshadows everything else. Michael Harrington established in his study of *The Other America* in 1963 a total of about 50 million poor in this country.

The new poor, as Harrington calls those left behind when the rest of the American society was moving ahead, are without aspiration, living in a system impervious to hope. This other America, he says, "does not contain the adventurous seeking a new life and land. It is populated by the failures, by those driven from the land and bewildered by the city, by old people suddenly confronted with the torments of loneliness and poverty, and by minorities facing a wall of prejudice."

Yet movingly enough, you read in Oscar Lewis' very authentic study *La Vida* (1965) how this forever hungry Felicita with her five children, tells the author:

> "What I'd like most for my children is for them to study and see if they can't make something of themselves. Not something very big, because I can't afford to send them to college. But I hope they at least finish high school and have a trade so that they can get good jobs. And I'd like my daughters to be virgins and marry with a veil and crown. I want them to be decent people, better than I am. One should always live with hope. But as long as I stay in Puerto Rico, I don't see how I can get ahead."

Here is, in the midst of the greatest poverty, a visualization of goals that reaches beyond the satisfaction of the most basic physical needs, of things that would allow for progress and that seem right to her.

As I said, I wish someone would make a research study on truly satisfactory degrees and kinds of need-satisfactions in people who truly feel good about their lives.

This study should include all types of physical pleasures that were not as yet mentioned, such as good physical exercise, sports and travels, and all sorts of manual and other physical activities. It also should include the study of those satisfactions of ego needs that come with the pleasure of prowess and good functioning as such.

While this study is still to be done, there is, however, one thing that more and more people are becoming aware of as perhaps the deepest need in human life and the one that is the hardest to realize. It is the need to get and to give true *love*. Love, this deepest of all feelings that everyone craves, seems at the same time the most elusive of all. It is just amazing to me how often I hear from my patients the statement that they believe they are in love, or they love, or they are being loved, but they are not sure. "I really don't know for sure what love is," is a statement I hear repeatedly. Personally I think that if a person really loves, they know it. But people have become extremely insecure in this area, particularly when sexual attraction, too much or too little of it, confuses the picture.

This subject of love is of course one which to discuss would fill more than a whole evening's time. All I can say at this point is that among all the need-satisfactions that would contribute to self-realization and fulfillment of life, the felt experience of genuine mutual love seems to me the most decisive. In the meantime, in the present confusion between sex and love many people would do well to read Erich Fromm's *Art of Loving* (1956).

But enough of this. I just wanted to mention, because at present this whole area is so much in the foreground, that while certainly psycho-physical *need-satisfaction*—as we will call it—is a basic tendency, it in itself has not been shown to bring about the fulfilling experience of self-realization. It can only contribute to it, in individually differing measure.

The area that seems to be most contributory to the experience of self-realization is that of *creative* activity. In the majority of biographies of persons whose lives are described as in some way admirable and frequently as fulfilled, some creative activity represents the central aspect of this life.

By creative is meant not necessarily only the ingenuous production of some great artist or scientist or other kind of world leader. Creative can be, as Americans particularly have emphasized, the imaginative handling of everyday life, the imaginative cooking of a housewife, the loving understanding with which a marital partner or a parent relates to his or her family, the well-planned development of a business, the imaginative skill of a salesperson, or also the handwork of a craftsman, the beautiful new rose created by a gardner. Creative can be the painting of a child or the poem of a teenager.

Of course, these creative talents and activities do not necessarily prevent a person from having an unhappy or a deeply disturbed life. But among all the experiences which may climax in ecstasy, or which lead to what Maslow calls "peak experiences," creativity reaches furthest and comes closest to the ecstasy of love. Maslow's examples of self-realizing persons are all very creative individuals.

In my own psychotherapeutic experience I found that all those who worked themselves through to any kind of creative doings, felt better about themselves and about life, even if some of their problems or conflicts remained unresolved. The reason is that any kind of creative activity is experienced by the person as a self-expression in which *feelings* are released in such a manner that the result is a *product*, which means something potentially valuable, useful also to others, contributing to the production on which human cultures are based. What makes people feel their producing is something of worth is that they put *effort* into this doing, and that the result of their mental and/or manual work either is something useful or beautiful or something of interest.

Interesting in this context is the story of one of my patients' radical change from complete preoccupation with self-pity, unhappiness, and hatred, to a creative concern with her family.

Zoe, a woman of about 33, married, with a family of two young children, had come to psychotherapy for about a year engrossed in complaints about her unhappy life. She felt her parents had never loved nor cared for her—which to a great extent was probably true, that the man she married, while loving her, was lazy, inefficient and earned only an insufficient salary, that she had to help with the income in doing part-time secretarial work and besides that take care of the house and the children without being able to do any of the things that really interested her due to lack of time and money.

After ventilating her resentments and hostilities for a good part of the year and vacillating between a complete rejection of everything and everybody in her life, with the wish to run away from it all on the one hand and on the other racking her brain about possibilities, how she could make her mother love her after all this time or make her husband be more ambitious and aggressive, and after she had come to the realization that all this would not work for one reason or another—the therapist asked her what exactly she thought human life was about. Did she think that her life, her future, any kind of satisfaction and fulfillment continued to depend on her mother finally accepting and loving her, which she seemed to have recognized as hopeless; on her husband becoming more ambitious and aggressive, which seemed unlikely; and on somebody taking her children and her household off her hands so that she could pursue other interests which still left open the question of what could be gained by this pursuit, like earning a college degree and teaching while somebody else raised her children.

At this point the therapist also expressed her opinion about the whole situation. She said that while it was very unfortunate to have had the kind of parents, particularly the mother she had grown up with, she had now a loving husband and had gotten acceptance and loving understanding from her therapist. So obviously she had worth in these persons' eyes and she was given emotional warmth.

She undid the effect of these, in constantly depreciating her husband's way of being and in taking for granted her therapist's acceptance. She also ignored the importance of having children who seemed willing to love her and who accepted a mother who did not impress as very loving herself.

The therapist felt that it was time that *Zoe* realized her own complete unwillingness to accept any unpleasant or difficult conditions of life, and that while demanding all the good things, she herself actually gave very little, was on the way to be as unloving as her own mother and was not grateful for anything at all.

This turning point in the therapist's attitude as well as the therapist's evaluating statement shocked *Zoe* immensely. She cried, expressed anger, and left, declaring she felt deserted and rejected.

The next week she returned and seemed a changed person. She said she realized that all she had done was complain about what had happened and was happening to her and that this was really no way of living, especially since her circumstances were not about to change. So maybe she could try to accept them and see what she herself could be doing with her life. She wanted to think what her life could be about.

Of course, the next time she returned, again in dismay over something that had happened between her and some friends, on whose acceptance and understanding she also depended obviously too much.

But the next time things had begun to clear up in a new way. In thinking about life, *Zoe* had come to the conclusion that she wanted life to be something that *she* took in hand, that *she* would form.

"My marriage, my children," she said, "I see suddenly it is like clay. Either it lies there, or you do something with it or not. In the morning, I wake up, this is for my son and I want to do it. This is a day in life and I can exercise some control and do something with it, instead of waking up angry and deprived. Seeing my children as my own, that I can hurt or do something good with it—you can do for and with it—in 5 years I will see what I have done for my children—I haven't been doing for them—I've never seen it though, I can do something with my life."

With all this I do not want to say that all planned production in the world is necessarily valuable. We all know that much production is ultimately useless, is of no benefit to humankind, or is even detrimental, and sometimes destructive.

But this is not the point in this present context. The point is the subjective experience of growth of *self-worth* that may be noticed in any previously retiring or passively hostile or lonely, depressed individual. It also can occur in persons with in all sorts of unresolved conflicts, if they can extricate themselves enough to write a poem, compose a song, or cook for once a decent meal, clean their home to their true satisfaction, or even only take the trouble to make themselves presentable and attractive in appearance.

Many of us find one of the saddest expressions of the hippies' devices is their physical appearance and physical being. With it, they demonstrate in the most pronounced way that they don't want to belong.

The wish to belong, on the other hand, is most strongly expressed in the productivity of any person who, even when lonely, does something constructive, particularly if this person shares this product with someone else.

Let me dwell on this a little longer and relate the life history of one of my patients who, after an extremely unhappy, depressed, and chaotic early development found self-worth in his creative work. This, as I said before, did not resolve all of his conflicts and problems, but at least it gave him great satisfaction and the certainty of doing something worthwhile in the world and of being worthwhile through doing it and dedicating himself to it.

The man may be called *Ellery.* He is now 51 years old, the creator and owner of a medium-size electronics factory which at present employs 150 persons.

I want to summarize briefly the experiences and motivations of this man's childhood and adolescence. Here we have:

A small mid-western town, a *mother* raised by an unloving stepmother, who married at 20 a boy of 18, with whom she takes off. A father, jolly, good-natured, earning his living by trucking. *Parental fights,* witnessed by the boy, an only child. He tries to get between the parents and protect mother.

Mother a *rigid* person, *conscientious,* but also *resents* this boy who caused her great suffering in childbirth.

Father probably bored by wife's seriousness and dislike of *sex,* takes off when the boy is five. Mother is left in *bitterness* and great *poverty.*

In Ellery's *emotional dynamics* of these and the following years, we can establish the following trends:

1. *Conflicted* feelings regarding both parents, mixed of *fear, attachment, resentment, protectiveness.* Vague feelings of *guilt,* regarding some coresponsibility for mother's suffering. He is close to no parent.
2. *Humiliation* and feelings of *worthlessness* due to poverty, poor treatment by people. *Incapacitation, isolation* due to much illness and constant moving.
3. *Conforming attitude,* identification with mother's *conscientiousness,* overwhelming feelings of *obligation to her* and indebtedness, instilled by her.

In his adolescence, Ellery feels and said later, when after 37 years he entered psychotherapy, a *deep depression* settled on him, which he could not shake.

Central to it was his feeling of *worthlessness* which had started early, as we saw, and never left him despite later scholastic successes; a feeling of *coresponsibility and guilt* regarding the father's leaving which so many children experience, *grief* about not having a father; *poverty and humiliation;* the mother's harping on his *obligation* toward her, failure in understanding how to integrate himself *socially,* poor beginnings of first *sex* relationships.

He went into *engineering* with a scholarship, his brilliant mind emerging increasingly in high school and college.

But now at about 28, after he had had several jobs, there came a *turning point* in his life, at which I like to pick up his development.

He realized now that *engineering* was only part of his interest, that making *money,* getting *security* for his mother and himself was not enough. Money and security would not help him to feel *worthwhile.* He felt different things were required to make him feel worthwhile. First, he wanted to create something, something that he knew would make him feel more expressive.

This was hanging together with another directive, something completely different which he gradually clarified for himself. Up to this point Ellery's life was about using skills he had learned for the purpose of making money and getting security for himself and his mother, thus fulfilling his obligations to her. *Other people* did not exist as essential parts of his life and his purposes.

The turning point at age 28 had to do with a certain degree of breaking free from the narrowness of his earlier directives and with the awakening to an outlook with far greater perspectives. What he felt vaguely, as he described it to me years later, was that he wanted a greater degree of *personal freedom* than he had in some job as an employee; that he began to feel he could be *creative,* that he was *ambitious,* and that he wanted to involve himself with *people* in a more personal way.

"I am," he said, "fascinated and *intrigued with complexity;* thus came to me the idea of a *business* as a *complex community of interests,* involving things, people, one of *the most total involvements* of physical things and human beings, highly intriguing of how do we do the mechanical grinding-out of products—beneficial, useful things to satisfy people's needs—the presenting of the products interestingly—the creating of the thing—and the relationships with the others who help to produce this and satisfying of the needs of these people—a fascinating intricacy of approaching the problem of monotony and boredom, of repetitive efforts.

I can deal with all this in a most creative way—I am aware of it. I tried to balance the relatedness of it all."

"Of course I knew," he says, "that when founding my business, I was completely inadequate with people, it was mostly the complexity of the enterprise that started me on it."

And this then is the motivation and the beginning of how Ellery decided to start a business of his own.

As an incidental, I like to mention that in the modern research on creativity (Eiduson, Taylor), this interest in complexity has emerged as one of the characteristics of the creative mind.

In terms of my theory of *phases* in my psychology of human life, Ellery had lived all the years from about 12 to 28 with a preliminary goal of life determined by the basic motives of *fear and obligations, special interests*, and the *reaching toward safety*.

Now with the beginning of a definitive self-determination toward a much more comprehensive and complete life goal, he made room for an expansive development of his *creativity* and he envisioned for the first time the working in—a still vaguely conceived of—*community of people*.

While struggling to find a way to realize his new goal, Ellery again met one of the two friends he had made in his college years, who revealed similar ambitions about starting a business of one's own; and since he had a little inheritance, Larry and Ellery started out with a very small workshop for electronics, which in the following twenty years developed into a relatively big business. Apart from their partnership in the matters of production and the development of the business, the two had little in common, in that Larry wanted mostly to become rich and powerful, whereas Ellery—as we heard—had much more complex intentions.

During the first ten years of struggle, Ellery felt bogged under, because there was still the fear of possibly not succeeding in life, there was still the pressure of his mother in the background and the fear of not finding *security*, there was still an inability to relate to people in more than business ways, and there was still no pleasure or happiness.

At 35, he married his secretary, 10 years younger than he, reasonably attractive, ambitious, and probably the initiator of their relationship, but pleasant and able to enjoy herself and seemingly able to bring joy into Ellery's life.

This marriage did not really succeed, partly because *Phyllis* was a rather superficial person who lacked interests as well as social skills, but also because Ellery was at that time still incapable of developing a deeper human relationship, and because the marriage was not based on true love for either of them. Phyllis enjoyed sex and reproached Ellery for his lack of ardor. Ellery was at that time too repressed a person to allow himself a free enjoyment of sex.

Ellery feels that in the years 28 to 37, he and his partner had succeeded in developing a small business to a reasonable degree of success and safety, but that he was completely dissatisfied with his development as a person and with his ability to deal with the people inside and outside his plant in the hoped-for closely cooperative ways.

"I deal with *people* at arms length," he said when at 37 he came into psychotherapy, which he had decided to enter at a meeting where he heard this therapist speak.

He felt he needed help. He was unable to free himself from the oppressive and depressive forces that had dominated his early development and prevented him from living a satisfactory personal life and from relating to people the way he envisioned it.

I think I will stop here, without continuing with the further details of this biography, and I will also skip the details of this interesting as well as painful therapy process which took place over ten years, during which it was interrupted twice by Ellery for long periods, once for a whole year.

I want to get to the point of the *human relationships* that Ellery developed with his employees, parallel with the progress of his own development as a person.

The present setup which Ellery described to me is that of a *"consolidated group"* of all the approximately 150 employees of a factory spread now over 120,000 square feet in four buildings.

In the designing and equipping of the buildings, Ellery's main consideration was for the people working in them. Everybody is important and everybody is included in monthly departmental meetings. Anyone can make complaints to Ellery, but the rule is that this person must also make suggestions for improvements, together with his or her complaint.

In the meetings, everybody may speak. Ellery says: "My own experiences as employee contributed to how I set things up—therapy made me more certain of the value of things I could include—like good warm personal relations, without being condescending. We interrelate at these meetings as human beings."

I ask for an example. He says:

> "Our truck driver is a gossipy old-maid type, he will take 25% facts and supply the rest, but he is still a good driver.
>
> Earlier in my Company, I might have kicked him out. Now I let everybody understand what we do, so nothing is unsaid and so he cannot gossip.
>
> Another man, the warehouse supervisor, is highly accurate talking about *functions*, but regarding *people* he exaggerates and gets emotionally involved. We spoke about that freely in a meeting."

No need to mention that there is employees' participation in gains and all sorts of desirable facilities for them. I speak here mostly of the human relationships which this man created in conjunction wtih a most rewarding production system.

Some time before he had the meetings arranged, he said:

> "I would like to devote most of my time to employee management and strategic planning for our company—it will be my next job in the company, when I have dictated the rest of planning to the computer.

The plant managers are consumed with daily working problems and production, etc.

We could have a fascinatingly close crew there—with feedback and enjoy it, giving people recognition—a relatedness based on something else but society rules—you got to deal with the individuals. I have been so grateful for therapy so often in my life, thank God for it. My enjoyment used to be things and abstracts, they are now way down as compared with people."

This man, in fact, has established in his factory encounter groups, or I feel, even more than that, namely truly human relationship-building groups.

This man himself, however, needed extensive and deep psychotherapy to be able to function with people and to do these things for people.

During the period of his creative work-development, Ellery had also found and established a deep personal love relationship with a divorcee whom he hoped to marry. However, he was still a somewhat inhibited person in the larger context of purely social relationships and gatherings and he did not as yet get involved in enough purely pleasurable activities, such as sports or travel.

He was too strongly dominated by his prevalent creative drive to extend himself sufficiently into other directions.

He knew he was too one-sided and he felt this was wrong. Yet he was not as yet able to allow for self-indulgence even in terms of sufficient recreation and easygoing activities. Planting roses in his garden was about as far as he would go.

I said he felt it was *wrong*. Now what exactly does he mean by that? It, of course, has nothing to do with morally wrongs in the traditional sense of morality. This is a new type of wrongness, which many people experience in themselves when they begin to become aware of themselves as persons.

This "wrongness" feeling comes out of the frame of reference of a new type of morality, namely the feeling for the *appropriateness of being a whole person.*

Appropriateness in whose eyes, according to whose judgment? Strangely enough in the person's own eyes and judgment. This appropriateness is a new concept of a person's being, different from the older concepts of so-called "goodness" and of "adjustment." Goodness which always has to do with unreachable ideals, La Mancha's "unreachable stars" was always a pursuit endangered by hypocrisy at the one end and Don Quixotism at the other end. We are not made to be holy, which does not mean that we could not have ideals somewhere at the distant horizon.

While "goodness" seemed always suspicious, "adjustment" became perfectly invalid in the light of society's blunders, such as the Nazi holocaust, other racial or social injustices, or to international law enforcements such as the Vietnam conflict which many responsible people refuted. "Adjustment" is desirable within the frame of reference of certain circumstances and conditions. It is not a goal of human life.

Many people feel that appropriateness of existence as a human being, as a whole person is something they want to accomplish. They want to live fully, they want to be whole, and they want to do this is a way they experience as right.

And what is this "right"? What is the "right" that *Marie* was searching for when she asked: "Should everyone *want* to be married?" It is the "right" that *Glen*, another young patient of mine, was searching for, when he asked: "Should not the state pay my livelihood and give me a chance to develop my creativity as a painter?" It is the "right" what the previously mentioned *Joe* was searching for, when he felt he should not go just by what his parents said, but should find himself.

The feeling of being now able to live "right" was experienced by *Arlene*, a 31-year-old homosexual and alcoholic patient of mine, when she finished psychotherapy after three years. She summarized in her last group therapy session what she felt about herself. She said:

"I am very much more independent, have the inner freedom I wanted, have a lot of self-worth, am aware of capabilities, while I always thought I was not even of average intelligence. I think now I am, and can get a college degree. I am not very creative and artistic, but am enough so for my yard and house. I am a loving and feeling, sympathetic person, also honest. I like myself now, and life.

On the negative side: I still have a tendency to be rather passive. For the first time in my life, I begin really to think; I want to think things through. Also my drinking is a negative. I have ambivalent feelings: it is not worth it to take a chance—I don't need it to be accepted—but I think about it at times.

My future goals: My relationship with Jenny is very important, and I look forward to a future. It is exciting, what could happen. I feel like reborn."

Now what had happened to this person in therapy?

First, as she says, she acquired an *inner freedom* she had been seeking, she also acquired the feeling of *self-worth* that she never had before. With this came *self-awareness, honesty*, and the certainty of being *loving and feeling*. She was not a very *creative* person, but was enough so to actively enjoy her home and garden and her work with her patients as a nurse. She also gained an outlook into the future which she never had before and she knew what mattered to her.

It did not make her perfect. She still had weaknesses and she felt it was too late to pull out of her homosexual pattern, which I had of course pointed out as unhealthy and as preventing her from developing completeness of life.

But apart from it, she had acquired valuable human characteristics, that because of their *attainability* I consider her representative of the new *image of humans*.

In the pattern that fulfills this image, is important that the person's *need-fulfilling, self-limitingly adaptive* and *creatively expansive tendencies* are *integrated* by an *order upholding self*. This order upholding tendency, which represents the innermost self, tells a person whether he or she is free or unfree, honest or not, and whether as a person he or she holds together. It also lets persons know when they are in *conflict* or *disorganized*.

In looking at life histories of people, we described them in terms of four basic tendencies directed toward fulfillment of life. The four tendencies were: need satisfaction, self-limiting adaptation, creative expansion, and upholding of the internal order. People seem to be most satisfied with themselves when they experience these tendencies as operating in a fair equilibrium and in integration, rather than in conflict or confused disorder.

Most people easily understand what these tendencies are about and can trace them in themselves. This is what I invite you to do with the help of *forms* which we have available for you here.

All in all, in this inner ordering process, persons know whether they live life to their own true satisfaction or not. And toward the end of life, older people whose histories I could not present wthin our limited space, will state whether their lives reached essentially a *fulfillment* or else were *failures*. These statements are sometimes not completely borne out by the facts, as the analyzing clinician may see them. Most people are very eager to feel, when the end is approaching, that they did not live quite in vain and without leaving something of value behind— some loving memory of somebody.

But within our frame of reference, the point is not primarily how many people evaluate their life as a whole objectively and correctly, but the point is that most human beings feel the need to *evaluate* their total existence in terms referring to fulfillment or failure of something; something, whatever it was that they ultimately believed in. Most people want desperately to believe in something, regardless of whether their lives have been ever so *disorganized* or *conflicted* or that they have found *integration* and *peace*.

4

Strategies of Adaptation:
An Attempt
at Systematic Description

ROBERT W. WHITE

At the outset of this inquiry we are confronted by four commonly used words with overlapping claims upon the territory to be discussed. The words are *adaptation*, *mastery*, *coping*, and *defense*. No attempt at systematic description is likely to prosper if these words are left in a state of free competition, jostling for the thinly scattered grains of truth that might nourish their meaning. Their peaceful coexistence requires, as in any well-regulated hen yard, the establishment of some sort of pecking order that everyone observes and fully understands. The first step in this direction is simple: clearly the boss hen is *adaptation*. This is the master concept, the superordinate category, under which the other three words must accept restricted meanings. Descriptions of mastery, of defense, or of coping alone cannot be systematic in any large sense, but they can become part of a system if they are ordered under the heading of *strategies of adaptation*.

PRELUDE ON TERMINOLOGY

The concept of *defense*, to take it first, is an obvious one, signifying response to danger or attack, but it comes to us with a somewhat swollen meaning because of the position it has been given in psychoanalytic theory. Freud's genius as an observer, so apparent in his unveiling of sexual and aggressive inclinations, never burned more brightly than in his perception of what came to be called the *mechanisms of defense:* repression, projection, undoing, and the other devices whereby danger was parried and peace restored in the frightened psyche. Psychoanalytic therapists, following this lead, became expert at scenting anxiety in the free associations of their patients; expert, moreover, at unraveling the ramified operations whereby security was achieved. Presently these operations were seen to have worked over long periods of time, producing such complex results as character armor and the protective organization of personality. Unwary theorists even jumped to the generalization that development was a simple counterpoint between instinc-

28

tual craving and defense. It became necessary after Freud's death for those who called themselves "ego psychologists" to restore explicitly the concept of adaptation and to confine defense to those instances of adaptation in which present danger and anxiety were of central importance.

The concept of *mastery*, perhaps an equally obvious concept, has never enjoyed the same vogue among psychologists. When used at all, it has generally been applied to behavior in which frustrations have been surmounted and adaptive efforts have come to a successful conclusion. The alternatives suggested by the word are not, as with defense, danger and safety, but something more like defeat and victory. This might imply a limiting definition, but in fact the concept of mastery has been used with no sense of limits. The English language, loved by poets for its flexibility, offers only pitfalls to the systematic thinker. There is nothing wrong with saying that danger and anxiety have to be mastered, which allows us to classify defense mechanisms as a form of mastery. It is equally correct to say that efforts at mastery serve as a defense against anxiety, which permits us to consider counteractive struggle a mechanism of defense. If mastery is to be used in any limited technical sense it should probably be confined to problems having a certain cognitive or manipulative complexity, but which at the same time are not heavily freighted with anxiety.

Where does the concept of *coping* stand? We can find out what we mean by it by noticing the kinds of situation chosen for studies of coping behavior. Sometimes these situations represent an acute dislocation of a person's life: serious crippling sickness, the death of close relatives, financial disaster, the necessity to live in a radically new environment. Sometimes the situation is less drastic, but it is still unusual in the subject's life: going to school for the first time, going to visit the child psychologist, or making the transition from high school to college. Nobody has chosen going to school for the sixty-third time as an occasion for coping. The freshman year at college, with all its new experience, clearly qualifies as coping, as does the sophomore year now that we are alert to the possibility of "sophomore slump" and dropping out, but nobody has yet detected any large-scale common problems that would justify choosing the junior year for an investigation of coping behavior. For "when the sea was calm," said Shakespeare, "all boats alike show'd mastership in floating"; only in a storm were they obliged to cope. It is clear that we tend to speak of coping when we have in mind a fairly drastic change or problem that defies familiar ways of behaving, requires the production of new behavior, and very likely gives rise to uncomfortable affects like anxiety, despair, guilt, shame, or grief, the relief of which forms part of the needed adaptation. Coping refers to adaptation under relatively difficult conditions.

This discussion of terms demonstrates the necessity of making *adaptation* the central concept. It may well be that in stressful situations things happen that have no counterpart in easier circumstances, but some of what happens is likely to come straight from the repertoire that is common to all adaptive behavior. There is a sense in which all behavior can be considered an attempt at adaptation. Even in the smoothest and easiest of times behavior will not be adequate in a purely mechanical or habitual way. Every day raises its little problems: what clothes to put on, how to plan a timesaving and step-saving series of errands, how to schedule the hours to get through the day's work, how to manage the cranky child, appease the short-tempered tradesman, and bring the long-winded acquaintance to the end of his communication. It is not advisable to tell a group of college students that they have no problems, nothing to cope with, during the happy and uneventful junior year. They will quickly tell you what it takes to get through that golden year, and as you listen to the frustrations, bewilderments, and sorrows as well as the triumphs and joys you will have a hard time conceptualizing it all as well-adapted reflexes or smoothly running habits. Life is tough, they will tell you, in case you have forgotten; life is a never-ending challenge. Every step of the way demands the solution of problems and every step must therefore be novel and creative, even the putting together of words and sentences to make you understand what it is like to cope with being a college junior.

Adaptation, then, is the only firm platform on which to build a systematic description. What is needed is an ordered account of *strategies of adaptation*, ranging from the simplest ways of dealing with minor problems and frustrations to the most complex fabric of adaptive and defensive devices that has ever been observed from the chair at the head of the psychoanalytic couch. If this can be done, the uses to be made of defense, mastery, and coping can be much more readily decided.

ADAPTATION AS COMPROMISE

There is another preliminary issue that is likely to get in the way if we do not deal with it at the start. Perhaps we can put a little blame on Freud for having started something that often crops up today as an unwitting tendency to think of adaptive behavior in a dichotomy of good and bad. Uncensorious as he was toward the neurotic behavior that circumstance and a repressive society had forced upon the patient, Freud was a stern and moral man who would not call a patient well until all neurotic anxieties were understood, all defense mechanisms abandoned, and all behavior brought under control of the clear-eyed ego that perceives everything exactly as it is. But this heroic prescription was meant to apply only to neurotic anxieties, legacies of childhood that did not correspond to present dangers. The ideal patient, issuing from his analysis cleansed of all anxiety, was really cleansed only of defenses against dangers that no longer existed. So we must attach less blame to the fastidious Freud than to the careless popularizers of mental health wisdom who have communicated the thought, utterly bizarre in one of the most frightening periods of human history, that the mentally healthy person is free from all anxiety and meets life with radiant confidence. Of course we all know better than that when we stop to think, but in the psychological and psychiatric literature there lies a concealed assumption that dangers must be faced because they are not really there, that any delay, avoidance, retreat, or cognitive distortion of reality is in the end a reprehensible piece of cowardice. We must march forward, ever forward, facing our problems, overcoming all obstacles, masters of our fate, fit citizens of the brave new world. Foolish as it is, this unwitting assumption sufficiently pervades our professional literature so that we really do have to stop and think. What are the transactions that actually take place between a person and his environment?

In actuality, of course, there are many situations that can be met only by compromise or even resignation. Events may occur that require us to give in, relinquish things we would have liked, perhaps change direction or restrict the range of our activities. We may have no recourse but to accept a permanent impoverishment of our lives and try to make the best of it. Furthermore, when dangers are real and information incomplete it is in no sense adaptive to march boldly forward. History provides many examples, none better than General Braddock in our own colonial days, who marched his column of British regulars through the forests of Pennsylvania straight into a French and Indian ambush. Described not inappropriately in military metaphors, adaptation often calls for delay, strategic retreat, regrouping of forces, abandoning of untenable positions, seeking fresh intelligence, and deploying new weapons. And just as recuperation from serious illness is not the work of a day, even though in the end it may be completely accomplished, so recovery from a personal loss or disaster requires a long period of internal readjustment that may not be well served at the start by forceful action or total clarity of perception. Sometimes adaptation to a severely frustrating reality is possible only if full recognition of the bitter truth is for a long time postponed.

The element of compromise in adaptive behavior can be well illustrated from that rich storehouse of information provided by Lois Murphy (1962) in her study of young children in Topeka. She describes a number of three-year-olds brought for the first time from their homes to her study center, where the business of the day is to meet a psychologist and engage in some activities that constitute a test of intelligence. Her first two illustrations, boys named Brennie and Donald, present us at once with a striking contrast. Brennie appears to be confidence incarnate. He climbs happily into the car, alertly watches and comments upon the passing scene, charms everyone with his smile, walks into the testing room with perfect poise, accepts each proffered task with eager interest, makes conversation and asks for appropriate help from adults, and finally leaves the scene with a polite expression of thanks. Brennie might be judged a paragon of mental health, and any three-year-old so easy to deal with is certain to be a psychologist's delight. In contrast, the day of Donald's visit is a taxing one for the staff. The child comes accompanied by his mother, described as "warm and ample," and he utters not a word either during the ride, when entering the building, or for some time after he enters the psychologist's office. Invited to sit down, he stands resolutely beside his mother, his feet spread slightly apart. He will string beads only when his mother has done so first, and once embarked on this operation, he refuses to be diverted by the psychologist, who would like to get on with the test. Slowly he warms up enough to dispense with his mother's mediation and deal directly with the psychologist, but the testing still drags because Donald becomes involved in, for instance, building-block constructions of his own instead of those required for the test. The session ends with the assessment far from complete.

It is easy to imagine what Donald's session would look like in the records of a typical guidance agency. He has displayed two highly disquieting symptoms. He has a bad case of separation anxiety, clinging to his mother when he should be facing reality, and he also displays withdrawal and introversion by building with blocks according to his fantasy instead of responding properly to social stimulation. But before we hurry Donald into psychotherapy let us look at the situation from a child's point of view. As adults we know something that he does not know: we know that Mrs. Murphy and her staff are full of kindness and patience and that they will go to great lengths to keep discomfort and anxiety at a minimum. Donald can know only that he is being taken to a strange place for a purpose he cannot fathom. Many children by the age of three have been to the pediatrician's office, to the barber, and perhaps even to the dentist, and they may well have noticed a credibility gap between parental assurances and the discomforts actually experienced during these visits. Now they are being taken to play games with a nice lady—a likely story indeed! If such conditions existed for Donald, he exhibits commendable common sense in sticking close to his mother, the one familiar object, until he can figure out the nature of the racket. It is his good fortune that his principal observer, Mrs. Murphy, understands his position, perceives him not as anxiously dependent but as a "sturdy boy," and appreciates his strategy of adaptation. She says:

Over the years we have seen Donald, this pattern has continued: cautious, deliberate, watchful entrance into a new situation, keeping his distance at first, quietly, firmly maintaining his right to move at his own pace, to make his own choices, to set his own terms, to cooperate when he got ready. These tendencies persisted long after he became able to separate from his mother (1962, p. 32).

And what of the perfectly adjusted Brennie? In reviewing Mrs. Murphy's book, I likened Brennie to a genial cocker spaniel who welcomes friend and burglar with equal joy. He seems to trust everyone without discrimination. This is fine as long as he stays in a highly restricted circle consisting of family, nursery school teachers, and sympathetic psychological researchers, who support him lovingly and demand a minimum amount of compromise. But eventually Brennie is going to find out that life is not a rose garden. Before long he will be entering what Harry Stack Sullivan described as the "juvenile era," a time when crude competition and aggression among peers are only slowly brought under the control of ripening social understanding. He will find that there are adults who do not respect children and may even take advantage of them. In his teens some of his contemporaries will urge him not to trust anyone over thirty. It is easy to project his career line further into the still competitive adult world with the self-seeking, scandals, and rackets that fill the daily newspapers. By that time Brennie may have been badly burned for his innocent credulity and thus learned to be circumspect, but if we compare him with Donald at the age of three, we reach the painful conclusion that it is the cautious Donald who is better adapted to the average expectable human environment.

This is a long introduction to the main task of this paper, but it will not have been wasted if we now start that task with a clear realization of these points: (1) that the described phenomena of coping, mastery, and defense belong in the more general category of strategies of adaptation, as part of the whole tapestry of living; and (2) that adaptation does not mean either a total triumph over the environment or total surrender to it, but rather a striving toward acceptable compromise.

THE TREND TOWARD
INCREASED AUTONOMY

The point of departure for a systematic description of strategies of adaptation should be the broadest possible statement. Let us put it this way: adaptation is something that is done by living systems in interaction with their environments. It is important to emphasize both the noun *systems* and the adjective *living*. Our whole enterprise can founder at the very start if the basic image is allowed to be mechanical rather than organismic. It is characteristic of a system that there is interaction among its various parts, so that changes in one part are likely to have considerable consequences in at least several other parts. A system, furthermore, tends to maintain itself as intact as possible and thus displays more or less extensive rebalancing processes when injured or deformed. This much is true of inanimate systems as well as animate ones, which makes it necessary to qualify the systems under discussion here as *living*. For it is characteristic of living systems that they do something more than maintain themselves. Cannon's historic studies of homeostasis have familiarized us with the remarkable mechanisms whereby animal and human living systems maintain internal steady states, such as body temperature and fluid content, and restore such states when circumstances have forced a temporary departure. But Cannon was well aware that maintaining homeostasis was not the whole story; he saw it as a necessary basis from which living systems could get on with their more important business. This further business consists of growth and reproduction. Living systems do not stay the same size. They grow dramatically larger: the puppy that you once held in your hands becomes the big dog that you can no longer hold in your lap. This increase eventually reaches its limit in any one system, but not until arrangements have been made to start a whole fresh lot of tiny living systems on their way toward maximum growth.

The fundamental property of growth in living systems was well described in 1941 by Andras Angyal. Looking for "the general pattern which the organismic total process follows," Angyal pictured the living system as partially open to the environment and as constantly taking material from the environment to become a functioning part of itself:

It draws incessantly new material from the outside world, transforming alien objects into functional parts of its own. Thus the organism *expands* at the expense of its surroundings. The expansion may be a material one, as in the case of bodily growth, or a psychological one as in the case of the assimilation of experiences which result in mental growth, or a functional one as when one acquires skill, with a resulting increase of efficiency in dealing with the environment (1941, pp. 27–28).

Thus the life process necessarily entails expansion, but Angyal carried the matter further. Living systems, he pointed out, exhibit *autonomy*. They are in part governed from inside, and are thus to a degree resistant to forces that would govern them from the outside. If this were not true, the whole concept of adaptation would be impossible. Angyal then describes the direction of the organismic process as one toward an *increase of autonomy:*

Aggressiveness, combativeness, the urge for mastery, domination, or some equivalent urge or drive or trait is assumed probably by all students of personality. All these various concepts imply that the human being has a characteristic tendency toward self-determination, that is, a tendency to resist external influences and to subordinate the heteronomous forces of the physical and social environment to its own sphere of influence (1941, p. 49).

It was an evil day, we may imagine, for the inanimate world when living systems first broke loose upon it. Conservative boulders doubtless shook their heads and predicted gloomily that if this subversive trend gained strength the day might come when living systems would overrun the earth. And this is indeed exactly what has happened. Most of the land surface is completely buried by living systems, and even the oceans are full of them. When we consider this outrageous imperialism it is small wonder that the expansion of peoples and of nations has been a besetting problem throughout human history. And even when we concentrate on strategies of adaptation, we must keep it in mind that human beings are rarely content with maintaining a personal homeostasis. Unless they are very old they are almost certain to be moving in the direction of increased autonomy. It can be a threat of disastrous proportions to discover in the midst of life that all avenues are blocked to further personal development.

Living creatures, in short, will constantly strive for an adaptive compromise that not only preserves them as they are, but also permits them to grow, to increase both their size and their autonomy. Consider an animal as it steps forth in the morning from where it has been sleeping and moves into its daytime environment. If all goes well, it will ingest a portion of that environment, maintain its visceral integrity by homeostatic processes and by eliminating waste material, add a tiny increment to its size, explore a little and thus process some fresh information about its environment, gain a bit in muscular strength and coordination, bask in the warm sunshine, and return at night to its den a little bigger, a little wiser, a little stronger, and a little more contented than it was in the morning. If the season is right, it may also have found an opportunity to set those processes in motion whereby a number of offspring will come into existence. A day like this can be described as one of maximum animal self-actualization. If all does not go well, the animal may return to the den hungry, cold, perhaps battered and bruised, yet still essentially intact as a living system, capable of recuperating during the night and setting forth again in the morning. Of course, it may have failed to keep itself intact or even alive, but we can be sure disaster occurred only because the animal's adaptive repertoire, employed with the utmost vigor, has not been equal to the circumstances. Animals try to go up; if they go down, they go down fighting.

SOME VARIABLES
OF ADAPTIVE BEHAVIOR

The adaptive capacities of any species of animal are to some extent represented in bodily structure, the product of natural selection. Protective coloring, great weight and strength, or such features as the rabbit's powerful hind legs that enable it to make bewildering hairpin turns in the course of its flight are part of the inherited equipment that favor certain styles of adapting. When we speak of strategies of adaptation, however, we are referring more particularly to the realm of behavior, the realm that is directly controlled by the nervous system and that is in various degrees open to learning through experience. This realm is traditionally broken down into receptive processes, central storage and organizing processes, and motor processes that lead to further sensory input. In the case of animals, whose inner experience, whatever its nature, remains forever closed to us, strategies of adaptation have to be described in behavioral language. They have to be described in terms of what can go on in a behavioral system of receptors, central structures, and effectors, not overlooking, of course, the contributions of the autonomic nervous system and the input of information from inside the body. How can we best describe the possibilities of adaptive control and regulation in an animal's behavioral system?

We could start with a flourish of analytic logic by talking sequentially about regulation in the sensory, the central, and the motor spheres. But this is a dangerous piece of abstraction; in actuality the whole thing operates not as a sequence but as a system. What happens when we surprise a squirrel feeding on the ground? There is a whisk of tail and before we know it, the animal has darted up a tree and is sitting on a branch chattering angrily at us. You might judge from a carelessly written mental health tract that the squirrel's behavior was neurotic and deplorable, inasmuch as it retreated instead of facing reality. But the squirrel is facing reality all right; it has simply elected to face it from a position of strength rather than from one of weakness. When you are on the cluttered ground and a huge creature is approaching, fear and flight are adaptive. When the cognitive field has thus been changed so that you are above the huge creature and have at your disposal all the escape routes provided by the branches of a tree, it is adaptive to sit down, be angry, and try the power of scolding. The squirrel has regulated the cognitive field, but has done so in large part by motor activity, and this is surely typical of adaptive strategies in the animal world.

Because the living animal is a system, adaptive behavior entails managing several different things at once. The repertoire by which this management is carried out can be conceptualized at this point in terms of action. One possibility is simply orientation with a minimum of locomotion. When locomotion is employed, it can consist of approach, avoidance while still observing the object of interest, or flight, and a final option is the complete immobility of hiding. Those are the possibilities stated in the most general terms. In order to behave adaptively the animal must use this repertoire to produce what prove to be, even in simple instances, fairly complex results. It seems to me that there are at least three variables that are regularly involved in the process, three aspects of the total situation no one of which can be neglected without great risk. If the animal is to conduct a successful transaction with the environment, perhaps leading to enhancement and growth, but in any event not resulting in injury or destruction, it must (1) keep securing adequate information about the environment, (2) maintain satisfactory internal conditions both for action and for processing information, and (3) maintain its autonomy or freedom of movement, freedom to use its repertoire in a flexible fashion.

I shall enlarge upon these three variables in a moment, but let us first place them in concrete form in order to secure the point that they must all be managed as well as possible at the same time. When a cat hears a strange noise in a nearby thicket, locomotion stops, eyes and ears are pointed in the direction of sound, and the animal's whole being seems concentrated on obtaining cognitive clarity. But if this were the only consideration, the cat might now be expected to move straight into the thicket to see what is there; instead, it explores very slowly and with much circumspection, for it is combining the third variable with the first, maintaining a freedom of movement that would be lost in the thicket. If the noise turns out to have come from a strange cat intruding on the territory, and there ensues a battle of vocal and hair-raising threats leading to an exchange of blows, the second variable becomes decisive. We know from the work of the ecologists that animal battles rarely go on to the death. The animal that sustains injury, feels incompetent, or is slowed by fatigue, shifts its tactics from approach to flight, and wisely lives to fight another day. This result is more probable if the first and third variables have been sufficiently heeded so that the animal is not cornered and has kept escape routes open.

Information

Securing adequate information about the environment is an obvious necessity for adaptive behavior. Action can be carried on most successfully when the amount of information to be processed is neither too small nor too great. If the channels are underloaded, there will be no way to decide what to do, as we would express it in adult conscious experience. If the channels are overloaded, there will again be no way to decide what to do, this time because the number of possibilities creates confusion. Of course this is not just a quantitative matter; what really counts is the meaning of the information in terms of potential benefits and harms. With this modification, however, it is permissible to use a quantitative metaphor and say that there is a certain rate of information input that is conducive to unconfused, straightforward action, and that both higher rates and lower rates will tend, though for different reasons, to make action difficult. Adaptive behavior requires that the cognitive field have the right amount of information to serve as a guide to action. Depending on circumstances, then, adaptation may take the form either of seeking more information or of trying to cut down on the existing input. The cautiously exploring cat illustrates the former process, behaving as though it asked the question, "What is it?" But if the same cat is in the nursery and is exposed to the affection and curiosity of several children, it will try to get away from some of the overwhelming input and might be imagined to ask, "What is all this, anyway?"

Departure in either direction from the preferred level of information is illustrated in Murphy's descriptions of the Topeka three-year-olds. There is likely to be a shortage of information before the children arrive at the testing center, and this is not easily dispelled by adult explanations. Once they have arrived, however, the children are flooded by an input that, because of its newness, they cannot easily put in order. There is a new room, a psychologist, an observer, and a collection of more or less unfamiliar materials. We have already seen how the sturdy Donald dealt with this situation, standing close to his mother, surveying the scene with alert eyes, and consenting to take action only when he had structured the cognitive field sufficiently to isolate an activity he felt competent to undertake. Another of Murphy's procedures was to have groups of children come to her home for a party, a situation quite new, strange, and bewildering to them and possibly a little odd even to adult eyes, inasmuch as each child had an observer assigned to keep account of everything he did. Donald faced this situation with his characteristic determination to get the cognitive field straight. After a long silent survey, he discriminated a zone of likely competence in the toys in the garage and went there to examine them. Later, he picked out a safe entry into the social scene and ended the afternoon in fairly active participation. In this he was more daring than another boy who found his first manageable zone to be building blocks in a corner of the garage and stayed with it the whole afternoon.

Internal Organization

Working on the cognitive field alone will not guarantee adaptive behavior if the internal organization of the system gets too far out of balance. This is crudely obvious if an animal is injured in a fight, weakened by loss of blood, or exhausted in a long struggle. It is clear also in the lowered alertness, curiosity, and effort of children who are feeling sick. Even in young children it is possible to detect another form of internal disorganization that can seriously hamper adaptive behavior: the disorganization produced by strong unpleasant affects such as anxiety, grief, or shame. Some of the Topeka children confronted their first session with the psychologist with a degree of emotion that made it difficult for them to make use of the available information. One little girl, for instance, became tearful and inert, as if drained of energy. When able to try the tasks at all, she could scarcely muster enough force to attend, handle objects, or speak above a whisper, and her most characteristic movement was to push the materials gently away. The inhibition vanished magically when she started for home. A normally active boy showed the paralyzing effect of anxiety first by keeping close to his mother, avoiding contact with examiner and test materials, and then by tentative work on the tasks with quick giving up in the face of difficulties. He was able by these tactics to control the anxiety and work up to an active part in the testing. As his internal organization came back to its usual balance, he spoke more loudly, moved more vigorously, explored the materials more boldly, initiated conversation, and became increasingly master of the situation.

Autonomy

Even if the internal organization is in good balance and the cognitive field is being dealt with competently, adaptive behavior may come to grief if freedom of action is not to some extent maintained. Animals, we may suppose, often enough get trapped in situations from which they cannot escape, but to a remarkable extent they seem to avoid this mishap, as if they were constantly monitored by a small built-in superego reminding them to keep their escape routes open. Once when I kept hens, I was worried to see a large hawk circling high above the yard, but my neighbor reassured me that a hawk would go without its dinner rather than drop down into a narrow, high-fenced pen that might hamper its return to the realms of safe soaring; and, sure enough, no hens were taken. Preserving space in which to maneuver is always an important consideration in strategy.

Among the Topeka children Donald again comes to mind as one who kept initiative in his own hands by refusing to be drawn into situations until he had given them a thorough scrutiny. Tactics of delay and refusals to participate, frustrating as they may be to the psychologist and thus all too readily given a derogatory tag like "anxious avoidance" and "withdrawal," may actually be in the highest tradition of adaptive behavior, following the adage to "look before you leap." Especially adept at maintaining autonomy was a girl named Sheila, not quite three, who after looking at the test materials announced that she did not want to watch them and instead would play with the toys on the floor. There was no sign of anxiety, and very quickly she involved the examiner in her game with the toys. Momentarily intrigued by a performance test set up before her, Sheila began to play with it, but when gently pressed to follow the examiner's rules rather than her own, she returned to the floor, announcing, "I want to do *this*. We don't like the game we had." Murphy comments as follows:

Here we see a child who in the face of continuing and skillfully applied adult pressures maintained her own autonomy. And it was not merely a matter of refusing and rejecting; it was a matter of doing this without allowing the pressures to depress her mood or to restrict her freedom of movement. Instead, during most of the time, the pressures served to stimulate her to her own best efforts in structuring the situation and obtaining enjoyment from it and from the relationship with the adult (1962, p. 82).

In adult life, Sheila possibly will become one of those who regard psychological tests as an invasion of privacy, and we should hesitate to criticize her for this because it may be part of a courageous career in the cause of civil rights.

Adaptive behavior, in short, involves the simultaneous management of at least three variables: securing adequate information, maintaining satisfactory internal conditions, and keeping up some degree of autonomy. Whatever the specific nature of the problem may be, those other considerations can never be safely neglected. But if we think in these terms, it becomes clear that strategies of adaptation typically have a considerable development over time. The temporal dimension is of the utmost importance for our problem.

THE TIME DIMENSION
IN ADAPTIVE BEHAVIOR

I doubt if any serious student of behavior has thought about the adaptive process without considering it to be extended over time. Yet it seems to me quite common in clinical assessments to look for samples of such behavior, for instance the client's initial reaction to the examiner or the way inkblots are dealt with on first meeting, and then jump to the generalization that these are the client's characteristic ways of meeting his problems. Undoubtedly this is one of the reasons for the well-known fact that psychological assessments based on tests picture everyone, even the healthiest, as a clinical case needing some kind of improvement. The client's characteristic ways of meeting a problem the first time may not be how he meets them the second and third times, still less the twentieth time. On their first visits to the study center Donald and Sheila would not have been recorded as secure children; in neither case could the psychologist come anywhere near to completing the examination. Fortunately, they were studied over a long period of time, and we know that both are strong sturdy specimens of humanity with sense enough to take their own time and deal with things in their own way. Strategy is not created on the instant. It develops over time and is progressively modified in the course of time.

If illustration of this principle were needed, the Topeka children could again furnish us with vivid examples. There is the little girl at the party, physically slowed by a slight orthopedic defect, who at the outset cannot manage the jumping board even with help, and at the end jumps joyfully entirely by herself. There are the two sisters, age five and three, who have to accommodate themselves to the awesome prospect of moving to another city. Their strategies are traced through the months of anticipation and preparation, through the move itself, and through the first few weeks of finding security and satisfactions in the new environment (Murphy 1962, pp. 69–75, 168–170, 178–185). But if we think in terms of the three variables just discussed, the importance of the time dimension becomes self-evident. The values of the variables are not likely to stay long unchanged. Perhaps clearer cognition will reveal danger, increase fear, and precipitate flight, but a good many of the situations encountered by children are simply new. There is, of course, always a little risk in newness, so what is required is a cautious approach allowing time to assess both the risk and the possibility of benefits. The input of information may lead to sharper discrimination of the field, discovery of areas of likely competence and enjoyment, quieting of disturbing affects in favor of pleasurable excitement, and a lowering of the premium on maintaining strict autonomy. All such rebalancing of the variables implies processes of learning extended over time. A profitable familiarity with the cognitive field can be gained simply by protracted inspection with no motor involvement beyond moving the eyes and head. Closer familiarity requires the making of behavioral tests, discovering one's competence to deal with promising portions of the environment. There are great individual differences among children in the speed and apparent ease with which they deal with the newness of the world around them. Considering the many and varied adaptations that have to be made, we should not hastily conclude that the quickest strategies are necessarily the best.

HUMAN COMPLICATIONS
OF THE ADAPTIVE PROCESS

Up to this point we have described strategies of adaptation almost wholly in behavioral terms. Illustrations have been confined to the behavior of animals and quite young children. The purpose of this maneuver has been to lay down a descriptive framework—one might say, a sort of biological grid—upon which to place the vastly more extensive strategies available to human adults. The human brain makes possible a transcendence of the immediate present that we do not suppose to exist in even the most intelligent subhuman primates. This is partly a matter of language and communication. As Alfred Kroeber memorably expressed it:

A bird's chirp, a lion's roar, a horse's scream, a man's moan express subjective conditions; they do not convey objective information. By objective information, we mean what is communicated in such statements as: "There are trees over the hill," "There is a single tree," "There are only bushes," "There were trees but are no longer," "If there are trees, he may be hiding in them," "Trees can be burned," and millions of others. All postinfantile, nondefective human beings can make and constantly do make such statements, though they may make them with quite different sounds according to what speech custom they happen to follow. But no subhuman animal makes *any* such statements. All the indications are that no subhuman animal even has any impulse to utter or convey such information (1948, p. 41).

The result of this capacity to talk about and think about things that are not immediately present is in the end an immense extension of the human horizon. Asch describes this in the following words:

Men live in a field that extends into a distant past and into a far future; the past and the future are to them present realities to which they must constantly orient themselves; they think in terms of days, seasons, and epochs, of good and bad times. . . . Because they can look forward and backward and perceive causal relations, because they can anticipate the consequences of their actions in the future and view their relation to the past, their immediate needs exist in a field of other needs, present and future. Because they consciously relate the past with the future, they are capable of representing their goals to themselves, to aspire to fulfill them, to test them in imagination, and to plan their steps with a purpose.

An integral part of man's extended horizon is the kind of object he becomes to himself. In the same way that he apprehends differentiated objects and their properties he becomes aware of himself as an individual with a specific character and fate; he becomes *self*-conscious. . . . Because he is conscious of himself and capable of reflecting on his experiences, he also takes up an attitude to himself and takes measures to control his own actions and tendencies. The consequence of having a self is that he takes his stand in the world as a person (1952, pp. 120–122).

It is in this vastly expanded world of experience that human beings must devise their strategies of adaptation.

One's first thought may be that the ensuing complexities are certain to drown us. I believe, however, that we stand to gain by fitting human strategies as far as possible into the three behavioral variables deduced from animals and young children. Take first the second variable, the maintaining, and if possible the enhancing, of the system's internal organization. It is here that awareness of the remote, the past, and the future, and especially awareness of oneself as a person, most dramatically expand the meaning of the variable. Clearly there is much more to be maintained than bodily integrity and control over disruptive affects. One thing that must be enhanced if possible, and desperately maintained if necessary, is the level of self-esteem. In part this shows itself as a struggle to keep intact a satisfactory self-picture, in part as attempts to preserve a sense of competence, an inner assurance that one can do the things necessary for a satisfactory life. Wide are the ramifications of keeping up one's self-esteem. Almost any situation that is not completely familiar, even casual and superficial contacts with new people, even discussing the day's news, can touch off internal questions like, "What sort of impression am I making?" "How well am I dealing with this?" "What kind of a person am I showing myself to be?" When self-esteem is tender or when the situation is strongly challenging, such questions, even if only vaguely felt, can lead to anxiety, shame, or guilt with their threat of further disorganization. No adaptive strategy that is careless of the level of self-esteem is likely to be any good. We certainly regard it as rare, unusually mature, and uncommonly heroic when after an unfortunate happening that diminishes his importance or shows him to be wrong, a person quietly lowers his estimate of himself without making excuses or seeking to lodge the blame elsewhere.

Less dramatic but still important are the expanded meanings of the other two variables. Securing adequate information is no longer confined to the immediate cognitive field. Information about things absent assumes increasing significance, especially when it bears on courses of action that extend into the future. Resources for information are also much richer: other people can be asked, relevant reading matter can be sought, and in some cases it is possible to send friends, employees, or students out to increase the scope of one's informational net. The maintaining of autonomy similarly gains a future dimension and a wider meaning. Looking ahead into the future and frequently making plans of one kind or another, we soon learn to be at least somewhat careful about committing ourselves. We feel better if things can be left a little open, if there are options; if, for example, in taking a job we see room for varying its duties or believe that in any event it will be a good springboard toward other jobs. "If I take this job," so many have asked themselves, "with its demands for teaching or medical service, will I have time for my own research?" Preserving an acceptable level of freedom of movement continues to be an important consideration even when the present physical field of the exploring animal has expanded into the imagined future social field of the human adult.

REFERENCES

Angyal, A. *Foundations for a science of personality.* New York: The Commonwealth Fund, 1941.

Asch, S. E. *Social psychology.* Englewood Cliffs, N.J.: Prentice-Hall, 1952.

Freud, A. *The ego and the mechanisms of defence.* London: Hogarth Press, 1937.

Hamburg, D. A., and Adams, J. E. A perspective on coping behavior: Seeking and utilizing information in major transitions. *Archives of General Psychiatry,* 1967, *17,* 277–284.

Kroeber, A. *Anthropology.* Rev. ed. New York: Harcourt, Brace & World, 1948.

Kroeber, T. C. The coping functions of the ego mechanisms. In R. W. White, ed., *The study of lives.* New York: Atherton Press, 1963.

Leventhal, H., Watts, J. C., and Pagano, F. Effects of fear and instructions on how to cope with danger. *Journal of Personality and Social Psychology,* 1967, *6,* 313–321.

Lindemann, E. Symptomatology and management of acute grief. *American Journal of Psychiatry,* 1944, *101,* 141–148.

Murphy, L. B. *The widening world of childhood: Paths toward mastery.* New York: Basic Books, 1962.

Silber, E., Hamburg, D. A., Coelho, G. V., Murphey, E. B., Rosenberg, M., and Pearlin, L. D. Adaptive behavior in competent adolescents: Coping with the anticipation of college. *Archives of General Psychiatry,* 1961, *5,* 354–365.

5

Adult Personality:

Toward a Psychology of the Life-Cycle

by Bernice L. Neugarten

A psychology of the human life-cycle has been slow in making its appearance. From one point of view, biological and sociological perspectives have not yet been integrated into an overarching theory of human behavior, nor have they been combined even in describing a meaningful context against which to view psychological change over the life-cycle. From a different point of view, the primary problem is that we lack a developmental psychology of adulthood in the sense that we have a developmental psychology of childhood. Because the term "development" has been used with such a wide variety of philosophical as well as scientific meanings, it will be strategic for purposes of the present discussion to avoid the awkward juxtaposition of the terms, "adult" and "development," and to speak of the need for a psychology of adulthood in which investigators are concerned with the orderly and sequential changes that occur with the passage of time as individuals move from adolescence through adulthood and old age, with issues of consistency and change in personality over relatively long intervals of time, and with issues of antecedent-consequent relationships.

Using this definition, the field of adult psychology and adult personality remains an underpopulated one among psychologists. The effect has been, to speak metaphorically,

that as psychologists seated under the same circus tent, some of us who are child psychologists remain seated too close to the entrance and are missing much of the action that is going on in the main ring. Others of us who are gerontologists remain seated too close to the exit. Both groups are missing a view of the whole show.

One of our problems lies in the fact that we are as yet without sufficient systematic data on adults. A few sets of data have been reported in which individuals have been studied from childhood into adulthood (Havighurst et al., 1962; Hess, 1962; Honzik and McFarlane, 1966; Kagan and Moss, 1962); but these studies are few in number, and despite the growing recognition of the importance of longitudinal research, there have been as yet no major longitudinal studies of men and women as they move from youth to middle age, or from middle age to old age. There have been even few carefully designed and well-controlled cross-sectional studies of adult personality in which age differences, to say nothing of age *changes*, have constituted a central axis of investigation (Kuhlen, 1964).

Not only is there a paucity of data, but more important we are without a useful theory. Personality theorists have not for the most part faced the questions of stability and change over the entire life-cycle. Attention has been focussed primarily upon the first two but not on the last five sevenths of life. Although Erikson's formulation of the stages of ego development is a notable exception (Erikson,

Adapted from a paper presented at meetings of the American Psychological Association, New York, September, 1966.

1950); and although Jung (1933); Buhler (1933, 1935, 1962); Fromm (1941); Maslow (1954); Peck (1955); and White (1963) have made important contributions, there is no integrated body of theory that encompasses the total life span.

At the same time we are aware that changes in personality occur in adulthood and that the personality is by no means fixed once the organism becomes biologically mature (Worchel and Byrne, 1964). There is evidence on all sides: the changes that occur in adults undergoing psychotherapy or religious conversions or brain-washings, or who live in concentration camps or prisons or ghettos or institutions for the aged. Nor need we look to such extreme situations. We are impressed with—although so far as I know, no one has yet systematically studied—the changes in personality that accompany motherhood in young women, for example, or that accompany career success in middleaged men.

To the psychologist, of course, like to any other scientist, much more is known than can be easily demonstrated. Confronted with the need to produce systematic evidence, the investigator who turns his attention to the study of adult personality is faced, first, with the problem of delineating those personality processes that are the most salient at successive periods in adulthood; then with the problem of describing those processes in terms that are appropriate; then to distinguish those changes that relate to increasing age from those that relate, say, to illness on the one hand or to social and cultural change, on the other; then—and only then—to interpret his findings in light of the question: Which of these processes and changes are orderly and sequential, and which are not? At the same time, because theory and observation must proceed simultaneously, he must always be concerned with the construction of a body of theory that will help account for his findings.

The present paper is addressed primarily to conceptual problems in relating childhood to adulthood, and in relating biological to social pacemakers of change in personality. In this connection we shall turn attention, first, to the delineation of salient issues in adult personality and the types of personality change that are measurable in middle-aged and old adults, mainly to illustrate some of the conceptual problems involved in predicating continuity or discontinuity over the life-cycle. Second, in describing an age-status system as one of the social contexts for viewing time-related changes, we shall comment upon the presence of social as well as biological time clocks.

I. The Salient Issues in Adulthood

First, with regard to the delineation of the salient issues. The criticism is sometimes made that psychologists focus on different phenomena and make use of different explanatory concepts for studying different age levels; and that they sometimes seem to regard children, adolescents, adults, and old people as members of different species. One implication is that if we were fortunate enough to have longitudinal data, the life span could be seen in more continuous and more meaningful terms and antecedent-consequent relations could more readily be investigated.

While this may be true, it is also true that longitudinal studies have thus far had a child-centered or what might be called a "childomorphic" orientation. The variables selected for study have been those particularly salient in childhood; or else those measured retrospectively from the data gathered when the subjects were children. In either instance, the investigator is confined to data and to concepts which may be only of secondary relevance when he attempts to explain the varieties or sequences in adult behavior. In this respect there are countless studies in the child-development literature that deal with dependence, aggression, cognition, the fate of the Oedipal—personality issues which, when projected into adulthood, lose much of their compelling quality.[1]

What, then, are the salient issues of adulthood? At one level of generality, it might be said that they are issues which relate to the individual's use of experience; his structuring of the social world in which he lives; his perspectives of time; the ways in which he deals with the major life themes of work, love, time, and death; the changes in self-concept and changes in identity as he faces the successive contingencies of marriage, parenthood, career advancement and decline, retirement, widowhood, illness, and personal death.[2]

To be more specific: One of our studies is based on lengthy interviews with 100 men and women aged 45 to 55, selected because they have been visibly successful in career or in civic participation. In this study, we moved

[1] Perhaps this point can be made more clearly and with less controversy if we move outside the area usually delineated as personality. A recent review of research on the relationship between college grades and adult achievement is summarized by the author's statement that "present evidence strongly suggests that college grades bear little or no relationship to any measures of adult accomplishment." (Hoyt, 1965)

It is widely acknowledged that school grades are a salient issue to the child or adolescent himself; and at the same time, they are important to the psychologist as an index of the child's intellectual progress and of his success in relating to the adult world. It is known also that school grades are excellent predictors of later school and college grades; furthermore, that there is a close relationship between grades and measures of intelligence in children. Finally, knowledge of the distribution of intelligence test scores and of school grades in large populations of children has led to constant modifications in our theories of the nature and growth of intelligence.

Yet when we move to adulthood, these relationships and the interpretations to be drawn from them become relatively useless. We cannot predict from school to later achievement; indeed, we have no well-established criterion of adult achievement. Next, lacking a criterion by which to standardize a test, we have no test of intelligence that will help us—except in the grossest sense—to predict adult accomplishment. Finally, of course, we have no theory of adult intelligence that is useful, in this sense, beyond the very first steps in the work career, namely *selection* of occupation.

We are even worse off when we come back to the field of personality and when we attempt to apply what we think we know about children to what we would like to know about adults.

[2] In commenting upon some of these problems I am drawing upon a set of studies that I and various of my colleagues have been carrying out in the Committee on Human Development at the University of Chicago over the past decade—studies of personality, of adaptational patterns, of career lines, of age-norms and age-appropriate behaviors in adults, and of attitudes and values across generational lines. Many of these studies have been reported earlier; some are just now being completed. While this line of inquiry does not involve longitudinal research on the same subjects (except for one group of 200 older persons who were followed over a 7-year period), it represents a related set of investigations in which the total number of adults who have participated now totals something over 2,000. Each study is based upon a relatively large sample of normal people, none of whom were volunteers. In some of the studies, samples have been drawn by probability techniques from the metropolitan community of Kansas City; in other instances, quota samples have been drawn from the metropolitan area of Chicago.

toward more and more naturalistic-phenomenological type data as we listened to what our subjects were saying and as we encouraged their introspection. As a result, we have delineated certain issues that seem to be typical of middle adulthood and which, if they appear at all, take quite different form in younger or older persons.

There is, for instance, the middle-ager's sensitivity to the self as the instrument by which to reach his goals—his sense of "self-utilization" as contrasted to the "self-consciousness" of the adolescent.

There is the shift in body cathexis and its relations to the self-concept. "Body-monitoring" is the term we use to encompass the large variety of protective strategies described by middle-aged people as techniques for maintaining the body at given levels of performance and in combatting the new sense of physical vulnerability. . . .

There is the striking change in time-perspective. Middle-aged adults restructure time in terms of time-left-to-live rather than time-since-birth. . . . They personalize death. . . . There is, also, in middle age, a "rehearsal for widowhood," which is more characteristic of women than of men, and an elaboration of the parenting-sponsoring theme, with regard to young associates as well as with regard to one's children. What we have called the "creation of social as well as biological heirs" appears to be the manifestation of what Erikson calls "generativity". . . .

There is the heightened self-understanding that comes to the middle-aged person from observing the aging parent, on the one hand, and the young adult child, on the other. One perceptive woman described it in these terms: "It is as if I'm looking at a three-way mirror. In one mirror I see part of myself in my mother who is growing old, and part of her in me. In the other mirror, I see part of myself in my daughter. I have had some dramatic insights, just from looking in those mirrors. . . . It is a set of revelations that I suppose can only come when you are in the middle of three generations."

There is the sense of expertise that accompanies middle-adulthood. One man said, "I believe in making decisions. . . . They may appear to others to be snap decisions, for I make them quickly and I don't look back and worry about what might have been if it had been done another way. I've had enough experience of my type. . . . I've been through it fifty times, so when I make decisions that seem to come out of the clear blue sky, they just represent a lot of experience. I've been over the ground before and I have the ready answer. . . ."

> There is also the sense that accomplishment is not only appropriate but is to be expected. Those who fail to achieve recognition have failed not to achieve the *extra*ordinary, but merely the ordinary. As one 45-year-old put it, "Middle age is when you're not really considered young anymore, by anyone. It's considered special when recognition and reward are given to the young businessmen, those in their 20s or 30's. But anybody who makes it after 40—well, that's expected. He's no long the young genius; he's just done what is par for the course . . ."

In pondering the data on these highly articulate men and women, we have been impressed (as with the findings from some of the earlier studies in this series) with the central importance of what might be called the executive processes of personality: self-awareness, selectivity, manipulation and control of the environment, mastery, competence, the wide array of cognitive strategies.

We are impressed, too, with the heightened importance of introspection in the mental life of middle-aged persons: the stock-taking, the increased reflection, and above all, the structuring and restructuring of experience—that is, the processing of new information in the light of experience; the use of this knowledge and expertise for the achievement of desired ends; the handing over to others or guarding for oneself the fruits of one's experience.[3]

It is perhaps evident that these psychological issues are ones to which the investigator comes unprepared, as it were, from his studies of children and adolescents. It is perhaps evident also why it is that to psychologists of adulthood most of the existing personality theories seem inadequate. Neither psychoanalytic theory nor learning theory nor social-role theory are sufficiently embracing of the data. Where, except perhaps to certain ego-psychologists who use terms such as "competence," "self," and "effectance," can we look for concepts to describe the incredible complexity shown in the behavior of a business executive, age 50, who makes a thousand decisions in the course of a day? What terms shall we use to describe the strategies with which such a person manages his time, buffers himself from certain stimuli, makes elaborate plans and schedules, sheds some of his "load" by delegating some tasks to other people over whom he has certain forms of control, accepts other tasks as being singularly appropriate to his own competencies and responsibilities, and in the same 24-hour period, succeeds in satisfying his emotional and sexual and aesthetic needs?

It is the incongruity between existing psychological concepts and theories, on the one hand, and the transactions that constitute everyday adult behavior, on the other, to which I am drawing attention.

II. Changes in Personality in the Second Half of Life

Although chance and consistency in adult personality is a problem area which has thus far attracted relatively few psychologists, evidence is nevertheless beginning to accumulate that systematic and measurable changes occur in the second half of life. While the series of studies carried out at Chicago have not been longitudinal, we have begun to delineate processes of change that are characteristic of individuals as they move from middle to old age (Neugarten, et al., 1964).

> As already implied, the middle years of life—probably the decade of the fifties for most persons—represent an important turning point, with the restructuring of time and the formulation of new perceptions of self, time,

[3] If confronted with the question of whether or not there are any "inherent" or "inevitable" changes in personality that accompany adulthood, there is at least one that would come at once to mind: the conscious awareness of past experience in shaping one's behavior. Psychologists are accustomed to the idea that experience is registered in the living organism over time; and that behavior is affected accordingly. But in the case of the human organism, it is not merely that experience is recorded; it is that the *awareness* of that experience becomes increasingly dominant.

and death. It is in this period of the life line that introspection seems to increase noticeably and contemplation and reflection and self-evaluation become characteristic forms of mental life. The reflection of middle-age is not the same as the reminiscence of old age; but perhaps it is its forerunner.

Significant and consistent age differences are found in both working class and middle class people in the perceptions of the self vis-à-vis the external environment and in coping with impulse life. Forty-year-olds, for example, seem to see the environment as one that rewards boldness and risk-taking and to see themselves as possessing energy congruent with the opportunities perceived in the outer world. Sixty-year-olds, however, perceive the world as complex and dangerous, no longer to be reformed in line with one's wishes; and the individual, as conforming and accommodating to outer-world demands.

Important differences exist between men and women as they age. Men seem to become more receptive to affiliative and nurturant promptings; women, more responsive toward and less guilty about aggressive and egocentric impulses. Men appear to cope with the environment in increasingly abstract and cognitive terms; women, in increasingly affective and expressive terms. In both sexes older people move toward more egocentric, self-preoccupied positions and to attend increasingly to the control and satisfaction of personal needs.

With increasing old age, ego functions are turned inward, as it were. With the change from active to passive modes of mastering the environment, there is also a movement of energy away from an outer-world to an inner-world orientation.[4]

Whether or not this increased "interiority" has inherent as well as reactive qualities cannot yet be established. It may be that in advanced old age, biologically-based factors become the pace-makers of personality changes; but this is a question which awaits further disentangling of the effects of illness from the effects of aging, effects which are presently confounded in most older persons who are the subjects of psychological research.

Another important finding in this series of studies is that, in the age-range 50 to 80, and in relatively healthy individuals, age does not emerge as a major variable in the goal-directed, purposive qualities of personality. In other words, while consistent age differences occur in covert processes (those not readily available to awareness or to conscious control and which have no direct expression in overt social behavior); they do *not* appear on those variables which reflect attempted control of the self and of the life situation.[5] Age-related changes appear earlier and more consistently, then, in the internal than in the external aspects of personality.

Nor is this all the evidence that exists of dynamic

[4] To this increased "interiority" of personality, we once gave the term psychological "disengagement," a term that accurately reflects the quality of some of these processes. The term has since become associated, in the field of gerontology, with issues of social role behavior, optimum patterns of aging, and even with the value systems of investigators as well as social policy makers who are concerned with the position of the aged in American society. Because the word has now taken on such a wide variety of meanings I prefer now to substitute the phrase "increased interiority of the personality."

[5] This differentiation reminds us of Brewster Smith's two personality subsystems—one which he has called adaptive or "external"; the other, the internal (Smith, 1959).

changes in personality in the second half of the life span. Lieberman, for instance, following a somewhat different line of inquiry, has found measurable changes in psychological functioning at the very end of life; changes which seem to be independent of illness and which seem to be timed, not by chronological age or distance from birth, but by distance from death (Lieberman, 1965). Similarly, Butler posits the universal occurrence in old people of an inner experience that he calls the life-review; a process that perhaps accounts for the increased reminiscence of the aged and which often leads to dramatic changes in personality (Butler, 1963).

It might be pointed out, parenthetically, that awareness of approaching death should perhaps not be viewed as a signal for the dissolution of the personality structure, but instead as the impetus for a new and final restructuring; an event that calls for a major readaptation, and which leads, in some individuals, to constructive, and in others, to destructive reorientations.

There is at least some evidence, then, that personality change can occur all along the life span; and that any personality theory which is to be useful to us in comprehending the life-cycle must take account of changes in advanced old age as well as in other periods of life.

III. Relations Between Biological and Psychological Change

This leads us back to questions of theory. Sometimes the very theories of developmental psychology hinder us in constructing a psychology of the life cycle. In this respect, the changes observable in behavior with the passage of short intervals of time—a month, six months, a year—are dramatic when one regards a young biological organism; and no less compelling are the overall regularities of biological change. It has been tempting for students of behavior to draw parallels between biological phenomena and psychological, and on this basis to establish a developmental psychology of childhood and adolescence. It has been relatively easy, if not always accurate, first to assume, then to look for ways of describing sequential and orderly progressions in psychological and social behavior. It has been easy to take growth as the model, to borrow from the biologist the concepts of increasing differentiation and integration, and the concept of an end-point toward which change is necessarily directed. It has been understandable, therefore, that we have used the biological clock as a frame of reference, looking to biological changes as the pacemakers of psychological; and taking for granted the intimate relationship between these two classes of phenomena.

The difficulty with this approach, however, can be illustrated from one of our investigations in which we proposed to study the psychological correlates of the biologic climacterium in middle-aged women. Along with other psychologists, we have been impressed with the changes in behavior that accompany puberty; and with the interpretation that the personality differences that are measurable in adolescents relate to major *developmental* components of biologic changes. We reasoned by analogy that there should also be biologically-based developmental components in the personality differences observable in middle-aged women—in short, that if puberty is an important developmental event in the psychology of females, so, probably, is the climacterium.

Accordingly we selected a sample of 100 normal women aged 43 to 53 from working-class and middle-class backgrounds, and obtained data on a large number of psychological and social variables. Using menopausal status as the index of climacteric status (presence or absence of observed changes in menstrual rhythm, or cessation of menses), we found climacteric status to be unrelated to our wide array of personality measures. Furthermore, there were very few significant relationships between severity of somatic and psychosomatic symptoms attributed to climacteric changes and these variables.

Granted that the question would be better pursued by a longitudinal rather than a cross-sectional method, nevertheless the negative findings were more largely due, we believe, to the fact that we were pursuing a certain parallelism between childhood and adulthood, a parallelism that probably does not exist.

This is not to say that the menopause is a meaningless phenomenon in the lives of women; nor that biological factors are of no importance in adult personality. Instead these comments are intended to point out: (1) that the menopause is not necessarily the important event in understanding the psychology of middle-aged women that we might have assumed it to be, from a biological model or from psychoanalytic theory—not as important, seemingly, as illness; or worry over possible illness; nor, even, as worry over possible illness that might occur in one's husband rather than in oneself; (2) that the timing of the biological event, the climacterium—at least to the extent that we could perceive it—did not produce order in our data; and (3) above all, that psychologists should proceed cautiously in assuming the same intimate relationships between biological and psychological phenomena in adulthood that hold true in childhood.

IV. The Age-Status System

As already suggested, the biological components of human development take a certain precedence in viewing personality change in childhood and early adolescence, and perhaps also in the very last part of the life span when biological decrement may overwhelm other components in the personality. There remains, however, the span of the adult years—a period of now approximately 50 years, beginning when the organism reaches biological maturity around age 20 and extending to approximately 70. In this long part of the life span the biological model is obviously insufficient, and we need a social framework for understanding the timing patterns that occur.

Psychologists have, of course, already looked at personality in one after another social context—the family, the school, the community, as well as in relation to social-structural variables in the society at large. Thus, social class groups, ethnic and religious groups, and now again, racial groups are studied with regard to the ways in which these groups create different subcultures and, through processes of socialization, the ways they produce both similarities and differences in personalities. One major context has been neglected, however: the age structure of

the society, the network of age-norms and age-expectations that govern behavior, and the ways in which different age groups relate to each other.[6]

Expectations regarding age-appropriate behavior form an elaborated and pervasive system of norms governing behavior and interaction, a network of expectations that is imbedded throughout the cultural fabric of life for the adult as much as for the child. There is a prescriptive timetable for the ordering of life events: a time when men and women are expected to marry, a time to raise children, a time to retire. This pattern is adhered to, more or less consistently, by most persons in the society, and even though the actual occurrences of these events are influenced by various life contingencies, it can easily be demonstrated that norms and actual occurrences are closely related.

Age norms and age expectations operate as prods and brakes upon behavior, in some instances hastening an event, in others, delaying it. Men and women are not only aware of the social clocks that operate in various areas of their lives, but they are also aware of their own timing and readily describe themselves as "early," "late," or "on time" with regard to family and occupational events.

Whether we identify ourselves as developmental psychologists or as social psychologists or as personality psychologists, we have perhaps taken the social dimension of age-status so for granted that, like the air we breathe, we pay it no attention. As soon as it is pointed out we agree, of course, that the society is organized by age—rights, duties and obligations are differentially distributed according to age; and the relations between age-groups change with historical time, as is so evident now, for instance, with the growth of political protest among college-age youth and with the changing age-base for political and social responsibility in our society.

Every encounter between individuals is governed, at least to some extent, by their respective ages. When we meet a stranger—indeed, when we first glance at any person—we think first in categories based on age and sex. We notice, first, "this is a male child," or "a young famale," or "an old man"; and we pattern our behavior accordingly—according, that is, to our own age and sex in relation to the other person's. So automatic and so immediate is this regulation of behavior that only when

---

[6] An analogy is appropriate: in sociology social stratification is a well-delineated field of study, and social class is recognized as one of the basic dimensions of social organization. Social classes, in turn, have been described as subcultures; and a tradition has developed of studying the behavior of both children and adults in relation to the social class to which they belong and in the context of the social-status structure of the community in which they live.

In similar fashion, some of us began several years ago to focus attention on the factor of age as another of the basic dimensions of social organization and the ways age groups relate to each other in the context of different social institutions. By a dimension of social organization, I refer to the fact that in all societies an age-status system exists, a system of implicit and explicit rules and expectations that govern the relations between persons of different ages. Certain behaviors come to be regarded as appropriate or inappropriate for each age group; and the relations between age groups are based upon dimensions of prestige, power, and deference. Older children have prestige in the eyes of younger; adolescents, in at least many ways, recognize the power of adults; and both children and adults, in at least some ways, show deference to the old. Each age group occupies a given status; and the system as a whole undergoes alterations in line with other social, economic, and political changes in the society.

the cues are ambiguous do we give it full awareness—as, for instance, when we face an adult of indeterminate age and when we fumble about in discomfort lest we make a blunder. Age, then, provides one of the basic guidelines to social interaction.

At the same time that psychologists have neglected the age-status dimension of social behavior, we have also neglected its relevance for providing an understanding of the various phenomena of personality internal to the individual. For example, although we always report the ages of the children whom we are studying, we seldom investigate directly the way in which the child himself thinks of his age or the way his perception of age colors his relations to other people. We have, for instance, talked at length about sex-role identity, but not about changing age-role identity. We have given very little systematic study to the way in which children, let alone adults, internalize age-norms and age-expectations. Nor have we even attended to the ages of the adults who deal with the child. In most of the studies of child-rearing no mention at all is to be found of the age of the parent, to say nothing of the way parental age might regularly be built into research designs as an important variable.

The saliency of age and age-norms in influencing the behavior of adults is no less than in influencing the behavior of children. The fact that the social sanctions related to age-norms take on psychological reality can be readily granted. One has only to think of the young woman, who, in 1940, was not yet married by age 25; or who, in 1966, is not yet married by 21; and who, if present trends continue over another few decades, will soon lie awake nights worrying over spinsterhood by the time she is 18. The timing of life events provides some of the most powerful cues to adult personality.

In our recent investigations we have perceived of age norms and of the age-status system as forming a backdrop or cultural context against which the behavioral and personality differences of adults should be viewed. Early in this line of inquiry, we began to study the outlines of the age-status system and the extent to which there was consensus in the minds of adults. We began with middle-aged men and women in the belief that, by virtue of their age, they would have relatively accurate perceptions of an age-status system (if such perceptions could be elicited at all); and we asked them a series of questions such as,

"What would you call the periods of life that people go through after they are grown up?" For instance, we usually refer to people first as babies, then as children, then as teen-agers.
"After a person is grown up, what periods does he go through?"
"At what age does each period begin, for most people?"
"What are the important changes from one period to the next?" (Neugarten and Peterson, 1957).

We discovered a commonly-held set of perceptions with regard to adult age periods, each with a distinguishing set of transition points and a distinguishing set of psychological and social themes. Thus, our respondents seemed to share a view that adulthood can be divided into periods of young adulthood, maturity, middle age, and old age, each with its distinctive characteristics and each

with its own psychological flavor.

At the same time there were sex differences in these perceptions, and differences between members of different social classes. The timing of middle age and old age occurs earlier to working-class than to middle-class men and women.

For instance, the typical upper-middle class man, a business executive or a professional, divides the lifeline at 30, at 40, and at 65. He considered a man "mature" at 40; at the "prime of life" and as "having the greatest confidence in himself" at age 40. A man is not "middle-aged" until almost 50; nor is he "old" until 70.
The unskilled worker, on the other hand, saw the life line as being paced more rapidly. For him, the major dividing points were placed at 25, 35, and 50. In his view a man is "middle-aged" by 40; "old" by 60.
In the eyes of upper-middle-class people, the period of young adulthood extending into the 30's—is a time of exploration and groping; a period of "feeling one's way," of trying out and getting adjusted to jobs and careers, to marriage, to one's adult roles; a period of experimentation. By contrast, the working-class man regards young adulthood as the period, not when issues are explored, but when issues are settled. They may be settled by giving up a certain type of autonomy—"when responsibility is *hung* on you," with an undertone of regret; or the issues may be settled by establishing one's independence—the "now you are a man" refrain—but in either case, young adulthood to the working man is the time when one gives up youth with a note of finality and takes over the serious business of life—job, marriage, children, responsibilities.

In these first studies the gross outlines of an age-status structure that seems to crosscut various areas of adult life were delineated. While their view of the life span was more implicit than explicit in the minds of many respondents, it seemed nevertheless to provide a frame of reference by which the experiences of adult life were seen as orderly and rhythmical. More important, progression from one age-level to the next was conceived primarily in terms of psychological and social changes rather than in terms of biological changes.

We also asked questions regarding age-appropriate and age-linked behaviors:

"What do you think is the best age for a man to marry? . . . to finish school . . . to hold his top job . . . to retire?"
"What age comes to your mind when you think of a young man? . . . an old man? . . ."

There was widespread consensus on such items. Among the middle-class middle-aged, for instance, 90 percent said the best age for a man to marry was from 20 to 25. Nor was the consensus limited to middle-aged persons or to persons residing in a particular region of the U.S. When responses to the same set of questions were obtained from other middle-class groups, essentially the same patterns emerged in each set of data.

When we looked at life history data with regard to the ages at which major events had actually occurred, we found striking regularities within social-class groups, with the actual occurrences following the same patterns described above. The higher the social class, the later each of the following events was reported by our respondents:

age at leaving school, age at first job, age at marriage, age at parenthood, age of top job, grandparenthood—even, in women, their reported age of menopause.

The perceptions, the expectations, and the actual occurrences of life events, then, are closely related; and the regularities within social class groups indicate that these are *socially* regulated.

Given this view that age norms and age expectations operate in the society as a system of social control, we undertook still another study of their psychological correlates, asking, How do members of the society vary in their perception of the strictures involved in age norms, or in the degree of *constraint* they perceive with regard to age-appropriate behaviors? We devised a questionnaire using items that relate to occupational career, some that relate to the family cycle, and some that refer to recreation, appearance, and consumption behaviors. For instance:

> Would you approve a couple who likes to dance the "Twist" when they are age 20? Would you approve if they are age 30? If they are age 55?
>
> What about a woman who decides to have another child when she is 45? When she is 37? When she is 30?
>
> A man who is willing to move his family from one town to another to get ahead in his company, when he's 45? when he's 35? 25?
>
> A couple who move across country so they can live near their married children—when they are 40? 55? 70?

We devised a score which reflected the degree of refinement with which the respondent makes age discriminations; then used this instrument with a group of 400 middle-class men and women divided into young (20–29), middle-aged (35–55), and old (65+). (Neugarten, Moore, Lowe, 1965) We found a significant increase in scores with age—that is, an increase in the extent to which respondents ascribe importance to age norms and place constraints upon adult behavior in terms of age appropriateness. The middle-aged and the old seem to have learned that age is a reasonable criterion by which to evaluate behavior; that to be "off-time" with regard to life events or to show other age-deviant behavior brings with it social and psychological sequelae that cannot be disregarded. In the young, especially the young male, this view is only partially accepted; and there seems to be a certain denial of age as a valid dimension by which to judge behavior.

> This age-related difference in point of view is reflected in the response of a 20-year-old who, when asked what he thought of marriage between 17-year-olds, said, "It would be OK if the boy got a job and if they loved each other. Why not?" While a 45-year-old said, "At that age, they'd be foolish. He couldn't support a wife and children. Kids who marry that young will suffer for it later."

We have begun also to study the correlates in personality and behavior of being "on time" or "off time." Persons who regard themselves as early or late with regard to a major life event describe ways in which the off-timeness has other psychological and social accompaniments. We are pursuing this line of inquiry now with regard to career timing. Thus, in a study of Army officers (the Army is one of the most clearly age-graded occupa-

tions available for study) the men who recognize themselves as being too long in grade—or late in career achievement—are also distinguishable on an array of social and psychological attitudes toward work, family, community participation, and personal adjustment.

These studies have relevance for a theory of the psychology of the life-cycle, in two ways: First, in indicating that the age structure of a society, the internalization of age-norms, and age-group identifications are important dimensions of the social and cultural *context* in which the course of the individual life line must be viewed;

Second, because these concepts point to at least one additional way of structuring the passage of time in the life span of the individual, and in *providing a time clock* that can be superimposed over the biological clock so that together they help us to comprehend the life cycle. The major punctuation marks in the adult life line (those, that is, which are orderly and sequential) tend to be more often social than biological—or, if biologically based, they are often biological events that occur to significant others rather than to oneself, like grandparenthood or widowhood.

If psychologists are to discover order in the events of adulthood, and if they are to discover order in the personality changes that occur in all individuals as they age, we should look to the social as well as to the biological clock, and certainly to social definitions of age and age-appropriate behavior.

V. Conclusion

In conclusion I would like to return once again to the problem of a personality theory that will encompass the life-cycle.

In commenting upon the salient issues of adulthood and in illustrating in particular from middle age, I have tried to illustrate the need for a theory which will emphasize the ego or executive functions of the personality; one which will help account for the growth and maintenance of cognitive competence and creativity, one that will help explain the conscious use of past experience. . .

In illustrating from our findings regarding differences between intrapsychic and adaptive aspects of personality as persons move from middle- to old-age, and from our findings with regard to biological climacterium in women, I have tried to illustrate some of the problems involved in any theory of personality that is based primarily upon a biological model of the life span.

Finally, in describing some of our studies regarding the age-status system and the pervasive quality of age-norms in influencing the psychology of adulthood, I have suggested at least one of the sociological components that, in addition to the biological, provides a view of the orderliness of change that underlies the total life-cycle.

References

Buhler, Charlotte. *Der Menschliche Lebenslauf als psychogiches Problem.* S. Hirzel, Leipzig, 1933.

Buhler, Charlotte. The curve of life as studied in biographies. *J. appl. Psychol.*, 1935, 19, 405–409.

Buhler, Charlotte. Genetic aspects of the self. *Ann. N.Y. Acad. Sci.*, 1962, 96, 730–764.

BUTLER, R. N. The life review: an interpretation of reminiscence in the aged. *Psychiat.*, 1963, *26*, 65–76.

ERIKSON, ERIK H. *Childhood and Society.* New York, Norton, 1950.

ERIKSON, ERIK H. Identity and the life cycle: Selected papers. *Psych. Issues*, 1959, I.

FROMM, E. *Escape from freedom.* New York: Rinehart, 1941.

HAVIGHURST, R. J., BOWMAN, P. H., LIDDLE, G. P., MATTHEWS, C. V., & PIERCE, J. V. *Growing up in river city.* New York: John Wiley, 1962.

HESS, R. D. High school antecedents of young adults performance. (mimeo)

HONZIK, MARJORIE, and McFARLANE, JEAN.

HOYT, D. P. The relationship between college grades and adult achievement: a review of the literature. *ACT Research Reports*, September, 1965, No. 7 American College Testing Program: P.O. Box 168, Iowa City, Iowa.

JUNG, C. G. *Modern man in search of a soul.* New York: Harcourt, 1933.

KAGAN, J., & MOSS, H. A. *Birth to maturity.* New York: John Wiley, 1962.

KUHLEN, R. G. Personality change with age. In P. Worchel & D. Byrne (Eds.), *Personality change.* New York: John Wiley, 1964. Pp. 524–555.

LIEBERMAN, M. A. Psychological correlates of impending death: some preliminary observations. *J. of Geron.*, 1965, *20*, 181–190.

MASLOW, A. H. *Motivation and personality.* New York: Harper, 1954.

NEUGARTEN, BERNICE L., & PETERSON, W. A. A study of the American age-grade system. *Proceedings of the Fourth Congress of the International Association of Gerontology*, Merano, Italy, 1957. Vol. 3, 497–502.

NEUGARTEN, BERNICE L., & ASSOCIATES. *Personality in middle and late life.* New York: Atherton, 1964.

NEUGARTEN, BERNICE L., MOORE, JOAN W., & LOWE, J. C. Age-norms, age constraints, and adult socialization. *Amer. J. Soc.*, 1965, *70*, 710–717.

PECK, R. Psychological developments in the second half of life. In J. E. Anderson (ed.), *Psychological Aspects of Aging.* Washington, D.C. A.P.A., 1956.

SMITH, M. B. Research strategies toward a conception of positive mental health. *Amer. Psychol.*, 1959, *14*, 673–681.

WHITE, R. W. Ego and reality in psychoanalytic theory. *Psych. Issues*, 1963, *3*, (3).

WORCHEL, P., & BYRNE, D. *Personality change.* New York: John Wiley, 1964.

II. The Bio-Physiology of Aging

Life is a continual process of differentiation, beginning with the division of the first germ cell in the embryo. Childhood is a process of increasing biological differentiation and growth, culminating in the attainment of physiological maturity. It is only recently that the more subtle processes of change through adulthood began to be studied, yet some of the consequences of these processes affect our psychological and social life. Herant Katchadourian presents a highly technical, but comprehensive, overview of the biological processes of development in adulthood, which allows us to see some of the underlying metabolic and physiological rhythms and changes that go on through life. Around age 30 people begin a steady but predictable biological decline, which is outlined by Bernard Strehler. The study of the aging process allows us to look carefully at some myths and some of the realities of aging. Arthur Galston talks about the most prevalent of these myths and its basis in reality: the search for immortality by reversing or slowing the aging process.

6

HERANT A. KATCHADOURIAN

Medical Perspectives on Adulthood

Confound not the distinctions of thy life which nature hath divided; that is, youth, adolescence, manhood, and old age: nor in these divided periods, wherein thou art in a manner four, conceive thyself but one. Let every division be happy in its proper virtues, nor one vice run through all. Let each distinction have its salutary transition, and critically deliver thee from the imperfections of the former; so ordering the whole, that prudence and virtue may have the largest section.

Sir Thomas Browne (1605-1682)[1]

CONTEMPORARY PHYSICIANS MAY NOT BE so articulate as their distinguished seventeenth-century colleague, but upon reflection they are likely to share Sir Thomas Browne's life-cycle perspective and to find it essential for the understanding of people and for dealing effectively with their ailments and infirmities. Such a holistic approach is more characteristic of the thoughtful clinician than of the technicians of medicine, for whom the parts of the body sometimes come to wag the whole.[2]

That physicians are aware of the significance of the life cycle is apparent in many aspects of medical practice: for instance, case histories, which constitute the fundamental units of clinical communication, always begin with a statement about the patient's age and sex. These two indices are essential for interpreting the history of an illness, the findings of the physical examination, and any laboratory tests. Because of the overlap between the signs and symptoms of various diseases, the identification of an illness is reached through a process of differential diagnosis whereby the physician makes probabilistic judgments that lead to a definitive decision. As diseases afflict people differently at different ages, the age factor becomes a significant clinical clue in the diagnostic process and an important epidemiological variable. Figures 1-4 illustrate this by showing the discrepant death rates from major illness and external causes at various stages of life.

At an even more fundamental level, a developmental aberration may constitute an illness, that is, the disease may be manifested by the untimely presence or absence of an age-related characteristic. Bed-wetting in an infant or the existence of immature blood cells in his circulation do not carry the pathological connotations that these same phenomena carry in adulthood. Treatment, too, can be age-dependent: choices of procedure and dosage, and even the expected outcome, are significantly linked to age.

Despite this pervasive awareness of the life cycle in medical practice, little formal attention has been paid to its various phases generally and to the concept of adulthood in particular. One searches in vain in medical dictionaries for definitions of adulthood. The term "adult" either does not appear at all or, when it does, it is usually defined as "fully grown and mature; a fully grown individual,"[3] or as someone who has ". . . attained full size, strength, and reproductive ability, or the ability to handle personal affairs."[4] The term "adult," like the term "adolescent," derives from the Latin "to grow." Simply put, an adolescent is someone who is growing up and an adult is someone who has grown up. But what does it mean to "grow up"? The answers found in medical texts are not very explicit. Though pediatric texts obviously deal with children, books on adolescence with adolescents, and most other texts with adults, the question of what an adult is is seldom raised.

The term "adult" does appear as one of the 8,500 subject headings in the *Cumulated Index Medicus*, which is the standard reference to the periodical biomedical literature. But of the 220,000 entries in 1974, it accounts for only two items ("adolescence," "adolescent psychiatry," and "adolescent psychology" fare better with a combined 125 entries).[5] In view of this apparent lack of concern specifically with adulthood, we shall have to consider medical notions about it in more general terms, as they are reflected in medical practice, in the perspectives of human biology, and in psychiatry.

Notions of Adulthood in Medical Practice

Throughout most of the history of medicine (which is almost commensurate with the human record generally), physicians have dealt with their patients in an all-inclusive system of general practice. Specializations based either on the nature of the illness and method of treatment or on the age of the patient are recent phenomena. The

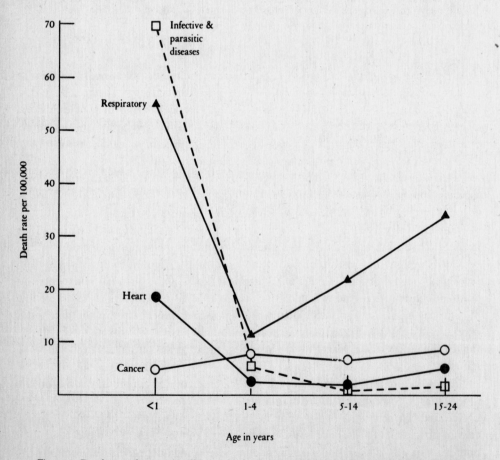

Figure 1. Death rates from major illnesses: birth to young adulthood. The plotted figures for each age group are the average numbers of deaths per year in each 100,000 persons of a given age in the total population. For example, in the four years included under age "1-4," the average number of deaths from respiratory disease was 11.4 per 100,000 children between the years of 1 and 4. The data are from the 1968 Mortality Statistics (Monthly Vital Statistics Report, U.S. Dept. of Health, Education and Welfare, 1971, Vol. 19, No. 12). (Redrawn from W. A. Marshall, Chapter 7, in R. R. Sears and S. S. Feldman, eds., *The Seven Ages of Man* [Los Altos, Calif., 1973]. © 1973 by William Kaufmann, Inc. All rights reserved.)

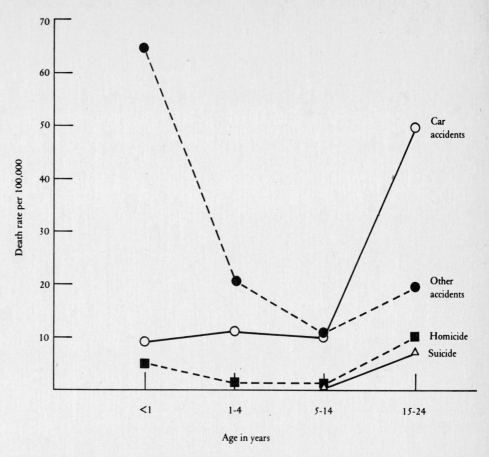

Figure 2. Death rates from major external causes: birth to young adulthood. The plotted figures are comparable to those in the illness chart. (Redrawn from W. A. Marshall, Chapter 7, in R. R. Sears and S. S. Feldman, eds., *The Seven Ages of Man* [Los Altos, Calif., 1973]. © 1973 by William Kaufmann, Inc. All rights reserved.)

first category of specialization includes most present-day medical disciplines. Fields are differentiated by their predominant method of treatment (e.g., the surgical specialties), the part of the body dealt with (e.g., cardiology), attention to a particular class of ailments (e.g., oncology), or even a specific illness (e.g., syphilology). The second category, based on age groupings, is more pertinent to our subject. The one solid offshoot from general medicine in this category is pediatrics. Far less well established are the fields of adolescent medicine and geriatrics (or gerontology).[6]

Pediatrics as a specialty dates back only to the middle of the nineteenth century; prior to that time it was included under internal medicine and, to some extent, obstetrics. But this is not to say that, earlier, physicians did not recognize the special problems of childhood. Even in Egyptian medical documents (such as the Papyrus Ebers of 1550 B.C.), there are sporadic references to diseases of infants and children. They are also found in Babylonian, Indian, and Talmudic texts.

Such references become even more plentiful in Greek and Roman medicine. Hippocrates (ca. 460-377 B.C.) had a good deal to say about childhood illnesses and devoted a whole treatise to dentition. He also noted a late advent of puberty in colder climates. The Roman physician Celsus admonished his colleagues that "children should not be treated as adults," and he pointed out the greater prevalence among youth of acute illnesses, epilepsy, insanity, and consumption.[7] Similar references can be found in the works of Galen (ca. A.D. 130-200), Oribasius (ca. A.D. 325-400), Rhazes (A.D. 850-923), and others. Another early landmark in the history of pediatrics was the publication in 1472 of the *Little Book on Diseases of Children* by Paulo Bagellardus (d. 1472), which was the first printed book entirely devoted to diseases of children.[8] About 1512-13, the *Rosegarten* by Eucharius Röslin (d. ca. 1526) ap-

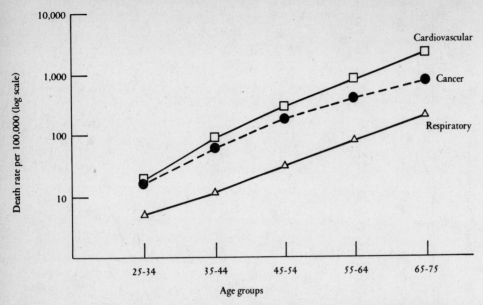

Figure 3. Death rates from major illnesses: young adulthood to later maturity. Note that the scale at left is logarithmic, the actual values would go off the page if they were plotted in conventional form. (Redrawn from W. A. Marshall, Chapter 10, in R. R. Sears and S. S. Feldman, eds., *The Seven Ages of Man* [Los Altos, Calif., 1973]. © 1973 by William Kaufmann, Inc. All rights reserved.)

peared, a work which eventually went through some forty known editions, the last of which was issued in 1730. This was a veritable textbook of pediatrics; all of its thirty chapters are devoted to diseases of children. Starting in the seventeenth century, the treatment of sick children steadily improved in quality, and events of significance in pediatric history become too numerous to mention here. By the mid-nineteenth century pediatrics was being taught in medical schools, and clinics and hospitals had been established for children; by the turn of the century pediatric associations had been founded both in Europe and in the United States.[9]

Adolescent medicine has emerged as a distinct field only during the past several decades, and at this stage of its development it is still being confronted with its own task of identity formation. The absence of a generally accepted label to designate specialists in adolescence is symptomatic. With varying degrees of euphonic abandon, terms like "teenologist," "teeniatrician," "hebiatrician" (Hebe, the goddess of youth), "ephebiatrician" (*ephebeios*, Greek for "youthful") have been put forth, but have so far mercifully failed to find favor.

The problem is real. The transition to adulthood occurs over the second decade: at its inception the individual is a child, at its conclusion, an adult, while in between he occupies biologically and psychologically ambiguous and fluid positions. Which specialist takes care of an adolescent patient often depends on the peculiarities of medical practice in the area, the particular relationship of a family to its family physician, the nature of the adolescent's illness, whether or not he has passed puberty, and other similar considerations. Currently, pediatricians, internists, psychiatrists, dermatologists, orthopedic surgeons, and, in increasing numbers, gynecologists are the specialists most likely to treat teenagers. When the biological process of puberty itself seems disturbed, endocrinologists are often consulted.

The field of geriatrics is also in the process of differentiating itself from general internal medicine. There is increasing recognition that special attention needs to be paid to the biological and psychosocial processes of aging and to the particular illnesses that afflict the elderly. Yet, here again there is some ambiguity as to when in the life cycle geriatrics becomes functional. Aging, after all, is a lifelong process which simply becomes more evident with the progress of adulthood. Nevertheless, just as pediatrics has seceded from internal medicine, so also it appears certain that the decade leading to

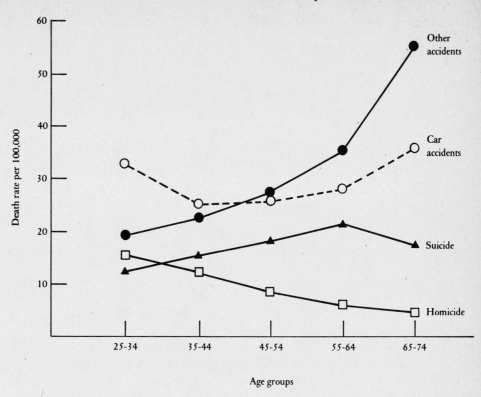

Figure 4. Death rates from major external causes: young adulthood to later maturity. (Redrawn from W. A. Marshall, Chapter 10, in R. R. Sears and S. S. Feldman, eds., *The Seven Ages of Man* [Los Altos, Calif., 1973]. © 1973 by William Kaufmann, Inc. All rights reserved.)

entry into adulthood and the last decade or two of adulthood itself will also become specialized provinces within medicine. Judging by the number of professional journals and associations of physicians available in these areas, this process is already well advanced. But to what extent the main span of adult life will itself become further subdivided for medical caretaking remains to be seen.

The Concept of Adulthood in Human Biology

Just as medical practice was—and remains—the domain of physicians, investigation of the human body also for a long time belonged exclusively to medicine. More recently, the enormous expansion of knowledge in these fields of research has produced a new type of medical specialist who is not a practicing physician but a research scientist trained in one or another of the basic medical sciences such as physiology or biochemistry.

Another distinction that has become profitably blurred is that between medicine and biology. Traditionally, physicians dealt with people, while biologists studied animals and plants. Today, however, physicians make extensive use of animals in their research, while biologists study human functions as well. It is quite legitimate, therefore, to think of all investigators of the human body as "human biologists" irrespective of their particular disciplinary background: the term is gaining wide currency, and we shall use it here to refer to the work of medical scientists who may or may not be physicians.

One need not be a human biologist to note with wonder the physical transformation of children into adults through the changes of puberty. This is a process crucial for the life of the species, and it is also a momentous event in the life of the individual. In biological terms one can say that adulthood has been achieved when puberty has been successfully completed.

But what is "puberty"? There is as yet no generally accepted definition. The term is often used synonymously with "adolescence" to refer to a vaguely defined transitional period between childhood and adulthood. Since biological and psychosocial developments during this phase of life have fairly distinct characteristics and do not entirely coincide, it would be preferable to use "puberty" for the former and "adolescence" for the latter. Unfortunately long usage has made this distinction difficult to maintain in practice.

The changes that constitute puberty have been classified by Marshall and Tanner as follows:

1) Acceleration and then deceleration of skeletal growth (the adolescent growth spurt).

2) Altered body composition as a result of skeletal and muscular growth together with changes of the quantity and distribution of fat.

3) Development of the circulatory and respiratory systems, leading, particularly in boys, to increased strength and endurance.

4) The development of the gonads, reproductive organs, and secondary sex characters.

5) A combination of factors, not yet fully understood, which modulates the activity of those nervous and endocrine elements which initiate and coordinate all these changes.[10]

There are two major biological consequences to these pubertal changes that have profound psychosocial repercussions. First, the child attains the physique and physiological characteristics of the adult, including reproductive capacity. Second, most of the major adult physical sex differences become established through this process.

The biology of puberty is the subject of an extensive and expanding literature. There is no need for us here to delve into its details, particularly since an account of these matters has been given by a leading authority in a relatively recent issue of this journal.[11] We shall therefore comment only briefly on the five categories of changes listed above.[12]

The pubescent growth spurt is among the more dramatic changes of puberty. Growth in stature is a continous process; by the age of 10, boys have already attained about 78 per cent and girls 84 per cent of their adult height.[13] What makes the growth spurt at puberty noteworthy, therefore, is not so much the amount of growth as its rate.

Among girls, the height spurt typically starts at about 10½ years, reaches peak velocity at 12, and is over by 14.[14] Among boys, the onset is usually at about 12 to 13, the peak at 14, and the end at 16.[15] During the year of peak height velocity a boy grows on an average of three to five inches and a girl somewhat less. In terms of rate of growth, this means an actual doubling in velocity compared to the period preceding puberty and approximates the rapid rate of growth of the two-year-old child.[16] With the culmination of the growth spurt, the rate of growth decelerates rapidly. Most girls at 14 years and most boys at 16 years have reached 98 per cent of their ultimate adult height.[17] Further noticeable growth in stature ceases at about 18 years in women and at 20 years in men.

Concurrent with the growth spurt, there are other changes that shape the adult physique. An important factor in the differences between male and female contours is the amount and distribution of subcutaneous fat. Young children gradually lose their chubbiness, but then, shortly before puberty, they regain some of it. With the growth spurt a negative fat balance is established among boys but not among girls, who usually enter adulthood with more body fat than males, particularly in the region of the pelvis and breasts.

Muscular development is more marked in the mature male. During puberty the muscles increase in size and even more in strength. Prior to puberty, there is no substantial difference in muscular strength between boys and girls, but distinct differences become established at puberty and persist into adulthood.[18] Boys also develop greater speed and coordination in bodily movements, and their reaction to sudden stimuli becomes quicker.

Changes in stature, musculature, and fat distribution constitute the more prominent alterations but by no means the only ones. Essentially, to varying degrees, the whole body becomes transformed. In addition to increased size, the shifts in bodily proportions shape the adult form. Some sex differences in proportion are present at birth: for instance, the forearm is longer relative to height in the male than in the female. But the broader shoulders of the male relative to his hips and his longer legs relative to his trunk are characteristics that emerge at puberty.

Other changes, such as those involving the face, are more subtle. Since the bones of the face grow faster than the cranium, in adulthood the face "emerges from under the skull," as it were. The profile of the adult is straighter, the nose projects further, and the jaw is more prominent. All these features are more marked in the male than in the female. Later in puberty the hairline of the male forehead recedes while that of the female does not change. All these factors, along with the growth of the beard, make the physical transformation of the male face in adolescence more marked than that of the female.

Equally important changes take place internally. The muscles of the heart, for instance, participate in the growth spurt along with the other muscles of the body. Puberty brings on an increase in the number of red blood corpuscles, the blood hemoglobin level, and blood volume. Once again, sex discrepancies are established in favor of males. The same is true for the respiratory system and its functions.

The net effect of these and related changes is to equip the adult with the necessary physiological mechanisms to allow for the effective exertion of his larger and more powerful body. As a result, post-pubescent individuals vastly outperform their pre-pubescent selves in all tasks requiring strength, endurance, and stamina: these changes are also more marked among males than among females.

A word of caution may be in order here. The physical discrepancies that puberty widens between male and female are real. But some extraordinary conclusions have been drawn from them. It is one thing to say that males have generally greater exercise tolerance and another to conclude that women therefore should not drive tractors or play football. While all the physical sex differences that emerge at puberty differentiate male and female populations, they do not equally affect all individuals within them. There are wide intrasex differences, and there is much overlap between the two groups: in other words, obviously women exist who are taller or stronger than many men. Furthermore, physical strength can be vastly increased by exercise and atrophied through disuse. A great many of the sex discrepancies that occur can be attributed to the selectivity by which males are pushed into physical exertion at work and play.

Much can be made of the male's physical advantages. But an advantage is meaningful only in relation to some specific purpose: to be big as a camel is no advantage if one needs to go through the eye of a needle. The physical attributes of the male are also generally present in other primates. Our evolutionary forebears differentiated the way they did because of some selective process. Quite plausibly, the male physique was better equipped for tasks such as hunting big game. But what use is this now? And what are the dangers of the male continuing to glory in the prowess of his striking arm and, by extension, in the potency of his weapons? Finally, before too much is made of the male's physical superiority, one should remember that statistically females outlive males, and survival is surely not a trivial test of physical fitness.

If puberty accomplished only what has been so far described, it would have done the preservation of the human species little good. For, tall and strong as adults may be, to preserve the species they must be able to reproduce. Reproductive capacity is thus the quintessence of biological adulthood, and, as shown by a comparison of various growth patterns (Figure 5), the reproductive system attains its greatest gains at puberty.

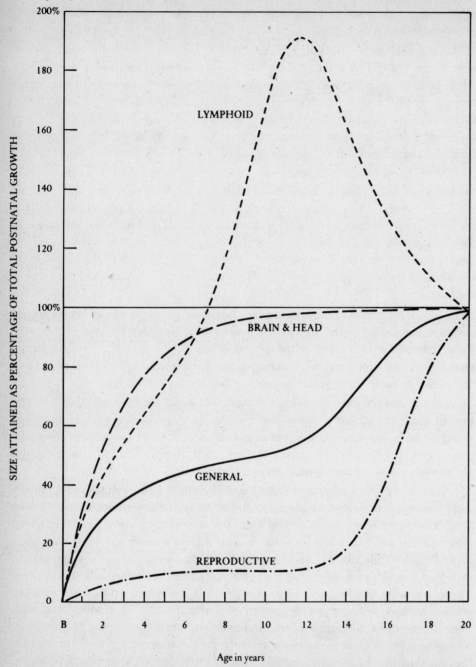

Figure 5. The main types of growth curves for various parts and tissues of the body. (Redrawn from G. A. Harrison, J. S. Weiner, J. M. Tanner, N. A. Barnicot, *Human Biology* [Oxford, 1964], p. 309. © 1964 by the Oxford University Press. All rights reserved.)

The reproductive system, like all other systems of the body, is already present in embryonal life. The genetic sex of the individual is immutably determined at conception: if the sperm that fertilizes the ovum carries an *x* chromosome, the issue is female; if it carries a *y* chromosome, the offspring is male. The genital system makes its appearance during the fifth to sixth week of intrauterine life when the embryo is about one-half to one centimeter long. It is quite undifferentiated at this stage: in both sexes there are a pair of gonads, two sets of ducts, and the rudiments of external genitals. Through an epigenetic process, the reproductive system develops and further differentiates sexually. In the seventh week, it becomes possible to tell if the gonad is going to become a testis or an ovary, and by the fourth month the sex of the fetus is unmistakable even by inspection of the external genitals alone. At birth, with very rare exceptions, a child is unequivocally male or female genetically, anatomically, and hormonally. Although the reproductive systems of male and female are built on the same basic plan, there is thus a progressive divergence throughout development in shape and function between the two. This sexual dimorphism is definitively established at puberty. A final installment occurs in women when they experience pregnancy, childbirth, and lactation.[19]

The maturation of the reproductive system in puberty involves the accelerated growth of the internal sex organs and the external genitalia. This is accompanied by the development of the so-called secondary sexual characteristics which include the development of the female breast, the sprouting of pubic and axillary hair, the lowering pitch of the voice, and the appearance of facial hair in the male. In physiological terms, the key events are the activation of ovulation and the menstrual cycle in females and the production of sperm and the ability to ejaculate in males (resulting from the development of the prostate gland which produces most of the seminal fluid).

It is not possible to assign simple age landmarks for these events, since both the onset and the duration of a given developmental event vary a great deal. For example, breast development, which often is the earliest visible sign of puberty in the female, is regarded as beginning normally at any time between the ages of 8 and 13 and ending normally between the ages of 13 and 18. Pubic hair appears at about age 11 (axillary hair follows a year later), and the adult pattern is established by age 14. Menarche usually occurs about two years after the start of breast enlargement: in the United States, most girls now begin to menstruate at around 12 or 13, but they may also perfectly normally do so as early as 10 years or as late as 16½ years. The early menstrual cycles tend to be irregular and often anovulatory, that is, a young woman does not become reliably fertile until a few years after the initial cycle.

In the male, testicular enlargement is usually the first pubescent change; it starts between 9½ and 13½ years and ends sometime between 13½ and 17 years. Pubic-hair growth occurs between 12 and 16.[20] The growth of the beard is often a later development. The first ejaculation usually occurs at 11 or 12, but mature sperm take a few more years to appear. This relative pubescent sterility in girls and boys, who have otherwise matured sexually, does not, however, amount to reliable contraceptive security, as some teenagers continue to discover to their grief.

In defining adulthood, an important distinction must be emphasized here between sex and reproduction. Whether one accepts Freud's broadly encompassing concept of the libido or Kinsey's far narrower definition of orgasmic "outlets," it can be reasonably asserted that sexuality starts and ends with life. Children are demonstrably capable of sexual arousal and orgasm (although one may question the propriety and wisdom of such demonstration). Sexual functions, like alimentary and eliminative functions, differ somewhat in children and adults, but these differences are not fundamental. The only significant change brought about by puberty is the male capacity to ejaculate during orgasm, and this is primarily of reproductive rather than sexual significance. Pre- and post-pubescent females, pre-pubescent males, and certain post-pubescent males experience orgasm without ejaculation.[21]

A similar statement can be made about sexual behavior. Anthropological and other evidence shows that children are quite capable of engaging in most forms of "adult" sexual activity.[22] That they do not do so overtly and in larger numbers in our culture is at least in part because of social inhibitions. It is not being suggested here that this ought not to be the case, but simply that behavioral differences between children and adults are not entirely biologically determined. Thus, although there are important biological factors that may influence adult sexual behavior, sexuality in itself is not a particularly refined criterion of adulthood. But reproductive capacity is.

A related and crucial developmental phenomenon is gender-identity differentiation. A model for the development of adult gender identity has been proposed by Money and Ehrhardt (Figure 6); it attempts to integrate genetic, hormonal, and social factors as they interact in sequentially defining this major aspect of adulthood.[23]

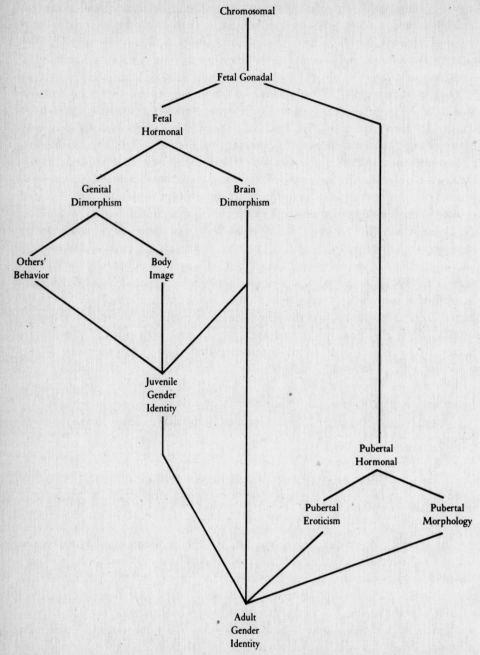

Figure 6. Diagram to illustrate the sequential and interactional components of gender-identity differentiation. (Redrawn from J. Money and A. A. Ehrhardt, *Man and Woman, Boy and Girl* [Baltimore, 1972]. © 1972 by the Johns Hopkins University Press. All rights reserved.)

The trigger that initiates the chain of events involved in puberty is located in the brain. So far as is known, the part of the brain that first stirs is the hypothalamus. The pituitary gland, the testes, ovaries, and the tissues of the body can be stimulated into activity long before the normal time of puberty. But, although potentially responsive, the rest of the body receives its marching orders from the hypothalamus, which issues them in its own good time and possibly under instructions from elsewhere in the brain.

To initiate puberty, the hypothalamus produces and releases higher concentrations of certain hormones which stimulate the anterior pituitary into increasing the output of two of its own hormones: FSH (follicle-stimulating hormone) and LH (luteinizing hormone). In the female, FSH stimulates the ovarian follicles to mature. These, in turn, produce estrogen which brings about most of the "feminizing" changes of puberty. The function of LH is related to ovulation and to the subsequent formation of the remnants of the ovarian follicle into the "corpus luteum," which produces the second female hormone, progesterone.

In the male, FSH initiates spermatogenesis and LH (which in the male is called interstitial cell-stimulating hormone: ICSH) activates certain cells in the interstices of the seminiferous, or sperm-bearing, tubules to produce the male hormone, testosterone. This, in turn, brings about the "masculinizing" changes of puberty. Although it is customary to refer to these gonadal hormones as "sex hormones" and to assign them gender, such designations must be understood mainly as manners of speech. Testosterone, for example, is as much a growth hormone as it is a sex hormone: it plays a central role in the growth spurt at puberty. Likewise, both classes of hormones are present in each sex; the difference is mainly a matter of relative concentration. (It may be sobering to note that estrogen is found even in the testes of bulls, and that the grand champion of estrogen production is the stallion, which is not the most effeminate creature by most conventional standards.)

Androgens (of which testosterone is only one) are produced in the female by the adrenal cortex and stimulate, for instance, the development of pubic and axillary hair. They also seem to have an erotogenic effect.

The production of these hormones is regulated through an intricate set of feedback mechanisms and follows a cyclical pattern in the female between menarche and menopause. One such feedback mechanism is hypothesized to keep the immature hypothalamus in check prior to puberty. Just as a house thermostat when it is set low does not trigger the furnace although the house is cool, so, prior to puberty, the hypothalamic "thermostat" is presumably set low and the pre-pubertal levels of circulating pituitary and gonadal hormones are insufficient to activate it (and the bodily tissues do not respond to such low concentrations of estrogen and testosterone). At puberty, the hypothalamus becomes more sensitive, as if its "thermostat" had been turned up. The low levels of circulating anterior pituitary hormones do not inhibit it any longer; thus, higher levels of hypothalamic hormones are produced which stimulate the anterior pituitary and, in turn, the gonads into greater activity, eventually raising the output of the sex hormones to a point where the body responds with the changes of puberty.[24] This negative feedback also controls the menstrual cycle in conjunction with other positive feedback systems that make it possible for increasing levels of a hormone to further stimulate its own production. These feedback loops operate at "short" and "long" ranges, linking the various components of the system. Thus, the neuro-endocrine mechanisms that trigger puberty and maintain the reproductive function of the adult are not so much a hierarchic as a cybernetic system, where the various constituent parts mutually regulate one another.[25]

Other changes in the brain during puberty remain something of a mystery. As was shown in Figure 5, the growth of the brain precedes the growth of other systems. The brain has already attained 25 per cent of its adult weight at birth; 50 per cent at 6 months; 75 per cent at 2½ years; 90 per cent at 5 years; and 95 per cent at 10 years, when the individual is on the threshold of puberty. In contrast, body weight at birth is only 5 per cent and at age 10 only 50 per cent of that of the young adult.

Given the cognitive differences between children and adults and the sequential development in cognition during development (as shown by Piaget, Kohlberg, and others), something other than the meager gain in brain size must account for the neurophysiological changes that underlie and limit the psychological gains. Since most, if not all, nerve cells in the adult are already formed during the first twenty to thirty weeks of intrauterine life, the answer must be sought in increased "connectivity" or communicative linkages between cells. In fact, for the first several years of life and possibly longer, there is a progressive increase in the number and size of dendrites in all layers of the cortex. Studies on myelination show that the brain continues to develop at least until adolescence and possibly into adulthood. Dendrites occupy very little space—even millions of them can be accommodated within the modest brain-weight increases of a few per cent that result in immense gains in the complexity of communicative networks and, hence, cognitive functions.[26] Plausible as this explanation might be, the more precise characteristics of the adult brain remain to be elucidated.

In our discussion so far, we have presented the orderly changes of puberty with only occasional references to its variabilities. Two illustrations will further underscore these variations: each set of three girls and three boys in Figure 7 represents precisely the same chronological age, yet the developmental achievements displayed are obviously wide apart. Figure 8 shows that some boys in their first year of grade school have already reached puberty while others in their last year of high school have not; this is also true for girls.

These are physiologically normal individuals. When one crosses the somewhat arbitrary border into pathologically early puberty, variations become even more extreme. Children, even mere infants, may be found with one or another of the manifestations of precocious puberty. The youngest mother on record, a Peruvian girl, was delivered by caesarian section of a healthy male infant when she was all of 5 years and 7 months of age on May 15, 1939. She had reached puberty at 3 and had become pregnant at 4 years and 10 months. Boys of comparable precocity may have fathered children, but, if so, it would be very much harder to verify. At the other extreme, puberty may be far delayed or its typical changes largely absent, as in the case of eunuchs. Disturbances of puberty result from precocious activity or interference with the function of the hypothalamus, anterior pituitary, or the gonads. They may be due to a wide variety of pathological factors, and sometimes they have no known or demonstrable cause.

The normal process of puberty is subject to a large number of genetic and environmental influences, including familial and possibly racial factors, and the effects of seasons, perhaps of climate, definitely of nutrition, illness, and emotional state.[27] Such

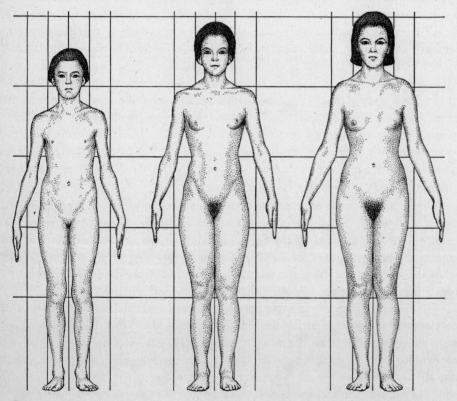

Figure 7.

THREE GIRLS, all with the chronological age of 12.75 years, differed dramatically in development according to whether the particular girl had not yet reached puberty (*left*), was part of the way through it (*middle*) or had finished her development (*right*). This range of variation is completely normal. This drawing and the one below are based on photographs made by author and his colleagues at Institute of Child Health of University of London.

factors combine to generate geographic and social class differences in the maturational patterns of puberty. A secular trend of a decline in the age at menarche has been in progress during the last century. In 1840, Norwegian girls on the average reached menarche at about 17 years; now the average is four years younger. Women who reached puberty around 1900 did so one to two years later than teenagers do now.[28] This general trend has progressed at a rate of about four months per decade, but it is beginning to level out in Western countries.[29] A similar pattern of early maturation is assumed to be occurring in boys, although it is more difficult to prove because males lack a comparably distinct event to mark the onset of reproductive maturation.

Another secular trend involves increased height. In successive decades since 1900, adolescents have become taller by 2.5 cm and heavier by 2.5 kg. But since this is a reflection more of earlier maturation than of a more protracted fever of growth, the net gain for adults has been 1 cm per decade: a race of giants is therefore not imminent.[30]

No formal subdivisions of adult life have been distinguished from a human biological perspective. Although aging is studied extensively from the cellular to the organismic level, this work has not as yet been translated into discrete life phases. Using reproductive maturity as the criterion, one could meaningfully divide the life span into three phases separated by puberty and the menopause or climacteric.[31] But the latter event is not so distinct an entity in the male as it is in the female. The landmarks of such a subdivision are also too far apart to provide us with sufficient rungs on the ladder to match the many other important events that characterize adult life. Nevertheless, the climacteric deserves some further comment both as an event of major significance and as a counterpoint to puberty.

A woman is born with several hundred thousand ova which begin to mature cyclically at puberty. Some 300-400 cycles later, ovulation becomes erratic and finally

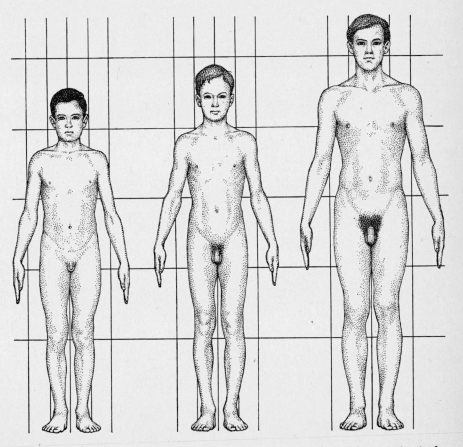

THREE BOYS, all of the chronological age of 14.75 years, showed a similar variation in the range of their development. As is indicated in the charts on page 40, evidently some boys have entirely finished their growth and sexual maturation before others even begin theirs.

stops as mysteriously as it began. The period of the menopause, which marks this event, usually occurs around the age of 47: about 50 per cent experience it between 45 and 50; 25 per cent before 45; and 25 per cent of women later than 50 years.

The cessation of ovulation results in infertility. Since the maturing ovarian follicle is the source of estrogen and progesterone, the post-menopausal woman also experiences the effects of withdrawal of these hormones. As increased levels of estrogen feminize the pubescent girl, decreased levels of estrogen have the opposite effect: they fail to counter the masculinizing effects of androgens which continue to be produced by the adrenal cortex. As a result, the pitch of the voice is lowered, for example, and the face becomes more hirsute. The other symptoms of the climacteric include "hot flashes," headaches, dizziness, palpitations, and joint pains. Almost all menopausal women experience these effects, but only about one in ten is significantly perturbed by them. Equally important are mood changes which occasionally culminate in the severe depressions of involutional melancholia. Although the reproductive system undergoes atrophic changes, the climacteric need not lead to sexual apathy or malfunction. Some women in fact experience an enhancement of erotic responsiveness, possibly due to the effect of androgen as well as to psychological factors such as freedom from the fear of pregnancy.

The male climacteric is a far more dubious entity. Gonadal function in the male does not generally cease as abruptly as it does in the female. Only rarely does a true male climacteric occur that includes symptoms such as hot flashes and similar signs of hormone withdrawal. More typically, there is a gradual decline in testicular function, with concomitant loss of fertility and potency, beginning in middle age. Nevertheless, males, too, can remain sexually active (and some even fertile) into old age.

In both sexes the hormonal decline in middle age is at the gonadal level. The pituitary hormones continue to be produced, but the testes and the ovary do not respond as before. Since estrogen can be readily administered, the biological changes of the climacteric can be significantly retarded and modified in women. Such hormonal replacement is of dubious value in males.

Psychiatric Viewpoints on Adulthood

Since its nineteenth-century emergence as a distinct medical specialty, psychiatry has been concerned with mental illness rather than with normative human development. Psychiatrists have traditionally labored in mental institutions, which for the most part have functioned as warehouses for the storage and custody of lost and unclaimed human beings. The great advances in the early history of psychiatry were thus in the more humanitarian treatment of the insane[32] and in the classification of mental illness.[33] It was Freud who brought psychiatry out of the madhouse.

Freud treated adults primarily, although his famous stages of psychosexual development were restricted to childhood. Even adolescence as a stage of life did not come into focus until the next generation of psychoanalysts, notably Anna Freud, August Aichhorn, Peter Blos, and, of course, Erik Erikson. Among the early psychoanalysts, Jung was one who addressed himself to life stages beyond adolescence;[34] in fact, he started with the stage of "youth" that he defined as spanning the period between post-pubescence and adulthood. Jung visualized this phase as one of disengagement from childhood aspirations, confrontation with the issues of sexuality and self-esteem, and a general broadening of life perspective. Between the ages of 35 and 40, according to Jung, personality changes slowly begin to occur: some childhood traits may reemerge, and a reshuffling of motivations and interests takes place. These changes gradually become stabilized, and attitudes and convictions begin to harden, so that by age 50 a tendency toward rigidity and intolerance is established.

Jung dwells at length on old age, which he sees as characterized by further deep-seated psychic reorganization. There may be a tendency to change in the direction of the opposite sex, such as when older men become more "feminine" and women more "masculine." Eventually, the main task becomes the confrontation of death. Rather than compete with the young or cling to the past, the individual must discover in death a meaningful goal to strive for rather than a peril to shrink from: ". . . an old man who cannot bid farewell to life appears as feeble and sickly as a young man who is unable to embrace it."[35]

The major effort so far to examine the entire life cycle has come from Erik Erikson. Given the fame of his work, the difficulty of summarizing his thoughts without greatly diminishing them, and his own contribution to this volume, it would be otiose of me to discuss his theories here in any detail, but we also cannot possibly omit all reference to them even in this brief account.[36]

Erikson's theory of psychosocial development postulates a sequence of eight phases or "ages of man." These phases derive in part from Freud's stages of psychosexual and libidinal development, but they also go beyond them and encompass the entire life span. Each stage is defined by a phase-specific task and follows a general chronology without being linked to specific, arbitrary age limits. The first four phases pertain to childhood, the fifth to adolescence, and the last three to adulthood.

These assignments hold true only in the sense that the phase-specific tasks reach their critical point of resolution during their respective phases. Otherwise, their solutions are prepared in previous stages and elaborated in subsequent ones. At each phase, components from each of the eight major tasks are present simultaneously as "pre-

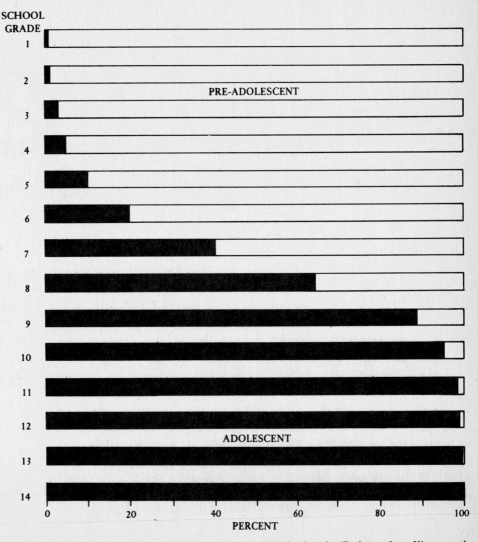

Figure 8. Per cent of adolescent (pubescent) boys in each school grade. (Redrawn from Kinsey *et al, Sexual Behavior in the Human Male* [Philadelphia, 1948], p. 187).

cursors," "derivates," and as the decisive "crisis" itself. Consequently, it is not possible to discuss any phase of development in isolation. Thus, childhood does not end nor adulthood begin with adolescence. Rather, the adult is anticipated in the child and the child persists in the adult. This is the thread that gives continuity to Erikson's developmental scheme.

The model for this scheme is epigenetic and based on a fundamental principle of embryonal development whereby the differentiation of each part progresses from the simple to the more complex, each part having its time of ascendance while all parts grow simultaneously. This process is also firmly rooted in a social context and relies on a coordination between the developing person and an average expectable environment. Through a "cog-wheeling" of life cycles, phase-specific needs of children are interlocked to those of caretaking adults as representatives of society. Added to the internal strands that hold an individual life cycle together are the external ties which link various life cycles in an expanding circle of interpersonal bonds.

The psychosocial transition to adulthood is accomplished during adolescence (Erikson's Stage V) through the achievement of a sense of ego Identity. This, in turn, permits the establishment of a sense of Intimacy by the resolution of the first phase-specific task of adulthood proper (Stage VI). Such intimacy involves relations with the other sex but also with others of the same sex, and one's own self as well.

The counterpart to intimacy is Isolation as manifested in the ability and willingness to repudiate, isolate, or even destroy forces and people inimical to oneself. Erikson defines these phase-specific tasks in terms of the polar opposites of successful outcome or failure. In this sense, isolation constitutes the failure of intimacy. But, in another sense, the negative outcome has its own desirable features: given the state of the world, a person with no ability or will to protect himself would soon be overwhelmed. The outcome of a given stage is thus never either one or the other alternative because such "pure forms" cannot exist and would be maladaptive if they did.[37]

The next phase of adulthood (Stage VII) confronts the issue of Generativity versus Stagnation. Continuing with the heterosexual paradigm, Erikson sees the central task here as the establishment, "by way of genitality and genes," of the next generation through the production and care of offspring. This same purpose may also be achieved by some who forgo parenthood and express their generativity through other altruistic and creative acts. Likewise the mere fact of biological parenthood or the desire for children does not in itself amount to true generativity. The failure to advance to this stage results in a stagnation that may take the form of obsessive pseudo-intimacy or a narcissistic self-indulgence whereby the person treats himself as if he were his "own one and only child."

The final phase of adult life must resolve the task of Integrity versus Despair and Disgust. Integrity is the "fruit of the seven stages" and the outcome of having taken care of things and people, adapted to triumphs and disappointments, originated others and generated things and ideas. It is the "acceptance of one's own and only life cycle and of the people who have become significant to it as something that had to be and that, by necessity, permitted no substitution."[38] If this "one and only life cycle is not accepted as the ultimate of life," the result is despair, since there is no time for fresh starts. Such despair leads to contempt of oneself and disgust with the world.

Adulthood in a more specific sense has so far received less attention in Erikson's work than adolescence. None of its phase-specific tasks would elicit the same recognition that the concept of Identity produces. Only those precursors of adult crises that appear in connection with adolescence (and none of the derivatives of the adult crises) have been spelled out. In his earlier presentation, Erikson designated the adolescent precursors of the three phase-specific adult tasks as Sexual Identity versus Bisexual Diffusion; Leadership-Polarization versus Authority Diffusion; Ideological Polarization versus Diffusion of Ideals.[39] In later versions of his table, these terms appear as Sexual

Polarization versus Bisexual Confusion; Leader-and-Followership versus Authority Confusion; Ideological Commitment versus Confusion of Values.[40]

In concluding his Jefferson Lectures, Erikson noted that we have had a century of the child and something like a century of youth, and he wondered when the century of the adult would begin.[41] This remark presages, perhaps, a shift in his own focus of interest.

In contemporary psychiatry a few other efforts dealing with normal adulthood in a developmental scheme deserve mention. Engel[42] and Lidz[43] have written thoughtful accounts bringing together insights from medicine, psychoanalysis, and the social sciences, but they are long on childhood and short on adulthood.[44] Grinker has studied normal young males whom he calls "homoclites."[45] Though the psychiatric literature on adulthood remains sparse, there is some evidence that increased attention is being directed to this phase of life: one encounters an occasional report of new research,[46] and middle age is now discussed in considerable detail as a distinct topic in standard texts of psychiatry.[47] There is also a substantial literature on the psychiatric aspects of old age.[48]

Since psychiatry draws heavily on research in the behavioral sciences, a full account of the psychiatric perspective on adulthood would also have to take account of this literature, which is a task we cannot take on here. By way of illustration, we might mention the monumental volumes of G. Stanley Hall on adolescence[49] and old age[50] which were published at the turn of the century. Currently, the work of Neugarten is particularly noteworthy,[51] and there are other contributors.[52]

Toward a Definition of Adulthood

Prerequisite to a clearer delineation of adulthood as a phase of life is a better understanding of what constitutes a "phase of life" in the first place. The presence of such stages can neither be taken for granted nor dismissed out of hand by the argument that "life is too complex to be pidgeonholed." Other things have been profitably classified that are not simple either; besides, "complexity" is as much a function of the level of analysis as it is inherent in the subject of study itself.

Taxonomy is the "law of arrangement" whereby, on the basis of certain characteristics, a group of objects, ideas, or phenomena is placed in a pattern for a particular purpose. Since there are many ways of classifying something, a single item can be part of any number of classifications: books, for instance, can be sorted out not only by author and subject, but also by size, shape, color, or weight. All such arrangements are artificial, but any one can be legitimate for some specific purpose. Still, they are not all equally relevant so far as the fundamental purpose of the objects being described is concerned.

In its attempts to look for order in the world, science assumes that, in addition to artificial categorizing of varying usefulness, there are also natural orders which, when elucidated, constitute natural laws. When Dmitri Mendeleyev (1834-1907) discovered that chemical elements show a periodic recurrence of properties when arranged in the order of increasing atomic weight, he laid one of the cornerstones of modern chemistry. This Periodic Table permitted him to detect errors in previously accepted atomic weights of elements based on their position, and the "gaps" that existed in the series permitted him correctly to predict the existence and properties of the elements gallium, scandium, and germanium fifteen years before their actual discovery. Similarly, after the discovery of helium and argon, the periodic law led to the prediction of the existence of neon, krypton, xenon, and radon. Classifications are thus not only convenient summaries; they can also be powerful research tools. Their "empty boxes" are part of their function and are not merely a reflection of incompleteness.

For a classification to be useful, it need not necessarily elucidate a fundamental natural law. Carl von Linne (1701-1778), for instance, relied on the number and arrangement of stamens and pistils in a flower for his placement of plants in various categories. Though an artificial system, it has proven enormously useful. But unlike his systematization of the animal and plant kingdoms, Linne's attempts at classifying minerals and diseases (he was trained as a physician) have not proved particularly useful.

The task of defining adulthood and its stages is basically a taxonomical venture. But it needs to be clarified if one is to "discover" divisions of the life cycle in the manner of "natural laws." Does one pick and choose certain aspects of adult life to fit into a schematic pattern or "invent" a pattern, as it were, for a purpose? The former presupposes the existence of life stages and subdivisions in an almost immutable sense. The latter model is far more modest and consistent with the notion that adulthood and its phases may be perceived differently at different times and places, depending on the aspects of adult biology and behavior that are chosen as the bases for assignment.

Since we are unlikely to find a single basic dimension, comparable to the atomic weight of elements, for defining life phases, the stages to be constructed must have various delineating limits. The nodal points must constitute significant landmarks that are appropriately spaced. If the rungs of the ladder are too far apart, the connectivity is lost and the system is not sufficiently differentiated. Likewise, if there is a profusion of stages, the scheme will be too fragmented. There are lessons to be learned in this regard from biology. For instance, one taxonomic pitfall is the fallacy of describing variant individuals as separate species by failing to account for intraspecies variability. There is likewise a danger in discovering "pseudostages" of the life cycle that are merely variants. Finally, for classification schemes to be useful, they must allow for continued correction or expansion, while leaving the essential character of the system intact. (For instance, to date, 330,000 plant and 1,000,000 animal species have already been named, 15,000 to 20,000 new species are discovered each year, and the Linnaean system still continues to assimilate them. Although the number of life stages is far fewer, the principle is the same.)

Any comprehensive definition of adulthood will have to be based on an understanding of our biological substrate and our psychosocial characteristics and be reflective of the mind and the spirit that lend meaning to life. Given the complexities of human nature and the pluralistic and rapidly changing nature of the world, to agree on such definitions is a difficult task. We are surely not going to arrive at a definition to end all definitions for all time. But we hope that approximations can be found that will be widely accepted, at least temporarily, within certain cultural confines and that will in turn perhaps reveal some universals.

Medicine has important bearings on several aspects of this problem. First, it contributes the indispensable dimension of normative biological development into and during adulthood. Second, it focuses on illness and debility which come progressively to preoccupy adult life. Third, it significantly alters the life span itself.

Biological maturity in the sense of the completion of growth and reproductive capacity is essential to any definition of adulthood. Yet this dimension may seem to be as much a source of difficulty as it is of help. At the ages when these biological gains are achieved, most persons in contemporary Western society are still hopelessly dependent, their identities nebulous, and their stations in life undetermined. Furthermore, like all biological phenomena, these changes follow a variable timetable which simply does not lend itself to the fixed and arbitrary schedules that society uses to certify people as adults. The result is the well known disparity between the biological and social imperatives of adulthood. To bridge this gap there is little point in espousing a return to a "natural" world where biological functions are allowed to be what they may. We may be primates, but we have also come down from the trees, and it would be difficult for us to climb back up again.

Yet it is also naive to expect that we can keep biological adults "on ice" until the social structure allows their full-fledged integration into the adult world and legitimization of the expression of their biological maturity. One solution to this dilemma may be a more differentiated response from society regarding which or what aspect of maturing functions are to be kept in check and which ones allowed reasonable expression.

A case in point is adolescent sexuality. In past times, because association between sex and reproduction was unpredictable, social inhibitions had to be imposed on sexual behavior, since no society could trifle with the welfare of its young and hope to survive for very long. Sex and reproduction are now reliably and safely separable; however, societal response remains ambivalent. Increasing numbers of young people are taking the matter in their own hands, but they frequently mismanage it and the relativistic morality which guides them in principle sometimes comes within whispering distance of amorality in practice.

There is no ready solution to this dilemma, but greater awareness of biological variation may temper the rigidity with which social schedules are set up in defining adulthood. It is a curious fact that we claim to put so much stock in the natural world, yet we either remain ignorant of it or disregard its true nature. From that bulwark of Catholic theology, Thomas Aquinas, to countless lesser figures, "rules of nature" and Natural Law have been invoked as guides to human behavior, yet there is often no discernible association between what we think exists and what actually does exist in nature, in terms both of our biological selves and of the living world at large.

The logistical problems involved in substituting a developmental for a chronological timetable in defining adulthood are enormous. It would certainly disrupt the pace of bureaucratic gymnastics and cause much administrative grief. Yet the current alternatives seem equally cumbersome: we assume young people to be what is convenient to adults for them to be and we then get upset when they are not. Neither does the answer lie in self-determination, however: for every youth truly more mature than his years, there are ten who are queue-jumping.

Serious questions can be raised as to whether our socially determined tempo of adult life is sufficiently linked to the concurrent progress of physiological processes. Our work schedules do allow us times to eat and rest, but, beyond such obvious accommodation, there is probably a great deal more that could be done to bring social schedules into step with biological rhythms. We are all aware of the alternation of sleep and wakefulness, but few realize that as many as a hundred other functions also follow daily cycles. These include the rates at which cells divide and metabolic processes fluctuate. For instance, body temperature drops at night, urinary output increases during the day, and other functions change rhythmically. As a result, the body's response to drugs, for example, is not uniform but depends, at least in some cases, on the time of administration (e.g., diabetics are far more sensitive to insulin at night). Likewise, experimental evidence shows that the time of exposure to a noxious agent may in part determine whether or not the organism will succumb to it. Such rhythmicity is characteristic of all living systems, including unicellular organisms. As Colin Pittendrigh has put it, "Gertrude Stein to the contrary notwithstanding, a rose is not necessarily and unqualifiedly a rose; that is to say, it is a very different biochemical system at noon and at midnight."[53]

The biological clocks ticking away in each of us are not restricted to the silent regulation of psychological processes. Such rhythms are also involved in behavioral regulation varying from fluctuations in the speed of problem-solving to shifts in mood. Much of the research in this field has involved circadian rhythms,[54] but biological rhythms, such as the monthly menstrual cycle, can also have shorter or longer "periods."[55] The longer the period of the rhythm, the harder it is to detect and study; the considerable variation of the same rhythm in different people further complicates its study. Such rhythms are not restricted to normal functions, but are also manifested in various medical and psychiatric conditions such as manic-depressive psychosis.

The study of metabolic rhythms and biological clocks is a fascinating field still in its infancy, but one with great potential to enhance our understanding of the biology of behavior—a subject with wide social ramifications.[56] One possible though partial explanation for the current plague of psychosomatic ailments and stressful lives is that the culturally set pace of life in industrialized societies is frequently out of phase with its basic metabolic rhythms. The entire evolution of man took place while he was a hunter. The agricultural way of life accounts for less than one per cent of human history, and no biological changes seem to have occurred during that time.[57] Thus, our bodies and the rhythms by which they oscillate are more or less the same as those of our remotest ancestors. But our societies and cultural determinants of behavior are quite obviously far from the same: hence the dysrhythmia.

Even prehistoric man must have been aware of the effects that significant disruptions had in his daily round of life: soldiers of all time have had to experience sleepless nights and forced marches. But these have been sporadic events, not ways of life. Today, such disruptions seem to have become routine. A case in point is long-distance east-west jet travel. The resultant symptoms of "jet lag" are well known; they constitute a physiological burden that has been widely imposed on people only during the past decade or two, but that we seem already to have accepted as if it were a preordained part of human destiny. The point is not to denigrate the tremendous advantages of jet travel but to indicate the uncritical willingness with which we expose our bodies to stresses whose long-term effects have yet to become fully manifest. When one moves from earthbound flights to travel in deep space, the dislocations entailed are difficult even to envisage.

All this perhaps has little bearing on adulthood except that adults set up the social schedules to which they then expose the rest of the populace as well, and that it is those adults in the most "adult" roles of leadership who are the most subjected to the effects of biological dysrhythmia. In fact, a willingness and seeming ability to defy the innate rhythms of the body for social or personal ends has become one of the hallmarks of adulthood in the Western world.

For medicine to contribute more significantly to this problem, considerable sifting and sorting of existing information as well as the acquisition of further data will be necessary. The stresses that result from the incongruous social demands on the body are serious, but we do not have to pay attention to them if we are willing to write off the toll in distress and casualties as part of the cost of modern life or of being adult.

Both personally and professionally we often harbor a rather curious attitude toward illness. Even though we know perfectly well that a great deal of life, especially adult life, will be afflicted by it, when we fall ill, we nevertheless have a tendency to feel slighted and aggrieved, or to be nagged by thoughts of failure and a sense of guilt. The "normal" state of being is assumed to be one of robust health, and death is a calamity whenever it comes.[58] If medicine could convey the notion that illness and death are part of life rather than aberrations imposed upon it, the conceptual and practical gains in understanding the life cycle would be considerable.

The impact of health measures on prolonging life hardly needs to be belabored. People in the West now have a life expectancy of 70 years and, by the end of the century, this figure will probably have reached 80 years. In contrast, life expectancy in classical Greece was 18 and in Rome 22 years. Much of this disparity is a reflection of the decline in infant mortality rates, but it is also true that more people are living longer today than ever before.

The impact of such changes on our concept of the life cycle is enormous. Napoleon was an army captain at 16, emperor at 32. Mozart died at the age of 35 years and 10 months.[59] Were Napoleon and Mozart "young adults" as we now understand the term when in their early thirties? These and countless other examples suggest that there is nothing fixed or immutable about life phases. They simply cannot be dealt with out of historical and cultural contexts. This is also why a purely biological definition of adulthood would be futile, quite aside from the fact that biology itself is subject to change.

Looking further into the future, there may even come a time when it will be possible to tamper with the biological clocks that regulate the very processes of growth and aging (or "ripening and rotting," as Hayflick puts it).[60] If and when that time comes, decisions may have to be made about what part of the life cycle to prolong. Within a life span of, say, one hundred years, would we want to foreshorten childhood or prolong it? If adulthood is to be stretched out, can it occur during our "prime" or will it simply prolong the period of decrepitude? And in relation to what function will "prime time" be determined? As we live longer, will we accomplish more and have fuller lives? Or will we simply stretch out what we do to fill up the time allotted according to some Parkinsonian principle?

Such problems and prospects have a way of suddenly catching up with us while we are preoccupied with one or another seemingly important matter. There are also plenty of life-cycle-related problems that are already urgent. Despite the rapid expansion of, and marked changes in, the older population, our notions of old age as a phase of life have undergone little revision. We go on marveling at the number of active, alert, "youthful" people in their seventies without recognizing that the same chronological age span now perhaps represents a different state than it did in the past (or may in the future). And if we keep piling "old people" upon "old people" as dependents on society, our welfare and supporting institutions will soon be pushed further toward the breaking point. But if we can reappraise who these people are, what their needs and capabilities are, and how this life phase should now be perceived, then matters can be quite different.

To deal with such issues, we need to confront them, perhaps, not so much with a grim determination to "solve" life's problems, but first with an attempt to understand them better. As Dostoevsky declared in his diary, his purpose as a writer was to "find the man in man." It is equally our task to try to find the adult in the adult in this day and age.

REFERENCES

[1]Sir Thomas Browne, *Religio Medici, Letter to a Friend, Christian Morals, Urn-Burial, and Other Papers*, Part III, Sect. 8 of *Christian Morals* (Boston, 1878).

[2]William Osler (1849-1919), the great clinician of our time, was so ardent an admirer of Sir Thomas Browne that a copy of the *Religio Medici* was placed in his coffin. Cited by J. H. Talbot, *A Biographical History of Medicine* (New York, 1970).

[3]Thomas Lathrop Stedman, *Medical Dictionary* (Baltimore, 1961).

[4]Blakiston's *New Gould Medical Dictionary* (Philadelphia, 1949).

[5]*Cumulated Index Medicus* (Chicago, 1974).

[6]Neither of these two fields yet constitutes a formal specialty in the United States as reflected by the existence of Specialty Boards. The credentials given by these Boards establish a physician as a specialist, but a certification for the practice of medicine is at the discretion of state licensing bodies. In principle, at least, any licensed physician is allowed to treat any and all illnesses.

[7]H. F. Garrison, "History of Pediatrics," *Abt-Garrison History of Pediatrics* (Philadelphia, 1965), p. 43.

[8]L. Clendening, *Source Book of Medical History* (New York, 1942), p. 261.

[9]The growth of modern pediatrics during the nineteenth century has been described by Abraham Jacobi (1830-1919), who himself contributed greatly to its development and is regarded as the "Father of American Pediatrics." Jacobi's collected works are in *Collectanea Jacobi*, W. J. Robinson, ed. (8 volumes; 1909). For Jacobi's biography, see Talbot, *op. cit.*, pp. 1119-21.

[10]W. A. Marshall and J. M. Tanner, "Puberty," *Scientific Foundations of Paediatrics*, J. A. Davis and J. Dobbing, eds. (London, 1974), p. 124.

[11]J. M. Tanner, "Sequence, Tempo, and Individual Variation in the Growth and Development of Boys and Girls Aged Twelve to Sixteen," *Daedalus* (Fall, 1971), pp. 907-30.

[12]For further details, see the references to Tanner. Also, F. P. Heald and W. Hung, eds., *Adolescent Endocrinology* (New York, 1970); B. T. Donovan and J. J. Van den Werff Ten Bosch, *Physiology of Puberty* (Baltimore, 1965); A. W. Root, "Endocrinology of Puberty," *The Journal of Pediatrics*, 83 (1973), pp. 1-19.

[13]D. Sinclair, *Human Growth After Birth* (London, 1973), p. 26.

[14]W. A. Marshall and J. M. Tanner, "Variations in the Pattern of Pubertal Changes in Girls," *Archives of Disease in Childhood*, 44 (1969), p. 291.

[15]W. A. Marshall and J. M. Tanner, "Variations in the Pattern of Pubertal Changes in Boys," *ibid.*, 45 (1970), p. 13.

[16]J. M. Tanner, "Physical Growth," *Carmichael's Manual of Child Psychology*, P. Mussen, ed. (3rd ed., New York, 1970), I, p. 94.

[17]Sinclair, *op. cit.*, p. 26.

[18]H. E. Jones, *Motor Performance and Growth. A Developmental Study of Static Dynamometric Strength* (Berkeley, 1949).

[19]See F. A. Beach, "Human Sexuality and Evolution," *Reproductive Behavior*, W. Montagna and W. A. Sadler, eds. (New York, 1974).

[20]Despite the chronological variability in onset, the progressive changes in breast, genital, and pubic-hair growth are consistent enough to be grouped into stages that act as developmental landmarks. For a discussion of these stages, see J. M. Tanner, *Growth at Adolescence* (2nd ed., Oxford, 1962).

[21]In the last category are males whose prostate gland has been removed (but without damaging the relevant nerves in the region). One could also include practitioners of the Indian technique of "Karezza" or "coitus reservatus" (not to be confused with "coitus interruptus"), although strictly speaking this may involve retrograde ejaculation into the urinary bladder rather than orgasm without ejaculation. This practice was commonly used as a means of birth control in the nineteenth-century communal Oneida colony in upstate New York. See N. Bishop, "The Great Oneida Love-in," *American Heritage*, 20 (1969), pp. 14-17, 86-92.

[22]For a cross-cultural review of childhood sexual behavior, see C. S. Ford and F. A. Beach, *Patterns of Sexual Behavior* (New York, 1951), and the relevant sections in A. C. Kinsey et al., *Sexual Behavior in the Human Male* and *Sexual Behavior in the Human Female* (Philadelphia, 1948 and 1953).

[23]J. Money and A. A. Ehrhardt, *Man and Woman, Boy and Girl* (Baltimore, 1972).

[24]For an extensive consideration of the mechanism of the onset of puberty, see M. M. Grumbach, G. D. Grave, F. E. Mayer, *The Control of the Onset of Puberty* (New York, 1974).

[25]One is reminded of the Roman general who claimed that his young son was the most influential person in the world because Rome controlled the world, the Emperor controlled Rome, the general himself controlled the Emperor, the general's wife controlled him and was in turn controlled by their little boy!

[26]J. M. Tanner, "Growth and Development of the Brain," *Carmichael's Manuel, op. cit.*

[27]For instance, randomly chosen and unrelated girls reach menarche at an average of 19 months apart. This difference is 13 months in sisters who are not twins, 10 months between nonidentical twins, and only 2.8 months between identical twins living together under average West European economic conditions.

[28]For a list of ages at the onset of menarche in various countries, see Table 7 compiled by Marshall and Tanner in Dobbing, *op. cit.*, p. 144.

[29]This phenomenon is ascribed in part to environmental factors, such as improved nutrition, but other factors may also be operative. Even increased exposure to light due to the widespread use of artificial lighting has been suggested as a cause (based on experimental work with animals), although the fact that blind girls reach menarche earlier than others would seem to contradict this. See N. A. Jafarey, "Effect of Artificial Lighting on the Age of Menarche," *Lancet*, 1 (1971), p. 707.

[30]F. Falkner, "Physical Growth," *Pediatrics*, H. L. Barnett and A. H. Einhorn, eds. (15th ed., New York, 1972), p. 239.

[31]"Menopause" refers to the permanent cessation of menstruation due to aging. "Climacteric" is a broader term that includes the various related changes experienced at this point. Strictly speaking, the latter term, but not the former, is applicable to males, although in current usage the two terms have tended to become synonymous.

[32]Pioneered by Philippe Pinel (1745-1826) in France, William Tuke (1732-1822) in England.

[33]The foundations of psychiatric nosology were laid down by Emil Kraepelin (1856-1926); Eugene Bleuler's (1851-1939) redefinition of schizophrenia was another major landmark.

[34]C. G. Jung, "The Stages of Life," in *The Collected Works of C. G. Jung*, Vol. 8 (New York, 1960).

[35]*Ibid.*

[36]The first detailed presentation of Erikson's concept of the life cycle is in "Identity and the Life Cycle," *Psychological Issues*, 1 (1959), pp. 50-100. Adulthood is dealt with in pages 95-99. See also *Identity, Youth and Crisis* (1968), and *Childhood and Society* (2nd ed., New York, 1963).

[37]This argument also holds well for Mistrust which is the opposite of Basic Trust, the phase-specific task of Stage I. But it is more difficult to see much virtue in the negative outcomes of some of the other stages such as Inferiority (II), Identity Confusion (V), Stagnation (VII), and Despair (VIII).

[38]Erikson, "Identity and the Life Cycle," *op. cit.*, p. 98.

[39]*Ibid.*, p. 120.

[40]Erikson, *Identity, Youth and Crisis, op. cit.*, p. 94.

[41]Erik Erikson, *Dimensions of a New Identity* (New York, 1974).

[42]G. Engel, *Psychological Development in Health and Disease* (Philadelphia, 1962).

[43]Theodore Lidz, *The Person* (New York, 1968).

[44]See Bernice L. Neugarten's review of T. Lidz's book in *Contemporary Psychology*, 14 (1969), pp. 409-11. See also John Romano in the *Journal of the American Medical Association*, 207 (1969), p. 244.

[45]R. R. Grinker, Sr., R. R. Grinker, Jr., and J. A. Timberlake, "A Study of the 'Mentally Healthy' Young Males (Homoclites)," *Archives of General Psychiatry*, 6 (1962), pp. 27-74.

[46]R. L. Gould, "The Phases of Adult Life: A Study in Developmental Psychology," *The American Journal of Psychiatry*, 129 (1972), pp. 33-J31. A project still in progress at the Psychophysiology Laboratory of the Institute of Living Hospital, Hartford, Conn., under the direction of C. F. Stroebel and B. Glueck, Jr., is also attempting to obtain daily records of life events, moods, and bodily changes from both patients and normal subjects.

[47]R. N. Butler, "Psychiatry and Psychology of the Middle-Aged," in A. M. Freedman, H. I. Kaplan, and B. J. Sadock, eds., *Comprehensive Textbook of Psychiatry*, 2 (2nd ed., Baltimore, 1975), pp. 2390-2404; B. L. Neugarten and N. Datan, "The Middle Years," in S. Arieti, ed., *American Handbook of Psychiatry*, Vol. 1 (2nd ed., New York, 1974).

[48]For an overview, see J. Weinberg, "Geriatric Psychiatry," in A. M. Freedman *et al., op. cit*, 2405-20.

[49]G. Stanley Hall, *Adolescence* (New York and London, 1904).

[50]*Idem, Old Age* (New York, 1922).

[51]B. L. Neugarten, *Personality in Middle and Later Life.* (New York, 1964); "Personality and Aging," in J. E. Birren and K. Warner Schaic, eds., *Handbook of the Psychology of Aging* (in press).

[52]See, for instance, C. Buhler, "The Course of Human Life as a Psychological Problem," *Human Development*, 2 (1968), pp. 184-200; D. J. Levinson *et al.*, "The Psychosocial Development of Men in Early Adulthood and the Mid-Life Transition," in D. F. Ricks *et al.*, eds., *Life History Research in Psychopathology*, Vol. 3 (Minneapolis, 1974); much of this research is discussed by D. C. Kimmel in *Adulthood and Aging* (New York, 1974).

[53]Quoted by R. R. Ward in *The Living Clocks* (New York, 1971), p. 278.

[54]The term "circadian" is derived from the Latin for "about" (*circa*) and "day" (*diem*). It is preferred to "daily" because these oscillations do not precisely coincide with the earth's daily rotation. "Diurnal" is also confusing since it is sometimes used in contradistinction to "nocturnal" and at other times in the sense of "daily." Pittendrigh in R. R. Ward, *op. cit.*, p. 276.

[55]For a review of psychological changes related to the menstrual cycle, see J. F. O'Connor, E. M. Shelley, and L. C. Stern, "Behavioral Rhythms Related to the Menstrual Cycle," *Biorhythms and Human Reproduction*, M. Perin *et al*, eds. (New York, 1974), pp. 309-24.

[56]For surveys in this field written for the general reader, see G. G. Luce, *Body Time* (New York, 1971); R. R. Ward, *op. cit.* The former has extensive bibliographical references.

[57]Sherwood L. Washburn and C. S. Lancaster, "The Evolution of Hunting," *Perspectives on Human Evolution*, S. L. Washburn and P. C. Jay, eds., Vol. 1, (New York, 1968), pp. 213-29.

[58]For reflections on this issue, see L. Thomas, "Biological Aspects of Death," *The Pharos of Alpha Omega Alpha*, 37 (1974), pp. 83-89.

[59]R. Tomlinson, *Demographic Problems: Controversy Over Population Control* (Belmont, California, 1967).

[60]L. Hayflick, "Why Grow Old?," *The Stanford Magazine*, 3 (1975), pp. 36-43.

7

A New Age
for Aging

*After 30, everyone begins a steady, predictable
decline toward death. Now we are on the brink of an alternative*

by Bernard L. Strehler

Growing old is a process that few people care to ponder; indeed, most people skirt the issue by spending a surprising amount of time and effort trying to remain youthful. We greet long-lost friends with comments about how well they look (meaning: you haven't aged much). We automatically categorize people according to whether they are younger or older than we are (meaning: I envy your youthful vigor and appearance or you have deteriorated more than I have). Billions of dollars are spent every year on cosmetics (meaning: we want to *look* young). Men dutifully jog around their suburban neighborhoods before leaving for the office (meaning: maybe this will slow down the deterioration of my circulatory system). We adulate youth and respect age (meaning: I would like to be young again; but there must be something good to look forward to—wisdom, perhaps). We advise friends to stop smoking (meaning: you may be shortening your life). The point is that every human being, whether he admits it or not, is at least vaguely apprehensive about the slow deterioration of his structure and functions that eventually ends in death.

Concern about aging and death is an important component of our sub-conscious life and may contribute more than is obvious to the increased mental disease among the middle-aged and elderly. Anxiety about the changed role in life that follows the female menopause or vague fears about potency in aging males are stresses that nearly everyone endures in silence despite the reassuring witticism of gerontologist Alex Comfort: "People give up sex for the same reasons they give up bicycling—it looks silly, arthritis makes it painful, or one has no bicycle!"

With all of the deep and hidden concerns about the processes that cause this sense of impermanence, it seems surprising that society has not invested more in trying to understand, control, arrest, or even reverse the underlying causes of aging. On the face of it, nothing would seem more appealing as a goal for the average person than an extension of the healthful years of life. Certainly most men are more curious about the reasons behind their own ephemeral existence on this globe than about the constitution of the rocks on the moon or whether life is present on Mars. But to date, less has been spent on the entire spectrum of research efforts in biological aging than on a single moon shot.

The reason, of course, is that men have become so accustomed to believing that their individual lives are finite, and that death is the inevitable price we pay for living, that they have refused to consider a biological alternative to individual extinction. After all, if death is inevitable—and unpleasant as well—why waste time, thought, and resources on a hopeless and depressing pursuit? Maybe if we don't think about it, it will go away.

Ironically, the same generation that learned to split and harness the atom, cracked the genetic code, and sent men to the moon may be the very one that will *not* benefit from the eventual amelioration of the aging process—a possibility that could become a practical reality before the end of this century. The control of the atom was the product of the urgencies of war; the understanding of how we are specified in long strings of genetic "beads," which each of our cells contains, was the culmination of a century of effort to understand the modes and mechanics of inheritance and gene expression; the conquest of space was prompted by the preceding successes of our competitors' Sputniks. But until now, the conquest of time itself has not been a social objective, and the President's recent

74

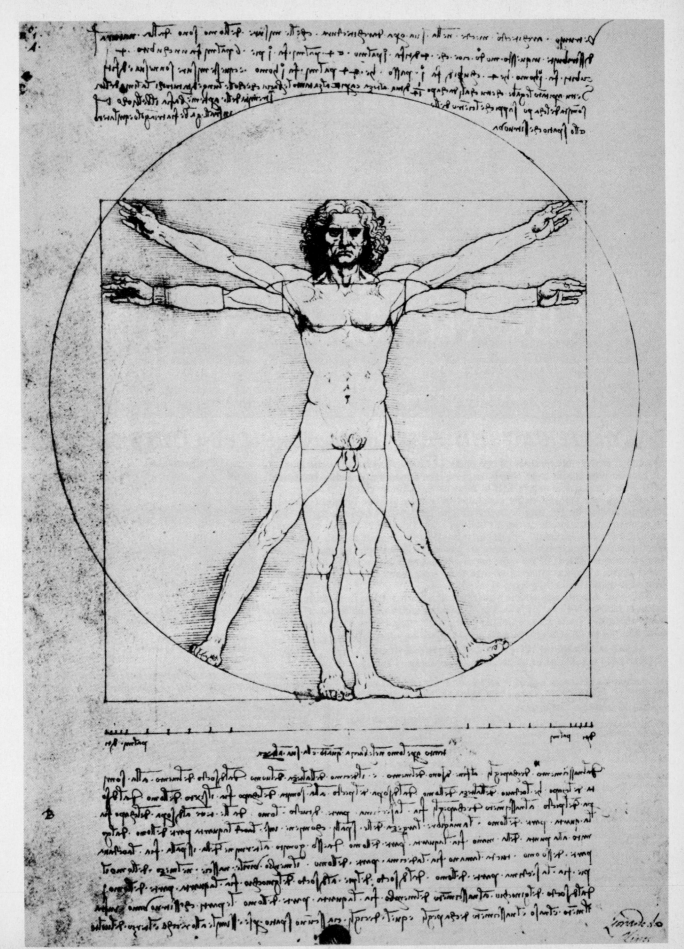

pocket veto of a bill to establish a National Institute for Research on Aging may postpone effective pursuit of this goal for another decade.

Implicit in the drive for federal support of research in this area is the possibility that men will be able to control—and perhaps reverse—part or all of the aging process. But the only way we can accurately predict what the chances are is to understand the nature of the events that lead to human aging. The transformation of life from a young state to an old one encompasses more than the mere passage of time, but the biological processes involved are not generally understood by the public. Perhaps if the basic principles and the rapidly growing body of new data were more openly discussed, there would be greater public support for the needed investment in fundamental research. Only such research, now or in the very near future, may make greatly extended lifetimes available for present generations of humans.

There are two generalizations to keep in mind about the events that occur as we age. The first is that many, although not all, bodily func-tions decrease gradually as aging takes place. This will not be news to anyone: all schoolboys know they can outrun their grandfathers and that the aged are less active, usually less alert, and more subject to disease than young adults. But this knowledge had not been put on a quantitative basis. During the last thirty years, however, Nathan Shock, the father of American gerontology, and his associates have described the exact rate at which different kinds of bodily functions fail. The essence of these findings is that most functions decrease gradually, at a rate of about 1 percent of the original capacity per year after age thirty. This means that the reserve ability to do all kinds of work will run out at about age 120. It is not surprising, therefore, that about 118 years is the greatest age attained by any human for whom good records of birth and death are available. There are occasional claims that individuals in certain parts of the Caucasus Mountains of the Soviet Union attain ages twenty or more years greater than this, but in the absence of records most such claims can probably be dismissed as folk fables. Once one attains great age, there is a great temptation to exaggerate it.

The second generalization is that the chance of dying does not increase in proportion to the amount of function lost. This was discovered and formulated into a simple mathematical law in about 1832 by an English insurance actuary, Benjamin Gompertz. The Gompertz law states that the chance of dying doubles about every eight years, irrespective of the environment in which one lives. This means that the chance of dying is about 1,000 times greater for a man of 100 than for a man of 25. If we did not age—that is, if we kept the physiology of a 15-year-old indefinitely—the average human life-span would be in excess of 20,000 years. This would mean that the oldest members among us could tell stories about the last Ice Age and give personal accounts of the entire span of recorded human history.

The basic question, of course, is not do we age, but what is the underlying mechanism. This can be summarized as follows: we age primarily because the cells in our bodies that cannot replace themselves either die or lose a small part of their function every year. This law applies to most of the tissues of the body, although some cells and tissues seem immune to the effects of the passage of time. These nonaging tissues include those covering the surfaces of the body (the skin and the lining of the digestive system) and the circulating cells in our blood. The skin forms a new layer of cells every four days or so, the lining of the gut is replenished every day or two, and the red blood cells are replaced on a regular schedule every four months.

Other body cells, such as those of the liver, replace themselves more slowly, although the liver (of experimental animals) can regrow to its original size within a week or so if part of it is removed surgically. Parts of the kidneys and the connective tissues are able to replace themselves more or less on demand.

Key organs and tissues in which cell replacement is either absent or inadequate are the muscles, heart, brain, and certain endocrine and immunity-conferring tissues. The nonreplenishing, or postmitotic,

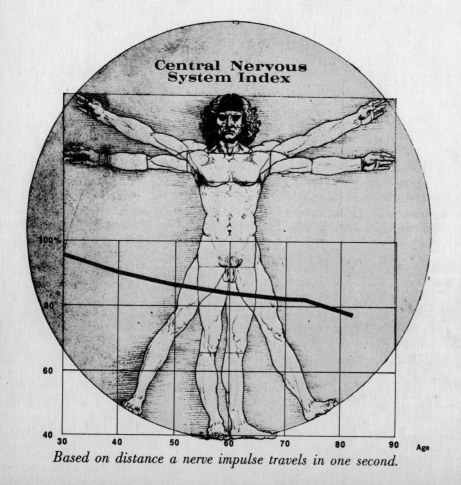

Central Nervous System Index

Based on distance a nerve impulse travels in one second.

cells involved exhibit two major differences from those in other parts of the body: many of the cells that remain in the tissues of an old animal are either larger or smaller than usual and the resultant irregular appearance of many old tissues is one of disorder; the second, obvious change is the accumulation of yellow-brown colorations known as age pigments. These materials accumulate slowly with age, and in the very old they may occupy nearly the entire cell body. They are believed to be produced by the reaction of oxygen with unsaturated fats in the membranes within cells. This reaction is similar to the one that causes varnish to harden and turn yellow as it dries and ages.

The rate at which it occurs can be reduced, in the test tube at least, by adding substances called antioxidants to the mixture. In this process the antioxidants trap intermediate molecules, called free radicals, and prevent such reactions from becoming self-perpetuating. Vitamin E is one antioxidant that occurs in nature, and BHT, a synthetic compound used to prevent various food products from turning rancid, has similar effects. One group of studies by Denham Harmon of the University of Nebraska indicates that it is possible to extend the lives of experimental animals by adding antioxidants to their diets. Whether the increased longevity is due to the suppression of antioxidative reactions within cells and tissues is not yet certain.

Recent studies also indicate that cells cultured artificially eventually lose their ability to divide or renew themselves. In his careful and imaginative work in this area, Leonard Hayflick of Stanford University has shown that human cells such as embryonic fibroblasts can only undergo about fifty divisions under artificial conditions. Whether such limitations occur in the body itself is not yet clearly settled. It seems likely that skin and gut cells, for example, are able to divide hundreds or thousands of times during the lifetime of a human. Some recent research suggests that all cells manufacture and accumulate materials that tend to prevent their division when the concentration of these substances is large enough. One class of such substances, called chalones, only inhibits the growth of the tissue from which it is extracted.

Lack of materials that inhibit cell division may contribute to the development of cancer—a disease that primarily affects the elderly. One reason that cancer develops could be that the natural inhibitors, perhaps "chalonelike" substances, are either not produced in adequate amounts or no longer have a growth-stopping effect on cells that have become malignant. This is an oversimplification of the origin of cancer, but several lines of evidence indicate that it is at least a part of the picture.

The key to understanding aging is to be found in the mechanisms that control and prevent the division of cells. Much information may fall out of the understanding of cancer, but it seems unlikely that all of the needed facts will result from the pursuit of studies directed toward other goals. What is needed is to focus an adequate research effort specifically on those processes that cause cells to lose vitality with age.

A law of nature states that all systems tend to become more disorganized as time passes unless energy is expended to generate order. Stars burn themselves out; untended gardens go to weed; social institutions become more unmanageable as they age. This also applies to the cells and molecules that make up the individual human being; unless molecules are stored at absolute zero and shielded from all kinds of radiation, they will gradually revert to less ordered arrangements of their atoms.

In one sense, living systems are an exception to this rule, for plants and animals do create order out of chaos. These living organisms are special kinds of machines, which harness the matter and energy about them in order to make more of their kind.

The basic reason that living things are mortal is that this must have favored their evolutionary success. One explanation for this paradox—the death of individuals favoring the perpetuation of the species—was suggested by Peter Medawar, a Nobel laureate in medicine and physiology, who pointed

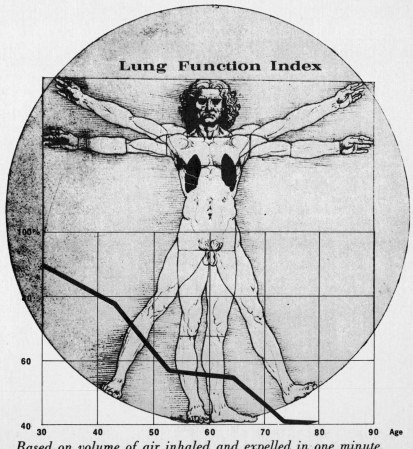

Lung Function Index

Based on volume of air inhaled and expelled in one minute.

out that some kinds of successful adaptations carry with them side effects that indirectly lead to aging and death. For humans, three such adaptations are particularly important: man is best able to function if he has a particular size; man's brain serves as an information storage device, as well as in other ways; our ancestors evolved in competitive environments, which placed a premium on the efficient use of raw materials. What unites these adaptations is that they all involve the "switching off" of certain inherited abilities at specific times in the lifecycle, and it is this process that ultimately causes the system to fail.

The limitation of the human body to a certain optimum size is achieved by the turning off of the genes that would lead to continued growth. The stabilization of memory elements in the brain is achieved, in part, by suppressing the ability of nerve cells in the brain to divide (nerve cell division is a great rarity after birth). Economy in the use of raw materials requires that only those parts that de-

teriorate rapidly—the skin, gut lining cells, blood cells—are regularly replaced. Tendons, muscles, heart, and brain cells stop replacing themselves as maturity is approached.

The consequence of this switching off of genes is to remove the affected cells from the "living system" category, as defined earlier, with aging and death eventually following. Yet all cells, whether in a functioning or switched-off state, contain the necessary genetic instructions to replenish themselves. When we discover how to unlock the information hidden in the DNA of each nonreplenishing cell, man may indeed possess the knowledge necessary to convert himself into an immortal.

Before the present revolution in biological thinking—the result of understanding how DNA stores the instructions to put the body's parts together—we had exceedingly cumbersome ideas about the regulation of gene expression. It had been thought that each specific event in each kind of cell was controlled by

a huge set of genetic instructions. It seemed inconceivable that man could devise nondestructive means for interfering with the enormous complexity of the regulating systems involved.

But it has now been demonstrated that the genetic code is really very simple. It was proved that it is a sequence of just three consecutive "beads," the nucleotide bases in the DNA, which code for a given kind of building block in the working parts of cells. (The building blocks are the body's total of twenty different kinds of amino acids, and the working parts are proteins, which are simply long chains of amino acids arranged in very specific ways according to the instructions provided by the DNA.)

It also has been shown that only two different types of control locations are involved in the regulation of which kinds of genes are expressed. These sites, on the surfaces of the DNA and of the ribosomes, control the copying of the information in specific segments of DNA—a process called transcription—and the decoding of this copied information—a process called translation. In other words, cells can select which of the many products they will make by either controlling the kinds of DNA copied or the kinds of messages decoded.

The importance of these discoveries in terms of the potential control of human aging is enormous. Instead of an imponderable array of control points, the number may be quite small, perhaps only a few dozen. This implies the possibility of producing chemical agents that will selectively change the controls of switched-off cells, thus releasing the latent genetic information needed to produce replacement parts—just as it is possible to produce antibiotics that will destroy infective bacteria without materially harming the body's functions. And far from being an unattainable goal in this generation of humans, selective production of new cells and tissues through pharmacological intervention is on the verge of being tested; at least the basic technology is at hand.

Whether this optimistic view is justified will depend on the results of experiments designed to test a

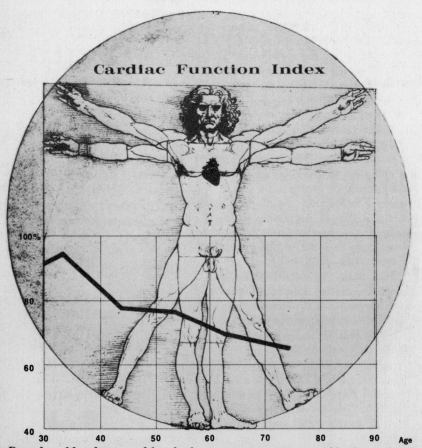

Based on blood pumped by the heart per square meter of body surface.

theory of gene regulation proposed about ten years ago. Harvey Itano, now a professor at the University of California at San Diego, suggested that certain genetic diseases are due to the inability of cells to translate some of the code words present in genetic messages. (He was interested in a blood disease, thallassemia, found in the Mediterranean region.) Itano proposed that the mutation responsible for this disease involved the substitution of a poorly translatable genetic code word for a readily translatable one in the defective gene. This idea was independently rediscovered by Gunther Stent, Bruce Ames, and the author, who applied it to aspects of development and aging.

The basic idea behind our thinking and experiments is that as cells mature they may shut off the ability to read, or decode, certain code words. The effect would be that all genetic messages written down in sequences that include nondecodable words could not be used to produce working parts of cells, including replacement parts.

If this idea were correct, one might expect different kinds of cells from the same individual to operate on different genetic languages. A genetic language is definable as a particular combination of code words that includes at least one word for each of the twenty amino acids. Because there are about sixty usable words in the genetic dictionary, it is obvious that a huge number of different kinds of languages are possible. In fact, because there are about three times as many code words as there are amino acids for them to specify, a sequence 100 amino acids in length (about average for a simple protein) can be written down in 3^{100} different ways within a given segment of DNA.

Even allowing for some inability to distinguish between certain words, it now appears that at least 10,000 different exclusive sets of code words could be used to specify 10,000 different kinds of cells. This is many times the number of different kinds of cells in the body.

One of the predictions implied in such a theory is that certain steps needed for the translation of a given word will be carried out by certain kinds of cells but not by others.

There are now at least fifty studies on various animals and plants that show some deficiencies in the translation machinery from one cell type to another. (Some cancer cells, it now appears, may have reacquired lost translating ability, perhaps as a result of "cancer virus" infection.)

Two findings by Michael Bick and the author are extremely pertinent in this regard. The first was that extracts from old soybean cotyledon tissue are unable to fully carry out the step involved just prior to the decoding of genetic information. (This step is the attachment of the proper amino acid to the right decoder molecule.) Young tissues, however, were perfectly capable of doing this.

The second finding was that old tissues contain a substance that specifically seems to block this step. These findings imply that the tissue is programmed to manufacture a "self-poison" (possibly similar to the chalones) late in its lifetime, and that such a "poison" effectively blocks the production of materials needed for an indefinite existence. The lifetime of this very tissue can be extended manyfold by applying a specific plant hormone, kinetin, to the tissue before it ages.

Equally important is an unpublished finding by Gerald Hirsch. He found that cellular material present in extracts of liver cells was unable to produce free soluble proteins if it was given a message from another tissue. These experiments imply that different cells do have different languages.

Roger Johnson and the author have recently made another promising discovery that may be the needed principle that will tie together many of the seemingly different effects of the aging process. Working with dog tissues, we found that nondividing cells lose a particular kind of DNA. This DNA is involved in the manufacture of the machinery needed to produce any kind of protein, the working parts of all cells. This genetic material, known as rDNA, codes for the ribonucleic acid that is part of the ribosomes—the machines through which the genetic messages are threaded as they are translated into working proteins.

It may be highly significant that, in the studies completed so far, this loss of rDNA occurs only in nondividing cells—brain, heart, skeletal muscle. Liver and kidney cells, for example, do not show such losses. The net effect of the gradual loss of some of this genetic material would be to reduce the maximum rate at which protein could be synthesized under stress. Thus, such different afflictions of the elderly as heart failure (which requires the manufacture of heart muscle proteins if it is to be prevented), inability to detect and reject cancer cells (which requires the rapid manufacture of antibody-like substances to kill off the aberrant cells), and a decrease in the efficiency of the hormonal systems (such as occurs in adult-onset diabetes) may all be ascribable to this fundamental loss of rDNA in nondividing cells. Studies are now under way to test a few of these implications.

It would be too sanguine to state at this time that vital functions could be regenerated simply by reinstating lost abilities to decode one or a few code words. What is needed, of course, is research to find out whether this simple, though versatile, mechanism really dominates the control of development and aging.

Predicting what will happen in, say, the next ten years in the field of understanding and controlling the biological aging process is about like giving a 10-day weather forecast. We know enough about the present situation and the main trends in this area of science to make an educated guess as to what will happen. Barring unforeseen breakthroughs in other areas of biomedicine that might provide important insights into the aging process, the key, limiting factor is whether the needed specific effort will be supported by society. This is an unsettled question right now.

One reason that research on aging has not received the emphasis it deserves has to do with the aging of bureaucracies themselves. New bureaus and institutes are often vital organizations; as they grow older they are concerned more with maintaining the status quo than with imaginative progress.

Within the government (the logical source of funds for basic research), two agencies have a prime interest and obligation toward the health of the elderly: the National Institutes of Health and the Veterans Administration. The National Institutes of Health has been charged with responsibility for support of research on medical problems; the Veterans Administration has responsibility for caring for the veterans of our wars. But both agencies are hampered by inadequate budgets.

Research on aging suffers from a particular disadvantage within the National Institutes of Health because of an absence of experts in decision making and advisory posts sufficiently aware of the details of the process. Instead research proposals are sent to groups of specialists in bacterial genetics, in epidemiology, cell biology, or general biochemistry. The members of each of these review panels or study sections are, almost without exception, leading members of the biomedical research community. But, if the review comments this author has seen

are representative, they are quite underinformed about the status of aging research—a field that is alien to their natural interests and, in fact, competitive with the professional objectives (funding) of most panel members.

For a brief time, just before the last election, it looked as though the starvation period for research on aging was about to end, for Congress had passed (by almost unanimous votes in both houses) a bill that would have established a National Institute for Research on Aging. It was jointly sponsored by leading members of both parties and supported by all of the research and service organizations concerned with the needs of the elderly. This bill created the institute that was unanimously called for by the representatives to the 1971 White House Conference on Aging (Research and Demonstration Section), convened by the President in December, 1971.

The euphoria in the aging research community was short-lived,

however, for the President killed the bill by pocket veto. The reasons given for the veto were: (1) it would cost $200,000,000 and (2) the work would duplicate work already being carried out within the government. Obviously, there has been some failure in communication, for it is hard to believe that a highly intelligent man would have made this decision if he had been apprised of all of the relevant facts. Perhaps the present governmental shake-up will open the lines of communication and give the President a more balanced view of the needs and opportunities in this field of research when the bill once again is passed and reaches his desk.

What happens in the next ten years thus depends directly on a total imponderable. If the institute is established and adequately and imaginatively funded and administered, it seems likely that by the year 1983 we will understand, in depth, the details of cellular and bodily aging. If no special effort is made to understand this most universal of all human afflictions, the date of understanding and possible control will be pushed back to the beginning of the twenty-first century, a date too late to benefit most of us alive today.

The eventual understanding and control of the aging process will cause a revolution in human affairs. Already a few studies are under way on the social consequences of greatly retarding or abolishing aging and death. A few misconceptions should, however, first be laid to rest. Some of the evidently misinformed opponents of greater, healthy life-spans seem to believe that the world would become populated with decrepit, patched-up, wizened, senile people, perhaps fed through tubes and moving with the aid of electronic prostheses. This ugly picture is totally false, for there is no way to appreciably increase life-span except by improving the body's physical state. Instead, humans that live for 150 years or more will be healthy for a much greater percentage of their total life-span. Men and women of highly advanced age will possess bodies like those of much younger people. In fact, their minds will be even more improved, for the greater

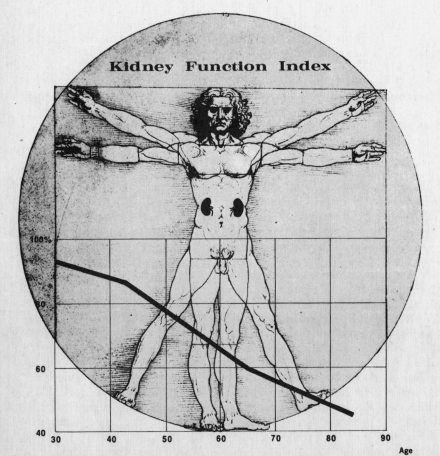

Based on blood flow through the kidneys.

years of optimum health will provide more opportunity to assimilate the world's wonders and lead to a greater measure of wisdom—the only intellectual commodity that often improves with age.

Because the healthy middle years of life will be doubled from the present 30 or 40 years, each individual will spend more time as a contributor to society. The average professional of today requires 25 to 30 years to acquire his training—mostly at the expense of the producing members of society. If the post-training years were doubled, every person could give much more back to the pool of resources from which he derived his start.

As the societies of the world evolve, there will be many changes in the kinds of creative activities open to men and women. People with many decades of optimum health will find it desirable, if not necessary, to move from one kind of occupation to another. One way in which continual retraining in new skills and professions could

well take place would be through a regular system of educational leaves-with-pay, much like the sabbatical system that now operates in universities. Every five or seven years, a person could take a year or so to acquire new skills and to refurbish old ones. Plans should be made now for the restructuring of educational institutions so that a continuing re-education will become the rule rather than the exception.

As machines take over the more onerous and repetitive tasks men have performed, opportunities for new careers in the so-called service area will evolve. It is unfortunate that there is not a better word than *service* (from the same root as the word *servant*) to describe the kinds of creative things people can do to make each other's lives enjoyable. Such efforts range from art, music, poetry, and beautiful gardens, to the care of children, entertainment, and creative conversation. As men escape from a subsistence society, in which work must be done to

provide for life's necessities, a much more fulfilling kind of work, one directed toward the improved enjoyment of life, will come to dominate.

In time, all of these joyous prophecies will probably come about anyway, provided we have wisdom, foresight, and a little luck. But they will be available to those who read these pages only if the minuscule investment needed to understand and perhaps control human aging is made in this coming decade. What is commonly termed the Protestant ethic encourages some sacrifice now (work, saving, investment, education, research) in order to derive greater benefits in the future. After nearly a decade of disparagement and eclipse, it seems once again to be revealing its wisdom. One can only hope that this resurgence in the appreciation of investment will extend to what is needed to assure a healthier, longer life for all—basic research on the most universal human affliction, aging itself.

8

In Search of the Antiaging Cocktail

by Arthur W. Galston

*Some cells nurtured in
an artificial medium seem to
have achieved immortality*

Life has been called a fatal disease. For all but a few organisms, death is an inevitable consequence of existence. From a biological point of view, this makes good sense, for death removes existing organisms and recycles their components, thus providing both environmental niches and basic chemicals for new life. The few exceptions to this almost universal rule include both the smallest and largest of living things.

Bacteria and similar microorganisms seem able to live indefinitely, granted only the availability of food, the removal of waste products and an opportunity for occasional genetic interchange. When cultured in this manner, such organisms reproduce by cell division at a constant rate that seems unaffected by the passage of time. The only sense in which death occurs is that the "mother" cell disappears in the process of giving rise to the two "daughter" cells. Among the larger forms of life, individual giant redwoods and bristlecone pines seem able to go on living and growing for thousands of years. Possibly they could live forever or at least until disease or some accident, such as lightning or fire, puts an end to their lives.

For most species of animals, there seems to be a built-in timer that dictates the maximum life-span. For humans, the average life-span may be approximately the biblical three score and ten years, although one

Quebec man is recorded as having lived to 113. (Stories of 160-year-old residents of the Caucasus and Azerbaijan must be treated skeptically because of the unavailability of birth certificates or other proof of date of birth.) Dogs generally die at the age of ten to twelve years, although several have lived beyond thirty, while houseflies last about seventy days.

As is widely known, advances in medicine have resulted in an increase in the average human length of life, but this is not due to an increase in the upper limit of the life-span. What preventive medicine and public health measures have done is reduce the number of early deaths from accidents and diseases associated with maternity, infancy, and childhood. As a result, the population profile, which used to look like a squat pyramid—with a large population base at birth and a sharp apex at the age of death—now looks more like a column of uniform width from birth until relatively old age, at which time there is a gentle taper to a point. Given contemporary medical advances, there is now no correlation between age and death rate below the age of thirty; beyond that point, the probability of death doubles with each eight years of increasing age. This is generally taken as meaning that the degenerative processes leading to death set in at about the age of thirty.

Within any given species, there is some variation in average life-span, and sometimes these variations can be traced to definite causes. The most obvious cause is the genetic background of the individual. Several decades ago, the American biologist and

biometrician Raymond Pearl showed a positive correlation between the age of an individual at death and the age of that person's parents at death. Pearl found that 45.8 percent of those who lived beyond age seventy had parents who did likewise, while only 13.4 percent of the septuagenarians had two short-lived parents. These figures seem to indicate that the best way to live to a ripe old age is to receive genes for longevity. And an obvious inference is that selective breeding among extraordinarily long-lived individuals might lead to an extension of the normal life-span. Unfortunately, children cannot choose their parents nor can individuals who wish to become parents sense the ultimate age of their mates.

Direct experimental proof of the connection between genetics and age at death has been demonstrated by several researchers. Working with rotifers—a simple animal—Albert Lansing, a specialist in the physiology of aging at the University of Pittsburgh School of Medicine, was able to modify the creatures' normal life-span of twenty-four days by simple selection. Eggs taken only from adolescent rotifers were grown, and the process was continued for more than fifty generations. The average life-span of the resultant individuals was found to have increased to more than one hundred days. Contrariwise, repeated selection of eggs from senescent rotifers for more than fifty generations decreased the life-span to fourteen days. The generalization seems clear: young mothers give birth to longer-lived offspring; older mothers to shorter-lived offspring.

Robert Sokal, a statistical biolo-

Arthur W. Galston teaches biology at Yale University.

82

gist at the State University of New York at Stony Brook, achieved the same result as Lansing but in a different way. Working with flour beetles, he killed all beetle mothers shortly after they had produced their first eggs. Within forty generations he succeeded in decreasing the average lifespan of the resultant population. Sokal reasoned that this change occurred because all those beetle mothers with potentially longer lifespans had had their lives cut short, while those with potentially short lifespans lived to their full life expectancy. The result, in a kind of testtube evolution study, was a drift of the population toward shorter lifespans.

In some species, including the human, there is a correlation between gender and longevity. Thus, in our society, women live an average of more than five years longer than men. Nobody yet knows whether this is due to the genetic difference between males and females (females have twenty-two pairs of autosomal chromosomes; males have the same number of autosomal chromosomes but substitute one longer Y chromosome for one of the X chromosomes) or whether the earlier death of men is related to a difference in their life styles. Whatever the cause, this differential mortality results in a marked excess of females in the older population.

Other factors affecting life-span in various species are the temperature at which young are reared (particularly in animals whose body temperature is not stable), diet (especially in early development), and exposure to radiation. Fruit flies, accordingly, live ten times longer at a temperature of 10° C. than at 30° C.; rats given a barely adequate caloric diet live longer than their well-fed siblings; and the life-span of mice exposed to whole body irradiation decreases progressively as the radiation dose increases. These experimental data have led certain experimenters to reason that aging is caused by some product whose concentration in the body is increased by high levels of nutrition, high rates of metabolism, and high doses of radiation. It has also led to attempts to ameliorate the harmful effects of these factors by dietary means, which might act as

a kind of fountain of youth. For example, radiation is known to cause the formation of free radicals, or molecules with unpaired electrons. Such molecules are extraordinarily reactive, and the harmful effect of radiation may result from the modification of nucleic acid and other important molecules by radiation-induced free radicals. One way to get around this trouble is to feed the body compounds that are known as "reducing agents," or antioxidants. The theory is that such ingested substances will react directly with the free radicals, thus keeping them from affecting important molecules in the cell. Vitamin E, a known antioxidant, has shown some promise in this regard.

One of the paradoxes of the aging process is its alteration when cells are removed from their natural positions in the body and are grown in artificial chemical media. The famous chicken heart culture experiments of Nobel laureate Alexis Carrel, in which Charles Lindbergh collaborated, implied that tissue from that organ could be artificially kept alive for more than thirty years—many times the normal life-span of the chicken from which it came. In fact, new, viable chick fibroblast cells were probably being introduced in the "embryo extract" periodically added to the culture medium.

Intimations of immortality are also gleaned from experiments with plant tissue cultures. As I have mentioned in several previous columns, cells removed from a carrot root in 1937 and put in an artificial medium are still dividing and show no sign of running down. In nature, by contrast, a carrot lives a maximum of two years.

Human cells also show evidence of extraordinary longevity when removed from the body. Henrietta Lacks, a woman with cancer of the cervix, provided cells for tissue culture in 1951. The donor has since died, but her cells, the noted HeLa strain used in laboratories all over the world, continue to grow. For such cells, it may be said that mortality is a consequence of being included in a differentiated body.

A different pattern is shown by human fibroblasts—the cells that form the connective tissues of the body.

Microbiologist Leonard Hayflick, of Stanford University School of Medicine, showed that fibroblast cultures were limited to about fifty divisions, accomplished over a period of about eight months. If the cultures were transferred to cold conditions in the middle of the experiment, thereby stopping cell divisions, the cultures would "remember" the number of divisions remaining before they ceased activity. In a companion study, Hayflick showed that the older the individual used as the source of the fibroblasts, the fewer the resulting divisions in culture. These data provided strong support for the "hourglass" theory of aging, in which the buildup of some harmful metabolite (or depletion of some essential substance) is envisaged as the cause of the aging process.

This research was recently shaken by the discovery by biochemist Lester Packer, and his colleagues in the department of physiology and anatomy at the University of California at Berkeley, that the inclusion of vitamin E in the culture medium extends the ability of fibroblasts to divide. In fact, vitamin E may even change cultured fibroblasts into indefinitely prolonged cultures, like those of HeLa cells and plant tissues. Whether this effect of vitamin E can be repeated by independent workers is not yet known.

In the human body, which contains nondividing as well as dividing cells, the phenomenon of aging is not likely to be attributable to a single cause. Nerve cells, for example, never divide after their formation. As life progresses, they suffer continual wear and tear until they die. At maturity, the brain has about one billion nerve cells. It is estimated that each day thereafter about 10,000 of them die and are irretrievably lost, never to be replaced. By the age of sixty-five, about 20 percent of all brain neurons are gone; this may account for the diminished mental acuity of some elderly people.

Muscle is another nondividing kind of cell in which wear and tear may be expected to play an important role. Much interest has recently been shown in collagen, the noncellular matrix that binds many cells together, forms the basis for connective tissue, and is the milieu in which bone calcification occurs. The collagen molecules in young persons are highly hydrated and quite flexible; the tissues of the young are accordingly supple. In advancing age, collagen becomes much more highly cross-linked and rigid, possibly as a result of oxidative changes. The resultant rigidity reduces the efficiency of muscles and such organs as the heart and lungs. Since collagen fibers cannot be renewed once they are laid down in the body, the loss of pliability leads to irreversible changes that are part of the total aging process.

But even tissues that can be renewed by cell division show diminished efficiency with increasing age. This may be related to an accumulation of perpetuated "mistakes" in the genetic apparatus. These could be in the form of extra chromosomes or errors at the level of DNA replication that cause mutations. As the load of accumulated errors becomes greater and greater, the rate of replacement of worn-out cells that need renewal (red blood cells, for example) diminishes progressively, and recovery from any injury becomes more difficult. Like the "wonderful one-hoss shay/that was built in such a logical way/it ran for a hundred years to a day" and then suffered total collapse (Oliver Wendell Holmes, *The Deacon's Masterpiece*), the body keeps functioning, all the parts suffering progressive attrition until some breakdown becomes the ultimate insult that terminates life. It is not likely that any single elixir will be able to retard all these degenerative changes. At the very least, the fountain of youth will have to be a complicated, multicomponent, antiaging cocktail.

III. Young Adulthood

C.H. ELDRIDGE '76

As recently as a century ago, people were considered adult and took on full responsibility for a family well before age 20. Then, as we demanded a longer period of compulsory schooling, the period known as adolescence was created, characterized by biological maturity (e.g., puberty), but in which the person was kept in a psychological limbo, waiting as it were at the door of adulthood. Now, with changing lifestyles and confusion over career choice and instability of the environment, as well as the inordinate length of the educational process for many types of work, the period of young adulthood, or youth, can be defined as a stage which many people (though by no means all) face after adolescence but before their achievement of full adulthood and its traditional responsibilities of family, job, and independence.

The turmoil of adolescence and young adulthood seems to be characteristic of cultures and periods of history like ours, which postpone adulthood and present the individual with a wide range of issues to integrate and choices to make. Young adulthood is a time riddled with questions of commitment, identity, and self-definition. The young adult must make choices in these areas that will be important determinants of his or her future life.

One of the major themes of young adulthood is the struggle to attain a sense of identity which is both durable and flexible enough to cope with the often bewildering changes offered by the environment, and the development of intimate relationships with people outside the family, a process described by psychiatrist Theodore Lidz. The way the young adult integrates childhood experiences into adult personality helps determine the sense of self. This process is superimposed on whatever unresolved issues and conflicts have already arisen in childhood, and has the potential to create future conflicts, or to resolve childhood conflicts decisively. To grasp the struggles of this period of life, it is important to understand the environmental context presented in this unique historical epoch, which includes the struggle with alienation described by Kenneth Keniston through the eyes of a young man who represents some of the conflicts of his generation.

Each generation, in addition to using the wisdom of past generations, creates new meanings and issues. As Vern Bengtson suggests, the nature of these age differences is often the source of conflict and creates difficulty and schisms between generations and pressure on the young adult. Next, Keniston presents an integrative article outlining the unique pressures and meanings which define the stage of life that he labels "youth." Gail Sheehy, in effect, has discovered yet another point of transition and conflict. The boundary line between youth and adulthood, she suggests, is no longer age 20, but closer to age 30. Mopsy Kennedy elaborates on these themes, offering a personal account of this transition point by a successful, creative young woman.

9

The Young Adult

by Theodore Lidz

THE LENGTHY developmental process as a dependent apprentice in living draws to a close as individuals attain an identity and the ability to live intimately with a member of the opposite sex, and contemplate forming families of their own. They have attained adult status with the completion of physical maturation, and, it is hoped, they have become sufficiently well integrated and emotionally mature to utilize the opportunities and accept the responsibilities that accompany it. They have reached a decisive point on their journeys. They have dropped the pilot and now start sailing on their own—but they have been taught to navigate and they have been provided with charts, albeit charts that can be but approximately correct for the currents and reefs change constantly. They have practiced under more or less competent supervision, taken trips in sheltered waters, and now they assume responsibility for themselves and must accept the consequences of their decisions. Usually couples decide to share the journey, and soon others join them, bidden and unbidden, whose welfare depends upon their skills and stability.

However, some will still tarry undecided about where they will journey, or the course they will take to an unfamiliar place, or whether to try out partners imaginatively or in actuality before setting forth. Some are still uncertain about where they will find their place in the scheme of things, whether they wish to find a place in the scheme, or whether there is a scheme of things at all. Those who delay are a minority, but include among them many who will be innovators, creators, and leaders, and therefore they require that we, too, pause to consider their transition through a period that Keniston (1970) has designated as *youth*, during which youths seek to reconcile potential conflicts between their emerging identities and the social order.

Still, the energies and interests of most young adults will now be directed beyond their own growth and development. Their independence from their parental families motivates them to achieve an interdependence with others and find their places in society. Through vocation and marriage they become united to networks of persons, find tasks that demand involvement, and gain roles into which they fit and are fitted and which help define their identities. They are virtually forced to become less self-centered through the very pursuit of their own interests.

The time when adult life starts is not set chronologically, for persons may have entered upon their vocations and selected spouses some time in adolescence, and others will remain tentative in their commitments through their twenties and may, in some respects, be considered still adolescent. If persons are still uncommitted, most make their occupational choices early in adulthood. Most individuals will also give up their much sought independence to share with another in marriage. Then the life cycle rounds to the point at which young adults are again confronted by the start of life, but now as members of the parental generation, and they often undergo profound personality reorientations as they become involved in the unfolding of a child's life. The period ends at a somewhat indefinite time, approximately when children's needs no longer form a major focus of attention, usually between thirty-five and forty, when persons have attained stable positions in society, or, at least, when they realize that they must come to terms with what they will be able to make out of their one and only life.

Young adults are at the height of their physical and mental vigor as they launch upon making their ways in the world; and their energies are usually expended more effectively than they were during adolescence. The expansiveness of adolescence had usually given way to efforts at consolidation in late adolescence, but young adults must focus energies and interests even more definitively as they commit themselves to a specific way of life; to marriage, with its libidinal investment in a single significant person; and to producing and nurturing a new generation. Now, more than ever, alternative ways of life must be renounced to permit the singleness of purpose required for success and to consolidate one's identity; and intimacy becomes reserved for a single person to make possible meaningful sharing with a spouse. Although commitment to another person entails the danger of being carried along in the other's inadequacies or misfortunes, its avoidance carries the penalty of lack of opportunity to be meaningful to others and have others become meaningful to the self.

Vocational choice and marital choice are two of the most significant decisions of a lifetime. Although they are sometimes made easily and even seemingly casually, they are both extremely complex matters that are resultants of the individual's entire personality development. They are two cardinal resultants of the lengthy process of achieving adulthood that we have been tracing; and now these decisions will become major determinants of the course of the individual's further personality development, of the satisfactions that will be gained from life, and of the trials and problems that will ensue and strain the integration of the personality and perhaps even warp it. The individual's own capacities and integration markedly influence the choices of occupation and spouse, and then influence how the person can cope with and gain fulfillment from both—and subsequently from being a parent. We shall, in the following two chapters, scrutinize the choices of vocation and spouse and then consider the tasks involved in adjusting to marriage and being a parent, but we shall first consider the period of youth and the integration of persons as they start adult life.

YOUTH

Keniston has suggested that a new stage in the life cycle, *youth*, has emerged with the growing complexities of postindustrial civilizations.* For many, the commitments of adult life do not follow directly upon adolescence. Indeed, in periods during which the assumption of adult status is delayed, there may be a prolongation of adolescence, and late adolescents and unmarried young adults are grouped together as "youth."*

Youth, in Keniston's usage of the word, does not designate such prolongation of adolescence, but rather a distinct stage in the life cycle through which only a limited number of people pass. These are persons who, having gained an ego identity or self-concept, become caught up in tensions between the self and society. "The awareness of actual or potential conflict, disparity, lack of consequence between what one is (one's identity, values, integrity) and the resources and demands of existing society increase. The adolescent is struggling to define who he is, the youth begins to sense who he is and thus to recognize the possibility of conflict and disparity between his emerging self-hood and his social order" (Keniston, 1974, p. 405). A central problem of the period is to find ways in which the self and society can become more congruent; and a critical task in personality development lies in achieving *individuation* (Jung, 1926)—the capacity to acknowledge reality and to cope with it, either through acceptance or through revolutionary opposition, but preserving a sense of "self," of intactness and

* Much as Ariès (1962) contends that prior to the industrial revolution "childhood" did not exist, and the idea that adolescence as a stage of life first developed at the start of the present century (Demos and Demos, 1969). There are, however, reasons to challenge these contentions. In most nonliterate (primitive) societies, though children may be expected to help with adult tasks, they are treated differently from adolescents and adults. The participants in the "Children's Crusade" were neither under six nor adults. As R. W. Beales (1975) has clearly documented, children were not considered competent to decide on conversion or fully responsible in seventeenth- and eighteenth-century New England. Jonathan Edwards placed the upper limits of childhood at fourteen; Thomas Hooker believed that a child of ten or twelve lived "the life of a beast" and could not consider the mysteries of salvation; etc. In the early days of Massachusetts only a person who was over sixteen could be executed for striking or cursing a parent.

Similarly, there is evidence of recognition of an adolescent period in nonliterate societies and in the early New England settlements. Among the Stone-Age peoples of Papua/New Guinea a boy does not become an adult after going through the pre-adolescent or adolescent initiation rituals, but spends many years learning the skills a man requires as well as the myths and rituals essential to the society; not until around the age of nineteen is he considered a man and ready to marry. A distinction is made between prepubescent and post-menarchal girls everywhere, and in Papua/New Guinea the postpubertal girls have special privileges until they marry. In early New England the period of apprenticeship, which did not end until the age of twenty or twenty-one, was, in a sense, equivalent to the period of adolescence. Beales (1975) notes that elements of a "youth culture" existed in colonial New England. In the early eighteenth century elders bemoaned the licentious ways of youth who frequented taverns, participated in lewd practices, frolics, and company-keeping. The term "youth" seems to have been applied to older adolescents and unmarried young adults.

* We find that in colonial New England "youth" for Benjamin Coleman (1720) was a "chusing time":

NOW O Young People is *your chusing time*, and commonly your *fixing time*; and as you fix it is like to last. Now you commonly chuse your *Trade*; betake your selves to your business for life, show what you incline to, and how you intend to be imploy'd all your days. Now you chuse your *Master* and your Education or Occupation. And now you dispose of your self in *Marriage* ordinarily, place your *Affections*, give away your hearts, look out for some *Companion* of life, whose to be as long as you live. And is this indeed the work of your Youth?

wholeness of self—distinct from society, even if engaged in fostering social reform or in revolutionary activity. *Individuation* is a psychological process or an "intrapsychic" matter in which one's ego identity is differentiated from the social system in which one lives. Failure to individuate properly leads to conformity to societal norms, which is, of course, simply the lot of most persons, but which can be scorned by youth as "selling out" or being "brain washed," and becomes a denial of the self when it is a matter of *overconformity*. The antipodal danger is *alienation*, in which efforts to preserve autonomy lead to the withdrawal from the social matrix that gives life substance, and perhaps even from interpersonal relations that give life meaning. A variant of alienation occurs when meaning and fulfillment are sought through psychedelic drugs.

It seems rather clear that *Youth* is not an altogether new stage of development. Over the ages many persons who were visionary, creative, or revolutionary passed through some such stage. In times of stress and change—as during the Great Depression of the 1930s—some young persons, because of their accurate perceptions of societal deficiencies, have been reluctant to enter into the adult world, for that seemed to be the way to stagnation if not simply an acquiescence in society's inequities and corruption. However, these were youths of superior cognitive capacities which permitted them to develop high ethical standards and to view matters from a perspective different from that of most of their contemporaries, and therefore they were usually, though not necessarily, persons who were highly educated. As currently about seventeen percent of young people in the United States complete college, a much higher proportion than heretofore, it is possible for a significant number of persons to experience the conflicts between self and society that lead to the developmental stage we are calling *youth*.

When we consider, the characteristics of *youth* depend upon the attainment of the stage of *formal operations* in cognitive development and then moving on to appreciation of the *relativity of social systems* and of the social roles and mores they encompass; to recognition of the *malleability of persons*, and how greatly who they are and what they become depend on how and where they are brought up; and to *transcend conventional morality* and even the postconventional morality of the social contract to attain a higher universal justice about which individuals can and must make their own judgments. The concepts of social relativity, developmental malleability, and universal abstract morality are not new, but they are interrelated matters that have of late taken on new pertinence. Becoming caught up in them opens new horizons for a youth, but in so doing creates developmental problems that can demolish the individual and not just one's individuation.

Relativism

The theory of relativity has affected thinking outside the physical sciences. We are concerned with the relativism that has arisen from gaining perspective through the study of other times, other civilizations, and other cultures that enables some persons to overcome their ethnocentricities and recognize the validity and utility of the ways of other peoples, even though they are very divergent from our own; and, consequently, that the ways and standards of our own society are more or less arbitrary. Persons may then believe that they have no obligation to adhere to societal norms, and claim that members of the society are simply indoctrinated or "brainwashed" to conform and preserve its constricting if not iniquitous ways. Particularly in times when societal ways run counter to a person's self-concept and ideals and lead to disillusionment in the society—as in the United States during the Vietnam war and the Watergate scandals—youths feel the schism between self and society intensely. The conflict need not lead to political activism to change society, or to a rejection of society with a dropping out into an "alternate culture" such as a communal way of life, but may lead to rejection of the self, with concomitant despair or even suicide, or to efforts to transform the self through study, meditation, Zen, psychoanalysis. Youths may also find a solution of the dilemma by choosing a career, such as medicine, that will permit them to preserve their ethical values within a social system they reject, or to embrace a legal career that will enable them to help correct injustice or change society.

Another consequence of relativism may be even more threatening. Recognizing the relativity of values as well as mores, youths may find themselves without a sense of meaning or purpose. The query "What difference does anything make if there is no meaning, no purpose, no God?" can lead to paralyzing existential anxiety or to an empty hedonism to counter despair, but for some it can open the way to a new freedom in directing their lives. A young man who was uncertain about his decision to study for the clergy took a moratorium of a year to reach a decision and spent much of it reading in a university library. His search after the nature of God led to a conviction that there could be neither a Deity nor a hereafter. However, after a period of personal disorientation and anxiety, he decided that if there were no general scheme of things and no meaning to the universe, that if he did not wish to be miserable, he would have to give meaning to his life. As he had no interest in bowing out of life, he decided that he could, as an American, make a game of his life and see what score he could make; or he might make a work of art of his life and strive to live an interesting tale of adventure, or a well-balanced introspective novel; or he might seek to help others live less troubled lives. He found that new ways of thinking about life had opened before him. He had, in a sense, learned that his life need not be empty because the world lacked purpose; it was up to him to provide meaning for his life. He had, in a sense, achieved what Perry (1970) has termed "commitment within relativism."

Human Malleability

The increased awareness of human malleability—the recognition of how greatly what persons become depends upon how and where they are brought up—has brought about a major social revolution that has greatly affected youth. Young people have been major movers in the civil-rights movement, the Peace Corps, Head Start, women's liberation, and other activities that seek to enable people to develop more fully and have better opportunities in life. It has also led some youths to believe in their own *omnipotentiality*—of their own capacities to change themselves and the direction of their lives. They need not follow in their parents' footsteps, or even in the patterns provided by the past; and they can, if they persevere, achieve beyond their earlier expectations for themselves. A young person may even believe that complete self-transformation is possible without regard to prior upbringing, education, and innate capacities. A college student, having learned that people can make of themselves whatever they wish, decided to become a harpsichord virtuoso, ignoring his lack of any musical training up to the age of twenty-one and his lack of any particular musical aptitude. Such persons have not yet overcome the egocentricity of formal operations and fail to differentiate between cognitive solutions of problems and the actualization of the imagined solution. However, at a more realistic level, young people have delayed, studied, and worked to change the direction and scope of their lives. Occasionally, the multiplicity of potential futures can virtually paralyze. A college student caught up in several divergent interests engendered by her courses and her extracurricular work in the inner city could not decide between them, and then came to realize that she might also be interested in areas in which she had not yet had experience. She spent hours asking friends why they had decided on one career or another. Eventually, she decided it mattered little what career she chose as long as it interested her and could be of benefit to others, and she then decided to study journalism because it could encompass many of her interests.

Abstract Morality

The attainment of the highest and most abstract level of morality also contains dangers. It will be recalled that according to Kohlberg's (1964) conceptualization of moral development, a limited number of persons move beyond conventional morality to define right and wrong in terms of the well-being of all members of a society, and of these some transcend such considerations to embrace more universalistic standards in which individuals must judge for themselves whether laws conform to higher principles such as the "golden rule." Persons can then become caught up in the relativism of laws and "justice," and reach idiosyncratic standards in which they take the law into their own hands; or even decide that, as everything is relative, the entire system of conventional morality is meaningless. They forget that societies have, at least to some extent, gradually developed moral systems that help preserve the integrity of the society and its members.* As Keniston (1974) has commented regressions from this highest form of morality can occur and lead to the amoral behaviors that are sometimes encountered in countercultures, and give license for orgiastic sex and unbridled drug usage; or to anarchy as the highest form of political morality.

Having entered into a relativistic world, youths can find it difficult to find solid footing, guidelines for their behavior, and directions for their

---

* In questioning conventional morality, some even see no reason for the incest taboo, not realizing how important it is to the emergence of the child from ties to parents and the family, as well as to the maintenance of the family. Many major dramatic works—*Hamlet, Oedipus Rex*, Aeschylus's *Oresteia*—concern the woes that follow upon incestuous behavior.

future lives. They are apt to question if not distrust conventional roles, values, and mores; and to turn their backs against lessons that can be gained from the past and seek to start afresh and make a new world. Clearing new trails through the jungle is a difficult task that does not get a person very far quickly. The youth makes forays into society and at commitments to other persons, seeking a workable way to relate to society and within society; or toward finding or founding a new and more congenial society; or searching for the right companion and to learn whether one is ready to form a permanent and exclusive relationship with another.

Many youths find direction, at least temporarily, by participating in movements that allow them to exercise their higher morality by combating some social ill. Marxism, antiwar movements, and civil rights have engaged generations of American youth. At a more individual level, they may decide on careers that will help lessen the woes of others or can enable them to improve society. They help bring about changes in society and its mores. Currently, the belief that sexual practices are the concern only of the individuals involved, rather than a matter of general moral values, has enabled young persons to live experimentally with one or more partners and delay marriage. During the Vietnam war, the youth in the United States were caught between their self-concepts and their country's unjust posture, and the young men found themselves in a dilemma concerning whether or not to avoid military service.

At present, young women may be having greater difficulties during *youth* than men. They are very apt to be caught up in tensions between their emergent ego identities and society's expectations and delimitations of women. Their conflict is further aggravated by their own ambivalent desires to achieve in careers and also to devote at least part of their lives to motherhood—a desire which, if not deeply rooted in women's biological makeup, has been deeply ingrained in most women during their formative years. As we have considered (Chapter 10) adolescent girls are entering womanhood at a time when women's roles in society have been changing profoundly. Most women now work before they have children, but do not become seriously engaged in pursuing careers: although they may be involved in the Women's Liberation movement, they are largely concerned with equal opportunity and pay at work, the condescending or sexual attitudes of employers toward them, having the freedom to pursue a career should they so wish, etc., but their basic orientation continues along traditional feminine lines of becoming a wife, helpmate, and mother. However, the highly educated women who move into and through the period of *youth* find a real conflict between their self-image as highly competent persons who wish to pursue careers and societal expectations for them. Their achievement orientation has conventionally been considered more masculine than feminine; and they may feel caught between their strivings to achieve and their own images of themselves as women. With relatively few models to follow, they are involved in changing both the way society regards and treats women and the way women regard themselves. They believe that women can be achievement oriented and still retain expressive characteristics, and that men should incorporate expressive as well as achievement-oriented instrumental characteristics. Women's liberation for them encompasses fundamental changes in the ethos of the society rather than simply the practical matters concerning equality of opportunity and treatment. However, as Martina Horner has found, bright, highly competent college women have feared success, considering that achievement requires competition, that competition is aggressive, and that aggression is unfeminine. She further found that two-thirds of college men did better in competitive than noncompetitive situations, as compared with fewer than one-third of the women subjects.* It is hoped that such anxieties concerning achievement have diminished under the impact of Women's Liberation movements, but it is unlikely that they will become extinguished in the near future.

The problems of female youth are also accentuated because they have greater freedom than men in the choice of future roles. They can decide to be primarily wives and mothers, and gain considerable gratification from it; but being a husband and father has not yet become a career for men. Here, as elsewhere, the ability to choose opens the way for inner conflict.

The awareness of the *relativism* of societal standards and roles as well as the feeling of *omnipotentiality* that is so much part of *youth* enables young women to move beyond the stereotypes of male and female roles, of the concept that instrumental functions are male and expressive functions essentially female, and to consider themselves doing almost anything that men can do. They can also go beyond objectivity and insist that sexual equality means the absence of any differences between the sexes,* and in the process deny the advantages of being a woman—rejecting any desire to have a child. They may also turn away from any need for a man, and find that they can gain sexual fulfillment through lesbian relationships. Perhaps, more unfortunately, they may become aggressively overcompetitive, identifying with the enemy, so to speak, and forgetting that they had objected to such aggressive competitive behavior in men.

Seeking new ways of being women, female *youth* usually remain away from home after college. They need the companionship of others who share their aspirations and encourage their strivings. They may live with a man while at college, encouraged to learn that there are men who find them attractive because of their abilities, but they must be certain that it is not that they are attractive despite their abilities. If they are to have a career they must find the proper man who will help them manage both career and marriage. They may also wish to be certain that having a career will continue to be more important than motherhood, or find ways of combining the two. It is important that they become aware of the difficulties of dual-career marriages from other colleagues, or at least recognize that a

* In a type of projective test given to ninety female and eighty-eight male first- and second-year college students, fifty-nine of the women but only eight of the men made up stories that reflected fear of success. The main trend of the women's stories indicated fear of being rejected, losing marital opportunities, and losing friends as a consequence of being at the top of the class. Others gave evidence that such success might mean they lacked femininity and might be abnormal. Some even denied that it would be possible for a woman to head a medical school class; and one woman gave the bizarre response "She starts proclaiming her surprise and joy. Her classmates are so disgusted with her behavior that they jump on her in a body and beat her. She is maimed for life" (Horner, 1968).

* As reflected in some writings of proponents of radical Women's liberation, the ultimate was seen in a first-year medical student (not at Yale) who called a professor of anatomy a male chauvinist and left the lecture hall when he sought to demonstrate (on a skeleton) the differences between the male and female pelvis.

woman must be extremely well organized to manage it. We shall return to consider such matters in the chapters on occupational and marital choice.

We have been considering *youth* as a stage in the life cycle of some particularly well-endowed and sensitive young people. We must, however, also realize that a period between the end of adolescence and the firm commitments of marriage and serious occupational involvement exists for graduate students and single persons in their twenties. It is often a time of trying out, trying occupations and partners, often an enjoyable time without serious responsibilities. Today, with the more or less socially approved practice of living with a member of the opposite sex in trial marriage or simply for convenience and enjoyment, the pressures to marry have diminished, and the duration of the period of youthful living is increasing.

THE INTEGRATION OF THE YOUNG ADULT

What does the young man or woman require within the self to make the essential decisions concerning career and marriage and have a reasonable chance of gaining strength and finding satisfaction from them? Fortunately, perhaps, psychiatrists are not required to sit in judgment and only very few persons seek their opinion and permission. We have followed the phasic preparation since birth for the assumption of adult status, and we shall not attempt to summarize here the steps by which a person integrates, achieves an ego identity and a capacity for true intimacy. We shall but attempt to state briefly some of the essential and some of the desirable aspects of a person's integration at this stage of life—concepts which will be amplified in subsequent chapters. Although it is simple to illustrate how deficiencies in achieving such capacities can lead a person into serious difficulties, we hesitate to call them requisites rather than desiderata, for few, if any, persons have all of these attributes, and the attainment of any of them always remains a matter of "more or less." We are considering an ideal, so to speak, to convey how a mature young adult might be integrated.

Young adults have, as we discussed in the preceding two chapters, become reasonably independent of their parents. They have established fairly clear boundaries between themselves and their parents; properly, they have not been burned in the process and become wary of ever relating intimately again, but they recognize that their paths and their parents' now diverge because they are moving toward different goals. If their early development went well, the revolt through which they gained their own identities has subsided and they can appreciate their parents on a fairly realistic basis. They no longer need their parents as essential objects who support and direct them, for parental figures have been internalized and are thus a salient part of their identities, and they do not need to attach themselves to another person immediately to ward off feelings of emptiness when they leave their parents, nor seek sexual relations primarily to counter loneliness. As they become spouses and parents themselves, they will continue to take on characteristics of their parents, but their identities will now also include derivatives from other significant persons. When the early family environment has been unfortunate, later relationships with teachers, friends, or friends' parents may have furnished stabilizing forces, more suitable objects for identification, and more hopeful objectives. In the process, they have learned to separate themselves and keep away those persons, including a parent, who are injurious to them, and perhaps even malignant if internalized as part of themselves. They do not confuse new significant persons in their lives with parents or siblings to the extent of repetitively reenacting old intrafamilial problems. A man does not, for example, awaken at night uncertain whether he is sleeping with his wife or mother, as did the son of a highly seductive woman; or a woman repeat with her daughter and husband an old rivalry with her sister for their father's affection.

As a result of the reorganization accomplished during adolescence, those components of the superego derived from internalization of the parents and their directives are less important. The individual may still follow parental dictates, but because they have been incorporated into one's own ethical system rather than because of fear of displeasing the parents. Indeed, as we have previously noted, much of what had been reasonable and useful in the superego now becomes part of the ego, and becomes more and more fully incorporated into the core of the ego—that is to say, into the basic orientation upon which decisions are made. The directives which help the individual to decide what is acceptable and unacceptable behavior now concern social and cultural norms and ideologic standards that are superordinate to parental dictates. The parents are no longer seen from the perspective of the child. They are no longer regarded as omnipotent figures who could take care of all difficulties if only they would, nor are they "split" into good parents who take care of one, and bad parents who do not. They are recognized as having both capabilities and inadequacies and more or less ambivalently as promoting both affection and anger; and concomitantly the superego now permits latitude for sexual outlets which, in turn, can help diminish the urgency of id impulsions. Although certain impulses, desires, and behavior arouse guilt, shame, or anxiety, these emotions are more likely to become signals to alter behavior or attitudes rather than leading to self-punitive depressions.

The ego tends to have greater control, considering one's ultimate well-being before giving in to immediate gratifications. A mass of data garnered from personal experience as well as from the person's cultural heritage can be utilized in reaching decisions. It can be manipulated imaginatively in an effort to try out alternative courses and their probable consequences, and also for fantasied gratifications; but the person distinguishes between pure fantasy and what it might be possible to realize. Magic and wishful thinking have given way before the need to turn fantasy into action so as to be able to gain the realization of wishes. Individuals appreciate that others perceive and experience events differently from the way they do, and both the limitations of their own views and the different ideas and feelings of others must be taken into account in seeking to bring ideas to fruition. Young adults now know enough about themselves and the world to decide whether the realization of a wish or a fantasy is a possibility worth pursuing.

A major aspect of a person's ability to carry out adaptive behavior concerns the capacities to tolerate tensions and the inevitable anxieties of life and still adhere to objectives and work through difficulties. The ability to adhere to commitments is usually taken as an index of "character," for it permits consistency and the avoidance of distraction by each attractive opportunity—whether it is an opportunity at work extraneous to one's own goals or a sexual distraction. Whereas at some periods in adolescence or young adulthood each fork in a road seems to require a decision, as the course of a life may be changed by following one path rather than the other, after commitments have been made, the objectives determine the ultimate direction and it matters little if one route or the other is followed for a stretch in progressing toward the goal.

Tensions and frustrations create anxiety and depressive spells but do not lead too often to a search for regressive solace in sensuality, in sleep, or in loss of self-awareness through the use of alcohol or narcotics. Frustrations are recognized as a part of life and, although avoided, they are accepted when necessary without mobilizing undue hostility and aggression—and such aggression as is aroused is directed toward overcoming the frustration rather than in vengeance or in hurting the self or those whom one needs. Various mechanisms of defense help control anxiety, but they are not called into play to an extent that markedly distorts the perception of the world or blinds one to realistic difficulties which must be faced and managed.

Now that problems of dependency and symbiotic strivings have been worked through, the boundaries of the self are secure enough for young adults no longer unconsciously to fear losing their identities when they seek after intimacy. They do not fear that a needed person will devour, engulf, or annihilate them, or that the loss of the self in orgasm will lead to obliteration; nor will they confuse themselves with a child, as does a mother who feeds her child when she is hungry. The young woman, however, needs to keep her boundaries sufficiently fluid to accept having a fetus within her, and to form a symbiotic bond with an infant.

A person is now secure enough in his or her gender identity not to need to prove his masculinity or her femininity to the self and others by repetitive compulsive sexual activity, or in undue masculine aggressivity or feminine seductiveness. And both men and women will realize that being a member of one sex or the other has both advantages and disadvantages, and are ready to make the most of the advantages rather than deplore their fate.

It has been customary in psychoanalytic literature to evaluate the stability and maturity of the progression to adult life in terms of the capacity for genital sexuality—properly, not simply the capacity for pleasure from orgasm in heterosexual relationships, but to enjoy sexuality in a meaningful intimate relationship. It is apparent, however, that some persons lead satisfactory and highly productive lives, even though they never achieve such genital sexuality, and that a person's maturity, including emotional maturity, may better be considered in terms of the achievement of a firm ego identity as well as the capacity for intimacy, recognizing that the capacity to come to terms with frustration or one's inadequacy can be a major aspect of maturity.

The developmental achievements that we have been considering as necessary for proper behavior in early adult life have been presented in rather black and white terms. In actuality, no one fully outgrows childhood needs and dependency strivings; no one progresses to adulthood unscarred by emotional traumata and more or less injurious relationships; no one manages to avoid being caught up in trying to solve some old problems; everyone continues to be somewhat motivated to gratify residual pregenital strivings; and we all utilize defenses of our ego that are no longer really necessary, and transfer characteristics of parents onto other significant persons. These are the things that color personalities and provide a distinctiveness and human frailty to all.

Still, such deficiencies, to sum up, should not lead persons to invest too much energy and effort in repetitively seeking after solutions to old problems poured ever again into new bottles, and should not prevent them from seeking completion in the present and the future rather than through the impossible task of remaking the past. Adults should also be capable of accepting the realization that many of the ways and rules of society are arbitrary, but that people need such regulations in order to live together— and they do not feel deceived and cheated by the arbitrariness of the rules; and they find their places in the social system, accepting it while hoping to improve it. Nor are they so readily disillusioned by other people, for faced by the difficulties in living they have become more tolerant of the failures and even deceptions of others.

Whatever their preparation, the time has come for young adults to make their own way in the world; they can delay and linger in the protection of the homes, or in the halls of their alma maters, where the storms of the world are filtered and refined, but they cannot tarry too long without commitment and the direction it provides. The choice of an occupation and the choice of a mate are the decisions that start them on their way. While both of these choices are often made as a rather natural progression in the path that a life has been taking, they are both highly *overdetermined*, tending to be resultants of the total developmental process together with the realistic opportunities available at the critical time of life. Although a single factor may clearly predominate in leading to a decision, a variety of factors virtually always enters consideration; and the conscious motives are often only rationalizations of unconscious forces that are exerting an indirect and disguised but powerful influence. The decisions may be no less useful and no less wise because of such unconscious influences, for unconscious motives may direct a person to significant and essential needs that are neglected or denied consciously, and because unconscious decisions can include repressed memories and intangible and nebulous perceptions and associations that may have considerable importance.

REFERENCES

ARIÈS, P. (1962). *Centuries of Childhood*. Alfred A. Knopf, New York.
BEALES, R. W. (1975). "In Search of the Historical Child: Miniature Adulthood and Youth in Colonial New England," *American Quarterly*, 27:380–398.
COLEMAN, B. (1720). "Early Piety Again Inculcated . . . ," p. 33. S. Kneeland for D. Henchman and J. Edwards, Boston.

DEMOS, J., and DEMOS, V. (1969). "Adolescence in Historical Perspective," *Journal of Marriage and Family*, 31:632–638.

HORNER, M. (1968). "A Psychological Barrier to Achievement in Women—The Motive to Avoid Success." Symposium presentation at the Midwestern Psychological Association, May, 1968.

—— (1969). "Fail: Bright Women," *Psychology Today*, 3:36 ff.

JUNG, C. G. (1926). *Psychological Types: The Psychology of Individuation.* H. G. Baynes, trans. Harcourt, Brace, New York, 1961.

KENISTON, K. (1970). "Youth as a Stage of Life," *American Scholar*, 39:631–654.

—— (1974). "Youth and Its Ideology," in *American Handbook of Psychiatry*, vol. 1. S. Arieti, ed. Basic Books, New York.

KOHLBERG, L. (1964). "Development of Moral Character and Moral Ideology," in *Review of Child Development Research.* M. L. Hoffman and L. W. Hoffman, eds. Russell Sage Foundation, New York.

PERRY, W. G. (1970). *Forms of Intellectual and Ethical Development in the College Years.* Holt, Rinehart & Winston, New York.

SUGGESTED READING

Group for the Advancement of Psychiatry (1975). *The Educated Woman: Prospects and Problems.* Mental Health Materials Center, New York.

KENISTON, K. (1974). "Youth and Its Ideology," in *American Handbook of Psychiatry*, vol. 1. S. Arieti, ed. Basic Books, New York.

10

An American Ishmael

by Kenneth Keniston

Inburn's appearance in no way set him apart from other undergraduates. Tall, with blue eyes and sandy hair, he wore the uniform of his classmates: baggy corduroys, a button-down shirt, horn-rimmed glasses, and a tie more often than not slid down from the collar. He walked with something of a slouch, hands deep in his pockets, his eyes mostly fixed on the pavement as if he were deep in some private thought. From the cafeterias he frequented, one versed in the ways of the college might have surmised that he was of literary bent and, from the fact that he so often ate breakfast at one particular cafeteria at 11:00 A.M. (having overslept the dining hall's more Spartan hours), that he was given neither to regular hours nor to impeccable attendance of lectures. But these qualities did not distinguish him from a goodly proportion of his fellow sophomores.

Nor did he create an unusual impression on others. The opinion of a woman of fifty who knew him casually can perhaps stand as typical: "I rather liked him. He is thin and pleasant—perhaps not a decisive, strong-willed person, but always agreeable, never obviously depressed, perhaps a little shy, as talkative as most men his age." A psychologist who knew him slightly commented, "He is a nice-looking fellow, with a deep voice that might go over well on the stage. He speaks hesitantly, but well despite pauses and hesitations—more like written prose than ordinary speech." His manner was polite, reserved, and even detached, which implied to some that he was proud and condescending, and to others that he tended to brood. Though he seldom looked directly at the person to whom he was speaking, occasionally, when caught up in a topic, he would gaze deeply and intently into his interlocutor's eyes, suggesting deeper feelings than his outward manner expressed.

On the surface, his background and interests were also altogether unextraordinary. Like many of his classmates, he came from a middle-class family outside of New England, and he had gone to a good high school where he had graduated near the top of his class and been editor of the school paper. His outstanding intelligence, however, did not distinguish him from his classmates, also of high talent; and while his grades in his freshman year were slightly uneven, they adequately reflected his ability and he made Dean's List. His father was an executive with a large Detroit corporation; and his mother, for a time a schoolteacher, had early abandoned her career for domesticity. Inburn himself had been undecided for a time as to his major, but had finally settled on English literature as a field which combined his interest in writing and his superior high school training in literature. Like other students of artistic interests, he had tried his hand at student dramatics and at writing, a career he sometimes thought of following. He was a student in good standing with the college authorities who had caused no one any trouble and who would not be easily picked out in a crowd.

In the most public sides of Inburn's personality, then, there was little to suggest what was the case: that he was deeply dissatisfied with society, the world, and himself, that he almost completely rejected the institutional forms within which he was living, that he would spend his first reading period for exams in platonic partnership with a call girl whose memoirs he was ostensibly recording for future use, and that, though he passed his exams, he would withdraw from the college never to return, heading instead on a motorcycle across the country to live with an "irredeemably dissolute" high school friend in San Francisco. Despite his conventional surface, indeed because of it, Inburn can stand as a prototypically alienated young man, separated by his own volition from the people, institutions, and beliefs which sustain most young men at his age in America, rejecting the forms by which most American men and women live, and condemned like the Biblical Ishmael by his past and like Melville's Ishmael by his own temper to live on the outskirts of society. In Inburn, we see alienation—the rejection of the roles, values, and institutions he sees as typical of adult American life—in unusually pure form; and the themes of his life stand as introduction to and summary of parallel and comparable themes in the lives of others like him.

An Endless and Featureless Countryside

Like seventy other volunteers for a psychological research project, Inburn took a battery of paper-and-pencil tests, many of which were designed to measure alienated outlooks. He first came to our attention even before the questionnaires were scored, because of his mordant marginal comments on items that he considered stupid or irrelevant. He scored among the highest scores on every index we then had of alienation—on distrust, pessimism, resentment, anxiety, egocentricity, the sense of being an outsider, the rejection of conventional values, rejection of happiness as a goal, and a feeling of distance from others. And had other subsequently developed measures of alienation been available, he would have scored high on them—on subspection (the desire to look beneath appearances), self-contempt, interpersonal alienation, dislike of conventional social groups, the rejection of American culture, the view of the universe as an unstructured and meaningless chaos. But even more revealing than test scores are some of the individual statements which he marked "strongly agree," often with exclamation points added; taken together, they constitute a kind of credo of disaffiliation: "The idea of trying to adjust to society as now constituted fills me with horror." "These are sad and depressing times when the whole world strikes the eye as a huge, heartless, impersonal machine, almost devoid of understanding, sympathy, and mercy." "I sometimes feel that I am the plaything of forces beyond my control." "I feel strongly how different I am even from some of my closest friends." "I have very little in common with most of the people I meet." "I don't think I'll ever find a woman who really understands me." "I have very little self-confidence." "I usually try to keep my thoughts to myself." "I sometimes wish I were a child again."

Soon after, when Inburn was asked to write a statement of his philosophy of life, he was unique among twenty-five students chosen for intensive clinical study in that he wrote an allegory instead of a formal statement:

> A group of men were motoring through an endless and featureless countryside in a tightly closed car, with all the windows rolled up. They reach a city, emerge from their vehicle, stretch their legs, and look around. They have a two-weeks stay ahead of them; after that they must move on into the wastes on the other side of the town, the same as before they arrived.
>
> "Well," I ask (being one of them), "what shall we do?" To all our surprises, each wants to spend his time differently. . . . "Personally," say I, "I would like to see the sights of this place."
>
> In this rather naïve allegory lies the ideal of my philosophy of life. If human (i.e., *my*) existence is looked on as a short time spent in a physical world with an inscrutable void on either side, it seems that the time can be most profitably spent in accumulating the most varied, the most valuable and most significant set of sense experiences it is possible to take in. . . .
>
> . . . one must not see the same sights over-frequently. What experiences are most valuable to fill this sixty to seventy year interlude are those that bring one into the closest contact with reality, with the ground, the bedrock of sheer existence. This, of course, involves living close to nature, outside of (or rather beneath) the superstructure of tin and shit and kite-paper man has built up to live in.
>
> . . . Rather obviously, I am not practicing what I preach to any extent at all now. I wouldn't be in this room writing this little essay if I were. So far, all I do is insult myself by saying it's a fine idea, in fact, it's the only idea in the universe, but you don't have the guts to put it into practice.

Inburn's statement is as noteworthy for what it excludes as for what it says. Unlike many other students, whose philosophies of life stress the importance of other people, Inburn mentions others only once, and then to state that he is different from them. Also unlike many of his classmates, he explicitly rejects the "superstructure" of society, and seeks above all the accumulation of sense experience, defined as that which will bring him into contact with "the bedrock of sheer existence."

Inburn's generally distrustful view of his fellow man was amplified when he was asked what harms and benefits he chiefly anticipated from his fellow men. He listed only "hostility, injustice, hypocrisy, slander, abuse." Asked whom he admired, he said "I never thought about it. Alexander maybe. Hemingway in Paris. Chopin," but asked whom he disliked, he responded with a long catalogue which begins "nearly everything, and everyone that's complacently midde-class," enumerates many specific examples, and concludes "I hate officious, supercilious, imperious, pompous, stupid, contented, or bigoted persons. I especially dislike opportuntists." And asked what his chief satisfactions and ambitions were he said, "I don't think I'll ever have a main source of satisfaction. Only to live so that I may have the truest picture of the world possible when I die. You mean vaulting ambition? Nobody strives for ideas anymore. It's hard enough just to strive." And asked how he would reform the world if he could, he said, "This is an unfair question. I guess I'd like to have us all go back to the womb."

Here, then, is a young man whose every attitude fits an alienated pattern—full of distrust, he expects only harm from his fellow men; he has few admired figures, but many he dislikes; he sees life as a meaningless interlude whose chief aim is the accumulation of varied sense experiences. He rejects society and conventional institutions; though he has no definite plans for his life, he clearly wants something different from the conventional life which draws most of his classmates; he denies all ambition; and his facetious Utopia is the womb.

More Than a Mere Mother-and-Only-Child

Inburn's autobiography, written for the research project for which he had volunteered, begins to provide some clues as to the development of his alienation. Like one or two of the more literarily ambitious research subjects, he began his autobiography in the third person:

> He came screaming and red-faced into the world on a December night in 1938, loath to leave his insensible

sanctuary. . . . It was in a hospital in St. Louis; his mother was a small, young woman and she never had a child again. His parents were both school-teachers and poor, after the ravages of the depression. His mother was particularly good looking when she was young—black hair, a good nose, strikingly large eyes, a sensuous lip and a delicate yet hard, vibrant, vivacious body.

Inburn goes on to describe his mother's Greek immigrant parents, her mother "a simple, exuberant, and cruel woman," and her father, who ran a small restaurant, "a strong man, and strongwilled," "tireless, too tireless."

His further description of his mother is extremely detailed. Despite her immigrant parents, "she made herself socially to nearly every family in St. Louis" [sic]. "Her petite and much-in-demand bottom was between two worlds. . . . She dropped her restaurant-owner's daughter's bad manners and grossness, and made herself, completely, at the cost of a great emotional and psychological complexity." She was ambitious, she taught herself to play the piano beautifully (she even gave recitals), "she *would* read poetry (though she never wrote it), she *would* paint, she *would* play tennis on the bank president's private court, and with his son." Despite her parents' lack of sympathy with her educational goals, she worked her way through high school and college, finishing each in three years. Elsewhere, Inburn notes that his mother is at the extreme end of the temperament scale: "volatile, passionate, typically Mediterranean"; and he adds that she "has a delicate constitution and has been warned against severe mental as well as physical strains."

In contrast to his full description of his mother, Inburn has little to say of his father. His father's family originally came from a farm in the Midwest, and Inburn's grandfather married his own brother's pregnant and cast-off girl friend, became a milkman in St. Louis, and was thereafter dominated by his wife, a "scolding, officious hypochondriac." The father's ancestry was primarily Welsh, with a mixture of German and Irish. Inburn's father showed early signs of intelligence and musical talent, and worked his way through high school and college where he met his wife-to-be. As a child, he seems to have been dominated by his mother, the "scolding, officious hypochondriac," who forced him to work in the evenings for the family landlord, "an idea he has recalled with bitterness at times." Awarded a scholarship to an Eastern college, Inburn's father was unable to accept it because he had to help support his parents—a responsibility that included helping pay his older half-brother's debts. Inburn describes his father now as a "phlegmatic, deliberate, steady-minded Welshman," noting the extreme contrast with his mother. "Father is pretty much of a failure in his own eyes," he comments, adding, "He's done pretty well as the world is concerned, though." Elsewhere he calls his father "a pillar in the community," adding parenthetically, "(Small pillar. Small community)." He describes "a great distance" between himself and his father, noting rather unenthusiastically, "We are friendly, though, except when my Greek side is up and I become disgusted with him and he annoyed at me."

His parents married immediately after graduating from college and both worked as high school teachers, his father occasionally holding two jobs to supplement the family income. Inburn's account continues:

This, then, is the situation (one might say predicament) Inburn was born into. By 1938 his parents had saved enough money to have a house of their own . . . they hired an architect and had the place built just as they wanted. The father is acquiescent and the mother has excellent taste, and it came out beautifully.

The first memories Inburn has are of this house—door knobs, the carpeting, the bright yellow and white kitchen, the apple tree in the backyard, the plum trees in the field beyond. It was in a fairly undeveloped suburban section, staunchly middle class.

He was pretty as a child, a little plump, with his mother's eyes and grace and quite curly blond hair. Mama tells me [sic] proudly how often people stopped her on the street and exclaimed about him. The closest friend he had in preschool days was a girl his own age. . . . He had nearly no male companionship until he entered school in the first grade, a year early, and he was somewhat precocious (not alarmingly so). He seems to have been quite well adjusted, pretty well liked by everyone, quite well liked by his teachers. Although he showed some intelligence, he was not remarkable. He liked his dog, his home, radio programs, soccer ball, brick walls, the janitor at school, trees, mornings, green lawns, walking, playing with toys, having imaginary adventures with the boy across the street in the orchard behind his house.

But as with most children his age, the Second World War profoundly affected Inburn:

When he was five years old, his father went into the war; he was gone for four years. In these four years he and his mother had the most intimate of relationships. They were one. Every thought, every action of one could be anticipated by the other. Somehow it seemed more than a mere mother-and-only-child relationship. We were in complete spiritual and mental and physical harmony with each other. Sometimes she was even shy with me. It was a strange relationship.

This description is as remarkable for the element of fantasy it contains as it is for the undeniable facts it must refer to. Inburn emphasizes the fusion of mother and child, the completeness of their understanding, their total anticipation of each other's thoughts and actions, their oneness. But in fact, such oneness and fusion can seldom occur after the first year of life; thereafter, mother and child assume an increasing separateness which usually eventuates in the child's independence as an adult. That Inburn thus describes his relationship with his mother at ages five through nine thus suggests a strong element of wish, perhaps on the mother's side but certainly on Inburn's, that all separateness between him and her be obliterated.

The end of the war brought a double dislocation for Inburn: first, his father returned from the war, and second, immediately thereafter his father left teaching and moved with his family to a more lucrative and more bureaucratic position in a Detroit corporation, where he is now, in his son's words, "a kind of minor official." Inburn himself makes little of either of these facts; but without noting the connection, he dates several changes in his behavior from the age of nine or ten. Of his state of mind, he writes, "From about nine or ten on, he got to be very moody, thinking too much or reading the wrong kind of books. The moodiness was always well within himself, though, and he was seldom snappish, perverse, or irritable." Elsewhere, he dates the beginning of intermittent constipation from the same age. And in a supplement to his autobiography, when recounting his sexual development, he writes:

> I was disturbed when I was finally convinced that children came out of women. I didn't want to believe it. It seemed base and carnal at the time. . . . I thought that if people wished for children strongly enough they would just come. I was first enlightened by some slightly older boys (9-10?); later and more clear-headedly by my parents, though sketchily (14).

After the move to Detroit, Inburn's family continued to travel during summer vacations, which he recalls with pleasure. But he also notes:

> But the summers away made it impossible for Inburn to play baseball. In that red-blooded American community baseball was a big thing. I was a little estranged from my fellows because of this.

Expanding on his subsequent relationships with his peers, he says:

> I was accepted, but made people indignant towards me because they felt I was not only superior to them but scornful of them. All but one friendship pretty casual, red-blooded. Few quarrels. It didn't matter that much. Frequent periods of extreme moodiness and solitariness. Disenchantment—estrangement.

In sum, his father's return and the family move to Detroit seem to have been a turning point in Inburn's life, marking the beginning of his moodiness, his constipation, his estrangement, and even coinciding with his disgust at the "base and carnal" nature of birth. But all of this is our surmise, for Inburn himself does not note the coincidence of dates.

When he was fourteen, Inburn first became interested in girls, describing himself as "struck dumb" by a girl "with eyes as blue as his, and deeper, framed in a simple kerchief, staring into his face in an autumn dusk." He continues,

> Not long later sex reared its ugly head. He fell in with some of his male contemporaries. And boys can be dirty. They can be vile. A hundred times we talked about the girls at school, describing with great vigor their proportions, or lack of them. Girls with breasts the size of five-cent ice cream cones. . . .

He reports "excessive masturbation," accompanied by "great clouds of guilt," and characterizes his major current feelings about sex as "anxiety, shame, disgust." He has never had intercourse.

Inburn reports no further events of outward importance until he was a junior in high school, when he met Hal, who played a major role in the development of his outlook:

> Hal was, and is, a cynical young man. Cynical, profound, skeptical, sarcastic, highly intelligent, casual in his manner, yet intense in his questioning. And he always questioned. His cynicism infected me: he became my very good, my best friend, the best and closest I ever had. What were we cynical about? You, for one thing, and ourselves, our teachers, our world, cynical about the very act of existence. Or rather, the fact of existence, for with us it was a passive experience. We let time and values and actions pass over us like a wash, like a coating of wax. We both had been raised as agnostics, but it was a mild sort of agnosticism, an unthought-about agnosticism. First of all we turned everybody's religion upside down and we shouted. We were roundly condemned, but Hal more, since he shouted more, and louder. That went by the board and we began on our contemporaries and on our society. We attacked everything, every person, every institution, with a bitter tooth. Our long secret conversations were rank with contempt. We were full of a magnificent disdain, and we fed it with all the knowledge we could get (and what wouldn't fit we disregarded)—Kafka, D. H. Lawrence, Hume, Rousseau, Voltaire, Shaw, Jung, Freud, Marx. We read voraciously, but not the right things, and not enough.
>
> . . . Hal is gone now. He went to college in Berkeley for a while, but now he is apparently irredeemably dissolute. . . . And he just doesn't give a damn. There was a great rift between us when I went to the College. He thinks now that it will ruin me, and now calls me a coward for not "finding out some things" on my own.
>
> Maybe he's right. If he means I'm becoming more complacent, I must plead guilty. As far as I can see, we both want knowledge; we want to know about the underpinnings of existence. I'm trying to do it through the institutions of my society, the college, for example. Hal is trying to "find out some things" on his own.

And on this inconclusive note, Inburn ends his autobiography.

In what he tells us about his life, certain themes and facts stand out. First is the marked contrast between his two parents. His mother emerges as "Mediterranean," ambitious, energetic, highstrung, driving, volatile, passionate, and, in her son's eyes, sensuous and physically attractive. Even her family is characterized as strong, tireless, simple, exuberant, and cruel. But he suggests that she has paid a high price in "complexity" and a "delicate" constitution and psychology for her efforts in "making herself." Inburn's father, in contrast, comes from North European stock, and from a long line of men who were dominated by women. Recall how his chances for a better education were limited by having to pay his half-brother's debts. And consider his move from his first love, teaching, to a more lucrative job where he now considers himself "a failure in his own eyes" despite contrary community judgment. Without fully stating it, Inburn clearly implies his father's weakness vis-à-vis his mother's drive ("The father is acquiescent and the mother has excellent taste . . ."). Inburn obviously finds his mother's vivid sensuousness far more interesting than his father's phlegmatic and taciturn nature. All of this makes Inburn's father a man difficult to emulate; and we would anticipate that this fact, coupled with Inburn's unusual past relationship with his mother, would cause Inburn difficulty.

In addition, several events stand out as having crucial importance in Inburn's life. One is his romanticized idyl with his mother during the war. The absence of any child's father for three or four years would be important to his development; but for Inburn, its importance must have been accentuated by his unique, "more than a mere mother-and-only-child relationship" with her. His friendship with Hal, too, was crucial. Until he met Hal, Inburn's life seems little different on the surface from that of most young men his age, with "his moodiness . . . always well within himself"; Hal acted as a catalyst for Inburn's alienation. Thirdly, Inburn's initial unwillingness to accept the fact of birth, his inability to overcome his not unusual first reactions to sex, and his current anxious attitudes are also worth underlining. While many a young man in our society has difficulty in reconciling himself to the "facts of life," it is remarkable at the age of nineteen to list "anxiety, shame, and disgust" as the only three emotions which sex evokes. And finally, Inburn's relations with his peers follows a familiar pattern for an alienated young man. He was not good at the games which mattered in his "red-blooded" community, his fellows considered him scornful, and he felt "frequent periods of estrangement." Even when he became editor of the school paper with his friend Hal, the two of them "managed to ruin it in three months." . . .

The Outsider Who Would Be Inside

We now have learned enough of the central themes in Inburn's life to enable us to try to reconstruct the origins and current functions of his alienation. In any such reconstruction, it is well to keep in mind that the principle of parsimony seldom applies in explaining individual lives; rather, only when we have begun to understand the subtle interweaving of themes, the "overdetermination" of any single act, belief, or fantasy, and the multiple functions that every dream, wish, action, and philosophy serves, do we begin to understand something of an individual. Thus, even with the best of intentions the psychologist must continually oversimplify, and by singling out one set of alienated beliefs and outlooks for special explanation, I here oversimplify Inburn the more.

To begin with, the outward circumstances of Inburn's life provided a setting within which his alienation became more than casually possible. As an only child, he was undoubtedly destined to feel more intensely about his parents than would a child with siblings or an extended family to dissipate the concentration of his affections and angers. Further, his father's absence for the four crucial years of the war must inevitably have intensified his preexisting feelings about his mother. And then, too, the son of a second-generation mother of Greek descent and a father of northern European stock is very likely to note a sharp temperamental contrast between his two parents and their

families. But these assured facts only provide a setting for the more central psychological events and fantasies which underlie Inburn's estrangement.

For further explanations, we must assume that Inburn's account of his parents is in many ways correct, at least as it describes their impact on him. His mother, as we have noted, emerges as a possessive, ambitious, driving woman, who, once she stopped teaching, devoted herself exclusively to domestic life. And at the same time, Inburn describes her as moody, passionate, highly sensuous, and physically attractive. The T.A.T. story in which a woman seeks to bind an unwilling man to her through sex again suggests that Inburn sees his mother as not only possessive, but as emotionally seductive, seeking from her son a kind of emotional fulfillment he could not provide and unconsciously attempting to use her attractiveness to bind him to her. Thus, even as a small child, Inburn probably felt torn between his dependency on his mother and his enjoyment of their extraordinary closeness on the one hand, and on the other her unwanted possessiveness and her unconscious needs that he be more to her than a son.

With a strong and vital husband, a possessive and seductive mother's effects on her son are usually limited; indeed, with such a husband, a woman is less likely in the first place to seek excessive fulfillment in her relationship with her children. But Inburn's father, at least as Inburn perceives him, was neither strong nor vital. "Taciturn," "phlegmatic," and "acquiescent," he had probably been better prepared by his own childhood for the role of the dominated than the dominant. Inburn also suggests that his father was disappointed with his own life, perhaps at least in part because he "acquiesced" to the extent of leaving his original vocation for a better-paying if less idealistic job. And finally, one can only wonder with what feelings the father could have greeted being denied an excellent education, struggling in the depression, or being taken away from his family, work, and country for four years during the war. In short, we have few grounds for believing that Inburn's father had qualities or zest enough to offset his mother's drive and sensuousness.

Even without Inburn's father's long absence during the war, such parents would have made for a rivalrous family triangle of singular intensity and equivocal outcome. More often than we generally acknowledge, husbands must struggle for their wives' affections with their children—and especially with only sons, who have but one rival between them and their mother's exclusive devotion to her child. And if the wife should come to find her husband dull or a failure in life, then the outcome is especially equivocal. But in Inburn's case, the wish to supplant his father must have been overwhelmingly reinforced by his father's sudden departure for the war. Few five-year-olds could resist the temptation unconsciously to consider such a four-year absence a token of their own triumph. We know something of the ensuing mother-son relationship from Inburn's idyllic account of his unique understanding with his mother; and we learn more from his T.A.T. stories in which the central relationships are peculiar intimacies between young men and women, with fathers and older men absent or somehow debased and scorned out of significant existence.

I have already noted the component of fantasy in Inburn's recollections of this idyl, which he endows with qualities more like those of an infant-mother symbiosis than those of a five-to-nine-year-old's relationship with his mother. Some of this he must of course have felt, perhaps encouraged by his mother's increased need of and responsiveness to him in her husband's absence. But some was clearly a fantasy, and time alone would have probably sufficed to break the illusion of perfect understanding and oneness. But his father's sudden return exacerbated, underlined, and made more traumatic Inburn's probably dawning awareness that he was less and less his Mama's pretty little child, and more and more a separate person, alone in crucial ways. It is from the age of nine or ten that he dates a variety of new feelings of moodiness and estrangement, and to the same age that his submarining hero traces his wish to slip forever downward in the deep warm sea. Again and again, Inburn as a college sophomore still expresses or symbolizes this overpowering wish for fusion with the maternal, for a blissful state without consciousness, for an "insensible sanctuary," in the last analysis, to be like a tiny infant in his mother's arms, who by gazing into her eyes enters her enveloping protection. What time and his increasing age has not accomplished in destroying the possibility of asylum, his father's return completed; therefore, as it were, the waters had receded and the submarine was beached.

For most children, such a loss, which is after all universal, can be assimilated without excessive backward yearning because there are active pulls into a future seen as better than what must be abandoned. For a boy, such forces are usually embodied in his father, who by the mere fact of an admired existence implicitly teaches his son that it is worth while to grow up to be a man. When there is no such father, when the mother's excessive devotion to her son undermines her husband's relative worth in the son's eyes, or when the father considers himself a failure and thus implicitly denies that the son should become a man like him—then the son's incentives to leave gracefully his ties with his mother are diminished, and physiological growth goes unmatched by psychological readiness.

For Inburn, then, there was an especially great deal to lose and especially little reason to give it up. Once he had been the apple of his mother's eye, fused at least in fantasy to her answering gaze, the child with whom she had been so strangely intimate as to be shy; but in his desire to retain his claustral estate he had, without wishing it, lost it, ended with a possessive and sensuous mother on his hands, and been left without a father to boot. Small wonder that his father's return brought moodiness, brooding, and constipation, and that when during the same year he learned the facts of birth, they seemed "base and carnal" compared with his own developing fantasies of regaining his former sanctuary. Henceforth, Inburn was to consider himself an outcast, dreaming of an Eden from which he perhaps dimly recalled he came, forever comparing his exiled realities of a dominating, seductive mother and a taciturn, psychologically absent father with the cozy cabin

But so far his inner feelings of estrangement were, he implies, "always well within himself," and he was "seldom in Noah's Ark and the downslipping submarine in the warm sea. snappish, perverse, or irritable." In the development of a more overt alienation, two further facts are crucial. This first is Inburn's sexual maturation and the accompanying psychological changes which he describes in his scornful account of "sex's ugly head" and the "dirtiness" and "vileness" of adolescent boys. Few boys in our culture, however enlightened their parentage, can pass through adolescence without further reassessing their closeness with their mothers; and for many, the acute fear of any sexual intimacy with anyone like her continues throughout life. But such fears, however normal a part of development for American men, can reach panic proportions in a youth who brings into adolescence an unresolved need to enter a woman not as a man but as a child seeking shelter. When these needs are coupled with a prior notion that sex and birth are base and carnal (undoubtedly transmitted in part by parents), deep anxieties about sex can last long into adulthood. And finally, if, as for Inburn, the prospect of becoming a man like one's father is deeply disconcerting and implicitly discouraged by mother and father alike, then the advent of manhood is even more disruptive. Adolescence must have further complicated Inburn's already tortuous relationship with this mother, adding to her possessiveness the new thread of that most "loathsome thing," incest.

In all young men and women the advent of adulthood releases immense new energies and potentials, which in most are centrally involved in establishing new intimacies with the opposite sex. This new learning is seldom smooth; but when it is severely blocked by unresolved needs and frustrations from the past, it takes but a slight catalyst—and often no catalyst at all—to transform these energies into rage, scorn, and aggression, often symbolically directed against those who have stood in the way of full adulthood. It was Hal, then, who provided the second crucial fact, the catalyst and vehicle for the transformation of Inburn's inward moodiness into an open and scornful alienation. From Hal, or with his help and encouragement, he learned cynicism, disdain, scorn, and contempt for the "superstructure of tin and shit and kite-paper" which represented society to them. Hal became for Inburn a kind of antisocial superego, so much so that Inburn puts his discontents with college into Hal's mouth, and when he finally leaves college, it is not to return to his parents, but to live with Hal and demonstrate that he has not, in fact, become "complacent." Further, with Hal he learned the vocabulary and logic of his instincts, culling from the works of the most alienated writers of the last two alienated centuries the diction of estrangement. The sense of alienation and exile, the rage and frustration which might have found outlet in delinquency in a youth of less intelligence, perceptiveness, and articulateness, in Inburn was aimed at targets sanctioned by usage and made meaningful by their personal symbolism, and thus found expression within a historical tradition. What had been contained was now released, and Inburn became overtly alienated.

Inburn's alienation in word and deed thus serves multiple purposes. Most centrally, it rationalizes his felt condition as an outcast from his first sanctuary: the feeling of exile is generalized, universalized into the human condition. . . . Furthermore, by condemning the society and the forms of society from which he himself came, Inburn states the partial truth that there is no sanctuary and that he does not wish to return. And by attacking society and all its authoritative concomitants, Inburn indirectly criticizes his father and all he stands for: conventionality, being a "small pillar in a small community," being "complacently middle-class," perhaps even being a "failure in his own eyes." Inburn's grievance against his father is a double one: his father disrupted Inburn's idyl with his mother, and probably more important, he was not strong enough to offer anything better than the mother-son intimacy which he disrupted. Inburn has accounts to render, and render them he does in his alienation.

11

THE GENERATION GAP

A Review and Typology of
Social-Psychological Perspectives

VERN L. BENGTSON
University of Southern California

Of those phenomena on which social scientists gather data and write analyses, there are few of more popular relevance today than discussions of the "generation gap." It is of course true that the problem of generations is one of the older issues in modern sociology; despite this, very few thorough studies have yet been made to illuminate the nature and extent of continuity or differences between age groups today. Even more importantly, there have been no empirical attempts to analyze the effect on social structure of such differences between generations. Indeed, all too often the discussion of such issues has been impressionistic, speculative, and even apocalyptic—not only in the popular press, but also in the pages of scholarly books and journals.

The purpose of this paper is to review some classical and some contemporary approaches to the problem of generations, and to order these perspectives in a typology reflecting some underlying dimensions of the social-psychological investigation of generations.

The term generation gap should be read as in quotation marks throughout this paper; for the phenomenon to which it refers is undoubtedly neither strictly generational nor is it a gap, using any reasonable definition of those terms. Be that as it may, the term has worldwide usage and a sort of connotative reality. The man on the street knows, in his own

AUTHOR'S NOTE: *With the collaboration of William C. Martin, Chico State College.*

The preparation of this paper was made possible in part by a grant from the Andrew Normal Foundation and from the Biomedical Sciences Research Grant FR-07012-02 to the University of Southern California. Support also came from the Gerontology Center of USC. The author is indebted to Sol Kobrin, LaMar Empey, and Marijo Walsh of USC, to Joseph Kuypers of the University of California, Berkeley, and to Reuben Hill of the University of Minnesota, for helpful suggestions in the preparation of this paper.

way, what the generation gap refers to, and social scientists have, rightly or wrongly, followed his lead in using the term.

THE GENERATION GAP AND MASS CULTURE TODAY

A fruitful way to begin this analysis is through a brief survey of the evidence of generational differences as portrayed in such everyday chronicles as the mass media and political rhetoric. For in the characterization of social movements and the identification of social problems, mass culture often antecedes social scientists by several years.

The message from the media is that differences between age groups are becoming a serious social problem, not only in America but in most Western industrialized countries (see Neugarten, 1970). Concern over the youth problem turns very often into outright hostility; and discrimination against the aged, more subtle but no less pervasive (see Butler, 1969), has serious implications in nations where increasingly longevity swells the ranks of the aged. One might say that *age-ism* has become a common theme in mass culture today, just as racism finally became acknowledged a decade ago in American society. Defined as prejudice by members of one age group against another age group (s), age-ism implies stereotyping, interpersonal distance, and often, conflict of interest. It describes the subjective experience implied in the popular definition of the generation gap (Butler, 1969; Neugarten, 1970).

Evidence for age-ism is found in almost any newspaper or mass distribution magazine picked at random during the past few months or years. For example, in one three-day period in the spring of 1970, the Los Angeles *Times* printed a variety of news items, editorials, and cartoons—and several advertisements—that portrayed relations between generations as cause for serious concern. One article explored the international ties of student protest movements; another reported the "get tough" reactions of several public officials toward campus demonstrations. A feature reporting the rapidly expanding commune movement and hippie subculture was presented on the same page as a brief article reporting on increasing drug arrests in an affluent suburb of Los Angeles. On the editorial page, a syndicated columnist described the immorality of student demonstrations, while the editorial urged that taxpayers not take out their grievances against student demonstrators at the polls by voting down school bond elections. One cartoon showed the President making a clumsy attempt to "rap" with youthful constituents, while another portrayed student protestors riding roughshod over Law, Order, and Justice. On the front page was a report of working class men assaulting student protesters; it was continued on an inside page next to a large advertisement suggesting that the purchase of a Mustang would "bridge the generation gap." Thus, in many ways, some humorous but most pensive, the mass-distribution newspaper reports sub-

stantial differences between youth and the mature generation today. The implication of most of this portrayal is that these differences lead to social disorganization: the nation is "coming apart at the seams" and an elite group of youth is doing most of the tearing.

Or to take another example, the alleged disorganization of the family by intergenerational tension is reflected in the titles of articles in American mass-distribution magazines between 1968 and 1970. *Life* discusses "The Gulf Between Parents and their Kids (Wider than Ever Before)"; *Look* analyzes "The Way Between Mother and Daughter"; *Saturday Review* wonders "What Are Our Young People Telling Us?" while the *Ladies Home Journal* suggests, somewhat tentatively, that "We Can Close the Generation Gap—IF."

A third example of generational relations as seen in popular culture is in the political arena. Not only has the gap become a political issue, it has been elevated to the level of a national problem. In one of his first addresses to the nation following his election in 1968, President Nixon characterized differences between youth and adults in our society as "a yawning gulf . . . between the two halves of our people, a great divide and misunderstanding that weakens our body politic" (Dougherty, 1968). He proposed and later implemented a National Youth Agency to "bring us together again in this area." Since then, the charge of discrimination against youth, or at least youthful protesters, has been leveled against the administration with growing fury. In the California gubernatorial election of 1970, an important campaign issue has been the warning of Governor Reagan that "there will be a bloodbath on our campuses" if protesters do not subside (Los Angeles Times, 1970). In the spring of 1970 thousands of campuses across the nation responded, in one way or another, to the deployment of U.S. troops in Cambodia, protesting not only on moral grounds but on the basis of discrimination against youth. The violence that has ensued is literally without precedent in American history; and· the traditional political ploy of "nothing but the best for our kids" has become unpopular. As the *Wall Street Journal* (1968) editorialized,

> Many middle-aged Americans are likely to feel that youth rebels not because it feels deep grievances, but because it has never felt any. What troubles the older generation is the nagging thought that this ill-mannered rebellion is reward not for its failures but for its success.

From the evidence available in the mass media, then, differences between age groups today are seen as an extensive social problem in contemporary society. Relations between the generations are seen as tenuous and often outright hostile. And the result of the differences and tensions between the generations is seen as an alarming disruption of present social organization.

When one turns to an analysis of the earlier sociological formulations of the problem of generations, however, an entirely different perspective is seen. In a tradition of research that was for the most part ignored in the United States, European sociologists made analyses of the cycle of generations to account for the inevitable ebb and flow of historical events.

CLASSICAL SOCIOLOGY AND THE PROBLEM OF GENERATIONS

Concern with discontinuity between generations dates as far back as recorded history goes (see Feuer, 1969, for an excellent review). Egyptian and Hebrew sages defined wisdom in terms that implied dire consequences for youth who forsook the way of their elders. The Maxims of Ptahhotep—the first document on ethics of which there is record—was, as Feuer notes, already concerned with the problem of generations. Plato and Aristotle incorporated generational struggle in their theories of political change. Aristotle suggested the cause of political struggle could be found in the conflict of fathers and sons.

In the late nineteenth century, Continental social historians—for the most part, followers of Hegel—began to systematically explore generations as a dimension of social organization and political change. As summarized by Mannheim (1952), Heberle (1951), and Marias (1968), the thesis they attempted to document was that the rhythm of changes in ideas and political institutions is associated with the emergence of new biological generations.

As Mannheim describes it, the goal of these early sociologists was to deal with the problem of social time to account for change in the nature of the social fabric from period to period. He contrasted the "positivist" with the "romantic-metaphysical" definition of generations—a distinction which is still useful when applied to current perspectives of generations. The early positivist school tied the movement of history to the fact that persons growing in an identifiable span of time under basically the same set of social events—wars, economic conditions, political movements—as they came of age. A new generation, arising with predictable regularity every 25 to 30 years, produces an identifiable historical era and serves as a link in the chain of progress. By contrast, the romanticists defined generations, not in terms of time span, but in terms of common sharing of experiences of a purely qualitative sort. A generation is defined by the shared *geist* of an era which colors all its products and is in a sense, independent of historical time. Thus the classical period in art lasted for three calendar generations, while the expressionism of the late nineteenth century only one; yet both can be seen as a generation of definite perspective in expressing artistic perception. From this viewpoint, then, a generation lasts as long as a single art form or mode of expression prevails.

The problem with both these positions is that they both fail to account for the "noncontemporaneity of the contemporaneous." This was Pinder's (1926) figure of speech referring to the contrasts in outlook that exist between two or three generational cohorts who live together as the same point in time. Mannheim proposes that the concept of generation be used as nothing more than a kind of identity of location in time, embracing related age groups who are embedded in a historical-social process. There is a "trigger action" of social and historical events which determine whether a new generation emerges every year, or every thirty or one hundred years, or whether it emerges at all. Thus during some periods, generations do not appear as social change agents because there has not been a catalyst to produce their consciousness as a generation: that is, a group differentiated from other generations and a unity despite the distinctions that usually occur within any age group (see the excellent discussions by Berger (1960) and Troll (1970) for contemporary perspectives of the Mannheim theme and the problems in generational analysis).

The classical sociological analysis of generations has been most often employed to explain political movements. Mentre (1920), Herberle (1951), and most recently Feuer (1969) have applied the concept to the rise of national parties and to political revolutions. Heberle suggested the concept of "decisive politically relevant experiences" to explain why succeeding generations may be oriented to interpret the institutions of society in different ways. However, he emphasizes that the entire generation will not have identical objective experiences, and a generation will include many subdivisions (social classes, for example) that create differences within them. Intragenerational divisions are still less pronounced than differences between generations. Such contrasts between generations will be greater in periods of rapid social change, and the longer a generation stays in power politically, the sharper will be the clash with the youngest generation (as in Germany in 1918 when the elderly leaders of old political parties blocked the rise of younger men). Feuer (1969), a contemporary writer in the Classical sociological tradition, suggests that the "moral deauthorization of the older generation" is a principal component of revolutionary change based on generational distinctions.

A final position in the classical tradition of sociology is that suggested by Davis (1940) in analyzing "the sociology of parent-youth conflict." Whereas Mannheim, Pinder, and Herberle focus principally on historical and structural conditions producing differences between generations, Davis focuses more on interpersonal and developmental issues. Whereas Mannheim considers conflict between age groups usual but not inevitable, Davis suggests that it is unavoidable, without commenting on the ultimate social gain or loss to be derived from such changes between generations.

For Davis, conflict between generations is the result of three universals in human development, modified by four variables having to do with the modern condition. The three universal factors leading to parent-child conflict are: (1) the basic birth cycle difference between parent and child; (2) the decreasing rate of socialization with the coming of maturity (that is, youth changes rapidly in personal orientations, while their parents change more slowly); and (3) the resulting intrinsic differences between parents and children in the physiological, sociological, and psychosocial planes of behavior.

These factors, according to Davis, may lead to conflict; but whether they do so, and to what degree, depends on the variables of: (1) the rate of social change; (2) the extent of the complexity of the social structure; (3) the degree of integration of the culture; and (4) the velocity of movement within the culture.

A review of the classical sociological analysis of generations, then, reveals many ideas that are relevant to the current social concern about the generation gap. How do these ideas compare with contemporary scholarly analyses of the nature of differences between age groups, and the effect of such differences on the stability and change of the social order? The next section presents a review of current perspectives in the scholarly literature to allow such a comparison.

CURRENT PERSPECTIVES ON GENERATIONAL DIFFERENCES AND SOCIAL CHANGE

In the past few years there has been a renaissance of scholarly interest in the problem of generations. The author has compiled a bibliography of over one hundred references to generational differences, though the number of empirical papers in this list is very small. To attempt to summarize these many orientations is difficult; however, one can posit some underlying issues which form dimensions useful in categorizing the current perspectives.

First, there is the issue of the *extent* of differences between age groups. Is there a very wide gap, a little gap, or none really at all? Is the gap serious and disruptive of the social order, or is it the natural mechanism of social change? In what dimensions of human behavior, values, or attitudes is the gap most manifest; in which areas is continuity the greatest?

Second is the question of the *novelty* of the current character of relations between generations. Has the gap always been there; has it always been as wide as it is today? What factors lead to the conflict being more pervasive at some periods in history than in others? Is such conflict the result, or the cause, of rapid social change?

Third, there is the issue of the *permanence* of difference between generations, in the life history of both the individual and the society. Will the differences so evident between today's youth and their elders dissolve as a natural correlate of achieving maturity; will youth grow out of it? Or will the currently observed difference in attitudes and behaviors become part of a mature personality, leading to decided change in the society when today's youth become the command generation? And, finally, is such change predictive and perhaps cyclical over long periods of time, or is it random? Is it true as in the old proverb, that what one generation builds the second rejects, leading the third generation to build the same sort of social mores as the first?

Such questions reflect the nature of the problem facing social scientists attempting to deal with generational differences, their correlates and consequences (see Aldous, 1965; Adelson, 1970; Troll, 1970). Using such issues as guides, one can organize the many current opinions regarding this problem in several ways. The simplest way is to proceed using one dimension to organize the literature, and then add another to form a more complete typology.

The dimension to be used first here is that of the extent of differences between age groups. Three rough categories of theorists and data appear: those that point to a "Great Gap" between age groups; those at the other end of the spectrum who suggest that the "Gap is an Illusion"; and those in between who infer "Selective Continuity and Difference" between age groups in today's society. All three positions are well represented in the current literature, and all three have some antecedents in classical treatment of the problem.

THE "GREAT GAP" POSITION

Some sociologists, anthropologists, and educators have published data and impressionistic essays that indicate profound differences between youth and adults today regarding value system, orientations toward social institutions, interpersonal relations and communication, and locus of control and authority. In its extreme, the message is that a social revolution along generational lines is sweeping the world, toppling established adult social structures. Richman (1968) suggests that the "bona fide generation gap, qualitatively different from those that have occurred before," finds its focus on overthrowing outdated political systems. Seeley (1969) views the present youth movements as the beginning of a transformation of society analogous to the Renaissance or Reformation--if they are not crushed by the Extablishment. One psychologist, educator Walter Angel (1968), summarizes his position with this quote: "the whole glacier of tradition is breaking up, and . . . a generation gap wider than we suspect has opened up under us." The gap appears, Angel adds, not at the extreme edges of society—the hippies and radicals—but throughout America where "a new madness, a new social but not necessarily ephemeral fad, a new psychological disease has gripped our nation." He labels the malignancy "gaposis" and suggests four strains: affluence, values, education, and communication as forces which are pulling apart age groups in our society.

Margaret Mead (1970) explains the pulling apart in terms of differential environmental experiences while young. It is no longer possible for the middle-aged parent to tell his son, "I was once a youth like you." The father never was just like him. Being twenty years old in 1970 is different from being the same age in the 1930s. Youth grow up in an environment of instant visual news, a threat of mass annihilation, and a growing concern with the credibility of establishment leadership.

Perhaps the most eloquent exponent of this perspective of youth-adult relations is Edgar Friedenberg (1959, 1965, 1969a, 1969b). He has argued prolifically that adult institutions have failed to listen to, let alone understand, a youth group which is progressively alienated. In his epigrammatic way he suggests that "young people aren't rebelling against their parents; they're abandoning them." Most recently, he has argued that the generation gap reflects "a real and serious conflict of interest" rather than mutual misunderstanding:

youth is a discriminated minority, he says, and the "genuine class conflict between a dominant and exploitive older generation and youth who are slowly becoming more aware of what is happening to them will escalate into open conflict before long" (Friedenberg, 1969).

Certain analyses of popular culture by social scientists substantiate the notion of significant differences between youth and the over-thirty group. A number of current films *(The Graduate; Wild in the Streets; Goodbye, Columbus)* portray variously exploitation, conflict, or simply difference in interpretation across generational lines. Herbert Goldberg (1968), a clinical psychologist as well as songwriter, has documented the revolution in popular music since 1962 in terms of the style and media employed, the youthfulness of the performers, and the thematic portrayal through lyrics of revolt, parent-child differences, humanistic values, and sensory stimulation. Korngold (1968) has similarly analyzed the burgeoning underground press movement as a new social institution serving the particular interests and needs of a youth subculture. These developments have led some sociologists to suggest that the culture gap between young and old is progressively widening (see Simmons and Winograd, 1967, Seeley, 1969) or at least that youth are fashioning a new, humanistic ethic to replace the protestant ethic of their elders (Myerhoff, 1969). Such cultural innovations may someday fulfill the prophesies of some current writers of an entirely new social order. (It is interesting to note, however, as Goldberg points out, how rapidly some cultural innovations of youth have been adopted by Establishment fashion—witness mod clothing and sideburned junior executives—and how easily youthful performers like the Beatles become sophisticated capitalists and behave in some respects much like the Jet Set their songs decry.)

From a psychodynamic perspective comes additional confirmation for the "Great Gap" view of relations between age groups. Freudians have long accepted the proposition that rebellion (challenging the power of an autocratic, authoritarian father-figure) is an essential step in the achievement of the power and independence essential to the masculine identity role. Bettleheim (1965) has observed that factors that traditionally have mitigated generational conflict even in this country have become feeble or inoperative. The family plays a decreasing role in the socialization of the young; the elder generation is no longer the resource it was for coping with the world. The result is that one simply has to rebel if one is to become socially as well as psychologically an adult.

In short, regardless of the many roots of generational difference, the "Great Gap" position emphasizes that there are basic and, in some sense, irreconcilable differences in behavioral predispositions between age groups in American society, and the force of these differences is resulting in rapid cultural transformation. Many would add that such transformations are all for the best. Margaret Mead (1970) has suggested that, in societies where there is rapid social change, generational discontinuity is more adaptive than is substantial similarity between cohorts, since old responses become inappropriate to radically new situations, and parents must learn from their children. Or, as Friedenberg (1969b: 42) has put it:

> If the confrontation between the generations does pose, as many portentous civic leaders and upper-case Educators fear, a lethal threat to the integrity of the American social system, that threat may perhaps be accepted with graceful irony. Is there, after all, so much to lose? The American social system has never been noted for its integrity. In fact, it would be rather like depriving the Swiss of their surfing.

THE "GAP IS AN ILLUSION" POSITION

At the opposite end of the spectrum, a second position emphasizes the continuities between generations, arguing that contemporary anxiety over the differences between age groups is greatly overplayed; it also draws on historical analysis to indicate the seemingly inevitable recurrence of periods of heightened conflict between age groups. In this sense, "the more things change, the more they stay the same" can be applied to relations between age groups as well as to political changes. Several contemporary analyses suggest that, though there are inevitably behavioral differences between age groups, the continuities in various aspects of behavior between one generation and the next, and the substantial solidarity between youth and their parents, take precedence over these differences (see Campbell, 1969, pp. 827-833, for an excellent review of the evidence for this position).

Four examples can be given. In the most comprehensive analysis to date of student protest movements, Feuer (1969) has presented voluminous historical documentation to the effect that the conflict of generations can be seen as both inevitable and recurrent. The intensity of the conflict varies, however, under such conditions as gerontocratic power structures and the obvious failure ("de-authorization") of the older generation to solve the problems facing the era. Current student movements are not to be considered simply as a manifestation of generational conflict: they have a more psychological base and end in failure unless attached to larger groups, defined not only on the basis of age. In short, youthful assault on the established structure is no more characteristic, nor revolutionary, in America in the 1960s than at other times and places within the modern era.

Similar findings are suggested in a second area, that of the so-called "sexual revolution," by Bell (1966) and Reiss (1968). The data of these studies may be interpreted to suggest that the greatest generational change in sexual behavior, at least with regard to premarital sex, occurred following World War I between the cohort born before, or after 1900, and not between today's youth and their parents. A survey by Walsh (1970) suggests that patterns of sexual behavior before marriage among current college students are remarkably similar to those characterizing their parents' generation.

Or, to give a third example, there are several studies which have touched on influence, sentiment, and interaction patterns between parents and youth. Some of these suggest that most adolescents and their parents perceive a decidedly satisfactory relationship in terms of communication, understanding, and closeness (Douvan and Adelson, 1966; Larson and Myerhoff, 1965; Adelson, 1968; Lubbell, 1968; Bengtson, 1969). Others indicated that parents are more important referent persons than peers for some aspects of decision-making in adolescence (Kandel and Lesser, 1969). Musgrove (1965) has suggested an interesting variation on this theme: in his samples, adolescents have generally favorable orientations toward adults, while the adults in his sample displayed decidedly less favorable descriptions of young people in general.

The fourth perspective comes from the research or political attitudes of students and their parents. In the main, such intergenerational research has indicated substantial continuity among both activists and nonactivists. For example, Thomas (1970), in a study of sixty politically active parents (thirty liberal and thirty conservative) and their college-age children, found that "children of highly politicized parents tend to be like their parents both in their political attitudes and their political behavior." Westby and Braungart (1968) found considerable similarity between members of the Young Americans for Freedom and their parents' political identification, and slightly less for SDS members; their conclusion is that a stratification theory explains political activism better than a generational hypothesis (the young are rebelling from the parents, and that's why they demonstrate). Gamson, Goodman, and Gurin (1967) studied radicals, bystanders, and moderates during the 1966 University of Michigan uprising and concluded that "discontinuity between background and present beliefs is an inhibiting factor, making action *less* rather than more likely. . . . Freed from the cost of sharply breaking with their background, the activists are willing to go further in support of their beliefs." Such examples could be used to argue that "the gap is an illusion."

There are, of course, several factors at work that make generational conflict more visible today, and perhaps different in nature—factors such as rapid social change (Davis, 1940); technological advances which decrease the span between generations (Berger, 1960); the revolutionary effects of the mass media on socialization experiences (Hayakawa, 1968); the changing population distribution with the "pinching" in the middle-age range (Birren and Bengston, 1969); and, finally, greater sensitization to differences between age groups brought about in part by the popular press. Despite factors such as the above, those who come down on the side of continuity in intergenerational behavior would hold that today's social conflict is not basically generational in nature at all. Perhaps, as Adelson (1968) has suggested:

> What we have tended to do is to translate ideological conflict into generational conflict; it may be easier to contemplate a rift between the generations than to confront the depth and extent of our current social discord . . . The feverish politics of the day do not align the young against the old, not in any significant way. Rather they reflect . . . the ideological differences in a deeply divided nation.

THE "SELECTIVE CONTINUITY AND DIFFERENCE" POSITION

A possible position can be suggested as intermediate between these two extremes. Like the second position, it maintains that in most respects, conflict between the generations is peripheral; solidarity, and continuity of values are substantial across generational lines within the family and across cohort lines in the broader social order. However, like the first perspective, it emphasizes that the rapid pace of social change has created new modes of behavioral expressions that may be quite different from those of the preceding generation.

Selective continuity from one arena of behavior to another is seen in the three-generational studies of Aldous and Hill (1965) and Hill and Aldous (1969). This is probably the most extensive study to date of intergenerational continuity and difference. Among the 84 three-generational lineages in their research (all adults and all living in separate households), the greatest continuity of behavior appeared in the transmission of religious affiliation. Less transmission from generation to generation appeared in the pattern of dividing marital household tasks, educational achievement, and the making of decisions within the family.

An interesting side note of this research, in the context of social change, is the suggestion of greater similarity between middle-aged parents and their married children than between the parents and the grandparents. Hill and Aldous comment that the historical period of the 1930s may have represented a watershed between generations in family decision-making behavior—a comment consistent with other observations about the "sexual revolution" and changes in religious patterns between generations (see Birren and Bengtson, 1968).

Additionally, Aldous has made some analyses of the *consequences* of continuity between generations. For example, continuity in religious affiliation over three generations is associated with less marital tension for the youngest generation; continuity in occupation (for white-collar groups) appears to have consequences in higher income for the younger generation than lack of such a tradition.

Such evidence of generational continuity in some aspects of behavior, and of differences in others, points to a contrast that may be made between overt behavior and covert value systems. Behavior as outwardly manifest may vary substantially from generation to generation, while values or personal philosophy may in fact be similar. Taking this as a hypothesis, the literature suggests some confirming evidence.

For example, Keniston (1968) has suggested a distinction between "core" and "formal" values in his sample of young radicals. He emphasizes that the young radicals come from liberal or radical families, but denies that what has been called the "red diaper baby" hypothesis adequately explains the radical differences in means displayed by them. The accumulating literature of student activists supports this notion: rather than rebelling from parental values, many activists, both of right and left, are in fact carrying them to their logical conclusion (Flacks, 1967; Keniston, 1968; Thomas, 1970; Block et al., 1970). For example, Troll, Neugarten, and Kraines (1969: 333) present data that shows considerable similarity between young adults and their parents in the domain of values:

> If one member of a family is dedicated to righting wrongs and changing the world (dedication to causes), it is likely that so will the others, even though the particular causes they espouse may not be the same; if one member values achievement (achievement need), probably so do the others; and so on. The salient values of this group of college students, whether they are activists or not, tend to be the salient values of their parents.

Troll's families exhibited greater similarity in the area of values than in other domains of personality—consistent with the "Selective Continuity" orientation.

Another way to look at the selective continuity is through the traditional value-norm differentiation proposed by Merton: specific values of the two cohorts—freedom, democracy, responsibility—may indeed be similar, but the norms, and therefore the behaviors, used by each age group to achieve the value ends may differ greatly (Bengtson, 1969). Or, to propose another perspective, differences in the structure and experiences of primary socialization agencies may account for the variability of the behavioral continuities present (see Larson and Myerhoff, 1967; Moriwaki and Bengston, 1969). Block has recently presented data to substantiate the hypothesis that family patterns may account for this determined rebellion and selective continuity, at least as perceived by the child. Larson and Myerhoff suggested that continuity in socialization techniques lead to continuity in value patterns; these in turn were predictive of school adjustment patterns of adolescent boys (Larson, 1967).

The problem with the selective continuity is that it doesn't say much that is useful unless further specification is added, as in Troll's distinction between similarity in personality and similarity in values and the Hill-Aldous differentiation among family behaviors. That some things change, and some things stay the same, is simply irrefutable; and to say that there is neither a great gap nor a complete congruence between generations may be points worth emphasizing in order to allay anxieties of parents and taxpayers. But, unless researchers will specify more clearly what the points of difference are, how extensive they may be, and propose models to demonstrate what the consequences of intergenerational differences are, this field of investigation may continue to add a sea of interesting facts gathered from ad hoc studies of campus demonstrations to our already entrenched speculations.

In concluding this review, one is struck with the value-laden flavor of many of these positions. The three perspectives presented above, one or the other of which seem to crop up in the conclusion section of almost every paper in this field, come close to being value statements, reflecting either radical or conservative or mixed preferences on the part of the investigator. As such, much of this scholarly debate has added little to the development of predictive knowledge in the area of intergenerational relations.

PERSPECTIVES FOR FUTURE RESEARCH: A TYPOLOGY OF THE NATURE AND EXTENT OF GENERATIONAL DIFFERENCES

In the search for more scientifically useful analyses of social problems, the course of events usually goes from the review of past work on the issue to the creation of typologies that allow for the identification of ideal types, and thence to the gathering of data suggesting the analytic utility of these constructs. In the analysis thus far, reviews of contemporary and traditional approaches to the problem of generational differences have been made, and the contemporary approaches have been organized around a dimension derived from mass culture approach to the problem: the extent of generational difference.

But to analyze the extent of differences betwen age groups is not a particularly productive enterprise when taken alone. More profitable, from a scientific perspective, is to add to this dimension some of the others discussed which have much broader sociological implications. When one considers the implication of social change in the light of the nature and the effect of generational difference, a number of interesting possibilities arise in terms of the effect of generational contrasts on the social structure.

Figure I presents a typology that combines an identification of the extent, nature, and effect of differences between generational cohorts. The vertical dimension, used to order the preceeding section, has already been discussed. The horizontal dimension dichotomizes the predominant nature of differences into structural factors which lead therefore to permanent social change, and developmental or maturational factors whose effect is thus temporary in the life of the society. Individual cells represent various views on the effect of generational differences. The bivariate possibilities may be characterized thus:

Nature and Effect of Generational Difference

		Structural Factors; permanent change	Developmental Factors; temporary change
	1. "Great Gap"	A. Social revolution	B. Normal rebellion
Extent of Generational Difference	2. "Selective Gap"	C. Social evolution	D. Nothing really new
	3. "Illusory Gap"	E. Social change, but not by generations	F. Solidarity will prevail

Figure 1. THE TYPES OF CONSEQUENCES FROM VARIOUS PERSPECTIVES OF GENERATIONAL DIFFERENCES

Type A: Social revolution. There are substantial differences between age groups; the differences are induced by primarily structural factors, such as age-status inequities or adherence to an outmoded ethic. Major social change will be the result as youth move into adulthood, permanently imprinted by the inequities they have experienced (Friedenberg; Mead; Seeley; Mannheim).

Type B: Normal rebellion. There are substantial differences between age groups in norms, values, and behaviors; but these differences are primarily due to maturational factors. When children grow up and assume adult responsibilities, the great differences will disappear. Social change, therefore, will be minor, and the rebellion largely individual (Freud; Bettleheim; Reiss; Davis).

Type C: Social evolution. There are major differences between age groups in some areas, and major continuity in others. Behaviors and norms are different, while values are not. The normative differences and the acting out lead to new styles of life and thus social change. A selective gap between generations will result in major changes on issues, such as sexual mores, racism, and the like, but the changes will be gradual and selective, rather than sudden and revolutionary, because the value system is transmitted more or less continuously (Keniston, Block et al).

Type D: Nothing really new. There are major differences in some areas because of normative contrasts, but continuity in others because the value system that youth will assume in adulthood is constant: responsibility, protection of home and family, necessary materialism. For example, youth become less permissive of premarital sex as they themselves become parents (Adelson; Bell).

Type E: Social change, but not by generations. There is great change evident in our society, but the change is not led primarily by generational conflict. All three generations are going through the social change, and to identify it with age group differences is to ignore the real ideological bases. Also, one must be aware of historical constancy in age group differences: there have always been certain differences, but today's are no greater and to call them a gap is a misnomer. The change is structurewide (Feuer, Adelson).

Type F: Solidarity will prevail over tangential differences. There are some apparent differences between children and their parents over largely peripheral issues that have to do with maturational factors. Despite such inevitable disagreements there is overwhelming solidarity between generations in most families; there is a basic, permanent, and constant solidarity between generations that will continue to develop (Campbell, Douvan and Adelson, Walsh).

THE POSING OF MORE REFINED RESEARCH QUESTIONS

As has been indicated, by now considerable work has been done in the study of generations; yet much of it is unsystematic and nonempirical. One can begin to build on what is accumulated and proceed to explore the uncharted areas. At the University of Southern California, a three-generational study is currently underway which will attempt to answer some of these questions.

It would seem that the first step toward collecting and ordering knowledge in this area would involve the systematic statement of important questions which remain to be answered. Perhaps the first question concerns the *nature and extent of differences between generational cohorts,* such investigations considered initially from outside the context of the family and its socialization implications. Despite imaginate cohort analyses using previously collected census and survey data such as Cain, 1967, 1968; Cutler, 1968, 1969; Glenn, 1968; Zody, 1969) and despite the growing body of social-psychological studies of student activists, it is simply not known how much the variation *within* a cohort on a given set of behavioral attributes compares with the variation *between* cohorts. Nor is it known which kinds of attitudes, values, or norms exhibit greatest variation between age groups; or what part aging plays in the causation of differences that are apparently generational.

Second, and perhaps even more important, is the dearth of knowledge concerning the *within-family differences* between generations. Building on the pioneering work of Hill and Aldous (1969), one might ask: To what degree do parents and children share a similar perspective of intergenerational interaction; is the definition of situation shared across generational lines? What are perceived as major sources of disagreement and discussion; why is solidarity higher in some families than in others?

Third, the *antecedents or correlates* of high or low generational similarity and high or low cross-generational solidarity await more systematic investigation. What are the family structure patterns of parent-child dyads evidencing high similarity in attitudes, values, and norms? Can model socialization patterns be found that characterize conformity or rebellion? What is the effect of social mobility between generations on cross cohort differences? What is the influence of nonfamily socialization agencies, such as strong peer group membership, on intergenerational continuity? What is the effect of immigration, as in those families where socialization of the grandparental generation occurred in another society?

Finally, the *consequences* of high or low generational similarity or difference have only begun to be investigated (Aldous, 1965) either in terms of effects on individuals or in terms of the shape of broader social change. What does it mean to a parent, for example, to have a son who is extremely different from himself in opinions and basic life values? Is denial, or guilt, or a feeling of betrayal, or cheerful acceptance the more likely response? What does it mean to the son, who loses what Keniston and Erikson suggest may be of central importance to optimal personal development, a sense of continuity with the past? How do families cope with the inevitable instances of intergenerational conflict that occur within the family? Is it likely that continuity is deleterious in rapidly changing societies?

REFERENCES

ADELSON, J. (1970) "What generation gap?" New York Times Magazine (Jan. 18): 10 ff.

——— (1968) "The myth of adolescence: a polemic." Presented at the meeting of the Amer. Psychological Assn., San Francisco, September.

ALDOUS, J. (1965) "The consequences of intergenerational continuity." J. of Marriage and the Family, 26, 5. 462-468.

——— and R. HILL. (1965) "Social cohesion, lineage type, and intergenerational transmission." Social Forces, 43: 471-482.

ANGEL, W. (1968) "Gaposis: the new social disease." Vital Speeches (August), 671-2.

BELL, R. R. (1966) Premarital Sex in a Changing Society. Englewood Cliffs: Prentice-Hall.

BENGTSON, V. L. (1969) "The 'generation gap': differences by generation and by sex in the perception of parent-child relations." Presented at the annual meeting of the Pacific Sociological Assn., Seattle, April 24.

BERGER, B. (1960) "How long is a generation?" British J. of Sociology 2: 10-23.

BETTELHEIM, B. (1965) "The problem of generations," pp. 76-109 in E. Erikson (ed.) The Challenge of Youth. New York: Anchor.

BIRREN, J. E. and V. L. BENGTSON (1961) "The problem of generations: emotions vs. reality." Presented at Senate Subcommittee on Aging, Santa Barbara, Calif. (Condensation in the Center Magazine, 2 (2), 84-87).

BLOCK, J. (1970) "Rebellion re-examined: the role of identification and alienation." Unpublished, Institute of Human Development, Univ. of Calif.

BLOCK, J., N. HAAN and M. B. SMITH. (1970) "Socialization correlates of student activism." J. of Social Issues, 26 (January): 25-38.

BUTLER, R. N. (1969) "Age-ism: another form of bigotry." Gerontologist 9 (4): 243-246.

CAIN, L. D. (1968) "Aging and the character of our times." Gerontologist 8 (4): 250-258.

——— (1967) "Age status and generational phenomena: the new old people in contemporary America." Gerontologist 7 (2): 83-92.

CAMPBELL, E. Q. (1969) "Adolescent socialization," pp. 827-835 in D. A. Goslin (ed.) Handbook of Socialization Theory and Research. Chicago: Rand McNally.

CUTLER, N. E. (1969) "Generation, maturation, and party affiliation: a cohort analysis." Public Opinion Q.

——— (1968) "The alternative effects of generations and aging upon political behavior: a cohort analysis of American attitudes toward foreign policy, 1946-1966." Oak Ridge, Tenn.: Oak Ridge National Laboratory.

DAVIS, K. (1940) "The sociology of parent-youth conflict." American Sociological Review, 5 (4), 523-534.

DOUGHERTY, R. (1968) "Nixon unveils plan for youth service agency." Los Angeles Times, Part 1 (Oct. 17): 6.

DOUVAN, E. and J. ADELSON (1966) The Adolescent Experience. New York: John Wiley.

ERIKSON, E. (1968) Identity: Youth and Crisis. New York: W. W. Norton.

——— (1965) "Youth: fidelity and diversity," pp. 1-28 in E. Erikson (ed.) The Challenge of Youth. New York: Anchor.

——— (1964) Insight and Responsibility. New York: W. W. Norton.

——— (1959) "Identity and the life cycle." Psychological issues 1 (1).

——— (1950) Childhood and Society. New York: W. W. Norton.

FEUER, L. (1969) The Conflict of Generations: The Character and Significance of Student Movements. New York: Basic Books.

FLACKS, R. (1967) "The liberated generation: an exploration of roots of student protest." J. of Social Issues 23 (July): 52-72.

FRIEDENBERG, E. (1969a) "Current patterns of generational conflict." Journal of Social Issues 25 (2), 21-38.

——— (1969b) "The generation gap." Annals of the Amer. Academy of Political and Social Science 382 (March): 32-42.

——— (1965) Coming of Age in America. New York: Vintage.

——— (1959) The Vanishing Adolescent. Boston: Beacon Press.

GAMSON, Z. F., J. GOODMAN, and G. GURIN (1967) "Radicals, moderates, and bystanders during a university protest." Presented at the meetings of the Amer. Sociological Assn., San Francisco, August.

GLENN, N. and M. GRIMES (1968) "Aging, voting and political interest." Amer. Soc. Rev. 33: 563-575.

GOLDBERG, H. (1968) "Contemporary cultural innovations of youth: popular music." Presented at the meeting of the Amer. Psychological Assn., San Francisco, August 31.

HAYAKAWA, S. I. (1968) "Mass media and family communications." Presented to the Seventy Sixth Annual Convention of the Amer. Psychological Assn., San Francisco, September 2.

HEBERLE, R. (1951) Social Movements. New York: Appleton-Century-Crofts.

HILL, R. and ALDOUS, J. (1969) "Socialization for marriage and parenthood," in D. Goslin (ed.) Handbook of Socialization Theory and Research. Chicago: Rand McNally.

KANDEL, D. and G' LESSER (1969) "Parental and peer influences on educational plans of adolescents." Amer. Soc. Rev. 34 (April): 212-223.

——— (1968) Young Radicals. New York: Harcourt, Brace, & World.

KENISTON, K. (1965) The Uncommitted: Alienated Youth in American Society. New York: Harcourt, Brace, & World.

KORNGOLD, B. (1968) "Contemporary culture innovations of youth: needs or symptoms?" Presented at the meeting of the Amer. Psychological Assn., San Francisco, August 31.

LARSON, W. R. (1967) Intrafamily Relationships and Adolescent School Adjustment. A final report submitted to the U.S. Office of Education, on cooperative Research Project no. 1353 and S-044. Youth Studies Center, Univ. of Southern Calif.

LARSON, W. R. and B. MYERHOFF (1965) "Primary and formal family organization and adolescent socialization." Sociology and Social Research 50 (Oct.): 63-71.

Los Angeles Times (1969) "Reagan denounces Berkeley demands." (May 12)

LUBELL, S. (1968) "That 'generation gap'," pp. 58-66 in D. Bell and I. Krislol (eds.) Confrontation. New York: Basic Books.

MANNHEIM, K. (1952) Essays on the Sociology of Knowledge. London: Routeledge & Kegan Paul.

MARIAS, J. (1968) "Generations: the concept." International Encyclopedia of the Social Sciences 6: 88-92. New York: Free Press.

MEAD, M. (1970) Culture and commitment: a Study of the Generation Gap. New York: Basic Books.

MENTRE, F. (1920) Les Generations Sociales. Paris: Bossard.

MORIWAKI, S. and V. L. BENGTSON (1969) "Influence of sex lineage on intergenerational continuities." Presented at the Eighth International Congress of Gerontology, Washington, D.C.

MUSGROVE, F. (1965) Youth and the Social Order. Bloomington: Indiana Univ. Press.

MYERHOFF, B. (1969) "New styles of humanism: American youth." Youth and Society, 1 (1), 151-177.

NEUGARTEN, B. (1970) "The old and the young in modern societies." American Behavioral Scientist, 14 (1).

PINDER, A. (1926) Das Problem der Generation in der Kunstgeschichte Europas. Berlin.

REISS, I. R. (1968) "America's sex standards—how and why they're changing." Trans-action 5 (4): 26-32.

RICHMAN, F. (1968) "The disenfranchised majority." Greater Occasional Paper 1 (1): 4-14.

SEELEY, J. (1969) "Youth in revolt." Britannica Book of the year. Chicago: Univ. of Chicago Press.

SIMMONS, J. L. and B. WINOGRAD (1966) It's Happening. Santa Barbara: Marc-Laird.

THOMAS, L. E. B. Neugarten and R. Kraines (1970) Family correlates of student political activism. Developmental psychology, Forthcoming.

TROLL, L. (1970) "The generation gap: conceptual models." Aging and Human Development, 1 (3).

TROLL, L. et al. (1969) "Similarities in values and other personality characteristics in college students and their parents." Merrill-Palmer Q. 15 (4): 323-336.

Wall Street Journal (1968) "What troubles the older generation?" October 4.

WALSH, R. (1970) "intergenerational transmission of sexual standards." Presented at the meetings of the Amer. Soc. Assn. Washington, D.C. September 2.

WESTBY, D. and R. BRAUNGART (1967) "Utopian mentality and conservatism: the case of the Young Americans for Freedom." Presented at the annual meeting of the Amer. Sociological Assn., San Francisco, August 30.

12

Youth: A "New" Stage of Life

KENNETH KENISTON

BEFORE THE TWENTIETH CENTURY, adolescence was rarely included as a stage in the life cycle. Early life began with infancy and was followed by a period of childhood that lasted until around puberty, which occurred several years later than it does today. After puberty, most young men and women simply entered some form of apprenticeship for the adult world. Not until 1904, when G. Stanley Hall published his monumental work, *Adolescence: Its Psychology and Its Relations to Physiology, Anthropology, Sociology, Sex, Crime, Religion, and Education,* was this further pre-adult stage widely recognized. Hall's work went through many editions and was much popularized; "adolescence" became a household word. Hall's classic description of the *sturm und drang,* turbulence, ambivalence, dangers and possibilities of adolescence has since been echoed in almost every discussion of this stage of life.

But it would be incorrect to say that Hall "discovered" adolescence. On the contrary, from the start of the nineteenth century, there was increasing discussion of the "problem" of those past puberty but not yet adult. They were the street gang members and delinquents who made up what one nineteenth-century writer termed the new "dangerous classes"; they were also the recruits to the new public secondary schools being opened by the thousands in the late nineteenth century. And once Hall had clearly defined adolescence, it was possible to look back in history to discover men and women who had shown the hallmarks of this stage long before it was identified and named.

Nonetheless, Hall was clearly reflecting a gradual change in the nature of human development, brought about by the massive transformations of American society in the decades after the Civil War. During these decades, the "working family," where children labored alongside parents in fields and factories, began to disap-

○ KENNETH KENISTON, author of *Young Radicals* and *The Uncommitted,* teaches in the department of psychiatry at the Yale University School of Medicine. A grant from the Ford Foundation helped support the research on which this article is based.

pear; rising industrial productivity created new economic surpluses that allowed millions of teenagers to remain outside the labor force. America changed from a rural agrarian society to an urban industrial society, and this new industrial society demanded on a mass scale not only the rudimentary literacy taught in elementary schools, but higher skills that could only be guaranteed through secondary education. What Hall's concept of adolescence reflected, then, was a real change in the human experience, a change intimately tied to the new kind of industrial society that was emerging in America and Europe.

Today, Hall's concept of adolescence is unshakably enshrined in our view of human life. To be sure, the precise nature of adolescence still remains controversial. Some observers believe that Hall, like most psychoanalytic observers, vastly overestimated the inevitability of turbulence, rebellion and upheaval in this stage of life. But whatever the exact definition of adolescence, no one today doubts its existence. A stage of life that barely existed a century ago is now universally accepted as an inherent part of the human condition.

In the seven decades since Hall made adolescence a household word, American society has once again transformed itself. From the industrial era of the turn of the century, we have moved into a new era without an agreed-upon name—it has been called post-industrial, technological, postmodern, the age of mass consumption, the technetronic age. And a new generation, the first born in this new era of postwar affluence, television and the Bomb, raised in the cities and suburbs of America, socially and economically secure, is now coming to maturity. Since 1900, the average amount of education received by children has increased by more than six years. In 1900, only 6.4 percent of young Americans completed high school, while today almost eighty percent do, and more than half of them begin college. In 1900, there were only 238,000 college students: in 1970, there are more than seven million, with ten million projected for 1980.

These social transformations are reflected in new public anxieties. The "problem of youth," "the now generation," "troubled youth," "student dissent" and "the youth revolt" are topics of extraordinary concern to most Americans. No longer is our anxiety focused primarily upon the teenager, upon the adolescent of Hall's day. Today we are nervous about new "dangerous classes"—those young men and women of college and graduate school age who can't seem to "settle down" the way their parents did, who refuse to consider themselves adult, and who often vehemently challenge the existing social order. "Campus unrest," according to a June, 1970, Gallup Poll, was considered the nation's *main* problem.

The factors that have brought this new group into existence parallel in many ways the factors that produced adolescence: rising prosperity, the further prolongation of education, the enormously high educational demands of a postindustrial society. And behind these measurable changes lie other trends less quantitative but even more important: a rate of social change so rapid that it threatens to make obsolete all institutions, values, methodologies and technologies within the lifetime of each generation; a technology that has created not only prosperity and longevity, but power to destroy the planet, whether through warfare or violation of nature's balance; a world of extraordinarily complex social organization, instantaneous communication and constant revolution. The "new" young men and young women emerging today both reflect and react against these trends.

But if we search among the concepts of psychology for a word to describe these young men and women, we find none that is adequate. Characteristically, they are referred to as "late-adolescents-and-young-adults"—a phrase whose very mouth-filling awkwardness attests to its inadequacy. Those who see in youthful behavior the remnants of childhood immaturity naturally incline toward the concept of "adolescence" in describing the unsettled twenty-four-year-old, for this word makes it easier to interpret his objections to war, racism, pollution or imperialism as "nothing but" delayed adolescent rebellion. To those who are more hopeful about today's youth, "young adulthood" seems a more flattering phrase, for it suggests that maturity, responsibility and rationality lie behind the unease and unrest of many contemporary youths.

But in the end, neither label seems fully adequate. The twenty-four-year-old seeker, political activist or graduate student often turns out to have been *through* a period of adolescent rebellion ten years before, to be all too formed in his views, to have a stable sense of himself, and to be much farther along in his psychological development than his fourteen-year-old high school brother. Yet he differs just as sharply from "young adults" of age twenty-four whose place in society is settled, who are married and perhaps parents, and who are fully committed to an occupation. What characterizes a growing minority of postadolescents today is that they have not settled the questions whose answers once defined adulthood: questions of relationship to the existing society, questions of vocation, questions of social role and life-style.

Faced with this dilemma, some writers have fallen back on the concept of "protracted" or "stretched" adolescence—a concept with psychoanalytic origins that suggests that those who find it hard to "settle down" have "failed" the adolescent developmental task of abandoning narcissistic fantasies and juvenile dreams of glory. Thus, one remedy for "protracted adolescence" might be some form of therapy that would enable the young to reconcile themselves to abilities and a world that are rather less than they had hoped. Another interpretation of youthful unease blames society, not the individual, for the "prolongation of adolescence." It argues that youthful unrest springs from the unwillingness of contemporary society to allow young men and women, especially students, to exercise the adult powers of which they are biologically and intellectually capable. According to this view, the solution would be to allow young people to "enter adulthood" and do "real work in the real world" at an earlier age.

Yet neither of these interpretations seems quite to the point. For while some young men and women are indeed victims of the psychological malady of "stretched adolescence," many others are less impelled by juvenile grandiosity than by a rather accurate analysis of the perils and injustices of the world in which they live. And plunging youth into the "adult world" at an earlier age would run directly counter to the wishes of most youths, who view adulthood with all of the enthusiasm of a condemned man for the guillotine. Far from seeking the adult prerogatives of their parents, they vehemently demand a virtually indefinite prolongation of their nonadult state.

If neither "adolescence" nor "early adulthood" quite describes the young men and women who so disturb American society today, what can we call them? My answer is to propose that *we are witnessing today the emergence on a mass scale of a previously unrecognized stage of life,* a stage that intervenes between adolescence and adulthood. I propose to call this stage of life the stage of *youth,* assigning to this venerable but vague term a new and specific meaning. Like Hall's "adolescence," "youth" is in no absolute sense new: indeed, once having defined this stage of life, we can study its historical emergence, locating individuals and groups who have had a "youth" in the past. But what is "new" is that this stage of life is today being entered not by tiny minorities of unusually creative or unusually disturbed young men and women, but by millions of young people in the advanced nations of the world.

To explain how it is possible for "new" stages of life to emerge under changed historical conditions would require a lengthy excursion into the theory of psychological development. It should suffice here to emphasize that the direction and extent of human development—indeed the entire nature of the human life cycle—is by no means predetermined by man's biological constitution. Instead, psychological development results from a complex interplay of constitutional givens (including the rates and phases of biological maturation) and the changing familial, social, educational, economic and political conditions that constitute the matrix in which children develop. Human development can be obstructed by the absence of the necessary matrix, just as it can be stimulated by other kinds of environments. Some social and historical conditions demonstrably slow, retard or block development, while others stimulate, speed and encourage it. A prolongation and extension of development, then, including the emergence of "new" stages of life, can result from altered social, economic and historical conditions.

Like all stages, youth is a stage of transition rather than of completion or accomplishment. To begin to define youth involves three related tasks. First, we need to describe the major *themes* or issues that dominate consciousness, development and behavior during this stage. But human development rarely if ever proceeds on all fronts simultaneously: instead, we must think of development as consisting of a series of sectors or "developmental lines," each of which may be in or out of phase with the others. Thus we must also describe the more specific *transformations* or changes in thought and behavior that can be observed in each of several "lines" of development (moral, sexual, intellectual, interpersonal, and so on) during youth. Finally, we can try to make clear what youth is *not.* What follows is a preliminary sketch of some of the themes and transformations that seem crucial to defining youth as a stage of life.

Major Themes in Youth

Perhaps the central conscious issue during youth is the *tension between self and society.* In adolescence, young men and women tend to accept their society's definitions of them as rebels, truants, conformists, athletes or achievers. But in youth, the relationship between socially assigned labels and the "real self" becomes more problematic, and constitutes a focus of central concern. The awareness of actual or potential conflict, disparity, lack of congruence between what one is (one's identity, values, integrity) and the resources and demands of the existing society increases. The adolescent is struggling to define who he is; the youth begins to sense who he is and thus to recognize the possibility of conflict and disparity between his emerging selfhood and his social order.

In youth, *pervasive ambivalence* toward both self and society is the rule: the question of how the two can be made more congruent is often experienced as a central problem of youth. This ambivalence is not the same as definitive rejection of society, nor does it necessarily lead to political activism. For ambivalence may also entail intense self-rejection, including major efforts at self-transformation employing the methodologies of personal transformation that are culturally available in any historical era: monasticism, meditation, psychoanalysis, prayer, hallucinogenic drugs, hard work, religious conversion, introspection, and so forth. In youth, then, the potential and ambivalent conflicts between autonomous selfhood and social involvement—between the maintenance of personal integrity and the achievement of effectiveness in society—are fully experienced for the first time.

The effort to reconcile and accommodate these two poles involves a characteristic stance vis-à-vis both self and world, perhaps best described by the concept of the *wary probe.* For the youthful relationship to the social order consists not merely in the experimentation more characteristic of adolescence, but with now more serious forays into the adult world, through which its vulnerability, strength, integrity and possibilities are assayed. Adolescent experimentation is more concerned with self-definition than are the probes of youth, which may lead to more lasting commitments. This testing, exacting, challenging attitude may be applied to all representatives and aspects of the existing social order, sometimes in anger and expectation of disappointment, sometimes in the urgent hope of finding honor, fidelity and decency in society, and often in both anger and hope. With regard to the self, too, there is constant self-probing in search of strength, weakness, vulnerability and resiliency, constant self-scrutiny designed to test the individual's capacity to withstand or use what his society would make of him, ask of him, and allow him.

Phenomenologically, youth is a time of alternating *estrangement and omnipotentiality.* The estrangement of youth entails feelings of isolation, unreality, absurdity, and disconnectedness from the interpersonal, social and phenomenological world. Such feelings are probably more intense during youth than in any other period of life. In part they spring from the actual disengagement of youth from society; in part they grow out of the psychological sense of incongruence between self and world. Much of the psychopathology of youth involves such feelings, experienced as the depersonalization of the self or the derealization of the world.

Omnipotentiality is the opposite but secretly related pole of estrangement. It is the feeling of absolute freedom, of living in a world of pure possibilities, of being able to change or achieve anything. There may be times when complete self-transformation seems possible, when the self is experienced as putty in one's own hands. At other times, or for other youths, it is the nonself that becomes totally malleable; then one feels capable of totally transforming another's life, or creating a new society with no roots whatsoever in the mire of the past. Omnipotentiality and estrangement are obviously related: the same sense of freedom and possibility that may come from casting off old inhibitions, values and constraints may also lead directly to a feeling of absurdity, disconnectedness and estrangement.

Another characteristic of youth is the *refusal of socialization* and acculturation. In keeping with the intense and wary probing of youth, the individual characteristically begins to become aware of the deep effects upon his personality of his society and his culture. At times he may attempt to break out of his prescribed roles, out of his culture, out of history, and even out of his own skin. Youth is a time, then, when earlier socialization and acculturation is self-critically analyzed, and massive efforts may be made to uproot the now alien traces of historicity, social membership and culture. Needless to say, these efforts are invariably accomplished within a social, cultural and historical context, using historically available methods. Youth's relationship to history is therefore paradoxical. Although it may try to reject history altogether, youth does so in a way defined by its historical era, and these rejections may even come to define that era.

In youth we also observe the emergence of *youth-specific identities* and roles. These contrast both with the more ephemeral enthusiasms of the adolescent and with the more established commitments of the adult. They may last for months, years or a decade, and they inspire deep commitment in those who adopt them. Yet they are inherently temporary and specific to youth: today's youthful hippies, radicals and seekers recognize full well that, however reluctantly, they will eventually become older; and that aging itself will change their status. Some such youth-specific identities may provide the foundation for later commitments; but others must be viewed in retrospect as experiments that failed or as probes of the existing society that achieved their purpose, which was to permit the individual to move on in other directions.

Another special issue during youth is the enormous value placed upon change, transformation and *movement*, and the consequent abhorrence of *stasis*. To change, to stay on the road, to retain a sense of inner development and/or outer momentum is essential to many youths' sense of active vitality. The psychological problems of youth are experienced as most overwhelming when they seem to block change: thus, youth grows panicky when confronted with the feeling of "getting nowhere," of "being stuck in a rut," or of "not moving."

At times the focus of change may be upon the self, and the goal is then to *be moved*. Thus, during youth we see the most strenuous, self-conscious and even frenzied efforts at self-transformation, using whatever religious, cultural, therapeutic or chemical means are available. At other times, the goal may be to create movement in the outer world, to *move others:* then we may see efforts at social and political change that in other stages of life rarely possess the same single-minded determination. And on other occasions, the goal is to *move through* the world, and we witness a frantic geographic restlessness, wild swings of upward or downward social mobility, or a compelling psychological need to identify with the highest and the lowest, the most distant and apparently alien.

The need for movement and terror of stasis often are a part of a heightened *valuation of development* itself, however development may be defined by the individual and his culture. In all stages of life, of course, all individuals often wish to change in specific ways: to become more witty, more attractive, more sociable or wealthier. But in youth, specific changes are often subsumed in the devotion to change itself—to "keep putting myself through the changes," "not to bail out," "to keep moving." This valuation of change need not be fully conscious. Indeed it often surfaces only in its inverse form, as the panic or depression that accompanies a sense of "being caught in a rut," "getting nowhere," "not being able to change." But for other youths, change becomes a conscious goal in itself, and elaborate ideologies of the techniques of transformation and the *telos* of human life may be developed.

In youth, as in all other stages of life, *the fear of death* takes a special form. For the infant, to be deprived of maternal support, responsiveness and care is not to exist; for the four-year-old, non-being means loss of body intactness (dismemberment, mutilation, castration); for the adolescent, to cease to be is to fall apart, to fragment, splinter, or diffuse into nothingness. For the youth, however, to lose one's essential vitality is merely *to stop*. For some, even self-inflicted death or psychosis may seem preferable to loss of movement; and suicidal attempts in youth often spring from the failure of efforts to change and the resulting sense of being forever trapped in an unmoving present.

The youthful *view of adulthood* is strongly affected by these feelings. Compared to youth, adulthood has traditionally been a stage of slower transformation, when, as Erik H. Erikson has noted, the relative developmental stability of parents enables them to nurture the rapid growth of their children. This adult deceleration of personal change is often seen from a youthful vantage point as concretely embodied in apparently unchanging parents. It leads frequently to the conscious identification of adulthood with stasis, and to its unconscious equation with death or nonbeing. Although greatly magnified today by the specific political disillusionments of many youths with the "older generation," the adulthood = stasis (= death) equation is inherent in the youthful situation itself. The desire to prolong youth indefinitely springs not only from an accurate perception of the real disadvantages of adult status in any historical era, but from the less conscious and less accurate assumption that to "grow up" is in some ultimate sense to cease to be really alive.

Finally, youths tend to band together with other youths in *youthful counter-cultures,* characterized by their deliberate cultural distance from the existing social order, but *not* always by active political or other opposition to it. It is a mistake to identify youth as a developmental stage with any one social group, role or organization. But youth *is* a time when solidarity with other youths is especially important, whether the solidarity be achieved in pairs, small groups, or formal organizations. And the groups dominated by those in this stage of life reflect not only the special configurations of each historical era, but also the shared developmental positions and problems of youth. Much of what has traditionally been referred to as "youth culture" is, in the terms here used, adolescent culture; but there are also groups, societies and associations that are truly youthful. In our own time, with the enormous increase in the number of those who are entering youth as a stage of life, the variety and importance of these youthful counter-cultures is steadily growing.

This compressed summary of themes in youth is schematic and interpretive. It omits many of the qualifications necessary to a fuller discussion, and it neglects the enormous complexity of development in any one person in favor of a highly schematic account. Specifically, for example, I do not discuss the ways the infantile, the childish, the adolescent and the truly youthful interact in all real lives. And perhaps most important, my account is highly interpretive, in that it points to themes that underlie diverse acts and feelings, to issues and tensions that unite the often scattered experiences of real individuals. The themes, issues and conflicts here discussed are rarely conscious as such; indeed, if they all were fully conscious, there would probably be something seriously awry. Different youths experience each of the issues here considered with different intensity. What is a central conflict for one may be peripheral or unimportant for another. These remarks, then, should be taken as a first effort to summarize some of the underlying issues that characterize youth as an ideal type.

Transformations of Youth

A second way of describing youth is by attempting to trace out the various psychological and interpersonal transformations that may occur during this stage. Once again, only the most preliminary sketch of youthful development can be attempted here. Somewhat arbitrarily, I will distinguish between development in several sectors or areas of life, here noting only that, in fact, changes in one sector invariably interact with those in other sectors.

In pointing to the *self-society relationship* as a central issue in youth, I also mean to suggest its importance as an area of potential change. The late adolescent is only beginning to challenge his society's definition of him, only starting to compare his emerging sense of himself with his culture's possibilities and with the temptations and opportunities offered by his environment. Adolescent struggles for emancipation from external familial control and internal dependency on the family take a variety of forms, including displacement of the conflict onto other "authority figures." But in adolescence itself, the "real" focus of conflict is on the family and all of its internal psychic residues. In youth, however, the "real" focus begins to shift: increasingly, the family becomes more paradigmatic of society than vice versa. As relatively greater emancipation from the family is achieved, the tension between self and society, with ambivalent probing of both, comes to constitute a major area of developmental "work" and change. Through this work, young people can sometimes arrive at a synthesis whereby both self and society are affirmed, in the sense that the autonomous reality, relatedness yet separateness of both, is firmly established.

There is no adequate term to describe this "resolution" of the tension between self and society, but C. G. Jung's concept of *"individuation"* comes close. For Jung, the individuated man is a man who acknowledges and can cope with social reality, whether accepting it or opposing it with revolutionary fervor. But he can do this without feeling his central selfhood overwhelmed. Even when most fully engaged in social role and societal action, he can preserve a sense of himself as intact, whole, and distinct from society. Thus the "resolution" of the self-society tension in no way necessarily entails "adjusting" to the society, much less "selling out"—although many youths see it this way. On the contrary, individuation refers partly to a psychological process whereby self and society are differentiated internally. But the actual conflicts between men and women and their societies remain, and indeed may become even more intense.

The meaning of individuation may be clarified by considering the special dangers of youth, which can be defined as extremes of *alienation, whether from self or from society.* At one extreme is that total alienation from self that involves abject submission to society, "joining the rat race," "selling out." Here, society is affirmed but selfhood denied. The other extreme is a total alienation from society that leads not so much to the rejection of society, as to its existence being ignored, denied and blocked out. The result is a kind of self-absorption, an enforced interiority and subjectivity, in which only the self and its extensions are granted live reality, while all the rest is relegated to a limbo of insignificance. Here the integrity of the self is purchased at the price of a determined denial of social reality, and the loss of social effectiveness. In youth both forms of alienation are often assayed, sometimes for lengthy periods. And for some whose further development is blocked, they become the basis for life-long adaptations—the self-alienation of the marketing personality, the social alienation of the perpetual drop-out. In terms of the polarities of Erikson, we can define the central developmental possibilities of youth as individuation vs. alienation.

Sexual development continues in important ways during youth. In modern Western societies, as in many others, the commencement of actual sexual relationships is generally deferred by middle-class adolescents until their late teens or early twenties: the modal age of first intercourse for American college males today is around twenty, for females about twenty-one. Thus, despite the enormous importance of adolescent sexuality and sexual development, actual sexual intercourse often awaits youth. In youth, there may occur a major shift from masturbation and sexual fantasy to interpersonal sexual behavior, including the gradual integration of sexual feelings with intimacy with a real person. And as sexual behavior with real people commences, one sees a further working-through, now in behavior, of vestigial fears and prohibitions whose origin lies in earlier childhood—specifically, of Oedipal feelings of sexual inferiority and of Oedipal prohibitions against sex with one's closest intimates. During youth, when these fears and prohibitions can be gradually worked through, they yield a capacity for genitality, that is, for mutually satisfying sexual relationships with another whom one loves.

The transition to genitality is closely related to a more general pattern of *interpersonal development*. I will term this the shift from *identicality* to mutuality. This development begins with adolescence* and continues through youth: it involves a progressive expansion of the early-adolescent assumption that the interpersonal world is divided into only two categories: first, me-and-those-who-are-identical-to-me (potential soulmates, doubles and hypothetical people who "automatically understand everything"), and second, all others. This conceptualization gradually yields to a capacity for close relationships with those on an approximate level of *parity* or similarity with the individual.

The phase of parity in turn gives way to a phase of *complementarity*, in which the individual can relate warmly to others who are different from him, valuing them for their dissimilarities from

---

* Obviously, interpersonal development, and specifically the development of relationships with peers, begins long before adolescence, starting with the "parallel play" observed at ages two to four and continuing through many stages to the preadolescent same-sex "chumship" described by Harry Stack Sullivan. But puberty in middle-class Western societies is accompanied by major cognitive changes that permit the early adolescent for the first time to develop hypothetical ideals of the possibilities of friendship and intimacy. The "search for a soulmate" of early adolescence is the first interpersonal stage built upon these new cognitive abilities.

himself. Finally, the phase of complementarity may yield in youth to a phase of *mutuality*, in which issues of identicality, parity and complementarity are subsumed in an overriding concern with the other *as other*. Mutuality entails a simultaneous awareness of the ways in which others are identical to oneself, the ways in which they are similar and dissimilar, and the ways in which they are absolutely unique. Only in the stage of mutuality can the individual begin to conceive of others as separate and unique selves, and relate to them as such. And only with this stage can the concept of mankind assume a concrete significance as pointing to a human universe of unique and irreplaceable selves.

Relationships with elders may also undergo characteristic youthful changes. By the end of adolescence, the hero worship or demonology of the middle adolescent has generally given way to an attitude of more selective emulation and rejection of admired or disliked older persons. In youth, new kinds of relationships with elders become possible: psychological apprenticeships, then a more complex relationship of mentorship, then sponsorship, and eventually peership. Without attempting to describe each of these substages in detail, the overall transition can be described as one in which the older person becomes progressively more real and three-dimensional to the younger one, whose individuality is appreciated, validated and confirmed by the elder. The sponsor, for example, is one who supports and confirms in the youth that which is best in the youth, without exacting an excessive price in terms of submission, imitation, emulation or even gratitude.

Comparable changes continue to occur during youth with regard to *parents*. Adolescents commonly discover that their parents have feet of clay, and recognize their flaws with great acuity. Childish hero worship of parents gives way to a more complex and often negative view of them. But it is generally not until youth that the individual discovers his parents as themselves complex, three-dimensional historical personages whose destinies are partly formed by their own wishes, conscious and unconscious, and by their historical situations. Similarly, it is only during youth that the questions of family tradition, family destiny, family fate, family culture and family curse arise with full force. In youth, the question of whether to live one's parents' life, or to what extent to do so, becomes a real and active question. In youth, one often sees what Ernst Prelinger has called a "telescoped re-enactment" of the life of a parent—a compulsive need to live out for oneself the destiny of a parent, as if to test its possibilities and limits, experience it from the inside, and (perhaps) free oneself of it. In the end, the youth may learn to see himself and his parents as multidimensional persons, to view them with compassion and understanding, to feel less threatened by their fate and failings, and to be able, if he chooses, to move beyond them.

In beginning by discussing affective and interpersonal changes in youth, I begin where our accounts of development are least precise and most tentative. Turning to more cognitive matters, we stand on somewhat firmer ground. Lawrence Kohlberg's work on *moral development,* especially on the attainment of the highest levels of moral reasoning, provides a paradigmatic description of developments that occur only in youth, if they occur at all.

Summarized over-simply, Kohlberg's theory distinguishes three general stages in the development of moral reasoning. The earliest or *pre-moral* stage involves relatively egocentric concepts of right and wrong as that which one can do without getting caught, or as that which leads to the greatest personal gratification. This stage is followed, usually during later childhood, by a stage of *conventional* morality, during which good and evil are identified with the concept of a "good boy" or "good girl," or with standards of the community and the concept of law and order. In this stage, morality is perceived as objective, as existing "out there."

The third and final major stage of moral development is *post-conventional.* It involves more abstract moral reasoning that may lead the individual into conflict with conventional morality. The first of two levels within the postconventional stage basically involves the assumption that concepts of right and wrong result from a *social contract*—an implicit agreement entered into by the members of the society for their own welfare, and therefore subject to amendment, change or revocation. The highest postconventional level is that in which the individual becomes devoted to *personal principles* that may transcend not only conventional morality but even the social contract. In this stage, certain general principles are now seen as personally binding although not necessarily "objectively" true. Such principles are apt to be stated at a very high level of generality: for example, the Golden Rule, the sanctity of life, the categorical imperative, the concept of justice, the promotion of human development. The individual at this stage may find himself in conflict with existing concepts of law and order, or even with the notion of an amendable social contract. He may, for example, consider even democratically-arrived-at laws unacceptable because they lead to consequences or enjoin behaviors that violate his own personal principles.

Kohlberg's research suggests that most contemporary Americans, young or old, do not pass beyond the conventional stage of moral reasoning. But some do, and they are most likely to be found today among those who are young and educated. Such young men and women may develop moral principles that can lead them to challenge the existing moral order and the existing society. And Kohlberg finds that the achievement of his highest level, the stage of personal principles, occurs in the twenties, if it occurs at all. Moral development of this type can thus be identified with youth, as can the special moral "regressions" that Kohlberg finds a frequent concomitant of moral development. Here the arbitrariness of distinguishing between sectors of development becomes clear, for the individual can begin to experience the tension between self and society only as he begins to question the absolutism of conventional moral judgments. Unless he has begun such questioning, it is doubtful whether we can correctly term him "a youth."

In no other sector of development do we have so complete, accurate and convincing a description of a "development line" that demonstrably characterizes youth. But in the area of *intellectual development,* William Perry has provided an invaluable description of the stages through which college students may pass. Perry's work emphasizes the complex transition from epistemological dualism to an awareness of multiplicity and to the realization of relativism. Relativism in turn gives way to a more "existential" sense of truth, culminating in what Perry terms "commitment within relativism." Thus, in youth we expect to see a passage beyond simple views of Right and Wrong, Truth and Falsehood, Good and Evil to a more complex and relativistic view; and as youth proceeds, we look for the development of commitments within a universe that remains epistemologically relativistic. Once again, intellectual development is only analytically separable from a variety of other sectors—moral, self-society and interpersonal, to mention only three.

In his work on *cognitive development,* Jean Piaget has emphasized the importance of the transition from concrete to formal operations, which in middle-class Western children usually occurs at about the age of puberty. For Piaget the attainment of formal operations (whereby the concrete world of the real becomes a subset of the hypothetical world of the possible) is the highest cognitive stage possible. But in some youths, there seem to occur further stages of cognitive development that are not understandable with the concept of formal operations. Jerome Bruner has suggested that beyond the formal stage of thought there lies a further stage of "thinking about thinking." This ability to think about thinking involves a new level of consciousness—consciousness of consciousness, awareness of awareness, and a breaking-away of the phenomenological "I" from the contents of consciousness. This breaking-away of the phenomenological ego during youth permits phenomenological games, intellectual tricks, and kinds of creativity that are rarely possible in adolescence itself. It provides the cognitive underpinning for many of the characteristics and special disturbances of youth, for example, youth's hyperawareness of inner processes, the focus upon states of consciousness as objects to be controlled and altered, and the frightening disappearance of the phenomenological ego in an endless regress of awarenesses of awarenesses.

Having emphasized that these analytically separated "lines" of development are in fact linked in the individual's experience, it is equally important to add that they are never linked in perfect synchronicity. If we could precisely label one specific level within each developmental line as distinctively youthful, we would find that few people were "youthful" in all lines at the same time. In general, human development proceeds unevenly, with lags in some areas and precocities in others. One young woman may be at a truly adolescent level in her relationship with her parents, but at a much later level in moral development; a young man may be capable of extraordinary mutuality with his peers, but still be struggling intellectually with the dim awareness of relativism. Analysis of any one person in terms of specific sectors of development will generally show a simultaneous mixture of adolescent, youthful and adult features. The point, once again, is that the concept of youth here proposed is an ideal type, a model that may help understand real experience but can never fully describe or capture it.

What Youth Is Not

A final way to clarify the meaning of youth as a stage of life is to make clear what it is not. For one thing, youth is not the end of development. I have described the belief that it is—the conviction that beyond youth lie only stasis, decline, foreclosure and death— as a characteristically youthful way of viewing development, consistent with the observation that it is impossible truly to understand stages of development beyond one's own. On the contrary, youth is but a preface for further transformations that may (or may not) occur in later life. Many of these center around such issues as the relationship to work and to the next generation. In youth, the question of vocation is crucial, but the issue of work—of productivity, creativity, and the more general sense of fruitfulness that Erikson calls generativity—awaits adulthood. The youthful attainment of mutuality with peers and of peerhood with elders can lead on to further adult interpersonal developments by which one comes to be able to accept the dependency of others, as in parenthood. In later life, too, the relations between the generations are reversed, with the younger now assuming responsibility for the elder. Like all stages of life, youth is transitional. And although some lines of development, such as moral development, may be "completed" during youth, many others continue throughout adulthood.

It is also a mistake to identify youth with any one social group, role, class, organization, or position in society. Youth is a *psychological* stage; and those who are in this stage do not necessarily join together in identifiable groups, nor do they share a common social position. Not all college students, for example, are in this stage of life: some students are psychological adolescents, while others are young adults—essentially apprentices to the existing society. Nor can the experience of youth as a stage of life be identified with any one class, nation or other social grouping. Affluence and education can provide a freedom from economic need and an intellectual stimulation that may underlie and promote the transformations of youth. But there are poor and uneducated young men and women, from Abraham Lincoln to Malcolm X, who have had a youth, and rich, educated ones who have moved straightaway from adolescence to adulthood. And although the experience of youth is probably more likely to occur in the economically advanced nations, some of the factors that facilitate youth also exist in the less advanced nations, where comparable youthful issues and transformations are expressed in different cultural idioms.

Nor should youth be identified with the rejection of the status quo, or specifically with student radicalism. Indeed, anyone who has more or less definitively defined himself as a misanthrope or a revolutionary has moved beyond youthful probing into an "adult" commitment to a position vis-à-vis society. To repeat: what characterizes youth is not a definitive rejection of the existing "system," but an ambivalent tension over the relationship between self and society. This tension may take the form of avid efforts at self-reform that spring from acceptance of the status quo, coupled with a sense of one's own inadequacy vis-à-vis it. In youth the relationship between self and society is indeed problematical, but rejection of the existing society is not a necessary characteristic of youth.

Youth obviously cannot be equated with any particular age-range. In practice, most young Americans who enter this stage of life tend to be between the ages of eighteen and thirty. But they constitute a minority of the whole age-grade. Youth as a developmental stage is emergent; it is an "optional" stage, not a universal one. If we take Kohlberg's studies of the development of postconventional moral reasoning as a rough index of the "incidence" of youth, less than forty percent of middle-class (college-educated) men, and a smaller proportion of working-class men have developed beyond the conventional level by the age of twenty-four. Thus, "youths" constitute but a minority of their age group. But those who are in this stage of life today largely determine the public image of their generation.

Admirers and romanticizers of youth tend to identify youth with virtue, morality and mental health. But to do so is to overlook the special youthful possibilities for viciousness, immorality and psychopathology. Every time of human life, each level of development, has its characteristic vices and weaknesses, and youth is no exception. Youth is a stage, for example, when the potentials for zealotry and fanaticism, for reckless action in the name of the highest principles, for self-absorption, and for special arrogance are all at a peak. Furthermore, the fact that youth is a time of psychological change also inevitably means that it is a stage of constant recapitulation, reenactment and reworking of the past. This reworking can rarely occur without real regression, whereby the buried past is reexperienced as present and, one hopes, incorporated into it. Most youthful transformation occurs *through* brief or prolonged regression, which, however benignly it may eventually be resolved, constitutes part of the psychopathology of youth. And the special compulsions and inner states of youth—the euphoria of omnipotentiality and the dysphoria of estrangement, the hyperconsciousness of consciousness, the need for constant motion and the terror of stasis—may generate youthful pathologies with a special virulence and obstinacy. In one sense those who have the luxury of a youth may be said to be "more developed" than those who do not have (or do not take) this opportunity. But no level of development and no stage of life should be identified either with virtue or with health.

Finally, youth is not the same as the adoption of youthful causes, fashions, rhetoric or postures. Especially in a time like our own, when youthful behavior is watched with ambivalent fascination by adults, the positions of youth become part of the cultural stock-in-trade. There thus develops the phenomenon of *pseudo-youth*—preadolescents, adolescents and frustrated adults masquerade as youths, adopt youthful manners and disguise (even to themselves) their real concerns by the use of youthful rhetoric. Many a contemporary adolescent, whether of college or high school age, finds it convenient to displace and express his battles with his parents in a pseudo-youthful railing at the injustices, oppression and hypocrisy of the Establishment. And many an adult, unable to accept his years, may adopt pseudo-youthful postures to express the despairs of his adulthood.

To differentiate between "real" and pseudo youth is a tricky, subtle and unrewarding enterprise. For, as I have earlier emphasized, the concept of youth as here defined is an ideal type, an abstraction from the concrete experience of many different individuals. Furthermore, given the unevenness of human development and the persistence throughout life of active remnants of earlier developmental levels, conflicts and stages, no one can ever be said to be completely "in" one stage of life in all areas of behavior and at all times. No issue can ever be said to be finally "resolved"; no earlier conflict is completely "overcome." Any real person, even though on balance we may consider him a "youth," will also contain some persistent childishness, some not-outgrown adolescence, and some precocious adulthood in his makeup. All we can say is that, for some, adolescent themes and levels of development are *relatively* outgrown, while adult concerns have not yet assumed full prominence. It is such people whom one might term "youths."

The Implications of Youth

I have sketched with broad and careless strokes the rough outlines of a stage of life I believe to characterize a growing, although still small, set of young men and women. This sketch, although presented dogmatically, is clearly preliminary; it will doubtless require revision and correction after further study. Yet let us for the moment assume that, whatever the limitations of this outline, the concept of a postadolescent stage of life has some merit. What might be the implications of the emergence of youth?

To most Americans, the chief anxieties raised by youth are over social stability and historical continuity. In every past and present society, including our own, the great majority of men and women seem to be, in Kohlberg's terms, "conventional" in moral judgment, and, in Perry's terms, "dualistic" in their intellectual outlook. Such men and women accept with little question the existing moral codes of the community, just as they endorse their culture's traditional view of the world. It is arguable that both cultural continuity and social stability have traditionally rested on the moral and epistemological conventionality of most men and women, and on the secure transmission of these conventional views to the next generation.

What, then, would it mean if our particular era were producing millions of postconventional, nondualistic, postrelativistic youth? What would happen if millions of young men and women developed to the point that they "made up their own minds" about most value, ideological, social and philosophical questions, often rejecting the conventional and traditional answers? Would they not threaten the stability of their societies?

Today it seems clear that most youths are considered nuisances or worse by the established order, to which they have not finally pledged their allegiance. Indeed, many of the major stresses in contemporary American society spring from or are aggravated by those in this stage of life. One aspect of the deep polarization in our society may be characterized psychologically as a struggle between conventionals and postconventionals, between those who have not had a youth and those who have. The answer of the majority of the public seems clear: we already have too many "youths" in our society; youth as a developmental stage should be stamped out.

A more moderate answer to the questions I am raising is also possible. We might recognize the importance of having a *few* postconventional individuals (an occasional Socrates, Christ, Luther or Gandhi to provide society with new ideas and moral inspiration), but nonetheless establish a firm top limit on the proportion of postconventional, youth-scarred adults our society could tolerate. If social stability requires human inertia—that is, unreflective acceptance of most social, cultural and political norms—perhaps we should discourage "youth as a stage of life" in any but a select minority.

A third response, toward which I incline, seems to me more radical. To the argument from social stability and cultural continuity, one might reply by pointing to the enormous *in*stabilities and gross cultural *dis*continuities that characterize the modern world. Older forms of stability and continuity have *already* been lost in the postindustrial era. Today, it is simply impossible to return to a bygone age when massive inertia guaranteed social stability (if there really was such an age). The cake of custom crumbled long ago. The only hope is to learn to live without it.

In searching for a way to do this, we might harken back to certain strands in socialist thought that see new forms of social organization possible for men and women who are more "evolved." I do not wish to equate my views on development with revolutionary socialism or anarchism, much less with a Rousseauistic faith in the goodness of the essential man. But if there is anything to the hypothesis that different historical conditions alter the nature of the life cycle, then men with different kinds of development may require or be capable of living in different kinds of social institutions. On the one hand, this means that merely throwing off institutional shackles, as envisioned by some socialist and anarchist thinkers, would not automatically change the nature of men, although it may be desirable on other grounds. "New men" cannot be created by institutional transformations alone, although institutional changes may, over the very long run, affect the possibilities for continuing development by changing the matrix in which development occurs.

But on the other hand, men and women who have attained higher developmental levels may be capable of different kinds of association and cooperation from those at lower levels. Relativism, for example, brings not only skepticism but also tolerance of the viewpoints of others, and a probable reduction in moralistic self-righteousness. Attaining the stage of personal principles in moral development in no way prevents the individual from conforming to a just social order, or even for that matter from obeying unreasonable traffic laws. Men and women who are capable of interpersonal mutuality are not for that reason worse citizens; on the contrary, their capacity to be concerned with others as unique individuals might even make them better citizens. Examples could be multiplied, but the general point is obvious: higher levels of development, including the emergence on a mass scale of "new" stages of life, may permit new forms of human cooperation and social organization.

It may be true that all past societies have been built upon the unquestioning inertia of the vast majority of their citizens. And this inertia may have provided the psychological ballast that prevented most revolutions from doing more than reinstating the *ancien régime* in new guise. But it does not follow that this need always continue to be true. If new developmental stages are emerging that lead growing minorities to more autonomous positions vis-à-vis their societies, the result need not be anarchy or social chaos. The result might instead be the possibility of new forms of social organization based less upon unreflective acceptance of the status quo than upon thoughtful and self-conscious loyalty and cooperation. But whether or not these new forms can emerge depends not only upon the psychological factors I have discussed here, but even more upon political, social, economic and international conditions.

13

CATCH-30

By Gail Sheehy

"What do I *want* out of this life, now that I'm doing what I ought to do?"

A restless vitality wells up as we approach 30. Almost everyone wants to make some alteration. If he has been dutifully performing in his corporate slot, he may suddenly feel too narrowed and restricted. If he has been in a long period of training, such as medicine, he may wonder at this point if life is all work and no play. If she has been at home with children, she itches to expand her horizons. If she has been out pursuing a career, she feels a longing for emotional attachments. The impulse to broaden often leads us to action even before we know what we are missing.

The restrictions we feel on nearing 30 are the outgrowth of the choices of the twenties, choices that may have been perfectly appropriate to that stage. Now the fit feels different. We become aware of some inner aspect that has been left out. It may make itself felt suddenly, emphatically. More often it begins as a slow drum roll, a vague but persistent sense of *wanting to be something more.*

Both the vagueness and the persistence, the unmistakable sound of a man in the Age 30 passage, pervade George Blecher's short story, "The Death of the Russian Novel": [1]

Sometimes I sit down with myself and say, "Look, you're thirty now. At best, you've got fifty years more. But what are you doing with it? You drag yourself from day to day, you spend most of your time wanting, wanting, but what you have is never any good and what you don't have is marvelous. Why don't you eat your cutlet, man? Eat it with pleasure and joy. Love your wife. Make your babies. Love your friends and have the courage to tell those who seek to diminish you that they are the devil and you want no part of them. Courage, man, courage and appetite!"

During this passage, which commonly spans the years between 28 and 32, important new choices must be made and commitments altered or deepened. The work involves great change, turmoil, and commonly, crisis —a simultaneous feeling of rock bottom and the urge to break out. The transition initiates the more stable and settled period of Rooting and Extending.

One common reaction to the transition into the thirties is tearing up the life one spent most of the twenties putting together. It may mean striking out on a secondary road toward a new vision. It often means divorce or at least a serious review of the marriage. People who have espoused the joys of singlehood or childlessness are often startled to find themselves wanting an old-fashioned marriage, or eager to stay home with a child.

Years later we wonder why so much confusion and doubt surrounded making changes that, in retrospect, seem obvious. That is because there is much more to this transition than changing the external circumstances. The voices from within become more insistent now. And in the thirties we begin to let down our guard. The iron gate we tried to shut against the Janus faces of the inner custodian when we were hell-bent on proving our identity to be wholly our own inspiration can now be opened a crack. On our side, we are a little more certain of ourselves. The other side, in turn, is beginning to lose some of its menace as a dictator and some of its seductiveness as a guardian. We can begin to see and hear its influence, little by little, to recognize it.

And so begins a courageous, though often clumsy, struggle with the gifts and burdens of our own inheritance. The challenge is to sort out the qualities we want to retain from our childhood models, to blend them with the qualities and capacities that distinguish us as individuals, and to fit all this back together in some broader form. The widening and opening up of our inner boundaries makes it possible to begin integrating aspects of ourselves that were previously hidden.

The combined evidence of many interviews, studies, and statistics suggests that the opening-up process starts in the late twenties and culminates in a restabilization and closing-off process that begins in the early forties. When Else Frenkel-Brunswik first delineated this broader phase, she characterized it as the most fruitful time in professional and creative work. A great deal happens at the beginning of it (nearing 30), so that its entrance is clearly defined, usually, by the final and definite choice of vocation. Although many personal relations are acquired before this time, she observed that they are usually only temporary. It is in the transition to the thirties that most people choose a definite personal tie and go on to establish a home.[2]

But not before they reappraise.

Almost everyone who is married will question that commitment. In some instances the real question is whether or not one wants to stay in any marriage. At the very least, the contract needs revising to allow for new things we know about ourselves. Or don't want to know, for our illusions die hard.

Nonetheless, the passage to the thirties stimulates a subtle psychological shift on all fronts. "Me" is just starting to take on as much value as "others." The urge to widen is beginning to overtake the need for safety. An aliveness is rising from within. And what about the change in sense of time?

Blecher speaking again: "The fear of death rivets me to the sidewalk. . . . Yet it doesn't make me live better."[3]

That is because death at this stage is still an abstract fear. There is still time to do it all. New continents of experience await discovery. We are impatient, yes, but not yet urgent.

Another surprise awaits all of us as the Trying Twenties draw to a close. Will power and intellect cannot overcome all obstacles, as we thought. As Bertrand Russell must have thought at the age of 27. By then he was well along in the analytical breakthroughs that eventually produced his *Principles of Mathematics*. He and his wife were living with Alfred North Whitehead. "Every day was warm and sunny," as Russell described it in his autobiography, and his nightly discussions with an older and wiser man were intoxicating. The autumn of his 27th year he felt to be "intellectually the highest point of my life." One day that winter everything changed, and a mysterious new dimension broke through the control of his mental powers. He returned home to find Mrs. Whitehead in agony from a recurring heart ailment. For five minutes, shaken to the core, he felt the impenetrable loneliness of the human soul.[4]

> At the end of those five minutes, I had become a different person. . . . Having for years cared for exactness and analysis, I found myself filled with semi-mystical feelings about beauty, with an intense interest in children, and with a desire almost as profound as that of the Buddha to find some philosophy which should make human life endurable.

The words of a fine writer put flesh on the sterile study. Frenkel-Brunswik found the passage into the thirties to be "the culmination period for subjective experiences," and Gould concluded from his study that a "marked subjective experience" reveals to people that life is much more difficult and painful than it was thought to be in the twenties.[5]

Life does indeed become more complicated, but it is in this complexity that we find possible a new richness. Russell was invigorated rather than depressed by his new awareness.

> A strange excitement possessed me, containing intense pain but also some element of triumph through the fact that I could dominate pain, and make it, as I thought, a gateway to wisdom. The mystic insight which I then imagined myself to possess has largely faded, and the habit of analysis has reasserted itself. But something of what I thought I saw in that moment has remained always with me.[6]

CATCH-30 AND THE COUPLE

If individuals sound baffled at this turning point, the confusion only increases when it comes to the couple. It makes itself loudly heard in the shattering of marriages. For the past fifty years, Americans have been most likely to break out of wedlock when the man is about 30 and the woman 28.[7]

What is this thing, this whirlpool of inconsistencies, that seems to catch so many? Catch-30, as I came to think of it.

The men and women we hear from in this chapter married in their early twenties. It was understood that she would stay out of anything but peripheral participation in the adult world and reproduce a family world for him. Roughly seven years later he is feeling competent as a man, an acknowledged, if still junior, adult. The press of the outside world has taught him how to maneuver around his professional illusions. He knows now, for instance, that vivid displays of intelligence are not as well rewarded as loyalty because many older men are afraid of younger men. But in his earlier twenties, when he wasn't sure about those professional illusions, he didn't dare tell his wife. To do so would have jeopardized the safety that both of them needed to believe he could provide.

Now, invigorated by his newfound confidence, no longer in constant need of having his loneliness taken care of, and becoming bored with a substitute mother, he changes the instructions to his wife: Now you must be something more, too. Be a companion instead of a child and mother. Be capable of excellence, like me.

"Why don't you take some courses?" is the way it usually comes out, because he still doesn't want her to stray too far from the caretaking of him (and children if they have or plan them). But what *he* sees as encouraging her, *she* perceives as threatening her, getting rid of her, freeing himself from her.

She is at war with her own Age 30 inner demons, feeling narrowed and impatient, although probably ill-equipped to be something more. As part of their original contract, she was told she didn't *have* to get out into the world in any full sense. So long as she does not make any strenuous efforts to individuate, she can partake of all those illusions that she brought along from her mother that make her feel safe. Anyone who pushes the other way is goading her toward danger. Therefore *he*, the husband who has suddenly changed the instructions to "You have to," must be the villain.

Now her experience is betrayal. She is being kicked out of her own house. She is 18 again, filled with all the anxieties that the 18-year-old has in leaving home. Little lessons in the culinary and creative arts lead nowhere except to the end of the course and back to the house. This is not being something more. It is being diverted into something else. She still has no impact on people and events in the larger realm, no access to the hierarchies of accomplishment, no *focus*. Her confidence has deteriorated. What does she have to offer the world? And even if there is a chance the world would take her seriously, is it worth leaving the security of home?

This is an important point: The willingness to risk is based on a history of accomplishment.

Her attention span shortens as the inner agitation builds. Women friends may be a consolation (so long as they're not achieving much of anything outside the home either). Maybe a lover is the cure for what ails her (and would serve to punish her husband at the same time). Business entertaining only rubs salt in the wounds. When the men talk in their knowing way of how to run things better—the country, the company, the union, the university—she feels she has nothing informed to add from her own experience. The easiest available diversion from her real problem is to pump all her hostile vitality into running a tight ship at home, because she is too fearful to attempt running things anywhere else.

Deep down her husband knows he could not tolerate her nonproductive life style. "I was concerned that Didi, who had an excellent mind and worked at the Guggenheim Museum when I married her, was not *doing* anything," one man recalled. Another businessman, whose wife had welcomed marriage as an excuse to stop answering casting calls, remembered a change in his attitude six or seven years later. "In that period I wanted from my wife a sense of her own independent contribution to the union." But he usually wants the contribution at no cost. It is hard for the man of 30 to imagine making enough room to allow for the serious training of his wife as a lawyer, designer, professor, actress, corporate hotshot. Even more forbidding, suppose she were to become just as preoccupied by and competent in her work as he?

The contradiction between what he wants and what he fears makes him feel guilty. Spinning into the whirlpool now is her envy, oppressive enough so that almost all men married to caregivers mentioned it. "I began at 30 to see a future for myself in the academic world, in a responsible position," is the way a burgeoning administrator described it. "I think there might have been some envy on my wife's part that I had a vision of myself. She stopped being supportive. Well, she still participated, but without showing much enthusiasm for the responsibilities of being my wife, such as entertaining. She still had nothing of her own. She was feeling frenzied."

He wants the problem to go away. It distracts him from his own Age 30 dilemmas. Having done all his shoulds as the apprentice, he is impatient to broaden his realm of responsibility.

First, he must begin honing his dream into definite goals, or discard the old dream for a new one, or broaden it or diversify it. Whatever the direction, it calls for major decisions. And it often calls for a move. There simply isn't enough time to play social worker to his left-behind wife. Or rather, he hasn't enough interest to make the time. He takes the necessity plea: "I'm too busy trying to build a future to solve your problems, too."

Later on (usually after the divorce) husbands will insist, "I *did* encourage her." And complain that she never followed through.

"Thirty was the time when I was on the make," recounts a man who made the vice-presidency of a major American corporation by the tender age of 35. "As long as the kids were taken care of I was happy; I wanted them out of my way. Suddenly you win an award, and you get this nice feeling—Jesus, people know my name.

"I thought my wife ought to do something. Be more structured. My wife had gone to art school, but she was turning out to be just a dull housewife. A bright girl who never does anything to capacity; whereas I was always pushing beyond capacity. She's a great weaver, great drawer, great cook—and never finishes anything! She'd start a project, drop it for six months, start something else. 'Let's make bread now.' So we'd have all kinds of great bread for a few months, and then we're through the bread kick. Drives me crazy! We discussed her getting a job, briefly, or going to school. I think she interpreted that as my wanting her to go out and earn money. My point was to make herself more interesting, more productive.

"On the other hand, I must have been one of the worst fathers around. Even when I was home, I was always working ahead. I remember once describing my life as a comic strip. 'I have this comic strip going, and I've got to keep ahead of publication. When I am home, I'm in my room, which is set up as a studio, and I'm working on what the hell am I going to do next week? next month? to keep the comic strip going.'

"My wife and kids just weren't that interesting. I told her my work was the most important thing to me. She took it okay. She's a nice, placid lady, and she was never on my back to earn more money.

"A dream of her own? If she has one, I'm not aware of it. I suspect that her dream was: Wouldn't it be nice to have a terrific husband?"

The same blind exasperations were expressed by a man called in the marketing world "a golden boy." Born poor, he married a Powers model and placed her in a suburban stage set. By the age of 30 he had become president of a major food-processing company.

"Oh, hell, the woods are full of courses my wife started. And the hospital groups, church groups, they all wash out—and how, I suggested them! Sure I criticized her. 'Don't start something you don't follow out on,' I told her. 'But more important, the reason you should do it is to broaden your interests. You're wasting your bloody life!' "

When the same man, several presidencies and twenty years later, looks back on what he really wanted from his wife at 30, the motives are clearer. And far less altruistic. "I guess I told her to take courses to buy peace. It's easy to say what I would have liked."

Would he have liked his wife to develop as a true peer back then, to have found a purpose in the world quite independent of her commitment to him?

"I'd like to say yes to that question. But I honestly don't think I could have handled it then."

Did he actually want a woman who was totally supportive without getting in the way or growing dull?

"Yes, exactly."

If the woman does not act on her own impulse to broaden during this passage, the bind doubles. Sensing that to give vent to any solid ambition—to devote the time, love, and discipline necessary to make it work—will invite a jealous backlash from her husband, she retreats instead to the safety of her un-grown-up stage. And tries to reel him back in with her: "Why don't you stay home more?" He senses that as a trap. What he formerly saw as safety, he now resents as danger. Now her whole effort is to hang on to the arrangement and hate him.

Who is right? They both are. The classic Catch-30.

The Testimonial Woman

Enter a third figure, who can offer the man a convenient lift out of his knot: the Testimonial Woman. Because the transition from the twenties to the thirties is often characterized by first infidelities, she is not hard to find. She is behind the secretary's desk, in the junior copywriter pool, in the casting call lineup, in the next lab coat. The root of the word *testimonial* is *testis* (plural *testes*). I read somewhere that when one aboriginal man bumped into another, he cupped the sexual parts of his tribesman in greeting. It was a "testimonial to manhood" and the original basis for the handshake. Whether or not it's true, the Testimonial Woman offers the same service: She fortifies his masculinity.

The wife bears witness to the embryo who was. Even if she doesn't confront him, he looks into those memory-bank eyes and recalls his faults, failures, fears. The new woman offers a testimonial to what he has become. She sees him as having always *been* this person. She is generally younger, subordinate but promising. He may be able to take the part of teacher. Then she can become more and more like him, further affirming him as admirable and worth emulating.

The traditional wife, at home with children and dependent on her husband, literally cannot afford to know what she half knows. It has the makings of a very angry situation.

A classic description of the Testimonial Woman spilled out of a 36-year-old advertising executive: "The big change in my life at the age of 29 was, I was no longer faithful to my wife. Everything started happening at once. I found out I could write copy, damn good copy. My salary climbed in one year from $10,000 to $24,000. Power comes with ability, and the more power you get, the more attractive you become to women. I began to screw around indiscriminately. It was terrific. Here I had a wife at home who was concerned only with the kids. Then a really significant thing happened. I met a girl who made me realize I would not stay married, although she ended our affair brutally. Two years later the lady came along. I hired her as my secretary. Used all the tricks there are to use with power. 'Go cash my paycheck.' I taught her how to write. I started her.

"What was tearing me apart was seeing what I was doing to my wife's life. Making it miserable without explaining it to her at all. Laying blame on her for not having made something of her life. You know, 'How many times have I asked you to go to school?'"

What did his wife say to his exhortations?

"She said, 'My life is devoted to the children.'"

If his wife suddenly *had* changed her whole mode of life, I asked him, would he have been able to take it?

"I can't answer that," he said gravely. "Because of things I now know about myself. And because, since we've divorced, she *has* changed."

After hearing that comment over and over again from men, I began to wonder if divorce is a *rite de passage*. Is this ritual necessary before anyone, above all herself, will take a woman's need for expansion seriously? The Changed Woman after divorce was a familiar figure to come out of the biographies, a dynamic figure, and one who usually held considerable allure for her startled former husband.

What's this? *She's lost weight, cut her hair, opened a shop, and from what I hear, seems to be playing around with all kinds of men. It kills me if I let it. She's not even trying to get married again! She says she doesn't want to be tied down.*

He would have you believe, as it is popularly assumed, that he outgrew his wife and that they had to divorce because she was a clinging, uninteresting person. Yet the Changed Woman is anything but dull. She has mystery. In fact he is amazed to see, several years out of their marriage, how

much dimension she has gained. The superficial reason for their split seldom holds up once he has learned more about himself. It has very little
to do with his wife, whoever she was.

With the advertising executive, it is a clear-cut battle with the powerful
mother on whom he allowed himself to remain financially dependent until
he was 27. It should be no surprise that the adman is having similar problems with the woman for whom he left his wife. After living with his
Testimonial Woman for four years, he says, "I can't promise her I'll be
faithful, either." His dream now, as he works feverishly to establish his
own agency, is to have a million dollars by the time he's 45. It is significant
that he projects 45 as the end of the dream period. Perhaps he won't be
capable of any deep mutuality with a woman until that time. Very likely
it will take him until then to work out his own autonomy. But not for the
reason he anticipates, that by the mid-forties he will be so rich he can't possibly be dependent on his mother. It will be because, if and when he faces
that emotional dependence, he will begin to understand himself.

When people become aware of their own complexities, they can see
a mate as more than their personal object of gratification. Only then can
they begin to understand that any mate is also a separate and complicated
person who comes with a history, who has a cycle of life to play out.

Divorce, however, is not a cure-all for the predictable disequilibrium
of this passage, as we shall see in the biographies.

Wives' Work

When the Age 30 passage stirs in a married woman the push from
within to expand, a struggle of massive proportions begins. Many counter-
forces oppose her expansion. The real needs and unrestrained possessiveness
of small children, for one. The thinly disguised jealousy of other women
who are too dependent to dare rocking the boat, for another. Often one's
own mother offers the cruelest disapproval. "My mother is practically
ashamed of me," lamented a 30-year-old who felt ready to put her training
into action. "She thinks I'm an inferior mother because I want to practice
medicine and have a housekeeper to help with the children."

And then there is the whole trick bag, part real and part imagined or
projected, of a husband's opposition. Some of the double messages he is
likely to send out are not unlike the contradictory wishes parents communicate to their adolescent children: *Take responsibility for yourself—but—
don't let that something take you away from me.* Husbands, like parents,
enjoy an irreplaceable ego boost from being idealized by their dependents.
If a woman begins to say to a man, in effect, "I'm no longer going to look
to you as the one who has the right answer all the time; I'm going to test
my own capacities and challenge you on issues," she is taking away a man's
free ride to feeling big.

But that is exactly where most woman have to begin. When the
husband has been made heir to the parental sovereignty, the wife, like the
adolescent wrestling for a sense of self, is going to have to place her world
view, her friends, her idea of a meaningful course to pursue in competition
with the presumptions of the person she has empowered as the Strong One.
It is a necessary precursor to her independence. And it must be seen as
necessary. Many women, by denying the necessity of this developmental
step, eventually blight the very marriages they are trying so hard to preserve.

And if she does act on her inner stirrings? If she declares her need for
an individual destiny and strikes out to find it? She may be astonished to
discover that her mate feels relieved. A man often finds himself delighted
not to have a wife waiting at home for him to bring her a world of accessible joys and money. But during the transition he may perceive malice
where none is intended. In her first clumsy attempts to sort out and declare

her individuality loudly enough so that she herself will believe it, he may hear himself being depreciated. Most men operate on the fantasy or at least the wish that their wives want what they want: *She should want to take care of me and the children because that's what I want from her.*

There is only one way to find out how much of the impediment is actually her husband and how much is her own mistrust of what lies on the other side of the status quo. And that is to take the risk. To do some serious thinking about how to increase herself, not just how to lose weight or jolly up her days with a lover. As psychoanalyst Allen Wheelis says, there is no question that the world will bend to a committed psyche. But the commitment must have the ring of reality.

If a woman in truth doesn't want to expand, that's another thing. Her out is easy. She can retreat at the first grunt of displeasure roused in her husband, or at the first setback in her efforts to finish a poem or complete her degree or carry off a boycott. She can take the cloak of victim. A mountain of current books, films, and magazine articles will back her up. And so long as she can convincingly blame the tedium of her life on men, she doesn't have to change.

Closed-Dyad Disease

Other problems beset the couple that has wallowed into the valley of the closed dyad: the in-turned husband-wife, mommy-daddy pair of the idealized American family. The closed couple is fine for rapid success and social climbing, but it tends to work against the building of community. What these pairs get in return for their upward mobility is a loss of lateral supports (real friends, neighbors, extended family). And without the support of the remainder of the community, the closed pair can become a *folie à deux*.

Anthropologist Ray L. Birdwhistell, a pioneer in the study of non-verbal communication between men and women, has spent tens of thousands of hours scrutinizing behavior within the closed dyad. He believes that the closed aspect is what makes this a diseased social form. The intensity that characterizes the early period of a relationship, the very thing that closes the dyad, is naturally reduced when two people face openness. But closed pairs regard it as illegitimate to have strong emotional feelings for *anyone* outside the family.[8] Haven't we heard it said a hundred ways?

HE: "You're always on the phone with your girl friends."

SHE: "Another business trip? You never spend any time with your family."

HE: "I can't bear another Thanksgiving with your mother."

SHE: "Why do you have to go out to dinner with people you see all day at the office?"

The individuals are only reaching out for lateral supports in friendship and vertical supports with kin. But if all such supports are considered flimsy or disloyal, the pair has nothing but each other and "associates" or "contacts," which means nothing but sanitized relationships. A deadly but familiar fix.

The usual defense is to justify all outside supports in terms of what they will do for the family. They must bring in money or prestige or possible opportunities for advancement.

HUSBAND: "I need the contacts I make on the golf course. You don't appreciate it, but I'm working my tail off out there!"

WIFE: I'm only going back to work so we can send Jennifer to private school. I'm sure I'll be a better mother for it."

So often a woman gives up her friends when she starts a family. Although the sisterhood cultivated by the women's movement has made friendships among women not only possible but precious, the old convention was to view women friends as fill-ins when there wasn't a man in her life. It is still common to let lapse the warm, nonsexual, buddy closeness she once had with a man friend because, well, her husband wouldn't understand.

Denials, justifications—the sad truth is, people are afraid to admit the satisfaction they derive from such outside relations.

ROOTING AND EXTENDING

Only in the early thirties do we begin to settle down in the full sense. Life becomes less provisional, more rational and orderly. Accomplishments are expected of us by now. As an actress put it, "After 30, there are no more advantages to be gained from simply being younger than other people."

And so most of us begin putting down roots and sending out new shoots. People make major investments in a home, both financial and emotional, and become very earnest about climbing career ladders. A major part of the settling process involves converting the dream into concrete goals. That is, assuming one has been lucky and the trials of the twenties have added greater substance to the dream.

An artisan who had spent six years "really scuffling'" to get his own business off the ground described "how that began to change about the time I was into my early thirties. By then the business was a fairly substantial one, not making a lot of money but a decent income, with good acceptance. My wife and I found the apartment we've been in for fifteen years. In that period everything seemed very cohesive and rational. The pieces all seemed to make some kind of sense. Friends were good. We went to a lot of parties, and we had a feeling of community. There was a lot of aspiring, too, but with goals in sight. That period was probably as close to the dream of my life as I've ever had."

The artisan was fortunate in being able to deepen his commitments in the passage to the thirties. He was his own boss; his business had not failed; nor was he dissatisfied with the direction he had taken in his twenties. He had waited until 29 to choose a wife. During the Rooting and Extending period marriage was a new extension for him, and friends took the place of the children this couple did not want to have.

For many men, the early thirties is the blue-suit period. They set a timetable for fulfilling their goals. It is of consuming importance to become acknowledged as a junior member of their occupational tribe. Men who continue to focus narrowly on their external goals can be, more than at any other time in their lives, shallow and boring.

Americans in corporate life run into a particularly mean conflict during the Rooting and Extending period. Settling down runs directly counter to the uprooting that is required of corporate gypsies. The man logs so many hours on airplanes, he can barely remember how to eat without pulling down a tray. He doesn't make friends; he makes contacts. The corporate wife, doing time on the "GE circuit" or with "I've Been Moved" (wives' vernacular for IBM), doesn't have an office to go to where she might find new acquaintances through her work. The neighbors she resolutely tries to cultivate vanish into the transfer pipeline. And before she has a chance to hang curtains in the new house, it's off to another town, another set of schools for the children, another Newcomers' Club. The only place in the world her name consistently appears is on property transfer lists.

Yet people will find ways to root that are instinctive. It is healthy to root. Those who felt the need to tear up the structure of their twenties are particularly keen to build a solid base. Says a divorcée of 34 who is redecorating her apartment, "I want to feel I'm a very stable citizen."

Another woman who divorced during the Age 30 passage and was just beginning to enjoy settling into her first decent apartment, with a room for her child that didn't look out onto a tenement wall, found out just how deep runs the need to root during this period. She was 32, but the man in her life had just passed 40. "Please, you've got to move in with me," he insisted all of a sudden. "There's plenty of time for that," she said in the calm of her stabilized period. "But we might all be dead tomorrow!" said he in the panic of his midlife crisis. Sensing his terrible urgency, but with vague misgivings, she did move in with him. A week later she felt like a letter that had been slipped under his door with no return address.

It is also unwise to ignore the Age 30 passage and attempt to move directly from the Trying Twenties into Rooting and Extending. Those who do so, often locked into their "secure" marriages, too fearful or self-indulgent to widen, may feel a lack of heroism in their daily lives and complain there are no more surprises. But rather than engage the inner impulse to broaden themselves, they bury the message in exterior changes: It's time to rearrange the furniture in their lives. And so they move from garden apartments to the suburbs or build houses or renovate brownstones, believing this in itself will give them a clear purpose in life. While the husbands concentrate on "making it," the wives are induced into what John Kenneth Galbraith calls "a competitive display of managerial excellence." [9]

Just as people find many routes into the turmoil of Catch-30, there are various ways to pull out: a few noisy but successful ways that address the problem directly, and the more common cooling techniques that keep the lid on while the fermentation continues.

14

32 Thoughts On Being 32

"After your twenties,
crisis and crunch and disappointment
are what make people interesting."

By Mopsy Strange Kennedy

1. I just read somewhere that 30 is the beginning of middle-age. Middle-age? Come on! I take that to be a challenge. This is the year I learned to do a backbend from a standing position. In my unathletic childhood I could never do that. In my teen-age years I was too preoccupied with keeping my girdle up (did I ever own such a thing?) to attempt anything so physically disruptive. I sometimes feel as if I've been given a free tank of gas.

2. Age, of course, really belongs to time. Whereas I once thought time was an absolute, it now seems to last forever only between two and four in the morning when I have insomnia. Because, you see, I remember the last ten years so clearly that if I were to hold them up in a beaker, I could see through this year to 1965.

Besides, there are different kinds of time. There's Puritanical time (to clean house); dark chocolate time (spent under a quilt, reading a book); or floating, wine-drinking time. There's also contrapuntal time (when you sit in a movie theater in the afternoon); mixed media time (when you read Napoleon's biography while listening to the Rolling Stones); inspirational time (when the literal ticking of the clock is mocked by an extraordinary surge of productivity); and cruel, congealed time (when the scowl lingers on your face).

Because time works differently for other people (as for my tortoise friend who finished medical school at the slowest metabolic rate), it is like pantyhose: one size fits all, but accommodates each person differently.

3. At times during my twenties, I began to think that there was nothing new under the sun. The bones of experience seemed to be picked dry. Now I realize what is new is approach, angle, mood, relationship to things, rather than just the things themselves. I'm discovering, for ex-

ample, a new subtext to the hours of the day. Formerly an inveterate morning person, I thought the middle of the night was for other people. Now I'm getting into those purple-bruised, aching night hours when, all energy and resistance spent, a new me swims to the surface: disillusioned, like a torch-singer, as dissipated as the deepening circles under my eyes. But wondrous enough, this person can read, write, converse, even watch television differently, living on a side of my mental moon I never knew existed.

4. When I saw the movie "Summer of 42" I was haunted by the sight of an actress my age portraying a woman dressed like my mother when I was little. As a child I spent hours dressing up in her pale-green velvet tea gowns, padded-shoulder dresses and fur stoles with little fox heads biting each other. I imagined that those same clothes would somehow wait for me, since I had no idea that styles changed. Those clothes evoked grown-upness and motherhood, but as it happened, a different adulthood, with different clothes, became mine. But seeing that movie, I had a brief illusion that I had precisely replicated my childhood dream of a grown-up self.

5. My attitude toward money, always unstable, has taken a new turn. I don't entirely support myself and I am not sure I ever could, so I tend to be more of the Guilt School. I wonder how I get things without seeming to deserve them. By the same token, I get irrationally mad when people without apparent special qualifications (training, brains, experience) earn a lot of money. And madder still when they arrogantly proclaim that a lot is "not enough." "More" suddenly becomes disagreeably less, and "less" becomes definitely more, to my way of thinking.

6. It used to be that worry, anxiety, anticipation scurried through me like a salty rat all day. That I

should be visited by such intense sensations was a sign that I was alive and not dormant. Telephone calls, unpaid bills, doorbell rings burned in my mind, and the calendar bristled with thumbtacks, fearful doctor appointments, and dreaded dinners.

But a small piece of information has given me a new perspective on anxiety. I discovered that the Chinese word for "crisis" combines two characters, one representing danger, the other opportunity. That idea was new to my Occidental, post-adolescent mind. I began to look with a sort of relish on all the million sources of worry (tangled waking dreams, paperwork, traffic) as an opportunity not to worry. As my dieting friend said, "I can't wait till the next meal so I can not eat."

About the same time, I began doing meditation at home. I was amazed and pleased to find a place of repose in my consciousness, where fragments, as in a film of breaking glass run backwards, could fly together, instead of apart.

7. It's extraordinary how gossip and anecdote inform our image of how our friends live: "After she heard about Jim, she gained 90 pounds," "He had so much trouble with his neighbors he had to move to Argentina," or best yet, "Go ahead and tell me the story, even if it's not true." People trade these pat headlines all the time. Once I heard such a life-judgment about myself ("I understood you were so miserable that you hardly saw anyone all year" I was? I did?). All of a sudden it threw into doubt my use of the same technique. I realized that the process of gossip is really a form of fictionalization—how can an outsider ever understand motives that remain ambiguous to their owner? So I object to these bite-size analyses that I once bought, and to their smug formulation of events, feelings, transactions. If that is what seeing myself as others see me means, I'd rather bumble along in my own way, thanks.

8. When I start my club, Society for the Prevention of Cruelty to Your Age, its main tenet will be: Never say anything degrading about your age. Why not own up to it for what it is? I hate to see my 60-year-old friend hesitate, blush and speak apologetically about older people. "Oh yeah, he's over the hill, sure. He isn't any spring chicken." Why not winter chicken?

To think that youth is all is a recipe for misery—every age has its different pleasures. Fifty knows more than twenty, after all.

9. Cleaning ladies still worry me, partly because I've had the exotic experience only once in my adult life. The week after this cleaning lady's visit, I tried to keep the house carefully balanced between clean-enough-to-bear (in case she didn't return) and dirty-enough-to-warrant-her-visit. Certain rugs, teetering over the edge of revolting, nearly made me drool with the desire to vacuum them, but my sybaritic side checked me.

Like all good patsys, I had bought some cottage cheese and diet cola for her lunch. (She had rejected as "too fattening" my offers of cold roast beef before.) I was gearing myself to apologize for whatever was wrong (the presence of dirt, the absence of dirt, the worn-out mops and sponges). This poised, apologetic balance was agonizing: worse than standing on one leg.

I waited and waited for her to show up—the slave of my servant—until it dawned on me she was not coming or even calling. I was so angry I found myself cleaning the house thoroughly for a change, pretending I was my own cleaning lady. Hours later, the house clean as a cat, I rested, basking in the fantasy that some kind person had done all this work for me. And miser that I am, I looked

on the $15 saved as a windfall, almost a present. I got an incredible kick out of the idea that the potentially maddening experience had so satisfied me in the end.

10. Having children has turned out to be one of the things I was really meant to do. Their pure, green energy amazes me; and I'm excited by their excitement. I watch them rough-housing around, sweet and luscious as marzipan. In my mind, I photograph them laughing, biting, singing, and screaming. I want to be able to remember all this was something that really did happen to me in my twenties and thirties.

11. When I got out of college, I felt so under-read that I went to the library like a starving girl, to concentrate on reading solid stuff. Ten years later, I still have a lot of catching up to do. To add to the load, many of the books I now want to read have been written since then. And of course I could re-read profitably almost every book I've ever read.

So I go to the library, wavering between Amusing and Improving. I want something that will pucker my brain, yet not beat me over the head with 100 wasted afternoons and a lot of prior knowledge I don't have. Often I make discoveries that spark others: thanks to Anne Sexton, I am reading poetry again; Margaret Drabble has reminded me of how well-disposed I am to reading contemporary English fiction; and certain books about cities have gotten me interested in a field I had once thought was not for me.

12. I quarrel in my mind with what used to be called "women's lib." The very phrase I find fishy: it has a have-you-stopped-beating-your-wife tinge to it. Like any set of beliefs which promises self-improvement ("clear" as in scientology, "saved" as in religion, "free" as in California) women's lib is a code for a particular dogma that actually usurps the real meaning of the words.

To me, "liberated" has many ringing associations removed from the subject of feminism: thinness after fatness, friendship after loneliness, release from painful infatuations, sky-diving, freedom from fear, etc. Sure, I also think it means being taken seriously and not made a slave or a doll. But it doesn't mean to me viewing sensuality, complex relations between the sexes, and certain chosen paths of passivity as bondage or backsliding.

My main annoyance with the movement is its niggardly, unvoluptuous view of children (try to defend staying home with small children to a die-hard liberationist, and see how "free to be you and me" we really are) and its aesthetic, which I find to be very unaesthetic.

Obviously the search for selfhood, even guerilla selfhood, is an admirable goal, but you don't need dogma to find yourself. Ironically, it's the most draped-in-the-flag feminists, relentlessly talking about oppression, that end up with a chip on their shoulders, burlap frowns, and pocketfuls of complaints and accusations that forbid real negotiation. The suggestion that pours off feminism is you can only go about experience in one way, or you aren't doing it right, which implies you can be a disgruntled Kate Millet but not, say, a happy Beverly Sills.

13. Someone said to me the other day, "After your twenties, crisis and crunch and disappointment are what make people interesting."

14. Six years ago, I came to grips with my hatred of exercise, especially my irritation with rackets, balls, partners, clubs, competition, and skills. I wrapped up all this loathing, threw it out, and became a jogger. Let's say instead I became a sidewalk-swallowing, weather-defying silver arrow of energy. I, who hate to walk (because you never bloody get there) love to run because it symbolizes getting there. And I discovered the notion of a "second wind"; that moment when you find yourself presented with a new pair of lungs willing to take on another mile. This discovery tells me I have other second winds to explore, in, say, playing the piano, reading, or making friends.

15. Food—cooking it, eating it, even looking at pictures of it—remains one of life's reliable pleasures. Nothing else (except perhaps reading) provides such a literal feast of color, opportunity and adventure. I feel that I address myself to food, cajoling and seducing it, and the food, in turn, flattered and inspired, returns the compliment. When I was younger and more impatient, I would cook food too quickly on too high a flame, resulting in hamburgers that clenched their blackened fists at me and jello that sunk in a rubber girdle at the bottom of a bowl. I've had impetuous food, crazy chilis, curries and mouthpuckering juxtapositions. Now I want soft-focus food: tender grapes, little squabs, pale green, clear soups: parsimonious but perfect.

16. The story of the cleaning lady reminds me of the category I call "victimology." My strong-willed friend Maura tells me she and I are often victims, so we like to pretend we work on "victim therapy." When I told her about the cleaning lady she replied, "Well, that's nice you ended up okay, but the fact is you let this woman victimize you. Now promise me if she calls back, you will not let her try to return?" This was the beginning of a deep, revengeful peace. Also the start of refusing religious salesmen entry into the house, of finding five delighted couples to help a worthy cause, and of inventing excuses for things I didn't want to do. Now I say to my oppressors, "I'm not going to have your damn in-law's godson visit me because I don't want to, that's why."

17. I met a psychiatrist at a party recently, and asked him if he didn't find living on the dark side of people's lives bizarre and fascinating. No, he said. "Everyone's dark side is pretty much the same, it's in the light side that people are incredibly different."

18. Now I'm going to say something nice about the women's movement. I admit it has called attention to certain abuses that were isolated, and taken sides with causes that were embattled. Now, the case of one man beating his wife in Tennessee is not just George mistreating Loretta. It also fits a category of unacceptable behavior—male chauvinism—which makes the diagnosis, if not the cure, much easier.

19. It seems some fiendish public relations man has divided life's stages in such a way that if you aren't in a certain slot, you are officially just-about-to-be, whether pre-senile, pre-teen, post-adolescent, mid-adult, or over-age. I wish someone would find a way to express what it means to be thirty-two that is not condescending or euphemistic. I guess what I really ask for is the impossible—a place in life that is free of definition, where neither the record salesmen, the denture cream companies, the layette manufacturers or the burial plot can find me. And I'm sure that is just the typical desire of a "pre-middle-aged, non-lactating, mid-married, para-professional college graduate" with the old 2.5 children and a beaten-up Volvo.

20. In the eighth grade, we had to write a letter to our future grown-up self. I remember what I wrote about: the treachery of becoming uptight, hypocritical, and the danger of concealing a lack of heart in a suburban veneer. Sad enough as it is, the grown-ups I wanted to not become were probably doing their best. How could I know the story of their lives? What I saw as a suburban veneer was probably the other side of "good wife, long-suffering mother." Youth is wasted on the young, as we all know, but I wonder if adulthood isn't wasted too on the adult.

21. And then there's sex—luring people together, Svengali-like, across supermarkets, rooms and impossible barriers. I find the secret, invisible communication of sexual attraction no less weird than the relations between the moon and the tides. Sometimes sex becomes so important that every other activity seems like a cruel diversion made up by a sadistic guidance counsellor to keep you from "it."

At other times, it seems about as irrelevant as golf. I heard the following story once, and thereafter I stopped thinking about other people's sex lives and only about my own (with an occasional side-trip to the letters column of *Penthouse*). A man I know (living, naturally, in California), found a girl on his doorstep one night asking to take a shower. Five minutes after this hokey shower, they were in bed together. "So you liked her?" I asked my friend, a little amazed, but willing to be converted by the story. "Who said anything about liking her?" "Ah, but you were instantly blazing with desire for her, then. . .?" "Who said anything about desire?" "Oh."

The thing I found so alarming about this story is the bad name it gives raw lust, or more accurately, the no name at all. Wasn't one of the purposes of the sexual revolution to connect motivation and availability? Here was availability all right, but where was the motivation? I am coming to the conclusion that mores don't necessarily tell you a thing about the way people feel.

22. When I was young, Françoise Sagan, at 18, wrote *Bonjour Tristesse*. It surprised me because no one I knew wrote a novel when they were 18. Many others now who I both know and don't know call themselves novelists. We seemed to have crossed the great divide between precocity and normal achievement in our sleep. A person I know who was to be "groomed as the crown prince" has now taken charge of a big newspaper. And some of those bald guys who got appointed to government jobs were my classmates. So the tick-tocks bump us forward, and finally the pendulum-broom sweeps us off the edge.

23. I find my friendships increasingly thematic. I talk about very specific things with certain friends. With one, we choose subjects, like the meaning of California fads, Barbra Streisand, social class, etc. With another, it's journalism and recipes. But with one friend, the dialogue centers on her lower back pain. Yet in this tiny boring subject a whole relationship—amazingly merry—seems to flower. And my best friend and I have a private language; our conversations occur in the subjunctive—"what if's," "let's look at it this way." Sometimes I am still surprised that my friends don't appreciate each other as much as I wish. Then I remember that friendships make the other person into a metaphorical Siamese twin—a sidecar personality—who is not the same with me as with others.

24. These are increasingly psychotherapeutic times. The introspective examination of what you do and what you think about it is accepted, moreover popular. People go around saying, "I'm working through this"; "My analyst says. . ."; "This is one of my big issues." I'm interested in the ways that people choose to live, see themselves, and discuss their self-revelations. But sometimes, the change in

self occurs on the talking-about-it level, rather than the living-it level.

25. A 19-year-old former student visited me for the weekend. I met him when I was an unusually juvenile twenty-six and he a grown-up fifteen: a blessed exception to the rule that you get along best with people your own age. Would I have gotten on with him if we were both nineteen? He'd already done things that would have seemed from-Mars to me when I was his age: he'd had the nerve and the exposure I lacked when I was nineteen. He represents the dark and terrifying world of adolescence behind closed doors that I will come to know through my children.

26. People talk about welfare chiselers, but not in reference to marriage, where, I for one, consider myself to be the lucky beneficiary of such a phenomenon. For instance, this house; it would be nice to think that my inspiration and hard work got me this Victorian cake of a house, but it's not so: it was my husband's hard work and inspiration. Marriage has a blessed economy about it: is this oppression that allows me to pursue my studies, play all afternoon with the kids, take odd jobs from time to time, write articles? I only hope the fellow who thinks marriage is so terrible is having as much fun in his efficiency apartment with his frozenette dinners as I am in this sprawl where I can move from room to room restlessly as in an indoor city.

27. A year is an eternity when you're little. The world turns a million times from birthday to birthday. But, as my math teacher pointed out, each year is proportionately a smaller and smaller part of the whole as you get older, and this explains why a year ago seems so sinisterly recent. This shocking speed of time will accomplish in the same interval that took me from puberty to motherhood a vanishing act on my children, and give them back as teen-agers. Then again, it amazes me that I am now the same age that my mother was when I first began to really know her.

28. Sometimes I think that living is like staying up all night, and seeing loops and loops of time and people and ideas come back, each time a slightly different color. I particularly notice this with people I've known for years who are now totally different than they once were. I swear some people die in their sleep and wake up the next day transformed.

29. A woman once asked me fiercely (hoping I wouldn't come up with a satisfactory answer) "What role models have you ever had?" I've admired my fair share of neurotic but endearing people over the years, shopping as much for style as for character or plot. I have some illusory sense I will get a sort of psychic suntan off them which will strengthen their admirable qualities in me.

The imaginary composite person I would like to become would have a profession (career sounds too dreary) of some respectability and scope, but which would also be playful at the edges. She would be an exceptionally devoted wife and mother, and live on the exotic side of the bourgeoisie, this side of hippiedom, but definitely this side of suburbia. I can see her now in a blue challis dress: she can play the piano very well, and knows a lot of poetry by heart. She does not share any of my obsessions, and yet it is possible for us to be friends.

30. The other day I heard myself barking at the children, "You'll just have to learn that you can't always get your way." One of them shouted back "You'll just have to learn to shut your mouth." Of course I wasn't going to learn to do that! Then I thought about this ridiculously pious phrase "You'll just have to learn." Whoever learns what they are taught? It occurred to me that this is probably why bankers beget hippies, and for all I know, hippies probably beget, in true cyclical and poetic manner, bankers in turn.

31. Which is real life—work or all that other stuff? I see work as a suit of armor, a role which because it is imposed, is not quite the real thing. Motherhood may too be a role, but to me it is bodily, emotionally **there.** I am troubled by the artificiality of work though I agree that it gives life flow and purpose. My friend argues it doesn't matter if you "become" your job. But that bothers me. I look for qualities in people that come from something else beside their work-identity. I once asked an engineer what else he'd like to do if he could live all over again. I expected him to say he would like to be a lawyer, but to my pleasure he said "I'd like to live again as a woman." That sounds like reality to me.

32. Thirty-one is a good age. Twenty-nine sounds like you're lying. Thirty is too full of meaning. But thirty-one is like a little sliver of a moon, just starting again. It has the promise of twenty-one, with an extra decade to hold it down and make it solid. But thirty-two is even better. It's your "early thirties."

IV. Relationships and Families
a. Couples

C.H. ELDRIDGE '76

As social animals, one of our greatest needs is to relate intimately and consistently with others. Through our significant relationships we create our personal sense of self-esteem and receive validation for who we feel we are. Our struggle to create and maintain these relationships is one of life's most essential tasks. The outcome of these relationships is one of the major yardsticks a person uses to evaluate his or her life. The style of relating a person adopts is, in effect, the way that person expresses his or her needs and experiences a sense of meaning in life.

In intimate relationships we express our sexuality, which forms an important aspect of our personality, as the article from SIECUS illustrates. Sexuality is not simply a physical performance. Rather, it represents and validates how we feel about ourselves as men and women. The central relationship in most people's lives is the sexual, household unit called the couple. Couples, like individuals, have unique individual styles, and also common patterns that may be seen in many relationships, as described by Allman and Jaffe. A couple's style is a major determinant of whether a person's most intimate relationship will be frustrating or gratifying. Carlfred Broderick next compares and contrasts a few of the often bewildering array of patterns, styles, and choices available to contemporary couples, which represent different values about life and sexuality. Carl Rogers, through an interview with a young woman who has been through several marriages, suggests some of the ways individual growth and family relationships are intertwined. Another interview study, this time by Thomas Cottle, presents some of the ways that social values and forces determine the behavior of a family unit.

As the couple unit expands into a family system, through creating children, new developmental tasks confront the system, as Reuben Hill's essay suggests. The roles of family members change as families confront the ever-changing demands of the different life stages, which can be seen from a family as well as an individual perspective. Families, too, have a life cycle and developmental process. Dennis Jaffe offers a case study of a new type of family, the commune, and how its process affects the development of the families and individuals within it. The choices and pressures of our time seem to have caused modern families to take a variety of directions, a diversity of choices which is similar to the situation we already saw with youth. In our time it seems that many of the pressures that we ordinarily expect to be settled by the onset of adulthood remain ongoing issues well into adulthood.

One of the primary functions of a family is raising children and socializing them to become participants in our culture, thus allowing our species to sustain itself. Sociologist Alice Rossi looks at the changing demands of parenthood, and how people learn them and take on parent roles. As demands on the parents and the family change, we see a corresponding change in the expected social roles and tasks of various family members, as Christian Beels depicts from the perspective of the father. The women's movement has made almost everyone sensitive to the implications for society of the changing roles of women and the need for the conventional roles and ideals of families to change to reflect women's growing equality and societal changes in work patterns.

15

Sexuality
and the Life Cycle
A Broad Concept of Sexuality

Introduction

As the Group for the Advancement of Psychiatry noted, the concept of sexuality generally accepted today is that described by Anna Freud: "...The sexual instincts of man do not suddenly awaken between the thirteenth and fifteenth year, i.e. at puberty, but operate from the outset of the child's development, change gradually from one form to another, progress from one state to another, until at last adult sexual life is achieved as the final result from this long series of developments." Today we recognize that we must concern ourselves with sexual feelings and behavior throughout the life cycle.

Most people are accustomed to thinking of sex as something involving merely the genital organs or as simple physical expression. To avoid this narrow and limiting conception of sex, we prefer to use the term *sexuality* as a recognition that sex expression is a deep and pervasive aspect of one's total personality, the sum total of one's feelings and behavior not only as a sexual being, but as a male or a female.

Thus, expressions of sexuality go much beyond genital responses, and are constantly subject to modification as a consequence of sexual experience and learning. Throughout the life cycle, physiological, emotional, social, and cultural forces condition sexuality in intricate and important ways, most expecially during early and late childhood. As individuals age, these influences may result in a widening range of possible sexual attitudes and expressions.

Simple Definitions No Longer Suffice

With the development of sophisticated research into sex and gender roles it is clear that the old simple definitions of male and female no longer suffice. Individuals may be classified as male and female on the basis of a growing number of criteria. These have been identified as follows:

1. *Genetic or chromosomal sex, determined at the moment of conception*. The normal female has two X chromosomes, while the normal male has one X and one Y chromosome. Recent research has discovered many types of sex-chromosomal anomalies.
2. *Gonadal sex*. The male has testes, while the female has ovaries.
3. *Hormonal sex*. The actions of the so-called male and female hormones may have important effects in bringing about feminization and virilization during critical periods of fetal development and puberty.
4. *Internal accessory reproductive structures*. The female has a womb, fallopian tubes, ovaries, etc., while the male has a prostate gland, sperm ducts, seminal vesicles, etc.
5. *External genital structures.*
6. *Sex of assignment and rearing.*
7. *Gender role and sexual orientation established while growing up.*

161

These variables may be independent of each other, resulting in incongruity between gender identity and other variables and creating special developmental and educational problems.

Prenatal Development

Male and female individuals begin their early embryonic development as forms which cannot be differentiated. Some researchers suggest that all embryos begin as females. According to Mary Jane Sherfey, "mammalian embryos, male and female, are anatomically female during the early stages of fetal life. In the human, the differentiation of the male from the female form by the action of fetal androgen (male sex hormone) begins about the sixth week of embryonic life and is completed by the end of the third month." So far as sexuality is concerned, more than the simple fact of differentiating male and female genitalia takes place during the prenatal period. Other organ systems and structures without which adult sexual responses would be impossible are developing also. The glandular system that will bring the childhood reproductive system into maturity during puberty is developing. The neural and muscular systems that make sexual responsiveness possible at various stages of life are also developing, as are the brain centers that later will send and receive sexual messages. As a consequence we can say that each human being is born with certain sexual capacities already present, and that these capacities looked at as a whole constitute a biological response system that can and does respond in an integrated and coordinated way to sexual stimuli.

Recent research with animals suggests the possibility that prenatal hormones affecting the nervous system may have important effects in making some individuals more or less ready than others to receive the definitions of masculinity and femininity from the parents. Freud proposed the theory of innate bisexuality; more recently a theory of psychosexual neutrality at birth has been put forward. On the basis of present knowledge, a more modest middle ground is indicated.

Sexuality in Infancy and Childhood

Prior to Freud, there was little understanding or acceptance of childhood sexuality. According to John Gagnon, "the shock for adults of Freud's discoveries was not that children might be involved in sexual activity, but that this activity was not confined to a few evil children and was, in fact, an essential precursor and component of the development of the character structure of the adult." Freud's theory of the stages of psychosexual development, which he called the oral, anal, and genital, has formed the basis of modern psychiatric thinking. These hypotheses, however, have never been subjected to sufficient scientific testing to be confirmed or disproven. Over the years this model of psychosexual development has been criticized on both empirical and theoretical grounds, primarily by learning theorists, who believe the whole theory is unnecessarily complex, and by anthropologists, who have attacked the idea that each of these stages, and particularly the stage of oedipal conflict, is necessary to normal personality development.

Carlfred B. Broderick, a leading researcher in preadolescent sexual behavior, has hypothesized that three primary conditions are necessary to normal heterosexual development: (1) the parent or parent substitute of the same sex must not be so punishing on the one hand or so weak on the other as to make it impossible for the child to identify with him; (2) the parent or substitute of the opposite sex must not be so seductive, so punishing, or so emotionally erratic as to make it impossible for the child to trust members of the opposite sex; (3) the parents must not systematically reject the child's biological sex and attempt to teach him cross-sex behavior. Thus, Freud's main contention, that normal heterosexual development is determined by a child's familial relationships and social experiences rather than by simple biological factors, seems to be borne out by the available data.

Children, even in infancy, clearly respond to stimuli which produce sexual reactions. Thus, infants of both sexes seem to experience pleasure from the stimulation of the genitals and other areas of the body which are commonly recognized as erogenous zones. Halverson demonstrated that male infants respond to certain internal or external stimuli with erections in the early weeks of life. There was a wide range in individual responsiveness—from 5 to as many as 40 erections daily. These were seemingly the consequence of body tensions rather than sexual reactions in the usual sense. The Kinsey studies showed that orgasmic experiences occurred in infants and children throughout the pre-adolescent period. Their data show an increase, with advancing age, in the percentage of children able to reach climax: 32% of the boys 2-12 months of age, 57% of the 2-5 year olds, and nearly 80% of the pre-adolescent boys between 10 and 13 years of age, reached climax. A recent study of 700 four-year-olds in an English urban community found that 17% of the children engaged in genital play at this age. Interestingly no class differences were found despite sharp differences in parental attitudes. Thus, punitive measures were apparently no more effective in discouraging such play than were either verbal discouragement or *laissez-faire* tactics.

The Learning of Gender Role

The establishment of gender role is of great importance to the developing child. John Money, who has made extensive studies of this aspect of sexuality, explains gender role as being "all those things that a person says or does to disclose himself or herself as having the status of boy or man, girl or woman, respectively. It includes but is not restricted to sexuality in the sense of eroticism. A gender role is not established at birth, but is built up cumulatively through experiences encountered and transacted — through casual and unplanned learning, through explicit instruction and inculcation. In brief, a gender role is established in much the same way as is a native language."

Money found it "definitely advantageous for a child to have been reared so that a gender role was clearly defined and consistently maintained from the beginning." Attempts to impose a change of gender role, in the case of hermaphrodites, after early infancy usually did not improve the child's life adjustment significantly. In fact it often made it worse. Money felt that the critical time for establishing a convincing awareness of gender on the part of the child was from around eighteen months until 3 or 4 years of age. It is important however, to recognize that role behavior is learned and that instruction in role behavior begins with birth.

In the process of establishing gender role or, to use another common term, of establishing a sexual identity, the parents and others around the child play an extremely important part. They convey to the child in both overt and covert ways what they consider appropriate role behavior. They do this through words they use, the name they give the child, the way they treat and dress the child, the kind of toys they buy, the games they encourage, the expectations they voice, the routines they establish, the kind of discipline exercised, and through their own examples. In this manner they give the child a concept of how he is to regard his own body, and how males and females relate themselves to each other.

"Big boys don't cry" and "little girls hug their daddies and mommies" are typical injunctions. They eventually result in the stereotyped and traditional American cultural pattern in which men deny their hurts and injuries and eschew crying as a sign of weakness, and women (who are commonly regarded as weaker than men to begin with) are encouraged to confirm this "weakness" by expressing tender and sentimental feelings. Men, to be "strong," renounce such expressions.

Patterns of individual interests are certain to be strongly influenced by gender, as is choice of leisure time activities, occupational choice, parental role, or mode of affectional expression (among many possible examples). These are, of course, mainly matters of cultural expectation and are learned reactions.

The child is aided in the development of gender role concepts by awareness and interpretation of responses which come from his own anatomy and physiology. Shuttleworth accounts for the greater male preoccupation with physical sex expression as compared to the female in this manner: Males, biologically, generally have more muscular power than females; they are better equipped for dangerous work or fighting. This physiological difference combined with social pressures which call for males to behave aggressively encourages them to be more active and forceful than females. This pattern of active, aggressive behavior logically carries over into their sexual behavior.

Differences in Male-Female Attitudes

Shuttleworth distinguished several factors which help to explain this difference in male-female attitudes toward sexual expression. The first is the male's greater awareness of genital responsiveness. Males from the very beginning and throughout their childhood years "...are more aware of their genitals and much more aware of the responsiveness of their genitals." Erections are an almost daily occurrence among all males. In his penis the male has an organ which can be seen, felt, named, and readily manipulated to bring about pleasure. Likewise his penis is the anatomical distinction which makes him clearly male. This greater awareness is intensified in adolescence with the production of semen in ejaculation. "Males behave as if they were under rather constant physiological pressures, strong in some individuals and weak in others, to obtain an orgasm which will release accumulated seminal fluids."

The development of an overt awareness of sexual feelings in the female is a more diffuse process, and generally comes at a later age. The learning is not so obviously associated with her physiology, but arises more clearly from her social and sexual contacts, particularly those with males. Nevertheless, a number of females do experience orgasm early in infancy or childhood. But the biological and social forces are intermingled in intricate ways and produce innumerable variations in behavior. Thus, one's role in the experience of intercourse and in the reproductive process is fixed in certain respects by one's biology, but even here learning and circumstance play an important part. Traditionally men have been the overt pursuers, women the coquettish, attracting, luring sex in the mating

process. These roles almost surely are conditioned by both physical and cultural factors. The sexual double standard (a standard which implies a differential according to sex membership, in the privileges and penalties extended to men and women) is suggested by many to be a cultural hangover from the past. According to Reiss, man's physical abilities afforded him economic, political, and military advantages that made it possible for him to define woman as inferior. Since he was in power in other areas, it is easy to conceive of his usurping special sexual privileges in addition.

The degree of passivity or aggressiveness which a male or a female exhibits in intercourse is also to some extent a matter of custom and desire regardless of the fact that the act of intercourse requires, biologically, penetration of the vagina by the penis. Of course, the experience of maturing a fetus in one's own body, carrying it through the period of gestation and finally giving life to the child in birth, provides an experience for women which is unavailable to men. Whether the biological experience of childbearing has any deep-seated or pervasive psychological consequences for male/female roles is a matter about which there are differing opinions, but no certainty. Biological differences, however, clearly make for certain unchangeable and divergent experiences that both differentiate the sexes and provide for a fascinating attraction and for complications in understanding and communication.

Childhood Learning About Sexuality

Children learn about their sexuality in many ways. Curiosity leads them to engage in exploratory activities involving themselves and other male or female children. They learn about their own bodies, the bodies of others, and what physiological reactions can be expected. They learn whether it is "safe" to experiment with sensations which adults call sexual and what sensations may come from experimentation. Adults commonly frown severely upon such activities. From parental reactions to these experiences children quite frequently derive their first deep-seated feelings toward sex.

The children may feel that adults cannot accept sexuality, or certain aspects of it, or, more likely, they develop a feeling that sex is threatening and that sexual expressions are to be regarded with guilt and shame.

Curiosity also prompts children to seek information about the reproductive processes, prenatal development and the roles of men and women in the sexual-procreative process. At this point more clearly than any other perhaps can be seen the divergence in the points of view of children and of adults concerning the children's intent. Many adults interpret the children's questions as "sex questions," but a more accurate interpretation is that they are questions designed to learn about life processes.

The Question of "Latency"

Traditionally, the years preceding puberty have been viewed as a period of "latency," as a phase of the child's psychosexual life when sexual development comes to a halt. However, this view is being increasingly challenged. Psychiatrist Harold I. Lief (in a private communication) has pointed out: "Latency does *not* involve an absolute decline of protosexual or sexual interests on the part of the post-Oedipal child, but a relative one at most. Between the ages of 5 and 11 (roughly) there is an enormous broadening of his range of interests as the child learns many things about the world in which he lives, and as he increases his contacts with his fellows. Curiosity about his family, including intense sexual curiosity, abates as he leaves the protective canopy of his family for the wider world. But his sexual interests are still there, somewhat masked by his involvement and commitment to the exploration of his milieu. If that environment is stagnant, or punitive, or otherwise inhibits his move outward to enlarge his horizons, the child's sexual curiosity and behavior may become active, even florid."

The research of Broderick and others has shown that, although there is a social segregation of the sexes in the middle grades which culminates at about age 12, there is *no* period in which the ma-

jority of boys and the great majority of girls are not interested in the opposite sex. This is shown by their conviction that they want to get married some day, by their reporting having a sweetheart, being in love (or having crushes), or liking love scenes in the movies. Only about 20% of the boys show the negative attitudes toward romance which are supposed to be typical of the latency period.

Is There a "Homosexual Stage?"

As youngsters move toward puberty, some go through a period (years 9–12 approximately) when their chief attachments are with members of their own sex. This has commonly been called the homosexual stage of development, but this concept, too, is questionable. There is no definite evidence that there is a homosexual stage during which all or most boys pass. During this period it is not uncommon, however, for exchanges of genital manipulation and exploration to occur. For most children probably the most traumatic part of such experiences is the horrified reaction of parents and/or other adults who may become aware of them, resulting in a conviction on the youngster's part that sex is dirty or evil. When they have an opportunity, children also engage in heterosexual play throughout prepuberty, but without the emotional commitment of love which comes later. The prepubertal age of "hating girls" is probably a period of consolidating masculinity more than of homosexual activity.

Puberty and Adolescence

A problem for children nearing the pubertal stage and those who have entered puberty is that they face physical and emotional changes and experiences for which they receive no explanation. Girls who are concerned about irregular menstruation or what they regard as atypical breast development, or boys who are concerned with masturbation or what they assume to be atypical penile size, experience difficulty in obtaining accurate and helpful information from parents, teachers or other adults. Most adults suppress or have forgotten their own childhood, or more often are too embarrassed to talk about it and consequently are neglectful of the extent to which worries and concerns about emerging sexuality trouble youth. Furthermore, many remain reticent about talking about these things.

Puberty arrives at different ages for different youth, ranging from ages 9—16 for girls and from 11—18 for boys. The average age is about two years earlier for girls than for boys. The available evidence suggests that the age of puberty has been lowering for both sexes over the past several decades. Ausubel notes a definite physical maturational sequence. "In girls the order is (1) initial enlargement of the breasts; (2) appearance of straight, pigmented pubic hair; (3) period of maximum growth; (4) kinky pubic hair; (5) the menarche; and (6) growth of axillary hair. In boys the corresponding order of pubescent phenomena is (1) beginning growth of the testes and penis; (2) appearance of straight, pigmented pubic hair; (3) early voice changes; (4) first ejaculation; (5) kinky pubic hair; (6) period of maximum growth; (7) axillary hair; (8) marked voice changes; and (9) development of the beard."

As the child enters adolescence he cannot be said to be fully mature sexually, yet he is reproductively and genitally mature and capable of reproduction. In our culture he now enters a period of stress. One source of stress is that he is physically ready for heterosexual genital expression, yet is denied it. In some other cultures this experience is more freely available to him than it has been in ours.

Masturbation becomes a central concern in early adolescence, particularly for the white middle class male, who almost universally engages in at least some masturbation during the teen years. Girls engage to a lesser extent. Although for a variety of reasons masturbation may become the focus of many anxieties and fears, the Committee on Adolescence of the Group for the Advancement of Psychiatry notes, it is essentially a "normal response to increased sexual development" which is "necessary to the control and integration of new urges and the working out of new relationships through trial acting and fantasy."

Their report on *Normal Adolescence* indicates how adolescent experiments with masturbation can serve normal development: "The adolescent learns that sexual excitement and engorgement and erection of the penis or the clitoris can be initiated at will, and that orgastic climax with the ensuing predictable subsidence of tension can be quickly brought about or repeatedly deferred by the manner of masturbation. This contributes to a developing sense of mastery over the sexual impulses and the new sexual capacities and helps the adolescent prepare for heterosexual relationships."

The ages at which children reach puberty and the time immediately following are likely to see a good many youth (almost certainly more boys than girls) involved in erotic play, genital examination, and experimentation with members of their own sex. These experiences are ordinarily referred to as homosexual experiences, but when the typical cultural stereotypes about homosexuality are applied, undue significance is given them. In the majority of cases, such experiences are likely to be simply a part of the development process. Curious about his own growth patterns and physical reactions and those of other youth, and denied the desired information, the adolescent in his desire to know may turn to sexual experimentation with others of the same sex. In this manner he learns something of what may be expected in the way of sexual manifestations in himself and others.

Most adolescents in the American culture are moving into some kind of heterosexual expression by the early teens. Actually, the age for moving into heterosexual activities is probably lowering, as the studies of Broderick and others show. The pattern of heterosexual expression seems ordinarily to follow a definite sequence, moving through embracing and kissing, and light caressing, to the more involved stages with heavy petting to intercourse itself. Of course unmarried youth vary in the extent and rapidity to which they progress through this pattern. In our culture many of the unmarried (more males than females) go through the entire sequence, ultimately experiencing intercourse; a few never begin until marriage. The timing of marriage, social class, religious and moral factors may influence their premarital experience.

Sexuality in Adulthood

In adulthood a wide variety and many combinations of sexual behavior patterns exist. Some persons will achieve heterosexual adjustment; others will be relying on masturbation or homosexual activities. Some may have come close to a renunciation of overt sexual expression. Those who have moved into heterosexuality, whether married or unmarried, will have developed a variety of patterns also. Some will have an adequate and satisfying sex life; others will find limited satisfaction. Some will be plagued with frigidity or impotence, or will be uninterested in sexual expression. Some will find sexual expression imposing intolerable burdens, or creating serious difficulties in human relations. Still others may be obsessive or compulsive in their sexual behavior. Former experiences and attitudes which the individual has sought to deny or repress may now crop out to interfere with effectiveness in the spousal or parental role.

Desirable, or desired, patterns of male and female interaction (role behavior) are often the source of confusion and conflict. This is particularly true since various social changes and technological developments have called long-standing patterns and practices into question. Education for women has resulted in giving them a competence which enables them to be self-supporting, and has opened opportunities in the business and professional world which were not available to them fifty years ago. At the same time it often requires readjustments in other family and spousal roles.

The perfection of contraceptive methods has given women the ability to control reproduction. The separation of sexual functioning from reproductive outcomes, if the sexual partners wish it, is now an accomplishable fact. This has made it more possible for women to concentrate directly and exclusively on the pleasure-sensory aspects of sex without the fear of pregnancy than ever before. The result is a blurring of former sharply and easily distinguishable gender roles, or an intrusion of one sex into the role practices commonly considered the prerogative of the other sex. This phenomenon is likely to increase in importance rather than to diminish.

Parental roles are structured around both biological and cultural differences between the sexes. The fact that the woman carries the child and has the mammary equipment for nursing the child (even though less and less often utilized) has cast her in the nurturant role, the father in a protective, supporting role. The fact that today's father is still prone to see himself as the disciplinarian, as the one to handle the family finances and to feel that he should be the family bread winner is partially a reflection of the extent to which traditional patterns become imbedded in current cultural attitudes. But here, too, role patterns are changing.

In marriage and parenthood the effects of immature, self-defeating sexual attitudes and experiences are often compounded. Parents have difficulties in teaching children because of their own unresolved feelings concerning sex or earlier sexual experiences. They are anxious about the incompetencies which they recognize in themselves, but at the same time are threatened by their children. For parents who have prided themselves on either their masculine prowess or feminine sexual attractiveness, the prospect of diminution or a fading of these qualities may be frightening; thus personal anxieties may be aroused by the emergent virility and sexual attractiveness of their children.

Menopause and Aging

Menopause for women and late middle age for men were formerly considered to signal the end of sex life. New attitudes and better knowledge of physiology and sexuality have changed this concept and have at the same time brought about a much more positive attitude among women toward the menopause. While men do not go through a definite or pronounced "change of life" as the female does, they do experience, but at different ages, a gradually diminishing virility and a slackening in their capacity to perform sexually. This is disturbing to many men, particularly to those who may have depended upon sexual performance to sustain their sense of masculinity and youthfulness. Their disturbance is even greater if the potency of their wives remains undiminished. Sexual expression in old age is more possible and more common than has usually been considered the case. Rubin has assembled research evidence indicating that so far as age is concerned there is no automatic cut-off to sexual relations, and that some individuals may continue their sex lives into the 70's, 80's, and even 90's. The frequency with which the 250 subjects of one study, age 60 to 90 years, engaged in sexual relations "ranged from once every other month to three times weekly." For some individuals frequency of intercourse actually increases in in the very late years.

Lawrence K. Frank has suggested that continued sexual functioning can come to have a very important psychological meaning in the later stages of life. He writes, in *The Conduct of Sex,* "Sex relations can provide a much needed and highly effective resource in the later years of life when so often men face the loss of their customary prestige and self-confidence and begin to feel old, sometimes long before they have begun to age significantly. The premature cessation of sexual functioning may accelerate physiological and psychological aging since disuse of any function usually leads to concomitant changes in other capacities. After menopause, women may find that continuation of sexual relations provides a much needed psychological reinforcement, a feeling of being needed and of being capable of receiving love and affection and renewing the intimacy they earlier found desirable and reassuring."

For both men and women hormonal replacement therapy and a new psychological outlook have proven useful in the later years.

Sexuality in the Family Life Cycle

Just as there is a cycle of sexual growth, development, and decline which characterizes individuals, so is there a cycle of sexual interaction which characterizes most married couples and their families. This pattern has its inception, for any particular couple, before marriage. In the premarital period couples necessarily respond to each other as sexual beings. They may respond by pretending that no sexual feeling exists between them. They may express their sexual feelings in varying degrees of physical intimacy, ranging from kissing and embracing through various degrees of petting to complete intercourse. They are also developing varying kinds of verbal and non-verbal communication patterns. Some may find it so difficult to talk about sex that all verbal references are avoided. Other couples—probably in increasing numbers as our culture becomes more open—are achieving satisfying and meaningful verbal communication about sexual matters.

With marriage comes the need for developing satisfying patterns of marital sexual relationships. For many couples this requires a considerable period of time. For most couples the frequency of marital intercourse is usually higher in the early months of marriage than it will be thereafter. The need for or the interest in dealing with variety in sexual expression commonly arises at this time and for some spouses variations are intolerable. So does planning for the coming and spacing of children and decisions upon the use or non-use of contraceptives. Adjustments in sexual patterns will be necessitated when pregnancy occurs. With many couples, as the Kinsey data revealed, changes and divergencies in the degree of sexual interest on the part of the partners must be faced. A common family cycle pattern is for wives, as they lose their inhibitions and feel more secure, to show more interest in intercourse than do their husbands. The declining interest on the part of men in the later years may be due to their absorption in business or professional activities, a declining physical capacity, taking wives for granted, the routine quality that has been allowed to creep into their lives, or a possible need of change and variety in sexual stimuli if they are to remain responsive.

Parent-Child Relations

The presence of children may have considerable effect on the parents' sexual patterns. Parents must become concerned with the problems and techniques of sex education. They are often so miseducated themselves and so ill at ease with questions that some children, becoming aware of the disquiet of their parents, never ask. Other children learn after an experience or two with their parents' uneasiness that such questions are better unasked. And so may begin a process which creates a communication chasm between children or youth and their parents so far as sexual matters are concerned.

By the time their children have reached adolescence, American parents typically find themselves unable to discuss intimate aspects of sexual behavior with them. This holds true whether it is their own children's sexual problems or questions which need discussion. This may add significantly to the strained relations that are likely to occur between parents and adolescent children, and in turn be related to the push on the part of children for economic independence and the conflicting need they feel for continuing to belong to their families. Then, too, children may not be able to discuss freely all aspects of their sex lives with their parents. They need to develop their own separate sense of sex identity as growing persons who will leave their own family and found a new one. Consequently for many families this period is one of uneasiness and tension for all. The parents hope that their sons and daughters will go through their adolescence without "getting someone into trouble" or "getting into trouble." The parents breathe a secret but a very real sigh of relief when their children are safely married.

The gulf between parent and child is to a large extent probably inevitable, with its roots perhaps lying in the difficulty that children have in accepting their parents as sexual beings. At any rate, it points up the fact that adults outside of the family can often be useful to young people in sex education and counseling, largely because they are not personally involved with each other. Many adults need guidance from professional sources, since new questions about sexual needs and expression arise as individuals move from one stage of life to another. As spouses go on in their marriage, or as single persons age (our society has never displayed any real concern for the sexual needs or problems of the middle-aged or older single person), cultural

inhibitions result in their sexual difficulties and needs becoming more and more exclusively their own private concern. They are seldom discussed even with physicians.

Conclusion

Certain developments seem to insure that our concepts concerning the nature and place of sex throughout the life cycle will continue to change. A feeling still exists among many that the only natural and proper use of sex requires its focus to be upon the reproductive process. The separation of reproductive outcomes from sexual functioning is certain to lay an increasing emphasis on the use of sex for communication, intimacy, and the enhancement of enjoyment. Over man's long history, his existence on the planet as a species was undoubtedly precarious and it is understandable that he should have been intensely preoccupied with the procreative aspects of sex. But today, the grave dangers reside in overpopulation. This, plus the fact that reproduction can now occur at will rather than by chance, necessitates a reassessment of the place of sex not only in the life cycle of individuals but in society as a whole.

The relation of sexual functioning to individual development and to fulfilling relationships, to leisure time, to full human functioning from childhood through old age, must be worked through in terms of a humane philosophy geared to our modern age.

Selected Bibliography

1. Ausubel, D. P.: "Physiological Aspects of Pubescence," *Theory and Problems of Adolescent Development*. New York: Grune & Stratton, 1954, p. 95.
2. Broderick, C. B.: "Sexual Behavior Among Pre-adolescents," *Journal of Social Issues*, 22(2), April 1966.
3. Broderick, C. B.: "Normal Socio-sexual Development," in Broderick, C. B., and Bernard, J., eds.: *The Individual, Sex, and Society: A SIECUS Handbook for Teachers and Counselors*. Baltimore: The Johns Hopkins Press, 1969.
4. Committee on Adolescence, Group for the Advancement of Psychiatry: *Normal Adolescence*, GAP Report No. 68, February 1968. (419 Park Avenue South, New York, N.Y. 10016, $1.50)
5. Gagnon, J. H.: "Sexuality and Sexual Learning in the Child," *Psychiatry*, 28(3), August 1965.

6. Halverson, H. M.: "Genital and Sphincter Behavior of the Male Infant," *Journal of Genetic Psychology,* 14:121-22, January 1966.

7. Money, J.: *Sex Errors of the Body.* Baltimore: The Johns Hopkins Press, 1968.

8. Money, J.: "Anomalies of Sexual Differentiation," in Broderick, C.B. and Bernard, J., eds.: *The Individual, Sex, and Society: A SIECUS Handbook for Teachers and Counselors.* Baltimore: The Johns Hopkins Press, 1969.

9. Peterson, J. A.: *Married Love in the Middle Years.* New York: Association Press, 1968.

10. Reiss, I. L.: *Premarital Sexual Standards in America.* New York: Free Press of Glencoe, 1960.

11. Rubin, I.: *Sexual Life After Sixty.* New York: Basic Books, 1965. (Paperback edition, New American Library)

12. Sherfey, M. J.: "The Evolution and Nature of Female Sexuality in Relation to Psychoanalytic Theory," *Journal of the American Psychoanalytic Association,* 14:28-128, January 1966.

13. Shuttleworth, F. K.: "A Bio-social and Developmental Theory of Male and Female Sexuality," *Marriage and Family Living,* 22:163-70, May 1959, (now *Journal of Marriage and the Family)*

16

Change, Conflict, and Couple Styles

by Lawrence R. Allman
and Dennis T. Jaffe

The couple is the basic building block of the central social system in society—the family. The family, in turn, is the social unit in which our most important relationships take place, the setting in which people grow, mature, and express themselves. Rather than conceptualizing human conflicts as belonging to individuals, and lying within a particular individual's psyche, a family systems perspective is emerging which views difficulty as taking place within a whole social unit. It is the whole system of relationships in a family, or the whole pattern of relating in a couple, which represents the problem or pathology, not a dysfunctioning or defective individual. This essay presents some of the basic problems facing the modern family social unit, and then looks at some of the basic issues, patterns, and styles facing the couple within the family. With this background, we explore the recurrent dysfunctional relationship patterns that can take place within a couple from the perspective of the family oriented psychotherapist, whose task is to help make relationships more functional. The application of a systems perspective to the development of couple difficulties offers an example of how developmental difficulties can be found in the growth of social systems, and need not necessarily be expressed or described from the perspective of the individuals involved, and their particular psychological dynamics and personalities.

The Family in Transition

Sociologist and family historian William Goode (1963) has summarized the recent history of the family. He feels that the industrial revolution, urbanization, and the increasing pace of social change have created a new set of social conditions, which in turn have created, or at least been reflected in, new styles of family relationship. These social forces have led to increasing isolation of the nuclear family from its extended kin and from integration into a consistent and enduring wider community. Families often migrate every few years, as the job marketplace demands, so that any friendships and relationships outside of its borders are only temporary. In addition, because of rapid cultural change, the wisdom of the previous generation, as Margaret Mead (1970) points out, becomes less relevant. Thus today, youth is more valued than wisdom. With the generation gap and the current dizzying pace of social change, children consider themselves "hipper," more aware and in the know, than their parents.

With all this change, a great emotional burden is placed on the marital couple, who must meet more and more of each other's emotional needs. The contemporary shift in relationships is away from a marital tie based on traditional obligations and roles, and often arranged by the family, to the situation in which the couples' main function is to be companions and helpmates to each other. Where previously a couple had many extended family relationships to lean on for support, companionship, and information, with the isolation and fragmentation of the nuclear family more and more pressure is placed on the couple. Increasingly, couples today move around, often far from other relatives and lifelong friends, and have only each other available.

In the past decade there has been another set of upheavals in the family, the outcome of which is uncertain. For a century there has been a movement for the social equality of women. While previously women were denied many political and social rights, and were felt to exist primarily as the subservient property of the breadwinner—husband—that situation is fast becoming obsolescent. Women now have full citizenship, and the women's movement has focused on gaining economic and social equality for women—equal work and equal pay with men, opportunity for employment at all stages of life, and an end to economic discrimination.

Such changes have consequences within the household and in the couple. Traditional social theory defined male and female roles. Men were said to be concerned with *instrumental* concerns—earning money, making decisions, and rational tasks. While the women's role was *expressive*—maintaining emotional bonds, especially with children, maintaining the house and a warm home environment, and providing support to the man who worked outside the home. Because such roles were common in many societies, social scientists often argued they were biologically determined, inevitable, and part of the natural order of things. All that is now in question, as women are demanding the right to choose their roles.

The male-female division of labor in the family, while still the norm, is challenged by many, and modified in many households. A majority of women now work outside the home, and many contribute substantial shares of the family income. With their financial contribution, they have demanded help with household and childrearing, either from society in the form of daycare and domestic help, or from the husband in the form of sharing tasks. Many families now have shared, or symmetrical, rather than divided, or complementary roles. However, in many households the male and the female hold different views of what ought to be. Thus the issue of household and marital roles is a source of conflict for many couples, and is a reason why many couples turn to counseling: they seek a mediator to help them redefine the terms of their relationship and the division of labor in the household. The conflict in the relationship may not stem from any personality of personal difficulties, but from a plain and simple conflict of interest and values, and can sometimes be conceptualized as similar to a labor dispute (Scanzoni, 1972).

The other social forces changing the family are the increasing openness of sexuality, leading to many forms of extramarital, premarital, and now post-marital sexual activity. Aided by improved contraceptive devices and liberalized abortion laws, sex and marriage no longer are believed to be inseparable (although the evidence is that more people believe this than actually practice it). Sexual expression is more and more being considered a personal need, and a personal right. Another change is the rise in divorce and separation. Now, a couple marrying has only a 50–50 chance of remaining together through their lives, although it is hard to project into the future. Most states have eased the restrictions on divorce, and no-fault divorce and nonpunitive property settlements are becoming the norm. It is getting to be as easy to divorce as to get married, and the social stigma and negative feelings about divorce are lessened. The adoption of these new family forms and lifestyles is increasing, even though the nuclear family remains the favorite of the wide majority. Many relationship issues stem from the difficulty of choice among the variety of alternatives, and the human tendency to want to try new things and to be confused by the changes that result from them.

The Changing Couple Contract

Each couple makes a series of agreements, some explicit and spoken, and some covert and unspoken. These agreements are their *contract*. It includes such elements as where they will live, who will work, how household arrangements will be made, financial sharing, whether they will have children, who will be responsible for what, and how will they relate to friends and family. While some couples spend a great deal of time together before marriage or some formally live together sharing their ideas and feelings, the marriage contract should not be thought of as a one-time event, which can be located in time and place. In fact, like everything else about relationships, the contract between a couple is an evolving entity, which can be reopened at any time by either mate. For example, a wife may decide that she no longer accepts the traditional housewife role, after bearing a child and several years of marriage. Her husband may want her to continue as she was, but they now will have a conflict and have to renegotiate. People enter into a couple for many reasons, such as to escape from their families of origin, to raise children, or to obtain money, security, sexual satisfaction, companionship, social status, or love. These reasons affect the nature of their couple contract.

Just as the individual has a life cycle, so too do a couple and a family. A couple and family are units continually adapting to new situations and crises by modifying their structures. For example, no change is so profound as the emergence of a third person out of a couple, and the birth of a child profoundly and permanently alters the nature of a couple. They must look to their future, and must adjust to the needs of a person outside themselves, who is at first totally dependent on them. After children are grown, a couple enters into yet another new situation, a post-parental stage of life.

In their couple and family relationships people tend to *replicate* or recreate the styles of adaptation and meeting their needs which they learned in their families of origin. This was first pointed out by Sigmund Freud, who noted that in their couples, and even in the relationship of the patient to the psychoanalyst, his patients tended to act out the patterns they used in relating to their own parents. The dysfunctional consequence of this pattern is that the therapist or mate is *not* one's parent, but a peer, a member of one's generation, and has different expectations. This replication of family patterns can lead to conflict. In addition, the other member of a couple is replicating the patterns *he* or *she* learned in his or her family, and the resulting interplay can lead to many levels of conflict. Each member of the couple may want his mate to act as parent, or may transfer feelings he had about his parents or family to the new situation, without regard to whether the same situation still exists. Thus, a man may get angry at little things his mate does, when in fact the anger results from a pattern of interaction he had with his parents. People who learn to make demands, throw tantrums, or inject their own needs without asking others for help, will transfer these patterns to their new couple relationships. One may also replicate previous situations outside the family; for example, a tragedy or rejection by a lover can lead to feelings that will create patterns in one's next relationship. Family therapists spend many sessions trying to help couples unravel the aspects of their relationship which involve replication of early family patterns, and aspects that arise out of their actual relationship.

The social context of one's life prior to the formation of the couple further shapes the needs we seek from our mate, and the patterns that result. For example, if a woman moves from her family home immediately into a couple out of fear of being alone, this fear may cloud her ability to see the other person clearly. Or if one falls in love immediately after the death of a parent, the new love may be based on the need to fill the emotional gap. Thus, the needs we seek in a couple have several sources:

1. Our personal history in our family of origin;
2. The nature of our individual social context when we form the relationship;
3. Our personal fantasies and expectations surrounding love.

Conflict in Couples

A couple relationship is a growing, changing entity, as each member strives to meet his or her changing needs, asking something from the mate and offering something in return. This give and take has been labeled "sexual bargaining"(Scanzoni, 1972), and the way in which the members communicate and meet their needs creates a unique style common to a couple.

The couple is at times a harmonious, stable organism, with each member giving and getting, feeling good and offering good feeling. However, just as commonly, couples find themselves in conflict. When any two people with different needs relate to each other, conflict can result. One person may want something that the other may not know about, or want to give, or not want to give without obtaining something in return. The issues in conflict may be sex, relations with in-laws, how money will be spent, what job one member may take, what to do in their spare time, how to raise the children, what to wear, how they should or should not have acted in a situation, personal aspirations and values, or even who will make decisions.

It is important to note that conflict in itself is neither unnatural nor pathological. Many people have been raised to feel that any open conflict is wrong, and that the presence of conflict signals trouble in a couple or family. Such families habitually sweep their differences under the rug. One can usually be sure that differences do exist, that no family can really exist without conflict among its members (Raush et al. 1974).

Indeed, conflict is the way people usually signal their need to negotiate, and it often serves as a mechanism for a family to begin to adapt to a new situation. Conflict is not necessarily destructive, or even an angry or emotional state of affairs. It merely signals a difference, and as such it needs to be aired.

The issue is the way in which conflict is part of the couple relationship. If a certain area is continually in conflict—for example, how to spend leisure time—then we might ask why there are always differences but never a resolution. We begin to suspect that the conflict is being used by the couple for a very different reason than to air differences of opinion. For example, one member of the couple may have inherited standards or attitudes from his family of origin and may be applying them to his wife. She may argue that she can do what she wants with her time. Another possibility is that couples are not aware of what they really are in conflict about. A fight over time together, for example, may be a fight over whether the husband really loves the wife. She equates time together with love, whereas he has a need to spend time apart, or with his men friends, which she in turn takes as a rejection. They fight over time because they do not see its underlying significance. The issue for a couple in conflict, then, may be simply to understand what they are fighting about, not to solve the overt reason for the conflict. That is why, for example, we often see a couple fighting continually about an issue that an outside person feels could be solved quickly and effortlessly by a logical compromise. Humor about couples often makes this point. Our comic strips and television shows continually make fun of marital conflict, and the laughter of the audience stems from the recognition of its universality.

Couples seek professional help when they feel that negotiation is not working, or that the relationship is not getting them what they want or need. There is usually a precipitating incident, or a focus for the complaint or conflict that a couple brings into therapy. However, these symptoms, complaints, or difficulties are simply the arena in which basic issues in their relationship are being expressed. The family therapist, marriage counselor, or psychotherapist thus shows them that his or her task is not simply to help them resolve the specific issue facing them at the time. The resolution of that difficulty depends on their understanding, how they express their needs to each other, and what they want from the relationship. Rather than fight about how to act, or what to do, then, a couple in family or marital therapy soon find themselves talking about what their basic needs are, how they feel about each other, and the covert contract or understandings that underlie their relationship. The process of family therapy, then, allows the couple to look at their own relationship, and the role of conflict within it, rather than simply finding a solution to a particular conflict.

Relationship Patterns

Family theorists have tried to define the various patterns of couple relationship, and to define couple problems using those basic patterns. Anthropologist Gregory Bateson noted that the patterns of communication and relationship within a couple could be thought of as a series of reciprocal interactions between two people. He found that certain patterns or differentiations of relationship could appear in a couple. And he noted two basic forms of interaction in relationship—*complementary* and *symmetrical* (Watzlawick et al., 1967).

A complementary relationship is characterized by inequality and maximization of differences, in which a statement of one member is followed by a different and opposite response by the other. This pattern is found in all superior-subordinate relationships, and is the classical couple pattern, wherein the male is dominant and the female subservient. These common roles have even been institutionalized as male and female roles, and until recently male power was a social imperative that was never questioned. A symmetrical relationship is characterized by equality and minimization of differences. Examples of such relationships are among peers, in social gatherings, where what one person says or does is repeated by the other person. The more modern companionship or shared role style of couple relationship is symmetrical rather than complementary. Symmetrical relationships may also be competitive, in cases where each person tries to make a similar response, but do it better. Games of one-upmanship are a certain kind of escalating symmetrical relationship, as each one tries to top the other.

It should be noted that a whole relationship does not have to be characterized purely by one pattern or the other. Complementarity or symmetry is a characteristic of a particular interaction, not necessarily a whole relationship. Many couples switch from one mode to the other in different situations. And in different situations one or another member may be dominant or subservient, depending upon in whose sphere of influence or expertise or power an interaction takes place. It should also be noted that neither pattern is better nor worse than the other. They each have their functions, and a flexible couple presumably will draw on both variations at different times in their relationship. A couple rigidly stuck in one pattern probably will have difficulty adapting to environmental demands. Many couples do have one or the other style which characterizes much of their relationship. This pattern determines the *structure* of their interactions, whereas particular issues such as household duties, sex, money, and children form its *content*. The structure or communication pattern determines the roles and power distribution which arise in the couple.

Psychiatrist Murray Bowen felt that the basic task facing a person in an intimate relationship is to differentiate his or her unique, individual self from the family unit. The first basic struggle is for the child and then the adolescent gradually to break free from the family of origin. Bowen viewed psychosis as the classic example of the inability or failure to differentiate a self. Within this basic framework, he redefined the problems faced by a couple in terms of relationship patterns. The major difficulties faced by a couple are:

1. For the individuals to feel whole and unique and independent while remaining within the context and security of the relationship. Couples that seem to do everything together, and can't exist on their own, for example, can be thought of as enmeshed, while those that never seem to be together or have anything in common except a name, could be called estranged. Either extreme presents difficulty for the maintenance of the equilibrium between the individual and the relationship.

2. The inability of the couple to differentiate between structural and content issues. For example, they will fight over many things, but the real issue is a struggle over who has the structural power to make decisions in the relationship.

3. The inability to see the patterns of the relationship, resulting in the feeling of being controlled in some way and unable to feel free and meet one's needs and goals within the relationship system. Such people talk as if they are victims of the relationship rather than partial creators of it, and they feel powerless to create change. They don't see ways out.

4. Problems posed by life stresses within the family as well as internal life stresses. All types of stress affect the equilibrium and functioning of the family unit and its relationships. Change in any part affects the whole.

5. Problems of differentiation between levels of communication. For example, a couple may be placing each other in double binds, or asking contradictory things of each other, or arguing past each other.

Thus, people experience the whole range of feelings within couple relationships. To the extent that the couple goes well, no individual problem or life stress is too big to be managed. Relationships are a form of "social dance" in which each person develops a style and pattern which he follows. Some move fast and are always on the go, some are constantly in contact and some never are, and others move slowly or always seem to let life pass them by. A healthy relationship is one in which the couple is able to adapt a relationship pattern which meets its individual needs, and the needs of the social environment. Functional couples are usually flexible, and do not have a rigid or stereotyped response to every situation, just as functional people are those who have a flexible range of individual responses to situations. Couples experience distress when they do not feel comfortable and safe in their relationships, when conflict or stress gets out of hand. While they select individual symptoms or signs as their specific problem by looking more deeply we can say that couple conflict results from problems in the structural patterns of relationship. We will now look at four specific couple relationship patterns, and present case studies which illustrate how they lead to difficulties.

The Cooperative Dilemma

The word *cooperate* has such good connotations that it is hard to think of how a couple could cooperate too much, or how cooperation could lead to difficulty. Yet it can be a potent source of personal alienation and boredom in a couple. In order to survive as a species we must be able to cooperate as a means of resolving conflict. In most conflicts, for example, there is cooperation framing the conflict in that the conflicting parties agree to a set of underlying rules which guides their conflict (Watzlawick et al., 1967). In couples, the rules might be to avoid physical violence or nasty threats, whereas among nations, the rules might be to avoid the use of nuclear weapons and not murder each other's ambassadors. But while cooperation underlies all of society, it presents a problem when it is allowed to overshadow all conflict, or all individual difference. When a couple lives in fear of any conflict, or any difference of opinion, then they may experience the relationship as personally deadening, because they negate themselves and their unique reactions in the name of cooperation.

The following is an example of a cooperating couple experiencing great psychological distress. First we will outline their presenting symptom, and then describe how that symptom fits into the context of their relationship.

The Browns were referred to an outpatient psychiatric clinic by their family doctor after Bernice Brown attempted suicide upon discovering that her husband, Harris, was having an affair with his secretary.

The Browns' met while attending a large midwestern university. They dated all through college and married a week after they graduated. They both came from large families in which the parents fought a lot. Since they "loved" each other so much, they promised each other never to fight as their parents had. They each were so afraid of conflict they adopted a style of relating in which they avoided saying or doing anything they thought the other would disapprove of. Before doing anything, each one would think what the other's reaction would be, and behave solely according to what he or she thought the other needed. They each lived for the other, but not for themselves. Thus, Bernice would be submissive to avoid conflict, and Harris would withdraw when he felt needy so he didn't upset or burden Bernice.

Their friends described them as an ideal couple. They lived an orderly, polite, predictable existence. Each clearly knew his or her own role and what to expect from the other. Their sexual life had dwindled from very active in their first year together, to a point now where they seldom had sexual relations. They never talked about this change in behavior.

The Browns exemplify the point at which the virtues of cooperation are overshadowed by the negative effects of avoiding the confrontation and expression of difference necessary to sustain an intimate relationship. The polite distance they maintained from each other, and their habit of assuming they knew the other's needs without voicing their assumptions, prevented them from really hearing each other's needs. They thus did not respond to changes in their lives. For example, when Harris had a business failure, he chose to bring his pain to his mistress rather than upset Bernice and possibly upset the order of his life. So each felt alone yet together, and was unable to share his or her innermost feelings. Over time, each built up resentment and frustration which culminated in Harris'

affair and the explosion that resulted in Bernice's angry attempt to kill herself, presumably both to get even and to express her own pain and frustration.

The Competitive Dilemma

Like cooperation, competition is also a necessary interaction pattern. In our highly competitive society, where competition for school grades and in sports starts early and continues through life, the notion persists that to be good is to be better or more powerful than anyone else around. One does not have merely to satisfy oneself, one has to satisfy oneself in relation to others. In competition a person seeks to maximize his gains by differentiating and surpassing the others around him. Such competition is necessary, to some extent, for species survival. However, as we noted before, competition exists within a backdrop of cooperation and basic agreement, otherwise it will get out of hand.

Competitive couples are in a continual struggle for power and supremacy over the other. Their communication is often sparked by "put-downs," "one-upsmanship," and "holier-than-thou" attitudes. While a couple can enjoy a competitive zeal, when the competition becomes endless it becomes a personal drain. Every arena of personal contact is a competitive game, involving striving and maneuvering, whether it be about who is more sexual, is a better worker, a wittier person, or just a better person in whatever category is in question. The following is an example of such a couple.

The Davises came to therapy after a massive fight that ended in Sid Davis beating up his wife Terry. Sid and Terry met shortly after college. They had both been campus leaders, and were both only children. They liked to play tennis, Monopoly, and any other form of competitive behavior. They had frequent disagreements, and confrontations, and enjoyed disagreeing and arguing. However, over time they fought more often, and the fights would escalate into full-scale conflict. Each of them felt he or she was "right" and the other "wrong," and wouldn't give in. Many fights focused on who was "boss" and "who knew more" about whatever they were arguing about. Their friends saw them as a lively, engaging couple who were fun to be around, although there was always an air of tension and playful hostility around them.

The Davises' interaction always involved power struggles and issues of control, struggles which neither could win decisively. Their relationship was often exciting and challenging, but was not a restful or safe place for either of them because everything was a competition. They could never let down their guard and loosen up. Being only children heightened their personal need to be the one and only in the relationship, and before they met, they each had lifestyles in which they were centers of attention and leaders. They couldn't relate to each other without one being in control, and the other would never allow that.

The Undifferentiated Family

In a relationship, differentiation is the degree to which members of the relationship experience themselves as both belonging to the relationship as well as being different from the relationship. The process of maturation is one of differentiation of the individual self from the family. The individual becomes more complex and differentiated as a system as he or she develops. Differentiation is important to a couple, because if one cannot experience oneself as different from one's mate, then one cannot be intimately involved with the other as a person. An undifferentiated person only relates to himself, and cannot be intimate with others, if they are experienced as only extensions of himself. The degree of differentiation of an individual from the family is used by Bowen and others as a measure of psychological health.

Minuchin and Montalvo (1967) looked at the interaction in families with emotionally disturbed children. They saw two polar family styles, which they called the *enmeshed* and the *disengaged* family. In the enmeshed family, "attempts on the part of one member to change elicits fast complementary resistence on the part of others" (Minuchin et al., 1967, p. 358). A change in any single person is experienced as a threat to the whole system, and the others act to block all change. Clinicians see this when one member of a family begins to improve, perhaps as a result of a hospitalization or individual therapy, the other members react to neutralize that change, doing such things as upsetting the person again or taking him out of treatment on some pretext. Thus things remain the same.

The enmeshed family lacks differentiation between individual members. They form what Bowen calls an "undifferentiated family mass." This deficiency is demonstrated by their inability to establish boundaries between each other as well as between generations. In such families, everyone acts as if they know what the other feels, wants, and likes, and the people regularly intrude upon each other's space and minds, all in the guise of being helpful. The following is such a family.

Sandra and Paul Williams came to therapy complaining that their sexual relations had become nonexistent. They also fought a lot about their relationships with their respective parents.

Sandra and Paul met in high school. They both had fathers who were alcoholic, and had experienced many family fights while children. They were both frightened of life and thought that love would overcome all. They were a clingy couple, going everywhere together. They felt they couldn't survive without the other. If Paul spent an evening with the boys, Sandra would be upset and angry, and Paul similarly would be angry if Sandra had a good time without him. They experienced themselves as a unit against the world. Even though they felt like one, they fought continually about the rules of their relationship as well as how to treat their in-laws. They basically could not establish themselves as distinctly separate individuals in their relationships to their parents or to each other. Their fights often ended with both crying and feeling like two desperate children, clinging to each other in the face of disaster. They had few close friends, because outside friendships threatened their relationship. They were like two symbiotic animals who needed each other to survive.

There is a lack of personal boundaries in the undifferentiated couple. The Williams' were unable to see

each other as separate, and further, could not separate their couple from each of their families of origin.

The Disengaged Relationship

The disengaged family is characterized as "an atomistic field; family members have long moments in which they move as in isolated orbits, unrelated to each other. They act as parts of a system so loosely interlocked that it challenges a clinician's notion that a change in one part of a system will be followed by compensating change in other parts (Minuchin et al., 1967, p. 354)." Such families show little interaction, intimacy, or even structure. Their boundaries are rigid and do not overlap; each person clearly knows his place and role. Such people often become enmeshed with social service agencies as a reaction against their isolation. However, their inability to form primary relationships within their families makes them likely victims of these institutions. They often are labeled "sick," "crazy," or pathological in other ways because of their lack of contact. Such families are so detached that the bonds fail to provide enough psychological nurturance to sustain the struggles fo life without external support systems. They are psychologically deprived, and if the deprivation is severe enough, the deficit will be hard to overcome in later life. They never know how to create a relationship because they have never experienced one.

The disengaged couple provide little nurturance for each other and their offspring. They show few signs of physical affection. How much they are aware of a need for closeness determines how much distress this type of relationship creates for those within them. For example, a woman in a disengaged couple who had previously experienced a close attachment in her family of origin would find it very unsatisfying, whereas someone with little primary contact in her family may find the distance of this kind of relationship comfortable. The amount of distress corresponds to the individual's need for closeness. People in such relationships often are so far apart that they don't even know what is wrong with the relationship, and even less about what feelings or events happen to other family members. Friends of such a family experience them as moving through life on separate courses, as in the following example.

Fred Smith was arrested for drunken driving. His wife, Ruth, never knew he had drinking problems. When he was in jail, Fred confessed to Ruth his feelings of being a failure in business and as a husband. She admitted she felt empty, and used medication to dull her psychological pain. They sought counseling not knowing what their problem was, but just feeling desperate.

Fred came from a family of seven while Ruth was an only child. Fred had constantly to escape to friends' houses to avoid the continual confusion in his house, while Ruth was the "star" of her family with all of her needs being met without her even having to ask. They went to junior college together and married after graduation. Fred did well in business, and Ruth quickly became pregnant and involved in the role of mother. Their life was routine and orderly. Each of them knew his or her role at home and rigidly adhered to it. There was very little give and take in their relationship. Over time they lived as if they were roommates, not even intimately involved with each other. They both had extramarital affairs, which were easy because the other would never probe or suspect.

They related to each other from a great distance. Both Fred and Ruth came from families in which they never learned to identify their own needs. The distance and size of Fred's family allowed him to find his place without engaging in conflict to differentiate his needs. Ruth's family was so busy taking care of her that she never learned to ask for what she wanted because she learned that others should know what she wanted. Each of them married with undifferentiated needs and a passive style of relating to their desires. Neither had a model of negotiating for their needs, so they fell into a relationship which maintained distance, satisfying their needs largely outside the relationship, Fred in business and Ruth as a mother. Each resented the other for not being more responsive, but they never confronted each other with their resentment.

Effective Relationships

We have seen that in each of the four clinical cases presented, the explosion or crisis that led to therapy was merely the outcome of long consequences of the couple's style and pattern of relationship. The crisis finally exposed the lifetime of dysfunctional relationship. None of the couples had its needs met in the relationship, and as a family, none was able to respond adaptively to environmental stress or demands.

It should be noted once more that there are no pure types of relationships. Every relationship can be defined along the scales of complementarity/symmetry, cooperativeness/competitiveness, and enmeshment/disengagement. Every couple stands somewhere on all three scales. Thus, a competitive couple might exhibit both complementary and symmetrical patterns, a certain degree of enmeshment or disengagement, and occasional flashes of cooperation. A healthy relationship has elements of all these patterns within the context of a *flexible* style. A pathological or dysfunctional relationship can be defined as the loss of this flexible, orderly balance, resulting in a rigidly fixed pattern of interaction or a disorganized, chaotic style. For example, a championship football team is one in which the members cooperate as a unit within the contest of a competitive interaction with another team. They show a high level of individual role differentiation, yet are enmeshed in a productive pattern of interaction called plays. There is also some competition among team members for scores and positions. Too much competition within the team is dysfunctional, as is too much disengagement among individuals. What is needed is a productive balance of all factors. It is the same with a couple or family, which must develop a system that adapts to the needs of each of the individuals within it, and of the demands of the environment around it.

The role of a therapist is to help the members of a couple see the dysfunctional, rigid, or inappropriate aspects of their pattern of relationship, and build in new responses toward greater flexibility. By looking beyond the particular issues that a couple brings to therapy, theorists have begun to define patterns and regularities of couple relationships as systems.

References

ACKERMAN, NATHAN. TREATING THE TROUBLED FAMILY. New York; Basic Books, 1966.

FERBER, A., MENDELSOHN, M., and NAPIER, A. THE BOOK OF FAMILY THERAPY. New York: Science House, 1972.

GOODE, WILLIAM. WORLD REVOLUTION AND FAMILY PATTERNS. New York: Free Press, 1963.

HALEY, J. and HOFFMAN, L., eds., TECHNIQUES OF FAMILY THERAPY. New York: Basic Books, 1967.

HALEY, J. and HOFFMAN, L., eds., TECHNIQUES OF FAMILY Stratton, 1971.

MEAD, MARGARET. CULTURE AND COMMITMENT. New York: Norton, 1970.

MINUCHIN, S., MONTALVO, B., GUERNEY, B., ROSMAN, B., and SCHIESNER, F., FAMILIES OF THE SLUMS. New York: Basic Books, 1967.

MINUCHIN, SALVADOR. FAMILIES AND FAMILY THERAPY. Cambridge, Mass.: Harvard University Press, 1974.

RAUSH, H., BARRY, W., HERTEL, R., and SWAIN, M., COMMUNICATION CONFLICT AND MARRIAGE. San Francisco. Jossey-Bates, 1974.

RAVICH, R. and WYDEN, B. PREDICTABLE PAIRING. New York: Peter Wyden, 1974.

RUBIN, ZICK. LIKING AND LOVING. New York: Holt, Rinehart and Winston, 1973.

SATIR, VIRGINIA. CONJOINT FAMILY THERAPY. Palo Alto, Cal.: Science and Behavior Books. 1967.

SCANZONI, JOHN. SEXUAL BARGAINING. Englewood Cliffs, N.J.: Prentice-Hall, 1972.

WATZLAWICK, P., BEAVAN, L., and JACKSON, D., THE PRAGMATICS OF HUMAN COMMUNICATION. New York: Norton, 1967.

17

Man + Woman

A Consumer's Guide to Contemporary Pairing Patterns Including Marriage

by CARLFRED B. BRODERICK

Now! At Last! The new fall lineup of the very latest plans and styles for satisfactory living together. The list includes a dazzling variety of sizes and shapes, options and accessories, never before made available to the general public, and the cost is surprisingly low. You pay your money and take your choice, and may you live happily ever after. Or at least until next Tuesday.

Dr. Broderick is Executive Director of the Marriage and Family Counseling Center at the University of Southern California and editor of the *Journal of Marriage and the Family*.

The man-woman relationship has always been a popular but variegated commodity and the behavioral sciences have never been loath to set up guidelines for consumers. Until recently the "rational" guidelines for choosing a suitable partner and developing a fulfilling relationship were pretty much agreed upon by the large body of "experts" with only an occasional dissenting voice to add color and provide a straw man for the main position.

Today all that has changed. The tide of books and articles advocating the widest variety of styles of pairing has reached flood proportions. As if this were not enough there are a seemingly infinite choice of lectures, classes, workshops, marathons and training sessions available to help the couple enrich their relationship (each according to its own lights).

Even the most enrichment oriented couple might get confused as to whether it was best to strive toward an Open Marriage, Mini-Marriage, Multilateral Marriage or Trial Marriage, or perhaps simply Honest Sex, Total Sex, or Desensitized Intimacy (in the latter case they get to watch several hours worth of filmed heterosexual and homosexual intercourse, masturbation, and fun and games in living color). Clearly there is need for a Consumers' Guide so that you can see at a glance just what the basic issues are that differentiate one approach from another.

After considerable sifting it is possible to reduce the number of key issues to five. The anatomy of most of the New Visions and also of most of the Traditional Wisdoms can be clearly viewed when their positions on each of these five issues are determined. To plot the profile of each movement would be too great a task for one brief article. Instead we will lay out each of the five issues and some of the most frequently discussed positions on each issue. The reader can then analyze the features of competing pairing patterns or even develop his own model, tailored to his own position on all five issues.

Dolls courtesy of Mattel, Inc. ©1972   Illustrations by Jackie Fukumoto

ISSUE #1

FREEDOM FROM PARENTHOOD
VS.
FULFILLMENT THROUGH PARENTHOOD

Position A: Anti-Natal (Utopian or Brave New World Variety)

In the best of all possible worlds children would be the wards of the state freeing all adults to pursue careers, fulfillment, etc. without encumbrance. Whether in the Huxlean fantasy where children are conceived in a test tube, developed in a bottle and decanted into a state nursery or in the more pragmatic mode advocated by Plato and Marx and Engels where the children are born to mothers but are immediately turned over to professional caretakers, this position holds that both children and adults profit from the elimination of the parent role in society. Freed from family ties the couple is free to be infinitely flexible in its arrangements, sex is free, commitments are open, etc.

Position B: Anti-Natal (Elitist or Jet-Set Variety)

This is not a societal philosophy but a personal preference to live an unencumbered life. Research shows that children compete with pair intimacy. These couples opt for an adult-centered life style of dual careers, travel, cultural enrichment, and exciting shared experiences. Moreover, with two incomes they can afford it.

Position C: Time-Limited Parenting

These couples commit 20 to 25 years of their marriage to childbearing but before and especially after attempt to achieve the life style of the Jet-set group in Position B. Often the parenting years themselves are characterized by a conscious determination not to let the children stifle the growth of the romance or of the career goals of the wife-mother.

Position D: Parenthood as Career

These couples have parenthood as a central focus of their pair relationship. The mother only works outside the home if she can justify it as "best for the family." Much of the father's spare time is spent with the family as a whole. Family rituals and traditions develop. After the children are officially launched important ties are maintained between the families. The relationship changes as the children raise families of their own, but the older couple never fully vacate their parental role while adding the grandparental role.

ISSUE #2

PAIR AS A SETTING FOR SELF ACTUALIZATION AND INDIVIDUAL GROWTH
VS.
PAIR AS A MUTUAL AID SOCIETY WITH DIVISION OF LABOR AND INTERDEPENDENCY

Position A: Whole-Soul (Utopian Orientation)

The "whole soul" point of view is that the man-woman relationship (or any other relationship, for that matter) only reaches its full potential when it facilitates its members' reaching their full human potentials. There are many versions of what constitutes "full human potential" and the vocabulary of each is, to some degree, unique.

Nevertheless there are several points common to nearly all versions of the movement. Everything is focused in the here and now. The past is dead, the

future may never be; it is what you are experiencing at the very moment which is real and getting in touch with it is your prime imperative if you would be whole. This has two aspects. First, it emphasizes keeping your current options open by not mortgaging your future with long range commitments. In this way you avoid getting "boxed in" or "closed minded." Secondly, *awareness* is all; for example, the couple must be absolutely honest with each other about their feelings and especially their most unacceptable feelings—anger, lust, fear, pain. The standard treatment for hung-up couples is sensitivity training or group confrontation—often on a marathon basis where barriers to emotional honesty erode under the stimulus of group pressure and physical exhaustion. Equally important is the development of sensory awareness, becoming intensely in touch with your own body and your senses of touch and taste and sight and smell. One branch of the movement is especially sensitive to the symbolic and actual defense against openness which clothes afford. For this group, at least, "letting it all hang out" is not just a vivid phrase.

One step further in the same direction is the ecstatic experience or the altered state of consciousness. This takes many forms both as to means and ends with each school defending its own mark of grace against all comers. Within the movement you may seek *satori* (the state of sublime detachment from all desire) through Eastern religious disciplines, *rebirth* through accepting Jesus, *astrotravel* through occult meditation, *grooving* through psychedelic drugs, *tranquility* through training your alpha waves with an electronic brain wave monitor and many, many more. Currently in fashion is pain as a royal road to the exalted state. Two of the most

chic versions are Primal Scream therapy (based on sensory deprivation and re-experiencing all pains back to the pain of birth) and Rolfing (where each part of your body is painfully massaged until you have worked through all of the meaning attached to each pain).

But whatever the approach, the key to this position is that the pair is only valuable if it facilitates the growth of the one. Constricting relationships should be exchanged for those in which the partners are helping each other to find their full Human Potential.

Position B: Mutual Enrichment

Midway between the thoroughgoing (and often expensive) personal renovations of the whole soul movement and the more traditional "strengthening marriage" position discussed below are a variety of mutual enrichment programs. Some are aimed impartially at both partners, laying out programs of improved communication, more effective arguing, better sex or whatever. Others are aimed primarily at the woman, urging her to develop in ways that will enrich both. Prescriptions vary from recipes for becoming a "fascinating" woman (mix equal parts canny Victorian matron and behavioral mod shaping technique) to brews designed to convert any housewife into a "sensuous" woman (add Masters and Johnson to a basic blend of grandpa's racier fantasies and then lace generously with women's lib).

Position C: Strengthening Marriage

Rather than personal enrichment (let alone achieving the "full human potential") this position

focuses on the institution of marriage itself. If emphasizes sacrifice, mutual support, and the traditional values of stability, exclusivity, and the fulfillment of conventional role expectations. The husband should be a good provider (steady pay check, provides the "advantages" to his family), a good father (spends time with the children, firm but understanding, backs up mother) and good husband (good leadership ability but emotionally supportive and personally gentle). The wife should be a good housekeeper (attractive home—neither too messy nor too compulsively neat, good manager), a good mother (warm, interested in children, informed on child development and applied psychology) and a good wife (warm, sexy, supportive). Books and articles on this view are less eye catching but nearly all of the mass media supply persuasive material supporting this "middle American" position.

ISSUE #3

INCLUSIVITY VS. EXCLUSIVITY

Position A: Multilateral Marriage

Marriage among three or more persons is held by many to be the ultimate expression of interpersonal maturity and openness. Everyone in the group is not married to everyone else but each person is married to at least two other persons.

This arrangement provides a broader base of intimate companionship within the marriage. In particular it includes unusual opportunity for closeness with adult members of one's own sex. Sexual life is enriched with variety in the context of commitment. Children receive the benefits of multiple parenting. And finally the whole group can become a continual encounter session with a unique combination of group support and group pressure for change.

The trouble with group marriage is that it makes heavier demands on individuals' discipline and selflessness than many can bear. Out of 20 that were followed in a study for two years only six survived that time period. Apparently pleasing two or three husbands or wives when compounded with trying to get along with two or three co-husbands or co-wives is not exactly a piece of cake.

Position B: The Commune

Although communes take many forms, all are an attempt to establish face to face intimacy with a larger circle of close associates. Most communes are more conventional in their sexual arrangements than multilateral marriages, but a few are based on open sexual patterns. Close association is always demanding and the communes that survive best are those based on common religions or ideological commitment and discipline.

Another stable form described by James Ramsey (he calls them "evolutionary" communes to distinguish them from the more radical "revolutionary" variety) is based on formal social contract (including legal incorporation more often than not). These groups band together to enable members to succeed better in the competitive American system through pooling their resources, living arrangements, etc. The least stable are the revolutionary or utopian communes which tend to resist organization and

structure and thus fail to sustain themselves or their boundaries.

Position C: Swingers

These couples are traditionally exclusive with respect to most things (living arrangements, care of children, holding of property, etc.) but involve themselves with other couples in sexual exchange or in group sex. Since they swing as a couple and by mutual consent they do not view this lack of sexual exclusivity as a threat to their own relationship. Many claim their marriages have been strengthened by this style of life although others do not survive. Studies indicate that most swingers return to a more traditional marital format after two or three years simply because it is such an emotionally taxing style of life.

Position D: Open Marriage

Couples committed to the human potential philosophy (see Issue #2 above) may maintain conventional living arrangements and yet be open to intimate friendships with other couples or individuals which may include sex. This differs from swinging in that swingers typically avoid close emotional ties with their partners, and tend to view sex recreationally. Proponents of the Open Marriage (or Honest Sex, or whatever name various authors chose to give it), on the other hand, exalt sexual intimacy as an ultimate sacrament of togetherness between persons who are already in deep communion in other dimensions.

Position E: Traditional Monogamy

"Forsaking all others, till death do us part." Still popular although on the defensive as a moral position in view of the enthusiasm of the advocates of alternative positions.

ISSUE #4

PERMANENT COMMITMENT VS. PERMANENT AVAILABILITY

Postion A: Universal Total Availability

Outside of the writings of a few Utopians (and also a few anti-Utopians such as Aldous Huxley, who were scared to death by the future they foresaw) the condition of universal total availability has never existed. There are individuals in our society committed to this principle, however.

Position B: Tentative Commitment — Options Open

The position that in the best of all possible worlds one could enjoy mutual love, trust and sexual satisfaction while avoiding marriage has been popular from ancient times. Formerly it was usually identified with the traditional male aversion to the "ball and chain," but in recent years it has become popular with both sexes and especially among college students. The rationale has both pragmatic and philosophical components. On the practical side these young people feel that their futures are too uncertain to make long range commitments. Moreover they are in a period of rapid personal development and they don't want to settle permanently on some-

one who may not "keep up" with their own growth. Finally, until they are settled in a job they may feel in no position to take on the commitments of home and family. From a philosophical viewpoint also they find this open ended relationship more attractive than marriage. For one thing, it is more sincere since there is no constraint against either person leaving if they tire of the arrangement. Moreover, it avoids the distasteful necessity of involving representatives of the establishment (clergy, magistrates, county registrars, etc.).

Research on this form of pairing is being done at several universities but the results are not all in yet. Early returns suggest that it seldom survives graduation and job placement. Couples either break up and go their separate ways or get married.

Position C: Time-Limited Commitments

The concept of a three or five year renewable marriage contract has been seriously suggested, although, so far as we know, it has never been put into practice anywhere. The notion is that the emotional and financial costliness of divorce could be avoided in this way along with the equally costly experience of a long term empty or destructive marriage. Certainly such an idea would necessitate a complete restructuring of modern romantic thought (try substituting "for three years" in place of "forever" in the standard romantic exchange). Also it would seem that bringing a child into the world with so tenuous a guarantee of partnership might be particularly taxing. Another variation would have a time-limited trial marriage contract to be followed (if the option were exercised) by a regular life-time commitment.

Position D: Open-Ended Marriage with Serial Polygamy

This is, in effect, our present system. California is the first state to grant divorce on a no fault, no contest basis. Either partner may end the marriage by filing for divorce. The judge's only job is to preside over the equal division of property and the assignment of custody of the children. Other states will follow. An increasing number of people will promise to "love, honor, and cherish till death do us part" more than once.

Position E: Life Long (or Even Eternal) Commitment

This traditional model is still the ideal of most Americans, even those who get divorced. Most people wouldn't believe it but despite the excitement about rising divorce rates, over two-thirds of us die married to the only spouse we have ever had. Surveys show that many believe (contrary to the doctrines of their own denomination) that their marriage will survive in after-life, as well. Curiously those who expect the most from marriage (in terms of personal growth and satisfaction) are often those most disappointed by it; marriages based on division of labor with mutual support appear to be the most enduring.

ISSUE #5

EQUALITY VS. COMPLEMENTARITY

Position A: Radical Women's Liberation

This position would settle for nothing less than the universal elimination of all social and economic

distinction based on sex. Most feminists do not reject what might be called stylistic differences as
long as they do not connote inferiority/superiority
but they would insist that responsibility for housework, child care, and income belong to each sex
equally. Moreover, each would have equal access to
the full range of economic, social and political activities available to the other. In order to achieve this,
many, but not all, adopt an anti-marriage or anti-
natal position.

Position B: Cake Eaters
(or Moderation in All Things)

These people want a world in which women can
compete succesfully with men in any field and be
rewarded equally for equal performance in any
field, but are committed also to the woman's right
not to compete with men at all. They would like
traditional sex roles to be an available option for
women and men who prefer that pattern.

Position C: Complementarity

This point of view is that men and women are
fundamentally different in their makeup and in their
relationship to society. Men are naturally more aggressive, sexual, cerebral, mechanical, etc. Women
are naturally more gentle, nuturant, expressive,
manually dextrous, etc. It does women and men
and society at large a disservice to attempt to suppress these differences in the name of equality. Men
and women are most fulfilled when teamed in a complementary coalition with each supplying strengths
the other lacks.

Well—there you are. Choose your pairing profile
and may you find what you seek.

As a parting service here is my own choice for

✔ BEST BUY

Although some customers may be happy to pay
a little extra for some of the special models available, years of laboratory testing indicate that the
model with the lowest maintenance costs and the
sturdiest performance record is the ever-popular,
traditional marriage (permanent, monogamous,
mutual support oriented, featuring parenthood as
career and optional cake-eating or complementary
stance in sex roles). In fact, I've had one for twenty
years myself and it's running better today than
when it was new. I recommend it.

Three Marriages— and One Growing Person

by Carl Rogers

A COUPLE WITH SEVERAL children, living in another part of the state, came to my knowledge through several social contacts. My wife and I were impressed by the obvious congeniality of the couple, and with the open and spontaneous relationship they had with the children as well as with each other. It seemed to be a genuinely healthy marriage—something not too often encountered these days. Consequently, I was surprised to learn from a few casual remarks on the part of the wife that this was her third marriage, and that the first two had not been happy ones.

When I began to work on [this article, it] occurred to me that if I could obtain an interview with this woman, I might be able to gain a few brief excerpts which would be enlightening. One reason for thinking of her was that she had seemed so very open and honest, a sort of healthily earthy person, who might be willing to talk freely about her experiences.

When I wrote to her, she was willing to be interviewed, to have it tape-recorded, and to have segments used for this book.

After the interview, as I listened to the tape, I found it so full of fascinating learnings—about marriage, about relationships in general, about sexual satisfaction, about the elements that change lives—that I simply could not take excerpts from it. I felt that it must be reproduced in full, with only the identifying details altered. So here is her account of her marriages. I believe it will repay rereading. At the conclusion I will comment on some of the psychological learnings it points up for me, but this by no means exhausts all its significant elements or the learnings it may stimulate in you.

As you will see, I spoke only once. From that point on, it is Irene's story.

ME: Tell me anything you want to about your three marriages, especially elements that you think might be of interest and use to young people. If you're sort of considering whether something is worth including or not, that would be the criterion, that if you feel, "God, I wish I had known of someone's experience like that when I was younger," then please include it. Not that you're talking *to* them—you will just be talking about yourself.

And include the mistakes, and the good choices and the good things you did, and the feelings in you in each situation, and whatever changes may have come about in you. Those are some of the things I have thought about, that I hoped you'd talk about. And then I have jotted down a few things which if you don't cover, I'll probably ask you about at the end. [They proved unnecessary.]

IRENE: You know, I was thinking about this appointment this morning, while I was sitting in the bathtub. (*Pause*) So, okay, starting with the kind of a person I was the first time, and reasons for being married.

Our family was really not a very friendly family. We had a lot of fun, we had a lot of problems, but we weren't very friendly, we weren't very real with each other. We didn't know much about that at all. There was great conflict between my mother and father and it sort of filtered down. None of us were very nice to each other. We didn't give each other room to be different, or to *be* at all. It wasn't a comfortable home to be in and the goal for most of us—there were seven of us—was to get out. That was the neat thing. And the only way to do that, that I knew of, was to get married. There wasn't money for college or anything like that. After we graduated from high school, we went to work. Anyway, that was my story. I did. And, I was anxious to get married, I wanted to get married and raise a family and settle down, and live happily ever after—storybook stuff.

You know, I think sex played an important role all along, even when I was very young. I was unaware, I was naïve, but sex was an important factor. There was never any discussion of sex in my family. I

185

remember once mentioning that a girl was pregnant and I was dismissed from the room for having used that word. So sex became something very interesting and very dirty.

I married probably, well, certainly, for all the wrong reasons. To get out of the house, and I not only really didn't know the man I married well at all, I didn't even know who *I* was. And so we really didn't do each other a favor. He didn't know who he was, and had had a very different upbringing, a very different family. He was very much loved and very sheltered and had always had financial security, which we didn't have. Those things were important to me, too. I thought, "Gee, here's a guy who has some money and a lovely family. . . ."

I was twenty-one, old enough to know better, but I was really like fourteen when it comes to understanding the world and me. Very naïve, and had had no sexual relations with anyone—had been terrified of it and fascinated by it all at the same time.

Another thing about my first husband is he had already been married once—this is an important factor—and divorced, and had had a child, whom he couldn't see any more. She was four at the time, and this really broke him up, a good deal more than I realized. His wife had threatened to kill their child if he so much as visited the girl, so he was not going to commit himself to marriage with the possibility of more children.

I wasn't tuned in to where he was, or who he was, or what was going on with him at all. It had been a terribly traumatic thing for him—he apparently loved his wife and loved his child. And she was sleeping with all his friends. He was the last one to find out and was divorced, and was terribly hurt by it, and felt really cheated, deceived, and didn't have a lot of trust. And I automatically assumed that that wouldn't apply to me, that I wouldn't be compared. I was a different person. But of course, I was compared. And he didn't trust me. I assumed a trust that didn't exist. He didn't want any more children, because he didn't want to lose any more. But very soon I got pregnant and we never really faced that. I know he was terribly unhappy about it, but we never really talked it out.

I really didn't pay any attention to anything he said, or any aspects of himself that he showed me that didn't fit in with some kind of stereotype I had for "my husband," you know, quote, whatever that is. And "my husband" was going to be strong and capable and a good father and love children and provide for me and satisfy me sexually—a storybook kind of thing. Of course, he turned out to be a human being and not a machine, and couldn't produce for me like that.

Okay, I didn't have any experience sexually, which was a great problem to us. He was fairly inexperienced, too, and apparently had had no problem with his first wife, and assumed again that there wouldn't be any with us, and if there was a problem it had to be me. I assumed it must be he. Sexually, I never had an orgasm. I put the blame on him. I felt that it was his fault that I wasn't sexually satisfied.

I always wanted sex, but it always left me completely unsatisfied.

I really had no idea what marriage was like. I had no idea at all, and jumped into it like we were playing a game—playing house. And, oh, another big factor I forgot to mention. Because he was divorced, my mother automatically labeled him unfit, and this was a big factor in pushing me to him. She liked him when she met him, she liked the kind of work he did, she liked his age, his appearance, all of those things, but as soon as she heard he was divorced, he was suddenly rotten, no good, bad, unfit, and it really rankled me. And marrying him was another means of defiance. By God, I was going to do this thing—and did, to my sorrow.

We had, as I said, serious problems sexually, and didn't know how to handle them. We'd talk about them in an accusative fashion instead of any kind of helpful way. I was ashamed of my inability to have an orgasm. It terrified me. It was, to me, a sign of not being a woman. And I blamed him as long as I could get away with it. And then I turned it inward on myself.

I'd never felt loved by my family or by my mother. I'd never had any real love from anyone. My mother told me when I was thirty-two years old, "I never loved you and I never can. I don't understand you, but I do respect you." I realized that she was really trying to give me something of a compliment, but my reaction was that I went to the bathroom and I vomited and vomited and vomited. That was just a terribly upsetting experience to know that not only had I *felt* that she never loved me, but she was saying *herself* that she never loved me.

I didn't feel worthy of being loved, just completely unlovable. And the sexual thing between my husband and myself just really validated those feelings. I wasn't worthy, I was not going to be able to experience this. But it was a terribly frustrating thing. I really let the sexual incompleteness get a hold on me and eat at me, and used it as a weapon on myself, and certainly on him, too.

It turned out that my husband wasn't a very strong man. He was an artist, somewhat effeminate and very sensitive, and as I said had been very sheltered and terribly hurt by his first marriage. None of these things did I consider. I expected him to be things that he wasn't, and he wasn't able to come across. So I hurt him, I did about everything wrong that I could, trying to work out *my* idea of what this marriage should be. It had nothing to do with two people trying to live together. I didn't even understand what *that* was all about. And he would—oh; he would start this project or that, spend money we didn't have, and not *finish* it. And I tried to support him, I thought, a good supporting wife, you know, "Honey, if this is what you want to do, why don't you *finish* it?" Not realizing that he was the kind of person that couldn't and that this pressure was ghastly for him.

And he wasn't a very sexy guy. He didn't need a lot of sex—he needed an occasional orgasm, that's all—just an ejaculation. He could have masturbated—

I'm sure it would have been just as satisfying to him. He didn't like my body, he didn't like to see me without any clothes on, and I had a lovely way of punishing him there. If things didn't go well or I was mad at him, all I had to do was appear at breakfast stark naked, you know! He'd gag on his egg, and leave for work—I did just cruel things. I'd tease him. I didn't help him—I didn't help him at all. I just pushed him deeper and deeper into his own private little hell, I guess.

And yet everything that I did to *him* hurt *me*. I realize that now, but I was so little aware of my own feelings that I really was scarcely aware of it then.

We presented a beautiful picture of marriage to our friends in the outside world. People thought, "Gad, aren't they marvelous? Don't they get along well, and isn't everything just grand?" And it's a game—a terrible game we played, and I think a lot of people do it. And we really could fool most of our friends, because they didn't want to know any more than that. We were fun to be with. Our home was a comfortable place to visit, and as soon as the doors were closed we began our own private *Virginia Woolf.* Yet we were both nice people. I think maybe we could have made it if I had had any of the understanding that I have now.

The children didn't help matters. I was pregnant all the time, had four children and lost two, even though I used contraceptives, and this was a responsibility he couldn't handle—an emotional responsibility as well as a financial responsibility. He just hated the thought of my being pregnant. He didn't want children. He didn't get any help from me on that, because husbands are *supposed* to be fathers, are *supposed* to love children, and all this nonsense. And sex was so awful, and became more and more awful.

This marriage lasted for eight years, and in the process I became really convinced that there was something physically wrong with me. And I don't mean physically, in the sense that it could be corrected surgically, or anything like that—that somehow when I was born, something was missing. I was beginning to believe that I simply could not be loved. This was a nagging thing with me. I had a lot of friends, but I sort of protected myself, I never really let myself get too close to people.

I even found myself holding back with my children. I would be uncomfortable if they wanted to, you know, really hold me or really get any kind of deep attachment. I didn't want that because I was just sure that if I allowed myself to love them and be loved by them, that they would find something out about me that they wouldn't be able to love. And I'd lose them, and so better not to love them than to love them and lose them. This didn't, of course, make it an easy time for my kids either, when they were little.

The whole household atmosphere was just ghastly. I thought I could live with it—be the martyr. I was the greatest martyr, I think, that ever lived. And I managed to go for eight years on that, with punishing and then consoling. I could just rip him to pieces, and then be his mother, and then criticize him for using me as a mother, and it was just a terrible, terrible thing. And neither one of us smart enough to know how to break out of this. We were really unaware of any other way of life, and stayed together mostly from pressures from family and society, and this silly game we played, not wanting *anybody* to know. That was very important.

Finally, as part of the sexual end of it—I don't know if you really want this, or not—but I'll tell you the point at which I felt the most degraded, the lowest, in our relationship. I used to want a lot of sex, because I just never was satisfied. I just needed more and more, and never got anything out of it, and I just drove him crazy, because he wasn't interested in it to begin with. And he finally told me that I was dull and uninteresting and I couldn't turn him on, and maybe if he had an affair with another woman, that would stimulate our relationship. And I even went along with that! He didn't want the responsibility of picking the girl, so I did *that* for him. And I couldn't very well punish him for something I'd set up, you know. It was just a sick, awful kind of thing we had going. I look back on that with a certain degree of horror.

I think that was a minor turning point. At any rate, I really took a good hard look at myself and what I was doing to myself. And to what end, you know. It was crazy, and I had thought I could live with it and I couldn't.

And his cruelty to my children—I mean, my husband really couldn't hurt me, he couldn't attack me, I was so well-shielded. He took it out on the kids, and so I could use that—this was my reason for divorce, he was cruel to the children. That was it. And I had the support of the whole world on that one.

I felt completely justified in the divorce. He just was not what a husband *should* be. I sentenced him and condemned him and I felt so *right* in doing so. I was a strong person, he was not so strong. I was just *right*, that's all, and he was a real bastard.

After the divorce I thought I was going to be in real good shape. I didn't have this worm hanging around my neck, and I could get a job and take care of things in a really super way. I had a lot of surprises in store for me there. I didn't drive, I had to learn how to drive a car. I got a job, a terribly dull job—office work in a factory, night shift. I had suddenly the realization of what it is to be alone. I had two children to raise. I was physically not well at all, recovering from a hysterectomy. That was another thing, in my decision to get a divorce, the timing couldn't have been worse. I was probably in the worst possible condition to make an important decision for myself. I was emotionally and physically just nowhere near tiptop.

I had to get a babysitter to watch the kids, and they were just running wild. My oldest boy was beginning to experience severe emotional problems as a result of me and his father and our marriage and everything. And I didn't know how to cope adequately with so many things at once. I was so, really, unfit to manage myself, let alone the other responsibilities—

the kids and the house and everything else.

I guess at that point I really thought I could have a successful sexual relationship with almost anyone, and I had great need for this. So I found myself bed-hopping for awhile. And to my utter amazement, it just wasn't any different. It didn't make any difference who I slept with—I still would just not be able to reach an orgasm. I'd go so far and stop. And I was so certain of my own worthlessness and unlovability that, for example, I never let any man know that I didn't have an orgasm. I put on a good show. The sexual excitement was real, I was sexually excited—but I'd also put on a good show of having an orgasm, just to make him feel better. I was just a complete shell. It was almost a driving obsession—if I could only have an orgasm, I would be a woman. It was so dumb. You know, that doesn't have anything to do with it at all, but that was it, and I wasn't measuring up, I just wasn't.

Working was a good thing. I met some new people and began to experience at least some sense of accomplishment, no matter how idiotic this work was, and easily moved up and began to supervise people, and that was a good feeling. But it was time-consuming.

I got into a little trouble with my neighbors. We lived in a tract area, we'd all moved in at the same time, and these people were all really my friends, I thought. But as soon as I was divorced, I found I wasn't welcome in any of the houses—that was a tough one for me to handle. I was a threat to all the women, I was after all the men—none of which was true, because I had a very strong moral code. A divorced woman is open for all kinds of things you just can't imagine until you're in that situation. It's like it's tattooed on your forehead, and you know, "Husbands, beware!"

Then I became involved with a man I worked for, one of the bosses. This was my second husband. He was twelve years older than I. He already had one degree, and he was working the second shift as well, because he'd changed his entire style of living. He was back in college, majoring in psychology. And he used everthing he'd learned on me, and I was easy bait, you know, "Wow, isn't he marvelous!" A good-looking man, stable, quiet-spoken, gentle (so he seemed), very bright, and he was interested in me, which just seemed astounding to me. You know, what in the world was there about me that could catch the eye of so marvelous a creature? And I was foolish enough to think that it had an awful lot to do with *me.* It didn't. It was strictly a sexual attraction. And since I didn't place any value on my appeal sexually, it just didn't compute with me, so it *had* to be something else. And so our relationship began from two different assumptions, again. I just assumed it had to be something other than sex, and he assumed I knew it was sex—it was dumb.

And, well he was married also, so I had terrible guilt feelings about the time we spent together. Eventually he divorced his wife and we married. And that sounds very simple, but it was a complicated procedure. I didn't really want to have anything to do with him, but his attention to me was something I couldn't resist. I was just drawn to it. I needed someone to care about me. I really desperately needed it, much as I thought I could get along without it. And I could sort of cheat myself in a hundred ways, and rationalize it away, because of, you know, his attention.

I tried to stop that relationship over and over and over again and couldn't do it. Even, you know, "My God, why don't you just go away and leave me alone?" and the more I held him off, the more attractive I seemed to him.

He was beautiful to the children, or it seemed to me he was, and that was so important to me. However, he never fooled the kids, because they told me right from the beginning, "He's just dreadful, Mother, and don't have anything to do with him." And in my superior position of knowledge and age, and as MOTHER, capital letters all, I just put aside everything they said and told them *I'd* make the decisions for the family, and at any rate. . . .

I thought *I* had broken up his home and felt like a dog. But, hell, he was going to get divorced anyway. If it hadn't been me, it would have been any little chick who came along. I've learned that since, and I don't punish myself for that much any more.

At that time I was just no one. I was so easily persuaded, anybody could talk me into anything. I didn't know who I was, except that I was a nobody. And the thing that I remember with real shock is that even before I married him, after he did get his divorce, I told a very good friend of mine, "The only way I'm ever going to get rid of him is to marry him and divorce him."

That shows various things. I felt that he couldn't possibly be interested in me and that sooner or later he'd find I was no good, and so I went into it on a very cynical basis, feeling, well, he's so hot for this—he has money, he'll give the children a father, and I won't have to work. I was so tired, and physically exhausted, and ready to stay home. Then another thing was that he seemed to have an interest in my oldest boy, and of course my children really were desperate for a father. And he gave that as one reason for persuading me to marry him—that he would be a good father to John, my oldest boy.

Well, our marriage lasted one year, and it was perfectly terrible. It turned out he didn't have a dime, he couldn't handle money, he was in debt, terribly in debt; I ended up losing most of my possessions to pay for his bills; I lost my car—well, everything I had that was of material value, and I didn't have very much. It was terrible! And all he wanted was sex, sex, sex. If I had been getting satisfaction from it, that probably would have been quite all right, but I wasn't. So, very soon, he became to me just a dirty old man. It was a ghastly scene.

Everyone was better off, really, when that ended. It's strange, too, because it's the part of my life that I recall the least. I find if someone says, "How long have you and Joe been married?"—this is my current husband—and I say six years, and my oldest child is eighteen, and they say, "Well, then, you've been divorced," and I always think only of two husbands. I never think of poor Ken, sandwiched in the middle. I really don't, very little.

I managed to get through it, somehow, but the important thing about this was that, again, I married for all the wrong reasons—I married so I could quit work and stay home with my children. I married for financial security which didn't exist, and I married for emotional security—the man was older, he seemed so capable, and wasn't. He was just a person too, like everybody else I know, and brought into the marriage his own problems and his own hangups, and I hadn't allowed any room for those. Once again I had had some nutty idea that as soon as we were married, then *my* idea of what marriage would be was going to happen, and, of course, it didn't.

Marriage was the one thing I really wanted, and failing at that *twice*, and so *completely*, was a very tough thing for me. I was at that time utterly and absolutely convinced that here was something about me that was unlovable, and I couldn't deny it any more. The pain of trying to love someone and trying to be loved, was really more than I could bear to try again.

I decided that I'd work and raise my kids and, you know, stay with them and do all those marvelous martyr things, and then I was going to kill myself. I had this plan all set up—that's the way it was going to be. And it gave me, oh, sort of an end to the misery, you know. I knew that eventually it was going to end. I wasn't going to have to wait through another thirty years of just terrible loneliness.

The loneliness would just eat away at me. And the knowledge that there was something wrong with me and that I wasn't going to be able to have any kind of sustained relationship—any relationship was going to be brief. And I'd make sure I kept it that way. Nobody was ever going to really know *me* again. I wouldn't show anything of myself, or darned little. Just as little as necessary. And learn to live without sex. I'd learned how to take care of myself. I'd masturbate and then I'd handle that guilt—just pile it on top, you know, one thing after another. Feeling guilty about what I'd done to my kids, what I'd done to two men, what I'd done to myself, and I could think two ways about that, either blame it on my mother—you know, poor old mother—or blame it on the fact that something was missing in me, which wasn't my fault, or I'd picked two peculiar men, which wasn't my fault, and half the time I could go that way and the other half I would just own it all, and, you know, punish myself.

I wonder sometimes how my third husband, whom I first met at a party and then at a meeting where we talked, ever managed to reach me through all of this stuff. It's kind of a miracle in a sense.

There were about three years between my first marriage and my second one, and there was about, oh, maybe a year and a half or two years between the second and the third one. Now in that period of time I really began to put aside my "shoulds" and my "ought tos," to put aside or somehow look at and own and come to peace with some guilt, by looking at the past and realizing, "It's past and I can't do anything about it, and I can really mess up my future if I mess around with the past."

So, first of all, I wanted to get acquainted with myself, and who I am and what are some of the things that cause me to behave the way I do—try to get in touch with some of my feelings, which were new things to me. I didn't think that anyone would care about those. Those had always been my own—and I guess those are some of the things I thought were the unacceptable things. If I felt suicidal or depressed, or if I felt unlovable, or if I felt any of the negative feelings I would have about myself, I must not let anybody see or anybody know about those things. It took me a long time to realize that those are the things that people can value and can care about. I wish I could remember clearly some of the process involved, and that's tough. I'm not very good at that. Joe had an awful lot to do with that.

Joe came into my life, and he's a man who has always been loved, knows it, accepts it without question, and I still feel in awe of that. He knows he has worth—that's something that is never questioned—and yet at the same time he could look at me, who had an almost exact opposite opinion of myself, and not be bothered by that or be put aside by that, and not encourage it either. He never confirmed my "sickness," he never confirmed my negative feelings about myself. He would hear them and accept them, and then, in his own way, say that they were kind of nonsense. "I realize you feel that way, but that's not the way you are."

And I began to try to look at myself. It was as if, just maybe, the way *he* sees me is closer to the way I am than the way *I* see me, and I began to sort of try that on a little bit. It's sort of an interesting thing. I found that it was a lot easier for me to put myself *down*, because then I didn't really have to perform. I didn't have to live up to anything. I was deprived and mistreated and unlovable and unacceptable, and *so* I didn't have to come out with any high order behavior at all. I could excuse myself for not coping, or not appreciating myself, or whatever.

I think if Joe had been fascinated by my horror story, I might have stayed in it a good deal longer than I did. He wasn't. He heard it and thought it was terribly sad, but he didn't want to hear it twice, and that was a little tough for me, because that was my ticket, kind of, with people—they'd be fascinated with anything ugly, and it would frighten 'em. I never frightened Joe. I could become so depressed, I'd sort of try on a suicide act. It would seem very real to me at the time, but he just never paid any attention. It just didn't exist for him, and it was, "Well, I hope you're over that now" or "My God, if you want to wallow in that, I'd better leave and come back when you feel better. Is there anything I can do to help you with this? I don't want to hear it again. If you want to beat yourself with your past, for the rest of your life, that's a trip you take all by yourself."

And a lot of it seemed kind of cruel, but it really snapped me out of it. I could go one or two ways. He cared about the person I was. He didn't give a goddamn about the person I had been or any of that. It was a part of me, true, but it was only a *part* of me. It wasn't all of me. And the more that I could look at myself through his eyes, the better I could feel about myself.

But an interesting thing about that was, I wasn't sure I wanted to. I didn't know whether I really *wanted* to be healthy, because there's a hell of a responsibility involved with that—just an enormous responsibility. I couldn't look forward to being a martyr, and dying in another ten years, and ending all the agony.

And I resented him, often, because still I believed, okay, buddy, you really care about me, but that's what *you* see. I don't let you see this little, black, rotten, ugly ball I have buried down inside that's really me, that's unlovable and unacceptable. And I was really terrified at that point in my life of attempting to—once again, you know—try to work on this exchange of love, the transaction of giving and receiving love.

I could maintain my status quo, you know, and feel sorry for myself, and put myself down and be a part-time martyr, and be safe, because it was known to me and I knew I could survive. It wasn't much of a life, but I was alive. Or I could really try once again to open myself up and let him see me and risk the possibility that that black ball inside of me really is so ugly that he's going to leave. And that's a terrible risk to take. For me, if I tried it again and failed at it again—and I'm not talking about marriage—I'm talking about a real relationship with another human being —I felt that I would go mad, that I *really* would lose my mind.

It wasn't worth the risk. But after a long time I realized that for me the greater risk—the greater risk was *not* to risk, and never really know whether I could be loved, and whether I could love.

I really had to reach that point. I held Joe off. I tried to shut him out every way I could think of. Joe was open, he was right there, he lived so much in the now, and I could find ways to criticize that. He was so very real it scared me. It fascinated me, I loved it, I really loved *him*, but I thought I knew how to do that and nobody else did. *I* could love; that was something I knew how to do, but nobody could really love me; there was going to be that terrible time.

But his interest in me did continue, and the relationship went on and on. We began to sleep together, and I got closer and closer to having an orgasm. And one thing was that Joe was never in a hurry. For me sex had always been a very quick thing. An ejaculation on the part of the man and that was it, and leaving me so frustrated that sometimes I'd go out and bang my head against the wall. And then I'd masturbate, and then I felt terribly guilty about that. I felt the masturbation was probably the reason I wasn't able to have an orgasm. So the whole scene was a very, very bad one for me.

But Joe was never in a hurry, and he was inter-

ested in what I enjoyed. What did *I* enjoy in our physical contact together? And I found that terribly hard for me to talk about. I just wasn't accustomed to that kind of interest and compassion. I really felt nobody could feel compassion for another person. But as I talked about it, and as we began to come closer and closer together, believe it or not, I began to have orgasms. And that made the whole relationship much more meaningful.

But I was certain that he would leave me just like all the rest. He'd get disgusted with me, he'd find out how unlovable I was. And so, for a while, I played the game of being attractive. I'd do anything in the world to please him. I never crossed him, never showed any negative feelings about what he did, because I felt I mustn't lose him. If he ever gets to know *me,* he'll leave me, so I've got to play the game of being an attractive woman. The thing I didn't realize is that I wasn't fooling him!

But it's not possible to play that kind of a game forever, so I finally decided—it wasn't a very conscious decision, but a gradual one—that, well, if he's really going to leave, maybe it'd better be now, so I'll find out. And I would sort of reach down in and peel off a layer of my ugly black ball and bring it out and put it on the table, and I thought, "Now this one will drive him away, and it had better happen now before I get too deeply involved."

And it just never made any difference to him, whatever it was. He would acknowledge it maybe, or ignore it, or shove it off on the floor, or whatever, but he never got up and left. Sometimes he would be very angry, sometimes he would weep, sometimes he would laugh, you know, he would just react. I would get his reaction to whatever it was, but he never left. And I couldn't understand this, because it's all I had ever known. And I'd try another layer, pull another one up. And I'd get a *real* reaction from him, some of it good, some of it not so good, but he'd stay, and that was the important thing.

You know, after several months it was the children who moved him into our house! And for a while he would, in the morning, leap up and go and sleep on the couch, or leave and go home at four or five in the morning—park the car down the block, things like that. And the stronger and the more real our relationship became, the more courage we had to let the world kind of see us living together, and it didn't matter so much how they judged us, but how we felt about *ourselves.*

Then there came the real turning point, and that was a strange experience. We'd been living together for close to a year, which seems unbelievable to me. How that ever worked in that neighborhood I don't know, but it did. An awful lot of it had to do with how I felt about myself. And how we felt about ourselves. At any rate, Joe was out of town—he was away on business and I was home—the kids were asleep, and I was sitting in the living room watching television, which was across the room from me, and next to the television set was a window, a big picture window. Normally, I had the curtains closed, but I didn't this night, and so when I looked across at the TV, I could see my reflection in the window. And I kind of had a conversation with myself. It was very important to me, and I don't know if you can hear what I'm saying, but it was sort of like this: "Hello. Here you are, thirty-four years old, and how *differently* life has turned out from what you expected." I had always had a very unreal picture of life. I thought I wanted to get married, settle down, have six children, God forbid, raise the family, and live happily ever after. It seemed like such a simple reasonable dream. And it really hadn't worked that way *at all.* I'd found a man, I'd loved him, I thought; I thought I was straight and open and honest, whatever that meant, and it really hadn't worked. There had been so much unhappiness. I'd had a lot of illness, I'd had so many problems with my children, I hadn't been able really to cope with life. I didn't know anything about it at all, it was really a devastating thing. Life had been pretty much *hell.*

I kind of talked to myself and listed all the things that had gone wrong. And then I began to wonder about some of the things that might be right. And one of the questions that came up—and, you know, these are questions from me to me—was, "What is it you really want? What is it that you're looking for?" And the answer turned out not to be a marriage, not to have six children, not to live happily ever after at all. It turned out to be that I wanted to learn how to love someone, just one person, and to be loved, and that's *all.* I didn't need the house, I didn't need anything else, but just really to know how to do that. To know how to experience that—both ways.

And my reflection in the window said, "Well, you jackass, what do you think you've got now?" And I sat there and thought, "Well, for crying out loud, you know, I really have a man I'm learning to love, and that means sharing myself. If that is my goal, to love and to be loved, I have it. Joe loves me, I love him, he loves the children. What do I want that I don't have?"

Up to that time I'd always had reservations about our relationship, because Joe had never seemed like he wanted to marry me. The piece of paper, that damned marriage certificate, was again my way of measuring his love, which is just dumb. He was living with me, he was sharing his life with me, he was marvelous with my children, very real with all of us. He accepted me just exactly the way I was, with all the crap, and I had exactly what I wanted, and I was denying it because I didn't have a piece of paper. I was cynical enough to be able to say, "Well, maybe Joe is just conning me, and what we have isn't real without a piece of paper." And I realized how *wrong* I was about that. And kind of a great thing happened to me, within me. I had a great talk with myself and felt a sense of peace that I'd never experienced before in my life.

I probably cried, I don't remember, it doesn't matter. But I also felt joy. Those were two things I didn't know anything about. I'm talking about a relationship with myself. I'd never experienced any peace

and I'd never experienced any joy. And that was the first time, and it was all by myself. I hadn't needed Joe. I hadn't needed anyone else to do this to me or for me. It was my own private experience and it was great. I can't overstress the importance of this conversation with my reflection. It was a real turning point.

And when Joe came back from his trip, I didn't have a need to share it with him, it wasn't a great big thing that had to be explained. It was mine and it was private and it was health and it was beautiful, and along with it came a lot of responsibility that suddenly didn't scare me—no suicide or any of the rest of it.

And apparently, I lifted—Joe and I have talked about this much after the fact—I apparently lifted all kinds of pressure from Joe to marry. I didn't say anything, but just my attitude changed. Suddenly, from his point of view, I was completely with him sexually and totally for the first time in my life. The peace that I felt about myself and the good feelings I had toward me and my own private joy were obvious, and were transmitted to him, and apparently it was something he was waiting for. It wasn't a very cognitive process he went through, but I seemed very much present to him, and in two weeks we were *married*, which was really kind of astounding! All of a sudden, Joe was absolutely positive that we ought to—only I use that in the nice sense—marry; that what we had going for us was working. And that it had every possibility, from his point of view, and certainly from mine, to continue to work better and better.

And I wasn't sure I *wanted* to get married. It was funny, because I was experiencing good things and didn't want to spoil them, and I didn't need it. And I really meant that. I could have visited his parents, my parents, all of the people who had been so frightening to me in their judgment of me before—suddenly I could have visited them, without marriage, with great pride. At any rate, we were married.

And it's been great, it really has. It changes every day, it changes constantly. And I really don't know that I've shared the last ounce or pound, or whatever it is, of my little black crap inside. But I'm not afraid to, and usually it comes out sort of naturally. I haven't reached a goal or an end of anything, but I'm in the process of reaching it. And for me it's just *being*, and it's not easy to do. A lot of times it would be a lot easier for me not to share some of the things that are going on with me. I think, "Oh, God, that's going to trigger this, which is going to trigger that, and as soon as I do that, you know, I'm in trouble, and our relationship is in trouble." I've *always* got to remember to share what I am *right now*, which is just being, and it's the *process*. And that works, and it's the only thing I've found that does. And it has given me joy, and sometimes I look in the mirror and really think I'm pretty, and that's *really* movement!

It seems a shame to wait until I'm forty, after an awful lot of years, but really, I don't regret one single thing that's happened to me. I don't punish myself any more, I really don't. I see it, and I'm sorry about a lot of things I've done. I'm sorry about a lot of things I've not done, and the way I've been, but I really don't punish myself any more. And I'm learning how to live in the now, and I'm beginning to understand what that word means. Our sex is absolutely fantastic. I find myself getting quite courageous sexually, which is kind of marvelous. Joe thinks I'm simply beautiful. And half the time I think he's got to be *blind*, but that's all right too. I have a good relationship with my kids and they have with each other. The thing snowballs, it moves from one to the other and to our friends. I keep Joe honest, he keeps me honest, we keep ourselves honest. No tricks, no games, and it's so wonderful to be able to live—to be just exactly who I am all the time, or *most* of the time, and find out it's okay. I really don't have to hide anything, I don't have to try to figure out what anybody wants and try to give it to him, in order to make friends or —It's *nice!* I'm sure I'm not that way twenty-four hours a day, by a long shot, but it's building, inching along, and it's kinda neat. And I'm glad to be alive. There aren't any guarantees, but I'm glad to be alive.

And you know, I've found that the little black ball inside of me is the most lovable part of me. The part of myself that I thought was ugliest is the most beautiful, because I've learned how to share it.

MEANINGS I FIND

A whole book of personality dynamics could be based on a study of Irene's life as she reports it. There are learnings about child development, about parent-child relationships, about the creation of one's self-concept, about the elements of bad relationships and good relationships, about the factors which make for personal change, about the sharing of oneself, about sexual adjustment (bad and good), about rationalization, and so on and on. At first I thought I would organize some of the meanings I find in Irene's experience under such headings. I came to feel that it might be more helpful if I simply listed some of my learnings, very briefly, in the order in which they occur in the interview. In that way you can check back to the document to see if you agree or disagree, and whether these suggest other elements to you. So here is a partial list.

The effect of destructive family relationships on the child and young person (p. 185).

The influence of early inhibitions regarding sex (p. 185).

The incredible gap which occurs in a relationship based on rigid expectations of the other and not on understanding (p. 186).

The disastrous effect which a failure to achieve a satisfactory sexual relationship can have on a marriage (p. 186).

The lasting influence of severe parental rejection (p. 186).

Some of the elements which can go into the building of a negative self-concept; maternal rejection (p. 186); sexual inadequacy (pp. 186, 188); failure in two relationships (p. 189); husband's dislike of her body (p. 186); etc. Some of these elements occur primarily in others, such as

"I never loved you." Others are experienced: "I've never had an orgasm." But when the person introjects the negative perceptions of others and values his own experience in terms of others' expectations ("I've never had an orgasm, so I'm not a woman"), then indeed the concept of self can become very negative.

The rising spiral of cruelty in a relationship based first on role expectations of the other and second on accusations for failing to live up to those expectations (pp. 186-187).

The strain of maintaining a mask in public which is totally different from the private reality (pp. 186-187).

The fear of relationships which is based on the belief that deep within the self there is something unspeakably awful which must never be revealed to others (p 187).

How a complete lack of experiential knowledge of living in a relationship with another, separate person can destroy a marriage (p. 187).

The bizarre behaviors which can gradually grow out of mounting frustration (such as soliciting another woman for her husband, p. 187).

The ease with which we adopt comforting rationalizations: "that was my reason for divorce, he was cruel to the children" (p. 187).

The difficulty of coping with the real world, a difficulty never realized until experienced (pp. 187-188).

The delicate complexity of a satisfactory sexual relationship between a man and woman (many references, but especially pp. 186, 188, 189, 190).

The need for attention and love which, when strong enough, distorts perceptions (p. 188).

The guilt over being a homebreaker, which added to her black self-concept (p. 188).

The weakness which grows out of the lack of any firmly grounded, positive, picture of oneself—the effect of being a "nobody" (p. 188).

A catalogue of dubious reasons for marriage: exhaustion, readiness to stay home, financial security, emotional security, good-looking partner, providing a father for the children, sexual attraction (on the part of the husband). Also rebellion against mother, wanting a home and children (pp. 188-189, and also pp. 186-187).

The way in which we suppress unpleasant memories (p. 188).

How life can become so unbearable, and how one's self can seem so awful that suicide and the destruction of the self seem desirable (p. 189).

The first dawnings of psychological health—looking at oneself (pp. 189-191, also pp. 187-188).

The ambivalence each of us feels about growth and health. They involve risk and responsibility. It is easier to be a martyr or a suicide (p. 189).

The strain that can go out of a relationship when one is being *real* (pp. 191-192).

The unimportance of social expectations and judgments, when a relationship is real (p. 191).

The meaning of life and relationships as a *process* of living, rather than as sets of role expectations (pp. 191-192, compared with all of the first two marriages).

The enormous value—and the risk—of openness in a relationship (pp. 191-192).

The overriding importance of the self-concept as the guide to a person's behavior. Compare the open, sharing behavior of a lovable, sexually adequate, non-guilty, "pretty" person, with beauty at the core (p. 191), with the behavior of an unlovable, sexually inadequate, fearful, unloving, basically defensive and ugly person (pp. 185-189). To be sure, many influences help to account for Irene's gradual change in her perception of herself, but it is not until she *does* gradually perceive herself differently, and has a different picture of herself which she accepts, that her behavior actually changes.

These are some of the meanings I find in Irene's experience. They seem rather pale beside the interview itself, but perhaps they will provoke some thoughts in you. I hope that her story has spoken to you in many personal ways, as well as provided food for thought about broader psychological principles.

19

Thomas J. Cottle

A MIDDLE AMERICAN MARRIAGE

"Two separate clocks, each ticking their own sweet time,
each heading off in a direction that would probably confuse the Almighty."

I HAD BEEN LATE ARRIVING at the Grazianos' house on Poplar Street. Some unexpected traffic, coupled with the uncongenial design of Boston's streets, was enough to put me almost forty-five minutes behind schedule. Theodore Graziano (his friends call him Mushy) had Tuesdays off from work; so the time I could spend with him and his wife Eleanor was precious. Normally, I would interview one of them alone.*

For about fifteen years, Ted Graziano has worked for a Boston newspaper. Starting as a stockroom "boy" (he was almost twenty-five at the time), he had worked his way up to where now, at thirty-nine, he was foreman of the shipping operation. Salaries had risen over the past years, bringing his take-home pay to where he could just about get by. The important thing for him was the security, a factor he had mentioned several times when we spoke at his office.

"This is not the time to be sitting on any gamble," he had said. "This is the time when the economy of the country demands that you get yourself a job that looks like it's got to hold out. Doctors, lawyers, judges, they got it best. The workingman, like always, he's going to be the first to get hit. Unemployment starts at the bottom and works its way up. It's like a disease that they can't find no cure for. You know it's out there and you just gotta do the best you can to avoid getting it. Stay warm, eat good food . . .

"You take a job like this." He waved his right arm about as if to take in the enormous shipping area, partitioned offices, and truck docks. "It's one hell of an operation. I got real responsibility here. You ask any man they got working here and they'll tell you about that responsibility. I tell you, though, in the beginning, ten years ago or so, it was one hell of a challenge. Couple nights there I got so damn excited with the prospect of it all, I could barely go to sleep. Now it's just another job to me.

"Man, there are times I'm working when I think about how nice it would be to be anywhere else. Sitting in the sun, or doing what you're doing. You know, walking around, talking to people. But most of the time I have to take those thoughts and crush 'em up like little paper balls and throw 'em away." He shook his head from side to side, crumpling an imaginary sheet of paper in one of his strong hands. Then he looked back at me. I had no answer for him.

---

*Theodore and Eleanor Graziano are fictitious names that have been used to hide the identity of a real family. For six years, my research has been devoted to working with families in various Boston communities. One purpose of this work is to describe the daily experiences of these families, and the history of their members, as well as my relationship with them. I met the Grazianos quite accidentally five years ago through a young man who worked for Ted Graziano. I soon met Eleanor, their children, and other members of their family.

As a methodological note, I work without tape recorder or prepared questionnaire, believing that both devices constrain interactions already made somewhat unnatural by my presence. In all instances, the families read my manuscripts and grant permission to publish them.

SINCE OUR HOME MEETINGS took place in the kitchen, I entered by the back door as the family members did. Alone in the house while his wife visited her mother, Ted had been sitting in the kitchen reading the newspaper. Eleanor had left us two glasses of milk and a cake covered with tinfoil on the kitchen table.

"Come on, let's eat," Ted said. "I've been dying with hunger waiting for you." He took great pleasure in cutting a slice of cake for me, and laid it gently on a plate. He reached over and placed a fork on the plate, then pushed one

Thomas J. Cottle is a member of the Education Research Center and the Medical Department of MIT. His books include Time's Children: Impressions of Youth, The Abandoners: Portraits of Loss, Separation and Neglect, and Out of Discontent: Visions of the Contemporary University (coauthor).

of the glasses of milk toward me. When I was taken care of he prepared a piece, considerably smaller, for himself. Ellie, I knew, would decline an invitation to eat with us. Baking this extra item affected their budget; the cake would have to last several days.

"So what do we talk about today, or shouldn't we say anything until Ellie gets here?" Ted asked, his mouth full of cake.

"Talk about anything you like, Ted," I said. "I'm not listening anyway with this cake here."

"Eat it up. There's lots more where it came from. Your wife cooks though, doesn't she?"

"Yes, she does."

"Well then, you aren't hurting too much." He sighed deeply, wiping some crumbs from his chin. "Lots of guys have it pretty bad. I told myself a long time ago, no wife of mine's going to work. Ever! No matter how bad it is, a man provides in his way, a woman in hers. Ellie doesn't need to go cleaning or secretarying, or work at the phone company like all her girl-friends. We'll manage. Eight thousand years and I'll have this house paid off, and when I die she'll be set up. She don't ever have to work if she don't want to. That's the way it's supposed to be. You agree?"

"Well, people have to work it out the way they want," I answered.

"You're not going to tell me you're one of those liberation people, are you?" he grinned at me.

"Well, I guess in a way I am. Men and women, it seems to me, have to enhance one another, support each other to be what they want."

"Now *that* I like. *That* I'll buy. That's all right. You know, now that you mention it, that's maybe like my biggest gripe. I never did have anyone enhance my life. I can look back at it now, forty years next July, I can't see a person anywhere enhanced me, helped me to get anything."

"You have Ellie," I suggested. His eyes were closed slightly as several thoughts seemed to touch him at once.

"Yeah, I got Ellie, all right. Probably a good thing for me too. But that's not the kind of support I'm talking about. A wife is a wife, she doesn't help you out there." He pointed at the window above the sink. "That's not what I mean."

"Can you talk about it?"

"Let me get the words first." He paused, looking into his glass. "The living day by day that women do is not what helps a man. There's a way a man has to get his whole life together. It's all got to fit somehow, make sense. You know what I mean?" He didn't wait for an answer. "It's got to be set up so that every move you make has some reason in a plan that you have to formulate somewhere along the line. It has to build toward something."

He looked at me. "You know about these things. You may be richer than I am, I'll bet you are too. And you may have a more interesting job, which I know you do. I even told you once, remember?"

"Yes. In the shop."

"At the office, right," he corrected me.

"Office."

"But the important thing is that a man knows what it means to arrange for his life. That, no woman knows! That I know for sure." A melancholy feeling was taking the place of anger. "There's a kicker in it though, you know?"

"Which is?"

"Which is that a life that asks us to make certain that pasts and presents and futures fit together in some logical way has a price. You know yourself, as time goes on it gets harder and harder to just live each day and get the most out of it. You don't live each day like that when you're a man. What you live is your work at the moment, your plans, what you call your prospects, *and* your regrets, what you should have done. You think about having bits of time back again to work with. You think how nice it would be to see what the future holds, even in a job like mine where I practically know how everything's going to turn out. Still, you'd like to take a little peek. Maybe just to know whether all those connections you're making are really sticking. You follow me?"

"Yes, I do," I answered.

"So you don't say the hell with what was and what will be. That's the way you think when you go out drinking. At least, that's the way it is for me. I go out and get a little in the bag," he started to smile. I smiled too as I saw his face take on, of all things, a look of pride. "That's when my future disappears, my past disappears, and I got once and for all my present moment and nothing else goddammit TO BE CONCERNED ABOUT!" He shouted the words as he straightened up in his chair. "But now, I ask you, how long's a man with any respect gonna run around in the bag? So you come home, and you sleep, and you drink coffee, and you make nice to your wife, and there you are the next day, thinking the same things all over again: how it all fits together, and how you wish you could be young again, and how great it would be to know what the future's got waiting for you."

"That's one hell of an analysis," I said.

"Well, I don't know as I'd call it an analysis, exactly," he said. "You just keep your eye on the future, because the name of the game is that since you don't have much to say about dying, you have to fill in as many of the empty spaces out there as you can. You don't leave things to chance. Ellie always talks to me, when I get in one sort of a huff or another, about God or about fate. 'Things will just happen,' she says all the time. 'Things are just going to happen.' Sure. They are. Lots of things are just going to happen.

"All you have is yesterday and today. That's all women have. Memories, tears, dreams, MOTHERS!"

Like the roof might fall in on our heads, right here in the kitchen. But the odds are against it because *I* fix the roof, because *I* make certain things like that *won't* happen.

"You know what it's like, Tom? It's just like football. There's a good reason why men like football. It's a man's game because it's played out the way men think. First, you got competition. Then you have a game plan. And you stick with it until you have to find a new one. And it's all leading up to something. Something you could practically predict. If you move here, I'll move there. You move here, I'll move there." He pushed his fingers against the tabletop, his right hand representing my team, his left hand representing his team.

"I can't say these things to Ellie. Of course, the kids don't want to hear about it. I talk with some of my friends, but not too many of them are as smart as you. I guess you know how little schooling we all have. Our kids, I hope, will be different. I'm starting to sound like the old lady. Hoping instead of arranging."

"Well," I tried to assure him, "there's got to be a place for hope in the plan."

"Sure," he said with resignation. "Of course there's a place for hope. But first you make preparations. Whatever is left over that you can't in any way control for, that falls over into the hope category. I don't need God or prayer, or hope."

W E HAD BEEN SPEAKING almost an hour when Eleanor Graziano entered the kitchen. She was flushed and out of breath.

"Please, please excuse me. I'm so late. I went over to my mother's for a minute. I didn't even take my coat off, and before you know it an hour's gone." I nodded to her and started to say something about my own lateness. "Did you find the cake?" she asked me.

"Did we," I replied.

"Was it all right?" she asked modestly. I grinned at her.

"Fair. It was fair, Ellie." She laughed and turned her face downward. Ted laughed too.

"A couple of jokesters I got here. Two little boys with no place to go and nothing to do but eat cake and get fat." I couldn't resist: "Oh, you love it and you know it, Mrs. G."

"You I love," she laughed. "Mushy I'm not so sure about." Ted and I laughed again and looked at one another.

"You better be careful, wife, or I'll tell *you* what I've been telling Tom here for the last hour about *you*."

"Yeah, and what's that?" she asked, removing her boots and throwing them in the back hallway.

"Oh," he started, "about people enhancing one another's lives. Game plans. You know, the usual . . ." He winked at me.

"Game plans?" she asked. "Football? Football! Is that it?"

"That's it," I said.

"Not quite," Ted said.

"Then what is it?" she wanted to know.

"Sit down, Ellie. You and Tom talk. I'm going to the corner for cigars. When I come back we'll continue with this. It's time for a commercial."

"Commercial? Tom, will you tell me please what he's babbling about?"

"I will."

"Go on then," she said to her husband. "I've got a few things for Tom you don't have to know about."

Ellie moved about the kitchen, peering into cabinets at canned goods and plates: "Can't seem to find . . . don't tell me I forgot to get . . . if I don't make a list when I go to the store I'm dead. Can you beat this? I'm not forty yet and my mother, who's almost seventy, has a brain in better shape than mine."

"I doubt that."

"No, it's true," she protested without looking back. "So what do we speak about today? Are you still asking the same questions?"

"Same questions, I suppose."

"Well, I don't know what else I can tell you. Mushy's the one with all the answers. There's nothing you could ask him that he wouldn't have some answer for. Some man, Mr. Graziano." I watched her lay out supplies and utensils in preparation for making dinner. The counter tops were spotless, the sink empty of dishes and garbage, the faces of the cabinets glistening. It was all quite a change from our first meeting four years ago, on the day actually when the Grazianos had moved from a four-room apartment less than a mile away. Suddenly Ted had gotten it in his head to buy a house. Ellie had argued that they couldn't afford it. But he was driven to buy, and on borrowed money they had managed. They had three bedrooms now, and they "could spread out," as Ellie said, finally admitting to her delight. "The children can stay in the same school, and I'm even closer to my mother. If we can just manage," she sighed, "it will be a blessing, *the* blessing of my whole life."

W HILE ELEANOR CHADWICK had never known poverty as a child, she also had never imagined that her marriage to Teddy Graziano, "the Mushy man," would ever lead to a home and a kitchen glowing with warmth and pride like this one. Her father had been an elevator operator and starter during the day, a warehouse inspector four nights a week. He had lived his entire life in Boston. His salary allowed his wife and five children to live comfortably enough in a three-story walk-up apartment. A screened-in back porch opened out from the kitchen of that apartment, and on hot summer evenings the family gathered there feeling as cool as one could during a Boston summer.

"That was ever so lovely, just to be together, even when it was so hot you thought you might die." Ellie and I had had a long conversation about her childhood when the Grazianos moved into their new home. We had sat in this same kitchen on cardboard boxes filled with supplies and clothes. "I would love to have those days back again," she had said. "Even before Mushy and all this. Even before. So many, many times, I wish that tomorrow would be the beginning of a change, a sort of change backward. It's not like you might think, that I fear getting older. No, it's just that wonderful feeling of worriless peace, childhood, being a little girl and having those long hours with my father. He was a delight to know. You would have liked him, Tom. 'Course that's not saying too much, since Dad never had an enemy. He got on with everyone. You know, in many ways, he was very much like Mushy. Mushy without the anger. Dad knew he would never be rich, that he'd never achieve anything special or wonderful in his life. He knew lots of rich people too, but I never heard him complain or compare himself with someone else. The world was the way it was and he was big enough to accept it.

"Mushy's the same way up to a point. I'm sure he feels that he's not going anywhere in his life, at his job, I mean, but he's not about to accept any of that. He'll always tell me that if next year's the same as this year, then he's been a failure. There's no other way. That kind of statement I never heard once from my father's mouth. Never once. For me, you see, that's the sign of a good man. If next year's the same as this one, then you thank God. You get down on your knees at night and you thank God that everybody is well, and that you have enough to eat, and a comfortable place to sleep. You know that everything is provided for. But Mushy doesn't want it that way. The comfortable things, of course, he wants. Like, he wanted this house." I remember Ellie looking about at the boxes lying everywhere and seeing in her face a look of, How are we ever going to get set up again? I saw excitement too, a controlled excitement as though one were not supposed to ask for such delicious treasures but could adore them if they came one's way.

"Well, I'm set here for life. I get used to something very quickly and don't ever want to change. You know something, I can feel in my hands the curtains we used to have in the apartment where I lived as a child. And the tables in the living room and the kitchen too. That's how strong my memory is, so that must be how strong my attachment to things is. To people too. It grieves me, it really does, that the good times are gone and by many, sad to say, forgotten. I think

Mush is that way. Something good happens, like maybe a party. He lives it as much as anyone. But then, when it's over, that's sort of the end of it. Me, I'm so different from him it's hard to believe we could have gotten along as long as we have. Something important happens, it doesn't matter whether it's good or bad, I hang on to it. It's just like the house. I love this, of course. But you give me the largest mansion you can find, a palace, and I'll sit in my bedroom, I mean bedrooms," she laughed, "and I'll be thinking of that little apartment I grew up in, the porch and summers, and all the rest of it."

THAT WAS PART of our conversation almost four years ago. Now, as we waited together in the same kitchen for Ted to return, I knew that we both felt a nostalgia, a longing for something, for the people of four years ago, for the people of our respective childhoods as well.

"You're pretty deep in thought, young man." Ellie surprised me.

"Yeah. I guess I was pretty deep into something there. I was remembering the discussion we had when you first moved. Remember that?"

"Yes." She strained to recover some of those earlier words. "Barely I do. About my childhood and the old place?"

"Yes. And your mother and father," I reminded her.

"Yes. I remember. I wonder what Mushy remembers of those days. I'll bet you very little. He sure likes to lock his past away. He thinks only of the future now. Every night in bed he's got another plan, another dream. Trips, property, real estate. The kids going to college. I have to tell him, 'Mushy, it's 1973, not 1993. Let time pass. You're living in an age that hasn't even been born yet. Give the world a chance to do what it's going to do. Mushy wants it to be 1993, that's fine with me, but he can damn well get there without me. I'll just take my own sweet time about it." She ended by pulling extra hard on the tie of her apron strings.

After sitting a while in silence, I rose from my chair. Through the window above the sink I saw Ted walking through a light rain. Ellie did not see him.

"I know one thing that makes me different from Mushy," she said. "I worry more than he does. I worry about what will happen. I worry there may not be ways to get things done as we want them to. But I don't worry about what I can't see, about what's not here yet. What's more, I believe you must live with a belief in God. Some things only God knows what to do with. Mushy thinks I'm nuts when I say this. So I've stopped saying it in front of him, and, for that matter, in front of the children when he's around. He worries too, but for him it's more that there won't be enough time to finish all

"Dad knew he would never be rich, that he'd never achieve anything special or wonderful in his life. . . . The world was the way it was and he was big enough to accept it."

the things he's planned to do. As for God, he's about as far from God as I am from . . . from . . . I don't know what. The President of the United States." I saw the top of Ted Graziano's head pass under the window

"Don't think for one minute I'm telling you little petty businesses in our lives," Ellie continued. "I'm telling you the most important things. We run, you might say, on different clocks. You know, like the East Coast and the West Coast. We're in the same country, speaking the same language most of the time, but we've got clocks inside of us that I'm sure run at different speeds, and in different directions as well." She hesitated again. She had more to say. The back door flew open and Ted entered the kitchen.

"A man with cigars," he began, "is a man halfway to heaven." He slammed the door shut so that the latch chain smacked loudly against the glass pane.

I had turned my body to greet him. Beside me I heard Ellie say quietly: "Two separate clocks, each ticking their own sweet time, each heading off in a direction that would probably confuse the Almighty."

HOW AND WHEN THE TENSION in their conversation grew to the proportions it would that rainy afternoon I cannot recall, or make myself recall. I was part of the tension, for I had asked the questions that aroused so many feelings. And I had split them apart by speaking intimately with each of them. Ellie was seated at the table across from me, Ted stood in the doorway between the dining space and living room, pacing in and out of our vision.

"You know, Ellie," he was saying, his anger rising, "that's probably where it all goes wrong, every time with every man and every woman."

"Where?" she asked. "Where does what go wrong?"

"Look. You and I may come from the same background," he pointed at his wife, "but there are times when we're so different it's almost laughable that we've made it this long."

"Are the kids upstairs?" Ellie questioned.

"Oh, the hell with the kids. Let 'em hear. What the hell's the difference if they hear? What do you want, children who don't know what's going on in their own house?"

"No, I don't." Ellie's voice sounded frightened.

"That's exactly what my parents always did. They tried to keep everything from us as though we didn't know what was going on. Let 'em hear for once.

"You've never been able to understand what my life is made of. I tell you plans, what might happen at work, I tell you my dreams, little that you could care."

"I listen to every one of them."

"Listening isn't enough, goddammit. It's like Tom here. He listens. But it isn't enough. You think my plans are nuts or that I live in the future somehow. Or that I got a lot of pipe dreams."

"I didn't say that."

"You do in your way. Here's a stranger come in this house is more sympathetic to the way I want to carve out my future than the woman I married. That's really a laugh."

"That's not fair, Ted," I said.

"I don't care about fair," he shot back. "We're way beyond talking about what's fair and what's not fair. I tell you things about my life, you don't come back with all the junk I have to hear from her!"

"*Her* is still in this room," Ellie said sharply. "Why don't you speak a little to *her*?"

"I *am* speaking to you. Who the hell you think I'm speaking to? The man in the moon?"

"I thought you might have been speaking to him," she nodded at me.

"When I want to speak with him, I'll speak with him. This is *our* business."

"Hey, maybe I should go," I suggested.

"No sir, you sit right there. You want to know about us, you listen to this part too. You stay around and see the seamy side too."

"Ted," Ellie broke in, "you're sounding foolish!"

"Oh shut up!" She didn't move. "You stay, Tom. I want you to hear. I work five hard days a week. That newspaper goes under, I'm out a job. I'd like you, Mrs. Know-it-all, to tell me just exactly what I'm supposed to do then. Huh? You got this philosophy you take every day one at a time? Isn't that your usual speech?"

"That's my usual speech," Ellie responded with resignation.

"Yeah. That's it. That's a terrific philosophy. You know where I'd be with that philosophy running my life? Do you *know*? *Do* you?"

"No, I don't, Ted. Where would you be?"

"I'd be with the same job I had when I was eleven years old. I'd be delivering for that McCrackle or McCarver or whatever the hell his name was." Ellie began to smile.

"Mencken," she corrected him.

"Mencken. McCracken. What the hell's the difference? You don't understand what I'm saying anyway."

"That's not true," his wife answered him. "I do."

"Yeah? Then what am I saying?" He looked at her smugly.

"That if you hadn't had some dream or goal you wouldn't have gone beyond the life you knew as a little boy."

"That's exactly right. So what I'd like to learn from you is, if you understand that, how can you be so . . . so . . . I don't know what, when it comes to listening to me?"

"I try to listen to you." Ellie's voice was kind.

"Maybe you do then. But our worlds are too different. You can't possibly understand what's in my head."

"I tell you what I believe in the best ways I can."

"That the God . . . you mean that God stuff?"

"Yes," she said firmly. "That God stuff, as you call it."

"That's where we part. I mean, that's where it all falls apart."

"Why? Where? What's falling apart, Ted?"

"Us. You, me. The whole thing. It falls apart. You rely on some set of beliefs that bring nothing." His anger, which had subsided, rose again. "God doesn't buy homes. God doesn't pay bills. Men do that. God don't provide! Love don't provide! You can go to church . . ."

"I realize that."

"You can go to church every day of the week, my friend, but if I don't work, or you don't work, you don't eat. You ever hear God throwing down food, or clothes? Or homes? Does your friend God do *that*?"

"Of course not. That's not why people . . ."

"You see you're wrong there. I'm sorry to correct you, but that's exactly what all those poor slobs go there on Sundays for. They march off to church and give their last pennies to God and beg Him to give them food or shelter, or whatever the hell they ask for."

Ted bent over and pointed at her, all the while keeping his distance. "That's why the poor are poor!" he yelled at her.

"Ted."

"C'mon, Ted," I joined in.

"Ted nothing," he came back. I made another gesture to leave. Ted came at me and grabbed my shoulder, pushing me back in the chair. "You wanna think of me as a madman, go ahead. But you'll leave here only when I'm finished."

"C'mon, Ted," I tried again.

"No, *you* listen! Both of you. The reason the poor stay poor is because of what *you* believe." He pointed at Ellie.

"You mean *I'm* the cause of people being poor," she said sarcastically.

"That's exactly right. *You're* the cause. All this business of living day by day, of wanting God to solve problems, of not doing things until they actually happen, until they actually fall into your goddamn lap, *you* believe that, and that's why people like you don't get anywhere. People are making it in this country every day of their lives. You still have a chance. But this business of laughing at someone 'cause he plans, or . . . praying—that's the end, boy. That's the living end. You hold onto your childhood, you've never let it go, and we're married almost twenty years. You see your mother as much as you see your husband. I'd love to know what in hell you two

can find to talk about every day. That's something for you to study, Tom." Ellie had placed her head in her hands. She made no sound. "But you don't hear me complain about what portion of my salary goes to supporting your mother, do you?"

"No, I don't hear you complain," Ellie whispered.

"WHAT'D YOU SAY?" Ted screamed at her. She lifted her head and answered him loudly: "I said, 'No, I don't hear you complain.' "

"No, I don't complain. I just shell out dough left and right for all those little things you bring her every day because that beautiful saint of a father of yours who loved everybody and everybody loved him, never planned, never dreamed. It ain't enough to be nice."

"Don't you dare speak about my father," Ellie said bitterly, staring at him.

"I'll speak about anyone I damn please. Who the hell's paying for this house anyway?"

"Yeah, well, you don't have to speak about the dead."

"I'm not speaking about the dead. I'm speaking about poor people; people who think love and niceness and praying in a church are what matter. It's all a lot of *shit*! Your parents were *full* of shit!"

"Ted!" she screamed at him. "Stop it!"

"And *my* parents were full of shit. None of 'em knew what was going on. They minded their own business and decided if this is what history brought them, then that's the way it had to be. Now you go ahead and look around at their children. Who's doing anything worthwhile? Huh? Who's dreaming about the future and not about the past? Huh? You and your mother cause poverty. You sit together like mentals dreaming of the good old days when your father was alive, and none of you gives a rat's ass that you were poor."

"Ted, please." Across from me, Ellie began to weep. My presence made it more difficult for her.

"Ted," I said, "I'm gonna go."

"You're not going. I'm not done." We looked at Ellie. "Let her cry. She cries all the time. Maybe we should call her mother over and they could have a good cry together about the old days. Maybe we could make an invention and bring back the dead." Ellie was sobbing.

"You're a monster."

"*I'm* the monster. Sure. *I'm* the monster, because I'm a little different from those idiots who run to church. I speak the truth. All you have is yesterday and today. That's *all* women have. Memories, tears, dreams, MOTHERS! You take a look at rich people someday. You know what they're doing?" He continued to pace up and back across the room. "They're planning so many things for their lives they ain't got time to go to church. They got the lives of their kids

"The rich work to make their lives work out. They've got things figured out you wouldn't even be able to dream of."

planned and their kids' kids. Jesus, you talk to some rich guy with his insurance policies and his trust funds. You ask them if they live day by day. They're an army, the rich. They march on the future and rip it up. They don't wait to see how their kids are turning out. They put 'em in the best schools, like these finishing schools, so's they can make sure the kids will *have* to turn out right."

He stopped, then pointed over his wife's shoulder. "You get windows over kitchen sinks like this one." I looked at him quizzically. "Windows over kitchen sinks," he repeated, nodding his head up and down. "The rich work to make their lives work out. They've got things figured out you wouldn't even be able to dream of. Believe me, I know. They think in enormous blocks of time. They're moving in decades, all the time left in this century. It's all big business. That's what their life is based on. Big business. Now, in this shitty little house, which is about the best I'm ever gonna be able to do, this woman here stands in front of a sink looking out the window all day worrying either ·about the weather, or whether it's daytime or nighttime. That's all women know. If it's daytime you make breakfast, if it's nighttime you make dinner. Bills, plans, what's going to become of us, they couldn't care less. Nighttime, daytime, all they want to know is what's in the cabinets to eat. Women and children. They're one and the same."

So what do you want of me, Ted? What do you want of me?" Ellie's voice and tears were frightening to Ted. He moved back, disappearing into the dining area. "Okay," she said, "you're a big man, you're doing a great job here in front of us, putting on this big show, probably for Tom. Now, just what is it that you want? Just what do you want me and my mother and *your* children to do? Why don't you answer that instead of carrying on here like a mental case. *You* answer, for once. You want me to work? Is that it? You want the kids to stop going to school and go to work? Here, give me the phone. I'll call up the schools and pull the kids out. That's what you want, isn't it? C'mon. C'mon. Here, big guy, gimme the phone. Come on!" She held her open hand out in front of her. "HERE!" she screamed. Ted walked toward her.

"Stop it, goddammit. The both of you," I heard myself yell.

"I'll give you," Ted was saying, "I'll give you the phone, across your fresh mouth is where I'll give you the phone."

"Go ahead," Ellie yelled. "You talk so much. Why don't you do something instead of babbling on like this, like some kind of an escapee from a mental hospital."

His mouth closed, he nodded sarcastically. "Escapee from a mental . . . This is what I gotta take. Every day of my life. I'm making it possible for four human beings to lead their lives with a little dignity." His voice had quieted somewhat. "Four ungrateful human beings. I don't have a soul to talk to in this house. I see the way people are living. I see the way people are dying, and we're not getting any of it. I can't even afford to get us ground in the cemetery. Has that, Mrs. Big Mouth, ever crossed that brilliant brain of yours? Where, exactly, would you like them to put my corpse when I die if I don't arrange for a plot? Here? Would you like it in the kitchen maybe? Just where do the poor die? You ever think of that?

"I see the future that you and your mother and all those idiots at church pray to God to take care of for you. I *see* that future. I'm already seventy years old and still working, still lifting Sunday papers, still dragging my ass around that goddamn hole. You're praying, and I'm working to have enough money to buy a place, and a way to get rid of my body which, if you'd really care to know, was dead a long, long time ago."

He glared at the two of us before continuing.

"Let me give you both a bit of a lesson. You," he said, pointing to me, "will have to excuse me if I don't sound like some important professor from MIT. A man doesn't die when his heart stops. That's not the only death a man has got to look forward to. There are lots of deaths . . ."

"Like when your parents die?" Ellie quietly interrupted.

"NO!" he yelled at her. "Wrong again. Those are the deaths that women fall apart with. Men don't die at the sight of death. You talk to soldiers. They fight with guys falling down all around 'em. Women go to cemeteries and fall apart. Men hold women together because they know more about death than women. They know more about death because they work. They work every damn day of their lives and so they know what it is to reach a point where you can't go any further. That's the death a man knows. The death of effort. You ever hear of the word incapacitated?" he asked his wife.

"Of course I did," Ellie answered.

"Of course I did," he mocked her in baby talk. "Of course you *don't*, you mean. You can't know 'cause women can't know the thought every day of your life something happening and you're not able to work again." He glared at Ellie, assured that I, a man, would have to agree. "That's death, my friend."

"And women don't know that?" she inquired.

"No, women don't know that. You don't know the feelings of these other deaths until you find yourself in a world where you don't have any choice, and you just stay at it, like it or not, knowing you better damn well stay healthy or a whole group of people are going to fall flat on their faces."

"You're talking through your hat," Ellie started. "How hard do you think it would be for all of us to go to work? We could all make up the difference. Did *you*, Mr. Bright Ideas, ever think of *that?*"

"Many, many, many times," Ted replied softly. "Many times I've thought about what it would be like having your wife and children working while you sat around the house, sick or tired or something. That, my friend, is another form of death. That may be the worst death of all. When women work it's a fill-in. They substitute, and brother, when they put in the substitutes it's because the first team either stinks or can't play. Or maybe," he smiled, " 'cause the first team's got a lead they'll never catch. If only it worked that way. If only I could ever get ahead of it, instead of always chasing, chasing, chasing. . . ."

"What are you chasing, chasing, chasing?" Ellie asked, looking up. "What is it that you're always after that you can know all these *special* deaths that no one else seems to know anything about? Huh?"

"I'm chasing life!" he yelled back at her. "I'm chasing the rich and the government and my bosses and taxes and bills. That's what I'm chasing. I'm a drowning man, chasing after a breath. After air. Is that enough for you? I don't take life day by day and sit back and dream about the beautiful past. Anybody does that has already drowned.

"How do you think it works out there? That somebody just *gives* you things? Things come to you because you work your goddamn ass off. And what's more, you can work your ass off every day of your life and end up with this!" He held his hand up making a zero sign with his thumb and index finger. "Zero!" he yelled. "Nothing! You can work just like your father did and end up with nothing!"

"He was a happy man on the day he died."

"The hell he was. You don't know anything about your father. You ask your brother about your father. Ask your mother. She knows. Maybe now that you're a big girl she'll tell you some of the real facts of life. Go ask her when you see her tomorrow. Go now, for Christ's sake, it's been almost an hour since you've seen the old lady. And ask your mother about his drinking."

"Shut up, Ted." Ellie was angered and embarrassed. She looked at me.

"I'm not supposed to be saying anything about that, eh? I'm supposed to keep my mouth shut so Tom can think that everything around us and our beautiful childhoods was perfect? You ask your mother about how many times your father died in his life before the Good Lord took him away. Ask her. She'll tell you. He died every night of his life. Every night he came home to that dump your family lived in, he died. You think it's easy for a man every day to look around at his life and be reminded of what a pitiful failure he is, and always will be? That's the death part, Ellie. And that's the part, re-porter, you better write about if you want to understand people like us. It's seeing every day of your life what you got and *knowing*, knowing like your own name, that it ain't never gonna get any better. That's what you live with, and that's what your father had in his mind and in his body every day, and every night. That's why a man drinks. Believe me, I know. You keep it from your children just so long. In this country, there ain't no one who fails and holds his head up. Any man who holds his head up after he loses is just trying to protect himself. No one likes a loser. That's why the rich can't stand us. That's why we moved here. What we had together all those years were *prisons*. They were advertisements of how much we didn't have. You got any doubts about it, you just turn on the TV and see the way people are living with their new cars and their boats, and with their homes in the country. How many times a day they gotta remind you of that, I'd like to know?"

FOR THE FIRST TIME, Ellie was nodding assent. I had seen her face show relief moments before when, unthinkingly, Ted had used the phrase, "the Good Lord took him away." Now she was her husband's wife, his woman. The direction of his anguish had shifted, and it was America, the rich, social classes, me, that he attacked and held responsible. No longer was it men against women; it was the poor against the rich, those who can, with a genuine sense, of autonomy and possibility underwriting it, achieve with dignity, and those who must sweat out the work, the waiting, and the decisions of bosses for bonuses and a chance to move ahead slightly.

Ted stood, not exactly next to his wife, but closer to her, leaving me, still seated, the third person. For long minutes the three of us were silent, Ellie and I staring at the tabletop, Ted standing near us, motionless. I could feel my eyebrows rising and falling as though something in me wanted to signal the two of them. Ted broke the silence, and turned to me. His voice was even and resolute. "Don't you worry about us. You go ahead and write whatever you feel you should." That was all he said the rest of that afternoon.

Two feelings had come over me, two feelings as distinct as shaking hands with both Grazianos simultaneously, Ted's right hand in my right hand, Ellie's hand in my left hand. I felt first, that I had been as moved by these two people as I had ever been by anyone or anything. But I felt, too, a desire to make all three of us special and unforgettable; famous, I suppose. I was halfway home, driving through an angry rain that made visibility almost impossible, before the one word that swirled in my head finally came to rest. Immortality.

"When women work it's a fill-in. They substitute, and brother, when they put in the substitutes it's because the first team either stinks or can't play."

IV b. Family Processes

C.H. ELDRIDGE '76

20

Decision Making and the Family Life Cycle

by Reuben Hill

The Family Developmental Approach

The family development approach emphasizes the time dimension neglected by the other conceptual frameworks dealing with the family, but its focus is on the family as a small group, the nuclear family occupying a common household. The time units employed encompass the family life span expressed in stages of development but subdivided into years of marriage.

The approach is eclectic in its incorporation of the compatible sections of several other approaches to the study of the family. From rural sociology the family development theorists have borrowed the concept of stages of the family life cycle which they have greatly elaborated, giving the phasing of the life cycle a theoretical rationale. From child psychology and human development have come the concepts of developmental needs and tasks. From the sociologists engaged in work on the sociology of the professions we have borrowed the concepts of career, viewing the family as a convergence of intercontingent careers of the positions of husband and wife, later of parents and children. From the structure-function and interactional schools has been borrowed the trio of concepts, position, role, and norms, particularly as these involve age and sex roles and changing family size. The many concepts associated with the family as a system of interacting personalities find their place in the modifications of the concept of role seen in role-playing, role-taking, reciprocity of roles, and role differentiation. These several concepts have been assembled together in a frame of reference that furnishes an opportunity for accretion of generalizations about the internal development of families from their formation in the engagement and wedding to their dissolution in divorce or death. The scope and organization of this framework may be described as follows:

"The family development approach views the family as a small group system, intricately organized internally into paired positions of husband-father, wife-mother, son-brother, and daughter-sister. Norms prescribing the appropriate role behavior for each of these positions specify how reciprocal relations are to be maintained, as well as how role behavior may change with changing ages of the occupants of these positions. This intimate small group has a predictable natural history, designated by stages beginning with the simple husband-wife pair and becoming more and more complex as members are added and new positions created, with the number in interpersonal relations reaching a peak with the birth of the last child, stabilizing for a brief period, to become less and less complex subsequently with the launching of adult children into jobs and marriage as the group contracts in size once again to the dyadic interactions of the husband-wife pair. As the age composition of the family changes, so do the age-role expectations for occupants of the positions in the family, and so does the quality of interaction among family members.

"Viewed social psychologically and developmentally, the family is an arena of interacting personalities, each striving to obtain the satisfaction of his desires. Parents often defer the satisfaction of their own immediate needs, however, in building complementary roles between themselves and their children. At some stages of development, parents and children are good company; at other stages, their diverse developmental strivings may be strikingly incompatible" (Hill, 1961, p. 63).

An immediate by-product of this conceptual framework has been its sensitizing effect upon researchers utilizing the family as the unit of study. Any research which seeks to generalize about families without taking into account the variation caused by the stages of family development represented in the sample will leave much variance unaccounted for, just as studies which ignore social class differences leave much unexplained. Buying patterns, saving patterns, and mobility patterns can be expected to vary greatly over the family life span, as will many other family behaviors as yet unassessed by family life-cycle categories.

Using the family developmental approach to behavior to analyze decision making in the family urges us to ask certain questions and to anticipate certain regularities. First of all, the approach divides the family cycle into stages of growth and development which have been demarcated by application of role theory to the changing positions in a family as it moves forward in time. The role content of the several positions in the family constitutes the *role complex* of the family at a given point in time. A stage of development would change, according to the framework, each time a fundamental change in the age role content in the positions making up the family occurs, or in other words each time the family's role complex changes.

The theoretically most sophisticated schemes for differentiating stages of the family life span today utilize three sets of data as indicators of change in role complex:

A first criterion used for dividing up the life span is the observable "number of positions in the family," which permits inferring stages of "expression," of "stability," and of "contraction" to be blocked off. Changes in stages of development (because fundamental changes in role complex occur) would be required by the birth of the first child, launching of first child into marriage, and launching of last child.

A second criterion involves the age composition of the family, which reflects indirectly the *family's complex of age role expectations in reciprocity* at any one time in the history of the family. This criterion requires that a stage be changed each time the role complex changes in any degree. If we were engaged in undertaking case studies of individual families, this procedure would be most interesting to follow, but in seeking to differentiate stages of development for large numbers of families it would be highly impractical to designate a new stage each time the complex of age role expectations changed, since there would be almost as many different combinations of stages (family careers) as there are families in the study. Duvall, reflecting the judgments of the various committees working on the problem since 1948, chose a simpler solution to the problem in her text (Duvall 1962). She suggests that it is sufficient to change stages of development each time the oldest child shifts from one significant age category to another. Of all the children, to be sure, the oldest child's development is the most significant for the shift in role content in the parents' positions, since his experiences present new and different problems which as yet the family has not encountered and bring about the most modification of role content in all other positions in the family. The significant age categories in which changes would be expected to occur in our society include: infant, preschool child, school child, adolescent, young adult, middle-aged adult, and aged adult.

A third criterion involves the change in the age role content in the husband-father position which occurs with his retirement from active employment. For the mother who has not been gainfully employed, her retirement from active mothering occurs with the launching of her last child into marriage and is captured in the shift in the family's role complex from the launching center to the post-parental stage.

Employing these three sets of readily available data of numbers of positions in the family, age composition of the family, and employment status of the father, several stages of the family life span can be differentiated, each representing a distinctive role complex, as follows: Stage I Establishment (newly married, childless); II New Parents (infant–3 years); III Preschool Family (child 3–6

years and possibly younger siblings); IV School-Age Family (oldest child 6–12 years, possibly younger siblings); V Family with Adolescent (oldest 13–19, possibly younger siblings); VI Family with Young Adult (oldest 20, until first child leaves home); VII Family as Launching Center (from departure of first to last child); VIII Post-parental Family, The Middle Years (after children have left home until father retires); IX Aging Family (after retirement of father).

Some generalizations which flow from the framework

The view of the stages of the family life cycle as distinctive role complexes opens up the way for anticipating the content of the family interaction for each of these stages. If we begin by looking at the focus of this conference on the aging family, we can readily see that the aged generation will be disproportionately found in Stage IX, with some representatives still in Stage VIII. The numerical composition of the family for both of these stages, in contrast with those which preceded them, is simple and stable —two positions with only one interpersonal relationship to maintain, a companionate dyad. This can be quite a contraction for large families. For the family of ten persons in which the author grew up, for example, there was a contraction from forty-five interpersonal relationships, which constituted the number the author's parents coped with before launching their eight children into jobs and marriage, to one in the post-parental period. The parental role content of the two positions which are left in the family in the post-parental stage (Stage VIII), as opposed to the spousal role content, is in the process of continuous redefinition, and by the time the couple enters Stage IX, almost fourteen years later, the nurturant, guiding, and socializing content will have largely disappeared in favor of a more symmetrical set of norms of mutual aid and reciprocity in exchanges between the generations.

The stages of family development are suggestive also of contrasts in needs, in volume of plans, and in willingness to take risks in the form of purchases and other commitments which affect the direction of decisions in the family. At the beginning of the family's life span, in Stages I–IV, the family tends to be future oriented, living with rapidly expanding needs for shelter spaces, for facilities, durable goods, and means of transportation. Needs press heavily on resources as the ratio of dependents to earners mounts, and we would accordingly expect that the volume of plans and decisions to make residential moves, to remodel, to purchase goods, to change jobs, and to purchase protective insurances to be very high. We would also expect concomitantly that the willingness to accept help from kin and peers as well as the utilization of credit from commercial sources would also be greater than at any other period in the life span.

In Stages V–VI, the stages of rearing school-age and adolescent children, we would expect the family to be more oriented to the here and now, to have achieved some equilibrium of interaction, but to be still heavily pressed with high needs for housing and added facilities.

In Stage VII, the stage of launching children into jobs and marriage, the family undergoes maximum contraction in size and experiences an irregular but slow decline in pressure of needs on resources. In many families the wife-mother has returned to the labor force, providing a double income to equalize the costs of higher education and of marrying off the children. The uncertainties and ambiguities of in-law roles and of grandparental roles are introduced into the positions of the family heads during this period. There are also complications of establishing mutually agreeable helping patterns for the newly married children through gift giving, exchanges, and loans.

In Stage VIII the family enters a stage of recovery financially, often with two earners, with disposable income for the first time since Stage I. The disposable income may be invested for retirement, but may also be turned to upgrading the level of living of the post-parental couple and helping both married offspring and their own aged parents. For some mothers it is a period of retirement from the protective roles that have been central to the career of wife and mother, so that they experience many of the adjustments to loss of functions which the breadwinner experiences at retirement. Mothers who have entered the labor force, on the other hand, experience the adjustments of loss of functions when retiring from their jobs years later. We would expect for the family as a whole that this would be a period of continued high volume of economic activity and, therefore, of decision making.

In Stage IX, with both spouses retired, we expect a net change in the direction of giving, restrictions on the helping of married offspring who are now economically established, and a reversal of roles with the aged receiving more help than they give. There will be sharply restricted economic activity over the years which remain. In this stage particularly we would expect the family to be more oriented to the past, making accordingly fewer attempts to structure the future.

From the standpoint of decision making, then, the framework has suggested a number of regularities which are relevant while leaving room for the discovery of many others. It has suggested that the sheer volume of economic activity will rise rapidly at the beginning of the life span of the family, level off, and then decline. Indeed, that is probably the excuse to call the family life span a life cycle, since so many behaviors are of this order: residental mobility, occupational mobility, complexities of family interaction owing to changing plurality patterns, and so on. Long-term as against short-run type planning will be expected to appear more in the early than in the middle and late stages of family development because of the different time orientations of the generations.

The framework does not tell us anything about the relative success the families will have in preplanning their economic activities at various points in the life span, nor whether families will be more or less rational in their decision making at the beginning, in the middle, or at the end of the life span. The framework tells us little indeed about expected changes in power allocation or the allocation of duties in the family over the life span, although some empirical studies using the framework have advanced some findings on these issues (Rollins, 1963, pp. 13, 20). These are among the discoveries we can anticipate in studying families empirically by stages of development.

Empirical findings

To answer the questions raised in this paper we should ideally have available longitudinal data on decision making over the entire life span of a cohort of couples who entered marriage in the same year. No such data have ever been collected in the history of family research, in part because of the cost and continuity of research organization required. The few data the we do have were collected in synthetic longitudinal studies of various types drawn from cross-sectional samples. A sample of couples of different durations of marriage is interviewed and the resulting responses aggregated as if they were drawn from a marital cohort moving over time. The study of decision making by Blood and Wolfe is of this type (1960, pp. 41–44). They demonstrate that the husband's power in the family structure increases from the honeymoon period, Stage I, where there are no children, to Stage II-III with young children, and declines slowly through the various subsequent stages of family development into the post-parental period, Stage VIII, after which it drops sharply as the husband retires in Stage IX. In recent years this same device of aggregating cross-sectional samples to construct the life cycle of families has been widely carried out in making generalizations about consumer behavior: the timing of home ownership, automobile ownership, the acquisition of television sets, automatic dryers, and so on (Clark, 1955, pp. 28–58, 61–66). The hazards of generalizing from such synthetic longitudinal studies have been covered in some detail elsewhere in which the author discusses the relative advantages and disadvantages of five methodological short cuts that have been devised to circumvent the costs and travail of longitudinal research with families (Hill, 1964).

In this paper we turn to the least unsatisfactory set of data available about decision making over the life cycle. We are drawing from data obtained from an intergenerational sample and are treating the data obtained from the youngest of three generations as representative of the early stages of the cycle, the data from the parent generation as representative of the middle stages, and the responses from the grandparent generation as depicting the last stages of development. By placing findings of the other two generations in juxtaposition with those from the grandparent generation, we can gain some idea of the distinguishing characteristics of decision making among older couples. The findings we cite are valuable in their own right but should be used cautiously when generalizing about changes in decision making over the life cycle. It would be more defensible to refer to our findings as changes in decision making over three generations.

The data which we shall use for an empirical description of decision making have been collected as part of the Minnesota Consumership Study. The areas of planning and decision making covered included eight recurring problems requiring long-range planning and fairly elaborate decision making: residential location, redecoration, remodeling, acquisition of durable goods and of automobiles, changes in the family's financial portfolio in savings, investments, insurance, provisions for retirement, and changes of occupation (change of job by husband, entering or leaving labor force by wife). Methods of data collection have included four semistructured interviews with wives, one joint interview with both spouses, tests and questionnaires filled out by both spouses, and direct observation of stress situations by interviewers.

The choice of intact families drawn from three generations of the same family line assures us relative homogeneity of family culture. Moreover, it provides us with three contrast groups to highlight the differences in decision making over the life span. A description of the families selected will make this even clearer. An intergenerational sample of intact families linked through three generations living within fifty miles of Minneapolis-St. Paul was obtained from area probability samples of the metropolitan area. Three hundred and twelve nuclear families, composed of 100 grandparent families, 105 parent families, and 107 young married families, survived four waves of interviews covering a year's observations. These families are ecologically dispersed within the metropolitan area and its hinterland; they are well distributed by social class and economic levels, but are somewhat more stable residentially than comparable families without three-generation linkages. The three generations have the following characteristics:

1. Age: Grandparents 60–80; parents 40–60; married children 20–30.
2. Ethnic make-up: Grandparents, ¼ Scandinavian, ½ other Northern European, balance Southern European; parents and children, similar.
3. Religious affiliation: ⅓ Catholic, ⅔ Protestant (Lutheran dominant), some Jewish. High continuity of religious affiliation from generation to generation.
4. Income: Grandparents, $1,000 to $6,000, ½ under $2,000; Parents, $1,000 to $20,000, ½ under $5,000; Married children, $2,000 to $10,000, ½ under $4,000.
5. Children in residence: Grandparents, no children at home; parents, ⅔ with children still at home; married children, 1/10 no children yet; ⅔ with children all below school age, 1/5 with children of school age under 12 years of age.

With this background let us turn to the performance of the three generations over a twelve-month period in 1958 to highlight the similarities and differences found among the three generations. We begin with a comparative picture of the financial and housing constraints operative on the three generations, as well as the types of problems perceived as requiring help over the twelve-month period. Second, we shall examine the location of power in decision making and degree of differentiation of sex roles by generation. Third, our research design permits us to examine within several areas of activity the volume of plans enunciated and actions taken, the planning horizons, the proportion of plans fulfilled, the degree of rationality in decision making, and the degree of satisfaction expressed with the actions taken. Our empirical overview will conclude with some of the correlates of planning, rationality, and satisfaction in the grandparent generation.

Situational constraints affecting decision making

We must remember that each of the three generations has had a different history before entering the twelve-month period of observation. The grandparent generation is educationally, occupationally, and financially handicapped compared with the younger generations. Educationally grandfathers averaged 6 years of schooling, fathers 9 years, and grandsons 12.6 years. Occupationally the grandfathers began lowest on the scale and have made the slowest movement upward. There has been an acceleration of occupational upgrading generation by generation when each is compared year by year since marriage. In each successive generation, more of the wives have worked during the first several years of marriage and more have returned to work after their children grew up. In all economic matters we can say that the married child generation is destined to outstrip the previous generations based on the achievements of each generation during the first ten years of marriage. In home ownership the married child generation has already exceeded the grandparent generation (80 percent homeowners) and is where the parent generation was only after twenty years of marriage. In acquisition of durable goods the married child generation has overtaken the grandparent generation and is at a point in its inventory where the parent generation was after thirty-five years of marriage—the same can be said for bathroom and bedroom spaces in the home and other amenities. This has not been done at the expense of protective insurances or retirement provisions, for the married child generation is well along in the acquisition of a portfolio of insurances and investments. Over 50 percent have retirement provisions over and beyond Social Security and 95 percent have life insurance. This married child generation starts its marriage with 82 percent covered, which is higher than their grandparents ever reached, and is as high as their parents achieved after thirty years of marriage.

The pressure of members on resources is greatest in the early stages of the life cycle. As the study began, the married children had the most children resident in the home (two) and had the fewest rooms per family (4.6). Grandparents had no children and had the next highest number of rooms (4.9). The parent generation had the most rooms (5.6) with two thirds of the families having a child still at home. In quality of housing, however, grandparents had the lowest rental values, and more of them lived in the lowest grade neighborhoods, two thirds in Class C and Class D areas compared with 50 percent among the parent generation.

We earlier indicated substantial differences in average income and in the range of income among the three generations, with grandparents averaging below-subsistence incomes (one-half under $2,000). We asked families for their subjective definition of the adequacy of their current income in terms of its sufficiency to buy necessities and luxuries. Table 1 tabulates the responses of the three generations in percentage form and suggests that the grandparent generation feel the financial squeeze more than the other two generations. Half of them are barely meeting the necessities, but 14.5 percent are on easy street. Three-fourths of the married child group checked the median expression, "We have the things we need and a few of the extras." Only one couple in this generation, however, feels really "flush." The parents are not only factually better off (in income, housing, and durable goods), but they feel more comfortable, distributing their answers towards the luxury end of the scale.

TABLE 1

PERCENTAGE DISTRIBUTION OF RESPONSES ON ADEQUACY OF
FAMILY INCOME BY GENERATION

Responses	Grandparents Percent	Parents Percent	Married Children Percent
Total	100.0	100.0	100.0
Do without many needed things	28.0	4.7	1.2
Have the things we need, but none of the extras	23.5	5.9	4.8
Have the things we need, and a few of the extras	30.5	61.0	76.0
Have the things we need and any extras we want, and still have money left over to save or invest	3.5	14.2	16.8
	14.5	14.2	1.2
Number of families	85	85	83

Degree of interdependence for mutual aid

We have indicated earlier in this chapter that family development theory anticipates some reversals in dependency-interdependency relations among the generations by stage of development. In the last of the four interviews respondents in each generation were asked to give an accounting of help given and received during the year from all sources including immediate and extended kin, peers, church, social agencies, private specialists, and commercial sources in the problem areas of illness, child care, household management, emotional gratification, and economic assistance.

When examined by vulnerability to problems requiring help, the parent generation was lowest in vulnerability (44.7 percent receiving no help of a stress or problem-area nature); the grandparent generation was next lowest (32.9 percent receiving no help due to crises). The married child generation with its infant-age dependents was most vulnerable (only 21 percent receiving no help of a crisis nature during the year).

The three generations reported an involvement in a vast nexus of transfers of one sort or another during the year, over five thousand, of which 3,781 were quite clearly help exchanges. Table 2 has been prepared to demonstrate the social networks within which help is exchanged. First of all, we note that help exchanges within the vertical kin (giving and receiving help, other generations) exceeds all other categories in the social networks for each of the generations. This is especially true for the grandparents for whom 65 percent of the instances of help received was familial (from children, the parent generation, or grandchildren) compared with 53 percent for the parent generation and 44 percent for the married grandchildren. The child generation operates in a wider flung network of exchanges with a less concentrated pattern especially of giving within the vertical kin line (only 28 percent) and giving proportionately more than the other generations to horizontal and vertical kin once removed (siblings, cousins, aunts, uncles, nieces, and nephews), 25 percent compared to 14 percent for the parent generation and only 9 percent for the grandparents. To all other sources (religious organizations, health and welfare agencies, and other specialists), the grandparents give proportionately

the most (29 pecent) followed by the other two generations at 25 percent each. Age mates are least likely to be recipients of help for the parent and child generation, whereas for the aged generation the horizontal and vertical kin once removed are least seen as targets for help.

In general we note that help instances given exceed those received for all generations and for virtually all categories of the social network. The level of giving is highest for the parent generation and lowest for the grandparents. The child generation leads in volume of receiving as might be expected, given its heavy needs.

In Table 3 we have looked much more intensively at the 1,674 exchanges which occurred exclusively among the three generations by type of help provided or received. The parent generation, within this narrower network, is again the most active in giving help and the married child generation the most frequent recipient of help. The grandparent generation both gave and received least of the three generations in help items of all kinds. The parent generation is the sociometric star of the interchanges, giving more to the married children and to the grandparents than either gives to the other. The parent generation also receives in exchange more from the grandparents and from the married children than either grandparents or grandchildren receive in their interchanges. By area of need grandparents required more help in the problem of illness (61 percent), household management (52 percent), and emotional gratification (42 percent), whereas the married child generation received help especially in the problem areas of child care (78 percent) and of economic assistance (49 percent).

Perhaps the most interesting findings in Table 3 are those which compare percentages receiving and giving help in five categories by generation. The parent generation quite clearly gives more help than it receives in all five areas of exchange. The grandparents, in sharp contrast, receive substantially more help than they give in all areas except child care where they have, obviously, no need of help. The married child generation gives more than it receives in three areas—emotional gratification, household management, and illness. This generation, on the other hand, receives more than it gives in the economic-assistance and child-care areas. We get from this table a most interesting picture of changes in symbiosis

TABLE 2

COMPARISON OF HELP INSTANCES GIVEN TO HELP INSTANCES RECEIVED BY
GENERATION AND BY VARIOUS SOURCES OVER A YEAR'S PERIOD*

Generation	Source or Recipient	Percent of Help Instances:		Total Instances of Help
		Given	Received	
Grandparent	Total	100	100	. . . .
	Other generations	47	65	521
	Peers	15	16	148
	Horizontal and vertical kin once removed	9	8	80
	All other agencies	29	10	206
		N = 574	381	955
Parent	Total	100	100	. . . .
	Other generations	44	53	637
	Peers	17	21	246
	Horizontal and vertical kin once removed	14	20	212
	All other agencies	25	6	252
		N = 890	457	1347
Married children	Total	100	100	. . . .
	Other generations	28	44	516
	Peers	22	20	316
	Horizontal and vertical kin once removed	25	27	380
	All other agencies	25	9	267
		N = 844	635	1479
	Total instances of help	2308	1473	3781

* Percents may not total 100 due to rounding.

over the generations. In the beginning of the life span the married child generation is apparently quite willing to receive various kinds of help and perceives itself more or less in equilibrium in its giving and receiving. It appears to benefit more from exchanges that are reciprocal than does the grandparent generation. The grandparents perceive themselves as both meager givers and high receivers, almost in a *dependency status,* whereas the parent generation, in contrast, is high in giving and modest in receiving, a *patron-type status.* Only the married child generation appears high both in giving and receiving, a *status of high reciprocity* and *interdependence* within its social network.

TABLE 3

COMPARISON OF HELP RECEIVED AND HELP GIVEN BY GENERATION
FOR CHIEF PROBLEM AREAS*

	TYPE OF CRISIS									
	Economic		Emotional Gratification		Household Management		Child Care		Illness	
	Gave Percent	Received Percent	Gave Percent	Received Percent	Gave Percent	Received Percent	Gave Percent	Received Percent	Gave Percent	Received Percent
Total	100	100	100	100	100	100	100	100	100	100
Grandparents	26	34	23	42	21	52	16	0	32	61
Parents	41	17	47	37	47	23	50	23	21	21
Married children . .	34	49	31	21	33	25	34	78	47	18

* Percents may not total 100 due to rounding.

21

The First Four Long Years of a Family Commune: A Case Study

by Dennis T. Jaffe

A small group of families living together now has an opening. We own our unusual home, share expenses, not incomes—we all hold outside jobs. We're beginning our fourth year of vegetable gardening. We tend toward organic methods and healthful diet. Membership requires no initial monetary commitment. Operating and food costs are billed monthly. If you are seriously interested in exploring community living as a more human life style, call us. On Friday nights we often have charades, poetry reading, or candlemaking. Saturdays—harvesting potatoes, building, or splitting logs.

Every year or so you can find an ad like this in the *New Republic* and other national magazines. Those who answer are invited to visit a communal settlement which defies almost every counter-cultural stereotype. About twenty people—toddlers, children, teenagers, unmarried and married couples, and a set of grandparents—live on a lovely estate in a wealthy suburban town. The families who started the commune had the same conventional roots as their neighbors, yet in five years the consequences of their decision to set up a joint household have been a chain of events that has altered every aspect of their inner and outer lives.

Those who call are invited to the Friday evening soup meal, made from the week's leftover food, which is followed by the community and its guests doing something together. The house lies just off the main road leading out of a small city, bordered on one side by a marsh and tidal river. Approaching it, one sees a blue mailbox with the names of the people currently in residence, and an old weathered barn and carriage house

facing on the river. Woods seclude the ten acre farm from the main road and its two neighbors. Beyond the driveway is the fifteen room main house, where kitchen, common rooms, and nine bedrooms are located. Around the huge lawn are several small outbuildings. The "loft" and the "coop" are built into the garage-workshop, and have several bedrooms. There are two other cottages—"utopia" and the "apple store"—and a study (originally built for the previous owner, a judge), and now a guest room, quiet space, and repository for several libraries. Behind it is a garden and grazing room for scores of chickens, ducks, geese, two goats, a pig, and a horse.

The entrance leads to the nerve center of the house, the huge kitchen and pantry area. To feed more than twenty residents and uncountable guests, the kitchen seems to need two of everything: pantries, refrigerators, freezers, stoves, dishwashers, sinks, washers, and dryers. The pantry shelves are neatly labeled and stocked like a small grocery, with large containers of grain, flour, sugar, and rice

on the floor. Pots are usually steaming on both stoves, cooking dinner, yogurt, and maybe dye for cloth; there usually is bread baking in the oven or cooling on the side. The large table is full of papers, magazines, and the day's snacks. Notes all over the cupboards carry messages, announcements, job rosters, menus, guests expected, and a few pictures and cartoons. This is where people hang out, from the first coffee at 6:00 A.M. until after midnight.

Breakfast, dinner, and cleanup are done each day by the people who sign up to do them on the weekly job list. Through the pantry there is a small dining room, but when there are a lot of guests, the breakfast table in the kitchen and another small table in an adjoining room (which is used for sewing, weaving, and crafts) are pressed into service as well. The community has not yet found a table that can seat everybody. Dinners are served informally, either by taking a plate from the kitchen or family style, depending on the whim of the cooks. A bell rings when dinner is ready, and people drift in from the cottages, from outside, from the living rooms or their bedrooms. Despite the low weekly meal charge of $11 per person, the garden, buying wholesale and in bulk, and other economies make it possible for the household to eat substantially.

The community calls itself a "family commune," which differentiates it from other urban communes. Five suburban families—nine adults and their thirteen children—bought the property in the summer of 1970. Only two adults, neither of them married any more, and two teenagers are left from the original group, so that the original traditional meaning of the word *family* has broadened somewhat. Also living there now are three married couples—one with three grandchildren who visit in the summer—as well as two other pairs of people more loosely defined as couples, and two single women, one of them with a child. The newest house members are a couple in their 40's with four children, who sold their home and altered their work patterns to live there. They first heard of the community when they answered the ad six months before.

The commune's origins stretch back to the Unitarian Fellowship and a visit to see the movie *If,* a surrealistic fantasy of the brutality of an English public school. Glenn and Toni Warren, and their five teenage children, had lived in the same town all their lives. Glenn was an executive, and Toni had been a housewife, but recently had gone back to college full-time, studying philosophy and education. They had always been more liberal and looser than their neighbors, had a lot of people in and out of their house, and allowed their children a great deal of responsibility and freedom. Derek and Betty Pennick left England because Derek had found a job with an aerospace company as an engineer. They were more traditional in their ideas than the Warrens. The movie reminded Derek of some families they knew who shared an old estate, and he mentioned that he might like to live like that. A day later the Warrens felt the same way. Toni called up Betty and suggested that they talk more seriously.

Their exploration might not have moved beyond fantasy had it not meshed with some disturbing questions coming up in their adult education group at the Unitarian Fellowship. They were looking at the role of moral education in their own and their children's lives. Toni recalls:

> We recognized that in a normal Sunday school you meet an hour a week, go to public school six hours a day, and you're at home most of the rest. If there was anything of value in the church school, it was worth more time. We felt that we needed to set up some sort of school so that these things could be incorporated more into our lives. We felt we were trying to say something different for an hour on Sunday than was being said at all times during the week. For example, you don't study hard to get good grades to get into Harvard, but because you're interested. When we saw *If* it acted as a catalyst. We asked ourselves how well we really knew the people our kids spent all day with.

They speculated about building or buying a huge house, where they could combine a new school with a community they all would live in.

To their surprise, everyone they approached with the idea was excited, and they quickly swelled to a core group of six families. The youngest couple, Dave and Joan Linden, were about to move so that Dave could take a teaching job in another city. But they were committed enough to the idea to drive 200 miles to attend meetings. "Since they were coming all that way, we had to have formal meetings," Toni explains. They met one weekend a month, often with kids and families camping at each others' houses. One of their first decisions was not to talk very concretely about what they would do, because they knew nobody else who had ever done such a thing, and had no conception of what would happen. Their purpose was simply to find a place, and in the process to get to know each other well enough so that by the time they had to make a definite commitment, they would be sure enough of each other to go through with it.

They received some advice from an architect who had lived in a cooperative house with his family for several years. They learned from him that they had neither the skills nor the resources to design and build a

place, so they began to scout existing places. They also dropped the idea of starting a school as too ambitious, feeling that if they could succeed in living according to their values, that in itself would be the kind of education they wanted for their children. They lost one prospective piece of property, an old country inn, and in the process one of the original families dropped out. Then they discovered their present place in their own community and bought it. Since it was already being used by a group of students, they readily saw its communal possibilities.

While they all had reservations and fears about taking such a step, each one found the advantages outweighed them. The new community seemed to mark progress toward greater closeness and connectedness in their personal relations. For example, Joan felt, "we would spend long evenings talking to the Warrens, go to an opera or an outing, or write poetry, and at 5:00 A.M. we would ask, why should we have to go home, why shouldn't we all live together?" Living together would be cheaper, reducing the amount of work they would have to do at unfulfilling jobs. The children would have many adults to relate to, and a great deal of space and independence. They explored their fears and reservations as well: losing contact with their children; lack of privacy; sharing a kitchen, food and housework; and differences of opinion about child-rearing and discipline.

They knew no other people who lived communally, and the experience of counter-cultural communes, heavily publicized in the year of Woodstock, seemed to have little relevance to them. Each family's financial commitment—over $20,000 made up of cash and loan—made them seem incurably affluent, and their children weren't much younger than the average hippie commune resident. Since they all had houses to sell, and longstanding jobs, there was no trouble obtaining a mortgage. Neither were zoning laws nor community hostility problems; they had several acres of land and several buildings, each zoned for a family, and were all pillars of the church and the town. Glenn had even been named Jaycee man of the year!

In the first months they spent $10,000 to improve the place. With the cream of the furniture of several families, in its first year the house had the elegant look of the English manor which was taken as its model. The fourth family—Roger Godfrey, at 75 a vigorous, retired demographer, and his wife Inez—had made their living by buying, living in, and restoring old houses, and offered their skills. Thus, at the start the commune was more an unconventional assault on a vision of gentility than a radical experiment in personal or social change.

Their odyssey began in late summer, 1970. The five families and their fourteen children, ranging in age from five to eighteen, divided up the rooms and moved in. The Warrens had five teenage children; the Pennicks had three, ages five, seven, and ten; the Godfreys had three very young children; and Lorraine Fine, a recently divorced schoolteacher, completed the contingent with three, ages 5, 10, and 13. Dave and Joan Linden, younger than the majority by at least ten years, had no children.

The physical organization of the household came about easily. Room assignments were made which did not reinforce family boundaries. Two outbuildings were winterized. The three teenage girls took the two room cottage "utopia," and the three ten-year-old boys took the loft. The kitchen and food buying were collectivized. Everybody took turns in meal preparation and cleaning, although it took a while to evolve a workable system.

The honeymoon lasted for a few months. Every meal was a banquet, served by candlelight, and every conversation was intense and meaningful. They wanted to build on the closeness that had grown up during the planning year. But very soon they also ran into the difficulties, which, in one way or another, are faced by any new domestic commune. Most striking, each family noticed a sudden shock as the commune reduced their physical and psychic space, as well as their control over their environment. The traditional family boundaries were roughly and suddenly open to other people, at the same time that one discovers a new sense of community. Glenn talks about these simultaneous discoveries:

Initially I had two distinct feelings. One was that I was losing my family. I was afraid of that. I liked the family setup, the closeness to the children. I felt that the nuclear family feeling, closeness, was going to be gone forever, and that turned out to be true. The other feeling was one of cameraderie. Here were many families I loved, setting out on a frightening, glamorous, together thing.. We had a chance of really experiencing close friendship that we couldn't get in other ways. So there was fear and optimism at the start.

Another difficulty was their differing commitments to nuclear family and traditional couple patterns. They were not rejecting the nuclear family; their name implied that families are the building blocks of their community. But living together seemed to be a catalyst for questioning and changing their customary ways of relating. Seeing each other relating to spouses, to children, and to each other made differences in style and values acutely obvious, and the comparisons, as we will see later, seem to lead almost inevitably to change.

Almost immediately traditional sex roles began to change, and with them the couple relationships. The commune was founded before the women's liberation movement, but from the start they began sharing sex roles. For example, it was simply assumed that cooking and cleaning would be shared equally, although all the families came from households where those tasks were primarily the wife's work. Also, some of the women wanted to learn house repair and construction, and donned dungarees and participated in that work from the start.

Two of the men, Dave, who was disillusioned with college teaching, and Roger, who was retired, did not have regular jobs, and thus became involved in daily work around the house. By the end of the year they were joined by Derek, who was laid off from his engineering job, and Glenn, who became disgusted with business. Since each family needed less money to live on, living on unemployment was feasible, and quickly led each man to question why he worked at such an unfulfilling job. Work became less important, because home was a community of friends and people to share things with. The

men soon found that it was more fun to stay home than to go to work. The women, often for the first time, not only received help with household tasks, but also found the home a place where they could grow, rather than a lonely and stifling place.

Each couple reacted differently to the demands of the new environment. The Godfreys found the unexpected conflict stressful to themselves and their children, and were disappointed that the closeness and intimacy of the community was not maintained. They left after six months.

The Pennicks quickly found that the commune's values conflicted with their very traditional sex roles. They often withdrew into their room with their children, forming a nuclear family within the commune. But the presence of other people with different values observing their relationship pressured them to change. Another of the women details one perspective on the process:

Derek would be very critical of Betty, put her down, and she tended not to stand up for her position very strongly, because after all he was a Ph.D. The whole relationship was that he was superior to her, especially in thinking, so her opinions weren't taken as seriously by either of them. She became aware of this, as she talked to others, and as she saw some of the other couples trying to relate differently. She began asserting herself more, confronting him. They had to come to terms with their relationship. The women would get together to talk, and she discovered that they reacted to Derek's autocratic ways in some of the same ways she did. This gave her support for standing up, insisting that she be considered. She saw other ways of dealing that she could adopt. Other people came down on Derek, helped him to see some of what he was doing, so she didn't have the whole job of changing the relationship. Because other people objected to the same things, he couldn't say it was her trip. It was difficult for him I think.

The Pennicks moved out at the end of the second year, but soon Lorraine and her children began living with them. The Pennicks and Lorraine shared a desire for a more structured, neater household, and were not comfortable with the looser, more laissez-faire attitudes evolving in the commune.

Collective living quickly exposed difficulties and contradictions in the marriages of the Lindens and the Warrens. Both couples soon drifted apart, and by the second year both couples had separated. The Lindens found themselves in a process opposite the Pennicks. They became totally immersed in the community, not taking time to tend or nourish their couple relationship. Joan Linden recounts how differences between them, and the satisfactions of the community, led them apart:

Dave was particularly concerned with privacy when we were having a discussion or argument or anything personal between us. More so than I. And he didn't really want to go into the conflicts we were having, but just to sweep them under the rug. Since both of us were pretty involved in community things it became harder to nourish our relationship. We didn't work at it hard enough. Our expectations and our interests diverged. We looked in the community to each follow our separate interests, so we didn't have to share. That was happening so nicely that we were spending less and less time together. Our time together would be with other people around so it wasn't time for us but for community, and didn't help our relationship. It became a substitute for the relationship.

At the same time, the Warrens began to discover that after 22 years of marriage and involvement in church, children, and community activities, they shared less than they thought. Their differences had been submerged in openness and friendliness. While neither had ever entertained the thought of separation, living communally soon brought up questions about their relationship. As they spent time together with others, they began to see, like the Lindens, this time had for long made up for the lack of time spent alone together, or alone apart.

The nature of the commune made these two separations complex, ambiguous, and unusual, provoking its most serious crisis. For the two years prior to the commune, the two couples had experienced a growing closeness. They spent many evenings together and the special relationship between all four formed a model for the relationships which everyone within the commune expected. During the first months of the commune they all remained close. Because they were the only adults without young children, they had free time after dinner and when the others were preoccupied with children. They would go for walks and spend hours talking, even exploring areas together that neither of the couples explored individually.

The others, struggling toward intimacy in the community, disapproved of the foursome going off alone, and placed pressure on them to extend their closeness to the rest. Conflict arose because these feelings were never discussed openly in the whole group, but rather simmered below the surface. It was hard for the whole group to get together and discuss such issues openly. Since the two factions did not deal openly with their feelings, the result was increasing distance, distrust, and alienation within the community. As the couples began to split, the community members were unable either to share their own feelings or to talk about what was happening. It became something everyone knew about, was upset, confused, and threatened by, but could not talk about, except in pairs.

Each couple became aware that their relationships lacked intensity when they were alone together. As they each began to explore separateness, each found support, closeness, and common interests with a member of the other couple. Dave and Toni, for example, neither of whom were working, were interested in old houses and fixing things. They liked to work with their hands, although it was a new experience for both of them. They helped fix up the house and then formed a company, Alternatives, to do repairs and construction work. They were both physically active, with a tendency to do something about feelings rather than just talk about them.

Glenn and Joan discovered shared interests as well. They each found their worlds slipping out from under them, and went through a period of intense personal conflict around their role, identity, and the future. Glenn had been the traditional dominant household head. He expected to be in control of everything, and until a few years before the commune, had done almost no housework. In the commune, his expectations were rudely shocked. No longer could he come down at a certain time and expect his breakfast to be in front of him. Toni began to confront him, demanding that he change, and stopped meeting his expectations. She withdrew suddenly; her dissatisfaction was a great surprise to him, since he felt they had a perfect marriage. He became upset, as his environment no longer responded the way he expected, but had no idea how to change. Under extreme stress at home and on the job, he quit work for the first time in his life, and went through a prolonged personal transformation. He read, did physical work, and spent time alone and time talking to others about his situation. He learned, for the first time in his life, to look at his feelings and to share them openly with others.

Joan too had expected that marriage would complete her identity, offering her traditional emotional support and fulfillment. As she saw her couple relationship deteriorating, she went into a period of panic and bewilderment. She sought out others in the commune to affirm herself as a person. She began the difficult task of discovering a sense of herself as an independent person, just as Toni was doing in her way. During this period of struggle, Glenn and Joan grew close and shared much of what was happening.

This process took two years and went through several ambiguous stages. The commune allowed the couple to keep their relationships fluid, ambiguous, letting them work themselves out and define themselves over time. In the commune a pair could feel distant, and still remain part of the community; there was no pressure for one or the other to move out. The first stage was a time of distance; each of the women initiated moving out of a shared bedroom. For a time, both Toni and Dave had literally no fixed bedroom. They slept in whatever room they happened to be. Each of them was growing and changing as an individual, and was wary and tentative about new relationships. The existence of new relationships was kept covert for a while, although most people in the house were aware of them. Their own uncertainty, and the unconventionality of the changes, seemed to keep anyone from wanting to make things more explicit. After the second spring, Dave and Toni very suddenly, within days of each other, left the commune for an indefinite period of travel. When they returned the next winter, their new relationship was open and accepted. Within the next year, both Glenn and Joan moved out of the commune permanently, each of them to live alone nearby.

It could be argued that the commune had little to do with this change process. However, the support for fluid relationships over a long period of time, and the particular outcome, seem to derive partially from the environment. Only in a commune can a couple separate yet remain together under the same roof. The commune offered each person help in working through his or her feelings. They were all able to remain members of a family and close to their children even though they left their marriages. The commune muted the shock of separation and lessened their isolation and loneliness.

A structural change that had far-reaching effects was the initiation of a weekly sensitivity session, in the fall of the second year, when the crisis was at its height. The first year was marked by tension; people would gossip about other people's behavior but were reluctant to share their feelings openly. There was no forum for settling such difficulties, other than the weekly business and housework meeting. Then Glenn and Joan wanted to attend an encounter group in town, and the others felt it was unfair for them to leave the community and talk about their inner experience to strangers. It made people ask, "why can't we do that here?" and begin to confront their fears of sharing. A local clinical psychologist was hired to attend a special weekly meeting designed to help share feelings and improve communication.

The meetings were difficult and strained at first. People talked very little about their feelings and the conflicts between each other, despite their desire to do so. Few of them were used to talking openly about such things. After a while some people began to talk about personal issues in their lives, their couples, and the community. Glenn and some of the others turned to this group for help during their personal crises. The meetings soon became a central focus of the community, and openness about conflict and feelings became the norm. Issues of childcare, couples, outside relationships, personal conflicts in style, work, feelings, drugs, and commitment all were aired.

The encounter group became the commune's forum for problem solving—a necessity in such a large family with no traditional or established patterns of communication. The meetings seemed to be an advance on encounter weekends or consciousness-raising groups in that the members of the group also lived with each other every day. Rather than being isolated from the world, the group was an integral part of community life, enabling its members to practice honesty and personal growth. Through the creation of the house meeting the commune moved toward a more open community, away from the isolation of individual families and the denial and avoidance of conflict.

Collective living forced alterations in the way the adults related to their children. This commune is most unique in that of the original fourteen children, more than half were preteens or teenagers. The initial impulse behind the commune came from a desire to create a better, freer, more creative and expressive, less repressive environment for their children. Quickly, after moving in, the families that agreed philosophically and knew each others' kids socially and in Sunday school, found that their ideas about freedom, sharing, discipline, and responsibility were very different.

Differences arose about responsibility for housework. Whereas some of the families felt that kids should do the same amount of housework and chores as adults, the Warrens believed strongly in individual freedom, so their kids joined only if they wanted to. Similar differences existed about snacks, bedtimes, and rules. The Warren's children were used to doing what they wanted, whereas other children their age had been heavily regulated. Neither family wanted to change, but it was difficult, for example, for two boys of the same age to share a room when one had a strict bedtime and the other none at all. There were weekly business meetings in which these issues were aired, but it was difficult for any of the families to drastically alter their styles.

A whole series of ideas emerged when the oldest Warren son came home from college during Christmas vacation with his girlfriend. They stayed together in the study. While this was fine with his parents, some of the others were highly upset. They feared its effect on their children, that the outside community would find out, or simply felt that it was wrong and they did not want it to happen in their house. At a house meeting called to discuss the issue, it was decided that since some people had strong feelings about it, the couple should stay somewhere else, which they did. Still, the differences between the more liberal and the more traditional families continued to be a sore spot. It was hard to compromise because the commune never intended to collectivize childrearing, even though some things were shared. So, the parents remained the final authority for their children, even if that led to conflict within the community.

Another reason for conflict concerning the role and responsibility of teenagers stemmed from their ambiguous position in society, which was carried over into the commune. Unlike their parents, they did not really choose to live in the commune or make an explicit commitment to the others. They went along with their family. Each of the families had one child who was against the move, while the others were positive but cautious. Because they did not actively choose to join the commune, it was hard to convince them to take a share of the responsibility without imposing sanctions. Some of the conflicts that exist between parent and teenager in traditional homes, around freedom and rules, were thus carried over into the commune. Their role as citizens of the community was ambiguous. They participated in business meetings, but were not invited to the sensitivity sessions. While they were urged to sign up for the jobs and do them, there was conflict about whether adults other than their parents should pressure them if they did not do their jobs. Since they were not present in meetings to be confronted, often conflicts between teenagers and adults remained simmering and unresolved, just as in traditional families.

The younger children seemed to enjoy the commune more. There were other children of all ages around, and also other adults, most of whom spent time with them. They were free to use any of the common rooms, including one set aside especially for them, and were less restricted than in nuclear households. They were encouraged to help out with chores, such as working in the garden or feeding the animals, which were opportunities to do things with adults and learn exciting activities. When a parent went out, there usually were others at home who could act as sitters or teachers. For example, Joan taught several children to play piano, and Dave, who helped organize the garden and livestock, always invited kids to work with him. Thus, people with no children (and no previous contact with them) could participate in a facet of family life that normally is closed to them, enriching the children's lives as well. At first, when there were so many kids, they ate earlier and separately from the adults, on their own at their own table. Later, when there were fewer of them, they ate with the adults.

The family orientation of the commune meant that the parents retained much of the responsibility of their traditional roles, although foodmaking and cleaning were collectivized. Thus, while the parent had responsibility for his or her children, control over their behavior was spread out. There was also some conflict about different styles of discipline, especially concerning excessive strictness which other members of the household, parents and nonparents, found difficult to uphold. However, when an adult was doing something and another person's child interfered or became a nuisance, there was an understanding that he or she could tell the child to go away. Because there were always other people and things to do, this did not become a source of friction. Fathers became more in-

volved in their young children's lives, as they became more involved in the household generally, taking on more of the cooking, feeding, cleaning, playing, and putting children to bed.

Childrearing is traditionally the arena in which many unconscious parental patterns cause difficulties. In the commune, there was a forum for other people to share what they saw the parent doing with the child and make alternate suggestions. Different styles thus became more than simply a source of friction; they became an opportunity for learning. In a communal situation, others can observe, make suggestions, and intervene in times of stress and tension. For example, one mother who felt that her youngest child was impulsive and difficult, was helped to relax around him, because others pointed out that they were not as concerned about his behavior. Thus, a parent learns a wider variety of responses to stress, and has others as cushions and helpers. This defuses certain family conflicts, thus making them easier on both parent and child.

The existence of diversity and pluralism in a commune, rather than the single model of the nuclear family, seems to generalize to other areas of life, which is one of the main reasons why people change when they live communally. Toni, for example, assesses the effects of the commune on her children:

> It affected everything about how they live and see the world. Instead of accepting things the way they are they ask questions. This sometimes got them into trouble in school. For example, whenever they were told anything, they would ask, "Why does that have to be?" Since they were familiar with the fact that there were many ways to do things, they knew that everything could be different, could be changed. I think that the most important affect of the commune on all of us is to carry that attitude through all areas of life, that things can be changed, that there are other ways, and we should not be so certain that our way is the only right one.

As some of the original families left they had to be replaced, to fill the house and help pay the bills. This meant going out into the world and recruiting new people. After the initial months, when people rarely left or

had guests, the residents began to get back in touch with their outside friends. People in the larger community were accepting, if somewhat curious, about their venture, and soon there was hardly an evening when there weren't several guests. Although it was difficult for some people to get used to the constant stream of visitors, eventually most became comfortable having other people around.

In some other senses the people decreased their community involvement in church, community, and political activities. Since their social needs were met at home, and their household was, in itself, a political experiment, most people felt a desire to cut down on other activities. The men's shift away from full-time work had a similar meaning. As they recognized the unfulfilling nature of their work, and found meaning and involvement in the commune, their life became house—rather than work—centered.

In their search for new members, and in order to share their vision of community with others, the commune members began to send speakers to conferences and to local groups. They also visited other communes in their area. Thus, although they started out oblivious to other communes, they eventually became very active in the commune movement. At their first gathering with people from other communes, they felt very different, in that they owned an elegant house, dined by candlelight, and contained families and many children. Yet they found common interests, and began to work with others to organize other gatherings. They held regular gatherings for people who called and expressed interest in their house and for people who answered their ad, both discussing communal living, and always, looking for new people. For a while, they had a difficult time finding new members because of the prohibitive cost involved, and because they still were looking for "families" rather than individual people to join.

But they did find other people like themselves, who were older and part of families, who wanted to live collectively. At one weekend conference they met Bert and Mary Sawyer. They were in their 50's, their children were all grown, and they were in a difficult life transition period. Their children had forced them to question their affluent middle-class lifestyle, and they had taken part in antiwar activities. When their children left, they had to acknowledge that their relationship was not as extensive as they had thought. Bert began to ask why he worked so hard at a dull job when he didn't need the money. Although it did not begin consciously, they became open to new ways of living.

The commune had decided to raise money by inviting guests to come live for "a week in a commune." The Sawyers had just gone on a long trip through Europe, and without even unpacking, they took up the invitation to visit. The commune, Bert felt on first impression:

> . . . seemed like a Quaker community. The adults welcomed us in the kitchen and we practically went single file into the library where we sat by a fire, spoke quietly about how they had started and the background, and about us. They seemed like a pretty subdued group, as well as a very strong willed group. What they had done was a big step. They were being put on the firing line by their actions. We began to visualize during our visit how this way of living would be. It got kind of scary and we went back to our house. But we found we missed it, as we started to go back to our individual work and community involvement. After two weeks we came back and said we wanted to become part of the community for another two weeks, and we never left. Two weeks later we said we wanted to live there, not necessarily permanently. We kept our house for a few months, as though we'd probably move back eventually. Soon we realized our life in that town was over, and sold the house. We were in a new phase, whatever it was. During the years there we had drifted apart, our interests in common were less and less. We had a feeling that the common interest in the commune would strengthen our personal relationship, it was something we would do together.

They bought the Godfrey's share of the commune with the money from selling their house.

Their relationship was altered drastically since living there, showing that altering sex roles is not only for young couples. Mary had gone back to work several years before, and through the women's movement had started to question some of her behavior. Bert had helped with the children more than other fathers, but always felt he was helping Mary to do her job. In the commune they were able to reach more equitable sharing. Their greatest change, however, was the acceptance of each other's differences. While they both felt that they came to have a lot more in common by sharing involvement in the commune, they also learned to follow their separate interests with others in the commune. For a period they even questioned their own relationship. It was the first time they questioned marital fidelity and exclusivity. In an atmosphere in which others were confronting similar problems, they asked other commune members to help them solve conflicts. Having another friend on hand, they found, made them more willing and able to listen to the other's point of view. Eventually, they grew beyond their original feelings of emptiness and depression to find a renewed commitment to personal growth within a meaningful community.

In the second and third years other new people came, and the commune began to be more open and flexible in its definition of membership and family. When the Pennicks left there was no new family to replace them, so a new category of resident, temporary renter, was created. People in periods of transition lived there for a while. A woman whose husband was away, a young man recently discharged from a mental hospital, a high school girlfriend of one of the teenage residents, and a recently divorced man all lived there for a few months. Because the commune was not explicitly set up to help people in transition, the others felt somewhat burdened. They began to ask for a longer-term commitment.

The next wave of people included a young couple with a child, who split up within a few months of their arrival. The wife moved out, and her husband began a relationship with a woman who felt uncomfortable with the commune. After a few months she asked him to decide between her and the commune, and he left as well.

The other new people were four single women, three of them with children. The commune represented another type of transitional community for them. They had been recently divorced, and found living alone difficult, lonely, and lacking in companionship for them and their children.

Accepting renters caused the commune to redefine the initial contract it asked of new members. The expectation that families move in and buy a share proved unrealistic. Not only did few people have the money, but it was hard to ask people to make such a financial sacrifice before they were sure the commune was the home they wanted. The residents found alternate ways of meeting payments, by increasing the mortgage paid by monthly assessments (about $75 per adult per month, less for children). But all residents, whether renter or owner, were considered full members.

The appearance and feel of the commune was much changed after four years. It had lost its look of middle-class tidiness, and had more of the clutter one would expect from twenty-two people following their separate interests. The furniture was older and more worn. The way things got done had also loosened up. Initially there were weekly business meetings to reach consensus on all issues—from who was neglecting chores to whether to buy a new can opener. Some people felt frustrated and powerless because a lone dissenter could block a decision, and endless hours were spent on minor details. As the people became more trusting of each other and more in general agreement as to how things should be done, people began to take the initiative to do things on their own. Eventually, if one wanted to do something, such as build a bicycle shed, have a party, or rearrange a room, a person simply asked if there were objections before acting.

The commune changed nearly all aspects of family life—household structures, sex roles, childrearing, openness about conflict and feelings, work versus home life, community involvement, values, and friendships —for the people who lived there. While there had been stress, conflict, and the breakup of couples, these took place within a context of adults struggling to grow and change the way they live. This commune is unique in that its membership was not drawn from adherents of the counterculture, yet over time their lifestyle moved toward these alternate values. While there are as yet no clear-cut criteria by which to evaluate communes, it is one of the longest lived and successful communes I have studied, and it seems to have created some viable structural alternatives to aspects of the nuclear family that have recently been under attack. It offers a structure for building more equal sex roles, sharing family and work responsibilities, developing more intimate personal relationships, decreasing one's consumption and cost of living, furthering personal growth, and building a meaningful community.

22

Divorce Fever: Is It an Epidemic?

By Erica Abeel

"...Marriages are succumbing because only a perfect relationship will do. No one wants accommodation—everyone wants *more*..."

"Five years ago, when our son started private school," a psychiatrist says, "there was only one divorced kid in the class. Today the application form routinely allows for separate addresses for the mother and father."

Glamour magazine interviewed Susan and Leo Braudy because they were a Model New York Couple. They were handsome, in love, and had a dual-career marriage. The following year Susan and Leo Braudy split.

"My God, not *them*," said Victor P. over his third brandy Alexander. "It's an epidemic." Since last week Victor himself has been sleeping on a couch across town.

The dearth of apartments in New York City, Pete Hamill suggested last summer, is due to the death of marriage. When a couple splits, a new apartment is needed, and another 2 rm/ct vw is snapped up.

"Sometimes when I go to Cobble Hill to pick up Amanda," says an estranged father, "I see the other fathers in the street looking shattered. Five out of seven couples on that block separated in the last six months."

There is no shortage of evidence: Divorce Fever is raging in New York City. The fever favors a particular subculture: middle- and upper-middle-class professionals, academics, business types, and media people, roughly 35 to 45 years old, who are overqualified, over-extended, overstimulated, and, now, with the support check in the mail, overdrawn.

Divorce has always been around, of course, but never so rampant. National figures show that the divorce curve soared 82 per cent between 1963 and 1972. New York City has had a phenomenal upsurge of divorce just in the past couple of years. Of all civil cases instituted here in 1973, 46 per cent were uncontested matrimonial matters, compared with 25 per cent the year before. Of course, the spread of divorce

fever in New York is even greater than statistics indicate, because statistics don't include the many couples who are split, but not legally separated or divorced.

The proliferation of splitters has made them suddenly super-visible, and now they seem the norm. He used to be an anomaly, one's Divorced Friend, feeding off cans of Hormel chili and rolling stiff sock balls around some furnished room. Quickly he was resocialized, recycled, and remarried to a newer model. But today almost anybody you talk to can think right off of *six* couples who have split in the last year. That means six husbands riffling through the *Voice* classified or checking in with A Man's Share, a new roommate agency catering to recently single men; and six wives with a lot of new closet space. "In Victorian times," says Abe the Shrink, "when the going got rough, people fainted. Now they get divorced."

Model Couples seem hardly less susceptible to the fever than the predictable casualties. The fighter pairs, the pots-and-pans slingers, Ms. and Mr. Macbeth, okay. But Victor and Sally, who cuddled in a single bed? Steve and Julie, who played duo piano? Peter and Sylvia, who seemed so interlocking, so *permanent?*

In the old scenario, the husband left, or slyly provoked his wife into throwing him out. And it's still mostly husbands who leave, according to Norman Sheresky, divorce lawyer and coauthor of *Uncoupling*. But there's a new scenario, emerging, though it's not yet statistically verifiable: a lot more wives are leaving, too. They storm out, crawl out, or usher to the door the father of three—with the Ethical Culture tuition statement following in the mail. Women have been the marital breakup victims so long it's hard to get a fix on this new image: the shell-shocked husband. On the Upper West Side or Bleecker Street Gardens, the wives are flourishing in freshly

painted apartments, and the husband/fathers on the sidewalk look—not bitter, but dumfounded. Like they don't know what hit them.

Everyone has his reasons, said Jean Renoir. But every couple's reasons for uncoupling are leavened by the culture's values, directives, and myths. Gone, for instance, is the stigma of "divorced." Divorce is now honorable, a part of the human condition—some proselytizers argue it's a condition of being human. "Sometimes outgrowing a relationship is obligatory," says Alex Comfort in *More Joy.* There is even talk of a divorce mystique. It's like getting a Ph.D., remarks a writer in the September *Atlantic*; it's an achievement in growth and self-analysis. For some, divorce represents a necessary rite of passage to Adulthood. You have suffered, you have acted, and now you stand alone, unbuttressed by a helpmate. You are free now to develop your potential, to come and go as you like, to get laid, to buy something hideous, to not cook dinner. You are free to Start Over, ideally positioned to discover the Perfect Relationship. In escaping a moribund marriage, you have eluded death —the deathliness of nonfeeling, of rote transactions. Singleman, says Joseph Epstein in *Divorced in America*, is the new American ideal. And Singlewoman is not far behind.

With the exception of Epstein's book, whose bias is on behalf of the nuclear family, the publishing theme of the year is how to re-enter Singlehood with a Panglossian optimism. Consider such tiles as *Creative Divorce* and *I've Had It, You've Had It.*

Doubling the lure of the free-and-single myth is the simultaneous decay of an older myth: marriage, and such ideals as family, a shared past, security, mutual dependence, and stability. Married is something for the folks out in the Heartland, where husbands are off

in the shop and wives are "the girls" gossiping over a second cup of coffee. Who in our New York subculture besides Anne Roiphe waxes romantic on the subject of the nuclear family? Her views, she has correctly observed, are considered "counterrevolutionary," even by her own children. Children, you say? Today their parents worry less about how to rear them than about where to deposit them.

The words My Wife, My Husband, stick in the craw hereabouts: they have unfashionable connotations of *ownership*. A long-term marriage is suspect, disreputable. Henry and Annette are plainly *stagnating*—in a swamp of orthodontia bills, mechanical sex, symbolic quarrels staged nightly like music hall routines, all the cues, all the one-liners known—for to grow (new myth) clearly means to grow apart. Over-fifteen-year marriages seem like some fusty corner of the Smithsonian.

The tepidness of married life is epito-mized in lousy sex, which is less cause than symptom of all else in the marriage that is lousy. A husband, in Erica Jong's *Fear of Flying*, is not all bad: he does pay the American Express bill so a wife can ball her way, economy class, through Europe. While a wife, in Alison Lurie's *The War Between the Tates*, lends herself, like an expensive library book that must be handled with care and returned promptly.

Ionesco came up with the most chilling image of all in his play, *Amédée, or, How to Get Rid of It*. A married couple is haunted by a Presence in the house: in the bedroom is a corpse which mushrooms out into the living room—first a foot, then the whole torso, etc. What is this corpse filling the house and Amédée and his wife with suffocating dread? Their marriage.

Some years back Amédée and his wife might have worked the corpse into the decorating scheme, or stepped over it, pretending it wasn't there. But now they might dissect the corpse, with the help of a couple of therapists, and get the hell out.

In New York City they'd get out several beats faster than they might in Savannah, Georgia. For we are all "possibilists" now, Joseph Epstein laments. Even if our marriage was good, "nothing any longer seems quite good *enough*." And New York teases our senses and strokes our ego and fires our fantasy of "better" like no other town.

Suddenly you hear people talking this special language, peppered with obsessively recurring words: More; Space; Growth; Intimacy; Constriction; Mobility; Autonomy; Dependence; Whole; Halves. (If they've been blanding-out in California, they'll throw in Alternatives; Scripts; Self-Actualizing.) What *is* this peculiar jargon? It's the slogans of people afflicted with split fever—and clues as to why they've got the bug:

More. Since they had the Depression to deal with, our parents worried about

"... Most fatal to the affair solution, the fifties philanderer is a romantic idealist. He may be horny, but he's also sentimental ..."

more eating, not more intimacy. (By the look of things, we may soon circle back to worrying about more eating.) Even in the very recent past, couples had a high tolerance for discord, and accepted compromise and a low-grade discontent. But now a low-grade fever has set in and marriages are succumbing because only a perfect relationship will do. No one wants to settle or accommodate—everyone wants *more*.

The push for "more" comes largely from psychotherapy. "It tells people, You can have more, you can have better, you can have everything," says medical writer Phyllis E., herself amicably separated from her husband of six years. Unfortunately for a marriage, though, "more" often means more for *me* rather than more for *us*. And a wife may have a very different conception of "more" than her husband.

Phyllis had a "loving and liberated marriage." Her work, her women friends, her activism in the movement rescued her from the clichés of coupleness—"Warren couldn't have dealt with a clinging person." But here she was, in her mid-thirties, and she felt she wanted more. Her idea of more happened to include marriage, unlike a consciousness-raising group sister who says, "I can't imagine anything more revolting than going hand in hand through life." But she wasn't getting it with Warren. She wanted a child; he didn't. She wanted more in the way of intimacy, but Warren, who has never been in analysis, was very closed off and uncomfortable with anything beyond low-level intimacy—"and who wants to live with a person like that?" Phyllis doesn't delude herself with fantasies of perfection. "Life is always a compromise," she says, "but I thought I could get a better compromise."

If for wives like Phyllis "more" frequently means great depth in a one-to-one relationship, for husbands it often has horizontal connotations: more sex with more women. "A whole group of my friends," says Abe the Shrink, "recently walked away from their marriages, saying, 'There's gotta be more to life than this.'" These husbands are leaving, according to Abe, not only in search of sexual stimuli, but because they have a utopian view of life. "Emotionally speaking, these men are badly educated. Their tastes are superficial. They want happiness. But for them happiness means no problems. They've

got the fantasy that if they Start Over there won't be any. Of course they can opt for an Uncommitted Relationship, like those launched in gay bars, and now very common among straights. Uncommitted is simpler—that's one of its attractions."

Space. In a marriage, people require psychological space—broom closets and secret inner rooms, strictly nonfunctional—long vistas, and possibilities for ruthless expansion. When they don't get the space, they start to give off those preseparation yelps and gasps of asphyxiation: "You're constricting me, sitting on me, crowding me out, blocking my development." Like Cathy, who is shy, talented, undeveloped, and in the orbit of Michael, who is gregarious, witty, one of the most successful copywriters in town. Cathy starts to read her twelve-year marriage as, "He's been taking up my air and sunlight; I can't flourish in his shadow, he's too big, he overwhelms me."

In Cathy's thinking there is a next logical step: "I'm not going to change him, I don't *want* to change him—but if *I'm* to grow and develop I'd better relocate in a new space where I won't be choked off." On his end, Michael is thinking, "There's gotta be more to life than this," and having fantasies about this dark, sensual, joyous cookbook writer he's met, who's just the opposite of his Cathy. Though they've come from such different places, the consensus is there: let's split.

An extraordinary thing happens during their trial separation. Transplanted, Cathy flourishes in her new open space. Her energy is released, she connects with people, women particularly, who offer a fretwork of emotional support. She also gets two great job offers in one week, a book contract, self-esteem.

For Michael, though, there is suddenly far too much space around him. He manages to avoid a breakdown. Barely.

Dependency. Depending on the person you were married to used to be respectable. Marriage, in fact, used to *mean* dependency. A couple was a symbiotic unit, a neurotic double-compensation. Now, thanks to psychotherapy, dependency is a double felony—against yourself (you're a cripple) and against your mate (he's got you around his neck). The Sullivanians, especially, are notorious for viewing marriage as "hostile integration." Visit Sullivan County,

between 77th and 82nd Streets on Broadway, and watch analysands leaving their "sessions," determined to get home and proclaim their autonomy.

Mimi is an architect, talented and domineering. Sam is charming and infantile. Mimi takes care of Sam—without her he might not be able to get out their front door. Not long ago Mimi shucked Sam, to everyone's disappointment—they were a perfect dinner party duo. Mimi sees it differently: "I couldn't stand being the only grownup in the family."

Peter is a designer, talented and domineering. Sylvia is charming and infantile. Peter and Sylvia are about to sign a separation agreement, and part of the reason for the demise of the marriage, according to Peter, is that he started to feel that he was carrying around dead weight. Why should he be responsible for someone else's life? Like Mimi, he couldn't stand being the only grownup in the family.

Mimi and Sam and Peter and Sylvia were all in couples therapy—where the key word is autonomy and where the important thing, said the resident matchunmaker, is not to save marriages but to save *lives*. If Mimi and Peter wanted to throw the dead weight off their backs, Sam and Sylvia were equally motivated—to throw down their crutches and walk. It all depends.

For 35- to 45-year-olds, it's the timing that queers it. People who are 40 or so are in crisis anyway: they reassess the past, find it wanting, realize they must Do It now instead of next week. For the first time, they see a classmate's picture on the obit page. But today's 40-year-olds are prime split material because, along with their other troubles, they got caught in a generational crunch. They came of age in the priggish, conformist fifties, when *McCall's* was selling Togetherness—but the rules they played by then no longer apply. Those rules have been revoked by the sexual and the feminist revolutions.

If you didn't marry, back in the fifties, you were defecting from the human race. Although some people married for love, many others pledged their lives for less promising reasons, frequently having to do with Mother. They had working against them, too, their sheer inexperience. As Peter puts it, "First marriages are like prisons. They happen before you know yourself very

well, or what you wanted. There are so many things you haven't tried. If the two of you can broaden your life experience together, fine." But soon Peter was falling back on another cliché, telling his parents that he and Sylvia were separating because they were "growing in different directions."

Much of their inexperience was due to generational puritanism—for they were courting at a time when "shacking up" was only for Bohemians and other misfits. The Sexual Revolution in the sixties may have delivered the *coup de grace* to many already wobbly unions. For "lacking a wide experience of life" could also be translated "lacking a wide experience of sex."

"We were very virginal when we married—even the men," says Peter, who is 41. "My friends and I had never sowed our wild oats." Sex with one's mate may be okay—superlative, for all one knows—but that's the trouble: it's all one knows. And suddenly, Out

There, there's a lot of action. In an Amish village it wouldn't be hard to be monogamous. But in New York? There's a *pressure* here to commit adultery, writer Susan Braudy feels; it's square *not* to. She would say to a man at a party, "But I'm married," and he would say, "I don't mind."

The trouble is, the fifties philanderer can't sustain a mistress-and-wife combo. "If they *could* have affairs, they might stay married," says psychiatrist Richard Rabkin, who believes that saving lives need not rule out saving marriages. But this is what happens: the affairs turn out to be not very satisfactory, because either they are one-dimensional, and offer just sex (Peter recalls that in six months, he'd never seen Nell in the daylight), or else the relationship flourishes and the lovers grow greedy for more of each other's time, putting the affair on a direct collision course with the marriage.

But—most fatal to the affair solution —the fifties philanderer is a romantic idealist. He may be horny, but he's also sentimental. As Peter puts it, "I found I couldn't separate sex and emotional involvement. I'd come home at 3 A.M. from Nell and climb into bed with Sylvia and it was . . . well, disorienting. I can't be involved with two women at the same time. I want it all with one woman." The solution soon becomes painfully obvious: pull up stakes, and move on in search of her.

The embattled couple straddling two generations may have managed to Self-Actualize in tandem, may have ridden out the sexual revolution. But can they survive the feminist revolution? Suddenly no one wants to be the wife. Not the wife, certainly, and not the husband, and not the baby-sitter, though she is usually in there pinch-hitting, sullen and dreaming of an island with 95-degree weather where there are crazy fruits instead of crazy people. As so-

"...Split fever rages in people turning 40 now. The next batch of 40-year-olds may take long-term cohabitation for granted..."

ciologist Jessie Bernard sees it, every marriage is really two marriages—the husband's and the wife's—and the wife now thinks she got a bum deal. She communicates this opinion to her husband. And suddenly, without realizing it perhaps, they've become a high-risk couple. For in questioning and then altering the Starting Line terms of the marriage, the wife is propelling them toward the Finish Line.

She started playing at marriage by the old division-of-labor rules: husband develops a career, wife tends home and children. The consensus between them on what each role entailed made for stability. But now, fifteen or so years later, the wife is caught short. She develops mad-housewife symptoms, and admits to the title "housewife" only with irony. For she feels herself a "failure." So what if her husband is the Martin Arrowsmith of Mt. Sinai? Surrogate success won't wash anymore.

The husband, meanwhile, is perplexed about this sudden Sturm und Drang polluting the atmosphere of his co-op. For he has given his wife what he has never had himself: time. The freedom to do what she wants. Their dialogue, repeated from Turtle Bay to Brooklyn Heights, from Gramercy Park to Riverdale, might run:

He: What's so terrible about having bed, board, Bonwit's, the shrink, plus a free-lance photography career subsidized by me?

She: It's like getting charity.

He: Just check out the Long Island Expressway any weekday at 5:30 P.M. Who's sitting there? Husbands. And what's so terrible about charity?

She: I have no control over my own life. I feel like a house nigger.

He: Damn nice house, too . . .

Joseph Epstein and his wife had a very nice house. But the woman Joseph Epstein married was no longer nice. In fact, she was alternately morose, sniping, and bored. She was spoiling everything by making this impossible *demand* on him. She was asking him to make her *whole*. It was infuriating.

She was furious, too. He was part of the system that reduced her to this sorry state—yet he didn't acknowledge one iota of responsibility. Their marital ties snarled into a Laingian knot that goes: he's angry at her for being angry at him for tacitly contributing to her crippling. In time the knot was cut.

But if many couples are splitting be-

cause the wife feels halved, even more are splitting because the wife has grown whole. One West Side couple, formerly a model marriage, are now a model for marital debacle. Like so many couples, they had this "contract" that she was a wreck and that he, the brilliant young critic, would take care of her. Little by little, with his collaboration, the wreck was rehabilitated. But as she grew stronger, more competent, more successful in her own work, he, in turn, felt diminished. The balance of power shifted. Try as they might, there was no way to renegotiate back. Maybe the real trouble is that God can't be kept waiting for dinner.

Eventually a marriage collapsing from within becomes susceptible to all the separation and divorce without. Sometimes a row of connecting marriages topples, in slow or quick succession, like a row of dominoes. In one such nexus, a row of brownstones in the West Eighties, the first to fall were Alex and Diana, who opened their marriage so wide it disappeared. After them went their best friends, George and Nina, who hated each other. Brad then decided to console Nina and leave his wife, Lore, pregnant with their second child. The most recent to go are the hub couple of the group, Dan and Betsy, who were perfect.

People with lurid imaginations speak of contagion and epidemics. They cite a sudden proliferation of Sullivanian rabbit warrens in a building on Broadway and 82nd, where matrimonial defectors are given safe-conduct. They also cite a divorce plague that wiped out the whole E line in the Eldorado. Movement women, it is rumored, are prime carriers and can transmit divorce fever over the phone. Joan K., a 45-year-old psychiatrist, who separated amicably from her husband, claims that her neighbors in Barnes Landing placed her in quarantine this summer to protect adjacent marriages.

Often the emulation of role-models is a key factor in the domino dynamic. Mina Superstar is very much admired by Phyllis and Karen. When Mina separated from her husband, Phyllis's pulse quickened, and she started a mental brief against her own marriage. But one reason she'd always hung in there was terror of living alone, and the low probability, so she imagined, of ever being with a decent man again. But here's Mina, cut loose, and she

seems to have lots of men. Mina is making a go of it. Why shouldn't it be the same for her, Phyllis?

Karen, married very young, feels sexually deprived and raring to range around a little, and she looks at Mina and Phyllis with their sexy new lives. Her temperature shoots up. Why shouldn't it be the same for her?

Some role-models blow up larger than life, like a Nana doll, and become myths. Like Carla Z., who walked out of her marriage, taking the three kids with her. Carla left behind (1) the upper ten percentile income bracket; (2) nine rooms on West 86th Street and the beach house in Seaview; (3) a husband who was a self-made V.P. with a company Lincoln Continental and who was such a wonderful father that his mother-in-law, permanently stricken by the desertion, is still cooking the erstwhile couple vats of fig compote and borscht. The story goes that *he* was conservative and inclined to workaholism, while *she* converted from Bendel's to the barricades. A detractor puts it, "Carla was always going with the latest revolution. First it was jail with the Berrigans and Grace Paley. Then it was feminism."

Whatever the reason for Carla's defection, she is the first domino in a seemingly endless row. Next thing you know, her best friend Sally is dumping Victor. "Carla showed Sally the way," Victor says. "There was Carla living out her liberation on her husband's money. She'd never been happier. She went back to college. She had a lover. And Sally got the message: shed me, but not my money."

But Carla's message reaches far beyond the circle of her close friends. She embodies the fantasies of women all over the city who scarcely know her. To them she is Brave New Woman. To their husbands she is the evil genie of Feminism, legitimizing and cheering on the wife walk-outs.

Carla is not unaware. "I seem to be the topic of much discussion," she says. "There's some kind of myth about me. A woman from my old building came up to me in the lobby and said, 'I wanna have lunch with you and pick your brain. You showed such chutzpah by walking out of this building and leaving your husband. And you looked like you had everything.'" The other day a woman she had never seen before told her, "I just left my husband,

thanks to you."

This kind of talk makes Carla uncomfortable. She says the women who claim they're emulating her have never seen her crying in her bed; she says they've never seen her pain.

Will the divorce epidemic rage a while longer and then, like some Biblical scourge, pass over? One reason to suspect its transitoriness is the accelerating obsolescence of all cultural artifacts. Moral styles may also flicker by at an accelerating speed, and the slogans of the subculture in '74 may seem, soon enough, so many fads. Split fever, too, is a phenomenon of people turning 40 now. The next generation of 40-year-olds may well take for granted some form of long-term cohabitation, and the challenge of the future, feels psychiatrist Richard Rabkin, will be to make a dual-career ménage that includes children really workable.

Then, too, there is already a reac-

tion setting in, a disillusionment with the life of Singleman and Singlewoman. Pain wasn't written into the Adult and Autonomous scenario. Yet here's the husband who walked out in search of More suddenly finding that *"la chair est triste,"* especially in an East Sixties studio; and here's Brave New Woman crying in her bed in the morning. Singles, male and female both, discover it's a mighty stressful life, this business of being "on" all the time. With a spouse, you could at least be a slob. And the turnover of lovers is dizzying. All you want suddenly is to turn over and go to sleep. Be forewarned: a strange nostalgia may set in. A recent casualty not yet on speaking terms with his wife dials her number in the hope she's out so he can listen to her voice on the answering machine. And the marrieds who left in the name of Autonomy find they wouldn't mind all that much if they could (1) depend on someone for maybe a week, and

(2) find someone who needed *them* a little. Can it be that Single really means Time Out? And the solution is *re*marriage?

For the rest of the country the answer is yes. The Bureau of the Census reveals that three-fourths of all divorced men and two-thirds of all divorced women remarry. And they do it fast, on the average of five years from the date of separation. (In the man's case, speed may be of the essence: according to the National Center for Health Statistics divorced men are four times as likely as married men to commit suicide.) Moreover, three-fourths of all remarriages are lifetime propositions. Which is all very instructive with regard to the rest of America, but not to the urban subculture: *its* tone is more temporizing.

After the fever highs and the glacial lows, there is a new need for caution, slowness, tentativeness. A lot of casualties are acting as if they're just home from the Magic Mountain and need to clear their heads a bit before rejoining the living. So there's no rush—even to legally divorce. Some observers go so far as to suggest cynically that permanent unavailability has a certain utility.

But the new temporizing is above all an admission of confusion. There's no next move prescribed, because, as sex therapist Helen Kaplan puts it, we don't know the essential bonding pattern of humans as we do those of gibbons or trumpeter swans. So rather than opt, with ill-founded confidence, for black-white solutions—i.e., together vs. separate—people are opting for half-tones. Thus people who are married may live apart and find they like each other better; or live apart *un*married, à la Jean-Paul Sartre and Simone de Beauvoir; or, most common of all (check the names on your building's mail boxes), live together unmarried.

In *The Future of Marriage*, Jessie Bernard predicts there will be more of these nuanced relationships, with *de-grees* of commitment between couples, on a one-to-ten scale. Perhaps there will even be some equivalent of frat pins and rings to indicate the degree. But Helen Kaplan's solution portends an even stranger new world. She likes being single again, she says, because she plans to remarry. Can it be that we'll wend our way back to that farthest-out design of all, the nuclear family?

IV c. Parents and Children

C.H. ELDRIDGE '76

23

Transition to Parenthood

ALICE S. ROSSI

A structural analysis of the parental role cycle pinpoints the factors which make the transition to parenthood more difficut than marital and occupational adjustment in American society: (1) lack of the cultural option to reject parenthood or to terminate a pregnancy when it is not desired, (2) the shift from marriage to the first pregnancy as the major transition point in adult women's lives, (3) abruptness of the transition at childbirth, and (4) the lack of guidelines to success-ful parenthood in our society. It is also suggested that every social role has the two independent axes of support and authority and that, contrary to expectation, the balance between expressive and instrumental activities is tipped toward a greater instrumental focus to the maternal role and to an excess of expressive activities in the paternal role, with the result that neither sex is ade-quately prepared for parenthood.

THE PROBLEM

THE central concern in this sociological analy-sis of parenthood will be with two closely re-lated questions. (1) What is involved in the transition to parenthood: what must be learned and what readjustments of other role commit-ments must take place in order to move smoothly through the transition from a childless married state to parenthood? (2) What is the effect of parenthood on the adult: in what ways do parents, and in particular mothers, change as a result of their parental experiences?

To get a firmer conceptual handle on the problem, I shall first specify the stages in the development of the parental role and then ex-plore several of the most salient features of the parental role by comparing it with the two other major adult social roles—the marital and work role. Throughout the discussion, special attention will be given to the social changes that have taken place during the past few decades which facilitate or complicate the transition to and the experience of parenthood among young American adults.

FROM CHILD TO PARENT: AN EXAMPLE

What is unique about this perspective on parenthood is the focus on the adult parent rather than the child. Until quite recent years, concern in the behavioral sciences with the par-ent-child relationship has been confined almost

Paper presented to the American Orthopsychiatric As-sociation, Washington, D.C., March 22, 1967. Grateful ac-knowledgment is made to the National Institutes of Health, sponsor of my work under a Research Career Development Award (USPHS-K3-MH23768), and to my friend and former colleague Bernice Neugarten, at the University of Chicago, whose support and stimulation were critical in supplementing my sociological training with the human development perspec-tive.

Alice S. Rossi, Ph.D., is Research Associate in the Department of Social Relations, The Johns Hopkins Uni-versity.

exclusively to the child. Whether a psychologi-cal study such as Ferreira's on the influence of the pregnant woman's attitude to maternity upon postnatal behavior of the neonate,[1] Sears and Maccoby's survey of child-rearing prac-tices,[2] or Brody's detailed observations of moth-ering,[3] the long tradition of studies of maternal deprivation[4] and more recently of maternal em-ployment,[5] the child has been the center of at-tention. The design of such research has as-sumed that, if enough were known about what parents were like and what they in fact did in rearing their children, much of the variation among children could be accounted for.[6]

The very different order of questions which emerge when the parent replaces the child as the primary focus of analytic attention can best be shown with an illustration. Let us take, as our example, the point Benedek makes that the child's need for mothering is *absolute* while the need of an adult woman to mother is *relative.*[7] From a concern for the child, this discrepancy in need leads to an analysis of the impact on the child of separation from the mother or inade-quacy of mothering. Family systems that pro-vide numerous adults to care for the young child can make up for this discrepancy in need between mother and child, which may be why ethnographic accounts give little evidence of postpartum depression following childbirth in simpler societies. Yet our family system of iso-lated households, increasingly distant from kins-women to assist in mothering, requires that new mothers shoulder total responsibility for the infant precisely for that stage of the child's life when his need for mothering is far in ex-cess of the mother's need for the child.

From the perspective of the mother, the question has therefore become: what does ma-ternity deprive her of? Are the intrinsic gratifi-cations of maternity sufficient to compensate for shelving or reducing a woman's involvement in non-family interests and social roles? The literature on maternal deprivation cannot answer such questions, because the concept, even in the careful specification Yarrow has given it,[8] has never meant anything but the effect on the child of various kinds of insufficient mothering. Yet what has been seen as a failure or inadequacy of individual women may in fact be a failure of the society to provide institutionalized substitutes for the extended kin to assist in the care of infants and young children. It may be that the role requirements of maternity in the American family system extract too high a price of deprivation for young adult women reared with highly diversified interests and social expectations concerning adult life. Here, as at several points in the course of this paper, familiar problems take on a new and suggestive research dimension when the focus is on the parent rather than the child.

BACKGROUND

Since it is a relatively recent development to focus on the parent side of the parent-child relationship, some preliminary attention to the emergence of this focus on parenthood is in order. Several developments in the behavioral sciences paved the way to this perspective. Of perhaps most importance have been the development of ego psychology and the problem of adaptation of Murray[9] and Hartmann,[10] the interpersonal focus of Sullivan's psychoanalytic theories,[11] and the life cycle approach to identity of Erikson.[12] These have been fundamental to the growth of the human development perspective: that personality is not a stable given but a constantly changing phenomenon, that the individual changes along the life line as he lives through critical life experiences. The transition to parenthood, or the impact of parenthood upon the adult, is part of the heightened contemporary interest in adult socialization.

A second and related development has been the growing concern of behavioral scientists with crossing levels of analysis to adequately comprehend social and individual phenomena and to build theories appropriate to a complex social system. In the past, social anthropologists focused as purely on the level of prescriptive normative variables as psychologists had concentrated on intrapsychic processes at the individual level or sociologists on social-structural and institutional variables. These are adequate, perhaps, when societies are in a stable state of equilibrium and the social sciences were at early stages of conceptual development, but they become inadequate when the societies we study are undergoing rapid social change and we have an increasing amount of individual and subgroup variance to account for.

Psychology and anthropology were the first to join theoretical forces in their concern for the connections between culture and personality. The question of how culture is transmitted across the generations and finds its manifestations in the personality structure and social roles of the individual has brought renewed research attention to the primary institutions of the family and the schools, which provide the intermediary contexts through which culture is transmitted and built into personality structure.

It is no longer possible for a psychologist or a therapist to neglect the social environment of the individual subject or patient, nor is the "family" they are concerned with any longer confined to the family of origin, for current theory and therapy view the adult individual in the context of his current family of procreation. So too it is no longer possible for the sociologist to focus exclusively on the current family relationships of the individual. The incorporation of psychoanalytic theory into the informal, if not the formal, training of the sociologist has led to an increasing concern for the quality of relationships in the family of origin as determinants of the adult attitudes, values, and behavior which the sociologist studies.

Quite another tradition of research has led to the formulation of "normal crises of parenthood." "Crisis" research began with the studies of individuals undergoing traumatic experiences, such as that by Tyhurst on natural catastrophes,[13] Caplan on parental responses to premature births,[14] Lindemann on grief and bereavement,[15] and Janis on surgery.[16] In these studies attention was on differential response to stress—how and why individuals vary in the ease with which they coped with the stressful experience and achieved some reintegration. Sociological interest has been piqued as these studies were built upon by Rhona and Robert Rapoport's research on the honeymoon and the engagement as normal crises in the role transitions to marriage and their theoretical attempt to build a conceptual bridge between family and occupational research from a "transition task" perspective.[17] LeMasters, Dyer, and Hobbs have each conducted studies of parenthood precisely as a crisis or disruptive event in family life.[18]

I think, however, that the time is now ripe to drop the concept of "normal crises" and to speak directly, instead, of the transition to and impact of parenthood. There is an uncomfortable incongruity in speaking of any crisis as normal. If the transition is achieved and if a successful reintegration of personality or social roles occurs, then crisis is a misnomer. To confine attention to "normal crises" suggests, even if it is not logically implied, successful outcome, thus excluding from our analysis the deviant instances in which failure occurs.

Sociologists have been just as prone as psychologists to dichotomize normality and pathology. We have had one set of theories to deal with deviance, social problems, and conflict and quite another set in theoretical analyses of a normal system—whether a family or a society. In the latter case our theories seldom include categories to cover deviance, strain, dysfunction, or failure. Thus, Parsons and Bales' systems find "task-leaders" oriented to problem solution, but not instrumental leaders attempting to undercut or destroy the goal of the group, and "sociometric stars" who play a positive integrative function in cementing ties among group members, but not negatively expressive persons with hostile aims of reducing or destroying such intragroup ties.[19]

Parsons' analysis of the experience of parenthood as a step in maturation and personality growth does not allow for negative outcome. In this view either parents show little or no positive impact upon themselves of their parental role experiences, or they show a new level of maturity. Yet many women, whose interests and values made a congenial combination of wifehood and work role, may find that the addition of maternal responsibilities has the consequence of a fundamental and undesired change in both their relationships to their husbands and their involvements outside the family. Still other women, who might have kept a precarious hold on adequate functioning as adults had they *not* become parents, suffer severe retrogression with pregnancy and childbearing, because the reactivation of older unresolved conflicts with their own mothers is not favorably resolved but in fact leads to personality deterioration[20] and the transmission of pathology to their children.[21]

Where cultural pressure is very great to assume a particular adult role, as it is for American women to bear and rear children, latent desire and psychological readiness for parenthood may often be at odds with manifest desire and actual ability to perform adequately as parents. Clinicians and therapists are aware, as perhaps many sociologists are not, that failure, hostility, and destructiveness are as much a part of the family system and the relationships among family members as success, love, and solidarity are.[22]

A conceptual system which can deal with both successful and unsuccessful role transitions, or positive and negative impact of parenthood upon adult men and women, is thus more powerful than one built to handle success but not failure or vice versa. For these reasons I have concluded that it is misleading and restrictive to perpetuate the use of the concept of "normal crisis." A more fruitful point of departure is to build upon the stage-task concepts of Erikson, viewing parenthood as a developmental stage, as Benedek[23] and Hill[24] have done, a perspective carried into the research of Raush, Goodrich, and Campbell[25] and of Rhona and Robert Rapoport[26] on adaptation to the early years of marriage and that of Cohen, Fearing *et al.*[27] on the adjustments involved in pregnancy.

ROLE CYCLE STAGES

A discussion of the impact of parenthood upon the parent will be assisted by two analytic devices. One is to follow a comparative approach, by asking in what basic structural ways the parental role differs from other primary adult roles. The marital and occupational roles will be used for this comparison. A second device is to specify the phases in the development of a social role. If the total life span may be said to have a cycle, each stage with its unique tasks, then by analogy a role may be said to have a cycle and each stage in that role cycle, to have its unique tasks and problems of adjustment. Four broad stages of a role cycle may be specified:

1. *Anticipatory Stage*

All major adult roles have a long history of anticipatory training for them, since parental and school socialization of children is dedicated precisely to this task of producing the kind of competent adult valued by the culture. For our present purposes, however, a narrower conception of the anticipatory stage is preferable: the engagement period in the case of the marital role, pregnancy in the case of the parental role, and the last stages of highly vocationally oriented schooling or on-the-job apprenticeship in the case of an occupational role.

2. *Honeymoon Stage*

This is the time period immediately following the full assumption of the adult role. The inception of this stage is more easily defined than its termination. In the case of the marital role, the honeymoon stage extends from the marriage ceremony itself through the literal honeymoon and on through an unspecified and individually varying period of time. Raush[28] has caught this stage of the marital role in his description of the "psychic honeymoon": that extended postmarital period when, through close intimacy and joint activity, the couple can explore each other's capacities and limitations. I shall arbitrarily consider the onset of pregnancy as marking the end of the honeymoon stage of the marital role. This stage of the parental role may involve an equivalent psychic honeymoon, that post-childbirth period during which, through intimacy and prolonged contact, an attachment between parent and child is laid down. There is a crucial difference, however, from the marital role in this stage. A woman knows her husband as a unique real person when she enters the honeymoon stage of marriage. A good deal of preparatory adjustment on a firm reality-base is possible during the engagement period which is not possible in the equivalent pregnancy period. Fantasy is not corrected by the reality of a specific individual child until the birth of the child. The "quickening" is psychologically of special significance to women precisely because it marks the first evidence of a real baby rather than a purely fantasized one. On this basis alone there is greater interpersonal adjustment and learning during the honeymoon stage of the parental role than of the marital role.

3. *Plateau Stage*

This is the protracted middle period of a role

cycle during which the role is fully exercised. Depending on the specific problem under analysis, one would obviously subdivide this large plateau stage further. For my present purposes it is not necessary to do so, since my focus is on the earlier anticipatory and honeymoon stages of the parental role and the overall impact of parenthood on adults.

4. *Disengagement-Termination Stage*

This period immediately precedes and includes the actual termination of the role. Marriage ends with the death of the spouse or, just as definitively, with separation and divorce. A unique characteristic of parental role termination is the fact that it is not clearly marked by any specific act but is an attenuated process of termination with little cultural prescription about when the authority and obligations of a parent end. Many parents, however, experience the marriage of the child as a psychological termination of the active parental role.

Unique Features of Parental Role

With this role cycle suggestion as a broader framework, we can narrow our focus to what are the unique and most salient features of the parental role. In doing so, special attention will be given to two further questions: (1) the impact of social changes over the past few decades in facilitating or complicating the transition to and experience of parenthood and (2) the new interpretations or new research suggested by the focus on the parent rather than the child.

1. *Cultural Pressure to Assume the Role*

On the level of cultural values, men have no freedom of choice where work is concerned: They must work to secure their status as adult men. The equivalent for women has been maternity. There is considerable pressure upon the growing girl and young woman to consider maternity necessary for a woman's fulfillment as an individual and to secure her status as an adult.[29]

This is not to say there are no fluctuations over time in the intensity of the cultural pressure to parenthood. During the depression years of the 1930's, there was more widespread awareness of the economic hardships parenthood can entail, and many demographic experts believe there was a great increase in illegal abortions during those years. Bird has discussed the dread with which a suspected pregnancy was viewed by many American women in the 1930's.[30] Quite a different set of pressures were at work during the 1950's, when the general societal tendency was toward withdrawal from active engagement with the issues of the larger society and a turning in to the gratifications of the private sphere of home and family life. Important in the background were the general affluence of the period and the expanded room and ease of child rearing that go with suburban living. For the past five years, there has been a drop in the birth rate in general, fourth and higher-order births in particular. During this same period there has been increased concern and debate about women's participation in politics and work, with more women now returning to work rather than conceiving the third or fourth child.[31]

2. *Inception of the Parental Role*

The decision to marry and the choice of a mate are voluntary acts of individuals in our family system. Engagements are therefore consciously considered, freely entered, and freely terminated if increased familiarity decreases, rather than increases, intimacy and commitment to the choice. The inception of a pregnancy, unlike the engagement, is not always a voluntary decision, for it may be the unintended consequence of a sexual act that was recreative in intent rather than procreative. Secondly, and again unlike the engagement, the termination of a pregnancy is not socially sanctioned, as shown by current resistance to abortion-law reform.

The implication of this difference is a much higher probability of unwanted pregnancies than of unwanted marriages in our family system. Coupled with the ample clinical evidence of parental rejection and sometimes cruelty to children, it is all the more surprising that there has not been more consistent research attention to the problem of *parental satisfaction,* as there has for long been on *marital satisfaction* or *work satisfaction.* Only the extreme iceberg tip of the parental satisfaction continuum is clearly demarcated and researched, as in the growing concern with "battered babies." Cultural and psychological resistance to the image of a non-nurturant woman may afflict social scientists as well as the American public.

The timing of a first pregnancy is critical to the manner in which parental responsibilities are joined to the marital relationship. The single most important change over the past few decades is extensive and efficient contraceptive usage, since this has meant for a growing proportion of new marriages, the possibility of and increasing preference for some postponement of childbearing after marriage. When pregnancy was likely to follow shortly after marriage, the major transition point in a woman's life was marriage itself. *This transition point is increasingly the first pregnancy rather than marriage.* It is accepted and increasingly expected that women will work after marriage, while household furnishings are acquired and spouses complete their advanced training or gain a foothold in their work.[32] This provides an early marriage period in which the fact of a wife's employment presses for a greater egalitarian relationship between husband and wife in decision-making, commonality of experience, and sharing of household responsibilities.

The balance between individual autonomy and couple mutuality that develops during the honeymoon stage of such a marriage may be important in establishing a pattern that will later affect the quality of the parent-child relationship and the extent of sex-role segregation of duties between the parents. It is only in the context of a growing egalitarian base to the marital relationship that one could find, as Gavron has,[33] a tendency for parents to establish some barriers between themselves and their children, a marital defense against the institution of parenthood as she describes it. This may eventually replace the typical coalition in more traditional families of mother and children against husband-father. Parenthood will continue for some time to impose a degree of temporary segregation of primary responsibilities between husband and wife, but, when this takes place in the context of a previously established egalitarian relationship between the husband and wife, such role segregation may become blurred, with greater recognition of the wife's need for autonomy and the husband's role in the routines of home and child rearing.[34]

There is one further significant social change that has important implications for the changed relationship between husband and wife: the increasing departure from an old pattern of role-inception phasing in which the young person first completed his schooling, then established himself in the world of work, then married and began his family. Marriage and parenthood are increasingly taking place *before* the schooling of the husband, and often of the wife, has been completed.[35] An important reason for this trend lies in the fact that, during the same decades in which the average age of physical-sexual maturation has dropped, the average amount of education which young people obtain has been on the increase. Particularly for the college and graduate or professional school population, family roles are often assumed before the degrees needed to enter careers have been obtained.

Just how long it now takes young people to complete their higher education has been investigated only recently in several longitudinal studies of college-graduate cohorts.[36] College is far less uniformly a four-year period than high school is. A full third of the college freshmen in one study had been out of high school a year or more before entering college.[37] In a large sample of college graduates in 1961, one in five were over 25 years of age at graduation.[38] Thus, financial difficulties, military service, change of career plans, and marriage itself all tend to create interruptions in the college attendance of a significant proportion of college graduates. At the graduate and professional school level, this is even more marked: the mean age of men receiving the doctorate, for example, is 32, and of women, 36.[39] It is the exception rather than the rule for men and women who seek graduate degrees to go directly from college to graduate school and remain there until they secure their degrees.[40]

The major implication of this change is that more men and women are achieving full adult status in family roles while they are still less than fully adult in status terms in the occupational system. Graduate students are, increasingly, men and women with full family responsibilities. Within the family many more husbands and fathers are still students, often quite dependent on the earnings of their wives to see them through their advanced training.[41] No matter what the couple's desires and preferences are, this fact alone presses for more egalitarian relations between husband and wife, just as the adult family status of graduate students presses for more egalitarian relations between students and faculty.

3. *Irrevocability*

If marriages do not work out, there is now widespread acceptance of divorce and remarriage as a solution. The same point applies to the work world: we are free to leave an unsatisfactory job and seek another. But once a pregnancy occurs, there is little possibility of undoing the commitment to parenthood implicit in conception except in the rare instance of placing children for adoption. We can have ex-spouses and ex-jobs but not ex-children. This being so, it is scarcely surprising to find marked differences between the relationship of a parent and one child and the relationship of the same parent with another child. If the culture does not permit pregnancy termination, the equivalent to giving up a child is psychological withdrawal on the part of the parent.

This taps an important area in which a focus on the parent rather than the child may contribute a new interpretive dimension to an old problem: the long history of interest, in the social sciences, in differences among children associated with their sex-birth-order position in their sibling set. Research has largely been based on data gathered about and/or from the children, and interpretations make inferences back to the "probable" quality of the child's relation to a parent and how a parent might differ in relating to a first-born compared to a last-born child. The relevant research, directed at the parents (mothers in particular), remains to be done, but at least a few examples can be suggested of the different order of interpretation that flows from a focus on the parent.

Some birth-order research stresses the influence of sibs upon other sibs, as in Koch's finding that second-born boys with an older sister are more feminine than second-born boys with an older brother.[42] A similar sib-influence interpretation is offered in the major common finding of birth-order correlates, that sociability is greater among last-borns[43] and achievement among first-borns.[44] It has been suggested that last-borns use social skills to increase acceptance by their older sibs or are more peer-oriented because they receive less adult stimulation from parents. The tendency of first-borns to greater achievement has been interpreted in a corollary way, as a reflection of early assumption of responsibility for younger sibs, greater adult stimulation during the time the oldest was the only child in the family,[45] and the greater significance of the first-born for the larger kinship network of the family.[46]

Sociologists have shown increasing interest in structural family variables in recent years, a primary variable being family size. From Bossard's descriptive work on the large family[47] to more methodologically sophisticated work such as that by Rosen,[48] Elder and Bowerman,[49] Boocock,[50] and Nisbet,[51] the question posed is: what is the effect of growing up in a small family, compared with a large family, that is attributable to this group-size variable? Unfortunately, the theoretical point of departure for sociologists' expectations of the effect of the family-size variables is the Durkheim-Simmel tradition of the differential effect of group size or population density upon members or inhabitants.[52] In the case of the family, however, this overlooks the very important fact that family size is determined by the key figures *within* the group, i.e., the parents. To find that children in small families differ from children in large families is not simply due to the impact of group size upon individual members but to the very different involvement of the parent with the children and to relations between the parents themselves in small versus large families.

An important clue to a new interpretation can be gained by examining family size from the perspective of parental motivation toward having children. A small family is small for one of two primary reasons: either the parents wanted a small family and achieved their desired size, or they wanted a large family but were not able to attain it. In either case, there is a low probability of unwanted children. Indeed, in the latter eventuality they may take particularly great interest in the children they do have. Small families are therefore most likely to contain parents with a strong and positive orientation to each of the children they have. A large family, by contrast, is large either because the parents achieved the size they desired or because they have more children than they in fact wanted. Large families therefore have a higher probability than small families of including unwanted and unloved children. Consistent with this are Nye's finding that adolescents in small families have better relations with their parents than those in large families[53] and Sears and Maccoby's finding that mothers of large families are more restrictive toward their children than mothers of small families.[54]

This also means that last-born children are more likely to be unwanted than first- or middle-born children, particularly in large families. This is consistent with what is known of abortion patterns among married women, who typically resort to abortion only when they have achieved the number of children they want or feel they can afford to have. Only a small proportion of women faced with such unwanted pregnancies actually resort to abortion. *This suggests the possibility that the last-born child's reliance on social skills may be his device for securing the attention and loving involvement of a parent less positively predisposed to him than to his older siblings.*

In developing this interpretation, rather extreme cases have been stressed. Closer to the normal range, of families in which even the last-born child was desired and planned for, there is still another element which may contribute to the greater sociability of the last-born child. Most parents are themselves aware of the greater ease with which they face the care of a third fragile newborn than the first; clearly, parental skills and confidence are greater with last-born children than with first-born children. But this does not mean that the attitude of the parent is more positive toward the care of the third child than the first. There is no necessary correlation between skills in an area and enjoyment of that area. Searls[55] found that older homemakers are *more* skillful in domestic tasks but experience *less* enjoyment of them than younger homemakers, pointing to a declining euphoria for a particular role with the passage of time. In the same way, older people rate their marriages as "very happy" less often than younger people do.[56] It is perhaps culturally and psychologically more difficult to face the possibility that women may find less enjoyment of the maternal role with the passage of time, though women themselves know the difference between the romantic expectation concerning child care and the incorporation of the first baby into the household and the more realistic expectation and sharper assessment of their own abilities to do an adequate job of mothering as they face a third confinement. Last-born children may experience not only less verbal stimulation from their parents than first-born children but also less prompt and enthusiastic response to their demands—from feeding and diaper-change as infants to requests for stories read at three or a college education at eighteen —simply because the parents experience less intense gratification from the parent role with the third child than they did with the first. The child's response to this might well be to cultivate winning, pleasing manners in early childhood that blossom as charm and sociability in later life, showing both a greater need to be loved and greater pressure to seek approval.

One last point may be appropriately developed at this juncture. Mention was made earlier that for many women the personal outcome of experience in the parent role is not a higher level of maturation but the negative outcome of a depressed sense of self-worth, if not actual personality deterioration. There is considerable evidence that this is more prevalent than we recognize. On a qualitative level, a close reading of the portrait of the working-class wife in Rainwater,[57] Newsom,[58] Komarovsky,[59] Gavron,[60] or Zweig[61] gives little suggestion that maternity has provided these women with opportunities for personal growth and development. So too, Cohen[62] notes with some surprise that in her sample of middle-class educated couples, as in Pavenstadt's study of lower-income women in Boston, there were more emotional difficulty and lower levels of maturation among multiparous women than primiparous women. On a more extensive sample basis, in Gurin's survey of Americans viewing their mental health,[63] as in Bradburn's reports on happiness,[64] single men are less happy and less active than single women, but among the married respondents the women are unhappier, have more problems, feel inadequate as parents, have a more negative and passive outlook on life, and show a more negative self-image. All of these characteristics increase with age among married women but show no relationship to age among men. While it may be true, as Gurin argues, that women are more introspective and hence more attuned to the psychological facets of experience than men are, this point does not account for the fact that the things which the women report are all on the negative side; few are on the positive side, indicative of euphoric sensitivity and pleasure. The possibility must be faced, and at some point researched, that women lose ground in personal development and self-esteem during the early and middle years of adulthood, whereas men gain ground in these respects during the same years. The retention of a high level of self-esteem may depend upon the adequacy of earlier preparation for major adult roles: men's training adequately prepares them for their primary adult roles in the occupational system, as it does for those women who opt to participate significantly in the work world. Training in the qualities and skills needed for family roles in contemporary society may be inadequate for both sexes, but the lowering of self-esteem occurs only among women because their primary adult roles are within the family system.

4. Preparation for Parenthood

Four factors may be given special attention on the question of what preparation American couples bring to parenthood.

a) *Paucity of preparation.* Our educational system is dedicated to the cognitive development of the young, and our primary teaching approach is the pragmatic one of learning by doing. How much one knows and how well he can apply what he knows are the standards by which the child is judged in school, as the employee is judged at work. The child can learn by doing in such subjects as science, mathematics, art work, or shop, but not in the subjects most relevant to successful family life: sex, home maintenance, child care, interpersonal competence, and empathy. If the home is deficient in training in these areas, the child is left with no preparation for a major segment of his adult life. A doctor facing his first patient in

private practice has treated numerous patients under close supervision during his internship, but probably a majority of American mothers approach maternity with no previous child-care experience beyond sporadic baby-sitting, perhaps a course in child psychology, or occasional care of younger siblings.

b) *Limited learning during pregnancy.* A second important point makes adjustment to parenthood potentially more stressful than marital adjustment. This is the lack of any realistic training for parenthood during the anticipatory stage of pregnancy. By contrast, during the engagement period preceding marriage, an individual has opportunities to develop the skills and make the adjustments which ease the transition to marriage. Through discussions of values and life goals, through sexual experimentation, shared social experiences as an engaged couple with friends and relatives, and planning and furnishing an apartment, the engaged couple can make considerable progress in developing mutuality in advance of the marriage itself.[65] No such headstart is possible in the case of pregnancy. What preparation exists is confined to reading, consultation with friends and parents, discussions between husband and wife, and a minor nesting phase in which a place and the equipment for a baby are prepared in the household.[66]

c) *Abruptness of transition.* Thirdly, the birth of a child is not followed by any gradual taking on of responsibility, as in the case of a professional work role. It is as if the woman shifted from a graduate student to a full professor with little intervening apprenticeship experience of slowly increasing responsibility. The new mother starts out immediately on 24-hour duty, with responsibility for a fragile and mysterious infant totally dependent on her care.

If marital adjustment is more difficult for very young brides than more mature ones,[67] adjustment to motherhood may be even more difficult. A woman can adapt a passive dependence on a husband and still have a successful marriage, but a young mother with strong dependency needs is in for difficulty in maternal adjustment, because the role precludes such dependency. This situation was well described in Cohen's study[68] in a case of a young wife with a background of co-ed popularity and a passive dependent relationship to her admired and admiring husband, who collapsed into restricted incapacity when faced with the responsibilities of maintaining a home and caring for a child.

d) *Lack of guidelines to successful parenthood.* If the central task of parenthood is the rearing of children to become the kind of competent adults valued by the society, then an important question facing any parent is what he or she specifically can do to create such a competent adult. This is where the parent is left with few or no guidelines from the expert. Parents can readily inform themselves concerning the young infant's nutritional, clothing, and medical needs and follow the general prescription that a child needs loving physical contact and emotional support. Such advice may be sufficient to produce a healthy, happy, and well-adjusted preschooler, but adult competency is quite another matter.

In fact, the adults who do "succeed" in American society show a complex of characteristics as children that current experts in child-care would evaluate as "poor" to "bad." Biographies of leading authors and artists, as well as the more rigorous research inquiries of creativity among architects[69] or scientists,[70] do not portray childhoods with characteristics currently endorsed by mental health and child-care authorities. Indeed, there is often a predominance of tension in childhood family relations and traumatic loss rather than loving parental support, intense channeling of energy in one area of interest rather than an all-round profile of diverse interests, and social withdrawal and preference for loner activities rather than gregarious sociability. Thus, the stress in current child-rearing advice on a high level of loving support but a low level of discipline or restriction on the behavior of the child—the "developmental" family type as Duvall calls it[71]—is a profile consistent with the focus on mental health, sociability, and adjustment. Yet the combination of both high support and high authority on the part of parents is most strongly related to the child's sense of responsibility, leadership quality, and achievement level, as found in Bronfenbrenner's studies[72] and that of Mussen and Distler.[73]

Brim points out[74] that we are a long way from being able to say just what parent role prescriptions have what effect on the adult characteristics of the child. We know even less about how such parental prescriptions should be changed to adapt to changed conceptions of competency in adulthood. In such an ambiguous context, the great interest parents take in school reports on their children or the pediatrician's assessment of the child's developmental progress should be seen as among the few indices parents have of how well *they* are doing as parents.

SYSTEM AND ROLE REQUIREMENTS: INSTRUMENTALITY AND INTEGRATION

Typological dichotomies and unidimensional scales have loomed large in the search by social scientists for the most economical and general principles to account for some significant portion of the complex human behavior or social organization they study. Thus, for example, the European dichotomy of *Gemeinschaft* and *Gesellschaft* became the American sociological distinction between rural and urban sociology, subfields that have outlasted their conceptual utility now that the rural environment has become urbanized and the interstices between country and city are swelling with suburban developments.

In recent years a new dichotomy has gained more acceptance in sociological circles—the Parsonian distinction between *instrumental* and *expressive,* an interesting dichotomy that is unfortunately applied in an indiscriminate way to all manner of social phenomena including the analysis of teacher role conflict, occupational choice, the contrast between the family system and the occupational system, and the primary roles or personality tendencies of men compared to women.

On a system level, for example, the "instrumental" occupational system is characterized by rationality, efficiency, rejection of tradition, and depression of interpersonal loyalty, while the "expressive" family system is characterized by nurturance, integration, tension-management, ritual, and interpersonal solidarity. Applied to sex roles within the family, the husband-father emerges as the instrumental rational leader, a symbolic representative of the outside world, and the wife-mother emerges as the expressive, nurturant, affective center of the family. Such distinctions may be useful in the attempt to capture some general tendency of a system or a role, but they lead to more distortion than illumination when applied to the actual functioning of a specific system or social role or to the actual behavior of a given individual in a particular role.

Take, for example, the husband-father as the instrumental role within the family on the assumption that men are the major breadwinners and therefore carry the instrumentality associated with work into their roles within the family. To begin with, the family is not an experimental one-task small group but a complex, ongoing 24-hour entity with many tasks that must be performed. Secondly, we really know very little about how occupational roles affect the performance of family roles.[75] An aggressive courtroom lawyer or a shrewd business executive are not lawyers and businessmen at home but husbands and fathers. Unless shown to be in error, we should proceed on the assumption that behavior is role-specific. (Indeed, Brim[76] argues that even personality is role-specific.) A strict teacher may be an indulgent mother at home; a submissive wife may be a dominant mother; a dictatorial father may be an exploited and passive worker on the assembly line; or, as in some of Lidz's schizophrenic patients' families,[77] a passive dependent husband at home may be a successful dominant lawyer away from home.

There is, however, a more fundamental level to the criticism that the dichotomous usage of instrumentality and expressiveness, linked to sex and applied to intrafamily roles, leads to more distortion than illumination. The logic of my argument starts with the premise that every social system, group, or role has two primary, independent, structural axes. Whether these axes are called "authority and support," as in Straus's circumplex model,[78] or "instrumental and expressive" as by Parsons,[79] there are tasks to be performed and affective support to be given in all the cases cited. There must be discipline, rules, and division of labor in the nation-state as in the family or a business enterprise *and* there must be solidarity among the units comprising these same systems in order for the system to function adequately. *This means that the role of father, husband, wife, or mother each has these two independent dimensions of authority and support, instrumentality and expressiveness, work and love.* Little is gained by trying to stretch empirical results to fit the father role to the instrumental category, as Brim[80] has done, or the mother role to the expressive category, as Zelditch has done.[81]

In taking a next logical step from this premise, the critical issue, both theoretically and empirically, becomes gauging the *balance* between these two dimensions of the system or of the role. Roles or systems could be compared in terms of the average difference among them in the direction and extent of the discrepancy between authority and support; or individuals could be compared in terms of the variation among them in the discrepancy between the two dimensions in a given role.

An example may clarify these points. A teacher who is all loving, warm support to her students and plans many occasions to evoke integrative ties among them but who is incompetent in the exercise of authority or knowledge of the subjects she teaches would be judged by any school principal as an inadequate teacher. The same judgment of inadequacy would apply to a strict disciplinarian teacher, competent and informed about her subjects but totally lacking in any personal quality of warmth or ability to encourage integrative and cooperative responses among her students. Maximum adequacy of teacher performance requires a relatively high positive level on both of these two dimensions of the teacher role.

To claim that teachers have a basic conflict in approaching their role because they are required to be a "bisexual parent, permissive giver of love and harsh disciplinarian with a masculine intellectual grasp of the world," as Jackson and Moscovici[82] have argued, at least recognizes the two dimensions of the teacher role, though it shares the view of many sociologists that role *conflict* is inherent wherever these seeming polarities are required. Why conflict is predicted hinges on the assumed invariance of the linkage of the male to authority and the female to the expressive-integrative roles.

It is this latter assumed difference between the sexes that restricts theory-building in family sociology and produces so much puzzlement on the part of researchers into marriage and parenthood, sex-role socialization, or personality tendencies toward masculinity or femininity. Let me give one example of recent findings on this latter topic and then move on to apply the two-dimension concept to the parental role. Vincent[83] administered the Gough Femininity Scale along with several other scale batteries from the California Personality Inventory to several hundred college men and women. He found that women *low* on femininity were higher in the Class I scale which measures poise, ascendancy, and self-assurance, and men *high* in femininity were higher in dominance, capacity for status, and responsibility. Successful adult men in a technological society are rarely interested in racing cars, soldiering, or hunting; they are cautious, subtle, and psychologically attuned to others. So too, contemporary adult women who fear windstorms, the dark, strange places, automobile accidents, excitement, crowded parties, or practical jokes (and are therefore high on femininity in the Gough scale) will be inadequate for the task of managing an isolated household with neither men nor kinswomen close by to help them through daily crises, for the assumption of leadership roles in community organizations, or for holding down supplementary breadwinning or cakewinning jobs.

When Deutsch[84] and Escalona[85] point out that today's "neurotic" woman is not an assertive dominant person but a passive dependent one, the reason may be found in the social change in role expectations concerning competence among adult women, not that there has been a social change in the characteristics of neurotic women. In the past an assertive, dominant woman might have defined herself and been defined by her analyst as "neurotic" because she could not fill the expectations then held for adequacy among adult women. Today, it is the passive dependent woman who will be judged "neurotic" because she cannot fill adequately the expectations now set for and by her. What is really meant when we say that sex role definitions have become increasingly blurred is that men are now required to show more integrative skills than in the past, and women more instrumental skills. This incurs potential sex-role "confusion" only by the standards of the past, not by the standards of what is required for contemporary adult competence in family and work roles.

Once freed from the assumption of a single bipolar continuum of masculinity-femininity,[86] authority-integration, or even independence-dependence,[87] one can observe increased instrumentality in a role with no implication of necessarily decreased integration, and vice versa. Thus, an increasing rationality in the care of children, the maintenance of a household, or meal planning for a family does not imply a decreasing level of integrative support associated with the wife-mother role. So, too, the increased involvement of a young father in playful encounters with his toddler carries no necessary implication of a change in the instrumental dimension of his role.

The two-dimensional approach also frees our

analysis of parenthood on two other important questions. Brim has reviewed much of the research on the parent-child relationship[88] and noted the necessity of specifying not only the sex of the parent but the sex of the child and whether a given parent-child dyad is a cross-sex or same-sex pair. It is clear from his review that fathers and mothers relate differently to their sons and daughters: fathers have been found to be stricter with their sons than with their daughters, and mothers stricter with their daughters than with their sons. Thus, a two-dimensional approach to the parent role is more appropriate to what is already empirically known about the parent-child relationship.

Secondly, only on a very general overview level does a parent maintain a particular level of support and of discipline toward a given child: situational variation is an important determinant of parental response to a child. A father with a general tendency toward relatively little emotional support of his son may offer a good deal of comfort if the child is hurt. An indulgent and loving mother may show an extreme degree of discipline when the same child misbehaves. Landreth found that her four-year-olds gave more mother responses on a care item concerning food than on bath-time or bedtime care and suggests, as Brim has,[89] that "any generalizations on parent roles should be made in terms of the role activities studied."[90]

Let me illustrate the utility of the two-dimensional concept by applying it to the parental role. Clearly there are a number of expressive requirements for adequate performance in this role: spontaneity and flexibility, the ability to be tender and loving and to respond to tenderness and love from a child, to take pleasure in tactile contact and in play, and to forget one's adultness and unself-consciously respond to the sensitivities and fantasies of a child. Equally important are the instrumental requirements for adequate performance in the parental role: firmness and consistency; the ability to manage time and energy; to plan and organize activities involving the child; to teach and to train the child in body controls, motor and language skills, and knowledge of the natural and social world; and interpersonal and value discriminations.

Assuming we had empirical measures of these two dimensions of the parental role, one could then compare individual women both by their levels on each of these dimensions and by the extent to which the discrepancy in level on the two dimensions was tipped toward a high expressive or instrumental dimension. This makes no assumptions about what the balance "should" be; that remains an empirical question awaiting a test in the form of output variables—the characteristics of children we deem to be critical for their competence as adults. Indeed, I would predict that an exhaustive count of the actual components of both the marital and parental roles would show a very high proportion of instrumental components in the parental role and a low proportion in the marital role and that this is an underlying reason why maternal role adjustment is more difficult for women than marital role adjustment. It also leaves as an open, empirical question what the variance is, among fathers, in the level of expressiveness and instrumentality in their paternal role performance and how the profile of fathers compares with that of mothers.

It would not surprise many of us, of course, if women scored higher than men on the expressive dimension and men scored higher on the instrumental dimension of the parental role. Yet quite the opposite might actually result. Men spend relatively little time with their children, and it is time of a particular kind: evenings, weekends, and vacations, when the activities and mood of the family are heavily on the expressive side. Women carry the major burden of the instrumental dimension of parenting. If, as Mable Cohen[91] suggests, the rearing of American boys is inadequate on the social and sexual dimension of development and the rearing of American girls is inadequate on the personal dimension of development, then from the perspective of adequate parenthood performance, we have indeed cause to reexamine the socialization of boys and girls in families and schools. Our current practices appear adequate as preparation for occupational life for men but not women, and inadequate as preparation for family life for both sexes.

However, this is to look too far ahead. At the present, this analysis of parenthood suggests we have much to rethink and much to research before we develop policy recommendations in this area.

Footnotes

[1] Antonio J. Ferreira, "The Pregnant Woman's Emotional Attitude and its Reflection on the Newborn," *American Journal of Orthopsychiatry*, 30 (1960), pp. 553-561.

[2] Robert Sears, E. Maccoby, and H. Levin, *Patterns of Child-Rearing*, Evanston, Illinois: Row, Peterson, 1957.

[3] Sylvia Brody, *Patterns of Mothering: maternal influences during infancy*, New York: International Universities Press, 1956.

[4] Leon J. Yarrow, "Maternal Deprivation: Toward an Empirical and Conceptual Re-evaluation," *Psychological Bulletin*, 58:6 (1961), pp. 459-490.

[5] F. Ivan Nye and L. W. Hoffman, *The Employed Mother in America*, Chicago: Rand McNally, 1963; Alice S. Rossi, "Equality Between the Sexes: An Immodest Proposal," *Daedalus*, 93:2 (1964), pp. 607-652.

[6] The younger the child, the more was this the accepted view. It is only in recent years that research has paid any attention to the initiating role of the infant in the development of his attachment to maternal and other adult figures, as in Ainsworth's research which showed that infants become attached to the mother, not solely because she is instrumental in satisfying their primary visceral drives, but through a chain of behavioral interchange between the infant and the mother, thus supporting Bowlby's rejection of the secondary drive theory of the infant's ties to his mother. Mary D. Ainsworth, "Patterns of Attachment Behavior shown by the

Infant in interaction with his mother," *Merrill-Palmer Quarterly*, 10:1 (1964), pp. 51-58; John Bowlby, "The Nature of the child's tie to his mother," *International Journal of Psychoanalysis*, 39 (1958), pp. 1-34.

[7] Therese Benedek, "Parenthood as a Developmental Phase," *Journal of American Psychoanalytic Association*, 7:8 (1959), pp. 389-417.

[8] Yarrow, *op. cit.*

[9] Henry A. Murray, *Explorations in Personality*, New York: Oxford University Press, 1938.

[10] Heinz Hartmann, *Ego Psychology and the Problem of Adaptation*, New York: International Universities Press, Inc., 1958.

[11] Patrick Mullahy (ed.), *The Contributions of Harry Stack Sullivan*, New York: Hermitage House, 1952.

[12] E. Erikson, "Identity and the Life Cycle: Selected Papers," *Psychological Issues*, 1 (1959), pp. 1-171.

[13] J. Tyhurst, "Individual Reactions to Community Disaster," *American Journal of Psychiatry*, 107 (1951), pp. 764-769.

[14] G. Caplan, "Patterns of Parental Response to the Crisis of Premature Birth: A Preliminary Approach to Modifying the Mental Health Outcome," *Psychiatry*, 23 (1960), pp. 365-374.

[15] E. Lindemann, "Symptomatology and Management of Acute Grief," *American Journal of Psychiatry*, 101 (1944), pp. 141-148.

[16] Irving Janis, *Psychological Stress*, New York: John Wiley, 1958.

[17] Rhona Rapoport, "Normal Crises, Family Structure and Mental Health," *Family Process*, 2:1 (1963), pp. 68-80; Rhona Rapoport and Robert Rapoport, "New Light on the Honeymoon," *Human Relations*, 17:1 (1964), pp. 33-56; Rhona Rapoport, "The Transition from Engagement to Marriage," *Acta Sociologica*, 8, fasc. 1-2 (1964), pp. 36-55; and Robert Rapoport and Rhona Rapoport, "Work and Family in Contemporary Society," *American Sociological Review*, 30:3 (1965), pp. 381-394.

[18] E. E. LeMasters, "Parenthood as Crisis," *Marriage and Family Living*, 19 (1957), pp. 352-355; Everett D. Dyer, "Parenthood as Crisis: A Re-Study," *Marriage and Family Living*, 25 (1963), pp. 196-201; and Daniel F. Hobbs, Jr., "Parenthood as Crisis: A Third Study," *Journal of Marriage and the Family*, 27:3 (1963), pp. 367-372. LeMasters and Dyer both report the first experience of parenthood involves extensive to severe crises in the lives of their young parent respondents. Hobbs's study does not show first parenthood to be a crisis experience, but this may be due to the fact that his couples have very young (seven-week-old) first babies and are therefore still experiencing the euphoric honeymoon stage of parenthood.

[19] Parsons' theoretical analysis of the family system builds directly on Bales's research on small groups. The latter are typically comprised of volunteers willing to attempt the single task put to the group. This positive orientation is most apt to yield the empirical discovery of "sociometric stars" and "task leaders," least apt to sensitize the researcher or theorist to the effect of hostile nonacceptance of the group task. Talcott Parsons and R. F. Bales, *Family, Socialization and Interaction Process*, New York: The Free Press, a division of the Macmillan Co., 1955.

Yet the same limited definition of the key variables is found in the important attempts by Straus to develop the theory that every social system, as every personality, requires a circumplex model with two independent axes of authority and support. His discussion and examples indicate a variable definition with limited range: support is defined as High (+) or Low (−), but "low" covers both the absence of high support and the presence of negative support; there is love or neutrality in this system, but not hate. Applied to actual families, this groups destructive mothers with low-supportive mothers, much as the non-authoritarian pole on the Authoritarian Personality Scale includes both mere non-authoritarians and vigorously anti-authoritarian personalities. Murray A. Straus, "Power and Support Structure of the Family in Relation to Socialization," *Journal of Marriage and the Family*, 26:3 (1964), pp. 318-326.

[20] Mabel Blake Cohen, "Personal Identity and Sexual Identity," *Psychiatry*, 29:1 (1966), pp. 1-14; Joseph C. Rheingold, *The Fear of Being a Woman: A Theory of Maternal Destructiveness*, New York: Grune and Stratton, 1964.

[21] Theodore Lidz, S. Fleck, and A. Cornelison, *Schizophrenia and the Family*, New York: International Universities Press, Inc., 1965; Rheingold, *op. cit.*

[22] Cf. the long review of studies Rheingold covers in his book on maternal destructiveness, *op. cit.*

[23] Benedek, *op. cit.*

[24] Reuben Hill and D. A. Hansen, "The Identification of a Conceptual Framework Utilized in Family Study," *Marriage and Family Living*, 22 (1960), pp. 299-311.

[25] Harold L. Raush, W. Goodrich, and J. D. Campbell, "Adaptation to the First Years of Marriage," *Psychiatry*, 26:4 (1963), pp. 368-380.

[26] Rapoport, *op. cit.*

[27] Cohen, *op. cit.*

[28] Raush *et al.*, *op. cit.*

[29] The greater the cultural pressure to assume a given adult social role, the greater will be the tendency for individual negative feelings toward that role to be expressed covertly. Men may complain about a given job but not about working per se, and hence their work dissatisfactions are often displaced to the non-work sphere, as psychosomatic complaints or irritation and dominance at home. An equivalent displacement for women of the ambivalence many may feel toward maternity is to dissatisfactions with the homemaker role.

[30] Caroline Bird, *The Invisible Scar*, New York: David McKay Company, 1966.

[31] When it is realized that a mean family size of 3.5 would double the population in 40 years, while a mean of 2.5 would yield a stable population in the same period, the social importance of withholding praise for procreative prowess is clear. At the same time, a drop in the birth rate may reduce the number of unwanted babies born, for such a drop would mean more efficient contraceptive usage and a closer correspondence between desired and attained family size.

[32] James A. Davis, *Stipends and Spouses: The Finances of American Arts and Sciences Graduate Students*, Chicago: University of Chicago Press, 1962.

[33] Hannah Gavron, *The Captive Wife*, London: Routledge & Kegan Paul, 1966.

[34] The recent increase in natural childbirth, prenatal courses for expectant fathers, and greater participation of men during childbirth and postnatal care of the infant may therefore be a *consequence* of greater sharing between husband and wife when both work and jointly maintain their new households during the early months of marriage. Indeed, natural childbirth builds directly on this shifted base to the marital relationship. Goshen-Gottstein has found in an Israeli sample that women with a "traditional" orientation to marriage far exceed women with a "modern" orientation to marriage in menstrual difficulty, dislike of sexual intercourse, and pregnancy disorders and complaints such as vomiting. She argues that traditional women demand and expect little from their husbands and become demanding and narcissistic by means of their children, as shown in pregnancy by an over-exaggeration of symptoms and attention-seeking. Esther R. Goshen-Gottstein, *Marriage and First Pregnancy: Cultural Influences on Attitudes of Israeli Women*, London: Tavistock Publications, 1966. A prolonged psychic honeymoon uncomplicated by an early pregnancy, and with the new acceptance of married women's employment, may help to cement the egalitarian relationship in the marriage and reduce both the tendency to pregnancy difficulties and the need for a narcissistic focus on the children. Such a background is fruitful ground for sympathy toward and acceptance of the natural childbirth ideology.

[35] James A. Davis, *Stipends and Spouses: The Finances of American Arts and Sciences Graduate Students*, *op. cit.*; James A. Davis, *Great Aspirations*, Chicago: Aldine Publishing Company, 1964; Eli Ginsberg, *Life Styles of Educated Women*, New York: Columbia University Press, 1966; Ginsberg, *Educated American Women: Self Portraits*, New York: Columbia University Press, 1967; National Science Foundation, *Two Years After the College Degree—Work and Further Study Patterns*, Washington, D.C.: Government Printing Office, NSF 63-26, 1963.

[36] Davis, *Great Aspirations*, *op. cit.*; Laure Sharp, "Graduate Study and Its Relation to Careers: The Experience of a Recent Cohort of College Graduates," *Journal of Human Resources*, 1:2 (1966), pp. 41-58.

[37] James D. Cowhig and C. Nam, "Educational Status,

College Plans and Occupational Status of Farm and Nonfarm Youths," U.S. Bureau of the Census Series ERS (P-27). No. 30, 1961.

[28] Davis, *Great Aspirations, op. cit.*

[39] Lindsey R. Harmon, *Profiles of Ph.D.'s in the Sciences: Summary Report on Follow-up of Doctorate Cohorts, 1935-1960*, Washington, D.C.: National Research Council, Publication 1293, 1965.

[40] Sharp, *op. cit.*

[41] Davis, *Stipends and Spouses, The Finances of American Arts and Sciences Graduate Students, op. cit.*

[42] Orville G. Brim, "Family Structure and Sex-Role Learning by Children," *Sociometry*, 21 (1958), pp. 1-16; H. L. Koch, "Sissiness and Tomboyishness in Relation to Sibling Characteristics," *Journal of Genetic Psychology*, 88 (1956), pp. 231-244.

[43] Charles MacArthur, "Personalities of First and Second Children," *Psychiatry*, 19 (1956), pp. 47-54; S. Schachter, "Birth Order and Sociometric Choice," *Journal of Abnormal and Social Psychology*, 68 (1964), pp. 453-456.

[44] Irving Harris, *The Promised Seed*, New York: The Free Press, a division of the Macmillan Co., 1964; Bernard Rosen, "Family Structure and Achievement Motivation," *American Sociological Review*, 26 (1961), pp. 574-585; Alice S. Rossi, "Naming Children in Middle-Class Families," *American Sociological Review*, 30:4 (1965), pp. 499-513; Stanley Schachter, "Birth Order, Eminence and Higher Education," *American Sociological Review*, 28 (1963), pp. 757-768.

[45] Harris, *op. cit.*

[46] Rossi, "Naming Children in Middle-Class Families," *op. cit.*

[47] James H. Bossard, *Parent and Child*, Philadelphia; University of Pennsylvania Press, 1953; James H. Bossard and E. Boll, *The Large Family System*, Philadelphia: University of Pennsylvania, 1956.

[48] Rosen, *op. cit.*

[49] Glen H. J. Elder and C. Bowerman, "Family Structure and Child Rearing Patterns: The Effect of Family Size and Sex Composition on Child-Rearing Practices," *American Sociological Review*, 28 (1963), pp. 891-905.

[50] Sarane S. Boocock, "Toward a Sociology of Learning: A Selective Review of Existing Research," *Sociology of Education*, 39:1 (1966), pp. 1-45.

[51] John Nisbet, "Family Environment and Intelligence," in *Education, Economy and Society*, ed. by Halsey *et al.* New York: The Free Press, a division of the Macmillan Company, 1961.

[52] Thus Rosen writes: "Considering the sociologist's traditional and continuing concern with group size as an independent variable (from Simmel and Durkheim to the recent experimental studies of small groups), there have been surprisingly few studies of the influence of group size upon the nature of interaction in the family," *op. cit.*, p. 576.

[53] Ivan Nye, "Adolescent-Parent Adjustment: Age, Sex, Sibling, Number, Broken Homes, and Employed Mothers as Variables," *Marriage and Family Living*, 14 (1952), pp. 327-332.

[54] Sears *et al., op. cit.*

[55] Laura G. Searls, "Leisure Role Emphasis of College Graduate Homemakers," *Journal of Marriage and the Family*, 28:1 (1966), pp. 77-82.

[56] Norman Bradburn and D. Caplovitz, *Reports on Happiness*, Chicago: Aldine Publishing, 1965.

[57] Lee Rainwater, R. Coleman, and G. Handel, *Workingman's Wife*, New York: Oceana Publications, 1959.

[58] John Newsom and E. Newsom, *Infant Care in an Urban Community*, New York: International Universities Press, 1963.

[59] Mirra Komarovsky, *Blue Collar Marriage*, New York: Random House, 1962.

[60] Gavron, *op. cit.*

[61] Ferdinand Zweig, *Woman's Life and Labor*, London: Camelot Press, 1952.

[62] Cohen, *op. cit.*

[63] Gerald Gurin, J. Veroff, and S. Feld, *Americans View Their Mental Health*, New York: Basic Books, Monograph Series No. 4, Joint Commission on Mental Illness and Health, 1960.

[64] Bradburn and Caplovitz, *op. cit.*

[65] Rapoport, "The Transition from Engagement to Marriage," *op. cit.*; Raush *et al., op. cit.*

[66] During the period when marriage was the critical transition in the adult woman's life rather than pregnancy, a good deal of anticipatory "nesting" behavior took place from the time of conception. Now more women work through a considerable portion of the first pregnancy, and such nesting behavior as exists may be confined to a few shopping expeditions or baby showers, thus adding to the abruptness of the transition and the difficulty of adjustment following the birth of a first child.

[67] Lee G. Burchinal, "Adolescent Role Deprivation and High School Marriage," *Marriage and Family Living*, 21 (1959), pp. 378-384; Floyd M. Martinson, "Ego Deficiency as a Factor in Marriage," *American Sociological Review*, 22 (1955), pp. 161-164; J. Joel Moss and Ruby Gingles, "The Relationship of Personality to the Incidence of Early Marriage," *Marriage and Family Living*, 21 (1959) pp. 373-377.

[68] Cohen, *op. cit.*

[69] Donald W. MacKinnon, "Creativity and Images of the Self," in *The Study of Lives*, ed. by Robert W. White, New York: Atherton Press, 1963.

[70] Anne Roe, *A Psychological Study of Eminent Biologists*, *Psychological Monographs*, 65:14 (1951), 68 pages; Anne Roe, "A Psychological Study of Physical Scientists," *Genetic Psychology Monographs*, 43 (1951), pp. 121-239; Anne Roe, "Crucial Life Experiences in the Development of Scientists," in *Talent and Education*, ed. by E. P. Torrance, Minneapolis: University of Minnesota Press, 1960.

[71] Evelyn M. Duvall, "Conceptions of Parenthood," *American Journal of Sociology*, 52 (1946), pp. 193-203.

[72] Urie Bronfenbrenner, "Some Familial Antecedents of Responsibility and Leadership in Adolescents," in *Studies in Leadership*, ed. by L. Petrullo and B. Bass, New York: Holt, Rinehart, and Winston, 1960.

[73] Paul Mussen and L. Distler, "Masculinity, Identification and Father-Son Relationships," *Journal of Abnormal and Social Psychology*, 59 (1959), pp. 350-356.

[74] Orville G. Brim, "The Parent-Child Relation as a Social System: I. Parent and Child Roles," *Child Development*, 28:3 (1957), pp. 343-364.

[75] Miller and Swanson have suggested a connection between the trend toward bureaucratic structure in the occupational world and the shift in child-rearing practices toward permissiveness and a greater stress on personal adjustment of children. Their findings are suggestive rather than definitive, however, and no hard research has subjected this question to empirical inquiry. Daniel R. Miller and G. Swanson, *The Changing American Parent*, New York: John Wiley & Sons, 1958.

The same suggestive but nondefinitive clues are to be found in von Mering's study of the contrast between professional and nonprofessional women as mothers. She shows that the professionally active woman in her mother role tends toward a greater stress on discipline rather than indulgence and has a larger number of rules with fewer choices or suggestions to the child: the emphasis is in equipping the child to cope effectively with rules and techniques of his culture. The nonprofessional mother, by contrast, has a greater value stress on insuring the child's emotional security, tending to take the role of the clinician in an attempt to diagnose the child's problems and behavior. Faye H. von Mering, "Professional and Non-Professional Women as Mothers," *Journal of Social Psychology*, 42 (1955), pp. 21-34.

[76] Orville G. Brim, "Personality Development as Role-Learning," in *Personality Development in Children*, ed. by Ira Iscoe and Harold Stevenson, University of Texas Press, 1960.

[77] Lidz *et al., op. cit.*

[78] Straus, *op. cit.*

[79] Parsons and Bales, *op. cit.*

[80] Brim, "The Parent-Child Relation as a Social System: I. Parent and Child Roles," *op. cit.*

[81] Parsons and Bales, *op. cit.*

[82] Philip Jackson and F. Moscovici, "The Teacher-to-be: A Study of Embryonic Identification with a Professional Role," *School Review*, 71:1 (1963), pp. 41-65.

[83] Clark E. Vincent, "Implications of Changes in Male-Female Role Expectations for Interpreting M-F Scores,"

Journal of Marriage and the Family, 28:2 (1966), pp. 196-199.

[84] Helene Deutsch, *The Psychology of Women: A Psychoanalytic Interpretation,* Vol. 1, New York: Grune and Stratton, 1944.

[85] Sibylle Escalona, "The Psychological Situation of Mother and Child Upon Return from the Hospital," in *Problems of Infancy and Childhood: Transactions of the Third Conference,* ed. by Milton Senn, 1949.

[86] Several authors have recently pointed out the inadequacy of social science usage of the masculinity-femininity concept. Landreth, in a study of parent-role appropriateness in giving physical care and companionship to the child, found her four-year-old subjects, particularly in New Zealand, made no simple linkage of activity to mother as opposed to father. Catherine Landreth, "Four-Year-Olds' Notions about Sex Appropriateness of Parental Care and Companionship Activities," *Merrill-Palmer Quarterly,* 9:3 (1963), pp. 175-182. She comments that in New Zealand "masculinity and femininity appear to be comfortably relegated to chromosome rather than to contrived activity" (p. 176). Lansky, in a study of the effect of the sex of the children upon the parents' own sex-identification, calls for devising tests which look at masculinity and femininity as two dimensions rather than a single continuum. Leonard M. Lansky, "The Family Structure also Affects the Model: Sex-Role Identification in Parents of Preschool Children," *Merrill-Palmer Quarterly,* 10:1 (1964), pp. 39-50.

[87] Beller has already shown the value of such an approach, in a study that defined independence and dependence as two separate dimensions rather than the extremes of a bipolar continuum. He found, as hypothesized, a very *low* negative correlation between the two measures. E. K. Beller, "Exploratory Studies of Dependency," trans., *N.Y. Academy of Science,* 21 (1959), pp. 414-426.

[88] Brim, "The Parent-Child Relation as a Social System: I. Parent and Child Roles," *op. cit.*

[89] *Ibid.*

[90] Landreth, *op. cit.,* p. 181.

[91] Cohen, *op. cit.*

24

Whatever happened to Father?

His roles are being usurped by teacher, policeman, social worker, therapist and mother

By C. Christian Beels

In the last generation, the position of the American father has begun to pale, to fade into the background of our society and our family life. He is still there, above the children and slightly to one side of the mother (is he still a little above?) but his figure begins to dissolve among other kaleidoscopic changes in the pattern.

What is the nature of this change, and what has caused it? How does it relate to other social trends? Answers are difficult, because fatherhood varies—lower-class family life presents father with different problems and solutions from those of middle-class family life. This is not only a matter of class culture; it is also a matter of straight economics. Whatever his ideals, a man will be one kind of father if he has no prospect of steady work, another if he is preoccupied with keeping his job and still another if he is mainly occupied with how to style his leisure and affluence.

And yet there is evidence that fatherhood is changing dramatically, and on a scale so vast that all classes are affected somehow. In fact, though many fathers must feel that the decline of their traditional role has been a relatively sudden, disruptive event, I will argue that fathers today are simply playing their indicated parts in the final act of a long historical process, one that they should understand and enter into, rather than work against.

C. Christian Beels, M.D., is a psychiatrist and family therapist at Bronx Psychiatric Center.

We have been saying good-by to one kind of old-fashioned father for a long time now. Our most explicit and fondest farewell came in 1939, when a play called "Life With Father" opened on Broadway and played for eight years. It said what the generation of the nineteen-forties remembered, with affection, regret and a little pity, about our common ancestor. I will use Clarence Day's "Father" as a figure to anchor our history, to show which way we have moved since the turn of the century. That was a time, we are told, when fathers were fathers—that is, when the myth to some extent agreed with the facts.

The time is 1890. Father is head of a Wall Street firm and lives in a town house on Madison Avenue with his wife, four sons, a cook and a maid. The maid (usually a new one every week; they keep leaving because of Father's tantrums) is hired by his wife. There have been a few cooks, too, but many years ago Father took matters into his own hands and hired this one, Margaret, on sight at a local agency. She has been cooking to his taste ever since, and she and mother are in collusion—they prepare him an especially good breakfast when Mother wants to talk him into something. They know they have him in a good mood when he summons Margaret from the kitchen below and bellows at her: "Margaret, these biscuits are good!"

He is not easy to persuade on matters of principle, however. He keeps a stern eye on his wife's spending for the household. He vetoes the visits of relatives: "I didn't buy this home to show hospitality—I bought it for my own comfort." He overrules her decisions on child-rearing:

WHITNEY (the third son): Well, Father, I'm going to pitch today and I promised to get there early, but before I go I have to study my catechism.

FATHER: What do you bother with that for?

VINNIE (Mother): Because if he doesn't know his catechism, he can't be confirmed!

WHITNEY (pleading): But I'm going to pitch today!

FATHER: Vinnie, Whitney's going to pitch today, and he can be confirmed any old time.

VINNIE: Clare, sometimes it seems to me you don't care whether your children get into heaven or not.

FATHER: Oh, Whitney'll get into heaven all right. I'll be there before you, Whitney, and I'll see that you get in.

Concerning his own business, the making of money, he consults no one—"Vinnie, this is a matter of dollars and cents, and that's something you don't know anything about." And he is absolute master over his own person. When it is discovered that he has never been baptized, he refuses to consider such a piece of nonsense. He laughs at his wife's despair that, unbaptized, he will never be able to join her and the children in heaven.

And yet, as the audience laughed, Mother spent what she wanted, the children learned the catechism, the relatives from Ohio stayed on, and in the last scene, tricked by a promise he made when he thought Mother was dying, he goes off to be baptized in the cab Mother has ordered (more expensive—the kind they use for funerals).

The fathers who laughed in the forties knew that they could never get away with roaring like that. They were feeling uneasy about the changes that were taking place in the roles of men and women and of parents and children. The generation of the forties thought they were very recent changes—that the world had changed in the twenties. But it had been changing for a very long time, and what had happened was not just a revolution of feminists against men, or of youth against age, but a much more insidious process in which these revolutions are late events. The process has involved our whole economy and way of life.

Max Weber, in tracing the history of our bureaucratic civilization, and in trying to account for bureaucracy itself, found that it grew steadily at the expense of familylike institutions and family-centered households. He noted that in the earliest families we know of, before there was anything like bureaucracy at all, "the chieftain of early history, the predecessor of kingship, is . . . on the one hand the patriarchal head of the family . . . and on the other, he is the charismatic leader of the hunt and war, the sorcerer, the rain-maker, the medicine-man, and . . . finally, the arbiter." "Charismatic" here means that the chieftain's power came from the loyalty he inspired in his followers because he was a good leader, and because he was the head of the family.

As kingship appeared and society grew larger and more complicated, some of the mysterious powers of kings and chieftains were delegated to overseers, ministers and stewards, who acquired their positions because they were able administrators. This shift of power from the inside to the outside of the king's person and family Weber called "rationalization." He meant by that a shift from command to administration, from inspiration to planning, from magic to science, from impulse to routine. It is the sort of shift that we in the West are fond of calling "progress."

The effect of rationalization on the family has been to deprive it steadily of functions. If, for example, you compare the warring households of Romeo and Juliet with the families of today, you can see the shift of function and authority from inside the patriarchal family to outside, to the impersonal routine of social institutions. Juliet's nurse has become the school system, the dueling family servants have become the police department, father's fortune and Juliet's dowry have become bank accounts, and, most important, the modern Romeo and Juliet could simply have gotten married without all the uproar. Their angry fathers would have been cooled out by a school psychologist or a social worker.

The family, which once was the center of the economy, with father presiding over lands or servants or apprentices, or at least over the farm animals or tools by which they lived, has now been reduced to an average of four people living in a house and getting everything they use from a bureaucracy. What has been the effect of rationalization on the people living in that house? An answer requires us to ven-

ture further into social-science theory, turning this time to anthropology.

In studying family customs and rules all over the world, anthropologists have confirmed the general idea that family members are economically dependent upon each other. That is, marriage and child-rearing are everywhere primarily an exchange of goods and services between the family members, and secondarily an exchange of sentiments, such as romantic love. In parts of Africa, a wife who does not cook is unsentimentally shipped back to her family, and a husband who does not support his wife has to deal with the sanctions of her brothers.

In the exchange of things, it is not that fathers always bring home the bacon and mothers always cook it. Rather, fathers always do X in exchange for mothers' doing Y. As Claude Lévi-Strauss and Morris Zelditch have pointed out, X and Y in that formula can stand for almost anything —there are societies where women do the food-gathering and men do the cooking, for example. But in general, X and Y are ritually defined as different, and the exchange of them makes husbands and wives economically dependent on one another. This is also true for parents and children: In all societies they have mutual obligations of rearing and teaching in exchange for

obedience and learning, so that they are in fact dependent on one another.

Now, what happens to the obedience and learning when, as in our society, the teaching and rearing are increasingly at the hands of teachers, media and the impersonal city? What happens to the contract between the parents when the X and Y of their exchange are nearly the same, and when in fact they do not exchange them with each other, but with impersonal bureaucracies outside the family?

The evidence is strong that, since the turn of the century, the process of rationalization has invaded the interior of the family and has affected it in much the same way that Weber described its affecting the world outside: The inspirational and traditional authority of father has been changed into a new rational form, and we will have to discover the results of this change. Weber noted that the "rise and fall of institutional structures, the ups and downs of classes, parties and rulers, implement the general drift of secular rationalization." And so it is with the rebellions in father's household. The children, no longer dependent for education, protection, patronage or the right to marry, have staged a fairly successful revolt. Most recently, Mother, no longer dependent for income and protection, has

declared her independence, all in the "general drift of secular rationalization."

In describing father at the turn of the American 19th century, then, we are seeing him near the end of his decline. There was, however, still something left of his role in the exchange of goods and services within the family. That had not yet been completely rationalized, and as we have seen from our look at Mr. Day, a lot of the manner of the old tyrant was still with him. Let us take a closer look at the economic and other obligations which he had at that time, in order to see what changes have brought us to the present.

He had the responsibility for making the money that supported the family. The income was supposed to increase steadily so that it could pay the bills for a number of children and their increasingly expensive outfitting or education or dowry. In America, where the children did not inherit a piece of the family land, but rather moved to a place of their own, the fortune amassed by the father in the ideal case was an inheritance to start the sons on families of their own, and to "provide for" the wife in her widowhood. Of such a father it was said, "He did very well by his family."

One thing that made it hard for the American father was that he was working alone as

the head of a small family, with responsibility for its economic survival. He was captain of a small ship in an uncertain sea, and he expected the crew to stay in line. The anthropologist Conrad Arensberg points out that his situation was different from that of the father in many parts of Europe who was *jointly* responsible with the men of his lineage for the management of the extended family's fortunes. The mythical American father was unsupported and untrammeled by mutual obligations of kinship—he had to "make it on his own." Indeed, he was most admired if he went out to found a new living as the "self-made man."

In exchange for waging this lonely battle, the father received service and support—domestic service from his wife, respect and help from his children. He owed his children, especially his sons, training in manliness, and in knowledge of the world. He was above all to be obeyed. The open challenge of disobedience or disrespect from children had to be put down with physical punishment if necessary, however distasteful that was to both parties. It was "to teach the child a lesson."

Now the first thing to notice about Father at this time is that although he appears to be surrounded by traditional obligations, he is

actually ripe for rationalizing. He had cut himself off from the traditions of kinship; he had submitted himself to the impersonal fortunes of the capitalist economy (and was about to protect himself from those vicissitudes with the rational institutions of life insurance, guaranteed pensions, labor unions and the civil service). He believed in the impartial administration of democratic government, and, above all, in efficiency in the conduct of life, by which he meant that, consistent with the demands of profit, it should be mechanized and scientific. The suffragettes in the first wave of feminism were already attacking his traditional control over education and the vote, using the same rationality that had been brought to bear on the freeing of the slaves.

The second thing to notice is that a shift of emphasis in the exchange *inside* the family could be seen. This is what the domestic comedy in "Life With Father" is really about. Listen as Father explains to Clarence something about the struggle between men and women:

FATHER: Clarence, if a man thinks a certain thing is the wrong thing to do, he shouldn't do it. If he thinks a thing's right, he should do it. Now, that has nothing to do with whether he loves his wife or not.

CLARENCE: Who says it has, Father?

FATHER: They do!

CLARENCE: Who, sir?

FATHER: Women! They get stirred up and then they try to get you stirred up too. If you can keep reason and logic in the argument, a man can hold his own, of course. But if they can *switch* you—pretty soon the argument's about whether you love them or not. I swear I don't know how they do it! Don't you let 'em, Clarence, don't you let 'em!

This theme is, of course, even older than Shakespeare, but it got a special laugh in 1939, from an audience that knew what Mr. Day was just beginning to figure out, that the contract between men and women had changed its emphasis from the exchange of goods and services to the exchange of love and understanding. This change had been a long time developing: Jane Austen had written about it a century before. But it began to get official notice in the nineteen-twenties when Ernest Burgess, the leading sociologist of the family, said that America was moving towards "companionship marriage." In such a family, skill in managing relationships can be more important than skill in earning money or running the household. A generation after Burgess, Talcott Parsons, noting the drift towards institutionalization of what the family used to do, looked for the irreducible functions of the family. He said there were two: the rearing of the children and the "stabilization of the adult personality," and he thought the American family was nearly reduced to doing just that.

To the extent, then, that the family has changed from a place characterized by the exchange of clear obligations between the sexes and between the generations to a place where a group of people live together for the sake of each other's emotional well-being and development, the father as we once knew him has become irrelevant. Child-rearing and the management of stable relationships were always mother's specialties. And, as we shall see, even her job has become increasingly rationalized. What has become of the position of father in this "irreducible" family? How has he continued to handle his three traditional jobs—as authority, as disciplinarian and as model?

The coloring of authority in father's image is almost washed out. The generation that laughed at Clarence's father's final impotence at the end of the

play, also laughed at Dagwood Bumstead's perpetual impotence in the funny papers. Clarence's father at least had a sort of ceremonial authority. When he comes down for breakfast in the morning at the beginning of the play, the maid and Mother have made sure that the cream and sugar are in front of his place, and that his coffee is piping hot.

Listen to a discussion of breakfast in the family of a contemporary father. He is, let us say, a middle-rank Wall Street lawyer. His wife is an instructor in mathematics at a city college. They have one son, George, who is 13. They are sitting in the office of a family therapist, who is trying to help them resolve the problems of their marriage.

HE: One of our troubles is, I can't get you to do a damned thing the way I want it.

SHE: Like what?

HE: Like breakfast. We don't have breakfast together. I remember breakfast as a really good time when I was a kid. Everybody talked about what they were going to do—it was a good way to start the day.

SHE: You mean, you want me to get up and fix your breakfast for you?

HE: Well, I think we don't see each other enough. By the time I'm home, George has eaten and he's busy. You teach classes two nights a week. Breakfast is our only time together except weekends, and then George is away or something.

SHE: If you want to see more of George, you'll have to make an appointment with him ahead of time. He's really booked up these days.

HE: I'm just talking about all of us being together once a day. It's not good for a family never to see each other together for a day at a time.

SHE: You have to get up so early to catch your train, and George and I—never mind. If it'll make you feel better—well, if we all have breakfast together, will you not make remarks about the dishes in the sink and all that? That's what really turned me off breakfast.

HE: I hate coming in with the kitchen in a mess in the morning. Why don't you do the dishes the night before?

SHE: Because I have time in the morning and I work the night before. Do you want to do the dishes the night before?

HE: Hell, no. What do you mean? You only work two nights.

SHE: I have papers to correct. Anyway, it's my kitchen. Shall I quit my job? Is that what's making you angry?

HE: No, no. I want you to work—you know that. It's the

way the time doesn't work out. [to therapist] What do you think?

THERAPIST: I think you're getting close to a solution.

Now, it is important to note that father is getting what he wants here — he only sounds as if he's losing and he may feel that way. But he has learned that being one-up is not the way to get ahead.

Where does this man's authority come from? From his job, and the money it makes? No—the job is something that makes him tired, that takes up his time, that alienates him from his family. He works hard, and because of depletion of energy he is negatively entitled to things that will compensate him and make him feel better, rather than positively entitled to dictate policy because of his authority as the breadwinner.

As David Schneider and Raymond Smith point out, the basis for decision in the middle-class family is really nobody's authority, but everyone's expertise and rationality. Husband and wife are seen as having equal access to these, depending on their experience. The husband knows more about the car, perhaps, but the wife knows more about the household machines and the strategies of the local shopping center. There is some ritual division of areas, such as inside-outside. He may take care of the car, the lawn and the shrubbery, deal with outside agents such as the insurance man; she may do the cooking and care for the inside of the house. He carries the trash out; she has a garden of flowers and vegetables which come into her domain. He does ritual cooking on the outside grill, etc. But there is enormous variation in these things, as well as in bureaucratic matters such as writing checks and keeping track of the budget. She may do that if she is better at it. Decision-making, even in large matters such as a move or a new car, where his knowledge of economic strategy may be seen as controlling, is nevertheless carried out with the rational etiquette of the budget conference.

In the crucial area of decisions concerning children's conduct, schooling, etc., decisions usually go to mother by default. These problems have to be worked out with the auxiliary child-rearing agencies such as teachers' conferences, P.-T.A. and the children's peers. If father wants something to say, he has to take extra time to be informed about all these things, because, of course, de-

cisions will be made rationally only on the basis of the facts and discussion.

Since life is not always so reasonable, what is the model in the middle class for decision-making where there is real conflict or distress? Recall that in the conversation above, the husband and wife are sitting in the office of a family therapist. This is an extreme degree of expert-consultation, perhaps, but it is only one end of the spectrum that includes advice columns, books about child-rearing, sex manuals, weekend conferences on family life, and so on. Authority to resolve conflict for the middle and professional classes resides increasingly with behavicral-science experts. And what do they propose?

To quote one of the most famous family mental-health experts, Virginia Satir: "Everyone must manifest uniqueness in himself and validate it in others, settle differences according to what works rather than who is right, and treat all differentness as an opportunity for growth."

Now there is a blueprint for conflict resolution without distinctions of age and sex. Following it, father stops exercising his authority and goes to therapy in order to improve his relationships.

It was into such an atmosphere that the latest wave of feminism, called Women's Liberation, arrived a few years ago — an atmosphere much more hospitable to liberation than the women thought from the initial outcry. After all, the new feminists are engaged in consciousness-raising dialogue, which, inspirational matter aside, is essentially a rational argument about the practicality of eliminating sex roles. Its main effect on the upper-middle class father, whose wife goes to her C.R. group while he minds the children, is to stimulate in him a guilty quandary: "Am I really doing enough? Maybe we should take separate vacations and I'll take the kids. After all, I go to conventions and business meetings without her. What the hell—let her try to get along on the salary *she* makes. How long would she last? Well, that's not fair..."

I have emphasized above that these are middle- and upper-middle class patterns. How do lower-class fathers manage their problems of authority? They have always had a harder challenge because the lower pay and insecurity of their jobs give them less to offer in an exchange. But they have clung to the old-fashioned ideal distinction between men's work and women's place much more strongly than the middle class

has. How has that worked for them?

Mirra Komarovsky, in "Blue-Collar Marriage," describes the paradoxes of this situation in white working-class families where a man's status is tied to his ability to support his family without his wife's help. The poorer and less educated the couple, the more strongly the husband insists that the wife not go out to work. The rub is that for these families especially, the extra income would often make the difference between bearable and unbearable living, so that the wife doubly resents the tedium and isolation of her situation. The only way out for the husband is to find a new job, which exposes them to the hazard of moving and making new friends, an especially difficult problem for this group to manage. "The sharp differentiation of masculine and feminine roles and the absence of the expectation of friendship in marriage...create difficulties for [both husband and wife]. Irritability, apathy, the desire for a job outside the home...are reactions of some women to the domestic routine unrelieved by companionship with their husbands.... The new social acceptance of working wives has not modified the husband's jealousy, his anxiety over the possible loss of power."

The couples who adjust best to this situation are the ones closest to the middle-class pattern, educated enough to accept the wife's need for work as a source of interest, confidants and friends outside the family.

Among the black, occasionally employed street-corner men described in Liebow's "Tally's Corner," the situation is even more distressing. These men are often on the move, have fathered children in other parts of the country whom they have never seen, help with the rearing of children in the families of the women they live with, and mostly hang out on the corner, looking for the next possibility to turn up. Most of them have been married and have tried to make marriage work. They *believe* strongly in a man's obligation to take care of his family, but their lives and incomes are such that they cannot realize the goal. They turn instead to other expressions of male dominance, trying to exploit women financially or sexually. Their women complain that they are "no good" as husbands. Various temporary, compromise living arrangements are worked out, none of which are satisfying in any permanent way because of poverty and the unworkable ideal.

For different reasons in different classes, then, the man who would be master of his house is a frustrated and retiring figure. He knows well he is a creature of the requirements of the job market. And the job itself has an effect. Daniel Miller, professor of psychology at Brunel University in Uxbridge, England, says, in concluding a study of the impact of men's jobs on their family lives: "What if the pressures of the job require relationships which are incompatible with the ones to which a person has been accustomed in earlier years? The results suggest that, in many cases, a man who conforms blindly to a foreman's instructions for 40 hours a week begins to establish similar relationships in the home, even if he was raised to question others' decisions and to take initiative. Even if his wife is inclined to show a traditional deference to her husband, she may have to take initiative in organizing an increasing number of familial activities as he gradually abdicates his roles."

We are now celebrating the coming of age of Dr. Spock's children. They are being judged very much as if he were their father. His advice not to spank or punish children is being called "permissive" by those who would blame our youth's troubles on him. Meanwhile, another generation of parents and another generation of child-rearing books are gratefully getting together to raise another generation of children.

What is important is that child-rearing in America is a psychological science, to which both mother and father have access, and that punishment, especially physical punishment, which used to be father's specialty, is out. In one of the best of the recent books, called "How to Father," by Fitzhugh Dodson, father is advised that he should give in occasionally to an uncontrollable impulse to spank his child, not for the child's good, but for his own. It clears the air, Dr. Dodson says, and the discussion can then proceed with father feeling calmer. Again, it is his mental health, not his duty, that is involved.

The instructions to father in this book are the same as those for mother: How to teach, guide, understand on the basis of developmental psychology, how to conduct a dispute using the new science of communication. The only differences are (1) it is understood that father is away a lot and can't do everything;

(2) he can expect to have a relationship with sons different from that with daughters, mainly because of the difference in the resolution of the Oedipus complex, and (3) he should expect to model male behavior for his sons, but he should not sex-type the interests of his children.

The chapters on adolescence in the book describe the parents as watching their children's explorations of the adult world with sympathy, interest and support, and urge them to face their own bewilderment at how things have changed. The kids have access to more money, drugs, sex and new ideas than any previous generation. The professional and middle-class families who read these books most are advised that the best thing they can do is know and communicate with their children.

Communication is handled by the person immediately involved, and the person involved is very often mother. In fact, many mothers resent that role as the "heavy"—with father the nice man who is home in the evenings and on weekends, whose time with the children is so precious that he should spend it developing his relationship with them and not hounding them to pick up their rooms. The discrepancy in discipline becomes even greater in the increasing number of divorced families where mother is the custodian, and where father is reduced to an every-other-weekend visitor whose visits are looked forward to as fun.

Divorced middle-class women often think their difficulties with managing the children come from "not having a man around." Lower-class women are quite sure of it, and often depend on the most available man literally to knock sense into their children—with much resultant conflict if the man is not the child's father.

In many situations, then, father is still needed to deal heavily with extreme provocations. But again, his authority is weakened by his isolation in the small family. The ultimate father in our society is an agency: family court or the policeman. About half the calls that patrol cars answer in New York City are for help

in settling family disputes, where the policeman finds himself in the role of substitute or back-up father, or mother's brother, or grandfather. Where the extended family and the ultimate patriarch once stood, here again stands an agent of society.

We come at last to the job at least half of which will always belong to father, the job of teaching his children what life is about by sharing it with them. The memoir on which "Life With Father" is based describes Clarence's recollection of trips to Father's office, watching him writing letters longhand at his desk, watching the clerks wait for him to leave the room before smoking, watching Father and the headwaiter at Delmonico's go through their greeting ritual. "I felt very important and grown-up on the days I went

> 'Today Romeo and Juliet could have married without all the uproar. Their fathers would have been cooled out by a school psychologist or social worker.'

to the office," he recalls, and everyone who has gone to watch Father work must remember something of that initiation into the world of men.

But the boy's identification with his father has to be followed by differentiation. When he was older, Clarence was proud to get one of Father's suits cut down for him, only to discover that he could not kneel in that suit to declare his love to his girl friend. He knew Father would never kneel: He had to get a suit of his own for that.

The psychologists have studied this aspect of fathering most thoroughly. One of the main criticisms they level at the American father is that he is not around enough to become an object of identification. He is "absent." This can mean either that he has deserted or separated, or that he is away on long business trips, that he hides behind the newspaper or that he does not make his presence felt through manly decision-making and comradeship.

In studies of absence in the sense of separation, desertion or divorce, there appears to be some correlation between total absence of the father during several years of childhood and subsequent delinquent behavior of the son. However, this sort of study

has the disadvantage of all single-factor investigations. This kind of absence is inseparable from low-income, high-crime environments and all the other "factors" which are said to produce delinquency. Children in these situations are brought up by mothers and a variety of other adults, including men who act as fathers to them, and if we look at their lives as a whole, the absence of a father seems the least of the influences that would send these boys astray.

There are a variety of other studies that appear to blame the father's failure (to make decisions, to be the breadwinner, etc.) for the shortcomings of the sons, but these conclusions are mostly based on dubious psychological tests of "masculinity" or "dominance"; in the world of liberated women and men that approaches, the less said about them the better.

Let us instead look at the American father as a role model in his natural habitat, the American family, and see what troubles he has there. What do "absence" and "presence" in fact mean in that life? How does it compare with family life in other cultures?

In small societies the world over, fathers are especially present as ceremonial leaders and as work leaders. They show up to preside over circumcisions, prayers, blessings, initiations, healing ceremonies, funerals, potlatches. At such times especially, children experience father's significance in the community and in their lives. And fathers teach children, particularly sons, how the men's work is done. In both these guises, father appears as the representative of the larger community, as the person who teaches the crafts, skills, endurances, politics and manners of public life in the small society.

This is precisely the part of life that is most obscure to the child in middle America, and most difficult for father to represent. Consider the problem: The middle-class American child lives not in a village but in a suburb or residential part of a city from which the society's most important work is excluded by zoning law. He lives in a school-and-camp world that is strictly age-graded, and that insulates him from the job market as long as possible. His teachers and counselors are defined as not doing men's work—indeed, they are likely to be women. Innocence of what goes on among adults is still a child-virtue in our culture. Father works at a job that may be alienating because it is drudgery, or so

bureaucratically abstract that it is incomprehensible to children (if not to father himself). And all this takes place in a culture that has almost completely renounced public ceremonies, as well as private. A child gets an occasional glimpse of father marching with his lodge in an ethnic-day parade, or giving the older sister in marriage and paying the bills for the wedding. Overheard conversations with mother about how he is being passed over at the office, or how he landed a contract, are probably the most truthful pictures of work. What does father do in order to appear as himself in this scenario?

He has established for himself, in fact, a rather rich ceremonial life, which is called "leisure activities" or "recreation," and which includes sports, home and car maintenance and hobbies. The controversy that has grown up in recent years around the sex-typing of some of these activities is understandable, since they once were the places to which father could absent himself from the domestic and child-rearing scene. And he could initiate his sons into these mysteries when they were of an age to join him. They were the separate arenas where father and sons could find both the language and the subject matter with which to communicate about the values, problems and solutions inherent in being a man.

In addition to strength and skill, competitive sports require control under pressure and often the exercise of two very closely paired traditional male abilities. One is called "sportsmanship," which is the ability to put the game before self. That is, to extinguish even the slightest show of a dominance battle—either exultation or humiliation—in competitive situations. The other is learning the strategic signals for dominance battles when they are called for. How to bluff to save face (fighting with the umpire), and how to bluff to win (poker, the deceptive strategies of basketball and football).

In the world of recreation, father appears as athlete, connoisseur-spectator or craftsman. These ceremonies have in common the celebration of a mythical past when a man pitted his skill and strength against the elements or other men and won or lost on fair terms. The contrast with the real world of the rationalized bureaucracy is obvious. That is the other world, besides the domestic one, from which the man wants to "get away"—the world of routine work and uncertain reward.

Now the women have invaded these activities one after another. Golf, tennis, fishing, hunting and camping, spectator sports—marvelous absences from the little house and its four people —are open to mother and daughter as well as father and son. There was a struggle, which went all the way to the courts, to keep girls out of Little League baseball, but the silliness of the arguments indicated all the more clearly that a ritual ground was being defended. Even automobile tinkering, which used to be man's most reliable refuge from women, as well as from the sense of being dominated by the machine, is now as coeducational as porno movie theaters. In both, women put up with a little ritual joking, but if they want in, they can come along. Women are in fact beginning to assert their rights to be plumbers and carpenters, and are organizing their own training courses. They have just started a sports magazine.

What has happened? Almost half of the mothers are working after their children reach school age, and at the same sort of routine, bureaucratic jobs that many men hold. Life is indeed much the same for the middle-class mother and father. Mothers are just as baffled as fathers by the changes in the world and in the children, just as frustrated and inarticulate at grasping what it all means, just as much in need of a place in their lives where they and their friends and children can do something immediate, active and exciting.

As these activities have become less male, they have moved into the family itself and have become the central focus of suburban leisured home life, especially of weekend and vacation time in the white-collar class. The activities of a family either together or as individuals become rather intensely associated with their identities, their special selves. A family is "into" water-skiing, a son has a rock band, a father is a Scoutmaster or an organist. Each exults in his craft, and the others respect him for it.

After all this, is there any reason to have father at all —does he have anything special to offer? The evidence of psychological research is not decisive. And one edge of libertarian social philosophy would say, no—not in the sense that a male parent is indispensable to a child's growing up. In permitting adoption by single women, courts and adoption agencies are beginning to agree with this philosophy.

On the other hand, my friend who is a roofer and lives in a bad neighborhood says, "Somebody has to teach a kid how to fight—how to take care of himself." And my son Alex, who is 8, says, "Fathers are important because they teach you when you are a child. They give you piggyback rides, so if you grow up to be a father, you'll know how to give your children piggyback rides." Those are compelling arguments. They remind us we have to look carefully at father's function because for the most part he is still very much around, and important to a lot of people.

It appears to those of us who work with troubled families that an essential part of the emotional repertoire of children is composed of behaviors and feelings taken up unconsciously from the relationships between others in the household. In the conventional household, the most important of those others are the parents, and it is likely that a child learns much of what he deeply knows about things like kindness, courage, failure and forgiveness from watching his parents with each other. And to the extent that conventional sex roles are easily learned, socially supported and temperamentally fitting, parents can use the conventions to help themselves enact these vital scenes with each other and their children.

But now we have come upon the crux of the problem. For every case I know in which the sex-typed conventions have given a mother and father ease and strength in being themselves, I can think of another where the opposite is true. A husband and wife who work together in a small service agency make each other miserable. She is a much better politician than he is, but he insists on taking the lead in meetings, and expects her to support him. A father has a rare accomplishment in playing games and joking with children, which he has turned into a way of putting his wife down. She cannot admit her distaste for such nonsense, and feels she is always losing in the competition for their affection, as well as in her efforts to be "a good mother." And there are many midlife divorces that are followed by a period of growth for the parents and relief for the children because, after the initial grief, the parents find a way of life that would not have been possible for either one while acting the dutiful spouse. To be sure, as a psychiatrist, I see more than the usual number of people whose temperaments and backgrounds do not fit their lives. But the statistical argument does not avoid the point: Fathers and mothers make their greatest contribution to their children and to each other when they have found a way to be most actively and expressively themselves, making the most of their gifts and skills. That is what the child should identify with, not with a sex role narrowly defined.

Father's main contribution, then, is to join mother in devising with generosity, and considerable ingenuity, a way of life that will permit them both to work together in whatever complementarity of careers they can make out. Two English books, "Dual-Career Families" by Rhona and Robert Rapoport, and "The Symmetrical Family" by Peter Willmott and Michael Young, suggest that there are several designs for this kind of life now being tried out not only by the professional class but by the middle class as well, and a recent article in The New York Times Magazine, "What do I do for the next 20 years?" by Susan Jacoby, described a model of it in blue-collar Flatbush.

Reading these reports leads me to conclude that even in the symmetrical family, father is overworked at work, played out and unable to give himself to full-time fathering when he gets home. His wife is also fed up with full-time mothering. Both seem to want part-time work and part-time parenting.

Perhaps we should redefine fatherhood altogether. It should not be the full-time job of one parent but the part function of both parents in accord with their ability and knowledge, and perhaps of people outside the family as well—friends, lawyers, mental health workers, politicians. It is the job of representing the perils and advantages of the larger world to a sheltered domestic group of children or old people or anybody who needs to know how to cope. A friend of mine, a woman lawyer, once suggested that single women —perhaps all women—need the services of an agency that would practice "preventive law"—would warn them of the pitfalls, financial and otherwise, they face as they thread their way through the bureaucracy—to provide them with the know-how and contacts that men get naturally from their association with one another. It is perhaps the ultimate in Weberian rationalization to call for such an agency as a replacement for the father-husband. But the idea does suggest that in the complex and hazardous world our rationality has produced, fatherhood is too important a function to be left only to the man in the family.

V. Work and Leisure

C.H. ELDRIDGE '76

One's career and work is also a central aspect of a person's sense of self, and the way he or she is seen by others. Work, career, and leisure activities take up a major part of our adult lives. Work, family life, leisure activities, and intimate relating are the major social contexts of an adult's life. Each contributes to a person's identity. Career choice determines much about our lives, from social class and lifestyle to how we feel about ourselves in relation to others. Work provides both economic support and an important part of our self-esteem. Also, many of the stresses in a family come from the stresses and demands placed on it by work and career demands. The traditional American family has been characterized by the husband having a demanding career and responsibility for the family's economic support and social standing, while the wife takes care of the home, raises the children, and provides emotional sustenance and nurture. As Hanna Papanek points out, this division of labor is presently undergoing change, and priorities and roles are moving in several new directions, particularly as more women become involved in careers. Jean Renshaw talks about how the work and family worlds interact. Robert Havighurst and Kenneth Feigenbaum explore how the styles in which people approach leisure parallel the way they approach their work.

25

An Exploration of the Dynamics of the Overlapping Worlds of Work and Family

JEAN R. RENSHAW, Ph.D.†

The relationship between the working lives and family lives of people in our society is a concern to both families and corporations. This article describes a research project that yielded theoretical statements about the interactions between organization life and family life for members of large corporations; grounded theory methodology and a systems theory approach were used. Data were obtained in a large multinational corporation from managers and their families who were undergoing three different kinds of organizational stress: international transfer, extensive travel, and job change to facilitator of personal and organizational change. The findings give reason for viewing organization and family as interacting systems and for considering the uniqueness of each individual's response to stressful events. They also indicate that an individual's feelings of influence over stressful events at the organization-family boundaries are significant for both organizational and family effectiveness.

THE RELATIONSHIP OF WORK AND FAMILY LIFE

OUR INCREASINGLY complex and rapidly changing environment puts in question many traditional ways of looking at ourselves. This is particularly true of the interaction between work and family life and the influence of this interaction on individuals in each setting. Three examples from the research project conducted by the author illustrate fairly typical difficulties that arise at this interface:

1. The manager of a large plant is worried. One of his brightest young executives is not living up to expectations. Erratic decisions and bad communication with his work team have contributed to missed deadlines and some unfortunate incidents with clients. The personnel manager suggests that the plant manager try to be patient for at least a few months and work around the executive because he is having family problems.

---

† Organization consultant, Santa Monica, California.

2. An international personnel manager is called into his department head's office. The subject of the meeting is a bright young supervisor who has been transferred to the United States as an upward step in his career. He has requested a transfer home at the end of the year, even though he was to have had a two-year tenure abroad. His family has not been happy in the States, and want to go home. The cost of interrupting the assignment at the end of a year is high, both in terms of employee morale and money.

3. The atmosphere in the office is somber as three department heads meet to discuss the complaints they have been receiving from one important work team. The focus of the complaints is the employees' travel schedules. Heavy travel during the summer season is a project necessity, but the complaints this year have been particularly bad, and the number of sick days and postponed travel schedules have been increasing.

These vignettes from the research data outline situations not uncommon in the corporate world today. In each incident the organization has a problem, and the problem is related to a family problem. More often than not, the organizational response is, "Yes, there is a problem, but it is the employee's family problem, and we cannot interfere in the personal lives of our employees."

When the scenes are viewed from the family perspective, the same incidents are described differently:

1. The nightly scene in the executive's home involves arguments and accusations about the amount of time the executive is spending on business problems and at the office. The wife believes they had an agreement in their marriage contract for joint responsibility for family and home. When the decision was made for her to go back to school after the baby was born, her expectation was for more participation by her husband in family maintenance. Their unresolved issues of priorities lead to discussions that invariably end in frustration and exhaustion.

2. In the case of the international transfer, the wife can be heard saying, "I left my career and family to come to the United States so that you could be successful in your job, but it really is too difficult for me, and I'm going home to have my baby."

3. In one of the families in which heavy travel was the issue, the wife makes a demand upon her husband. "The teacher told me today it's very important for you to spend more time with our son. She thinks a lot of his disturbed behavior can be traced to wanting more attention from his father, since he told her you're never home." The husband's response is, "But you know I have to finish up this assignment. Things will be better in the fall."

The dynamics of such family meetings are similar to those taking place in the corporation. The predominant responses in both settings are feelings of impotence and regret over not being able to change the circumstances. From the family viewpoint, such situations are often seen as resulting from organizational decisions and policies over which the family has no control or interest. In the organization, they are often seen as resulting from family situations over which the organization has no control or interest.

Contemporary organizational life makes many demands upon its members, as well as upon their families. Promotions, transfers, requirements for travel, demands for creativity and innovation all subject the employee to stresses. Correspondingly, each stress causes implicit demands for change in the supporting family. Promotions often require a different life style and entertainment pattern for the family, transfers obviously uproot and change the family system, and extended business travel requires changes in family roles and functions.

These potential stresses are not new, but they occur with increased frequency. At the same time that employees are requiring more support, many families are moving away from the supportive role. A variety of societal forces, such as the increased demands for self-determination by women, children and minorities and the changing roles of husband and wife are shaping new family roles and structure. While work and family sometimes support each other, at other times their goals and processes are in conflict. That the "corporation man" manages his family as well as his job is a myth held by both organizations and families and one that is becoming increasingly harder to maintain.

Many students of family life have investigated the impact of industrialization on the structure and functioning of the family. Sociologists who have studied the family, Parsons (16), Goode (9), Linton (13), generally agree that industrialization has moved a number of traditional functions away from the family. Social scientists disagree, however, on whether industrialization has weakened the nuclear family or made it more important. Some, Parsons (16) and Goode (9), believe that industrialization has in fact strengthened the nuclear family as the important affective, relational domain for the individual. Others, Linton (13), Slater (22), believe that the increasing pressures that industrialized society places on the nuclear family combine with a lessening of societal sanctions against dissolution of marriage to weaken the nuclear family. In either case, there is general recognition that the world of work is an important force influencing family stability. Parsons (9, p. 53) goes so far as to state that the world of work in effect defines the husband's role in the family.

While it is clear to those working with families that the world of work has an impact on family life, *there is little official recognition of the family world from the organization's perspective*. Until recently, organizational researchers have been able to ignore, or neutralize, the effects of family functioning upon organizational effectiveness. An often-cited work, Katz and Kahn (12), has one index reference on family, which refers to organizational family rather than conjugal family; March (14) also talks about organizational families but not about conjugal families. Organizations suffer from the same myopia that organizational researchers sustain. While many managers recognize informally the impact of the family lives of employees upon organizational functioning, the work-family boundary has not been considered a legitimate area of concern for organizations, save for one issue, the "fit" of an executive's wife in the company. There are popular cartoons, as well as literature and organizational manuals, that describe the appropriate role for an executive's wife—e.g., Burger (4).

Although work-family issues have not generally been of concern for the organization, societal trends make it more difficult to ignore work-family interactions. There are increasing pressures on the corporation, both from outside and from within, to take more responsibility for the impact of corporate life on families. For example, the 1970 White House Conference on Children and Youth (23) made the following recommendations having to do with working life:

> To an extent not generally recognized, the patterns of life of American families are influenced by employment policies and practice. Employers, both public and private, can make a significant contribution to placing families and children at the center rather than the periphery of our national life by:
>
> —recognizing their role in influencing the way American families live.
>
> —changing the organization and demands of work in ways which will enable children and parents to live and learn together.
>
> *At both central and local levels, industries, businesses and government offices should examine present policies and practices of the organization as they affect family life.* (Italics in original)

But what about the industrial and governmental organizations that are being asked to examine their policies and practices as they affect family life? If the organization is seen as solely responsible for a shift in practices and attitudes, the paternalistic assumptions that have traditionally clouded organization life may simply be reinforced further. Societal transitions toward self-determination, new marital role structures, and increased awareness of the need for job satisfaction all contribute to the view that the work-family boundary is relevant to organizational effectiveness as well as to family stability and that it is not a subject an organization should consider simply for the sake of the families. The motivation for examining and hopefully changing some of these policies and practices is not altruistic; there is something in it for organizations as well.

However, the manager, family member, researcher, or consultant who is convinced that the interactions between the work and the family systems deserve explicit consideration finds little theory to direct him in understanding how the organization and family affect one another. The literature on family and organization that is available has generally viewed the organization from the family perspective. While the family perspective is essential, it is only a fraction of the picture and leaves out a broad range of issues related to family influences on organizational effectiveness. The research on which this article is based was undertaken to determine whether theory could be formulated to relate family and organizational influences on one another. Family influences on organizational effectiveness were studied as well as organizational influences on family effectiveness.

THE RESEARCH PROCESS

The interactions between work and family are ongoing, but periods of high stress accentuate these interactions and make people more aware of them. These are also the periods when organizations and families tend to seek outside consultants. For this reason the research focused on people at periods when the organization was placing greater than usual demands upon them as employees and as family members. Periods of high organizational demand chosen for study were heavy business travel, international transfer, and the learning of new affective and relational skills in the organizational context.

The research utilized grounded theory methodology, Glaser and Strauss (10), combined with a systems approach, Buckley (3), Emery (8). The methods of grounded theory were chosen because they structure the research process and data collection toward the discovery of theory useful as a framework to people coping with the phenomena being studied. The two salient characteristics of all grounded theory research are:

1. The focus, or principal objective, of the research is to *generate* relevant theory which is not speculative, but based on the data of the research.

2. The research uses a constant comparative method of analysis of multiple comparison groups to discover and formulate theory. (Glaser and Strauss [10])

The process of grounded theory research is akin to anthropological investigation. In the present research, the objective was an increased understanding of the culture of families and organizations. The informants for a family were, in a majority of cases, the husband and wife. On a few occasions, the researcher talked with and observed children of these families during home interviews. One hundred twenty-six people were interviewed in the course of the two-and-one-half-year research project. The characteristics of the population are summarized in Table I.

The managers included in the first four groupings were members of one large, diversified, multinational corporation. There was a basic shared organizational culture among the groups, although the degree to which it was shared varied from group to group. The corporation was chosen because of the variety of types of stresses experienced by its managers and because of its rare willingness to accept the work-family interface as a legitimate area for investigation. The nature of the research and voluntary participation tended to attract the more liberal members of a fairly conservative, established organization.[1]

The experiences with the research population led to a view of the organization and the families as separate social systems. This in turn led to a systems approach, which takes a holistic rather than linear approach to problems. The term, *system,* is used to define a social

---

[1] The methodology and population characteristics are described more fully in the author's doctoral dissertation (17).

TABLE I

Type of Stress and Characteristics of People Providing Data for the Work-Family Research

Grouping	Type of Stress	Number of People	Characteristics
I	Extensive business travel	14 (8 employees, 6 wives)	The employees in this group were research scientists, largely chemical and agricultural background. Between May and September they spent approximately 70 percent of their time traveling. Participated in a workshop with spouses on stresses associated with travel.
II	Extensive business travel	12 (6 employees, 6 wives)	Backgrounds similar to people in first grouping. Food and chemical products. Heavy business travel.
III	Psychological stresses associated with being a staff facilitator of change, including periods away from home	12 (6 employees, 6 wives)	Internal organization consultants, functioning as change agents. Backgrounds in line management and other staff roles.
IV	Transfer temporarily (one to two years) to the U.S. from another country.	23 (12 employees 11 wives)	Backgrounds in engineering—civil, and chemical. All employees spoke English, but about one-third of wives had trouble with English. Workshops with wives looked at stresses associated with international transfer.
V	Transfers to a different national culture	66 (employees and relatives)	All other persons sampled are included in this grouping. Includes internationals transferred temporarily to the U.S. (other than engineers); U.S. citizens transferred abroad; U.S. and other foreign nationals living temporarily in India.

entity with certain prescribed characteristics. Ackoff (1, p. 332) says: "Initially we can define a system broadly and crudely as any entity, conceptual or physical which consists of interdependent parts." Living systems are defined as "open systems" rather than "closed systems," i.e., they are open to energy-matter exchanges with an environment. A useful compilation of the characteristics common to open systems is found in Katz and Kahn, (12, p. 17): "All social systems, including organizations, consist of the patterned activities of a number of individuals. Moreover, these patterned activities are complementary or interdependent with respect to some common output or outcome; they are repeated, relatively enduring, and bounded in space and time."

These definitions can be applied equally well to the family and to the organization. In the field of family therapy, the term, "family homeostasis" is used to refer to the systemic nature of the interaction among family members. Satir (18, p. 1) says: "According to the concept of family homeostasis, the family acts so as to achieve a balance in relationships. Members help to maintain this balance overtly and covertly. The family's repetitious, circular, predictable communication patterns reveal this balance."

Consequently, while individuals were the principal sources of data, the research focused on what the experiences of individuals revealed about groups of people who constitute social systems. Commonalities discovered among individual experiences were the bases of the theoretical statements about systems. Data were collected by interviews, participant observation, and questionnaires. Company records were used to obtain information about other aspects of organizational life such as business travel patterns.

The product of research using grounded theory methodology is theory *generated* by the data of the research, not theory "proven" by the data. The findings (theory) of this research provide a way of looking at problems rather than solutions to problems. While they do not tell the reader what to do in a given situation, they provide a way of viewing the situation.

The criterion used to judge grounded theory is that "the theory must fit the situation being researched, and work when put into use. By 'fit' we mean that categories must be readily (not forcibly) applicable to, and indicated by, the data under study; by 'work' we mean that they must be meaningfully relevant to and be able to explain the behavior under study" (Glaser and Strauss [10, p. 3]). The theory that evolved in this research meets this criterion by its initial testing with members of the population from which the sample was drawn.

FINDINGS

The findings of the research reported here comment on the daily interactions between work and family life. However, people have become so skilled at coping with many of the day-to-day pressures that the latter are not discernible at first glance, even by the participants themselves or by skilled observers. (See Culbert [5] for an amplification of the dynamics of this type of coping.) For this reason, situations were chosen in which the stresses are highlighted and obvious, as in instances of transfer, heavy travel, and unusual roles in the organization. The dynamics of stress creation and coping are similar for these unusual events and for the ordinary, daily, ongoing interactions between organization and family life, but they are more observable.

The Creation of Stress

This study attempted to understand the process of interaction and how stress is created between organizational and family life. All persons interviewed saw themselves as members of both a work and a family system. The married employees saw themselves as functioning concurrently in the two social systems of work and family. The wives thought of themselves first as family members but also as significantly affected by, and members of, their husband's work system. This was expressed in statements such as, "When *we* came to the company," or "When the company transferred *us*." Even the unmarried persons interviewed had family or intimate system memberships that affected their work system activities in some significant way.

However, while all thought of themselves as members of work and family systems concurrently, they often behaved as if the system in which they were operating at the moment was the only system in which they lived. Many instances were observed or cited in which persons, both policymakers and employees, appeared to forget all about the forces operating in the family system while functioning in the work system. There were also instances in which organizational forces were ignored by the family. Failure to keep the fact of their concurrent membership in a work system and a family system in conscious recognition created problems over and over for people interviewed.

For example, one husband-employee was offered and accepted a new position that involved a great deal of responsibility and a transfer to a different location within the United States. The job excited him and involved an upward step, so he took it gladly. At the same time his wife became pregnant and had to give up her studies at the local college, as well as change her place of residence. At the end of a year and a half, the husband seemed bewildered that his wife had moved to her parent's home, and much of the spark and motivation he had felt for his new job disappeared with her. He reflected, "My job doesn't seem as important now as it did before she left."

In another family interviewed, the work system was the one apparently ignored for a time. When they realized that the wife was feeling trapped by her total immersion in family responsibilities, they decided that she would return to a profession she had given up at marriage. Her husband and the children would then take on more of the family responsibilities. This change was exciting for their family, and although the wife's returning to her profession after many years required extra effort and energy, she stretched to meet the challenges, greatly improving her life. In their planning, however, they had neglected to take account of the fact that the husband was about to receive a significant promotion with changed and heightened responsibilities. With this new promotion, the simultaneous expansions in the work and family systems placed enormous strains on all of them.

In another part of the company, the members of a work team engaged in heavy business travel were almost unanimous in their view that the travel placed a heavy burden both on them and their families. The exceptions were a single woman who said she enjoyed the travel and that it had very little impact on her family life. Her major problem was the distrust she experienced from the wives of men with whom she traveled. The other exception was a man who said the travel was irrelevant to his family life, and his family life was not related to his work. In interviews and questionnaires at the time, he expressed ambivalent feelings about his marriage, and in the work situation he generally volunteered for the heaviest travel assignments. Upon further questioning, it appeared that his travel served as an escape from a difficult family situation. In this instance, family events affected choices made in the work system and temporarily gave support to the organization demand for heavy business travel. Since it was not possible to interview this employee's wife, the effects of this situation upon her and the family were not verifiable.

For the other members of this work group, the stresses of travel were manifested in their organizational functioning. For some, there were fatigue and increasing uneasiness as they traveled. Some attempted to cut trips as short as possible. For one couple the pressures on their family life were greater than they were willing to bear, and they considered the husband's leaving the work group and perhaps the organization.

All the husbands and wives interviewed listed stresses they experienced as a result of the business travel. For the family, these stresses included the effect of disconnected relationships, increased responsibilities for the wife, and guilt feelings for the husband, as well as personal fatigue, fears of being alone, and worry for one another. Organizational stresses included disrupted communications, disconnected relationships, and fatigue.

The connection between organization and family events is even more obvious in the case of the families who were transferred. Thirteen families were interviewed who were on temporary transfer (one to four years) to the United States from another country. For each of these families, the transfer meant a disruption of their normal lives and restructuring of their family lives in a new environment. For each wife, there was an increase, at least initially, in the degree of dependence upon her husband as she adjusted to a new environment, which was, in essence, his environment. This dependency was especially marked for the wives with a language problem. Concomitant pressures were then placed on the husband to assume additional responsibilities such as shopping, finding a home, and dealing with all the medical and utilitarian needs of a family, as well as the demands of his new job. For families with children, there was the additional complication of finding and adjusting to schools with differing philosophies of education and sometimes different languages. The organizational changes for the husbands were not as extreme since many elements of the work culture were common to both countries, but some adjustments were inevitable.

That these events had an effect on organizational functioning is attested to by the concern of the head of the department and the personnel manager, whose interests in making the transfer a better experience included consideration for the individual as well as the primary concern for seeing that the organizational job got done. They were troubled about resistance to transfers, especially when the transfer meant an upward movement for the employee, and they cited instances of marital disruption and disturbed children as being organizational problems.

The data indicated that there were interactions between the work system and the family system in all of the cases. A rash of articles has been published recently in the popular press—*Cosmopolitan* (21), *Wall Street Journal* (2), *Ms.* (7), etc.—on the deleterious effects of transfers on the wife (see also Seidenberg [19]). In the short term, the wife may carry a disproportionate share of the physical and emotional burdens associated with an organizational event such as transfer. However, the findings of the study point to the fact that the impact of these events is systemic, that it involves both the work system and the family system, and the effects are apparent eventually in both systems.

The common stance for both the organization and the family is to ignore the interactions between the two systems unless or until they become a problem. The author had extreme difficulty finding a company that was willing to allow research on the relationship of organization and family life. The prevailing organizational norms maintaining the separateness of work and family were stronger for most companies than their initial interest in the subject. Management seems unable to envisage any other approach to the problems of organization-family interaction than the usual one of ignoring one system, usually the family system. Only when the stresses become unbearable are the interactions recognized.

When people do acknowledge the interaction of events in the organization and family systems, their natural inclination is to assign causality from one system to the other. Organizational events are blamed for family problems, and family events are blamed for organization problems. This is consistent with our cultural orientation, which tries to establish the cause for events, particularly if they are problem events, so that they can be remedied. This is reflected in our classical scientific method and is an ability highly rewarded in our society, especially in industrial organizations. One manager articulated this attitude explicitly when he said, "Let's find out what's wrong with the families so we can fix it up and get on with the job." Some examples from the research data illustrate this phenomenon.

In the group doing heavy travel, one man's travel status was seen as the cause of his wife's nervous stomach condition. Another's heavy travel was blamed for his children's social behavior. One man felt his miserable trips and consequent reluctance to travel were caused by his wife's difficulties and complaints, while another said his trips were miserable because his wife did not complain, and consequently he imagined the worst. There were stories of families in which the husband's long absences caused the marriage to deteriorate, or the husband's absences caused the wife to be unfaithful or the husband to be unfaithful, or a child's drug problem was attributed to the family's frequent moves on company business.

Administrators and personnel department people talked in general and specific terms about employee distractions and lower levels of performance that they thought were caused by family stresses. The family was also blamed for employee resistance to travel, transfer, and other organizational events.

A multitude of examples gathered through observations, interviews, and questionnaires corroborate the proposition that left to their own natural inclination, people tend to blame work stresses for family problems and family stresses for work problems.

However, the causality assigned to the interactions between organizational and family life often had little objective foundation but was rather based on an individual's idiosyncratic perceptions and needs. Repeatedly, it was found upon closer examination that events in the two systems were related, but the stated cause and effect relationships were an inadequate explanation for the situation.

For instance, one couple attributed the wife's ulcer and stomach problems to the anxiety created by the husband's business travels.

But when interviewed separately, the wife revealed that her nervous stomach condition was not a new symptom for her. In fact, she had exhibited some manifestations of psychosomatic illness since high school, and these symptoms had occurred periodically throughout her married life. In spite of this fact and his knowledge of it, her husband took responsibility for her anxiety and illness. His assignment of blame to himself and his job fit into his perception of himself as the responsible person, the "Rock of Gibraltar" for everyone. It enabled them to explain the situation in a way that maintained their accustomed ways of being together, but it did not deal with the underlying problems, either of the couple's relationship or the company's personnel policies.

Another couple separately and jointly attributed an especially difficult time in their marriage to his participation in a workshop sponsored by the company that had triggered some important personal change for him. A concurrent event, which they both ignored, was the wife's return to a career after many years of being at home. It is clear that both these events were interacting to contribute to the totality of the situation with the presenting cause-and-effect relationship being only one piece of it.

While assigning causality from one system to another allowed people to simplify highly complex situations, the process of simplification often led to incomplete and dysfunctional problem-definitions. In many cases, the simplified explanation satisfied the individual's need for understanding, but after defining the problem as causal, people often withdrew from further exploration of contributing circumstances. More often than not, they defined the causes as outside their control and withdrew with feelings of powerlessness and frustration.

For example, in the case of the employee whose wife went back to Europe after six months of a planned, two-year stay, the cause-and-effect relationships he and his co-workers assigned to the situation actually got in the way of effective problem-solving. The couple had decided to transfer to the United States from Europe as an important step in the husband's career, even though for his wife it meant giving up her profession, friends, and family. She returned to Europe at the end of six months for a temporary visit that was extended indefinitely. At the time the husband was interviewed, his wife had returned to their home in Europe, and he was having an extremely difficult time here in the United States, both personally and in his job. He insisted, however, that the problems were caused by the nature of his job and the organization policies affecting him and that his family system and his wife's actions were irrelevant to his job behavior. On the other hand, his co-workers, as well as his supervisor, felt that his family situation was the cause of the difficulties he was having on and off the job. Both causal explanations had some validity, but neither was an adequate explanation of the situation, and neither explanation in isolation led to an effective situation.

The problem was experienced by the employee and affected his co-workers, but each system (family and work) had, in effect, located the cause in the other system and placed it beyond its control. In this case, both systems remained immovable in their chosen causal definition, and there was little communication and no solution. The employee left after one year of his projected two-year stay, carrying feelings of failure and resentment toward the organization. The organization perceived him as not being able to manage effectively his job or his family. In this situation, each system's definition of the problem served as an escape from examining its own contribution. The employee did not look at what he was doing to contribute to the complexity of his family/work problems. The organization, on the other hand, did not have to look at the manner in which transfers and employee career decisions were handled. The failure to formulate more complex explanations exacted a high toll in terms of employee relations and transfer costs.

The case of the employee whose wife suffered from ulcers is another instance in which the agreed-upon causal explanation did not lead to solutions. Placing the blame for her anxiety and illness on his travel and the organization's travel policies provided an escape from looking at the complexities of their relationship, their family system, and its interactions with the work system. Having defined his absences as the cause of their problem, he then spent much energy worrying about the effects of his travel, envisaging the only solution as giving up traveling, and ultimately his present job. Until they participated in a workshop focused on the stresses of travel, (Culbert and Renshaw [6]), they were stuck with that causal explanation, which led to a dead end. During the workshop, they were each able to question their causal definition of the situation and entertain alternative solutions.

There were many other instances in which the causal explanations cited by the individuals got in the way of effective problem-solving. This is not to say that causal explanations are never useful. In the course of daily living, cause and effect are often assigned to concurrent events in work and family life. Often this simplification is functional. It can remove the need for making many minor decisions. The employee who attributed his family's mood to whether he was on time for dinner found that explanation functional. He made great efforts to be on time, and it seemed to work. The wife who attributed her husband's grumpiness at the end of the day to his boss's behavior in the office found this explanation functional. It allowed her to maintain her own focus and cope with her husband's moodiness. However, many of the problems observed occurred when causality was assigned too early to work-family interactions and clung to thereafter. The interactions continued to create stress, and the causal definition got in the way of seeking more effective ways of coping with the situation.

The preceding section has discussed the forces and dynamics operating to create potentially stressful situations at the organization-family boundaries. The next section describes the process of coping with these stresses.

Coping With Stresses

Initially in the research an attempt was made to categorize people into typologies of family and organizational career stages, hypothesizing that this would reveal patterns of ability to cope with organizational pressures. There are certainly patterns of particularly stressful events associated with different stages of family life—i.e. families with young children have different stresses than those with teen-age children or no children. In the organizational system, managers entering the career ladder tend to have different sets of stresses than those who have "made it." There was no consistent pattern, however, in ability to cope with these stresses relative to the typologies. These findings led to the conclusion that no two individuals and no two families can be expected to react in the same way to a similar set of potentially stressful events in organizational or family life.

Although the conditions of travel were similar for most of the twenty employees involved in extensive business travel, their perception of the experience and its associated stresses, as well as their adaption to the stresses, was different, ranging from the man who found travel a useful escape from a difficult family situation to the husband who was considering changing jobs because the travel created such hardships for him and his wife.

Similarly, for some of the families on a temporary transfer from another country, the experience was an exciting challenge, an opportunity to learn or practice their English and to travel in another country. For others, the experience was almost a traumatic upheaval, and they spent the two years recovering. In one family, the parents described the learning their children had acquired in their two-year stay in the U.S., while in another family, the parents described only the disruption and emotional problems created for their children by the transfer.

It became apparent that the objective events in themselves were not a sufficient indicator of the outcome of the situation. An individual's experience of stress is composed of two elements—the objective properties of the event and the subjective meaning the events hold for the individual. This statement is consistent with medical theories relating stress and physical illness (cf. Selye [20], Hinkle, *et al.* [11]), which state, in effect, that whether illness results from a given stressor (stressful happening) is dependent on the individual stress response triggered in an individual by that stressor. Hinkle, *et al.*, state: "The clue to the relationship between life experiences and illness . . . appears to be not so much in the nature of the life situations themselves as in the way that these situations are perceived by those who experience them" (11, p. 279).

What variables, then, are significant in predicting the outcome of potentially stressful situations? One factor emerged across the groupings in the population and across typologies of work career and family career patterns as significant in determining the subjective meaning a particular event held for an individual and consequently his ability to cope with that situation. The research data indicate that *the amount of influence an individual perceives he has over the events in a stressful situation is central to explaining why one individual is able to cope successfully with stressful events and another has difficulty with similar events. It also explains why a person is able to cope at one time and has difficulty with a similar stressful situation at another time.*

An investigation of perceived influences as a relevant factor in coping with stress grew out of the previously cited workshop conducted for managers and their wives who were engaged in extensive business travel. The initial hypothesis of the research during this workshop was that family and organizational effectiveness in coping with the stresses of travel could be improved by means of a husband-wife seminar directed toward increasing problem-solving skills used in coping with the stresses of business travel. Changes in behavior were assessed by a variety of means: interviews of participants and co-workers, examination of expense records for travel, participant assessment of the intensity of stresses experienced before and after the workshop, and consultant observations. An attitude questionnaire was administered at intervals to both the experimental group and a comparison group whose members were traveling extensively for business reasons but who did not participate in a problem-solving workshop.

The author hypothesized that if the workshop were successful, travel behavior would change and the attitudes toward travel, the job, and the organization would improve. After the workshop, the participants and their co-workers, as well as supervisory personnel, reported improvements in the job situation related to travel, including such things as rescheduling the necessary travel to meet both organizational and personal requirements, better experiences by employees when they did travel, cooperating and sharing of travel by several employees, planning on the part of families for the periods of absence and enjoying them, and shorter travel periods. Some of the reported changes by individuals were striking and beyond the expectations of the consultant and the participants. The participants reported improved effectiveness in coping with the stresses of business travel. All except one couple rated the workshop as extremely valuable. The one couple's rating was neutral.

However, even though improvements in family and organizational effectiveness were reported by all the participants, the hypothesized changes in attitude toward travel, the organization, and the family did not take place. The participants had considered travel a nuisance before the workshop, and they felt the same after the workshop. They had valued their families and the organization before the workshop, and they still valued them after the workshop. The only significant attitude change was in their attitude toward themselves. They viewed themselves as more potent, and they evaluated themselves more positively. Comparing this group with the people who had not participated in the workshop, the attitude change was statistically significant ($t = 3.62$, $df = 22$, and $p = .05$)—and unexpected.

When integrated with other data and theory, the results contributed to a theory of perceived influence. The participants in the workshop on travel did not appear to change their basic attitudes toward the idea of necessary job-related travel. *What they did change was their view of their own strength and ability to make it a better experience.* In addition, the wife's feelings of influence were augmented by the organizational sponsoring of the workshop to include the wives. This legitimized the family's interactions with the organizational issue of travel and thus strengthened the inputs the wives were able to make to increased problem-solving effectiveness.

Similarly, exploring the experience of transfer with those living temporarily in the United States, many instances of perceived influence as a factor in coping with stress were found. A few case examples will be cited here.

Two families were roughly matched on the basis of country of origin, ages of children, fluency in English of the wives, and career stage of the husbands. One family described its experience in the United States as challenging and exciting, although not without difficulties. The wife and husband had had some problems in adjusting to the United States, but their children now spoke English like natives and were happy. Generally, they all felt it had been a good experience. In the other family, however, the wife still felt her English was inadequate and therefore didn't go out much. Some of the wives in the international community spoke of their concern about her. In her interview, she talked mainly about how difficult the experience had been and how much she wanted to return to her home.

Both families were queried as to how the decision had been made to come to the United States. In the first family, the husband and wife both stated in separate interviews that the process of decision-making originated in the husband's initial assessment that a transfer to the United States would be helpful to his work career. At that point, he told his wife about the possibility, and the family discussed at great length the anticipated effects the transfer would have on each of them. They eventually made the decision together. In the second family, the husband said he had become aware over a period of time that in order for him to have the kinds of experience and knowledge he needed to advance, he would have to spend time in the United States. He had been thinking about such a move for at least a year and a half before the opportunity arose, so he was prepared to come immediately when the offer was made. When his wife was asked how the decision had been made, she said that her husband had come home from work one night and told her that they must transfer to the United States in two months. This had been her first knowledge of the possibility; she had had no feelings of influence over the decision. While the husband's adjustment to the United States had been relatively smooth, his family had, and was having, an extremely difficult time and were living only for the day when they could return home.

Another somewhat different orientation toward the decision to transfer explains further the role of perceived influence. In this family the wife blamed organizational policies for her husband's not receiving a promotion, and the supervisor blamed the characteristics of the man himself for the situation. The wife described a family decision-making process in which the children participated. After some hard choices, they all decided they would like to come to the United States. The children and wife became involved in activities, and for them it had been a good experience. The husband also described the family decision-making process, but prior to that he said the decision to take the job in the United States had not been a choice for him at all. A new director had wanted to bring in some of his own assistants, and it had seemed expedient to have this employee transfer to the United States temporarily while the new organization was being established. So in this family, the wife and children had felt a part of the decision to transfer, while the husband had not; their contrasting experiences in the United States reflected this difference.

The researcher then asked each individual involved in facilitating organizational and personal change about the decision to enter this profession, since in this company it is possible to change from a consulting role to a technical role, and vice versa. In this group, a similar pattern emerged relating the degree of influence each individual felt he had over becoming involved in the profession to the feelings of satisfaction and ability to cope with the stresses associated with it. In one family, the wife had been instrumental in her husband's becoming interested in the organizational consulting area. She had participated in a number of workshops similar to ones used in organizational consulting. Her experiences had been extremely positive, and when the opportunity came for her husband to move into the profession, she had been a strong force in his decision, reinforcing his own inclination toward consulting. In her interview with the researcher, she was extremely positive about the effects of her husband's profession on his family life. In fact, she would have liked him to be able to devote more of his time to this profession.

Their experience was in direct contrast to another family in which the wife had been extremely reluctant to see her husband move into the role of a facilitator. She had been happy with his technical position and found the values and practice of the new profession threatening to their relationship and their jointly valued way of life. They continued to have a close relationship, but his professional life was difficult for her to accept. She served as a brake against his exploration of new behaviors, such as more direct conflict-management and greater openness in expressing feelings, and ensured that he would not move completely into the mode of his new profession.

The experience of other families also reflected differences in the amount of influence the wives felt they had in a decision to become involved in a profession that was seen, particularly in the wife's opinion, as a threatening type of profession. In one family, the transition to the role of organization development consultant had been particularly painful. The wife had felt out of control, as she saw frightening changes in her husband. He seemed to devalue much of their life style as he moved away from rigid routine and toward more flexibility. They were able to work through this period of transition to the point where the husband now served as her "consultant" in her job. But the first years in which she felt she had no influence over what was happening to her husband and their relationship were described as extremely difficult for both of them.

While many questions are raised about the meaning of influence to different individuals and the factors contributing to an individual's assessment of his own degree of influence, the general concept of perceived influence as relative to the ability to cope with stresses was evident in the three study groups. It appears that no matter what formal or informal agreements people think they have with each other regarding the division of influence, each individual makes his own estimate of the degree of influence he can exert relative to the rest of the system.

For instance, the group of people traveling extensively for business had a shared norm that they did have influence over the travel situation. This belief was held also by their bosses. Organizational policies in this company were quite enlightened regarding travel. However, there were also powerful, but less defined, pressures that militated against making the most of some of the allowances such as the norm that status was lost if families interferred with organizational scheduling. In the face of ambiguity and conflicting messages from the organization each person made an individual assessment of the degree to which he could influence the travel situation.

SUMMARY

This article has set forth some preliminary theoretical statements about the relationship between organizational life and family life. Over a spectrum of organizational and family events studied, the two systems were found to be interdependent. Although there was a tendency to ignore this interdependence, over a period of time the interactions were forced into awareness by the emergence of problems. Stress is created between organizations and families by the fact that people live simultaneously in both systems, and the pressure of events in the two systems is cumulative. Stresses in one system are not caused by events in the other system but are a function of the interactive nature of the relationship. The common tendency to blame one system for events in the other system neither correlates with reality nor is useful in coping with the stresses.

The key factor in coping successfully with stress was found to be the amount of influence an individual perceived himself as having over the events. While it may not always be possible to change the objective events, it may be possible to restructure them and discover new avenues of influence or freedom for a given individual.

As a result of the study, it is recommended that organizations and families take a more open stance toward the areas of decision-making where the two worlds overlap, rather than accept the traditional, passive role of mutual blame. The family consultant can be aware of the causal explanations family members give to describe work-related problems and can question these assumptions. Organizations must develop mechanisms for integrating the family perspective into relevant organizational decisions. One example of how this has been done is described in Culbert and Renshaw (6). A joint, problem-solving approach on the part of both systems is suggested. Ultimately, the organization must take responsibility for including the family system in certain areas of organizational decisions. There are other areas, however, where the family and those working with families can take the initiative in influencing decisions that affect the family's quality of life.

REFERENCES

1. ACKOFF, R. L., "Systems, Organizations and Interdisciplinary Research" in F. E. Emery (Ed.), *Systems Thinking*, Penguin Books Ltd., Middlesex, England, 1969.

2. BRALOVE, M., "The New Nomads," *Wall Street Journal*, August 1, 1973.

3. BUCKLEY, W., *Modern Systems Research for the Behavioral Scientist*, Chicago, Aldine Publishing Co., 1969.

4. BURGER, N. H., *The Executive's Wife*, London, Collier Books, 1968.

5. CULBERT, S. A., *The Organizational Trap*, New York, Basic Books, Inc., 1974.

6. CULBERT, S. A. and RENSHAW, J. R., "Coping With the Stresses of Travel as an Opportunity for Improving the Quality of Work and Family Life," *Fam. Proc.* 11: 321–337, 1972.

7. DIENSTAG, E., "Those Whither-Thou-Goest Blues," *Ms Magazine*,

8. EMERY, F. E. (Ed.), *Systems Thinking*, Middlesex, England, Penguin Books, Ltd., 1969.

9. GOODE, W. J., *World Revolution and Family Patterns*, Glencoe, Ill., Free Press, 1963.

10. GLASER, B. and STRAUSS, A. L., *The Discovery of Grounded Theory: Strategies for Qualitative Research*, Chicago, Aldine Publishing Co., 1967.

11. HINKLE, L. E., CHRISTENSON, F. D., KANE, A., OSTFEL, W. N., THETFORD, W. N., and WOLFF, H. G., "An Investigation of the Relation Between Life Experience, Personality Characteristics, and General Susceptibility to Illness," *Psychosom. Med.*, 20: 278–295, 1958.

12. KATZ, D. and KAHN, R. L., *The Social Psychology of Organizations*, New York, John Wiley & Sons, Inc., 1966.

13. LINTON, R., "The Natural History of the Family" in R. N. Anshen (Ed.), *The Family: Its Function and Destiny*, New York, Harper & Row, 1945.

14. MARCH, J. G. JR., *Handbook of Organizations*, Chicago, Rand McNally & Co., 1965.

15. OSGOOD, C. E., SUCI, G. J., and TANNENBAUM, P. H., *The Measurement of Meaning*, Urbana, Ill. Univ. of Ill. Press, 1967.

16. PARSONS, T., "The Family in Urban Industrial America" in T. Parsons and R. F. Bales, *Family Socialization and Interaction Process*, New York, Free Press, 1955.

17. RENSHAW, J. R., "Explorations at the Boundaries of Work and Family Life," Unpublished Ph.D. dissertation, University of California, Los Angeles, 1974.

18. SATIR, V., *Conjoint Family Therapy: A Guide to Theory and Technique*, Palo Alto, Calif., Science and Behavior Books, Inc., 1964.

19. SEIDENBERG, R., *Corporate Wives—Corporate Casualties?*, New York, American Management Association, Inc., 1973.

20. SELYE, H., *The Stress of Life*, New York, Toronto, London, McGraw-Hill Book Co., 1956.

21. SHABER, D., "The Sexual Behavior of the (Traveling) American Male," *Cosmopolitan*, pp. 136–145, April, 1970.

22. SLATER, P., *The Pursuit of Loneliness. American Culture at the Breaking Point*, Boston, Beacon Press, 1970.

23. THE WHITE HOUSE CONFERENCE ON CHILDREN AND YOUTH, "Children and Parents: Together in the World," Forum 15, Washington, D.C., Government Publications Printing Office, 1971.

Reprint requests should be addressed to Jean R. Renshaw, Ph.D., Department of Electrical Engineering, OHE 530E, University of Southern California, Los Angeles, California 90007.

26

Men, Women, and Work: Reflections on the Two-Person Career

by Hanna Papanek

Our viewpoints as social scientists, no less than as novelists and poets, are developed through what we are, where we have come from, and where we have been. Our choice of research problems reflects concerns which often underlie our own lives, and even our accidentally chosen problems come to define our later work. Other points of view become foreclosed through the cumulative effect of specialized knowledge and of concepts which we have found congenial. Much of American sociology, for example, reflects the world of men, most often the world of white men in industrial society. But even where the concerns of women are considered, the focus is often exclusively on the American middle class. Such a restricted perspective not only damages our collection of relevant data but also constrains the analysis of what we find. From my specific viewpoint, as a woman born in Europe, most of whose professional work has been done in Muslim South Asia where women are secluded or segregated, much current sociological analysis suffers from the neglect of relevant comparisons with other societies. More subtly also, the life experiences of American women—including professionals married to fellow professionals—have been left out of systematic consideration in much of the analysis of our own society.

In this paper, I discuss some of the aspects of American women's "vicarious achievement" (Press and Whitney 1971; Lipman-Blumen 1972) through their husbands' jobs in a special combination of roles which I call the "two-person single career." This combination of formal and informal institutional demands which is placed on both members of a married couple of whom only the man is employed by the institution is particularly prevalent in middle-class occupations in the United States but is not restricted to them, or indeed to the United States. The pattern plays a particularly significant role, however, where an explicit ideology of educational equality between the sexes conflicts with an implicit (and now often illegal) inequality of occupational access. This particular American dilemma is resolved in a very American style—by providing a social control mechanism

which serves to derail the occupational aspirations of educated women into the noncompetitive "two-person career" without openly injuring the concept of equality of educational opportunity for both sexes. The social control mechanism comes into full force after the educational process is completed, although it is of course anticipated by many years in which children learn conformity to sex roles and sex-role stereotypes. The "two-person career" pattern is fully congruent with the stereotype of the wife as supporter, comforter, backstage manager, home maintainer, and main rearer of children. The timing and nature of this particular resolution of the dilemma in which educated American women are placed is illuminated more clearly through comparisons with other societies in which sex segregation is more consistent, more open, and more pervasive.

Incidentally, the concept of the "two-person single career" should not be confused with that of the "two-career family" (Holmstrom 1972), although elements of the "two-person career" pattern clearly present major problems for the family in which both husband and wife follow independent careers. In fact, women often find the demands of their husbands' jobs to be a major factor in their own reluctance or inability to develop independent careers at levels for which their education has prepared them, and move instead into patterns which may be highly productive and innovative and in which the demands of the husband's job are incorporated into the wife's own work in a career.

The deliberate focus in this discussion on the role played by women in the orbit of men's occupations raises several sets of questions. It should by now be obvious that the sociological and anthropological study of women is not very advanced, even in societies where women are accessible to researchers and not isolated by *purdah* (seclusion) as they are in much of South Asia. It is clear that data about the life of women are generally insufficient, especially if compared with what is known in the same society about the life of men. This insufficiency reflects a lack of interest on the part of predominantly male social scientists, but also speaks to the problems of access and empathy with people who are felt to be very different from oneself. Of course, the challenge of learning about a very different culture, to penetrate into very different worlds, is often a major element in the underlying motivation of sociologists and anthropologists, who have made a professional virtue out of what is otherwise considered a vice—intense curiosity about other people. But for some reason, the challenge of learning about another sex is less clearly part of our professional motivations and is hedged in by so many external social restraints and internal psychological complications that it tends to play only a small role in the published literature. Its role in the less formal pattern of interaction between professionals and co-workers is, of course, another story.

In the case of studies of women, there is also the additional problem that public written materials, such as historical records, literary works, and codes of law, usually do not directly reflect the life experiences of women. Knowledge about women's lives in societies to which one is a stranger, either in space or in time, is too often derived from what men have written—and perhaps we do not fully understand some of the problems which this entails. What role do male fantasies play in what is written about women, both in novels and in legal codes? What kinds of women do men feel free to discuss among themselves? There have certainly been times and places where men have only spoken about women outside their own families, or women who were somehow in the public domain. At the same time, there has been a dearth of women writers, as Virginia Woolf (1929) and Tillie Olsen (1965) among many others have pointed out. What women might have written about women's lives must be found in oral materials, unpublished diaries, stories, and direct observation. Again, this is particularly important if one studies societies, or segments of societies, to which one is an outsider.

At another level, the insufficiency of data about women's lives also contributes to an inaccurate understanding of societies where little is known about half the population, its women. Studies often report on "the people" of an area, without necessarily specifying whether women have been included, and whether their customs and manners differ in any way from those of the men. Such differences are most likely to occur in societies which are highly sex segregated, and where access to women is particularly difficult for male researchers; but such societies may also be particularly instructive about the operation of sex distinctions.

One moves to another point in the argument if it is suggested that knowledge about the lives of men, and the transactions between them, does after all include most of the significant truths about a society. From much of sociological theory one could, indeed, gain this impression, since there is a very definite focus on public acts and public actors—in political systems, bureaucracies, religious institutions, the economy. In some societies more than in others, women do participate to significant degrees in some of these sectors, as, for example, the market women of West Africa participate in the economy; but these public spheres of action tend to be male dominated in many societies. The consumers of the products of public action and the persons with whom interaction occurs on other levels are often excluded from the sociological domain.

In a very general way, the distinction between public and private worlds corresponds to the differences which have long been established in sociology through such concepts as primary and secondary groups, or *Gemeinschaft* and *Gesellschaft* types of association. But the study of sex segregation in South Asian societies suggests that some very specific factors may be involved in such systems, and that the public-private distinction may be particularly useful in an exploration of women's roles.

While societies differ sharply from each other in the extent to which women are restricted in their access to the world outside the home, this is the defining characteristic of sex segregation in much of South Asia. There are differences between Muslims and Hindus in the actual operation of seclusion practices, and these are consistent with the value systems associated with the two religions (Papanek 1971, 1973). Both reflect a preoccupation with the dimension of sexual and reproductive behavior, especially as it affects women. Sexuality, and its implications for reproductive behavior, purity of descent, contacts between males and females, child rearing, economic behavior, and so on, must be obvious elements in any study of sex segregation. And the family group, however it is defined, tends to be the focus for much sexual and reproductive behavior, particularly its systematic and sanctioned aspects. This point makes it important to develop a valid system of analysis which takes account of the special nature of sexuality, and the relationships based upon it, in a study of women's lives.

It is probably useful to begin with this assumption, rather than to use analogies to other forms of association, such as caste. While the concept of "women as a caste" may have obvious advantages in calling attention to the many inequities of sex discrimination, it is not useful in the development of social theory as it affects women. If sexual relationships and reproductive behavior are used as points of departure for analyzing the place of women in most societies, relevant concepts must include distinctions between social groups within which it does or does not occur in systematic, sanctioned ways. There are obvious problems connected with using a public-private distinction based on this point, of course. Large areas of sexual behavior are indeed private but occur outside the family setting. They constitute very important areas of social behavior which have been studied far too little by sociologists (see Marcus 1966; Humphreys 1970). Homosexual relationships—that is, sexual relationships not connected with reproductive behavior—also require integration into an analytical system.

The specific topic of this discussion—"vicarious achievement" in the two-person single career—is concerned with transactions which occur at the boundary between public and private spheres. They involve a three-way relationship, between employer and two partners in a marriage, in which two sets of relationships are of the "secondary" type and one is of the "primary." Usually, the wife of the employee is inducted into the orbit of her husband's employing institution not because of her own, or the institution's, specific choice but because she is related to her husband through sexual, economic, and emotional bonds. The relationship between the wife and the employer also tends to be maintained and expressed through dimensions which are somewhat different from those used in the relationship with the employee. While terms such as instrumental and expressive relationships have been very useful in some studies, they are not the most appropriate terms for the two-person career, since elements of both are involved in the relationships.

The induction of the wife into the husband's work orbit may take the form of adding new types of work to her activities as a housekeeper or mother, or as someone with a career of her own. Or it may take the form of modifying only slightly the activities which she already carries on as part of her complex of roles, such as influencing her life style, adding to her role as a hostess, and so on. This makes it difficult to distinguish specifically which activities result from her involvement with her husband's work, except through reference to the goals of the work or the group of people whom it concerns. In general, it is also true that the institution which employs the husband proceeds on the assumption that the alternative uses of the wife's time are neither important nor productive, in the economic sense of the term, and that her "opportunity costs" are therefore low. This is, of course, consistent with the general view of housework and women's work, in general, as a low-status nonproductive activity. Oddly enough, few suggestions have been made for getting along without it.

"Vicarious Achievement" in the Two-Person Single Career

"Vicarious" is defined by Webster as "experienced or realized through imaginative or sympathetic participation in the experience of another . . . acting for a principal . . . having the function of a substitute . . . taking the place of something primary or original." Its use in current research on women tends to be asymmetrical, being applied only to women who fulfill "their achievement needs either completely or predominantly through the accomplishments of their husbands" (Lipman-Blumen 1972, p. 36). Presumably, the concept would also lend itself to application in the sense of men being "vicarious homemakers," or bringing up their children "vicariously" through their wives' activities in these spheres. Interestingly enough, the distinctions which have been made tend to follow other lines. Tresemer and Pleck (1972) in their study of men's reactions to women of achievement point out that American men "are simultaneously living through their wives' emotionality [while the] women live vicariously through their husbands' achievement." The complementarity indicated in this study between expressive and instrumental relationships of men and women must be considered in light of the fact that, at least in some instances, instrumental activities tend to be more highly valued in American society than expressive ones. The terms are so closely attached to behavioral and gender stereotypes that they should be used with caution.

"Vicarious achievement" is probably most typical of the American middle class, since the employing institutions which foster it and the educational preparation which makes it possible function mainly at this level. There appear to be class distinctions in the extent to which the occupational worlds of men affect the lives of women. Rainwater, Coleman, and Handel (1962) point out that working-class wives are much less involved with their husbands' occupational roles than are the wives of middle-class men in their study. There are probably also differences between ethnic and racial groups. In any case, the type of participation in "two-person careers" described in this paper differs in many important respects from the situations where wives must also hold jobs to support the family, or those in which they are working partners, as on small farms, in small businesses, mama and papa stores, and other joint enterprises. In the middle-class two-person career pattern, the wife is neither formally employed nor remunerated in any direct sense.

But there are sharp differences between middle-class occupations in the extent to which the participation of wives is elicited; in Rose Coser's terms, some institutions are more "greedy" than others (Rose Coser and Rokoff 1971). At the same time, the vicarious achievement pattern is structurally a part of the middle-class wife's role, rather than being a matter of choice, accident, or conflict. Some parallels can be drawn with the ways in which ambivalence has been found to be structurally inherent in some occupational roles. Some of the ambivalent aspects of the physician's role, for example, were seen as "conflicting normative expectations socially defined for a particular social role associated with a single social status" (Merton and Elinor Barber 1963, p. 96). Similarly, conflicting normative expectations are part of the middle-class married woman's role; and structured ambivalence is associated with her participation in the two-person career on the part of all three participants—the wife, the husband, and the employing institution.

Some indications of the relative importance of two-person careers is given in Helena Lopata's study of Chicago-area housewives in 1956 and 1962 (Lopata 1965, 1971), which clarifies some of the varieties of role orientations of women in different income levels, backgrounds, and places of residence. Among the group of "husband-oriented wives" in her classification, she singles out the "more highly educated woman who has herself worked in complex organizations" as the one most likely to be "interested in her husband's job, its problems and social relations" (1971, p. 104). This is the relatively small group which is most likely to be involved in the two-person career. Lopata concluded that, in her sample, "few women expressed an interest in what the man does when he is outside the home" (1965, p. 121); but the specific wording of her questionnaire may have contributed to this view. Possibly, the question "Does a wife have a great deal of influence on her husband's job? Why? How?" may contradict the prevailing ideology that women should not do so. Perhaps, if women had been asked about the kinds of modifications in their lives which had been brought about through the man's career demands, the proportions might have been different. In any case, Lopata's study does indicate that husband-oriented women were most likely to occur among women with "successful husbands," with professional degrees or Ph.D.'s and comparatively high incomes (1971, p. 65). This group also includes those women, such as a group of Air Force officers' wives, who had "a strong dependence upon their husband's job" (1965, p. 123), and whose husband-orientation could be the result of the man's external commitments.

Many of the examples of two-person careers described in this paper fit the Lopata categories, although the focus of the analysis is somewhat different.

The best-known two-person career pattern is that of the corporate executive's wife described by Whyte (1952, 1956) and many others. Of course, the pattern is not confined to business executives but occurs particularly often in the case of large, complex institutions employing highly educated men. Colleges and universities, large private foundations, the U.S. government (particularly the armed forces and the foreign service), and similar institutions all develop their own version of the two-person career pattern among their employees. They all communicate certain expectations to the wives of their employees. These expectations serve the dual function of reinforcing the husband's commitment to the institution and of demanding certain types of role performance from the wife which benefit the institution in a number of ways. A pattern of pressures is generated for both members of the couple which is closely related to social mobility, mobility within the employing institution, loyalty, and interpersonal rivalry.

While this pattern is typical of the United States, it probably exists in many other industrial societies to some degree. In some societies, such as Japan (Vogel 1967), the pattern of lifetime commitment by the employee to the employing institution may accentuate some elements of the pattern, such as involvement in social activities with colleagues, and possibly diminish some others involving specific contributions by the wife. Similarly, in the bureaucracies of some former British colonies, as for example the Civil Service of Pakistan and the Indian Administrative Service, wives are deeply involved in the rank distinctions of their husbands; and in the social life they share almost exclusively with fellow civil servants but they may be barred from more specific helpmeet activities by the social customs which segregate men and women.

The wife's involvement with her husband's career frequently begins before the career itself, during the stage when he is undergoing the advanced training so typical of these middle-class careers, while she is working in a temporary job to support them both, having abandoned or interrupted her own studies. The process of induction into the two-person career pattern proper begins when the husband is interviewed for a job or considered for a fellowship. It is called "finding out whether the wife is suitable." The most important aspect of this suitability is related to social mobility, that is, whether the wife is able to maintain a certain kind of life style and to change it along with her husband's changes in rank, but no faster or slower.

The most general characteristics, in fact, of the two-person career pattern focus on the status and rank aspects of the man's job. Wives are enlisted in the institutional pressures connected with mobility in the organization and with the hazing of low-ranking members. It is the wives who are most closely involved with the institutionalized perquisites of rank outside the office—housing, level of consumption, friendship circles, clothes, sociability, manners, club memberships, and so on. It is no accident, of course, that the most clear-cut application of these pressures occurs in situations where the employing institution operates in a social enclave, as in overseas diplomatic missions, army posts, college towns, and company towns. A recent State Department directive, reported in the *New York Times* (January 26, 1972), illustrates both the rank and hazing aspects. It was stated that "the wife of a Foreign Service employee who has accompanied her husband to a foreign post is a 'private person' and 'not a Government employee.' " She could no longer be required to perform services, including menial work, for the wives of her husband's superiors. It is, of course, clear that such services had previously been required, and that many of them are likely to continue to be customary. For example, volunteer work, participation in the entertainment of guests, holding children's parties, and so on are all nominally optional activities, but participation is strongly expected. A wife who does not participate risks injuring her husband's career, in much the same way that it is likely to be injured by a wife who drinks too much, talks too much, or has strong independent aspirations. Wives of overseas personnel of the U.S. government are also expected to participate in formal courses of training before going overseas.

Pointing up the contrast between the role of such training in the participation of men and women in direct and vicarious achievement is the practice of many institutions of barring wives from the "serious" training programs developed for men. It has been the practice, for example, at the Harvard Business School's advanced management training programs to stipulate that the wives of participants may not live on campus (and preferably not in Cambridge) during the intensive course, since it is felt that their presence would distract the men from their immersion in course work and contacts with other executives.

The fact that the women's activities are labeled as being outside the men's work orbit, while being within their ranking system, reinforces the ambivalence which characterizes most aspects of the two-person career. This ambivalence is particularly destructive to the self-esteem of many participants, since it often emphasizes activities which women personally reject but are expected by their husband's colleagues to perform (see Evelyn Riesman 1958). This is consistent with the low valuation which employing institutions normally place on the time as well as the work performance of wives. This low "opportunity cost" placed by institutions on the time of wives assumes that they have no alternative earning opportunities, but is clearly destructive of developing such alternatives. The lowest opportunity costs are often assumed to exist in those institutions which are most prestigious and competitive for men, as is indicated to some extent by the dearth of equal-level careers among the wives of high-status academics.

The high degree of ambivalence which accompanies the induction of women into the institutional orbits of their husbands is based on the need to enlist the women's participation and loyalty without letting their actual contributions decrease the importance which the institution places on the husband's work. This is very similar to the ambivalent valuation placed on the work of women in the male-female complementary pairs which are so typical of many Western societies but absent in sex-segregated societies (Papanek 1971). These pairs include doctor and nurse, executive and secretary, principal and teacher, editor and research assistant, among many others. In each, the division of labor stresses the indispensability of the woman along with the man's higher status and higher salary. In each of these pairs, there are also obvious incongruities between expected and recognized areas of responsibility, as the woman's potential responsibility in her complementary job is tacitly recognized by all concerned to be very large, while neither her status nor her salary recognizes this potential in formal terms. For instance, nurses are tacitly expected to take over several important medical functions in cases of emergency, as is also the case in the roles of many secretaries, assistants, and teachers. There is usually very little reciprocity, however, as well as a greater tendency to replace the female member of the pair with a substitute female.

Other types of involvement by women in two-person single careers concern other elements of the man's job in addition to its status dimensions. Many activities are aimed at increasing the husband's competitive advantage in the actual work situation. These helpmeet activities are usually not specifically required by the institution, although they are rarely rejected when performed. They include typing and editing manuscripts, collaborating in the laboratory, taking notes in classes and meetings, and participating in fieldwork. Judging from the frequency of authors' acknowledgements to their wives—"without whom I would not have been able to work with the women in *X* community"—there exists a large group of para-professional sociologists and anthropologists in the United States. They do not publish independently and are not usually co-authors, and their professional recognition tends to be informal and vicarious.

There is often a high degree of tension surrounding the contributions made by wives to the work of their husbands, and there are many possible alternatives. In an older generation of academics, for example, one can find many wives who worked productively for many years as their husbands' private or acknowledged research assistants. They may have exerted considerable influence on their husbands' work, which was acknowledged both by the husband and his closer colleagues but rarely by the profession at large. In other cases, academic wives combined their unofficial colleagueship with professional activities, such as editing a professional journal. As Helen Hughes (1973) points out, some of these jobs lent themselves to considerable expansion in terms of professional influence when they were occupied by faculty wives for a long period rather than a succession of graduate students.

On the other hand, many of these older wives suppressed or diverted their own professional ambitions and chose occupations which would not bring them into their husbands' professional orbits, such as real estate agents in college towns or teachers in local private or public schools. Such women sometimes report that they would have liked to work more closely with their husbands, as official or unofficial colleagues, but that this would not

have been acceptable or would have created too many tensions. The alternative jobs which they chose may not have been helpmeet activities in the sense of this discussion, therefore; but their choices do illustrate some of the factors involved in accepting or rejecting a vicarious achievement role.

Some of the tensions inherent in the vicarious achievement role are dramatically illustrated in the life of Zelda Fitzgerald (Milford 1970). In her case, rejection of the vicarious role demanded by her husband created serious conflicts between them both as artists and as husband and wife. Her biography indicates many of the profound questions which a discussion of women as vicarious achievers cannot even begin to answer. For example, the complex emotional and intellectual exchanges which may occur in a marriage or any similar kind of long-range relationship make obvious contributions to the work of both members of the couple. Usually, however, the institutional pressures which help to define the job of the husband tend to emphasize a more public presentation of ideas and skills than is usually the case for the wife. Prevailing social stereotypes tend to require her to be satisfied with knowing the extent of her contribution to her husband's work and to the growth and development of her children. And who, indeed, should measure published output in books and journals against such tangibles as children? In fact, men who are under heavy pressures from their employing institutions often express overt or covert jealousy toward women who face different sets of pressures, while attempting to maintain their intellectual and emotional development at high levels. This jealousy—usually expressed in such terms as "be glad you don't *have* to be in the rat race"—is often a factor in the development of independent careers for women and should be distinguished from the exploitative attitudes which often are expressed in similar terms.

Once the discussion of wives' contributions to their husbands' work goes beyond the obvious and simple levels of direct assistance of the kind which could also be performed by a substitute, such as a laboratory assistant, research assistant, secretary, and so on, it is clear that many complicated problems arise. Leaving these aside for the moment, it is probably correct to say that openly acknowledged collaboration, in the context of a two-person career, is not very frequent. This ambivalence surrounding the wife's contribution suggests that many institutions, again particularly in the academic world, recognize the fragility of male self-esteem in American society and have adopted a number of ways of safeguarding it. Acknowledged collaboration can more often be expressed in the case of a team of professionals who are also married, but even in these cases both institutional and personal problems are considerable. It is, of course, clear that employing institutions, run mainly by men in these cases, usually recognize the problems of male colleagues more clearly, and that safeguards built into career patterns, hiring practices, and reward systems are geared to men rather than women, whether wives or potential female colleagues.

A third type of two-person career emphasizes the man's public image. These jobs include some where the wife's participation is almost, but not quite, formally institutionalized—the ambassador's wife, the mayor's wife, the wife of a large foundation representative abroad, the wife of a company president, the First Lady, and so on. All of these women are expected to give acknowledged public performances, as are also the wives of political candidates (McCarthy 1972). The rejection of such public roles by the wife requires considerable effort and is generally seen as injuring the husband's work performance. On the other hand, some wives may be used as overt or covert excuses to reject a male candidate, as personnel reports and newspaper stories often indicate. The limits to acceptable participation by the wife in the husband's public image are illustrated by those cases where the wives become public personalities themselves and no longer operate only in the context of the husband's role. The key expression which indicates that these stereotyped limits have been exceeded is the statement "she is a . . . in her own right," indicating that an exceptional achievement has occurred. This expression is not used in the case of husbands of exceptional women, even where there are stereotyped expressions of disdain, as in the case of actresses' husbands who may be referred to as "Mr. her-name." Women who develop their own public image, starting from their base as the wives of prominent personalities, usually evoke fierce attacks and loyalties which are partly based on their having violated stereotyped standards of proper behavior in the vicarious achievement role. The complex career of Eleanor Roosevelt illustrates the development of this pattern especially well, particularly the process of rejecting the shadow role (Lash 1971, 1972). In her case, it is perhaps possible to speculate that her husband's disabling illness made it first possible for her to develop a more activist role in the public eye and to be accepted in such a role, at least at the beginning, by those who later became detractors. It must also be noted that, until recently, the widows of public figures have had a much better chance of independent election than other women in the United States (see Dreifus 1972).

The kinds of contributions which wives in these careers make to their husbands' work thus include status maintenance, intellectual contributions, and public performance. All of them are uniformly required by the man's employing organization, but their acceptance is accompanied by very high degrees of ambivalence by the employer, the husband, and the wife. In all cases, the induction of the wife into the orbit of the husband's employing institution is intended to increase the couple's commitment to the employer, to raise the husband's motivation to achieve in order to maintain a high level of consumption, and to increase his competitive advantage.

Needless to say, the wife's contribution is usually not directly acknowledged, nor it is directly remunerated. For example, the entertainment allowances given by some firms for the home entertainment of business guests do not include the wife's labor as an expense, while that of a hired maid can usually be reimbursed. Travel costs incurred by wives attending their husbands' business meetings, unless specifically required by the organization, are considered part of the husband's taxable income if they are paid for by the employer. This ruling transforms the wife's participation in her husband's business convention into a fringe benefit for him. It is instructive to examine the rulings and court cases which have been concerned with the application of this concept, despite their vagaries, for they illustrate many of the prevailing notions connected with the two-person career.

Wives who participate in two-person careers, therefore, can expect to be paid for their work only vicariously through the husband's income. Their reward, as is clearly implied by their involvement in rank distinctions, comes through raises in salary and perquisites granted to the husband. In another sense, the wife can consider that her activities enable the husband to devote additional time and energy to his institutional employer. The concept which might be applicable here is that she is "gainfully unemployed"—that is, not considered "'employed" in the economists' or census-takers' sense but nevertheless "gainfully" occupied in the context of a two-person career. At the same time, of course, the wife's participation in a two-person career can cost the couple considerable money, if she is thereby prevented from developing an independent, and independently remunerated, career. It is only if the wife's opportunity costs are in fact as low as the husband's employer considers them to be that the couple benefits financially from her participation in the two-person career.

Tax rulings concerning the tax-deductibility of "substitute" child care and housekeeping expenses indicate that the prevailing conception of very low opportunity costs for wives characterizes the entire pattern of women's access to equal opportunities in employment. While the stereotypes affecting the rulings are derived from the middle-class conceptions of judges, tax lawyers, and government bureaucrats, they affect all women, most harshly those who are heads of households or who are in the labor market because they help to support their families. In this sense, the derailing pattern which the two-person career represents for middle-class women has serious consequences for women outside the middle class in its widespread effects on general conceptions of how women should be employed.

Finally, a small semantic point should be made which is relevant to the entire pattern of women's employment. It is still customary, even among writers who profess to be sympathetic to the needed changes in women's lives, to differentiate between "women who work" and "women who do not work." It should be obvious that if any such distinctions must be made, they should be made between "women who work in the home," "women who work outside the home," and perhaps for a small category, "women who do not work." This would eliminate some of the invidious comparisons which continue to be made between different groups of women. It might also advance, by a very small amount, the accurate understanding of women's roles in American society.

Training for Women's Work

The two-person career has been described as a derailment solution of an American women's dilemma, produced by the ideology of equal educational opportunity for both sexes, which is often in conflict with continuing inequalities of opportunity in employment. There are many aspects to the educational component of this dilemma, some of which can be clarified by comparisons with the upbringing and education of women in a highly sex-segregated society of South Asia (India, Pakistan, and Bangladesh).

In the United States, the preparation of women for participation in the middle-class two-person career remains the barely latent function of many colleges. It is an important aspect of the role of colleges in American social mobility and consists not only of providing the great meeting grounds for the American middle class but also of perpetuating an existing sex-role ideology through formal and informal practices. Training suitable wives for important men is a function which is only now beginning to be challenged—not only by students but also by some women's colleges and coeducational institutions themselves.

The crucial aspect of the role of the college in the development of two-person careers is that it combines two otherwise separate functions. First, in its narrowly defined educational role, it serves to channel the educational aspirations of women students through available course offerings, possible role models, and career counseling. These often modify existing egalitarian commitments and serve to channel women students into fields which are conventionally regarded as more suitable for them. Second, the American college has been notable among universities throughout the world for its specific social mobility functions. More than is usual in many other countries, the American college experience tends to define the class and occupation into which students intend to move, rather than those from which they come. Friends and acquaintances at college tend to remain crucial in the later personal and occupational orbits of many students, especially among men, and particularly in elite colleges and in those large state institutions whose constituency comes from within the state and remains within it later. The importance of meeting one's future marriage partner at college is affected to some degree by all of these functions of the American college. The choice of college often serves to express certain intentions and ambitions, and a shared college experience may express some degree of shared expectation, which affects the importance of making marriage choices in college. A similar concern with shared life styles is evident also in the criteria used by parents arranging their children's marriages in the Pakistani middle class.

The importance of secondary and advanced education for women, moreover, is one of the keys to the prevalence of the two-person career, since it brings women into the potential recruitment patterns of many professions and middle-class occupations. Not only do women become possible entrants into many fields on the basis of their training, but the same training also means that they become available to assist their husbands in the various ways that have been mentioned for two-person careers. The contrast with more highly sex-segregated societies is very striking in this regard. While secondary and advanced education is available to women in South Asia, and they are participating in it in increasing numbers, special occupations for women have developed (particularly in Pakistan) for female clienteles. The importance of these specialized occupations and the prestige which they gain for

women deeply affect the career choices made by educated women. The values of a purdah society also keep women from participating in two-person careers with their husbands to a very large extent. With a few exceptions, women participate little in the public image of their husbands, and social contacts between business or professional colleagues most often exclude or downgrade the participation of wives. Since the complementary occupations which are usually filled by women in industrialized countries (secretaries, nurses, assistants, etc.) are usually filled by men in sex-segregated societies, wives also tend to participate less in formal or informal helpmeet activities with their husbands. The South Asian situation is very different from the American one in the sense that a few definite career opportunities are open for educated women, and these lead to high prestige and high accomplishment. The two most prevalent special women's occupations are medicine and teaching, although it should be made clear that "lady doctors" are acceptable while female nurses generally are not, because of the menial connotations of their work and their contact with male patients. Sex segregation similarly excludes many other occupations from consideration by women, although the system operates far more stringently in Pakistan and Bangladesh than in India. The lack of advanced education—or indeed any education—for most Muslim women in South Asia until quite recently has also meant that very few adult women are available to help their husbands in those ways for which formal education is necessary.

At the same time, there are outstanding women with unusual careers in South Asia; in some instances, their participation is either actually greater, or perceived more frequently, than is the case in the United States. Women in politics, in careers in the communications media (particularly radio), and in the civil service (in the case of India) are some specific examples. It is likely that such women, having overcome many social pressures in the process of attaining their education and training, move freely into available careers without being derailed by considerations of possible two-person careers. Both their own guilt feelings and public opposition of them may be less than would be the case in the United States.

Despite the important role played by sex-role stereotypes in the United States, comparison with the highly sex-segregated societies of South Asia does clarify some of the points about women's education in the United States which have led me to characterize it as at least ideologically equal for male and female students. In Pakistan and Bangladesh, for instance, most of the education of girls takes place in segregated institutions, especially between the ages of 11 and 18. The overall values of the purdah system result in a sharp separation between the worlds of men and women, even for those who do not observe seclusion in their own families (Papanek 1973). Competence is learned and achieved within the separate world of each sex, usually from a teacher of the same sex. There is relatively little competition between the sexes, since the ideals to be achieved by men and women are seen as very different from each other. Complementarity between the sexes is seen as very important, and the highly specific allocation of labor between the sexes produces a high degree of dependency between them, especially for services defined as strictly men's or women's work. Independence and self-reliance are not seen as virtues in the sense that they are understood in the United States. Continued reliance on parental guidance is considered appropriate long after the age at which it would be considered acceptable in North America. The most obvious example is the prevalence of the arranged marriage in South Asia, but other examples can also be seen in occupational choice, educational goals, business decisions, and so on.

Illustrating this process even in a highly unusual situation, a young Bengali university teacher with an American Ph.D. described how her father had deliberately turned his three daughters away from feminine pursuits toward masculine occupational goals and achievement standards. She recalled that "when he once found us playing with dolls, at a dolls' wedding, he snatched away a doll and tore it up, and when we wore bangles on our arms, he made us take them off. My elder sister was told she would be a teacher, and I was to become a doctor until my father decided this was not a good idea when a cousin started to talk about the difficult anatomy courses he was taking at the medical college. . . . We read a lot of books in my house and talked about all these things too, of course."

Training for women's work is a key underlying factor in the development of the vicarious achievement pattern, as has already been noted; but two different kinds of education are really involved in this distinction—education in a formal setting and training for women's work in the home. In the South Asian case, both ascriptive group membership and traditional learning "at the mother's knee" tend to be very important, even for the educated urban middle class. Other kinswomen are teachers, models, and critics, while men are consumers of the work products but are not generally skilled in the same proceses. In the American setting, the traditional feminine activities of cooking, sewing, and housekeeping are much more likely to become incorporated into the school curriculum and into the activities of nonfamily agencies, such as Girl Scouts, church groups, 4-H clubs. Of course, similar clubs also exist in South Asia, especially in the cities, and domestic science is an important part of the curriculum of women's educational institutions; but the balance of the emphasis seems to be somewhat different.

In South Asia, the pattern of family training for women's work is reinforced further by the separateness of the women's world and by the central role of food in the society. Food preparation in both Muslim and Hindu society is surrounded by many sets of rules. Both raw materials and modes of preparation make food the medium through which regional, linguistic, caste, religious, and status differences are often expressed. Food exchanges between men play a crucial role in the ranking aspects of the caste system (Marriott 1968). While women do not necessarily play central roles in these transactions —although they are likely to be the preparers of food, and it would be interesting to find out if it plays a role in their ranking—food remains part of a very important complex of emotions and practices for women. In the American setting, the analogies which come to mind would include the Jewish example, in which a long tradition of orthodox concern with food purity combined with a long history of persecution and food anxieties to produce a pattern in which food becomes a central symbol in the woman's relationship with her family. The preparation of food is learned in the context of the woman's family in South Asia—that is, in the private sphere—while in American middle-class society some impersonal agencies in the public domain may also be involved. In addition to the ones already noted, there are cookbooks, advice columns in newspapers and magazines, friends, "gourmet clubs," and other sources from which a woman can learn to overcome her family and ethnic heritage, if she chooses.

One of the consequences of these differences in the learning process is that changes in the definition of women's work and in the allocation of labor between the sexes is easier in the United States. Family size is also a factor in this regard. Large extended families are usually the ideal, if not always the practice, in many parts of South Asia, and changes in women's work may be quite difficult in such a setting. In Indonesia, on the other hand, family groups tend to be nuclear, with only limited relationships to bilateral kin (Hildred Geertz 1961). Outside influences and other languages may be easier to introduce in such a situation, possibly including modifications in the pattern of women's work. It may be only through comparisons with many other societies, however, that these differences can be clarified and the very large possibilities for change in the American woman's role can become apparent.

Early marriages are customary in South Asia, although this is changing as a result of legislation, education, and other factors. As a result, learning in the context of family life is likely to occur quite early in the girl's life. Once a woman has learned her basic skills, there is little occasion for much further learning, especially if her life circumstances and basic diet remain unchanged. The learning process becomes associated with youth and low status in a society where age is honored, especially in the case of women's learning. There is little occasion to emphasize continuing education throughout life, although change-oriented outside agencies in fields like family planning and adult education are beginning to emphasize these new ideas. The family-based mode of learning is, in effect, at the heart of what we consider "tradition"— customs embedded in a complex pattern of relationships, not readily detached from them or changed. In this sense, there are also beliefs in the "immutability" of persons and their work skills; such beliefs are often referred to in the large literature dealing with the difficulties of changing people's food, health, and work habits.

In the case of women, there are apparently some situations in which this "immutability" is particularly important. For instance, Saghir Ahmad (1967) has noted that in a Punjabi Muslim village members of the cultivators' group tended to marry outside their occupational grouping (*quom*) more readily than members of artisan groups (p. 88). In this area, it is not customary for women to work in the fields, although they do assist men with specific tasks, such as the drying of crops, in the home. The wives of artisans generally have customary tasks which supplement their husbands' performance. This is an example of joint work, carried out within the limits of the purdah system. Zekiye Eglar, writing about another Punjabi Muslim village (1960), probably provides an explanation for this difference in marriage patterns in her comment that the village barber must marry a woman brought up in a barber family, so that she can perform the important work of a barber's wife (p. 34). Otherwise, he cannot be a satisfactory village barber and must leave the village. It seemed to be assumed that these specific skills could not be learned by some other woman—as indeed they could not, if they were customarily taught only to a growing girl in her own family.

It is also in this context that the congruence between natal and affinal family life styles is examined very closely in South Asia when marriage arrangements are made. This emphasis is based not only on the importance of congeniality in a situation where love is expected to develop after the wedding, not before, but also on the unspoken assumption that early family learning is crucial and that there is no substitute for it.

These differences parallel the distinctions made by Hall (1959) among formal, informal, and technical learning. "Formal activities are taught by precept and admonition. . . . [It] is a two-way process [which] tends to be suffused with emotion. Informal learning is largely a matter of the learner picking others as models . . . most commonly it occurs out-of-awareness. . . . Technical learning, in its pure form, is close to being a one-way street. . . . The knowledge rests with the teacher [and] is usually transmitted in explicit terms" (pp. 93–95).

In these terms, what girls practice in the setting of their family to prepare them for "women's work," in the South Asian case is both formal and informal learning. Very little of it is technical. Technical learning occurs in the formal educational institution, and more boys than girls go to school in South Asia. The boys are more likely to experience technical learning, which they later elaborate in formal and informal ways in the social system of their work with colleagues. It is possible that lack of experience with technical learning in an impersonal environment is of major importance in the generally assumed tendency of women to be "more traditional" than men. It is the lack not only of what educational institutions teach but also of the way in which it is taught that may affect the future possibilities of changing women's lives in societies similar to those in South Asia. In the United States, on the other hand, both boys and girls have access to technical learning, in Hall's sense; the significant differences between the sexes are likely to occur on the level of formal and informal learning. It is at this level that appropriate sex-role behavior is taught. The later choices made by American women of vicarious achievement roles, or of failure (see Horner 1970), are likely to be nominally voluntary; in the South Asian case, there is much less room for personal choice.

All of these factors make it very unlikely that women's training in South Asian society would prepare them for roles of vicarious achievement through their husband's work if this entailed any kind of active participation. The men's work orbit remains largely male, especially in Pakistan—as is made graphically clear by the usual index: a total absence of toilets for women in most employment premises. But changes are occurring very rapidly in all South Asian countries, as the result of changes in both employment and education. The future of women's employment, and women's lives more generally, is likely to take very different directions in Bangladesh, Pakistan, and India. As these changes occur, new social control patterns will also develop, most probably in connection with educational systems and problems of unemployment.

Changes in the American pattern, on the other hand, are most likely to occur at those points where divergences are greatest between legally granted equality of access to educational opportunities by both sexes and the actual denial of equal access through the informal control mechanisms, which include the vicarious achievement pattern and its related sex-role ideology. For one of the results of the ideology of equality is that women have become motivated to achieve and perform in the same spheres and with the same skills as men. The elements in the two-person career pattern which have been discussed in this paper indicate some aspects of ideology, conflict, and change. The combination of achievement motivation and education in the skills through which men satisfy their achievement needs in American society is one of the powerful forces illustrated in the two-person career. The addition to these forces of continuing ambivalences, ambiguities, and derailment practices indicates a series of underlying stresses which many women have long experienced and which some are now making more visible. It is in this context of making things visible that it becomes useful to reflect on personal experiences, informal observations carried on over many years, and to speculate on past and future developments.

References

Ahmad, Saghir. 1967. "Class and Power in the Punjabi Village." Ph.D. dissertation. Michigan State University, East Lansing.

Coser, Rose L., and Gerald Rokoff. 1971. "Women in the Occupational World: Social Disruption and Conflict." Mimeographed. Presented at the annual meeting of the Eastern Sociological Society, New York.

Dreifus, Claudia. 1972. "Women in Politics: An Interview with Edith Green." *Social Policy 2* (January-February): 16–22.

Eglar, Zekiye. 1960. *A Punjabi Village in Pakistan*. New York: Columbia University Press.

Geertz, Hildred. 1961. *The Javanese Family*. Glencoe, Ill.: Free Press.

Hall, Edward T. 1959. *The Silent Language*. New York: Doubleday.

Holmstrom, Lynda Lytle. 1972. *The Two-Career Family*. Cambridge, Mass.: Shenkman.

Horner, Matina S. 1970. "Femininity and Successful Achievement: A Basic Inconsistency." In *Feminine Personality and Conflict*, by Judith M. Bardwick, Elizabeth Douvan, Matina S. Horner, and David Gutman. Belmont, Calif.: Brooks/Cole.

Hughes, Helen M. 1973. "Maid of All Work or Departmental Sister-in-Law." *American Journal of Sociology* 78 (January): 767–72.

Humphreys, Laud. 1970. *Tearoom Trade: Impersonal Sex in Public Places*. Chicago: Aldine.

Lash, Joseph P. 1971. *Eleanor and Franklin*. New York: Norton.
———. 1972. *Eleanor: The Years Alone*. New York: Norton.

Lipman-Blumen, Jean. 1972. "How Ideology Shapes Women's Lives." *Scientific American* 226 (1): 34–42.

Lopata, Helena Z. 1965. "The Secondary Features of a Primary Relationship." *Human Organization* 24 (2): 116–23.
———. 1971. *Occupation: Housewife*. New York: Oxford University Press.

McCarthy, Abigail. 1972. *Private Faces—Public Places*. Garden City, N.Y.: Doubleday.

Marcus, Steven. 1966. *The Other Victorians: A Study of Sexuality and Pornography in Mid-nineteenth Century England*. New York: Basic.

Marriott, McKim. 1968. "Caste Ranking and Food Transactions: A Matrix Analysis." In *Structure and Change in Indian Society*, edited by Milton Singer and Bernard S. Cohn. Chicago: Aldine.

Merton, Robert, and Elinor Barber, 1963. "Sociological Ambivalence." In *Sociological Theory, Values and Sociocultural Change*, edited by E. A. Tiryakian. Glencoe, Ill.: Free Press.

Milford, Nancy. 1970. *Zelda*. New York: Harper & Row.

Olsen, Tillie. 1965. "Silences: When Writers Don't Write." *Harper's Magazine* (October), pp. 153–61.

Papanek, Hanna. 1971. "Purdah in Pakistan: Seclusion and Modern Occupations for Women." *Journal of Marriage and the Family* 33 (3): 517–30.

———. 1973. "Purdah: Separate Worlds and Symbolic Shelter." *Comparative Studies in Society and History*, in press.

Press, M. Jean, and Fraine Whitney. 1971. "Achievement Syndromes in Women: Vicarious or Conflict Ridden." Mimeographed. Presented at the annual meeting of the Eastern Sociological Society, New York.

Rainwater, Lee, R. P. Coleman, and Gerald Handel. 1962. *Workingman's Wife*. New York: McFadden-Bartell.

Riesman, Evelyn T. 1958. "Pouring Tea." *Southwest Review* 43 (3): 222–31.

Tresemer, David, and Joseph H. Pleck. 1972. "Maintaining and Changing Sex Role Boundaries in Men (and Women)." Paper presented at the Radcliffe Institute Conference on "Women: Resource for a Changing World," Cambridge, Mass.

Vogel, Ezra F. 1967. *Japan's New Middle Class: The Salary Man and His Family in a Tokyo Suburb*. Berkeley: University of California Press.

Whyte, William H. "The Wife Problem," *Life,* January 7, 1952. Reprinted in *The Other Half*, edited by Cynthia F. Epstein and W. J. Goode. Englewood Cliffs, N.J.: Prentice-Hall, 1971.

———. 1956. *The Organization Man*. New York: Simon & Schuster.

Woolf, Virginia. 1929. *A Room of One's Own*. New York: Harcourt Brace.

27

Leisure and Life-style by Robert J. Havighurst
and
Kenneth Feigenbaum

Leisure has generally but vaguely been seen as a source of satisfaction and even of delight. In a society in which most people had to work, and to work hard and long, leisure was scarce and was regarded either as a reward to be earned by work and to be enjoyed because one had worked so hard for it or a good thing conferred by inherited wealth or by marriage to wealth.

With the coming of more leisure in the lives of the common people, not all the rosy promises have been realized. Some people have found themselves with more leisure than they really wanted. The values of increased leisure to welfare and the quality of living of society as a whole have been seriously questioned. It is clear that modern leisure is not an unmixed blessing. This suggests the desirability of studying the uses that people make of

their leisure, what satisfactions they get out of it, and how it fits into the rest of their lives.

Using the concept of "life-style" to describe a person's characteristic way of filling and combining the various social roles he is called on to play, we may see how leisure fits into it. To do so, the Kansas City Study of Adult Life interviewed a sample of men and women aged from forty to seventy to get an account of the way the person spent his time and the significance to him of his major social roles—those of parent, spouse, homemaker, worker, citizen, friend, club or association member, and user of leisure time. About a quarter of the interview was devoted to leisure. The individual was asked about his favorite leisure activities, what they meant to him, why he liked them, whom he did them with, as well as a number

of questions about vacations, reading, television, radio, and movies, and what he did around the house.

On the basis of this interview, ratings were made of the competence of the individual in his social roles. Rating scales were devised to represent the general American expectations or definitions of these roles.[1] The rating scale for user of leisure time follows:

a) *High (8–9)*.—Spends enough time at some leisure activity to be rather well known among his associates in this respect. But it is not so much the amount of leisure activity as its quality which gives him a high rating. He has one or more pursuits for which he gets public recognition and appreciation and which give him a real sense of accomplishment.

Chooses his leisure activities autonomously, not merely to be in style. Gets from leisure the feeling of being creative, of novel and interesting experience, sheer pleasure, prestige, friendship, and of being of service.

b) *Above average (6–7)*.—Has four to five leisure activities. Leisure time is somewhat patterned, indicating that he has planned his life to provide for the satisfaction of the needs met through these activities.

Leisure interests show some variety. Displays real enthusiasm for one or two—talks about them in such a way as to indicate that he has put considerable energy into acquiring proficiency or the requisite understanding and skills and prides himself on it.

c) *Medium (4–5)*.—Has two or three leisure activities which he does habitually and enjoys mildly—reading, television, radio, watching sports, handwork, etc. May do one of these things well or quite enthusiastically, but not more than one. Gets definite sense of well-being and is seldom bored with leisure.

Leisure activities are somewhat stereotyped; they do not have a great deal of variety.

d) *Below average (2–3)*.—

(1) Tends to take the line of least resistance in leisure time. Needs to be stimulated. Looks for time-fillers.

May have one fairly strong interest but is content with this one which brings him some sense of enjoyment. Leisure time is usually spent in passive spectatorship. *Or:*

(2) May have very little spare time. What time he has is taken up with activities related to his job or profession or with work around the house viewed as obligatory and not as a pastime.

e) *Low (0–1)*.—

(1) Apathetic. Does nothing and makes no attempt to find outside interests. *Or:*

(2) Tries anxiously to find interesting things to do and fails to find them. Is bored by leisure and hurries back to work. Dislikes vacations and cannot relax.

The procedure in studying life-style was based upon the use of the scores for performance in the eight social roles. A life-style was defined as a pattern of role-performance scores shared by a group of people.

Among 234 persons in the Kansas City Study of Adult Life, there were twenty-seven specific patterns, or life-styles, each characterizing from 8 to 34 members. The specific patterns were grouped into four major groups,

[1] For the other role-performance scales and for the pattern analysis mentioned later see Havighurst, 1957.

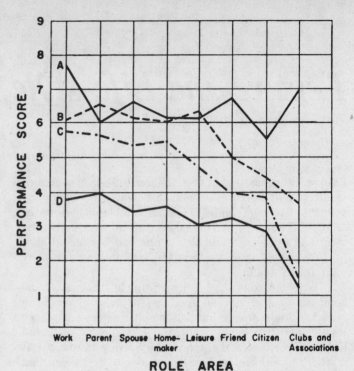

Fig. 1.—Life-styles of middle-aged people: *A*, community-centered; *B*, home-centered high; *C*, home-centered medium; *D*, low level.

and these four groups may be regarded provisionally as life-style groups. Their characteristic role-performance scores are shown in Figure 1. The names given to the life-style groups, and a brief description of each, follow:

A. *Community-centered*.—This is a pattern of uniformly high performance scores in all eight social roles. It is called "community-centered" for the sake of contrast with the following group, though the performance scores in the community roles of citizen, club or association member, and friend are not higher than those in the family areas. The social class distribution of these people in the Kansas City Metropolitan Area is shown in Table 1.

B. *Home-centered high*.—These people have performance scores in the roles of parent, spouse, homemaker, worker, and user of leisure time which are about the same as those of the community-centered, but they fall far below in the roles of friend, citizen, and club or association member. These people and the community-centered group have the highest personal adjustment scores and the highest scores on a rating of manifest complexity of life-style.

C. *Home-centered medium*.—These people have a family-centered pattern, though below that of the home-centered high group in role-performance scores.

D. *Low level*.—This is a pattern of generally low role-performance scores, with the family and work roles somewhat above the other roles. This group has very low scores on personal adjustment and on complexity.

The community-centered style of leisure emphasizes activities engaged in away from home. The individual uses entertainment institutions, such as the theater or the concert or social institutions, such as the country club,

TABLE 1

SOCIAL CLASS DISTRIBUTION OF LIFE-STYLES
(Percent)

Social Class	Sex	Community-centered	Home-centered High	Home-centered Medium	Low Level	Un-grouped	Total Group
U & UM	M	7	3	1	0	2	13
	F	6	3	3	0	1	13
LM	M	8	11	10	3	1	33
	F	5	4	17	3	4	33
Working	M	4	8	18	8	2	40
	F	2	5	23	7	3	40
Lower	M	0	0	6	7	1	14
	F	1	0	5	7	1	14
Total group	M	19	22	35	18	6	100
	F	14	12	48	17	9	100

NOTE: The actual distribution of individuals in the Study Sample was the basis for this table, but the figures have been adjusted to fit the true social class distribution of adults in the Kansas City Metropolitan Area, as determined by Richard Coleman (unpublished working paper in the files of the Committee on Human Development, The University of Chicago).

Rotary, chamber of commerce, Red Cross, etc., as the context for a major part of it. People employing the community-centered style of leisure tend to be autonomous, that is, to "choose activity with purpose and regard for its function in one's personal life" and to engage in activities that have some element of novelty. They are more instrumental and more inclined to "play a game or participate in an activity for some goal beyond the game or activity (philanthropic activity, etc.)." "Benefit for society" was given quite often as the motive.

Community-centeredness is the favorite leisure style of upper-middle-class people. Being successful in business or a profession induces them to join business and social organizations where they interact with each other to form wider circles of social and business contacts. Membership in the country club is part of their proper and accepted style of living. The community-centered individuals also tend not to have young children at home, which allows freedom for outside activity.

In contrast are the home-centered people whose leisure is spent mostly around the house. This style is strongest in lower- middle- and working-class individuals and falls off in the lower-class, where family values lose some importance and the few pastimes become sex-differentiated, the men going fishing alone or to the bar or poolroom with the "boys."

Leisure activities are engaged in jointly by the members of the family for the majority of the home-centered, whether it be a church outing, a fishing trip, or watching television. Sex-differentiated activities, such as sewing and embroidering for the women and carpentry and "fixing around the house" for the men, still allow for conversation and interaction between the spouses. Friendship and sociability are cultivated by visits from neighbors rather than through any membership other than church or perhaps a fraternal organization. For some people the family-centered style was not one of choice but of necessity, owing to the presence of young children.

A number of activities such as fishing and traveling during vacations were common to both leisure styles, with some differentiation as to the manner of them. In the community-centered style travel consists of going to resorts and sightseeing, while for the people engaged in home-centered leisure travel consists of a car trip to visit working-relatives in other cities. For the working-class members of the home-centered style travel may be quite circumscribed; one spoke of "taking a trolley trip to see the city."

In spite of the relationship between life-style and social class position, there were people whose life-styles did not correspond with their class positions, as would be expected in a society with a considerable degree of social mobility. From Table 1 it appears that some ten percent of the population may have patterns above their class level and five percent below it.

Two examples, one of a community-centered man with a high rating as a user of leisure and the other of a high leisure home-centered man, may further the reader's image of the difference between the two styles of leisure.

Mr. X is a fifty-year-old executive vice-president of a bank, with a pattern of leisure activities which is the prototype of the community-centered style of leisure. He is president of one country club, a member of another, a Shriner, and a member of the executive council of a national Boy's Club movement and of a number of charity organizations. Mr. X's favorite leisure activity is to go on trips during his vacation, to New York City to see the Broadway theater, and to see exhibitions of modern art. He is active in encouraging the local art museum to acquire examples of modern art. He enjoys playing golf once or twice a week at the country club, playing cards, painting his garage, and entertaining business people both at home and at the club. He does not own a television set, preferring the good music on the radio. He goes with his wife to the movies and to all the musical comedies that come to Kansas City. As for friends, Mr. X calls ten to twelve couples "close." He met them through various activities: "My business connections here at the bank, civic clubs, church, etc." With his wife he goes out to eat once a week and entertains other couples.

In contrast to Mr. X, Mr. Y, a fifty-eight-year-old social worker, is an example of an individual who employs the home-centered style of leisure. His favorite activity is gardening, in which he spends one-half hour to an hour a day during the growing season. Mr. Y's hobby is model railroading, which he engages in with his wife in the basement of his home. He also does some woodworking and woodcarving and manual work around the home. Once in a while he reads historical fiction. The television set plays for two hours an evening, showing sports events, quiz shows, and plays. With his wife he reads, plays cards, does model railroading, and takes walks. Living in a neighborhood of younger adults, he claims that he has few friends and that a large part of his time is spent taking care of the two children of his son. Mr. Y's "going out" consists only of movies (with wife) and American Legion meetings once a month.

The differences between the home-centered high, home-centered medium, and low-level life-styles as far as leisure is concerned are mainly those between high, medium, and low ratings on the scale of competence as a user of leisure. A higher role performance is associated with the following variables: autonomy, creativity, getting strong pleasure from the activity, instrumental, high energy input, ego integration, vitality, and expansion of interests and activities.

Have those whose leisure is home-centered different personalities from the community-centered? Or is the difference caused by some external factor, such as residence in a suburb versus residence in an apartment area in the center of the city, or having several young children versus having one or none? It has been suggested by David Riesman (1957) and by Margaret Mead (1957), among others, that the trend toward suburban living and the trend toward larger numbers of children are making for values and leisure activities that are more home- and family-centered.

Riesman speaks of "suburban styles of life and thought" and stresses the suburban constriction of leisure to the family and the living-room–garden–television set, at the expense of theater, concert hall, downtown meetings, country clubs, and heterogeneous social groups. Margaret Mead says that the generation which has married since the war is much more concerned with home and family life than earlier generations and is busy trying to turn home life into "a self-rewarding delight."

To explore the differences between home-centered and community-centered people, we compared a community-centered group with a similar number of home-centered people, equating the groups for age and socioeconomic status. There was no difference between the two groups in the proportions of suburban dwellers and the proportions who lived in single-family houses with gardens and recreation rooms. However, the home-centered had more children living at home. This suggests that the presence of children in the home, together with the desire to have children and to have a home-centered life, are more influential than the actual physical location of one's house in determining leisure style. It should be borne in mind, however, that Kansas City does not have many apartment dwellings for upper-middle-class people near the city's center.

The foregoing facts point to the conclusion that the personality, more than the situation, determines the leisure style.

It has been assumed up to this point that there was a close correlation between personal adjustment and performance in the leisure role. The correlation coefficient is .32 for men and .33 for women, with socioeconomic status partialed out. Clearly, there are some exceptions to this rule. Study of these exceptions may teach us something more about the value of leisure.

Accordingly, we selected the cases which showed most markedly a high adjustment–low leisure performance combination and those who combined low adjustment with high leisure performance. There were nine of the former and twelve of the latter in the sample of 234 people. The criterion for the high adjustment–low leisure combination was an adjustment score of 6 or above on the ten-point adjustment scale and a score of 5 or below on the ten-point leisure performance scale. The criterion for the low adjustment–high leisure group was an adjustment score of 4.5 or below and a leisure score of 6 or above.

The content of the leisure and the significance ratings of the leisure activities of the low leisure–high adjustment people were similar to the general pattern of people with low leisure and low adjustment scores. There are low significance ratings as to the autonomy of the leisure activity, the creativity expressed in it, some apathy with respect to the activity, and either a decline in leisure interests or no expansion of interests.

These are people who get along very well with little or no leisure. They show a great deal of vitality in the instrumental activities of life. The men are busy with their jobs and the women with their children, allowing little time for leisure and restricting them to leisure activities near home. Six out of the nine in the group are females and follow this pattern. Their leisure activities are centered either at home, where they sew, watch television, and take care of the children, or in the church. The relationship between the spouses is good, and there is a general feeling of contentment and emotional security. It is this basically which accounts for the high adjustment scores of the group.

The group of individuals with high leisure scores and low adjustment tend as a whole to be maladjusted socially or occupationally and attempt to get through leisure what they cannot get in the other roles. They use their leisure as a compensation to make up for their deficiencies and to give their life some meaning.

The men in the group, often alienated from work, from spouse, or from the "community," attempt to adjust to this alienation by engaging in leisure activities where they invest a lot of energy and through which they can enjoy themselves and see themselves as socially acceptable. One is a factory manager. He finds no satisfaction in this position but rather pictures himself as an intellectual and therefore spends a great deal of time reading. A second, an amateur pilot, directs his leisure away from a home where some emotional difficulties exist. Another man was trained as an engineer and has shifted over the years from one job to another, finally going into a business with his wife, which he does not enjoy. Like the factory manager, he pictures himself as a scholar and spends his leisure time reading oriental history.

The women in the group have difficulty in relating to their husbands and are emotionally insecure; there are degrees of feelings of unwantedness and not being loved. They concentrate their energies into a single activity which they engage in alone and where they can achieve a great deal of proficiency, such as sewing, embroidery, or petitpoint, or in church activities where they can spend time with the "women" and achieve the feeling of "doing something worthwhile."

Conclusions

1. The most successful life-styles, as judged by the level of role-performance scores, have concomitant patterns of leisure activity. The community-centered life-style includes a leisure pattern which spreads from the home out through a variety of community circles. On the other hand, a successful home-centered life-style contains a home-centered leisure pattern. These successful leisure patterns tend to be autonomous, creative, instrumental, vital, and ego integrative, whether they be community-centered or home-centered.

The lower-level life-styles are lower in performance in roles external to the home than in the home roles. They also have lower-level leisure styles, with lower scores on the values listed in the preceding paragraph.

2. The two major types of leisure style, the community-centered and the home-centered, appear to be equally accessible to middle-class people, but rarely are working-class people community-centered. An individual with a large family of children is more likely to be home-centered. However, his place of residence—whether in a suburb, single-family home, or city apartment—does not seem to affect his leisure style to any great degree. The personality of the individual appears to find its own leisure style.

3. There are a few exceptional cases where the life-style and the leisure style are not in close relation. One group of such cases consists of about five percent of adults. They are people with little or no leisure activity who have a successful life-style and good personal adjustment. These men and women generally invest most of their energy in work or in home and children, with little time and inclination for leisure.

Another group consists of about six percent of adults. They have a high level of leisure activity but are dissatisfied or inadequate workers or parents or spouses who attempt to compensate with a high leisure performance.

VI. Middle Life

C.H. ELDRIDGE '76

With the increasing life span, one's children can be grown and out of the house before a person has lived even half his or her life. The second half of life was traditionally thought to be simply a continuation of family and work contexts in a chain of repetition. Now, upon closer examination, and due to the changes we have already looked at in relation to previous life stages, the person in the middle stage of life, age approximately 40 and beyond, is seen to experience a range of changes and psychological development that can be as drastic and vast as the changes of youth. This middle life stage is the focus of a number of new studies which are reported here.

At middle life the person often hits a period of crisis, when he begins to assess the realities of his life and evaluate his position. The immediate problems of establishing a career and raising young children are past, and as Carl Jung suggested, the person faces an internal stirring, a questioning of values and inner, existential questions which he or she may not have had the time or inclination to think about previously. A study by Yale psychologist Daniel Levinson, reported by Maggie Scarf, looks at how this midlife crisis and transition point strikes men. The way that our society views the aging process, and the roles to which middle-aged people are consigned, are important factors in the way an individual experiences aging. Susan Sontag suggests that our society has been characterized by a double standard of aging, in which women are treated more shabbily than men, with unfortunate results. A classic study by Marjorie Lowenthal and David Chiriboga looks at the "empty nest" situation, in which a couple that has spent their married life oriented around their children are faced with a transition when their youngest child leaves home. This can either be traumatic, or a point of opportunity. In addition to its social and psychological transitions, middle life for the woman, as Bernice Neugarten documents, is beset with the biological/hormonal changes of menopause, which have a range of psychological consequences. The interaction between the aging body, and the social conceptions and expectations of aging people, creates a situation for the person in middle life that complicates and often exacerbates whatever psychological and identity conflicts are brewing. One aspect of middle life is the confrontation with mortality and the imminence of death, which Elliot Jacques explores.

28

THE DOUBLE STANDARD OF AGING

An instrument of oppression, says the author, is the social convention that aging enhances a man but progressively destroys a woman. Accordingly, to liberate themselves, women must "disobey the convention." BY SUSAN SONTAG

"How old are you?" The person asking the question is anybody. The respondent is a woman, a woman "of a certain age," as the French say discreetly. That age might be anywhere from her early twenties to her late fifties. If the question is impersonal—routine information requested when she applies for a driver's license, a credit card, a passport—she will probably force herself to answer truthfully. Filling out a marriage license application, if her future husband is even slightly her junior, she may long to subtract a few years; probably she won't. Competing for a job, her chances often partly depend on being the "right age," and if hers isn't right, she will lie if she thinks she can get away with it. Making her first visit to a new doctor, perhaps feeling particularly vulnerable at the moment she's asked, she will probably hurry through the correct answer. But if the question is only what people call personal—if she's asked by a new friend, a casual acquaintance, a neighbor's child, a co-worker in an office, store, factory—her response is harder to predict. She may

Susan Sontag wrote and directed the recently released film Brother Carl. Styles of Radical Will *is her latest book of essays.*

side-step the question with a joke or refuse it with playful indignation. "Don't you know you're not supposed to ask a woman her age?" Or, hesitating a moment, embarrassed but defiant, she may tell the truth. Or she may lie. But neither truth, evasion, nor lie relieves the unpleasantness of that question. For a woman to be obliged to state her age, after "a certain age," is always a miniature ordeal.

If the question comes from a woman, she will feel less threatened than if it comes from a man. Other women are, after all, comrades in sharing the same potential for humiliation. She will be less arch, less coy. But she probably still dislikes answering and may not tell the truth. Bureaucratic formalities excepted, whoever asks a woman this question—after "a certain age"—is ignoring a taboo and possibly being impolite or downright hostile. Almost everyone acknowledges that once she passes an age that is, actually, quite young, a woman's exact age ceases to be a legitimate target of curiosity. After childhood the year of a woman's birth becomes her secret, her private property. It is something of a dirty secret. To answer truthfully is always indiscreet.

The discomfort a woman feels each time she tells her age is quite independ-

ent of the anxious awareness of human mortality that everyone has, from time to time. There is a normal sense in which nobody, men and women alike, relishes growing older. After thirty-five any mention of one's age carries with it the reminder that one is probably closer to the end of one's life than to the beginning. There is nothing unreasonable in that anxiety. Nor is there any abnormality in the anguish and anger that people who are really old, in their seventies and eighties, feel about the implacable waning of their powers, physical and mental. Advanced age is undeniably a trial, however stoically it may be endured. It is a shipwreck, no matter with what courage elderly people insist on continuing the voyage. But the objective, sacred pain of old age is of another order than the subjective, profane pain of aging. Old age is a genuine ordeal, one that men and women undergo in a similar way. Growing older is mainly an ordeal of the imagination—a moral disease, a social pathology—intrinsic to which is the fact that it afflicts women much more than men. It is particularly women who experience growing older (everything that comes *before* one is actually old) with such distaste and even shame.

The emotional privileges this society

confers upon youth stir up some anxiety about getting older in everybody. All modern urbanized societies—unlike tribal, rural societies—condescend to the values of maturity and heap honors on the joys of youth. This revaluation of the life cycle in favor of the young brilliantly serves a secular society whose idols are ever-increasing industrial productivity and the unlimited cannibalization of nature. Such a society must create a new sense of the rhythms of life in order to incite people to buy more, to consume and throw away faster. People let the direct awareness they have of their needs, of what really gives them pleasure, be overruled by commercialized *images* of happiness and personal well-being; and, in this imagery designed to stimulate ever more avid levels of consumption, the most popular metaphor for happiness is "youth." (I would insist that it is a metaphor, not a literal description. Youth is a metaphor for energy, restless mobility, appetite: for the state of "wanting.") This equating of well-being with youth makes everyone naggingly aware of exact age—one's own and that of other people. In primitive and pre-modern societies people attach much less importance to dates. When lives are divided into long periods with stable responsibilities and steady ideals (and hypocrisies), the exact number of years someone has lived becomes a trivial fact; there is hardly any reason to mention, even to know, the year in which one was born. Most people in nonindustrial societies are not sure exactly how old they are. People in industrial societies are haunted by numbers. They take an almost obsessional interest in keeping the score card of aging, convinced that anything above a low total is some kind of bad news. In an era in which people actually live longer and longer, what now amounts to the latter *two-thirds* of everyone's life is shadowed by a poignant apprehension of unremitting loss.

The prestige of youth afflicts everyone in this society to some degree. Men, too, are prone to periodic bouts of depression about aging—for instance, when feeling insecure or unfulfilled or insufficiently rewarded in their jobs. But men rarely panic about aging in the way women often do. Getting older is less profoundly wounding for a man, for in addition to the propaganda for youth that puts both men and women on the defensive as they age, there is a double standard about aging that denounces women with special severity. Society is much more permissive about aging in men, as it is more tolerant of the sexual infidelities of husbands. Men are "allowed" to age, without penalty, in several ways that women are not.

This society offers even fewer rewards for aging to women than it does to men. Being physically attractive counts much more in a woman's life than in a man's, but beauty, identified, as it is for women, with youthfulness, does not stand up well to age. Exceptional mental powers can increase with age, but women are rarely encouraged to develop their minds above dilettante standards. Because the wisdom considered the special province of women is "eternal," an age-old, intuitive knowledge about the emotions to which a repertoire of facts, worldly experience, and the methods of rational analysis have nothing to contribute, living a long time does not promise women an increase in wisdom either. The private skills expected of women are exercised early and, with the exception of a talent for making love, are not the kind that enlarge with experience. "Masculinity" is identified with competence, autonomy, self-control—qualities which the disappearance of youth does not threaten. Competence in most of the activities expected from men, physical sports excepted, increases

---

> For a woman to be obliged to state her age, after "a certain age," is always a miniature ordeal.

---

with age. "Femininity" is identified with incompetence, helplessness, passivity, noncompetitiveness, being nice. Age does not improve these qualities.

Middle-class men feel diminished by aging, even while still young, if they have not yet shown distinction in their careers or made a lot of money. (And any tendencies they have toward hypochondria will get worse in middle age, focusing with particular nervousness on the specter of heart attacks and the loss of virility.) Their aging crisis is linked to that terrible pressure on men to be "successful" that precisely defines their membership in the middle class. Women rarely feel anxious about their age because they haven't succeeded at something. The work that women do outside the home rarely counts as a form of achievement, only as a way of earning money; most employment available to women mainly exploits the training they have been re-

ceiving since early childhood to be servile, to be both supportive and parasitical, to be unadventurous. They can have menial, low-skilled jobs in light industries, which offer as feeble a criterion of success as housekeeping. They can be secretaries, clerks, sales personnel, maids, research assistants, waitresses, social workers, prostitutes, nurses, teachers, telephone operators—public transcriptions of the servicing and nurturing roles that women have in family life. Women fill very few executive posts, are rarely found suitable for large corporate or political responsibilities, and form only a tiny contingent in the liberal professions (apart from teaching). They are virtually barred from jobs that involve an expert, intimate relation with machines or an aggressive use of the body, or that carry any physical risk or sense of adventure. The jobs this society deems appropriate to women are auxiliary, "calm" activities that do not compete with, but aid, what men do. Besides being less well paid, most work women do has a lower ceiling of advancement and gives meager outlet to normal wishes to be powerful. All outstanding work by women in this society is voluntary; most women are too inhibited by the social disapproval attached to their being ambitious and aggressive. Inevitably, women are exempted from the dreary panic of middle-aged men whose "achievements" seem paltry, who feel stuck on the job ladder or fear being pushed off it by someone younger. But they are also denied most of the real satisfactions that men derive from work—satisfactions that often do increase with age.

The double standard about aging shows up most brutally in the conventions of sexual feeling, which presuppose a disparity between men and women that operates permanently to women's disadvantage. In the accepted course of events a woman anywhere from her late teens through her middle twenties can expect to attract a man more or less her own age. (Ideally, he should be at least slightly older.) They marry and raise a family. But if her husband starts an affair after some years of marriage, he customarily does so with a woman much younger than his wife. Suppose, when both husband and wife are already in their late forties or early fifties, they divorce. The husband has an excellent chance of getting married again, probably to a younger woman. His ex-wife finds it difficult to remarry. Attracting a second husband younger than herself is improbable; even to find someone her own age she has to be lucky, and she will probably have to settle for a man considerably older than herself, in his sixties or seventies. Women become sexually ineligible much earlier than men do. A man, even an ugly man, can remain eligible well into old age. He is an acceptable mate for a young, attractive woman. Women, even good-looking women, become ineligible (except as partners of very old men) at a much younger age.

Thus, for most women, aging means a humiliating process of gradual sexual disqualification. Since women are considered maximally eligible in early youth, after which their sexual value drops steadily, even young women feel themselves in a desperate race against the calendar. They are old as soon as they are no longer very young. In late adolescence some girls are already worrying about getting married. Boys and young men have little reason to anticipate trouble because of aging. What makes men desirable to women is by no means tied to youth. On the contrary, getting older tends (for several decades) to operate in men's favor, since their value as lovers and husbands is set more by what they do than how they look. Many men have more success romantically at forty than they did at twenty or twenty-five; fame, money, and, above all, power are sexually enhancing. (A woman who has won power in a competitive profession or business career is considered less, rather than more, desirable. Most men confess themselves intimidated or turned off sexually by such a woman, obviously because she is harder to treat as just a sexual "object.") As they age, men may start feeling anxious about actual sexual performance, worrying about a loss of sexual vigor or even impotence, but their sexual eligibility is not abridged simply by getting older. Men stay sexually possible as long as they can make love. Women are at a disadvantage because their sexual candidacy depends on meeting certain much stricter "conditions" related to looks and age.

Since women are imagined to have much more limited sexual lives than men do, a woman who has never married is pitied. She was not found acceptable, and it is assumed that her life continues to confirm her unacceptability. Her presumed lack of sexual opportunity is embarrassing. A man who remains a bachelor is judged much less crudely. It is assumed that he, at any age, still has a sexual life—or the chance of one. For men there is no destiny equivalent to the humiliating condition of being an old maid, a spinster. "Mr.," a cover from infancy to senility, precisely exempts men from the stigma that attaches to any woman, no longer young, who is still "Miss." (That women are divided into "Miss" and "Mrs.," which calls unrelenting attention to the situation of each woman with respect to marriage, reflects the belief that being single or married is much more decisive for a woman than it is for a man.)

For a woman who is no longer very young, there is certainly some relief when she has finally been able to marry. Marriage soothes the sharpest pain she feels about the passing years. But her anxiety never subsides completely, for she knows that should she re-enter the sexual market at a later date—because of divorce, or the death of her husband, or the need for erotic adventure—she must do so under a handicap far greater than any man of her age (*whatever* her age may be) and regardless of how good-looking she is. Her achievements, if she has a career, are no asset. The calendar is the final arbiter.

To be sure, the calendar is subject to some variations from country to country. In Spain, Portugal, and the Latin American countries, the age at which most women are ruled physically undesirable comes earlier than in the United States. In France it is somewhat later. French conventions of sexual feeling make a quasi-official place for the woman between thirty-five and forty-five. Her role is to initiate an inexperienced or timid young man, after which she is, of course, replaced by a young girl. (Colette's novella *Chéri* is the best-known account in fiction of such a love affair; biographies of Balzac relate a well-documented example from real life.) This sexual myth does make turning forty somewhat easier for French women. But there is no difference in any of these countries in the basic attitudes that disqualify women sexually much earlier than men.

Aging also varies according to social class. Poor people look old much earlier in their lives than do rich people. But anxiety about aging is certainly more common, and more acute, among middle-class and rich women than among working-class women. Economically disadvantaged women in this society are more fatalistic about aging; they can't afford to fight the cosmetic battle as long or as tenaciously. Indeed, nothing so clearly indicates the fictional nature of this crisis than the fact that women who keep their youthful appearance the longest—women who lead unstrenuous, physically sheltered lives, who eat balanced meals, who can afford good medical care, who have few or no children—are those who feel the defeat of age most keenly. Aging is much more a social judgment than a biological eventuality. Far more extensive than the hard sense of loss suffered during menopause (which, with increased longevity, tends to arrive later and later) is the depression about aging, which may not be set off by any real event in a woman's life, but is a recurrent state of "possession" of her imagination, ordained by society—that is, ordained by the way this society limits how women feel free to imagine themselves.

There is a model account of the aging crisis in Richard Strauss's sentimental-ironic opera *Der Rosenkavalier*, whose heroine is a wealthy and glamorous married woman who decides to renounce romance. After a night with her adoring young lover, the Marschallin has a sudden, unexpected confrontation with herself. It is toward the end of Act I; Octavian has just left. Alone in her bedroom she sits at her dressing table, as she does every morning. It is the daily ritual of self-appraisal practiced by every woman. She looks at herself and, appalled, begins to weep. Her youth is over. Note that the Marschallin does not discover, looking in the mirror, that she is ugly. She is as beautiful as ever. The Marschallin's discovery is moral—that is, it is a discovery of her imagination; it is nothing she actually *sees*. Nevertheless, her discovery is no less devastating. Bravely, she makes her painful, gallant decision. She will arrange for her beloved Octavian to fall in love with a girl his own age. She must be realistic. She is no longer eligible. She is now "the old Marschallin."

Strauss wrote the opera in 1910. Contemporary operagoers are rather shocked when they discover that the libretto indicates that the Marschallin is all of thirty-four years old; today the role is generally sung by a soprano well into her forties or in her fifties. Acted by an attractive singer of thirty-four, the Marschallin's sorrow would seem merely neurotic, or even ridiculous. Few women today think of themselves as old, wholly disqualified from romance, at thirty-four. The age of retirement has moved up, in line with the sharp rise in life expectancy for everybody in the last few generations. The *form* in which women experience their lives remains unchanged. A moment approaches inexorably when they must resign themselves to being "too old." And that moment is invariably—objectively—premature.

In earlier generations the renunciation came even sooner. Fifty years ago a woman of forty was not just aging but old, finished. No struggle was even possible. Today, the surrender to aging no longer has a fixed date. The aging crisis (I am speaking only of women in afflu-

A man can remain eligible well into old age. Women, even good-looking women, become ineligible at a much younger age.

ent countries) starts earlier but lasts longer; it is diffused over most of a woman's life. A woman hardly has to be anything like what would reasonably be considered old to worry about her age, to start lying (or being tempted to lie). The crises can come at any time. Their schedule depends on a blend of personal ("neurotic") vulnerability and the swing of social mores. Some women don't have their first crisis until thirty. No one escapes a sickening shock upon turning forty. Each birthday, but especially those ushering in a new decade—for round numbers have a special authority—sounds a new defeat. There is almost as much pain in the anticipation as in the reality. Twenty-nine has become a queasy age ever since the official end of youth crept forward, about a generation ago, to thirty. Being thirty-nine is also hard; a whole year in which to meditate in glum astonishment that one stands on the threshold of middle age. The frontiers are arbitrary, but not any less vivid for that. Although a woman on her fortieth birthday is hardly different from what she was when she was still thirty-nine, the day seems like a turning point. But long before actually becoming a woman of forty, she has been steeling herself against the depression she will feel. One of the greatest tragedies of each woman's life is simply getting older; it is certainly the *longest* tragedy.

Aging is a movable doom. It is a crisis that never exhausts itself, because the anxiety is never really used up. Being a crisis of the imagination rather than of "real life," it has the habit of repeating itself again and again. The territory of aging (as opposed to actual old age) has no fixed boundaries. Up to a point it can be defined as one wants. Entering each decade—after the initial shock is absorbed—an endearing, desperate impulse of survival helps many women to stretch the boundaries to the decade following. In late adolescence thirty seems the end of life. At thirty, one pushes the sentence forward to forty. At forty, one still gives oneself ten more years.

I remember my closest friend in college sobbing on the day she turned twenty-one. "The best part of my life is over. I'm not young any more." She was a senior, nearing graduation. I was a precocious freshman, just sixteen. Mystified, I tried lamely to comfort her, saying that I didn't think twenty-one was *so* old. Actually, I didn't understand at all what could be demoralizing about turning twenty-one. To me, it meant only something good: being in charge of oneself, being free. At sixteen, I was too young to have noticed, and become confused by, the peculiarly loose, ambivalent way in which this society demands that one stop thinking of oneself as a girl and start thinking of

oneself as a woman. (In America that demand can now be put off to the age of thirty, even beyond.) But even if I thought her distress was absurd, I must have been aware that it would not simply be absurd but quite unthinkable in a *boy* turning twenty-one. Only women worry about age with that degree of inanity and pathos. And, of course, as with all crises that are inauthentic and therefore repeat themselves compulsively (because the danger is largely fictive, a poison in the imagination), this friend of mine went on having the same crisis over and over, each time as if for the first time.

I also came to her thirtieth birthday party. A veteran of many love affairs, she had spent most of her twenties living abroad and had just returned to the United States. She had been good-looking when I first knew her; now she was beautiful. I teased her about the tears she had shed over being twenty-one. She laughed and claimed not to remember. But thirty, she said ruefully, that really is the end. Soon after, she married. My friend is now forty-four. While no longer what people call beautiful, she is striking-looking, charming, and vital. She teaches elementary school; her husband, who is twenty years older than she, is a part-time merchant seaman. They have one child, now nine years old. Sometimes, when her husband is away, she takes a lover. She told me recently that forty was the most upsetting birthday of all (I wasn't at that one), and although she has only a few years left, she means to enjoy them while they last. She has become one of those women who seize every excuse offered in any conversation for mentioning how old they really are, in a spirit of bravado compounded with self-pity that is not too different from the mood of women who regularly lie about their age. But she is actually fretting much less about aging than she was two decades ago. Having a child, and having one rather late, past the age of thirty, has certainly helped to reconcile her to her age. At fifty, I suspect, she will be ever more valiantly postponing the age of resignation.

My friend is one of the more fortunate, sturdier casualties of the aging crisis. Most women are not as spirited, nor as innocently comic in their suffering. But almost all women endure some version of this suffering: A recurrent seizure of the imagination that usually begins quite young, in which they project themselves into a calculation of loss. The rules of this society are cruel to women. Brought up to be never fully adult, women are deemed obsolete earlier than men. In fact, most women don't become relatively free and expressive sexually until their thirties. (Women mature sexually this late, certainly much later than men, not for innate biological reasons but because this culture retards women. Denied most outlets for sexual energy permitted to men, it takes many women *that* long to wear out some of their inhibitions.) The time at which they start being disqualified as sexually attractive persons is just when they have grown up sexually. The double standard about aging cheats women of those years, between thirty-five and fifty, likely to be the best of their sexual life.

That women expect to be flattered often by men, and the extent to which their self-confidence depends on this flattery, reflects how deeply women are psychologically weakened by this double standard. Added on to the pressure felt by everybody in this society to look young as long as possible are the values of "femininity," which specifically identify sexual attractiveness in women with youth. The desire to be the "right age" has a special urgency for a woman it never has for a man. A much greater part of her self-esteem and pleasure in life is threatened when she ceases to be young. Most men experience getting older with regret, apprehension. But most women experience it even more painfully: with shame. Aging is a man's destiny, something that must happen because he is a human being. For a woman, aging is not only her destiny. Because she is that more *narrowly* defined kind of human being, a woman, it is also her vulnerability.

To be a woman is to be an actress. Being feminine is a kind of theater, with its appropriate costumes, *décor*, lighting, and stylized gestures. From early childhood on, girls are trained to care in a pathologically exaggerated way about their appearance and are profoundly mutilated (to the extent of being unfitted for first-class adulthood) by the extent of the stress put on presenting themselves as physically attractive objects. Women look in the mirror more frequently than men do. It is, virtually, their duty to look at themselves—to look often. Indeed, a woman who is not narcissistic is considered unfeminine. And a woman who spends literally *most* of her time caring for, and making purchases to flatter, her physical appearance is not regarded in this society as what she is: a kind of moral idiot. She is thought to be quite normal and is envied by other women whose time is mostly used up at jobs or caring for large families. The display of narcissism goes on all the time. It is expected that women will disappear several times in an evening—at a restaurant, at a party, during a theater inter-

a compact mirror and touches up her make-up and hair without embarrassment in front of her husband or her friends.

mission, in the course of a social visit —simply to check their appearance, to see that nothing has gone wrong with their make-up and hairstyling, to make sure that their clothes are not spotted or too wrinkled or not hanging properly. It is even acceptable to perform this activity in public. At the table in a restaurant, over coffee, a woman opens

A man doesn't need to tamper with his face. A woman's face is the canvas on which she paints a revised portrait of herself.

All this behavior, which is written off as normal "vanity" in women, would seem ludicrous in a man. Women are more vain than men because of the relentless pressure on women to maintain their appearance at a certain high standard. What makes the pressure even more burdensome is that there are actually several standards. Men present themselves as face-and-body, a physical whole. Women are split, as men are not, into a body and a face—each judged by somewhat different standards. What is important for a face is that it be beautiful. What is important for a body is two things, which may even be (depending on fashion and taste) somewhat incompatible: first, that it be desirable and, second, that it be beautiful. Men usually feel sexually attracted to women much more because of their bodies than their faces. The traits that arouse desire—such as fleshiness—don't always match those that fashion decrees as beautiful. (For instance, the ideal woman's body promoted in advertising in recent years is extremely thin: the kind of body that looks more desirable clothed than naked.) But women's concern with their appearance is not simply geared to arousing desire in men. It also aims at fabricating a certain image by which, as a more indirect way of arousing desire, women state their value. A woman's value lies in the way she *represents* herself, which is much more by her face than her body. In defiance of the laws of simple sexual attraction, women do not devote most of their attention to their bodies. The well-known "normal" narcissism that women display—the amount of time they spend before the mirror—is used primarily in caring for the face and hair.

Women do not simply have faces, as men do; they are identified with their faces. Men have a naturalistic relation to their faces. Certainly they care whether they are good-looking or not. They suffer over acne, protruding ears, tiny eyes; they hate getting bald. But there is a much wider latitude in what is esthetically acceptable in a man's face than what is in a woman's. A man's face is defined as something he basically doesn't need to tamper with; all he has to do is keep it clean. He can avail himself of the options for ornament supplied by nature: a beard, a mustache, longer or shorter hair. But he is not supposed to disguise himself. What he is "really" like is supposed to show. A man lives through his face; it records the progressive stages of his life. And since he doesn't tamper with his face, it is not separate from but is completed by his body—which is judged attractive by the impression it gives of virility and energy. By contrast, a woman's face is potentially separate from her body. She does not treat it naturalistically. A woman's face is the canvas upon which she paints a revised, cor-

rected portrait of herself. One of the rules of this creation is that the face *not* show what she doesn't want it to show. Her face is an emblem, an icon, a flag. How she arranges her hair, the type of make-up she uses, the quality of her complexion—all these are signs, not of what she is "really" like, but of how she asks to be treated by others, especially men. They establish her status as an "object."

For the normal changes that age inscribes on every human face, women are much more heavily penalized than men. Even in early adolescence, girls are cautioned to protect their faces against wear and tear. Mothers tell their daughters (but never their sons): You look ugly when you cry. Stop worrying. Don't read too much. Crying, frowning, squinting, even laughing—all these human activities make "lines." The same usage of the face in men is judged quite positively. In a man's face lines are taken to be signs of "character." They indicate emotional strength, maturity—qualities far more esteemed in men than in women. (They show he has "lived.") Even scars are often not felt to be unattractive; they too can add "character" to a man's face. But lines of aging, any scar, even a small birthmark on a woman's face, are always regarded as unfortunate blemishes. In effect, people take character in men to be different from what constitutes character in women. A woman's character is thought to be innate, static—not the product of her experience, her years, her actions. A woman's face is prized so far as it remains unchanged by (or conceals the traces of) her emotions, her physical risk-taking. Ideally, it is supposed to be a mask—immutable, unmarked. The model woman's face is Garbo's. Because women are identified with their faces much more than men are, and the ideal woman's face is one that is "perfect," it seems a calamity when a woman has a disfiguring accident. A broken nose or a scar or a burn mark, no more than regrettable for a man, is a terrible psychological wound to a woman; objectively, it diminishes her value. (As is well known, most clients for plastic surgery are women.)

Both sexes aspire to a physical ideal, but what is expected of boys and what is expected of girls involves a very different moral relation to the self. Boys are encouraged to *develop* their bodies, to regard the body as an instrument to be improved. They invent their masculine selves largely through exercise and sport, which harden the body and strengthen competitive feelings; clothes are of only secondary help in making their bodies attractive. Girls are not particularly encouraged to develop their

bodies through any activity, strenuous or not; and physical strength and endurance are hardly valued at all. The invention of the feminine self proceeds mainly through clothes and other signs that testify to the very effort of girls to look attractive, to their commitment to please. When boys become men, they may go on (especially if they have sedentary jobs) practicing a sport or doing exercises for a while. Mostly they leave their appearance alone, having been trained to accept more or less what nature has handed out to them. (Men may start doing exercises again in their forties to lose weight, but for reasons of health—there is an epidemic fear of heart attacks among the middle-aged in rich countries—not for cosmetic reasons.) As one of the norms of "femininity" in this society is being preoccupied with one's physical appearance, so "masculinity" means *not* caring very much about one's looks.

This society allows men to have a much more affirmative relation to their bodies than women have. Men are more "at home" in their bodies, whether they treat them casually or use them aggressively. A man's body is defined as a strong body. It contains no contradiction between what is felt to be attractive and what is practical. A woman's body, so far as it is considered attractive, is defined as a fragile, light body. (Thus, women worry more than men do about being overweight.) When they do exercises, women avoid the ones that develop the muscles, particularly those in the upper arms. Being "feminine" means looking physically weak, frail. Thus, the ideal woman's body is one that is not of much practical use in the hard work of this world, and one that must continually be "defended." Women do not develop their bodies, as men do. After a woman's body has reached its sexually acceptable form by late adolescence, most further development is viewed as negative. And it is thought irresponsible for women to do what is normal for men: simply leave their appearance alone. During early youth they are likely to come as close as they ever will to the ideal image—slim figure, smooth firm skin, light musculature, graceful movements. Their task is to try to maintain that image, unchanged, as long as possible. Improvement as such is not the task. Women care for their bodies—against toughening, coarsening, getting fat. They *conserve* them. (Perhaps the fact that women in modern societies tend to have a more conservative political outlook than men originates in their profoundly conservative relation to their bodies.)

In the life of women in this society

the period of pride, of natural honesty, of unself-conscious flourishing is brief. Once past youth women are condemned to inventing (and maintaining) themselves against the inroads of age. Most of the physical qualities regarded as attractive in women deteriorate much earlier in life than those defined as "male." Indeed, they perish fairly soon in the normal sequence of body transformation. The "feminine" is smooth, rounded, hairless, unlined, soft, unmuscled—the look of the very young; characteristics of the weak, of the vulnerable; eunuch traits, as Germaine Greer has pointed out. Actually, there are only a few years—late adolescence, early twenties—in which this look is physiologically natural, in which it can be had without touching-up and covering-up. After that, women enlist in a quixotic enterprise, trying to close the gap between the imagery put forth by society (concerning what is attractive in a woman) and the evolving facts of nature.

Women have a more intimate relation to aging than men do, simply because one of the accepted "women's" occupations is taking pains to keep one's face and body from showing the signs of growing older. Women's sexual validity depends, up to a certain point, on how well they stand off these natural changes. After late adolescence women become the caretakers of their bodies and faces, pursuing an essentially defensive strategy, a holding operation. A vast array of products in jars and tubes, a branch of surgery, and armies of hairdressers, masseuses, diet counselors, and other professionals exist to stave off, or mask, developments that are entirely normal biologically. Large amounts of women's energies are diverted into this passionate, corrupting effort to defeat nature: to maintain an ideal, static appearance against the progress of age. The collapse of the project is only a matter of time. Inevitably, a woman's physical appearance develops beyond its youthful form. No matter how exotic the creams or how strict the diets, one cannot indefinitely keep the face unlined, the waist slim. Bearing children takes its toll: the torso becomes thicker; the skin is stretched. There is no way to keep certain lines from appearing, in one's mid-twenties, around the eyes and mouth. From about thirty on, the skin gradually loses its tonus. In women this perfectly natural process is regarded as a humiliating defeat, while nobody finds anything remarkably unattractive in the equivalent physical changes in men. Men are "allowed" to look older without sexual penalty.

Thus, the reason that women experience aging with more pain than men is not simply that they care more than men about how they look. Men also care about their looks and want to be attractive, but since the business of men is mainly being and doing, rather than appearing, the standards for appearance are much less exacting. The standards for what is attractive in a man are permissive; they conform to what is possible or "natural" to most men throughout most of their lives. The standards for women's appearance go against nature, and to come anywhere near approximating them takes considerable effort and time. Women must try to be beautiful. At the least, they are under heavy social pressure not to be ugly. A woman's fortunes depend, far more than a man's, on being at least "acceptable" looking. Men are not subject to this pressure. Good looks in a man is a bonus, not a psychological necessity for maintaining normal self-esteem.

Behind the fact that women are more severely penalized than men are for aging is the fact that people, in this culture at least, are simply less tolerant of ugliness in women than in men. An ugly woman is never merely repulsive. Ugliness in a woman is felt by everyone, men as well as women, to be faintly embarrassing. And many features or blemishes that count as ugly in a woman's face would be quite tolerable on the face of a man. This is not, I would insist, just because the esthetic standards for men and women are different. It is rather because the esthetic standards for women are much higher, and narrower, than those proposed for men.

Beauty, women's business in this society, is the theater of their enslavement. Only one standard of female beauty is sanctioned: the *girl*. The great advantage men have is that our culture allows two standards of male beauty: the *boy* and the *man*. The beauty of a boy resembles the beauty of a girl. In both sexes it is a fragile kind of beauty and flourishes naturally only in the early part of the life-cycle. Happily, men are able to accept themselves under another standard of good looks—heavier, rougher, more thickly built. A man does not grieve when he loses the smooth, unlined, hairless skin of a boy. For he has only exchanged one form of attractiveness for another: the darker skin of a man's face, roughened by daily shaving, showing the marks of emotion and the normal lines of age. There is no equivalent of this second standard for women. The single standard of beauty for women dictates that they must go on having clear skin.

The system of inequality is operated by men, but it could not work if women themselves did not aquiesce in it.

Every wrinkle, every line, every grey hair, is a defeat. No wonder that no boy minds becoming a man, while even the passage from girlhood to early womanhood is experienced by many women as their downfall, for all women are trained to want to continue looking like girls.

This is not to say there are no beautiful older women. But the standard of beauty in a woman of any age is how far she retains, or how she manages to simulate, the appearance of youth. The exceptional woman in her sixties who is beautiful certainly owes a large debt to her genes. Delayed aging, like good looks, tends to run in families. But nature rarely offers enough to meet this culture's standards. Most of the women who successfully delay the appearance of age are rich, with unlimited leisure to devote to nurturing along nature's gifts. Often they are actresses. (That is, highly paid professionals at doing what all women are taught to practice as amateurs.) Such women as Mae West, Dietrich, Stella Adler, Dolores Del Rio, do not challenge the rule about the relation between beauty and age in women. They are admired precisely because they *are* exceptions, because they have managed (at least so it seems in photographs) to outwit nature. Such miracles, exceptions made by nature (with the help of art and social privilege), only confirm the rule, because what makes these women seem beautiful to us is precisely that they do not look their real age. Society allows no place in our imagination for a beautiful old woman who does look like an old woman—a woman who might be like Picasso at the age of ninety, being photographed outdoors on his estate in the south of France, wearing only shorts and sandals. No one imagines such a woman exists. Even the special exceptions—Mae West & Co.—are always photographed indoors, cleverly lit, from the most flattering angle and fully, artfully clothed. The implication is they would not stand a closer scrutiny. The idea of an old woman in a bathing suit being attractive, or even just acceptable looking, is inconceivable. An older woman is, by definition, sexually repulsive—unless, in fact, she doesn't look old at all. The body of an old woman, unlike that of an old man, is always understood as a body that can no longer be shown, offered, unveiled. At best, it may appear in costume. People still feel uneasy, thinking about what they might see if her mask dropped, if she took off her clothes.

Thus, the point for women of dressing up, applying make-up, dyeing their hair, going on crash diets, and getting face-lifts is not just to be attractive.

They are ways of defending themselves against a profound level of disapproval directed toward women, a disapproval that can take the form of aversion. The double standard about aging converts the life of women into an inexorable march toward a condition in which they are not just unattractive, but disgusting. The profoundest terror of a woman's life is the moment represented in a statue by Rodin called *Old Age:* a naked old woman, seated, pathetically contemplates her flat, pendulous, ruined body. Aging in women is a process of becoming obscene sexually, for the flabby bosom, wrinkled neck, spotted hands, thinning white hair, waistless torso, and veined legs of an old woman are felt to be obscene. In our direst moments of the imagination, this transformation can take place with dismaying speed—as in the end of *Lost Horizon,* when the beautiful young girl is carried by her lover out of Shangri-La and, within minutes, turns into a withered, repulsive crone. There is no equivalent nightmare about men. This is why, however much a man may care about his appearance, that caring can never acquire the same desperateness it often does for women. When men dress according to fashion or now even use cosmetics, they do not expect from clothes and make-up what women do. A face-lotion or perfume or deodorant or hairspray, used by a man, is not part of a disguise. Men, as men, do not feel the need to disguise themselves to fend off morally disapproved signs of aging, to outwit premature sexual obsolescence, to cover up aging as obscenity. Men are not subject to the barely concealed revulsion expressed in this culture against the female body—except in its smooth, youthful, firm, odorless, blemish-free form.

One of the attitudes that punish women most severely is the visceral horror felt at aging female flesh. It reveals a radical fear of women installed deep in this culture, a demonology of women that has crystallized in such mythic caricatures as the vixen, the virago, the vamp, and the witch. Several centuries of witch-phobia, during which one of the cruelest extermination programs in Western history was carried out, suggest something of the extremity of this fear. That old women are repulsive is one of the most profound esthetic and erotic feelings in our culture. Women share it as much as men do. (Oppressors, as a rule, deny oppressed people their own "native" standards of beauty. And the oppressed end up being convinced that they *are* ugly.) How women are psychologically damaged by this misogynistic idea of what is beautiful parallels the way in which blacks have

been deformed in a society that has up to now defined beautiful as white. Psychological tests made on young black children in the United States some years ago showed how early and how thoroughly they incorporate the white standard of good looks. Virtually all the children expressed fantasies that indicated they considered black people to be ugly, funny looking, dirty, brutish. A similar kind of self-hatred infects most women. Like men, they find old age in women "uglier" than old age in men.

This esthetic taboo functions, in sexual attitudes, as a racial taboo. In this society most people feel an involuntary recoil of the flesh when imagining a middle-aged woman making love with a young man—exactly as many whites flinch viscerally at the thought of a white woman in bed with a black man. The banal drama of a man of fifty who leaves a wife of forty-five for a girlfriend of twenty-eight contains no strictly sexual outrage, whatever sympathy people may have for the abandoned wife. On the contrary. Everyone "understands." Everyone knows that men like girls, that young women often want middle-aged men. But no one "understands" the reverse situation. A woman of forty-five who leaves a husband of fifty for a lover of twenty-eight is the makings of a social and sexual scandal at a deep level of feeling. No one takes exception to a romantic couple in which the man is twenty years or more the woman's senior. The movies pair Joanne Dru and John Wayne, Marilyn Monroe and Joseph Cotten, Audrey Hepburn and Cary Grant, Jane Fonda and Yves Montand, Catherine Deneuve and Marcello Mastroianni; as in actual life, these are perfectly plausible, appealing couples. When the age difference runs the other way, people are puzzled and embarrassed and simply shocked. (Remember Joan Crawford and Cliff Robertson in *Autumn Leaves?* But so troubling is this kind of love story that it rarely figures in the movies, and then only as the melancholy history of a failure.) The usual view of why a woman of forty and a boy of twenty, or a women of fifty and a man of thirty, marry is that the man is seeking a mother, not a wife; no one believes the marriage will last. For a woman to respond erotically and romantically to a man who, in terms of his age, could be her father is considered normal. A man who falls in love with a woman who, however attractive she may be, is old enough to be his mother is thought to be extremely neurotic (victim of an "Oedipal fixation" is the fashionable tag), if not mildly contemptible.

The wider the gap in age between

partners in a couple, the more obvious is the prejudice against women. When old men, such as Justice Douglas, Picasso, Strom Thurmond, Onassis, Chaplin, and Pablo Casals, take brides thirty, forty, fifty years younger than themselves, it strikes people as remarkable, perhaps an exaggeration—but still plausible. To explain such a match, people enviously attribute some special virility and charm to the man. Though he can't be handsome, he is famous; and his fame is understood as having boosted his attractiveness to women. People imagine that his young wife, respectful of her elderly husband's attainments, is happy to become his helper. For the man a late marriage is always good public relations. It adds to the impression that, despite his advanced age, he is still to be reckoned with; it is the sign of a continuing vitality presumed to be available as well to his art, business activity, or political career. But an elderly woman who married a young man would be greeted quite differently. She would have broken a fierce taboo, and she would get no credit for her courage. Far from being admired for her vitality, she would probably be condemned as predatory, willful, selfish, exhibitionistic. At the same time she would be pitied, since such a marriage would be taken as evidence that she was in her dotage. If she had a conventional career or were in business or held public office, she would quickly suffer from the current of disapproval. Her very credibility as a professional would decline, since people would suspect that her young husband might have an undue influence on her. Her "respectability" would certainly be compromised. Indeed, the well-known old women I can think of who dared such unions, if only at the end of their lives—George Eliot, Colette, Edith Piaf —have all belonged to that category of people, creative artists and entertainers, who have special license from society to behave scandalously. It is thought to be a scandal for a woman to ignore that she is old and therefore too ugly for a young man. Her looks and a certain physical condition determine a woman's desirability, not her talents or her needs. Women are not supposed to be "potent." A marriage between an old woman and a young man subverts the very ground rule of relations between the two sexes, that is: whatever the variety of appearances, men remain dominant. Their claims come first. Women are supposed to be the associates and companions of men, not their full equals—and never their superiors. Women are to remain in the state of a permanent "minority."

The convention that wives should be younger than their husbands powerfully enforces the "minority" status of women, since being senior in age always carries with it, in any relationship, a certain amount of power and authority. There are no laws on the matter, of course. The convention is obeyed because to do otherwise makes one feel as if one is doing something ugly or in bad taste. Everyone feels intuitively the esthetic rightness of a marriage in which the man is older than the woman, which means that any marriage in which the woman is older creates a dubious or less gratifying mental picture. Everyone is addicted to the visual pleasure that women give by meeting certain esthetic requirements from which men are exempted, which keeps women working at staying youthful-looking while men are left free to age. On a deeper level everyone finds the signs of old age in women esthetically offensive, which conditions one to feel

> Women have another option. They can age naturally and without embarrassment, actively protesting.

automatically repelled by the prospect of an elderly woman marrying a much younger man. The situation in which women are kept minors for life is largely organized by such conformist, unreflective preferences. But taste is not free, and its judgments are never merely "natural." Rules of taste enforce structures of power. The revulsion against aging in women is the cutting edge of a whole set of oppressive structures (often masked as gallantries) that keep women in their place.

The ideal state proposed for women is docility, which means not being fully grown up. Most of what is cherished as typically "feminine" is simply behavior that is childish, immature, weak. To offer so low and demeaning a standard of fulfillment in itself constitutes oppression in an acute form—a sort of moral neo-colonialism. But women are not simply condescended to by the values that secure the dominance of men. They are repudiated. Perhaps because of having been their oppressors for so long, few men really *like* women (though they love individual women), and few men ever feel really comfortable or at ease in women's company.

This malaise arises because relations between the two sexes are rife with hypocrisy, as men manage to love those they dominate and therefore don't respect. Oppressors always try to justify their privileges and brutalities by imagining that those they oppress belong to a lower order of civilization or are less than fully "human." Deprived of part of their ordinary human dignity, the oppressed take on certain "demonic" traits. The oppressions of large groups have to be anchored deep in the psyche, continually renewed by partly unconscious fears and taboos, by a sense of the obscene. Thus, women arouse not only desire and affection in men but aversion as well. Women are thoroughly domesticated familiars. But, at certain times and in certain situations, they become alien, untouchable. The aversion men feel, so much of which is covered over, is felt most frankly, with least inhibition, toward the type of woman who is most taboo "esthetically," a woman who has become—with the natural changes brought about by aging— obscene.

Nothing more clearly demonstrates the vulnerability of women than the special pain, confusion, and bad faith with which they experience getting older. And in the struggle that some women are waging on behalf of all women to be treated (and treat themselves) as full human beings—not "only" as women—one of the earliest results to be hoped for is that women become aware, indignantly aware, of the double standard about aging from which they suffer so harshly.

It is understandable that women often succumb to the temptation to lie about their age. Given society's double standard, to question a woman about her age is indeed often an aggressive act, a trap. Lying is an elementary means of self-defense, a way of scrambling out of the trap, at least temporarily. To expect a woman, after "a certain age," to tell exactly how old she is— when she has a chance, either through the generosity of nature or the cleverness of art, to pass for being somewhat younger than she actually is—is like expecting a landowner to admit that the estate he has put up for sale is actually worth less than the buyer is prepared to pay. The double standard about aging sets women up as property, as objects whose value depreciates rapidly with the march of the calendar.

The prejudices that mount against women as they grow older are an important arm of male privilege. It is the present unequal distribution of adult roles between the two sexes that gives men a freedom to age denied to women. Men actively administer the double standard about aging because the "masculine" role awards them the initiative in courtship. Men choose; women are chosen. So men choose younger women. But although this system of inequality is operated by men, it could not work if women themselves did not acquiesce in it. Women reinforce it powerfully with their complacency, with their anguish, with their lies.

Not only do women lie more than men do about their age but men forgive them for it, thereby confirming their own superiority. A man who lies about his age is thought to be weak, "unmanly." A woman who lies about her age is behaving in a quite acceptable, "feminine" way. Petty lying is viewed by men with indulgence, one of a number of patronizing allowances made for women. It has the same moral unimportance as the fact that women are often late for appointments. Women are not expected to be truthful, or punctual, or expert in handling and repairing machines, or frugal, or physically brave. They are expected to be second-class adults, whose natural state is that of a grateful dependence on men. And so they often are, since that is what they are brought up to be. So far as women heed the stereotypes of "feminine" behavior, they *cannot* behave as fully responsible, independent adults.

Most women share the contempt for women expressed in the double standard about aging—to such a degree that they take their lack of self-respect for granted. Women have been accustomed so long to the protection of their masks, their smiles, their endearing lies. Without this protection, they know, they would be more vulnerable. But in protecting themselves as women, they betray themselves as adults. The model corruption in a woman's life is denying her age. She symbolically accedes to all those myths that furnish women with their imprisoning securities and privileges, that create their genuine oppression, that inspire their real discontent. Each time a woman lies about her age she becomes an accomplice in her own underdevelopment as a human being.

Women have another option. They can aspire to be wise, not merely nice; to be competent, not merely helpful; to be strong, not merely graceful; to be ambitious for themselves, not merely for themselves in relation to men and children. They can let themselves age naturally and without embarrassment, actively protesting and disobeying the conventions that stem from this society's double standard about aging. Instead of being girls, girls as long as possible, who then age humiliatingly into middle-aged women and then obscenely into old women, they can become women much earlier—and remain active adults, enjoying the long, erotic career of which women are capable, far longer. Women should allow their faces to show the lives they have lived. Women should tell the truth.

29

Transition to the Empty Nest

Crisis, Challenge, or Relief?

Marjorie Fiske Lowenthal, MA, and David Chiriboga, PhD, San Francisco

The present study examines evidence for and against a midlife crisis in an intensively studied sample of 54 middle and lower-middle class men and women whose youngest child is about to leave home. While some members of the sample had serious problems, the confrontation of the empty nest, when compared with retrospections of the low points in the past and expectations of the future is not of a nature to justify use of the term "crisis." The departure of the youngest child, indeed, was generally anticipated with a sense of relief.

THE suggestion of a midlife crisis, especially at gatherings of middle-aged professionals, provokes about as many generalizations as does the ubiquitous generation gap. Psychiatrists speak of marital disasters and involutional depressions. Physicians note dramatic increases in ulcers, hypertension, and coronary disease, especially among executives who realize that they have reached their highest level in the corporate hierarchy. Psychoanalysts suggest that a midlife crisis may be a developmental stage. Judd Marmor,[1] for example, describes it as essentially a separation loss involving the giving up of the fantasy hopes of youth and a confrontation with personal mortality. He cites four modes of coping: (1) denial by escape (frantic activity); (2) denial by overcompensation (sexual adventures, for example); (3) decompensation (including anxiety states, depression, and diffuse rage); and, finally, (4) integration at a higher level, including a lessening of narcissistic self-involvement

From the Adult Development Research Program, Langley Porter Neuropsychiatric Institute, University of California, San Francisco.

Presented in condensed form at the annual meeting of the American Psychological Association, Miami Beach, Fla, September 1970.

Reprint requests to Langley Porter Neuropsychiatric Institute, University of California, 401 Parnassus Ave, San Francisco 94122 (Mrs. Lowenthal).

resembling Erikson's[2] postulated final stage of ego integrity. Psychoanalysts Jane Pearce and Saul Newton,[3] finding support for a midlife crisis in their clinical experience, conclude that "the decision to grow or to die is the crisis of middle age" (p 135). Jacques,[4] on the basis of an historical study of the lives of artists and writers, supplemented by his own clinical findings, pinpoints 35 as a critical age, often followed by illness or death on the one hand, or by radical change in the content of creative output on the other.

Social science research thus far has focused primarily on normative midlife stages such as the menopause or the empty nest, or on trends in work achievement or marital satisfaction. These data do not lend much support to such a thesis. Neugarten et al[5,6] point out that neither the menopause nor the "empty nest" are experienced as crises among middle-aged women; rather, for men as well as women, the middle years may bring an enriched sense of self and an enhanced capacity to cope.[7] Brim,[8] summarizing a number of sociological and psychological studies of marital adjustment, finds happiness at its peak in the first year of marriage, decreasing gradually for the next 15 years, then rising again to level off at a higher plateau. Paraphrasing Deutscher,[9] he concludes that

The postparental period is one of greater satisfaction in marriage than before. For most this is not a crisis period but rather a "golden period" in which there is an increase in shared activities with the spouse, a decrease in mutual concerns about money. . . . There is possibly a "discovery" of the personality of the marital partner as it has evolved during the 25- to 30-year-period of child-rearing.

Blood and Wolfe,[10] on the other hand, suggest that preoccupation with children may temporarily engulf dissatisfactions with the spouse, which then rise to the surface after the children have departed.

The exploration of the "empty nest" stage reported here is part of a longitudinal study of transitional stages in the adult lifespan. The analytic framework for the overall study developed from the concept that a significant component of the adaptive process in adulthood consists of efforts directed toward achieving, restoring, or maintaining equilibrium between one's aims in life (intentionality, goals) and one's behavioral pattern or style.[11] A major objective of the broader study is to determine whether transitions in the adult lifecycle which are normatively viewed as incremental (such as going to college, acquiring a first job, marriage, parenthood) reinforce growth-promoting processes and the establishment of a new equilibrium between intentions and behavior at a higher level of complexity; and whether transitions normatively viewed as decremental (the empty nest, widowhood, retirement) result in constriction or equilibrium at a lower level of complexity. We are further interested in how these adaptive processes relate to more conventional indicators of adaptation.[12] The full explication of this model must await the posttransition follow-up field work. In this communication, we are concerned with a portion of it. Our interest is in determining how the period of anticipation of the empty-nest or postparental stage is experienced, in comparison with retrospections of past periods and anticipations of the future, and how these perceptions relate to self-concept and mood. Since the empty-nest stage is generally construed as more problematic for women than for men, we shall pay close attention to sex differences.

The data for this analysis derive from depth interviews, averaging about nine hours, with 27 men and 27 women approaching the "empty nest" stage of parenthood; that is, their youngest child was about to graduate from high school. Average ages were 51 for men and 48 for women. They are primarily Anglo-Americans in the higher blue-collar and clerical occupations, with a few on the middle level of management; about half of the women are working and have worked much of their adult lives. We shall first describe their evaluations of the present period in comparison with their recollections of earlier adult stages and their expectations for the future. This will be followed by an examination of how the present appears in the context of "turning points" in adult life, and of how present problems and satisfactions compare with those of earlier periods. We shall conclude with a brief review of the current marital relationship, of morale, and of self-concept.

Evaluations of the Present as Compared With Past and Future

In the course of the interview, respondents filled in a life evaluation chart where they rated each year of their lives from 1 to 9, 9 being "absolute tops" and 1 being "rock bottom." (This chart is an adaptation of one developed by Professor Jean MacFarlane of the Institute of Human Development, University of California, Berkeley.) In the analysis of this chart, we have delineated six life stages: adolescence (ages 12 to 20), young adulthood (21 to 29), "midlife" (30 to 38), early middle age (age 39 to four years before the present period), the "empty nest" (four years before and four years after the interview year), and the retirement transition period (60 to 68). Coding of the various stages was based on a 5-point scale, called the Stage Evaluation Code (SEC); scores ranged from 1, one or more points within the period being the highest of the entire life-span evaluation, through 5, one or more points within the period being the lowest of the entire chart. (Coding of these charts was undertaken independently by two judges, with a Pearson reliability coefficient of 0.99.) Each individual received one score per stage, but we are here concerned only with the extreme highs and the extreme lows.

Among men, all life stages are characterized by similar proportions of high points, with the present (along with adolescence) having a slight edge. Among the women, the period of early marriage and parenthood clearly surpasses all others, but the present period, encompassing pre- and postempty nest, is more likely to have highs than early middle age, and more than twice as likely to include high points as the (anticipated) pre- and postretirement stage. Among men for whom the present period encompassed high points, the emphasis was on work (Table 1). For a 52-year-old brewery worker a challenge came from a promotion: "I got the new job of being supervisor I feel these two years are the best, they present a new challenge . . . something I could get hold of." For others, the theme was job stability or financial security. Though half of the women worked too, work was not mentioned as accounting for a high point. Among them, the emphasis was on personal relationships, especially familial. As the wife of a bank clerk and mother of two put it:

Things are coming up now. . . . I am athletic and healthy and I have a strong heart. These will be great years if Bob's health holds out too. We are both interested in our home and we look forward to taking a trip by boat.

The present phase, which we expected to be critical at least for the women, encompassed the *lowest* points in the life charts for only five persons (three women and two men). For none of them did the explanations for these low ratings have anything to do with the pending departure of the youngest child from home. One was a woman whose husband had just left her (temporarily, as it turned out); a second woman's husband had been mortally ill for a year; and the third was herself suffering from a serious illness. One of the two men lends some support to the Blood and Wolfe[10] hypothesis: He had just come to the realization that his marriage had been a failure all along. The second man had a multi-

plicity of problems, none of them having to do with the "empty nest": His eldest daughter was a hippie, he had had financial reverses, and he felt that sociopolitical conditions, local and national, had become untenable.

As Table 2 indicates, there are considerably fewer lows in the present and future than in the past, tending to confirm findings reported from a similar life chart study by Back and Bourque[13] conducted among a cross-section sample. Lows are most frequent in adolescence and for the period we have called early middle age (age 39 to four years prior to the present, average age 46) followed by young adulthood. The period surrounding Jacques'[4] postulated critical age of 35 is singularly free of low points. In accordance with Jacques'[4] thesis about the midlife point, it may be that the critical year has moved up. In any case, age 39 to four years prior to the interview included nervous breakdowns, physical illnesses, financial crises, and marital problems. For women, the lows for this latter period were sometimes also connected with child-rearing problems (or with spouse over problems with children). These ranged from instances where children were dropouts, runaways, or entangled with the law, to concerns with such matters as hair or skirt length, use of the family car or time when expected home after a date. Regardless of the severity of problems, the present empty-nest period is perceived as promising:

I feel my job with them is done. I don't have to discipline them anymore, it's their problem. . . . I hope I can always be a mother, but we'll treat each other as adults. I have a much more relaxed feeling now.

Aside from providing little evidence for an empty-nest crisis, Tables 1 and 2 also reveal some very striking sex differences. While looking across the lifespan, both men and women report more highs than lows, the ratio is more than 3 to 1 among men and considerably less than 2 to 1 among women.

It also should be noted in passing that if, instead of using highs and

Table 1.—Distribution by Life Stage of SEC Scores Highest or Equal to the Highest of the Entire Life Span*

	Adolescence (12-20)	Young Adulthood (21-29)	Midlife (30-38)	Early Middle Age (39-Present)	Empty Nest (Present Period)†	Retirement Transition (60-68)	Total Mentions, High Periods
Men	13 (19%)	11 (16%)	11 (16%)	11 (16%)	12 (17%)	11 (16%)	57 (100%)
Women	8 (18%)	15 (34%)	7 (16%)	4 (9%)	7 (16%)	3 (7%)	37 (100%)

Note: χ^2 by period = 10.421, df = 10, $P < 0.50$
  χ^2 (men) = 0.278, df = 5, $P < 0.99$
  χ^2 (women) = 10.143, df = 5, $P < 0.10$
  Binomial test, by sex
  $z = 2.257$, $P < 0.025$, two-tailed test

* A maximum of one entry per stage per respondent.
† Four years before and four years after the time of interview.

Table 2.—Distribution by Life Stage of SEC Scores Lowest or Equal to the Lowest of the Entire Life Span*

	Adolescence (12-20)	Young Adulthood (21-29)	Midlife (30-38)	Early Middle Age (39-Present)	Empty Nest (Present Period)†	Retirement Transition (60-68)	Total Mentions, Low Periods
Men	4 (24%)	6 (35%)	0 (0%)	5 (29%)	2 (12%)	0 (0%)	17 (100%)
Women	8 (33%)	4 (17%)	1 (4%)	8 (33%)	3 (13%)	0 (0%)	24 (100%)

Note: χ^2 by period = 11.227, df = 4, $P < 0.05$
  χ^2 (men) = 5.681, df = 2, $P < 0.10$
  χ^2 (women) = 5.546, df = 2, $P < 0.10$
  Binomial test, by sex
  $z = 0.937$, $P < 0.1736$, two-tailed test

* A maximum of one entry per stage per respondent.
† Four years before and four years after the time of interview.

lows from the Stage Evaluation Code, raw scores from the life evaluation chart are averaged by stage, the results are essentially similar. The period we have called early middle age continues to represent a low point for the women, while young adulthood represents the lowest point for the men. The empty nest, in comparison, is a period of ascendancy, as is the retirement transition period, for both men and women. (Tables not presented here are available upon request from the authors.)

The Empty Nest as Turning Point, Frustration, or Satisfaction

As they reviewed their lives, these middle-aged parents were also asked, without reference to the life chart, to describe periods of major change or turning points. Most frequently evoked were normative role changes in the past, such as completion of education (men and women equally divided on this score), the acquisition of a first job or a better job (half again as many men as women), marriage, establishing a

home, and having children. Some women, but no men, spoke of beginning to date, meeting their future spouse, or having an affair, as crucial. Relatively few members of either sex mentioned political or social circumstances, the exceptions being a few men who mentioned World War II, and one man and one woman who recalled the severe impact of the Depression in their childhood. Fifteen women, but only four men, spoke of separations from others due to divorce, moves, illness, or death. As in their life chart review, women were far more negative in reporting turning points than men. Yet, though most of these women had older children who had already left home, only one spoke of such an event as a turning point. And even in this instance, it was not the child's departure per se but the fact that she had left after a major argument that had made the event traumatic.

For very few was the present (for most, a few months before the youngest child was to leave high school) singled out as a turning point. The exceptions were three of

the five persons described earlier, for whom the present period included the lowest point on their life charts for reasons quite unrelated to the empty nest. One (a woman) singled out the present as a positive transition because of the pending arrival of a grandchild (an additional 15 members of the sample have grandchildren, but did not mention grandparenthood as a turning point).

In this life review section of the interview, subjects were also asked to pinpoint and describe periods and circumstances that they found particularly frustrating, and those they found especially satisfying. Frustrations tend to be as distant as the major turning points for most and fewer than one in five reported frustrations in the present. In these relatively few instances where frustrations were current, men tended to cite occupational or monetary problems, and women to speak of interpersonal difficulties, largely marital and parental. Conversely, no men pointed to marital or child-rearing problems as a source of frustration and no women pointed to occupational problems. No man or woman cited the past or pending departure of a child as frustrating.

While frustrating periods were largely in the rather distant past, the things people were proud of in their lives tended to continue into the present. The matters for pride were not the converse of the sources of frustration for men, though they were for women. Men's frustrations were usually connected with work or money, but they, like the women, singled out circumstances which reflect expressive, interpersonal values in talking about what they were proud of, referring to their marriages, their children, or more generally their families. For women, frustrations often involve parenthood, but they are in the past. For men and women alike, the satisfactions of parenthood continue, the empty nest notwithstanding.

Respondents were also asked to focus only on the present and discuss their major *current* difficulties and satisfactions. In this context, men once more reverted to instrumental, largely occupational and financial concerns as they had in reviewing lifespan frustrations. Some women (but no men), reported problems with the youngest child as their major current difficulty, often leading to problems with spouse:

I get frustrations every day but I learn to live with them, to cope with them. I'm having difficult times now. It's because my husband and I have sort of lots of misunderstandings. I couldn't call them quarrels. Differences of opinion I would say. We always had them. The greatest was when my youngest daughter started to date. Also there are differences of opinion about school work. These are the greatest problems.

Six women (and no men) cited marital woes per se as their main current problem; these were seen as threatening to the marriage in three instances, while the remaining three were in effect saying merely that their marital life could be more pleasant.

With one exception, neither men nor women singled out the pending departure of the youngest child as a current problem. Interestingly, the

exception was a man, and he comes closer to describing an empty-nest "crisis" than anyone else in the sample—though crisis seems scarcely the apt term for it:

There was the day that my older daughter got married and I thought here I am losing my pet. I figured this was just the natural reaction. My youngest son just said to me he is getting married in February and my youngest daughter said, "Daddy, are you going to give me a wedding, too?" At the other extreme, two fathers wished they had had their children earlier and that they were already out on their own. As one of them explained:

I wish now that my children were older, and already out of the house and living their own lives. I would like to be rid of that particular responsibility. I would like to have the accomplishment of raising my children, but also to be discharged of the responsibility of maintaining them. . . . I would prefer that (my son) had already been able to take care of himself a few years earlier, so that I would be able to enjoy my last years at work and also my retirement without being responsible for him.

Current satisfactions for both men and women, like the things they were most proud of or satisfied with from a lifespan perspective, tended to be of an expressive or interpersonal rather than an instrumental or material nature. For nearly half, it continued to be children or "family," for some it was friends. For only three (two men and one woman), however, was it marriage. Interestingly enough, among those who did report current satisfaction in instrumental or material areas, there were more women than men. Perhaps one might more reasonably call this satisfaction with one's competence or effectiveness, since it was just as likely to include gratification in managing a home well, in dressmaking, or in cooking, as to include gratification from paid work. It is, perhaps, a sad commentary on the lives of middle-class, middle-aged men in our society, most of whom have reached their peak occupational level, that fewer than one fourth of them reported work as a source of current satisfaction; moreover,

only five considered their past occupational achievements a matter of pride. Among women, few were dissatisfied with their achievements either in paid occupations (half of these women worked) or in homemaking tasks, and many found satisfaction in both.

It may be that the apparent reversal of sex differences at this life stage reflects an attempt at compensation or substitution among those women facing the empty nest. Conversely, the expressive concerns of men may be a kind of anticipatory adjustment to their pending retirement, which several expect to occur in the not too distant future. That these may be developmental changes is suggested by the findings of Neugarten and Gutmann[14] in their study of age and sex shifts in projective test material. Comparing successive age groups, they report a strong tendency for women to move from expressive to instrumental responses and a reverse trend among men.

Marital Relationship

Thus far, while we have reported some evidence for the existence of problems during the empty-nest period, with only a few exceptions, they do not seem to be of a nature to warrant use of the term crisis, and they rarely suggest that the pending departure of the youngest child is a cause of distress. There may be problems with that child, but they will be resolved (or overlooked) when he goes to college or gets his first job, or is no longer physically present on a day-to-day basis.

We now turn to an exploration of the thesis that the departure or pending departure of children may activate latent problems between spouses. In a section of the protocol devoted to perceptions of close others and of social networks, respondents were asked to describe their spouses, their agreements and disagreements, and their sexual attitudes and expectations. Perceptions of the spouse were grouped into two categories: positive or indulgently ambivalent, and negative.

Consistent with their generally optimistic stance, the men spoke positively of their wives in a ratio of two to one, whereas women were twice as likely to describe their husbands in negative terms as to give positive appraisals. The majority of men described their wives in both expressive and instrumental terms, usually stressing their capacity for warmth and understanding, and then going on to discuss their competence as homemakers. Though more than half of these middle-aged men had wives who were working, their competencies or contributions in this area were not mentioned. Their few complaints about their wives had to do with extravagance or being too easygoing with the children. Women, on the other hand, tend to criticize their husbands for poor interpersonal relations, outside of the family, with the children, and, frequently, with themselves:

He doesn't mix at all with people. He is not friendly . . . maybe it's shyness but I don't think so. He doesn't like people, period. He is . . . not a fighter. That annoys me sometimes. . . . If you want to argue, you just have to argue by yourself—he gets up and leaves.

We don't have fights, we are past that stage. That's the reason I live from day to day.

He is a master of passive resistance. He doesn't argue, he just keeps quiet. . . . he . . . can just turn people off.

Men and women were each equally divided between those who said they have no disagreements or only mild ones and those who reported moderate-to-severe disagreements and, not surprisingly, those whose descriptions of spouse were most critical were more likely to report severe disagreements. It should be added, however, that many wives volunteered the information that they do not have disagreements because they, the wives, placate their husbands. "I give in to him," as one put it; or "You have to learn to live with him and not do those things which upset him." While the most frequent area of disagreement between spouses had to do with child-rearing, there was no consistent pattern to these disagreements: men and women alike were as likely

to believe that their spouses were too strict with the children as they were to consider them too permissive. The general tenor of these observations, however, was flat, without affect. They seem to be saying what is done is done, implying that once the last child has departed marital harmony will be restored:

. . . the main thing we really have our big arguments about is over our daughter. You know, because he feels that I'm taking her side too much, and more or less going against him. And I feel that I sort of want to protect her from him, because I think he gets too belligerent to her, instead of trying to talk sensibly; his temper gets away from him. . . . Because I don't want to be so strict that she'll feel she wants to run away from home or something. Whereas the way he acts toward her, it makes her want to feel that way. So I've got to be the sort of buffer in between. And that really gets his goats (sic), you know. . . . But then we keep telling each other, "Well, let's not get ourselves all upset over this." Because you know, we don't think she will be living at home all that much longer.

The generally more cheerful perspective of the men was further reflected in their reports on changes in sexual activity and satisfaction. The majority report that their sex life is about the same or better than it used to be. "We are freer now," says a 61-year-old carpenter, "it has grown better from year to year." And a 48-year-old policeman elaborated with a kind of lifecycle perspective:

Oh yeah. When you are young, you're wild, just concerned with your own self-satisfaction. You don't know what it's all about but you think it's something that should be done. And most kids in their teens, it's just an accomplishment, a feat, something to brag about. But as you get older, you realize there's more to it. It's something not to be abused. It should occur at a happy time.

The majority of women, on the other hand, report a decline in frequency or quality or both. For many, however, this does not so much represent a disappointing change as a relief. One woman reports a complete cessation of sex life and goes on to say, "I'm happy about it. I am not a sexy person and

I never have been." Others are content with a decline:

It's probably dwindled. Probably more on my part. I never got much out of sex personally.

I don't have as much interest as I used to. . . . You have so many things to do you don't have the time . . . the desire is still there but it's just not so often. Jack is nice and sometimes he does things that are just as good as sex relations.

While at first glance this difference in attitude might be interpreted as a reflection of menopausal problems in women, we find little support for such a thesis in these data. None reported severe menopausal problems, only four reported moderate ones, and the rest only mild difficulties or none at all. Like the middle-aged women studied by Neugarten,[5] they are very matter-of-fact if not offhand about the matter, several of them expressing gratitude for the advances of modern medicine.

Morale and Self-Concept

To recapitulate, though a few of these middle-aged parents were having serious problems, there is little indication that they were specific to middle age, or triggered by confrontation with the postparental life stage. Some women, to be sure, seemed concerned about the uses of their time, saying that they "ought to do more" (paid work, voluntary activities), but they elaborated on such possibilities in rather vague or ambivalent terms. The wife of a sales engineer reflected this rather common ambivalence, noting that one of her problems right now is thinking about

. . . getting a job instead of putting it off. Always have a reason to do it next week or next month. I ought to go back to school and brush up on something. Actually nothing is too convenient, everything is far away, way downtown. Driving downtown is a major operation.

Those (relatively few) who are pursuing interests and activities outside the home will no doubt continue to do so; it seems unlikely that many of those who are not will radically change their behavioral pattern after the youngest child departs. As one of our respondents explained, you opt for a family-centered versus a more broad-gauged existence when you marry or when you have your first child. Once that choice has been made, paths for reentry into the larger world become blocked or obscured.

Working or not, the majority of these women were primarily home-and-family centered. One would therefore expect the prospects of the postparental phase to influence their mood more than that of men. To explore their subjective feelings about themselves and their lives more directly, we asked our subjects about their current mood and about positive and negative emotional experiences during the past week. Nearly half reported themselves (in Bradburn's terms[15]) as "pretty happy," and twice as many (a third or more) reported themselves as "very happy" as "not too happy." Despite their prevailing tendency to be more optimistic, men did not differ from women in these self-appraisals. In more detailed reports on a list of the following 12 feeling states experienced in the past week, women reported greater frequencies of both positive and negative states.

  On top of world
  Very lonely or remote from other people
  Angry at something that usually wouldn't bother you
  That you couldn't do something because you just couldn't get going
  Particularly excited or interested in something
  Depressed or very unhappy
  Pleased about having accomplished something
  Bored
  Proud because someone complimented you on something you had done
  So restless you couldn't sit long in a chair
  That you had more things to do than you could get done
  Vaguely uneasy about something without knowing why

While this mutability on the part of the empty-nest woman may reflect problems resulting from their life stage, we suspect it mainly reflects a sex difference in affective proclivities. Bradburn[15] combining ages 21 to 59, reports similar (though nonsignificant) differences between the sexes, and we find them in our other age groups. The generally cheerful self-rating was echoed throughout the protocols. In ratings of hope, made by three members of the interdisciplinary research team, nearly three times as many of these subjects were rated hopeful (a rating of 3 or 4 on a 4-point scale) as were rated not hopeful. (Interrater reliability for the measure is 0.73; all cases were triple rated, with ratings averaged.) Men, however, were more likely to be given a 4 rating, women to be given a 3.

Turning to another source for gauging morale, we have examined the discrepancy between real and ideal self-concept and positive versus negative self-descriptions. Subjects were given a 70-item adjective self-rating list, with the instruction to rate each adjective according to whether it was like them, unlike them, or in-between. (Adjectives were those in the Block Adjective Q Set for Non-Professional Sorters.[17]) They were also asked to circle those adjectives which were like them but which they wished were not. At the next interview session the interviewer asked for a rating of the ideal self as well. A discrepancy score was developed from comparisons between the real and ideal self, and a count of the number of items circled as undesirable self-attributes formed the basis for a Self-Criticism Index. A two-way analysis of variance indicated that empty-nest women reported more traits they wished they did not have than did the men ($F = 6.34$, $P < 0.025$). Similarly, a greater discrepancy for women was found between real and ideal evaluations ($F = 13.08$, $P < 0.01$) than was true among men.

A more detailed analysis of particular qualities accepted or rejected as descriptive of themselves further supports this tendency among men to project a positive image: They accept many more favorable adjectives as descriptive of themselves, and reject many more negative ones than do women, in a ratio of about two to one. A paired comparison shows men describing themselves as competitive, competent, and restless, the women describing themselves as disorderly, easily embarrassed, sarcastic, and worried.

Conclusions

Neither responses to specific questions about critical periods and problems nor the content of these detailed protocols as a whole convey the impression that the prospects of the departure of the youngest child are in any way threatening for this preempty-nest sample. On the contrary, to speak in terms of the basic paradigm for the research[12] it appears that they are looking forward to establishing a somewhat less complex lifestyle, and the anticipatory relaxing or re-orienting of child-rearing goals affects their morale only favorably. The present is only rarely a low point or even a turning point of any kind in their lives and when it is, the pending empty nest is not one of the reasons cited. While several women (and no men) report marital difficulties ostensibly thus supporting the Blood and Wolfe hypothesis,[10] none of them indicate that these problems have in any way been triggered by the pending empty nest.

Viewed in the context of the past and the anticipated future, the present period appears to be a favorable one for both men and women. Comparing the views of the two sexes, however, women do tend to have a somewhat more negative and pessimistic orientation. They are, for instance, more critical of their spouses, of themselves, and of many other dimensions of their lives than are the men. At this stage of the research, there are two possible interpretations of this finding: that this reflects a lifelong difference between men and women (suggested by the fact that we find similar sex differences among high school seniors), or that the more negative stance of the women presages a "crisis" that may become manifest after the child has actually left home. We lean toward the former interpretation, that women, perhaps for sociocultural reasons, feel freer to express complex or ambivalent attitudes and feelings, but this by no means reflects less satisfaction with life or less overall happiness (the findings of Bradburn[15] and of Gurin et al[16] tend to support this interpretation). The implications for the men are somewhat more speculative. They seem either to have a conscious reluctance to report negative circumstances or affect, or to repress them altogether. The cost of this effort to live up to a strong male image may be great, for in the population at large it is the men who have serious difficulties in midlife, as reflected by sex differences in alcoholism rates, admissions to mental hospitals, suicide rates, and serious physical illness. While we have no evidence that the pending empty nest is in itself problematic for these men, it may trigger off deep-seated anxieties about their next transition, retirement, which in turn may reinforce the denial mechanism.

The present study is part of a longitudinal study of transitional stages in the adult lifespan supported by grant No. HD-03051 from the National Institute of Child Health and Human Development.

References

1. Marmor J: The crisis of middle age. Read before the annual meeting of the American Orthopsychiatric Association, Washington DC, March 1967.

2. Erikson E: *Childhood and Society*. New York, WW Norton & Co Inc Publishers, 1963.

3. Pearce J, Newton S: *The Conditions of Human Growth*. New York, Citadel Press, 1963.

4. Jacques E: Death and the midlife crisis. *Int J Psychoanal* 46:502-514, 1965.

5. Neugarten BL, Wood V, Kraines RJ, et al: Women's attitudes toward the menopause, in Neugarten BL: (ed): *Middle Age and Aging*. Chicago, University of Chicago Press, 1968, pp 195-200. (Also in *Vita Humana* 6, 1963.)

6. Neugarten BL: Adaptation and the life cycle. *J Geriat Psychiat*, to be published.

7. Neugarten BL: Awareness of middle age, in Neugarten BL (ed): *Middle Age and Aging*. Chicago, University of Chicago Press, 1968, pp 93-98.

8. Brim OG, Jr: Adult socialization, in Clausen JA (ed): *Socialization and Society*. Boston, Little Brown & Co, 1968, pp 182-226.

9. Deutscher I: *Married Life in the Middle Years*. Kansas City, Community Studies, 1959.

10. Blood RO Jr, Wolfe DM: *Husbands and Wives: The Dynamics of Married Living*. New York, The Free Press of Glencoe Inc, 1960.

11. Lowenthal MF, Spence D, Thurnher M: Interplay of personal and social factors at transitional stages, discussion in Rosow I: *Socialization to Old Age*. National Institute of Child Health, to be published.

12. Lowenthal MF: Intentionality: Toward a framework for the study of adaptation in adulthood. *Aging and Human Development*, to be published.

13. Back KW, Bourque LB: Life graphs: Aging and cohort effect. *J Geront* 25:249-255, 1970.

14. Neugarten BL, Gutmann D: Age-sex roles and personality in middle age: A thematic apperception study, in Neugarten BL (ed): *Personality in Middle and Late Life*. New York, Atherton Press, 1964, pp 44-89.

15. Bradburn NM: *The Structure of Psychological Well-Being*. Chicago, Aldine Publishing Co, 1969.

16. Gurin G, Veroff J, Feld S: *Americans View Their Mental Health*. New York, Basic Books, Inc Publishers, 1960.

17. Block J: *The Q-Sort Method in Personality Assessment and Psychiatric Research*. Springfield, Ill, Charles C Thomas Publisher, 1961.

30

HUSBANDS IN CRISIS

Most men change as they approach middle age—in ways that can pose a threat to marriage. An important new study reveals *how* they change, and why, and what their wives can do about it /By Maggie Scarf

Why does a rising corporation executive suddenly, in his early forties, quit his job and go off with his family to a new kind of life on a farm? What makes a seemingly happy husband leave his wife for a girl not much older than his daughter? Why do so many men, at about this time in their lives, begin to drink too much, become discontented and depressed for no clear reason, undergo what appears to be a distinct personality change?

Wives usually know, or sense, that something mysterious comes over a man as he approaches his middle years—not a physical change, such as they themselves experience in menopause, but a psychological one. But what, exactly, brings this change about? Why does it so often erupt in crisis? And how are women to understand and deal with it?

According to a group of six researchers at Yale University, now involved in the third year of a four-year study of males between the ages of thirty-five and forty-five, this ten-year period is often the strategic turning point in a man's life. Led by Dr. Daniel J. Levinson, a psychologist of fifty-one, the research team has been conducting intensive interviews

with a carefully selected group of forty men in this critical time of their lives. Ten of the men are executives, half recruited from a large, settled firm, half from a smaller, more experimental company; ten are blue- and white-collar workers from the same two companies; ten are writers, some well known, some not; ten are biologists at different stages of their academic careers.

Acknowledging that what will emerge from these interviews is not going to be *universally* true for men in their middle years, the Yale team nevertheless started out with a few general questions. Were all the men in the study group heading toward, or going through, or just recovering from, some experience of

crisis? If so, did this crisis tend to vary in intensity for men in different occupations? Or—despite differences in type of work, degree of success, and so on—were their problems basically similar, and linked (like those of early adolescence) to their age?

Now, with all of their major interviewing completed, and the follow-up interviews (two years later) well under way, the researchers have come to several tentative conclusions.

"We're always asked whether or not we've found that there is such a thing as a 'male menopause,'" Dr. Levinson says. "But as far as I'm concerned, this phrase is misleading. The period we're studying is some ten years earlier than the female

psychological reorientation between thirty-five and forty-five, the Yale team reasoned, there ought to be earlier, clearly identifiable stages in their adult development that led them to that point.

In analyzing their interviews, the researchers found that there appear to be three such stages. The first, which they call "Getting into the Adult World," starts around the time a man is in his early twenties. At this point, the men interviewed had all been exploring sexual and marital opportunities, different work possibilities, varying kinds of adult group memberships—but had not made firm internal commitments. Quite often, during this exploratory phase, they pursued contradictory goals—one man was working toward success as a businessman and as a writer at the same time. Later, as he integrated his life into a meaningful pattern—and firmly committed himself to it—he let go of those half-formed goals and dreams that did not fit in.

"Getting into the Adult World" might, for one man, last throughout the entire period of his twenties, while for another the phase could be extremely brief. But the common experience was that by the age of thirty to thirty-two, a man had moved into the next stage of adult life, which the research group called "Settling Down." During this period, he became absorbed in the major tasks of his early adult life: proving himself in an occupation, establishing a family, working out a set of values and beliefs that would cement and give meaning to the "life" he was creating. During this phase, he was obviously far less free to explore alternate occupational or sexual options. Those aspects of his personality that had no place in the life he had built for himself tended to be pushed aside or left dormant.

During this "Settling Down" phase, he was deeply influenced by the values and judgments of those around him: He wanted to "make it" in terms of beliefs he shared with his group at large. Spurred on by some vaguely perceived goal (for many of the biologists in the study, it was related to dreams of someday winning the Nobel Prize), he struggled forward toward a satisfaction that always lay ahead, just over the horizon.

"But by age forty," points out Mrs. Charlotte Darrow, the one sociologist in Dr. Levinson's group, "a man has reached his horizon. Whatever illusions he might have had before, this is, inevitably, a time of assessment. He knows fairly clearly just where he has placed in life's battles—and just about how much farther he can go."

If he has failed, either in his own eyes, or in others', or in both, there is the pain of making peace with that knowledge. But even when he has *not* failed—when he has won the very professorship or high executive position he set out to achieve—he often must come to terms with feelings of futility

change of life. Still, as to whether a male 'crisis' exists, I would say that if one means this in the sense of 'turning point,' then such a thing does take place.

"It generally begins somewhere in the late thirties, and the most fundamental thing about it is that it's a part of normal development: a man at this stage *can't* go on unchanged. He's at the end of something, his early adulthood, and moving toward another period—middle age. There's a discontinuity at this point in his life. He's coping with a variety of new circumstances, like the first indisputable signs of aging; and at the same time, he's assessing old things—fantasies and illusions about himself which he's sustained up until this point."

How men respond to mid-life stress varies, according to Levinson, as widely as does the degree of stress itself. At one extreme would be someone like Gauguin—who, in his midthirties, shed his wife, family, and career as a bank clerk to become a painter and go off to live in the South Seas. At the other extreme would be the man who feels depressed and upset as he moves toward forty, but does nothing, makes no change in his occupation, marriage, or way of living. In between is the man who perhaps takes flight in a series of extramarital affairs, does poorly in his work for awhile; then the flurry dies down, he stays put and doesn't change anything in his life at all.

Yet, regardless of what a man does or doesn't do during this decade, he emerges from it "different"—restabilized, in his mid- or late forties, on another personality level. "Even if nothing whatsoever in his external life is different," Dr. Levinson observes, "*he* is, and it's all going to have a different meaning for him."

If men do undergo some profound

and meaninglessness. In reality, the dream he has achieved turns out to be far more limited than was his original vision.

"At this point," Mrs. Darrow explains, "many beliefs and values—all of those obvious 'truths' that support a man while he is Settling Down—may suddenly come into question. For he's been engaged in a huge effort, working toward the thing that was supposed to make him happy in some glorious distant future. And now here he is, and things suddenly don't seem so clear. And he starts asking himself: Is this what I really wanted? Was it worth all I had to give up? Do I want to go on doing these same things for the years I have left?"

At the same time, those inner voices that he silenced or ignored earlier now make themselves heard again, and with a new urgency. "After all," Mrs. Darrow notes, "in order to do this masculine thing—I mean, to move out and to achieve in the external world—he simply has had to sacrifice, to neglect or suppress certain parts of his self. For example, some of the research biologists felt they had had to emphasize the more rational, consciously intelligent, tough-minded aspects of their personality. This often meant defending against another whole area having to do with more emotional, softer, less masculine wishes and feelings."

The restlessness and discontent that a man may begin to experience more and more intensively toward the close of his thirties is, in the view of the Levinson team, a forerunner of normal personality growth and change. At this stage, a man begins to feel a new kind of freedom from external pressures: the long work of making an identity and place in the world is almost completed. But at the same time, an often painful process of reevaluation and reappraisal is getting under way. Now he wants to find out who *he* really is, what *he* really wants—and, perhaps, what doors are still left open to him.

This process of self-questioning, affecting not only his view of himself but of those about him, brings with it profound inner changes. These changes may take place quietly, almost unnoticed. The biologists mentioned earlier might, on nearing forty, feel a new desire to be related to *people* rather than ideas or things—and shift undramatically into more administrative jobs. Or, such inner changes might be reflected in a man's profound modification of his own ideas about himself. As one thirty-nine-year-old writer taking part in the study put it: ". . . Phrasing it melodramatically, I feel a weakening of the need to be a great man. And an increasing feeling of: 'Let's just get through this the best way we can. Never mind hitting any home runs; let's just get through the ball game without being beaned.' " He noted that his whole early adult career had been guided by a dream of success and fame, which had never been realized,

but now, ". . . when I think of giving these things up it doesn't pain me any more . . ."

The changes may be more fundamental, as they appeared to be for one forty-four-year-old businessman, whose marriage was flowering after twenty years of what he called "dormancy." As he said, "From an emotional standpoint, ours has probably been a very one-way relationship, with my wife doing most of the giving. I suspect . . . it hasn't gone very far in terms of enrichment. I know I'm the one who's contributed most of the control, kept us on this lousy monotonous plateau. But I'm going through some kind of change, becoming less 'intellectual' about feelings and so on. Like, the other night my wife had her menstrual period, and we got into bed, and well, she was just very nervous. You know, rolling and tossing. I don't know why, but I just started rubbing her back, and soothing her. And then I just held her face to face. I put my arms around her, and we just stayed that way. And this seemed to comfort her quite a bit, and she quieted down and had a good night. . . . You see, I felt this might do her good, and I tried it. Which I'm not sure I would have thought of six months or a year ago. In fact, I suspect a year ago I might have lain there for awhile and then said, 'Well, I'm going to have a cigarette.' And then I'd have gotten a blanket and gone to sleep on the couch . . ."

The mid-life decade, like adolescence, appears to be a crossroads—a time when new personality growth is possible, and some degree of personality change inevitable. A man may now move toward a new kind of intimacy in marriage, toward a greater self-fulfillment in his work life, toward deeper, more realistic relationships with his children. Or, he may be stopped at this point, suffer a developmental defeat. For this period of a man's life holds its threats also: in this decade the incidence of alcoholism, hypochondria, and obesity—all connected to depression—show a marked rise. Sexual difficulties, if they existed before, are exacerbated. The divorce rate leaps. As long ago as 1965, statistics indicated that nearly one-fourth of all persons filing for divorce in this country had been married for longer than fifteen years. And the incidence of marital breakup, in what experts have dubbed the "twenty-year slump," appears to be increasing every year.

What, then, are the specific problems a man is dealing with in this transitional period between early adulthood and middle age? And if he can be expected to emerge from the decade "different," to some degree, in what way is he likely to change?

The clearest and most obvious difficulties a man goes through at this time have to do with the simple fact that he has lost the sense of growing up; he

has begun growing old. He is no longer in the stage of "apprenticeship," of being the young man with promise. As he approaches forty, he moves into a new position. And beyond, as he perceives with a fresh and painful clarity, lies old age—and his own death.

The knowledge that one will someday die is difficult to deal with psychologically. As Freud observed: "No one believes in his own death . . . in the unconscious, everyone is convinced of his own immortality." But death's reality presses on a man now in a host of new ways: through the aging or dying of parents, through the deaths of friends, through obvious signs of his own aging. He must inevitably confront the growing evidence that his control over his own body is limited.

As one forty-four-year-old taking part in the study recalled: ". . . I understood (suddenly, waking up after a party one morning) that I could not, that I did not have an absolute capacity for sleeplessness and alcohol. . . . It was a very dramatic and distinct change, because up until then I could stay up until dawn or 7 or 8 A.M. . . . But in the summer of my thirty-seventh year I realized I could no longer do that. I felt terrible. I got the message very radically. I suddenly realized I was no longer twenty-four years old. I was getting on toward forty."

As the same man related in a subsequent interview: "I tend to notice it in the newspapers nowadays when people my own age die. Which is something you don't seem to remark on much when you're in your thirties. But then, people at that age die in accidents; in their forties they start to keel over from heart attacks. . . . Hardly a day goes by when I don't say—I don't mean it preoccupies me, by any means—but I play the awful game. I'm sure many people do. Where you say: "God, in six years I'll be fifty. . . .""

Here is the way another man, a black industrial worker in his early forties, expressed it: "I'm working in the business, hard. And I'm getting older, and the energy I started with is running out. Sooner or later I'm not going to be able to work as hard, and I really haven't gotten any place. As you get older, you begin to think of yourself as a man in a hurry. The years are going by, and you want to know your life meant something . . ."

Another man, who had thrown over a successful business career a few years earlier in order to go into full-time writing, described himself this way: "I don't make love as much, I play doubles instead of singles. I try to substitute technique for that earlier, animal energy." He often suffers from bouts of insomnia, and "when I'm awake, alone in the night that way, I think about my own death."

The paradox of these years, the time of a man's "prime" and his "fulfillment," is that they bring with them an ineluctable realization of how fleeting are those years, and that prime. It is this new and vivid encounter with Death, taking place at mid-life, that lends the period its painful tone and precipitates its often critical nature.

Another central set of problems has to do with a man's changing experience of fatherhood. During this decade of his life there are generally new, sometimes overwhelming cries and criticisms and demands coming from his own near-adult children. Here, for example, is what four men, chosen at random from the study sample, faced.

An executive: His oldest daughter had just had what he termed a "tantrum" and dropped out of college. His "Number One Son" was not working up to the level of his ability.

An industrial worker: His oldest child, a stepson, "cannot seem to learn . . . He's not as smart as he might be." His own son could get all A's, but "doesn't cooperate . . . seems emotionally unstable, never hears what you say, can't keep his mouth shut."

A novelist: His oldest son, age thirteen, was in a "terror of a rebellion." He was a "dropout," had "run away," was "into drugs," and was doing no work at school.

Another writer: His oldest child, an eighteen-year-old boy, was "tall, handsome, swinging away. . . ." But he was a political revolutionary, had been picked up by the police three times. He was attending a private boarding school: "That is, *when* he is there. . . ."

According to Dr. Edward Klein, one of the three psychologists on the research team, "As father to a baby, you can entertain all kinds of illusions about your own power and omnipotence: there is that child whose very fate depends upon you, whom you're going to mold and shape into some ideal being." But during his children's adolescence, a man must inevitably compare that fantasy with what is now becoming reality—and accept the limited nature of his own influence.

Almost simultaneously, his relationship to his own father is changing. The fathers of the four men quoted earlier, for example, were either dead, frail and helpless, or—in one case—slowly dying. (" 'Painful' is the way I would describe my own feelings. . . . This isn't the man of my childhood.") The man at mid-life thus seems to be caught in a generational cross fire: as well as being father to his own children, he often must be, in effect, father to his aging or dying parents as well.

"The essence of what is happening," observes Dr. Klein, "is that as a man is having to let go of his own dependency, he's getting a lot of new problems and flak from his sons. And by that I don't mean only from his real sons, but his 'symbolic sons' also. Because his paternity, at this point, doesn't extend only to his own children, and perhaps to his parents. It comes to be expected of him by other, younger adults."

That this is so can in itself come as a shock: Many men in their late thirties retain the illusion that they are still young, or, as Klein says with a smile, "simply ageless." A chance word, however, a remark made by a younger colleague, may bring to them the sudden realization that people in their late teens and early twenties see them as vaguely parental—as middle-aged or even old.

A man between thirty-five and forty-five is moving (perhaps feeling shoved) into a variety of new relationships that involve, in the widest sense of the word, "bringing up" the succeeding generation. This is what the psychoanalyst Erik Erikson calls the stage of generativity. Erikson views this development of a newer, more altruistic, more "fathering" stance toward younger adults, as a normal stage of emotional growth. "Individuals who do not develop generativity," he has written, "often begin to indulge themselves as if they were their one and only child."

The difficulty is, however, that assuming fatherhood in its fullest sense involves letting go of certain fantasies about the self. As Dr. Klein puts it, "In a way, this final taking-on of responsibility is like the last bite of the Biblical apple. You're no longer the 'son,' the one who can't do certain forbidden things without full awareness of the consequences: you're the guy who's in charge of the whole show, the one who's entrusted to *take care* of others. The trouble," he adds with a rueful laugh, "is—who wants to let go of the apple?"

Concerns about sexuality—fears about the possibility of waning virility, allusions to worries about declining sexual attractiveness—were another of the major problem areas emerging from the Yale interviews. Less than one third of the men taking part in the study were actually involved in extramarital relationships; but there was much fantasy about possible affairs, and a good deal of psychological conflict around the issue. A number of the men were, for the first time, consciously and seriously considering a relationship with some other woman. Said one man who had recently made a small beginning toward a liaison of this kind: "I haven't had the nerve (to begin a physical sexual affair with her). I set these things up, and then I don't go through with it . . . (but) I cannot pass her house, I cannot think of her without the most excitement and an energy change coming over me."

Another man described the way in which his thought processes were diverted by fantasies of women. Even at home, while telling a story to his children, he found that a woman often appeared on the horizon of the tale, interjecting herself between the "King" and the "Queen," and laying claim to the male. "I'm rarely at peace inside," he remarked. "What I'm torn about is whether my commitment to my wife is the thing I really want . . ."

According to Dr. Ray Walker, psychiatric resident working on the Yale team, the commonness of sexual fantasy among men in this decade is related to a heightened sense of loneliness. For most men this doesn't have to do simply with a search for sexual variety or adventure. The whole question of one's marriage and family are part and parcel of the far more general question of one's life. And in the midlife period, when a man is searching for goals which are more true to his inner self, then he may come face to face with something fairly disquieting: an awareness of what is missing in his relationship with his wife."

(These remarks were virtually paraphrased by a biologist taking part in the study: "I feel much more lonely now than I did in the earlier years of marriage. There is this feeling I have, yes, that maybe out there there is someone who might share a more intellectual kind of life with me.")

Dr. Walker notes that during the first half of a man's life his dominant feminine image is related to the ideal of the Mother: "the Nurturer, the one who feeds him, builds up his ego, makes his life easier." At the time when a young man chooses a wife, this feminine ideal prevails strongly in his unconscious thought: He projects onto the woman he marries many of the wishes and illusions and feelings that relate to the archetype of the Mother.

But, as he approaches middle age, his overriding feminine image begins to change: He now wants to relate to a woman much less as Mother and far more as Lover and Companion. As this change occurs, Dr. Walker explains, a man becomes ready to stop projecting his own more childish wishes and feelings upon his wife. At this point, the entire relationship will either go through a phase of restructuring and change, or the husband will feel "stuck." He will begin to experience his wife in a new way: "She'll remain the Mother, but now it will be the Dark Mother—the negative feminine, the one who is holding him back from realizing himself. At this juncture, she starts becoming in his mind, at least—the personification of the Entrapper."

In an interview with a forty-one-year-old executive who described his marriage as "solid, one that would go on forever," the coexistence of conscious loyalty and an unconscious movement in a totally different direction, were demonstrated in a striking way: "My wife isn't an oversexed individual," he began comfortably. "I think we've got a good match there. If it wasn't, either one way or another, my attentions would have turned a long time ago. Still . . . you know, sometimes I see a movie or read a book and I think, Gee, she's frigid compared to what I'm seeing, or this thing I'm reading. . . . But in my evaluation, she's not a frigid person. She has deep feelings, she's warm, she's a devoted mother. . . . (But) you never know what will happen as you get older. They say once the kids grow up, then divorces occur. I can't predict that something won't happen once the kids are gone . . ."

Perhaps the most fascinating and suggestive phenomenon to emerge from the study thus far has been the appearance, in the case histories of most of the men interviewed, of a kind of relationship that the Yale group has come to call the "mentor relationship." Almost every man who had achieved a degree of success in the world had had, during the period of his early adult life, one or more "mentor" figures.

A mentor, explains Dr. Braxton Mc-Kee, who is the only practicing psychiatrist in the study group, "is a person who is at least a bit older, usually eight to ten years, and who has some expert knowledge or wisdom, or personal qualities or skills, which he offers to share with the younger man. A mentor could be someone like a professor, a more established executive, an older relative —but he is usually someone connected with a guy's occupation."

For the younger man, the mentor represents a point of development that is higher than his own, and to which he himself aspires. The mentor is in this sense a parental figure, and yet he is also a friend. He is someone who, by his attitude, more or less says to the younger man: "Here is the world, of which I am a part; and into which I invite you—to become my peer and colleague." He offers, as the actual parent never can, the possibility of a real equality with him.

"Generally speaking," observes Mc-Kee, "it is assumed that once a person separates from his father, and leaves home, he is independent. But that's simply not true. What seems to be consistently overlooked is the parental function of the organization the man becomes involved with—and also the fact that, despite his newfound 'independence,' he starts almost immediately to seek out these semiparental mentor figures. And develops much further, by the way, if he succeeds in finding them."

Mentor relationships, the Levinson group believes, may be a crucial part of early adult development—possibly *the* crucial part. A break with the mentor is very often the signal that a man has come to the third stage of early adult life, which the researchers call "Becoming One's Own Man."

In this phase, a man does just that —he assumes more responsibility for himself in the world, insists on speaking with his own voice, becomes more autonomous, less dependent, more authoritative in his work and family life. This new state of being is brought about in part by external happenings: He may have just reached the top of the ladder in his job, received his professorship, won a prize. On the other hand, the new feeling he has about himself can also be self-generated. Explains Dr. McKee: "For a sizable number of individuals, there just seems to be this sense that one ought to be making a step toward something a little better, more responsible, or creative. Something that comes out of a man's own inner goals—perhaps a new kind of job he goes after now. There is this sudden reaching toward something that is in some way different—independent of the tasks he's been working on, and independent of the mentor."

After "Getting into the Adult World" —the period of exploration—and "Settling Down"—the phase of intense commitment to building an identity and a life for himself—"Becoming One's Own Man" marks the conclusion of a man's struggle to adapt to and conquer his external environment. It sets the stage for the more internal battles and self-questionings that follow—for the period of crisis and change that characterize the mid-life transition.

A flurry of letters always reaches the Yale group's research offices shortly after any public mention of their project. Says Maria Levinson, one of the team's psychologists and wife of its director, "Most of the mail we receive is fairly typical. Wives who write in— from 'the two of us'—on behalf of a husband who seems to have caught some kind of virus, something which attacks men at mid-life. The wife's initial response is often a kind of frenzy of mothering: Her husband is sick with this thing and her question is, how can she cure him?"

What if a woman has lived happily with a man for some fifteen or twenty years and he suddenly begins changing. What can she make of it?

"She should view it as a stage in the developmental process," Mrs. Levinson says, "not as a kind of flu. As a period during which a man is going to go through some painful changing of gears. When he s starting to experience himself as 'older,' and having come to terms with that, and with the task of making way for the upcoming generation. In brief, as a time when a serious transition is being made—which involves feelings of unsettlement, and sometimes turmoil."

But what advice might one offer to a woman whose husband is going through this period of turmoil?

"In some of our cases," Mrs. Levinson remarks thoughtfully, "it was the wife, not the husband, who upset the equilibrium, who made demands for him to get out of his rut and start changing. In general, however, what she does depends very much on the stage she herself is at—and on her capacity to tolerate her husband's depression. And, of course, it depends on the amount of understanding and intimacy that has existed between them.

"You know," she observes, "in the love of young adults there is a great deal of projection and fantasy: A young wife projects onto her husband many of her feelings about her father, and a young husband projects onto her his feelings and fantasies about his mother. But now, in the mid-life period, when one is being freed of many of these earlier illusions, the question is: Can that younger love become something more adult? If there is good communication between the two people, then they are probably developing in parallel ways. In that case, there will be change on both parts: they'll reintegrate at a higher, more honest level."

But suppose a man becomes disturbed and won't talk about it to his wife? Suppose he can't show his weakness to her? Or that his dissatisfaction with himself has something to do with a dissatisfaction with her—*and he finds some other woman to talk to?*

"You are not talking about something so simple as mere dissatisfaction," Mrs. Levinson says firmly. "You are talking about an existential condition. A man comes to feel disappointed, humiliated, violated by what he has done with his life and the part he feels his wife has played in this process. What can *she* do, if she doesn't happen to feel the same way—if she feels, instead, that their life is tolerable if not ideal, and if she feels that he, in seeking an illusory change, is betraying her and abandoning their children?

"To the extent that the wife is in the grip of feelings of moral outrage and victimization by him," she continues, "there is probably nothing she can do to keep the marriage together. And perhaps, if they have been moving apart over a period of years, the marriage isn't worth saving; it might be liberating for both, and a relief for the children, if they simply went their separate ways. A real reconciliation would have to involve important changes in the relationship; the choice would be between renewal or stagnation.

"If a man can leave his marriage with little or no pain," she adds, "then obviously it has become empty, without real meaning for either partner. But in our experience, where a man seriously considered breaking up his family, he went through enormous suffering.

"In such a case," Mrs. Levinson says, "it would not be enough for his wife to be sympathetic, or to try to make herself more 'alluring.' She would have to be prepared to grasp the magnitude of his despair, to share in it in whatever ways she could, to come to terms more fully with her own suffering, and to see their joint plight as containing also the possibility for their further development."

The crisis that confronts a man at mid-life is, by its very nature, a turning point for his wife as well. It almost goes without saying that the more fully they both understand the changes, the better they will be able to weather them. This decade by no means represents the beginning of the end: It often signals a movement into something newer, stronger, and more profound for both partners.

31

By Bernice L. Neugarten

A New Look at Menopause

IN THE PAST FEW YEARS advances in medical and biological sciences have led to a new point of view toward medical treatment of so-called menopausal symptoms in middle-aged women. In addition to the growing medical literature, a number of popular books and a proliferation of articles in women's magazines have reported the accumulating evidence on the value of estrogen-replacement therapy, not only for the treatment of temporary symptoms but for long-term gains in health.

Dr. Robert A. Wilson, for example, is one of the new "extremists." His book, *Feminine Forever*, urges that the menopause be regarded as a hormone-deficiency disease, to be treated and cured like any other disease, and that estrogen be given to the vast majority of women past 40. Dr. M. Edward Davis of Chicago's Lying-In Hospital is another medical authority whose research over the past 30 years has led him to a similar position. While the few investigators whose views on this topic mark them as innovators are gaining widespread attention, they constitute a small minority. The majority of physicians have not yet relinquished the more traditional view that menopause is a natural process, one that is best not interfered with, and only a few women currently are finding their way to physicians' offices to ask for prescriptions for estrogen.

As is true of many other medical and psychological problems, the adoption of new practices depends upon a wide network of attitudes and beliefs: in the present instance, upon attitudes toward menstruation as well as menopause, toward sexuality, femininity, and appropriate sex-role behavior in women of various ages. The extent to which the new ideas are accepted and acted upon depends, of course, upon the speed with which attitudes can be expected to change both in women themselves and in the physicians who treat them.

This leads, then, to the fields of psychology in general and of attitude measurement in particular, fields which have

thus far produced no systematic studies of the belief-systems that surround the menopause or of its psychological significance to women.

The terms *climacterium* and *menopause* often are used interchangeably, even though there is a worthwhile distinction between them. The term *climacterium* denotes the gradual involution of the ovaries and the various biological processes associated with that involution. The climacterium usually encompasses several years, during which women lose the ability to reproduce. The menopause, the cessation of menses, is but one sign, though the most readily identifiable sign, of the climacterium.

The term *menopause* is more familiar and has come to be used loosely to refer to the wide array of biological and psychological symptoms presumed to be associated with the climacterium. More colloquially still, women refer to "the change of life," and middle-aged women speak of being "in" the change, or not yet in it, or past it, implying thereby that they are referring not merely to the cessation of menses but to the whole period of the climacterium.

Although there are wide individual variations, the average age at which menstruation ceases is a little under 50. (In a national survey of women in the United States during 1960-62, 50 per cent reported that by age 49 their menstrual periods had stopped.) In some women the menstrual cycle ceases very abruptly, but more often its disappearance is gradual. A period or two is skipped, then menstruation recurs more or less normally from one to several times, then there is again a period of amenorrhea which may last several months, and so on until complete cessation. This "dodging period" of the menopause may go on for a year or two, sometimes longer. The amount and duration of the menstrual flow may be normal until the very end, but frequently there is a gradual diminution of both.

The loss of the childbearing function is brought about by progressive and ir-

reversible changes which occur in the ovaries as a result of that mysterious process called aging. While aging itself is by no means understood, it is nevertheless well established that the human ovary has a functional life of about 35 years. Over this period of time, the ability of the ova to mature gradually diminishes, and finally ovulation stops. The production of ovarian hormones decreases, and then falls below the level capable of producing bleeding from the walls of the uterus.

The underlying hormonal activities are extraordinarily complex, and various endocrine glands are involved in the maintenance and then the disappearance of the menstrual cycle; in brief, we can say that with age the ovary loses its function of controlling certain activities of the pituitary gland. Certain hormones produced by the pituitary then rise to high levels, affecting the vasomotor system, which in turn produces certain physiological symptoms, primarily the so-called "hot flash" or "hot flush" that is regarded as the most characteristic symptom of the menopause.

Over time the lowered level of estrogen in postmenopausal women has widespread effects, some of which are damaging to the cardiovascular system, the skin, and the musculature and bone structure of the body, as well as to the reproductive organs.

Replacement of estrogen by artificial means (usually by oral administration) is not new in the field of medicine, and it long has been used by at least some gynecologists for the relief of so-called menopausal symptoms, especially the discomfort of the hot flush. What *is* new is the evidence that long-term administration of estrogen offers other benefits for middle-aged and older women, particularly by countering atherosclerotic changes in the blood vessels and by preventing osteoporosis, the brittleness of bones. The once-held opinion that estrogen, if used continuously, might be a carcinogenic agent has been pretty well disproved. Dr. Davis, for example, has

	Per cent
The worst thing about middle age	
Losing your husband	52
Getting older	18
Cancer	16
Children leaving home	9
Menopause	4
Change in sexual feelings and behavior	1
What I dislike most about being middle-aged	
Getting older	35
Lack of energy	21
Poor health or illness	15
Feeling useless	2
None of these	27
The best thing about the menopause	
Not having to worry about getting pregnant	30
Not having to bother with menstruation	44
Better relationship with husband	11
Greater enjoyment of sex life	3
None of these	12
The worst thing about the menopause	
Not knowing what to expect	26
The discomfort and pain	19
Sign of getting older	17
Loss of enjoyment in sexual relations	4
Not being able to have more children	4
None of these	30
How menopause affects a woman's appearance	
Negative changes	50
No effect	43
Positive changes	1
No response	6
How menopause affects a woman's physical and emotional health	
Negative changes	32
No effect	58
Positive change or improvement	10
How menopause affects a woman's sexual relations	
Sexual relations become more important	18
No effect	65
Sexual relations become less important	17

INTERVIEWS   When middle-aged women were interviewed about their attitudes toward menopause — their own and in general — they gave these responses.

	Per cent who checked "agree"
Menopause is an unpleasant experience for a woman.	58
Women should expect some trouble during the menopause.	59
Menopause is a disturbing thing which most women naturally dread.	57
The thing that causes women all their trouble at menopause is something they can't control — changes inside their bodies.	78
Women often get self-centered at the time of the menopause.	67
Women worry about losing their minds during the menopause.	51
A woman in menopause is apt to do crazy things she herself doesn't understand.	53
Menopause is a mysterious thing which most women don't understand.	59
Women are generally calmer and happier after the change of life than before.	75
After the change of life, a woman feels freer to do things for herself.	74
After the change of life, a woman has a better relationship with her husband.	62

CHECKLISTS   When the women were asked to check "agree" or "disagree" on an attitude check list, their responses were considerably more negative than they had been in interviews.

been following a group of women on estrogen over many years, some for as long as 28 years, and reports only favorable outcomes. In another recent study, the very small but measurable decrements in height that occur in old age (which reflect loss of calcium from the bones and consequent realignment of the vertebrae) were halted in a group of older women to whom estrogen was administered in therapeutic dosages.

What remains now is an educational problem: to inform large numbers of women and large numbers of physicians of the benefits of estrogen replacement and to alter long-held contrary attitudes about letting nature take its course. The new information will be of maximum value if acted upon by women relatively early in their lives, that is, for the average woman, in her late 40's. But it can be predicted confidently that the 45-year-old woman will be quick or slow to act, depending not only upon the extent to which she clings to the folklore but upon the extent to which she suffers from menopausal symptoms.

Attempts to delineate the symptoms characteristic of the menopausal phase of the climacterium have aroused considerable debate with regard to the very existence of a menopausal syndrome. For some women, the so-called menopausal symptoms (hot flushes, tingling sensations, vertigo, insomnia, headaches, irritability, anxiety, depression) occur early, before the actual cessation of menses; for other women, they coincide with the menopause; for others, they do not appear until several years later. Still other women seem to remain free of such symptoms altogether.

Symptoms ascribed to menopausal change by one or another investigator over the years have embraced every body system and a good portion of all the vasomotor, cardiovascular, metabolic, sensory, digestive, skeletal, muscular, glandular, central nervous system, mental, emotional, and temperamental manifestations known to medicine and to psychology. At the same time, other investigators object to the inclusion of symptoms which may be due to coincidental pathologic changes, to concomitant cardiovascular change, to other age-related changes, or to social and psychological stresses; they hold that only the hot flush is to be regarded as a true menopausal symptom—and even the hot flush occurs in women of other ages. Some of the latter group maintain that the menopausal syndrome

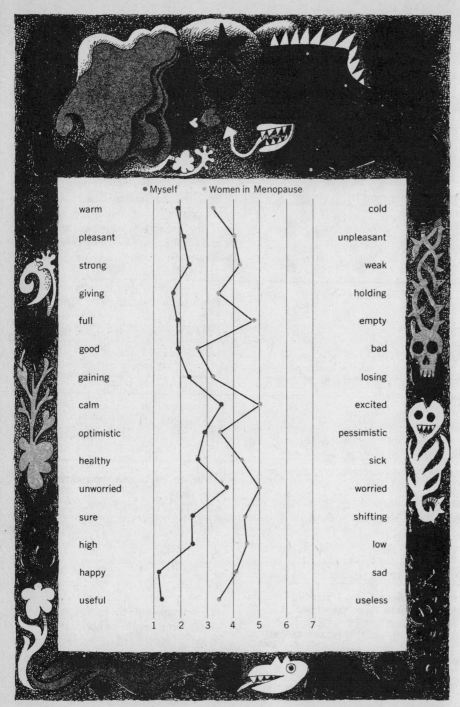

	• Myself	• Women in Menopause	
warm			cold
pleasant			unpleasant
strong			weak
giving			holding
full			empty
good			bad
gaining			losing
calm			excited
optimistic			pessimistic
healthy			sick
unworried			worried
sure			shifting
high			low
happy			sad
useful			useless

1 2 3 4 5 6 7

PROFILES When the women were asked to indicate their own position and that of menopausal women in general, they consistently showed more positive attitudes toward themselves.

is an artifact created by the traditional method of clinical history-taking, which places undue emphasis upon those symptoms toward which the physician directs the patient's attention.

Most of the research evidence on this point has been guided by one or another of two points of view regarding etiology: an endocrine-factor theory, which attributes menopausal symptoms to the disturbance in hormonal balance, and an emotional-factor theory, which em-phasizes the premenopausal personality of the patient. The emotional-factor theory says, in short, that only those women who are so predisposed, on the basis of earlier psychosexual trauma, will suffer with menopause.

The Lack of Evidence

In truth, there is little evidence for evaluating either point of view. Although there is much medical literature regarding the symptoms of the meno-pause and their treatment, the studies have been confined largely to clinical or problem cases—those that come to the attention of the physician or, more rarely, the psychotherapist. The conspicuous lack of research regarding the psychological effects of the climacterium upon normal women is due in part to the fact that middle age is a period in the life cycle that has been largely neglected by psychologists.

Accurate information is lacking with regard to the *incidence* of symptoms, let alone their significance, for these same reasons. One study carried out in England in the 1930's on a large community population indicated that 85 per cent of women had some symptoms at menopause, but that only 10 per cent were incapacitated on one or more occasions. More recent estimates are that perhaps 75 per cent of all women experience some disturbance or discomfort during the climacterium, even though, in the absence of disease, relatively few seem to bring these troubles to the doctor.

Some psychologists have written that, because it is a visible sign that her reproductive life has come to an end, the menopause is a critical event in the life of the middle-aged woman and a major threat to her adjustment. Some psychotherapists have observed that the menopause presents a particular threat to a woman's self-concept if reproduction and motherhood have been her primary symbols of worth; or if the symptoms provoked by internal hormonal changes themselves create undue emotional tensions or anxiety; or if the menopause signifies a loss of sexual attractiveness or sexual interest.

One noted woman psychoanalyst, Helene Deutsch, described the mastering of psychological reactions to the menopause as one of the most difficult tasks of a woman's life. Another woman psychoanalyst, Therese Benedek, on the other hand, has described it as a developmental phase in which energy used earlier for coping with the fluctuations of the menstrual cycle and for reproductive tasks is released for new forms of psychological and social expansion. But these opinions too are based upon those few middle-aged women who have made their way to the psychotherapist's office or to the psychoanalyst's couch.

The significance of the menopause has been defined but hazily, too, through studies of women who are hospitalized for what loosely is called involutional depression or involutional psychosis. As is true with so many psychiatric categories, the label means different things to different diagnosticians. More important, the relationship between endocrine changes and mental illness remains obscure. Thus it is not clear whether, even in the small number who are hospitalized, the climacterium has been truly influential, or whether these women's illnesses were triggered instead by a constellation of social and psychological changes in their lives.

A large proportion of women have an artificial rather than a natural menopause, as the result of a surgical operation. The striking statistic here, based on data from the National Health Survey, is 25 to 30 per cent among American women presently aged 50 to 64. Hysterectomy, the removal of the uterus, is the most common procedure involved. Because these operations, whether remedial or preventive, are associated with disease, and usually with malignancy, women in whom artificial menopause occurs can be presumed to have quite different psychological reactions from those women in whom the menopause is a natural event.

Even leaving aside the number in whom disease is either present or suspected, however, the psychological effects of the natural menopause are clearly difficult to assess.

What Do the Women Say?

We began our own studies by gathering a large number of exploratory interviews. Middle-aged women from varying backgrounds were asked to assess their own climacteric status (to state whether they regarded themselves as premenopausal, "in" the change of life, or postmenopausal). Each woman was then asked for the basis of this assessment. What, if any, symptoms had she experienced? What had her anticipations of menopause been and why, what had she heard and read about it, what changes had she observed in other women (mother, sisters, friends)? What did she regard as the worst and the best aspects of menopause? What, if any, changes in her life did she attribute to it?

It soon was apparent that women varied greatly in both their attitudes and their experiences. Some, particularly at higher educational levels, vehemently assured the interviewer that the menopause was without any social or psychological import. Indeed, they said, the enlightened woman does not fear nor—

even if she suffers considerable physical discomfort—does she complain about the menopause.

"Why make any fuss about it?"

"I just made up my mind I'd walk right through it, and I did."

"I saw women complaining, and I thought I would never be so ridiculous. I would just sit there and perspire, if I had to. At times you do feel terribly warm. I would sit and feel the water on my head, and wonder how red I looked. But I wouldn't worry about it, because it is a natural thing, and why get worried about it? I remember one time, in the kitchen, I had a terrific hot flush . . . I went to look at myself in the mirror. I didn't even look red, so I thought, 'All right . . . the next time I'll just sit there, and who will notice? And if someone notices I won't even care . . .'"

A few confessed to considerable fear.

"I would think of my mother and the trouble she went through, and I wondered if I would come through it whole or in pieces."

"I knew two women who had nervous breakdowns, and I worried about losing my mind."

"I thought menopause would be the beginning of the end . . . a gradual senility closing over, like the darkness."

"I was afraid we couldn't have sexual relations after the menopause—and my husband thought so, too."

"When I think of how I used to worry! You wish someone would tell you—but you're too embarrassed to ask anyone . . ."

Other women seemed to be repeating the advice found in women's magazines and in newspaper columns:

"I just think if a woman looks for trouble, she'll find it."

"If you fill your day with constructive things—like trying to help other people—then it seems to me nothing can enter a mind already filled."

"If you keep busy, you won't think about it, and you'll be all right . . ."

Underlying this variety of attitudes were two common themes. First, whether they made much or little of its importance, middle-aged women were eager to talk about the menopause. Many volunteered that they seldom dis-

cussed it with other women, that they wanted more information and more communication. It seemed that the menopause, unlike menstruation and certainly unlike pregnancy and childbirth, was a relatively taboo topic, one which did not often provide material for the typical coffee-klatsch with friends and neighbors or for conversations between husbands and wives. In other words, there seem to be neither the informal nor the formal social supports around the menopausal woman that are so strikingly evident around the pregnant woman and the new mother. A few women went on to comment that their physicians had brushed aside their questions and their complaints, saying, "Oh, it's just the menopause. You must expect these things. You'll get over it."

The second thing which impressed us in these early interviews was that, although many women professed not to believe what they termed "old wives' tales," most women nevertheless had heard about the "dangers" of the menopause and could recite them easily: menopause often results in mental breakdown; it marks the end of a woman's sexual attractiveness as well as her desires; and so on. Many women used the "I have a friend" approach, saying that although they themselves had neither fears nor major discomforts, they knew other women who had many irrational fears or who had suffered greatly.

We interpreted such responses as indicative, at least in part, of the psychological mechanism of projection. That is, these women might be attributing to others unpleasant feelings, problems, or anxieties which they were unwilling or unable to acknowledge in themselves.

After the exploratory interviews, we selected for more careful study a group of 100 white women aged 45 to 55. These women were drawn from lists of mothers of recent graduates from two public high schools in the Chicago metropolitan area, one of them a high school in a working-class area, the second in an upper middle-class area. None of these women had had surgical or artificial menopause, and all were in relatively good health. All were living with their husbands, and most had at least one younger child at home. Two-thirds were housewives, the rest working at part- or full-time jobs. Two-thirds were Protestants of varying degrees of devoutness and the other one-third included Catholics, a few Jews, and a few agnostics.

Based on subsequent interview material, these women turned out to be divided about equally among the three climacteric statuses, with 28 reporting themselves to be premenopausal; 41, menopausal; and 31, postmenopausal (that is, having had no menstrual periods within at least the past two years). It also turned out that climacteric status did not differentiate among this group of women on any of a large number of social or psychological measures, except for reported frequency and **severity of menopausal symptoms** (where, naturally enough, symptoms were reported more frequently by the menopausal subgroup than by the other two subgroups).

This last fact led us to conclude that climacteric status as we had defined it is relatively insignificant to women aged 45 to 55, and that instead women in this age group regard themselves as falling within a general life period during which the climacterium occurs. In other words, the single index of presence or absence of the menstrual cycle was imbedded in a larger context of biological, psychological, and social cues which together signified movement from one life stage to another. In this sense, the 100 women demonstrated greater similarities than differences and can be regarded as a single "climacteric" group.

Wishing to follow up, in particular, the implication of a projection of attitudes, we used various techniques from the psychologist's stock in trade: a free-flowing interview, conversational in tone; a formal check list, asking for agreement or disagreement with a set of prestructured statements; and certain indirect methods of asking for comparisons between the self and other women.

The variety of approaches was designed to elicit both overt and covert attitudes. As is well known, answers to psychologists' questions depend upon the form in which the questions are asked. Sometimes there are limits imposed by the measuring instrument itself which prevent people from giving an accurate report of their perceptions and feelings. Sometimes the individual gives "socially desirable" responses to direct questions but then proceeds to respond to indirect questions in ways which are more self-disclosing.

What They Say in Interviews

The interviews began with questions regarding middle age, the changes the women had recognized in themselves over the past ten years, and their present concerns and gratifications. Compared with other events of middle adulthood, most women tended to minimize the significance of the menopause in producing anxiety or stress. When asked what changes in middle age worried them most, only four women out of the 100 mentioned the menopause. More than half indicated instead that their greatest concern was widowhood. For the others, it was, generally, getting older, or fear of cancer, or children leaving home. When asked what they disliked most about middle age, most women repeated "just getting older," or cited lack of energy, or poorer health. Only a few attributed these changes to the menopause.

When the focus was narrowed further, and the women were asked to identify the most positive and the most negative aspects of the menopause itself, the responses become more differentiated. Almost three-fourths agreed that not having to worry about getting pregnant or not having to bother any more with menstruation was a decided advantage. A small number said that the menopause brought about a better relationship with their husbands or greater enjoyment of sexual relations. Typical responses were: "Believe me, I wouldn't want a 'change of life' baby! That's a fear we all have"; "I'm so happy about not menstruating any more, I could dance with joy. I was looking forward to it for years"; "It's great not having to bother with menstruation. I'm old enough and I've had all the children I want." Only 12 of the 100 women were unable to see any gain or advantage.

On the negative side, most of the women complained that the worst things about the menopause were not knowing what to expect, or the pain and discomfort, or the fact that the menopause is a sign of getting older. Only a few women regarded loss of sexual enjoyment or the inability to have more children as being important. And only a few made such comments as "The worst thing is the tension that builds up. You don't have the release you used to have from the menstrual period"; "I expected the worst and I got it. One minute you feel fine and free as air and all of a sudden you get terribly nervous"; "The thing you fear is that you're going out of your mind. Sometimes you get so depressed!" A sizable proportion said they could think of no particular losses. Some went on, instead, to report an improvement in state of mind or state of health. "Since

my menopause I feel like a teen-ager again. I can remember my mother saying that, too. After the menopause she really became vigorous, and I can say the same about myself. I'm never tired now." Another said, "I had been extremely nervous all my life, but now I've changed for the better."

Later in the interviewing sessions, each woman was asked to describe the frequency and intensity of her own symptoms. Some reported many somatic and psychological symptoms and others reported very few, but there was no consistent relationship between severity of symptoms reported and negativity of attitudes expressed about the menopause in general or about its overall importance. Some women reported great discomfort but at the same time made light of the importance of the menopause; others did the reverse.

A lack of relationship between attitudes and actual physical or emotional status is by no means limited, of course, to middle-aged women. The same general finding often has been made before, and it has emerged again in a recent study of pregnant women, in which positive and negative attitudes toward pregnancy were found to be unrelated to the severity of physical complications surrounding the pregnancy.

In part, this lack of relationship may reflect the tenacity of belief-systems that are formed before the actual occurrence of an event like pregnancy or menopause and are maintained even after personal experiences which may be contrary to one's anticipations. One mode of reconciling attitude and experience may be the projection that we have been suggesting here; for example, a woman may anticipate difficulty with the menopause, fail to experience it, and then attribute difficulty to other women instead. If this is so, then projection probably includes at least two components: the tendency to deny unpleasant feelings in the self even when they exist; and the tendency, when no unpleasant feelings do arise, to regard oneself as an exception and go on believing that the rule fits other people instead. In either instance, the general belief-system may persist relatively unaltered.

Although most women minimized the negative aspects of their own menopause, they responded somewhat differently when asked about changes attributable to the menopause in other women. These questions were deliberately worded more indirectly, and the responses began in turn to have a projective quality. For example, when asked how the menopause affects a woman's appearance ("a" woman, not necessarily oneself), half the women attributed to the menopause undesirable changes in weight, skin texture, hair color, and other physical characteristics. When asked about physical and emotional health, one-third of the women came forth with various lists of negative changes: "I've noticed that many women go to the hospital for operations at this time"; "Most women become irritable"; "I guess it's really a desperate time for many women, emotionally as well as physically."

Even here, however, the responses of the group as a whole did not show a marked shift toward the negative. Almost half the group maintained that changes in appearance in other women were coincidental with, but not attributable to, the menopause. As one woman put it, "In my circle, a woman keeps up her appearance from the time she's young until the day she dies. The menopause has nothing to do with it." And a majority maintained that any changes in the physical health or emotional status of women were idiosyncratic, related not to the climacteric itself but to other types of illness or to a reduced capacity to tolerate stress generally. "A complainer complains about the menopause, just like anything else. She can always find something to worry about."

Similarly, most of these women maintained that there was no predictable relationship between the climacterium and changes in a woman's sexual behavior, saying instead that alterations in sexual activity were a function of the woman's attitudes towards sexuality and of her earlier patterns of sexual behavior. (Of the 35 women in this study who indicated that there was likely to be some change in sexual activity as a result of the climacterium, half took the view that sexual activity becomes less important; the other half said that sex relations become more enjoyable and more important.)

What They Say on Check Lists

The general picture shifted when the form of the inquiry shifted. We had devised a check list of attitudes toward menopause in order to provide a different order of data from that obtained from the more open-ended interview questions. The statements on the check list were culled from our earlier explora-

tory interviews, from the medical and psychological literature, and from folklore regarding the menopause.

Each woman was asked to check whether she agreed or disagreed with each statement. The statements were worded in terms of "other women" or "women in general" rather than in terms of "self." The check list included items that concerned feeling states (feeling better, feeling depressed); the temporary nature of the menopause and the possibility of recovery and relief thereafter; the extent of discontinuity or change produced by the menopause; the degree of control women have over their symptoms; the nature and extent of real or imagined losses associated with the menopause; the degree of unpredictability of behavior; and changes in sexual interest or sexual behavior. [See illustration page 44, bottom]

Responses from these 100 women showed a less positive set of attitudes than had been expressed in the earlier interviews. Now the majority viewed the menopause as a disagreeable, disturbing, depressing experience, and as an unpredictable and mysterious event. Half went so far as to agree that women worry about losing their minds during the menopause, a fairly strong statement. Furthermore, by attributing recovery to the postmenopausal period, these women seemed to be saying that the menopausal period itself is burdensome and upsetting. It is true that responses to certain other items on the check list were more favorable than these, but our overall conclusion was that underlying negative attitudes were breaking through on this instrument and that it was easier for many of these women to express themselves negatively —and perhaps in ways they regarded as unacceptable—when the questions were presented in this less direct, less personal fashion. Many, though not all, seemed to feel safer about acknowledging unenlightened, even superstitious, beliefs which they otherwise disowned.

What They Say Indirectly

With a third method of inquiry, the picture shifted further. Each woman was handed a sheet of paper with the word "myself" written at the top, followed by 15 pairs of bipolar adjectives such as pleasant-unpleasant, worried-unworried, strong-weak. She was asked to place a check mark on a line between the two words in each pair to indicate where she thought she belonged between the

two extremes. She then was handed another sheet of paper with the same pairs of adjectives, but this time with the phrase "women in menopause" at the top of the page, and she was asked to make the same type of assessments — did she regard menopausal women as being relatively pleasant or unpleasant, worried or unworried, and so on?

In this set of data there was one striking consistency. All the women rated themselves more favorably than they rated "women in menopause" [See illustration page 45]. Here again is a phenomenon familiar to psychologists, for people questioned this way often tend to put their best foot forward, so to speak. It is, however, the consistency with which these assessments differentiate between the self and other women which is noteworthy here. We interpreted these differences as further evidence of projection, and as confirming the ambivalence of attitudes regarding menopause.

Psychologists always are plagued (or should be) with the problem of generalizing their findings to groups they have not studied. It is very likely that belief-systems regarding the menopause would be found to vary according to many factors. Single or childless women may be different from this group of mothers. Women whose menopause has been induced surgically are likely to be different. In addition, women's attitudes probably vary with educational level, with ethnic background, and with religious beliefs. We have some evidence from the present study, for instance, that women with high-school educations or less are more anxious about the menopause than women who have attended college. There is also good evidence that the frequency of surgically induced menopause is higher, nationwide, among Negro women than among white. This fact may reflect differences in health conditions and perhaps also differences in the medical services now extended to different racial and socioeconomic groups; it probably influences attitudes toward both artificial and natural menopause in both Negro and white women.

In all, the study reported here is a relatively modest one. It does demonstrate, however, some of the complex and ambivalent attitudes that come into play when a woman picks up a newspaper and reads about estrogen-replacement therapy. If the prevailing attitude is "It's not me who needs help; it's the other women," and if anxiety rises and denial operates, then not all women are likely to reach for the telephone to call their physicians.

To restate the obvious, women (like men) have complex attitudes; accordingly, they (like men) behave in complex ways. Attitudes toward the menopause and the use of medical services for the treatment of menopausal symptoms will depend upon changes in the vast network of attitudes that surrounds the process of aging, sexuality, and the increasing freedom of middle-aged women. The newspaper columnist, the professional educator, and the adult counselor, along with the physician and the psychologist, can help bring about these changes. The eagerness for information on the part of the middle-aged woman will speed change, too. And finally, as longevity increases, the menopause is likely to become less closely associated with old age and thus to lose some of its negative connotations.

32

By ELLIOTT JAQUES

DEATH AND THE MID-LIFE CRISIS

In the course of the development of the individual there are critical phases which have the character of change points, or periods of rapid transition. Less familiar perhaps, though nonetheless real, are the crises which occur around the age of 35—which I shall term the mid-life crisis—and at full maturity around the age of 65. It is the mid-life crisis with which I shall deal in this paper.

When I say that the mid-life crisis occurs around the age of 35, I mean that it takes place in the middle-thirties, that the process of transition runs on for some years, and that the exact period will vary among individuals. The transition is often obscured in women by the proximity of the onset of changes connected with the menopause. In the case of men, the change has from time to time been referred to as the male climacteric, because of the reduction in the intensity of sexual behaviour which often occurs at that time.

Crisis in Genius

I first became aware of this period as a critical stage in development when I noticed a marked tendency towards crisis in the creative work of great men in their middle and late thirties. It is clearly expressed by Richard Church in his autobiography *The Voyage Home*:

There seems to be a biological reason for men and women, when they reach the middle thirties, finding themselves beset with misgivings, agonizing inquiries, and a loss of zest. Is it that state which the medieval schoolmen called *accidie*, the cardinal sin of spiritual sloth? I believe it is.

This crisis may express itself in three different ways: the creative career may simply come to an end, either in a drying-up of creative work, or in actual death; the creative capacity may begin to show and express itself for the first time; or a decisive change in the quality and content of creativeness may take place.

Perhaps the most striking phenomenon is what happens to the death rate among creative artists. I had got the impression that the age of 37 seemed to figure pretty prominently in the death of individuals of this category. This impression was upheld by taking a random sample of some 310 painters, composers, poets, writers, and sculptors, of undoubted greatness or of genius. The death rate shows a sudden jump between 35 and 39, at which period it is much above the normal death rate. The group includes Mozart, Raphael, Chopin, Rimbaud, Purcell, Baudelaire, Watteau. . . . There is then a big drop below the normal death rate between the ages of 40 and 44, followed by a return to the normal death rate pattern in the late forties. The closer one keeps to genius in the sample, the more striking and clearcut is this spiking of the death rate in mid-life.

The change in creativity which occurs during this period can be seen in the lives of countless artists. Bach, for example, was mainly an organist until his cantorship at Leipzig at 38, at which time he began his colossal achievements as a composer. Rossini's life is described in the following terms:

His comparative silence during the period 1832–1868 (i.e. from 40 to his death at 74) makes his biography like the narrative of two lives—swift triumph, and a long life of seclusion.

Racine had thirteen years of continuous success culminating in *Phèdre* at the age of 38; he then produced nothing for some twelve years. The characteristic work of Goldsmith, Constable, and Goya emerged between the ages of 35 and 38. By the age of 43 Ben Jonson had produced all the plays worthy of his genius, although he lived to be 64. At 33 Gauguin gave up his job in a bank, and by 39 had established himself in his creative career as a painter. Donatello's work after 39 is described by a critic as showing a marked change in style, in which he departed from the statuesque balance of his earlier work and turned to the creation of an almost instantaneous expression of life.

315

Goethe, between the ages of 37 and 39, underwent a profound change in outlook, associated with his trip to Italy. As many of his biographers have pointed out, the importance of this journey and this period in his life cannot be exaggerated. He himself regarded it as the climax to his life. Never before had he gained such complete understanding of his genius and mission as a poet. His work then began to reflect the classical spirit of Greek tragedy and of the Renaissance.

Michelangelo carried out a series of masterpieces until he was 40: his 'David' was finished at 29, the decoration of the roof of the Sistine Chapel at 37, and his 'Moses' between 37 and 40. During the next fifteen years little is known of any artistic work. There was a creative lull until, at 55, he began to work on the great Medici monument and then later on 'The Last Judgement' and frescoes in the Pauline Chapel.

Let me make it clear that I am not suggesting that the careers of most creative persons either begin or end during the mid-life crisis. There are few creative geniuses who live and work into maturity, in whom the quality of greatness cannot be discerned in early adulthood in the form either of created works or of the potential for creating them: Beethoven, Shakespeare, Goethe, Couperin, Ibsen, Balzac, Voltaire, Verdi, Handel, Goya, Durer, to name but a very few at random. But there are equally few in whom a decisive change cannot be seen in the quality of their work—in whose work the effects of their having gone through a mid-life crisis cannot be discerned. The reactions range all the way from severe and dramatic crisis, to a smoother and less troubled transition—just as reactions to the phase of adolescent crisis may range from severe disturbance and breakdown to relatively ordered readjustment to mental and sexual adulthood—but the effects of the change are there to be discerned. What then are the main features of this change?

There are two features which seem to me of outstanding importance. One of these has to do with the mode of work; the second has to do with the content of the work. Let me consider each of these in turn. I shall use the phrase 'early adulthood' for the pre-mid-life phase, and 'mature adulthood' for the post-mid-life phase.

Change in Mode of Work

I can best describe the change in mode of work which I have in mind by describing the extreme of its manifestation. The creativity of the twenties and the early thirties tends to be a hot-from-the-fire creativity. It is intense and spontaneous, and comes out ready-made. The spontaneous effusions of Mozart, Keats, Shelley, Rimbaud, are the prototype. Most of the work seems to go on unconsciously. The conscious production is rapid, the pace of creation often being dictated by the limits of the artist's capacity physically to record the words or music he is expressing.

A vivid description of early adult type of work is given in Gittings' biography of Keats:

Keats all this year had been living on spiritual capital. He had used and spent every experience almost as soon as it had come into his possession, every sight, person, book, emotion or thought had been converted spontaneously into poetry. Could he or any other poet have lasted at such a rate? . . . He could write no more by these methods. He realized this himself when he wished to compose as he said 'without fever'. He could not keep this high pulse beating and endure.

By contrast, the creativity of the late thirties and after is a sculpted creativity. The inspiration may be hot and intense. The unconscious work is no less than before. But there is a big step between the first effusion of inspiration and the finished created product. The inspiration itself may come more slowly. Even if there are sudden bursts of inspiration, they are only the beginning of the work process. The initial inspiration must first be externalized in its elemental state. Then begins the process of forming and fashioning the external product, by means of working and re-working the externalized material. I use the term sculpting because the nature of the sculptor's material—it is the sculptor working in stone of whom I am thinking—forces him into this kind of relationship with the product of his creative imagination. There occurs a process of interplay between unconscious intuitive work and inspiration, and the considered perception of the externally emergent creation and the reaction to it.

In her note 'A Character Trait of Freud's', Riviere (1958) describes Freud's exhorting her in connexion with some psycho-analytic idea which had occurred to her:

Write it, write it, put it down in black and white . . . get it out, produce it, make something of it— *outside you*, that is; give it an existence independently of you.

This externalizing process is part of the essence of work in mature adulthood, when, as in the case of Freud, the initially externalized material is not itself the end product, or nearly the end product, but is rather the starting point, the object of further working over, modification, elaboration, sometimes for periods of years.

In distinguishing between the precipitate creativity of early adulthood and the sculpted creativity of mature adulthood, I do not want to give the impression of drawing a hard and fast line between the two phases. There are of course times when a creative person in mature adulthood will be subject to bursts of inspiration and rapid-fire creative production. Equally there will be found instances of mature and sculpted creative work done in early adulthood. The 'David' of Michelangelo is, I think, the supreme example of the latter.

But the instances where work in early adulthood has the sculpted and worked-over quality are rare. Sometimes, as in scientific work, there may be the appearance of sculpted work. Young physicists in their twenties, for example, may produce startling discoveries, which are the result of continuous hard work and experimentation. But these discoveries result from the application of modern theories about the structure of matter—theories which themselves have been the product of the sculpted work of mature adulthood of such geniuses as Thomson and Einstein.

Equally, genuinely creative work in mature adulthood may sometimes not appear to be externally worked over and sculpted, and yet actually be so. What seems to be rapid and unworked-over creation is commonly the re-working of themes which have been worked upon before, or which may have been slowly emerging over the years in previous works. We need look no farther than the work of Freud for a prime example of this process of books written rapidly, which are nevertheless the coming to fruition of ideas which have been worked upon, fashioned, reformulated, left incomplete and full of loose ends, and then reformulated once again in a surging forward through the emergence of new ideas for overcoming previous difficulties.

The reality of the distinction comes out in the fact that certain materials are more readily applicable to the precipitate creativity of early adulthood than are others. Thus, for example, musical composition, lyrical poetry, are much more amenable to rapid creative production than are sculpting in stone or painting in oils. It is noteworthy, therefore, that whereas there are very many poets and composers who achieve greatness in early adulthood—indeed in their early twenties or their late teens—there are very few sculptors or painters in oils who do so. With oil paint and stone, the working relationship to the materials themselves is of importance, and demands that the creative process should go through the stage of initial externalization and working-over of the externalized product. The written word and musical notation do not of necessity have this same plastic external objective quality. They can be sculpted and worked over, but they can also readily be treated merely as a vehicle for the immediate recording of unconsciously articulated products which are brought forward whole and complete—or nearly so.

Quality and Content of Creativity

The change in mode of work, then, between early and mature adulthood, is a change from precipitate to sculpted creativity. Let me now consider for a moment the change in the quality and content of the creativity. The change I have in mind is the emergence of a tragic and philosophical content which then moves on to serenity in the creativity of mature adulthood, in contrast to a more characteristically lyrical and descriptive content to the work of early adulthood. This distinction is a commonly held one, and may perhaps be considered sufficiently self-evident to require little explication or argument. It is implied, of course, in my choice of the adjectives ' early ' and ' mature ' to qualify the two phases of adulthood which I am discussing.

The change may be seen in the more human, tragic and less fictitious and stage quality of Dickens's writing from *David Copperfield* (which he wrote at 37) onwards. It may be seen also in the transition in Shakespeare from the historical plays and comedies to the tragedies. When he was about 31, in the midst of writing his lyrical comedies, he produced *Romeo and Juliet*. The great series of tragedies and Roman plays, however, began to appear a few years later; *Julius Caesar*, *Hamlet*, *Othello*, *King Lear*, and *Macbeth* are believed to have been written most probably between the ages of 35 and 40.

There are many familiar features of the change in question. Late adolescent and early adult idealism and optimism accompanied by split-off and projected hate, are given up and supplanted by a more contemplative pessimism. There is a shift from radical desire and impatience to a more reflective and tolerant conservatism. Beliefs in the inherent goodness of man are replaced by a recognition and acceptance of the fact that inherent goodness is accompanied by hate and destructive forces within, which contribute to man's own misery and tragedy. To the extent that hate, destruction, and death are found explicitly in early adult creativeness, they enter in the form of the satanic or the macabre, as in Poe and in Baudelaire, and not as worked-through and resolved anxieties.

The spirit of early adult creativeness is summed up in Shelley's *Prometheus Unbound*. In her notes on this work, Shelley's wife has written:

The prominent feature of Shelley's theory of the destiny of the human species is that evil is not inherent in the system of the Creation, but an accident that might be expelled . . . God made Earth and Man perfect, till he by his fall ' brought death into the world, and all our woe '. Shelley believed that mankind had only to will that there should be no evil in the world and there would be none. . . . He was attached to this idea with fervent enthusiasm.

This early adult idealism is built upon the use of unconscious denial and manic defences as normal processes of defence against two fundamental features of human life—the inevitableness of eventual death, and the existence of hate and destructive impulses inside each person. I shall try to show that the explicit recognition of these two features, and the bringing of them into focus, is the quintessence of successful weathering of the mid-life crisis and the achievement of mature adulthood.

It is when death and human destructiveness—that is to say, both death and the death instinct—are taken into account, that the quality and content of creativity change to the tragic, reflective, and philosophical. The depressive position must be worked through once again, at a qualitatively different level. The misery and despair of suffering and chaos unconsciously brought about by oneself are encountered and must be surmounted for life to be endured and for creativity to continue. Nemesis is the key, and tragedy the theme, of its recognition.

The successful outcome of mature creative work lies thus in constructive resignation both to the imperfections of men and to shortcomings in one's own work. It is this constructive resignation that then imparts serenity to life and work.

The Divine Comedy

I have taken these examples from creative genius because I believe the essence of the mid-life crisis is revealed in its most full and rounded form in the lives of the great. It will have become manifest that the crisis is a depressive crisis, in contrast to the adolescent crisis, which tends to be a paranoid-schizoid one. In adolescence, the predominant outcome of serious breakdown is schizophrenic illness; in mid-life the predominant outcome is depression, or the consequences of defence against depressive anxiety as reflected in manic defences, hypochondriasis, obsessional mechanisms, or superficiality and character deterioration. Working through the mid-life crisis calls for a re-working through of the infantile depression, but with mature insight into death and destructive impulses to be taken into account.

This theme of working through depression is magnificently expressed in *The Divine Comedy*. This masterpiece of all time was begun by Dante following his banishment from Florence at the age of 37. In the opening stanzas he creates his setting in words of great power and tremendous psychological depth. He begins:

In the middle of the journey of our life, I came to myself within a dark wood where the straight way was lost. Ah, how hard it is to tell of that wood, savage and harsh and dense, the thought of which renews my fear. So bitter is it that death is hardly more.

These words have been variously interpreted; for example, as an allegorical reference to the entrance to Hell, or as a reflection of the poet's state of mind on being forced into exile, homeless and hungry for justice. They may, however, be interpreted at a deeper level as the opening scene of a vivid and perfect description of the emotional crisis of the mid-life phase, a crisis which would have gripped the mind and soul of the poet whatever his religious outlook, or however settled or unsettled his external affairs. The evidence for this conclusion exists in the fact that during the years of his early thirties which preceded his exile, he had already begun his transformation from the idyllic outlook of the *Vita Nuova* (age 27–29) through a conversion to 'philosophy' which he allegorized in the *Convivio* written when he was between 36 and 38 years of age.

Even taken quite literally, *The Divine Comedy* is a description of the poet's first full and worked-through conscious encounter with death. He is led through hell and purgatory by his master Virgil, eventually to find his own way, guided by his beloved Beatrice, into paradise. His final rapturous and mystical encounter with the being of God, represented to him in strange and abstract terms, was not mere rapture, not simply a being overwhelmed by a mystical oceanic feeling. It was a much more highly organized experience. It was expressly a vision of supreme love and knowledge, with control of impulse and of will, which promulgates the mature life of greater ease and contemplation which follows upon the working-through of primitive anxiety and guilt, and the return to the primal good object.

Dante explicitly connects his experience of greater mental integration, and the overcoming of confusion, with the early infantile relation to the primal good object. As he nears the end of the 33rd Canto of ' Paradiso ', the climax of his whole grand scheme, he explains:

Now my speech will come more short even of what I remember than an infant's who yet bathes his tongue at the breast.

But the relationship with the primal good object is one in which reparation has been made, Purgatorio has been traversed, loving impulses have come into the ascendant, and the cruelty and harshness of the superego expressed in the inferno have been relieved. Bitterness has given way to composure.

In Dante, the result of this deep resolution is not the reinforcing of manic defence and denial which characterizes mystical experience fused with magic omnipotence; but rather the giving up of manic defence, and consequent strengthening of character and resolve, under the dominion of love. As Croce has observed:

What is not found in the ' Paradiso ', for it is foreign to the spirit of Dante, is flight from the world, absolute refuge in God, asceticism. He does not seek to fly from the world, but to instruct it, correct it, and reform it . . . he knew the world and its doings and passions.

Awareness of Personal Death

Although I have thus far taken my examples from the extremes of genius, my main theme is that the mid-life crisis is a reaction which not only occurs in creative genius, but manifests itself in some form in everyone. What then is the psychological nature of this reaction to the mid-life situation, and how is it to be explained?

The simple fact of the situation is the arrival at the mid-point of life. What is simple from the point of view of chronology, however, is not simple psychologically. The individual has stopped growing up, and has begun to grow old. A new set of external circumstances has to be met. The first phase of adult life has been lived. Family and occupation have become established (or ought to have become established unless the individual's adjustment has gone seriously awry); parents have grown old, and children are at the threshold of adulthood. Youth and childhood are past and gone, and demand to be mourned. The achievement of mature and independent adulthood presents itself as the main psychological task. The paradox is that of entering the prime of life, the stage of fulfilment, but at the same time the prime and fulfilment are dated. Death lies beyond.

I believe, and shall try to demonstrate, that it is this fact of the entry upon the psychological scene of the reality and inevitability of one's own eventual personal death, that is the central and crucial feature of the mid-life phase—the feature which precipitates the critical nature of the period. Death—at the conscious level—instead of being a general conception, or an event experienced in terms of the loss of someone else, becomes a personal matter, one's own death, one's own real and actual mortality. As Freud (1915) has so accurately described the matter:

We were prepared to maintain that death was the necessary outcome of life. . . . In reality, however, we were accustomed to behave as if it were otherwise. We displayed an unmistakable tendency to 'shelve' death, to eliminate it from life. We tried to hush it up. . . . That is our own death, of course. . . . No-one believes in his own death. . . . In the unconscious everyone is convinced of his own immortality.

This attitude towards life and death, written by Freud in another context, aptly expresses the situation which we all encounter in mid-life. The reality of one's own personal death forces itself upon our attention and can no longer so readily be shelved. A 36-year-old patient, who had been in analysis for seven years and was in the course of working through a deep depressive reaction which heralded the final phase of his analysis some eighteen months later, expressed the matter with great clarity. ' Up till now,' he said, ' life has seemed an endless upward slope, with nothing but the distant horizon in view. Now suddenly I seem to have reached the crest of the hill, and there stretching ahead is the downward slope with the end of the road in sight—far enough away it's true—but there is death observably present at the end.'

From that point on this patient's plans and ambitions took on a different hue. For the first time in his life he saw his future as circumscribed. He began his adjustment to the fact that he would not be able to accomplish in the span of a single lifetime everything he had desired to do. He could achieve only a finite amount. Much would have to remain unfinished and unrealized.

This perspective on the finitude of life was accompanied by a greater solidity and robustness in his outlook, and introduced a new quality of earthly resignation. It reflected a diminishing of his unconscious wish for immortality. Such ideas are commonly lived out in terms of denial of mourning and death, or in terms of ideas of immortality, from notions of reincarnation and life after death, to notions of longevity like those expressed by the successful 28-year-old novelist who writes in his diary, ' I shall be the most serious of men, and I shall live longer than any man.'

Unconscious Meaning of Death

How each one reacts to the mid-life encounter with the reality of his own eventual death—whether he can face this reality, or whether he denies it—will be markedly influenced by his infantile unconscious relation to death—a relationship which depends upon the stage and nature of the working through of the infantile depressive position, as Melanie Klein discovered and vividly described (1940, 1955). Let me paraphrase her conclusions.

The infant's relation with life and death occurs in the setting of his survival being dependent on his external objects, and on the balance of power of the life and death instincts which qualify his perception of those objects and his capacity to depend upon them and use them. In the depressive position in infancy, under conditions of prevailing love, the good and bad objects can in some measure be synthesized, the ego becomes more integrated, and hope for the re-establishment of the good object is experienced; the accompanying overcoming of grief and regaining of security is the infantile equivalent of the notion of life.

Under conditions of prevailing persecution, however, the working through of the depressive position will be to a greater or lesser extent inhibited; reparation and synthesis fail; and the inner world is unconsciously felt to contain the persecuting and annihilating devoured and destroyed bad breast, the ego itself feeling in bits. The chaotic internal situation thus experienced is the infantile equivalent of the notion of death.

Ideas of immortality arise as a response to these anxieties, and as a defence against them. Unconscious fantasies of immortality are the counterpart of the infantile fantasies of the indestructible and hence immortal aspect of the idealized and bountiful primal object. These fantasies are equally as persecuting as the chaotic internal situation they are calculated to mitigate. They contain omnipotent sadistic triumph, and increase guilt and persecution as a result. And they lead to feelings of intolerable helplessness through dependence upon the perfect object which becomes demanding of an equal perfection in behaviour.

Does the unconscious, then, have a conception of death? The views of Melanie Klein and those of Freud may seem not to correspond. Klein assumes an unconscious awareness of death.

Freud assumes that the unconscious rejects all such awareness. Neither of these views, taken at face value, is likely to prove correct. Nor would I expect that either of their authors would hold to a literal interpretation of their views. The unconscious is not aware of death *per se*. But there are unconscious experiences akin to those which later appear in consciousness as notions of death. Let me illustrate such experiences.

A 47-year-old woman patient, suffering from claustrophobia and a variety of severe psycho-somatic illnesses, recounted a dream in which she was lying in a coffin. She had been sliced into small chunks, and was dead. But there was a spider's-web-thin thread of nerve running through every chunk and connected to her brain. As a result she could experience everything. She knew she was dead. She could not move or make any sound. She could only lie in the claustrophobic dark and silence of the coffin.

I have selected this particular dream because I think it typifies the unconscious fear and experience of death. It is not in fact death in the sense in which consciously we think about it, but an unconscious fantasy of immobilization and helplessness, in which the self is subject to violent fragmentation, while yet retaining the capacity to experience the persecution and torment to which it is being subjected. When these fantasies of suspended persecution and torture are of pathological intensity, they are characteristic of many mental conditions: catatonic states, stupors, phobias, obsessions, frozen anxiety, simple depression.

A Case of Denial of Death

In the early adult phase, before the mid-life encounter with death, the full-scale re-working-through of the depressive position does not as yet necessarily arise as a part of normal development. It can be postponed. It is not a pressing issue. It can be put to one side, until circumstances demand more forcibly that it be faced.

In the ordinary course of events, life is full and active. Physiologically, full potency has been reached, and activity—social, physical, economic, sexual—is to the fore. It is a time for doing, and the doing is flavoured and supported to a greater or lesser degree—depending on the emotional adjustment of the individual—by the activity and denial as part of the manic defence.

The early adult phase is one, therefore, in which successful activity can in fact obscure or conceal the operation of strong manic defences. But the depressive anxiety that is thus warded off will be encountered in due course. The mid-life crisis thrusts it forward with great intensity, and it can no longer be pushed aside if life is not to be impoverished.

This relationship between adjustment based upon activity in the early adult phase, and its failure in mid-life if the infantile depressive position is not unconsciously (or consciously, in analysis) worked through again, may be illus-

trated in the case of a patient, Mr N, who had led a successful life by everyday standards up to the time he came into analysis. He was an active man, a ' do-er '. He had been successful in his career through intelligent application and hard work, was married with three children, had many good friends, and all seemed to be going very well.

The idealized content of this picture had been maintained by an active carrying on of life, without allowing time for reflection. His view was that he had not come to analysis for himself, but rather for a kind of tutorial purpose—he would bring his case history to me and we would have a clinical seminar in which we would conduct a psycho-analytic evaluation of the case material he had presented.

As might be expected, Mr N had great difficulty in coping with ambivalence. He was unconsciously frightened of any resentment, envy, jealousy, or other hostile feelings towards me, maintaining an attitude of idealized love for me and tolerant good nature towards every attempt on my part to analyse the impulses of destructiveness, and the feelings of persecution which he was counteracting by this idealization.

When we finally did break through this inability to cope with ambivalence—indeed a pretty complete unfamiliarity with the experience —it emerged that, in all his relationships, his idealization was inevitably followed by disappointment—a disappointment arising out of failure to get the quality of love he was greedily expecting in return, and nursed by the envy of those whom he idealized.

It was out of the analysis of material of this kind that we were able to get at the reflection in the analysis of his early adult mode of adjustment. He admitted that he was ill, and that unconscious awareness of his illness undoubtedly was the main reason for his seeking analysis. Being active, and over concerned for others, were soporifics, to which he had become addicted. Indeed, he confessed, he had resented my analysis taking this defensive addiction away from him. He had secretly entertained ideas of stopping his analysis ' because all this thinking about myself, instead of doing things, is no good. Now I realize that I have been piling up my rage against you inside myself, like I've done with everyone else.'

Thus it was that during the first year of his analysis, the patient lived out many of the techniques which had characterized his early adult adjustment. It was with the onset of the Christmas holiday that the unconscious depressive anxiety, which was the main cause of his disturbance in mid-life, came out in full force. It is this material that illustrates the importance of the depressive position and unconscious feelings about death in relation to the mid-life crisis.

He had shown definite signs before the holiday

of feelings of being abandoned, saying that not only would he not see me, but his friends were to be away as well. Three days before the end of the holiday, he telephoned me and, in a depressed and tearful voice, asked if he could come to see me. I arranged a session that same evening.

When he came to see me, he was at first afraid to lie on the couch. He said that he wanted just to talk to me, to be comforted and reassured. He then proceeded to tell me how, from the beginning of the holiday, a black gloom had settled upon him. He yearned for his mother to be alive, so that he could be with her and be held and loved by her. ' I just felt completely deserted and lost ', he said. ' I sat for hour after hour, unable to move or to do any work. I wanted to die. My thoughts were filled with suicide. Then I became terrified of my state of mind. That's why I 'phoned you. I just had never conceived it as even remotely possible that I could lose my self-control like this.' Things were made absolutely unbearable, he then explained, when one of his children had become nearly murderously aggressive towards his wife a few days before. His world seemed to have gone to pieces.

This material, and other associations, suggested that his wife stood for the bad aspect of his mother, and his son for the sadistic murderous part of himself. In his fear of dying, he was re-experiencing his own unconscious fantasies of tearing his mother to pieces, and he then felt abandoned and lost. As I interpreted on these lines, he interjected that the worst thing was the feeling of having gone to pieces himself. ' I can't stand it ', he said, ' I feel as though I'm going to die.'

I then recalled to him a dream he had had just before the holiday, which we had not had time to analyse, and which contained material of importance in the understanding of his infantile perception of being dead. In this dream he was a small boy sitting crying on the kerb in his home town. He had dropped a bottle of milk. It lay in jagged shattered bits in the gutter. The fresh good milk ran away, dirtied by contact with the muck in the gutter. One of his associations to the dream was that he had broken the bottle by his own ineptness. It was no use moaning and crying over the spilt milk, since it was himself, after all, who had caused the damage.

I related his dream to his feeling of being abandoned by me. I was the bottle of milk—containing good milk—which he destroyed in his murderous rage because I abandoned him and went dry. He unconsciously felt the Christmas holiday as losing me, as he felt he had lost his mother and the good breast, because of his ineptness—his violence and lack of control—and his spoiling me internally with his anal muck. He then felt internally persecuted and torn to pieces by the jagged bits of the bottle, representing the breast, myself, and the analysis; as Klein (1955, p. 313) has expressed it, ' the breast taken in with hatred becomes the representative of the death instinct within.'

I would conclude that he had unconsciously attempted to avoid depression by paranoid-schizoid techniques of splitting and deflecting his murderous impulses away from me, through his son against his wife. These techniques had now begun to fail, however, because of previous analytical work with respect to his splitting and denial. Whereas he had been able to deny what in fact turned out to be a pretty bad situation in his home, by perceiving it merely as the product of his own projections, he now became filled with guilt, anxiety, and despair, as he began to appreciate more that in reality the relationships at home were genuinely intolerable and dangerous, and were not just a projection of his own internal chaos and confusion.

During the succeeding months, we were able to elaborate more fully his attitude towards death as an experience of going to pieces.

A connexion between his phobic attitude to death and his escape into activity was manifested, for instance, in his recalling one day a slogan that had always meant so much to him—' Do or die '. But now it came to him that he had always used his own personal abbreviation of the slogan—simply ' Do '. The possibility of dying just did not consciously exist for him.

On one occasion he demonstrated at first hand how his fear of death had caused him always to retreat from mourning. A friend of his died. The patient was the strong and efficient one, who made all the necessary arrangements, while friends and family stood about helplessly, bathed in tears and paralyzed with sorrow. He experienced no feeling—just clear-headedness and a sense of action for the arrangements which had to be made. He had always been the same, had done the same when his father and his mother had died. More than that, however, when I interpreted his warding off of depression by means of denial of feeling and refuge in action, he recalled an event which revealed the unconscious chaos and confusion stirred within him by death. He remembered how, when a cousin of his had suddenly collapsed and died a few years before, he had run back and forth from the body to the telephone to call for a doctor, oblivious of the fact that a small group of people had gathered about the body, and not realizing that everyone but himself was perfectly aware that his cousin was quite dead, and had been for some time before he arrived upon the scene.

The chaos and confusion in the patient in connexion with death, I would ascribe to his unconscious infantile fantasies equivalent to death—the fantasies of the destroyed and persecuting breast, and of his ego being cut to pieces.

Mainly, I think, because of the love he got from his father, probably reinforcing his own innate good impulses and what he has had described to him as good breast-feeding in the first five weeks with his mother, he had been able to achieve a partial working through of the infantile depressive position, and to develop his good intellectual capacities. The partial character of his working through was shown in the extent of his manic denial and activity, and his excessive use of splitting, introjection and projection, and projective and introjective identification.

During the period of early adulthood—the twenties and early thirties—the paranoid-schizoid and manic defence techniques were sufficiently effective. By means of his apparent general success and obsessional generosity, he was able to live out the role of the good mother established within, to nurture the good part of himself projected into others, to deny the real situation of envy and greed and destructiveness expressed by him as his noxiousness, and to deny the real impoverishment of his emotional life, and lack of genuine love and affection in his behaviour as both husband and father.

With the onset of mature adulthood in his mid-thirties, his defensive techniques began to lose their potency. He had lost his youth, and the prospect of middle-age and of eventual death stimulated a repetition and a re-working through of the infantile depressive position. The unconscious feelings of persecution and annihilation which death represented to him were re-awakened.

He had lost his youth. And with both his parents dead, nobody now stood between himself and the grave. On the contrary, he had become the barrier between his children and their perception of death. Acceptance of these facts required constructive resignation and detachment. Unconsciously such an outlook requires the capacity to maintain the internal good object, and to achieve a resigned attitude to shortcomings and destructive impulses in oneself, and imperfections in the internal good object. My patient's unconscious fantasies of intolerable noxiousness, his anxieties of having polluted and destroyed his good primal object so that he was lost and abandoned and belonged nowhere, and his unconscious fantasies of the badness of his internalized mother as well as his father, precluded such detachment and resignation. The psychological defences which had supported his adjustment in early adult life—an adjustment of a limited kind, of course, with a great core of emotional impoverishment—failed him at the mid-life period when, to the persecutory world in which he unconsciously lived, were added his anxieties about impending middle and old age, and death. If he had had a less well established good internal object, and had been innately less constructive and loving, he might have continued his mature adult life along lines similar to his early adult type of adjustment; but if he had, I think his mid-life crisis would have been the beginning of a deterioration in his character, and bouts of depression and psychosomatic illness, due to the depth and chronicity of his denial and

self-deception, and his distorted view of external reality.

As it has worked out, however, the positive factors in his personality make-up enabled him to utilize his analysis, for which he developed a deep sense of value and appreciation. The overcoming of splitting and fragmentation first began to show in a session in which, as out of nowhere, he saw two jagged edged right-angled triangles. They moved together, and joined to make a perfect square. I recalled the dream with the broken bits of bottle to him. He replied, ' It's odd you should mention that; I was just thinking of it. It feels like the bits of glass are coming together.'

Evasion of Awareness of Death

One case history does not of course prove a general thesis. It can only illustrate a theme, and the theme in this instance is the notion that the circumstances met by this patient at the mid-life phase are representative of a general pattern of psychological change at this stage of life. The extent to which these changes are tied up with physiological changes is a question I am not able to tackle. One can readily conjecture, however, that the connexion must be an important one—libido, the life-creating impulse, represented in sexual drive, is diminishing, and the death instinct is coming relatively more into the ascendant.

The sense of the agedness of parents, coupled with the maturing of children into adults, contributes strongly to the sense of ageing—the sense that it is one's own turn next to grow old and die. This feeling about the age of parents is very strong—even in patients whose parents died years before there is the awareness at the mid-life period that their parents would then have been reaching old age.

In the early adult phase of life, contemplativeness, detachment, and resignation are not essential components of pleasure, enjoyment and success. Manically determined activity and warding off of depression may therefore—as in the case of Mr N—lead to a limited success and pleasure. Splitting and projection techniques can find expression in what are regarded as perfectly normal patterns of passionate support for idealized causes, and equally passionate opposition to whatever may be felt as bad or reactionary.

With the awareness of the onset of the last half of life, unconscious depressive anxieties are aroused, and the repetition and continuation of the working-through of the infantile depressive position are required. Just as in infancy—to quote Klein again (1940, p. 314)—' satisfactory relations to people depend upon the infant's having succeeded against the chaos inside him (the depressive position) and having securely established his " good " internal objects ', so in mid-life the establishment of a satisfactory adjustment to the conscious contemplation of one's own death depends upon the same process, for otherwise death itself is equated with the depressive chaos, confusion, and persecution, as it was in infancy.

When the prevailing balance between love and hate tends more towards the side of hate, when there is instinctual defusion, there is an overspill of destructiveness in any or all of its various forms—self-destruction, envy, grandiose omnipotence, cruelty, narcissism, greed—and the world is seen as having these persecuting qualities as well. Love and hate are split apart; destruction is no longer mitigated by tenderness. There is little or no protection from catastrophic unconscious fantasies of annihilating one's good objects. Reparation and sublimation, the processes which underlie creativeness, are inhibited and fail. And in the deep unconscious world there is a gruesome sense of invasion and habitation by the psychic objects which have been annihilated.

In primitive terms, the process of sculpting is experienced partly as a projective identification, in which the fear of dying is split off and projected into the created object (representing the creative breast). Under the dominance of destructiveness the created object, like the breast, is felt to

remove the good or valuable element in the fear of dying, and to force the worthless residue back into the infant. The infant who started with a fear that he was dying ends up by containing a nameless dread (Bion, 1962).

The conception of death is denuded of its meaning, and the process of sculpted creativity is stopped. It is the experience of a patient who, having created a work of art by spontaneous effusion, found that 'it goes dead on me; I don't want to have anything more to do with it; I can never work on it further once it is outside, so I can never refine it; it completely loses its meaning for me—it's like a strange and foreign thing that has nothing to do with me.'

The ensuing inner chaos and despair is unconsciously fantasied in terms akin to an inferno: ' *I came to myself within a dark wood . . . savage and harsh and dense.*' If this state of mind is not surmounted, hate and death must be denied, pushed aside, warded off, rejected. They are replaced by unconscious fantasies of omnipotence, magic immortality, religious mysticism, the counterpart of infant fantasies of being indestructible and under the protective care of some idealized and bountiful figure.

A person who reaches mid-life, either without having successfully established himself in marital and occupational life, or having established himself by means of manic activity and denial with consequent emotional impoverishment, is badly prepared for meeting the demands of middle age, and getting enjoyment out of his maturity. In such cases, the mid-life crisis, and the adult encounter with the conception of life to be lived in the setting of an approaching personal death, will likely be experienced as a period of psychological disturbance and depressive breakdown. Or breakdown may be avoided by means of a strengthening of manic defences, with a warding off of depression and persecution about ageing and death, but with an accumulation of persecutory anxiety to be faced when the inevitability of ageing and death eventually demands recognition.

The compulsive attempts, in many men and women reaching middle age, to remain young, the hypochondriacal concern over health and appearance, the emergence of sexual promiscuity in order to prove youth and potency, the hollowness and lack of genuine enjoyment of life, and the frequency of religious concern, are familiar patterns. They are attempts at a race against time. And in addition to the impoverishment of emotional life contained in the foregoing activities, real character deterioration is always possible. Retreat from psychic reality encourages intellectual dishonesty, and a weakening of moral fibre and of courage. Increase in arrogance, and ruthlessness concealing pangs of envy—or self-effacing humbleness and weakness concealing fantasies of omnipotence—are symptomatic of such change.

These defensive fantasies are equally as persecuting, however, as the chaotic and hopeless internal situation they are meant to mitigate. They lead to attempts at easy success, at a continuation on a false note of the early adult lyricism and precipitate creation—that is, creation which, by avoiding contemplation, now seeks not to express but to avoid contact with the infantile experience of hate and of death. Instead of creative enhancement by the introduction of the genuinely tragic, there is emotional impoverishment—a recoil away from creative development. As Freud incisively remarked: ' Life loses in interest, when the highest stake in the game, life itself, may not be risked.' Here is the Achilles heel of much young genius.

Working through the Depressive Position

When, by contrast, the prevailing balance between love and hate is on the side of love, there is instinctual fusion, in which hate can be mitigated by love, and the mid-life encounter with death and hate takes on a different hue. Revived are the deep unconscious memories of hate, not denied but mitigated by love; of death and destruction mitigated by reparation and the will to life; of good things injured and damaged by hate, revived again and healed by loving grief; of spoiling envy mitigated by admiration and by gratitude; of confidence and hope, not through denial, but through the deep inner sense that the torment of grief and loss, of guilt and persecution, can be endured and overcome if faced by loving reparation.

Under constructive circumstances, the created object in mid-life is experienced unconsciously in terms of the good breast which would in Bion's (1962) terms moderate the fear component in the fear of dying that had been projected into it and the infant in due course would re-introject a now tolerable and consequently growth stimulating part of its personality.

In the sculpting mode of work the externally created object, instead of being experienced as having impoverished the personality, is unconsciously re-introjected, and stimulates further unconscious creativeness. The created object is experienced as life-giving. The transformation of the fear component in the fear of dying into a constructive experience is forwarded. The thought of death can be carried in thinking, and not predominantly in projective identification, so that the conception of death can begin to find its conscious realization. The reality-testing of death can be carried out in thinking, separated partly from the process of creating an external object. At the same time the continuing partial identification of the creative sculpting with the projection and reintrojection of the fear of dying gives a stimulus to the sculpting process because of its success in forwarding the working through of the infantile projective identification with a good breast.

Thus in mid-life we are able to encounter the onset of the tragedy of personal death with the sense of grief appropriate to it. We can live with it, without an overwhelming sense of persecution. The infantile depressive position can be further worked through unconsciously, supported by the greater strength of reality-testing available to the nearly mature individual. In so re-working through the depressive position, we unconsciously regain the primitive sense of wholeness—of the goodness of ourselves and of our objects—a goodness which is sufficient but not idealized, not subject to hollow perfection. The consequent feeling of limited but reliable security is the equivalent of the infantile notion of life.

These more balanced conditions do not, however, pre-suppose an easy passage through the mid-life crisis. It is essentially a period of purgatory—of anguish and depression. So speaks Virgil:

Down to Avernus the descent is light. But thence thy journey to retrace, there lies the labour, there the mighty toil by few achieved.

Working through again the infantile experience of loss and of grief, gives an increase in confidence in one's capacity to love and mourn what has been lost and what is past, rather than to hate and feel persecuted by it. We can begin to mourn our own eventual death. Creativeness takes on new depths and shades of feeling. There is the possibility, however, of furthering the resolution of the depressive position at a much deeper level. Such a working-through is possible if the primal object is sufficiently well established in its own right and neither excessively idealized nor devalued. Under such circumstances there is a minimum of infantile dependence upon the good object, and a detachment which allows confidence and hope to be established, security in the preservation and development of the ego, a capacity to tolerate one's shortcomings and destructiveness, and withal, the possibility of enjoyment of mature adult life and old age.

Given such an internal situation, the last half of life can be lived with conscious knowledge of eventual death, and acceptance of this knowledge, as an integral part of living. Mourning for the dead self can begin. alongside the mourning and re-establishment of the lost objects and the lost childhood and youth. The sense of life's continuity may be strengthened. The gain is in the deepening of awareness, understanding and self-realization. Genuine values can be cultivated —of wisdom, fortitude and courage, deeper capacity for love and affection and human insight, and hopefulness and enjoyment—qualities whose genuineness stems from integration based upon the more immediate and self-conscious awareness and acceptance not only of one's own shortcomings but of one's destructive impulses, and from the greater capacity for sublimation which accompanies true resignation and detachment.

Sculpted Creativity

Out of the working through of the depressive position, there is further strengthening of the capacity to accept and tolerate conflict and ambivalence. One's work need no longer be experienced as perfect. It can be worked and re-worked, but it will be accepted as having shortcomings. The sculpting process can be carried on far enough so that the work is good enough. There is no need for obsessional attempts at perfection, because inevitable imperfection is no longer felt as bitter persecuting failure. Out of this mature resignation comes the serenity in the work of genius, true serenity, serenity which transcends imperfection by accepting it.

Because of the greater integration within the internal world, and a deepening of the sense of reality, a freer interaction can occur between the internal and the external worlds. Sculpted creativity expresses this freedom with its flow of inspiration from inside to outside and back, constantly repeated, again, and yet again. There is a quality of depth in mature creativity which stems from constructive resignation and detachment. Death is not infantile persecution and chaos. Life and the world go on, and we can live on in our children, our loved objects, our works, if not in immortality.

The sculpting process in creativity is facilitated because the preparation for the final phase in reality-testing has begun—the reality-testing of the end of life. For everyone, the on-coming years of the forties are the years when new starts are coming to an end. This feeling can be observed to arise in a particularly poignant way by the mid-forties. This sense of there being no more changing is anticipated in the mid-life crisis. What is begun has to be finished. Important things that the individual would have liked to achieve, would have desired to become, would have longed to have, will not be realized. The awareness of on-coming frustration is especially intense. That is why, for example, the issue of resignation is of such importance. It is resignation in the sense of conscious and unconscious acceptance of inevitable frustration on the grand scale of life as a whole.

This reality-testing is the more severe the greater is the creative ability of the individual, for the time scale of creative work increases dramatically with ability. Thus the experience is particularly painful in genius, capable of achieving vastly more than it is possible to achieve in the remaining years, and therefore frustrated by the immense vision of things to be done which will not be done. And because the route forward has become a cul-de-sac, attention begins its Proustian process of turning to the past, working it over consciously in the present,

and weaving it into the concretely limited future. This consonance of past and present is a feature of much mature adult sculpting work.

The positive creativeness and the tone of serenity which accompany the successful endurance of this frustration, are characteristic of the mature production of Beethoven, Goethe, Virgil, Dante, and other giants. It is the spirit of the ' Paradiso ', which ends in words of strong and quiet confidence:

But now my desire and will, like a wheel that spins with even motion, were revolved by the Love that moves the sun and other stars.

It is this spirit, on a smaller scale, which overcomes the crisis of middle life, and lives through to the enjoyment of mature creativeness and work in full awareness of death which lies beyond—resigned but not defeated. It is a spirit that is one criterion of the successful working through of the depressive position in psychoanalysis.

REFERENCES

BION, W. (1962). *Learning from Experience.* (London: Heinemann; New York: Basic Books.)

FREUD, S. (1915). 'Thoughts for the times on war and death.' *S.E.,* **14.**

KLEIN, M. (1935). ' A contribution to the psychogenesis of manic-depressive states.' In: *Contributions to Psycho-Analysis.* (London: Hogarth, 1948.)

—— (1940). ' Mourning and its relation to manic-depressive states.' In: *Contributions to Psycho-Analysis.*

—— (1955). ' On identification.' In: *New Directions in Psycho-Analysis.* (London: Tavistock; New York: Basic Books.)

RIVIERE, J. (1958). ' A character trait of Freud's.' In: *Psycho-Analysis and Contemporary Thought,* ed. J. D. Sutherland. (London: Hogarth.)

VII. Old Age

C.H. ELDRIDGE '76

As a person enters old age, life takes on yet another set of new significances—one becomes aware of imminent death as one's friends and loved ones begin to die. The body becomes more limited and frail, and diminishing capacities place one in a dependent situation. The often callous way that society regards and treats old people affects the way they feel about themselves and their worth to society. We don't seem to value the wisdom of the aged the way other cultures do. In old age, a biological, psychological and social upheaval creates a final period of rapid change in a person's life.

Robert Butler discusses how the aged set about reviewing their lives, extracting its significance and meaning. Irene de Castillejo talks about some of the psychological roles that old people play, for themselves and in society. Sexuality is affected by aging, but French philosopher Simone de Beauvoir challenges the common notion that sexuality is no longer an aspect of the life of an old person. The societal denial of sexuality in the aged often compounds their despair and loneliness. Elaine Brody documents some of the emotional changes experienced by an older member of a family and how these changes affect the whole family unit as other family members change in relation to the aging member.

33

The Life Review: An Interpretation of Reminiscence in the Aged

Robert N. Butler*

THIS PAPER POSTULATES the universal occurrence in older people of an inner experience or mental process of reviewing one's life. I propose that this process helps account for the increased reminiscence in the aged, that it contributes to the occurrence of certain late-life disorders, particularly depression, and that it participates in the evolution of such characteristics as candor, serenity, and wisdom among certain of the aged.

Allusions to a life-reviewing process are common in the literature of various historical periods:

They live by memory rather than by hope, for what is left to them of life is but little compared to the long past. This, again, is the cause of their loquacity. They are continually talking of the past, because they enjoy remembering. — ARISTOTLE, *Rhetoric* [367-347 B.C.].[1]

Mem'ry's pointing wand, that calls the past to our exact review.—COWPER, *Task* [1784].[2]

What makes old age hard to bear is not a failing of one's faculties, mental and physical, but the burden of one's memories.—MAUGHAM, *Points of View* [1959].[3]

Intimations of the existence of a life review in the aged are also found in psychiatric writings—notably in the emphasis upon reminiscence—and the nature, sources, and manifestations of the life review have been studied in the course of intensive psychotherapeutic relationships.[4] But often the older person is experienced as garrulous and "living in the past," and the content and significance of his reminiscence are lost or devalued. Younger therapists especially, working with the elderly, find great difficulties in listening.[5]

The prevailing tendency is to identify reminiscence in the aged with psychological dysfunction and thus to regard it essentially as a symptom. One source of this distorted view is the emphasis in available literature on the occurrence of reminiscence in the mentally disordered and institutionalized aged. Of course, many of the prevailing ideas and "findings" concerning the aged and aging primarily stem from the study of such samples of elderly people. Since the adequately functioning community-resident aged have only recently been systematically studied [6] and intensive study of the mentally disturbed aged through psychotherapy has been comparatively rare,[7] these important sources for data and theory have not yet contributed much to an understanding of the amount, prevalence, content, function, and significance of reminiscence in the aged.

Furthermore, definitions and descriptions of reminiscence—the act or process of recalling the past [8]—indicate discrepant interpretations of its nature and function. Reminiscence is seen by some investigators as occurring beyond the older person's control: It happens to him; it is spontaneous, nonpurposive, unselective, and unbidden. Others view reminiscence as volitional and pleasurable, but hint that it provides escapism. Thus purposive reminiscence is interpreted only as helping the person to fill the void of his later life. Reminiscence is also considered to obscure the older person's awareness of the realities of the present. It is considered of dubious reliability, although, curiously, "remote memory" is held to be "preserved" longer than "recent mem-

* A.B. 49, M.D. 53, Columbia Univ. Intern, St. Lukes Hosp., N.Y. 53-54; Res., Langley Porter Clinic, San Francisco 54-55; Rsc. Psychiatrist, NIMH, Bethesda, Md. 55-62; Res. and Clin. Administrator, Geriatric Service 58-59, Consultant 59-, Chestnut Lodge Sanitarium, Rockville, Md.; private practice, Washington, D.C. 56-; Faculty 59-, Rsc. Psychiatrist, Study Center 62-, Washington School of Psychiatry. Member: Amer. Med. Assn., Amer. Psychiatric Assn., Amer. Gerontological Assn.

ory." In consequence, reminiscence becomes a pejorative, suggesting preoccupation, musing, aimless wandering of the mind. In a word, reminiscence is fatuous. Occasionally, the constructive and creative aspects of reminiscence are valued and affirmed in the autobiographical accounts of famous men,[9] but it must be concluded that the more usual view of reminiscence is a negative one.

In contrast, I conceive of the life review as a naturally occurring, universal mental process characterized by the progressive return to consciousness of past experiences, and, particularly, the resurgence of unresolved conflicts; simultaneously, and normally, these revived experiences and conflicts can be surveyed and reintegrated. Presumably this process is prompted by the realization of approaching dissolution and death, and the inability to maintain one's sense of personal invulnerability. It is further shaped by contemporaneous experiences and its nature and outcome are affected by the lifelong unfolding of character.

THE SIGNIFICANCE OF DEATH

The life review mechanism, as a possible response to the biological and psychological fact of death, may play a significant role in the psychology and psychopathology of the aged.

The following dream, related by a 70-year-old-man, illustrates the awareness of approaching death:

> I dreamt that I had died and my soul was going up and when I did reach the top I saw a great, huge statue—or living man—sitting there, and then a second man came over to me and asked, "What do you want?" I answered, "I want to get in here." So the big man said, "Let him in." But then the second man asked, "What did you do in the other world?" I told him a great deal about myself and was asked, "What else?" I told of an occasion in which I helped an old lady. "That's not enough. Take him away." It was God judging me. I was very afraid and woke up.

The interrelationship of awareness of impending death and recall of past inadequacies is shown in the following case history.

A 70-year-old retired and widowed mother came from another city to visit her son and showed no inclination to return home. Six months later, the son, anxious about his depressed, irritable mother, brought her to me. She reluctantly accepted a psychotherapeutic relationship: Frightened and guarded, overly suspicious, she continually described her worthlessness; she considered herself so un-

worthy that she was not able to attend church. I had two impressions—that she was wrestling with guilt concerning past wrongs, acts both committed and avoided, and that she was afraid of death and judgment.

In one interview, she suddenly appeared to confirm these impressions, which up to then had not been presented to her. She asked about privileged communication—that is, whether I would testify in a court of law against her if she were indicted for her past misdeeds, an unlikely event. Later in the hour she said, "I am worried about my granddaughter—that something does not happen to her." She did not explain but added, "I wonder if she will be able to face her final examinations and graduation day." [Since her granddaughter is an excellent student, she had little reason to worry.] Still later in the hour she said, "My doctor referred to these black spots on my head as God's subpoenas." [She was referring to brown, not black, senile freckles on her scalp.] She went on to explain that she had been having difficulties getting her hair done properly and perhaps this was because she was contagious.

The significance of death is often inappropriately minimized by psychiatric writers, reflecting the universal tendency to deny its reality; it is also sidestepped by some writers through the use of such psychoanalytic constructs as castration anxiety, which has been held to be the basic fear. Fear of death is often conceptualized as merely manifest and not authentic.[10]

The relation of the life-review process to thoughts of death is reflected in the fact that it occurs not only in the elderly but also in younger persons who expect death—for example, the fatally ill[11] or the condemned. It may also be seen in the introspection of those preoccupied by death, and it is commonly held that one's life passes in review in the process of dying. One thinks of the matador's "moment of truth" during the *faena*. The life review, Janus-like, involves facing death as well as looking back. Lot's wife, in the Bible, and Orpheus, in Greek mythology, embodied an association of the ideas of looking death in the face and looking back.

But the life review is more commonly observed in the aged because of the actual nearness of life's termination—and perhaps also because during retirement not only is time available for self-reflection, but also the customary defensive operation provided by work has been removed.

In extreme cases, severe consequences of the life review seem to be quantitatively related to the extent of actual or psychological isolation. The writings of Cannon, Richter, Adland, Will, and others.[12] suggest a relationship between isolation, or loneliness, and death. "The feeling of unrelatedness is incompatible with life in the human being," writes Will.[13]

Reviewing one's life, then, may be a general response to crises of various types, of which imminent death seems to be one instance. It is also likely that the degree to which approaching death is seen as a crisis varies as a function of individual personality. The explicit hypothesis intended here, however, is that the biological fact of approaching death, independent of—although possibly reinforced by—personal and environmental circumstances, prompts the life review.

MANIFESTATIONS OF THE LIFE REVIEW

The life review, as a looking-back process that has been set in motion by looking forward to death, potentially proceeds toward personality reorganization. Thus, the life review is not synonymous with, but includes reminiscence; it is not alone either the unbidden return of memories, or the purposive seeking of them, although both may occur.

The life review sometimes proceeds silently, without obvious manifestations. Many elderly persons, before inquiry, may be only vaguely aware of the experience as a function of their defensive structure. But alterations in defensive operations do occur. Speaking broadly, the more intense the unresolved life conflicts, the more work remains to be accomplished toward reintegration. Although the process is active, not static, the content of one's life usually unfolds slowly;[14] the process may not be completed prior to death. In its mild form, the life review is reflected in increased reminiscence, mild nostalgia, mild regret; in severe form, in anxiety, guilt, despair, and depression. In the extreme, it may involve the obsessive preoccupation of the older person with his past, and may proceed to a state approximating terror and result in suicide. Thus, although I consider it to be a universal and normative process, its varied manifestations and outcomes may include psychopathological ones.

The life review may be first observed in stray and seemingly insignificant thoughts about oneself and one's life history. These thoughts may continue to emerge in brief intermittent spurts or become essentially continuous, and they may undergo constant reintegration and reorganization at various levels of awareness. A 76-year-old man said:

My life is in the background of my mind much of the time; it cannot be any other way. Thoughts of the past play upon me; sometimes I play with them, encourage and savor them; at other times I dismiss them.

Other clues to its existence include dreams and thoughts. The dreams and nightmares of the aged, which are frequently reported,[15] appear to principally concern the past and death. Imagery of past events and symbols of death seem frequent in waking life as well as dreams, suggesting that the life review is a highly visual process.[16]

Another manifestation of the life review seems to be the curious but apparently common phenomenon of mirror-gazing, illustrated by the following:

> I was passing by my mirror. I noticed how old I was. My appearance, well, it prompted me to think of death—and of my past—what I hadn't done, what I had done wrong.

One hospitalized 80-year-old woman, whose husband had died five years before her admission, had been discovered by her family berating her mirror image for her past deeds and shaking her fist at herself. She was preoccupied by past deeds and omissions in her personal relationships, as evidenced by this excerpt from nursing notes:

> Patient in depths of gloom this morning—looking too unhappy for anything. Patient looked angry. I asked her with whom. She replied, "Myself." I asked, "What have you done that merits so much self-anger so much of the time?" She replied, "Haven't you ever looked yourself over?" In the course of conversation I suggested she might be too harsh with herself. At this she gave a bitter laugh and stuck out her chin again.

Later in her hospitalization she purposely avoided mirrors.

Another patient, 86 years old and periodically confused, often stood before the mirror in his hospital room and rhythmically chanted either happily or angrily. He was especially given to angry flare-ups and crying spells over food, money, and clothes. When angry he would screech obscenities at his mirror image, so savagely beating his fist upon a nearby table that the staff tried to protect him by covering the mirror. But in contrast to the first patient he denied that the image was himself, and when an observer came up beside him and said, "See, this is me in the mirror and there you are in the mirror," he smiled and said, "That's you in the mirror all right, but that's not me."

Adaptive and Constructive Manifestations

As the past marches in review, it is surveyed, observed, and reflected upon by the ego. Reconsideration of previous experiences and their meanings occurs, often with concomitant revised or expanded understanding. Such reorganization of past experience may provide a more valid picture, giving new and significant meanings to one's life; it may also prepare one for death, mitigating one's fears.[17]

The occasions on which the life review has obviously been creative, having positive, constructive effects, are most impressive. For example:

> A 78-year-old man, optimistic, reflective, and resourceful, who had had significantly impairing egocentric tendencies, became increasingly responsive in his relationships to his wife, children, and grandchildren. These changes corresponded with his purchase of a tape recorder. Upon my request he sent me the tapes he had made, and wrote: "There is the first reel of tape on which I recorded my memory of my life store. To give this some additional interest I am expecting that my children and grandchildren and great-grandchildren will listen to it after I am gone. I pretended that I was telling the story directly to them."

Ingmar Bergman's very fine, remarkable Swedish motion picture, *Wild Strawberries*, provides a beautiful example of the constructive aspects of the life review. Envisioning and dreaming of his past and his death, the protagonist-physician realizes the nonaffectionate and withholding qualities of his life; as the feeling of love reenters his life, the doctor changes even as death hovers upon him.

Although it is not possible at present to describe in detail either the life review or the possibilities for reintegration which are suggested, it seems likely that in the majority of the elderly a substantial reorganization of the personality does occur. This may help to account for the evolution of such qualities as wisdom and serenity, long noted in some of the aged. Although a favorable, constructive, and positive end result may be enhanced by favorable environmental circumstances, such as comparative freedom from crises and losses, it is more likely that successful reorganization is largely a function of the personality—in particular, such vaguely defined features of the personality as flexibility, resilience, and self-awareness.

In addition to the more impressive constructive aspects of the life review, certain adaptive and defensive aspects may be noted. Some of the aged have illusions of the "good past"; some fantasy the past rather than the future in the service of avoiding the realities of the present; some maintain a characteristic detachment from others and themselves. Although these mechanisms are not constructive, they do assist in maintaining a status quo of psychological functioning.

Psychopathological Manifestations

As indicated earlier, the many and varied behavioral and affective states resulting from the life review can include severe depressions, states of panic, intense guilt, and constant obsessional rumination; instead of increasing self-awareness and flexibility, one may find increasing rigidity. The more severe affective and behavioral consequences apparently tend to occur when the process proceeds in isolation in those who have been deeply affected by increasing contraction of life attachments and notable psychosocial discontinuities, such as forced retirement and the death of the spouse. But, again, while environmental circumstances are important, it is in character and its lifelong unfolding that the unfortunate manifestations of the life review mainly originate.

In a recent series of articles on the aged appearing in a national magazine, a 70-year-old woman in a mental hospital is quoted, "Some nights when I can't sleep, I think of the difference between what I'd hoped for when I was young and what I have now and what I am." [18] The most tragic situation is that of the person whose increasing—but only partial—insight leads to a sense of total waste: the horrible insight just as one is about to die of feeling that one has never lived, or of seeing oneself realistically as in some sense inadequate. [19]

Because the affective consequences are not all readily attributable to definitive losses, the painful accompaniments of the life review are often hard for the observer to understand. It is often extremely difficult for the reviewer to communicate his insights because of their unacceptability to him. When he can communicate them, it is also extremely difficult for the observer to comprehend and face them. The more tragic manifestations are the most difficult—at times impossible—to treat. I believe that this situation is one contribution to the increased suicide rate found in old age. [20]

One group of persons who seem to be especially prone to anxiety, despair, depression, or the extreme kind of total catastrophe outlined above, consists of those who always tended to avoid the present and to put great emphasis on the future. These people made heavy investments in and commitments to the future: The future would bring what they struggled to achieve, and it would be free of that which they dislike but have tolerated in the present. This places a considerable strain upon old age, which cannot often deliver; the wishes cannot be met. The poet Adah I. Menken clearly stated this idea in the line, "Where is the promise of my years, once written on my brow?" [21]

Another group that appears to be especially prone to some of the more severe manifestations and outcomes of the life review consists of those who have consciously exercised the human capacity to injure others. These people, in whom guilt is real, can see no way of reversing the process; they do not imagine forgiveness and redemption. Still another group that appears especially vulnerable to the consequences of the life review may be best described as characterologically arrogant and prideful. This group may overlap with the previous group, but not all its members necessarily have undertaken directly hurtful actions. Their narcissism is probably particularly disturbed by the realization of death.

The following case illustration concerns a person whose life and personality probably involves a merger of all of the factors predisposing one toward psychopathological complications resulting from the life review. [22]

Mrs. G, a 69-year-old married woman, developed a depression six months prior to hospitalization; her depression had been unsuccessfully treated by electroshock, tranquilizers, and heeded recommendations that she take vacations and move to a new environment. She was agitated, suspicious, delusional, nihilistic ("This is the end of the world"), self-derogatory, and self-accusatory, and revealed suicidal ideas. She was embittered and hostile, particularly toward her husband, with whom she was often combative. She was preoccupied with thoughts of death. She had lived for nearly 20 years across the street from a hospital morgue; her physician had sensed this to be disturbing to her and had therefore recommended moving, which she did. She refused psychological testing, explaining, "Why should I be uncomfortable during the little time remaining?" She had a fear of cancer, and once stated, "You can see your funeral go by but still not believe it." She viewed her situation as futile and increasingly refused to talk in any detail about herself to others, including members of her family.

She was in good physical health although she showed increasing preoccupation with her gastrointestinal tract. Upon admission, symptoms suggesting the possibility of a malignancy required investigation. The examinations were all negative, but the patient became increasingly "fixated" upon her lower bowel.

There was no evidence of organic mental changes, including confusion. She became essentially mute several weeks after her admission; she refused to recognize her psychotherapist as a therapist and refused to cooperate with nursing personnel or the ward administrator. She felt no one "could understand." She assaulted others and herself; she would smash her fist at her head and body until she was a frightful sight to behold, with extensive eccymoses and hematomas all over her body. She refused to eat or drink and continued to lose weight; she rarely slept, day or night. Upon the firm insistence of the administrator that she would be sedated and fed intravenously or by tube, she responded by maintaining a minimum intake of food and fluid. Occasional sedation interrupted her sleeplessness. Otherwise, she did not materially change at that time, and continued to be assaultive toward family members and staff, and to be self-abusive. Because of her years and the remarkable amount of self-destructiveness, she created considerable anxiety and despair in the staff, which eventually was reflected in terms of considerable anger and rage at her. It was exceedingly difficult to break through this kind of bind. Her threat of suicide made the situation for the professional staff even more difficult. However, during the course of a year she improved to the extent that she was no longer as self-punitive or assaultive.

On one occasion she communicated to the Director of Psychotherapy her concern with "God's wrath" and at various times gave intimations of her severe and intense sense of guilt about both past actions and past omissions. Her wish to kill herself seemed quite clear in both direct and indirect statements.

Her past history strongly suggested that she had never realized her potentialities as a person and had never achieved an individual sense of identity. Her premorbid personality was characterized by dependency, indecisiveness, self-centeredness, stubbornness, and a lack of generosity, despite the fact that she had stayed home to care for her mother and father after the other siblings had married. An attractive woman, she did not marry until a year and a half after her mother's death, when she was 47; her husband was then 60. Behind a dignified and passive façade lay a formidable character. She was the quiet but potent center of opposing family forces; her gift was the masterly regulation of these forces. Moreover, she had become increasingly isolated in the three years prior to admission.

In addition to whatever irrational and unconscious feelings of guilt the patient may have experienced, it appeared quite clear that she had in fact done or omitted to do things that justified her sense of guilt. From indirect intimations and direct communications, it became apparent that she was engaged in a process of reviewing her past life but that despite the presence of professional people she was unwilling to review her life with them.

Her therapist concluded that "all of these changes, especially the more restricted life, might have brought on an opportunity for the patient to inquire about herself; that is, to do some introspective thinking. Such introspection might have led to some thoughts about the uncertainty of her future, as well as some unpleasant traits of her personality, and it is this kind of inquiry that might have led to her depression."

The terrifying nature of some of the insights accompanying aging can also be seen in the following illustration from James's *The Beast in the Jungle*.[23] In it James delineated the nature of the "beast" of insight, and of detached, egotistic, intellectualizing John Marcher, upon whom the beast descended. In this profoundly disturbing creation, Marcher's illumination grows to the point of "gazing at [what] was the sounded void of his life," and "leaving him stupefied at the blindness he had cherished."[24]

John Marcher had earlier been reminded by his friend, Mary Bartram:

You said you had had from your earliest time, as the deepest thing within you, the sense of being kept for something rare and strange, possibly prodigious and terrible, that was sooner or later to happen to you.

She theorized,

Isn't what you describe perhaps but the expectation—or at any rate the sense of danger, familiar to so many people—of falling in love?[25]

As the story progressed, and life passed by,

He felt in these days what, oddly enough, he had never felt before, the growth of a dread of losing her by some catastrophe—some catastrophe that yet wouldn't at all be *the* catastrophe.[26]

They aged:

He had been struck one day, after an absence exceeding his usual measure, with her suddenly looking much older to him than he had ever thought of her being; then he recognized that the suddenness was all on his side—he had just simply and suddenly noticed. She looked older because inevitably, after so many years, she *was* old, or almost; which was of course true in still greater measure for her companion.

His surprises began here; when once they had begun they multiplied; they came rather with a rush. It was as if, in the oddest way in the world, they had all been kept back, sown in a thick cluster, for the late afternoon of life, the time at which for people in general the unexpected had died out.[27]

The possibility of losing Mary through death troubled him.

It would represent, as connected with his past

attitude, a drop of dignity under the shadow of which his existence could only become the most grotesque of failures. What did everything mean—what, that is, did *she* mean, she and her vain waiting and her probable death and the soundless admonition of it all—unless, that, at this time of day, it was simply, it was overwhelmingly too late? [28]

Since it was in Time that he was to have met his fate, so it was in Time that his fate was to have acted; and as he waked up to the sense of no longer being young, which was exactly the sense of being stale, just as that, in turn, was the sense of being weak. . . .[29]

He had in this later time turned nervous, which was what he in all the other years had never been; and the oddity was that his nervousness should have waited till he had begun to doubt, should have held off so long as he was sure.[30]

When his friend died, he found he had no special position or admission to the social situation of mourning. He didn't have:

. . . the distinction, the dignity, the propriety, if nothing else, of the man markedly bereaved. It was as if in the view of society he had not *been* markedly bereaved . . . . he found himself wondering if he oughtn't to have begun, so to speak, further back.[31]

He visited her grave monthly.

It thus grew for him, in the oddest way, a positive resource; he carried out his idea of periodical returns, which took their place at last among the most inveterate of his habits. What it all amounted to, oddly enough, was that in his finally so simplified world this garden of death gave him the few square feet of earth on which he could still most live. It was as if, being nothing anywhere else for any one, nothing even for himself, he were just everything here, and if not for a crowd of witnesses or indeed for any witness but John Marcher, then by clear right of the register that he could scan like an open page. The open page was the tomb of his friend, and *there* were the facts of the past, there the truth of his life, there the backward reaches in which he could lose himself. He did this from time to time with such effect that he seemed to wander through the old years with his hand in the arm of a companion who was, in the most extraordinary manner, his other, younger self; and to wander, which was more extraordinary yet, round and round a third presence—not wandering she, but stationary, still, whose eyes, turning with his revolution, never ceased to follow him, and whose seat was his point, so to speak, of orientation. Thus in short he settled to live—feeding all on the sense that he once *had* lived, and dependent on it not alone for a support but for an identity.[32]

But the realizations increased.

No passion had ever touched him, for this was what passion meant; he had survived and maundered and pined, but where had been

his deep ravage? . . . He had seen *outside* of his life, not learned it from within, the way a woman was mourned when she had been loved for herself. . . . Now that the illumination had begun, however, it blazed to the zenith, and what he presently stood there gazing at was the sounded void of his life. He gazed, he drew breath, in pain; he turned in his dismay, and, turning, he had before him in sharper incision than ever the open page of his story. The name on the table smote him as the passage of his neighbor had done, and what it said to him, full in the face, was that *she* was what he had missed. This was the awful thought, the answer to all the past, the vision at the dread clearness of which he grew as cold as the stone beneath him. Everything fell together, confessed, explained, overwhelmed; leaving him most of all stupefied at the blindness he had cherished.[33]

This remarkable story was written in 1903 when James was 60. Other writings of James's contain similar content. *The Ambassadors* is about a man superbly equipped to react to the experiences which came to him too late.[34] The titles of his two unfinished novels are also pertinent to the life review: *The Sense of the Past* and *The Ivory Tower*. As Van Wyck Brooks has written, James's fiction became increasingly tragic with age.[35]

Discussion

It is evident that there is a considerable need for the intensive detailed study of aged persons in order to obtain information concerning their mental functioning, the experience of aging, approaching death, and dying. Behavior during aging may be clarified by the revelations of subjective experience. Because of the garrulity, repetitiveness, and reminiscence of the aged, it is not always easy for investigators or therapists to listen; but for those who will listen there are rewards. The personal sense and meaning of the life cycle are more clearly unfolded by those who have nearly completed it. The nature of the forces shaping life, the effects of life events, the fate of neuroses and character disorders, the denouement of character itself may be studied in the older person. Recognition of the occurrence of such a vital process as the life review may help one to listen, to tolerate and understand the aged, and not to treat reminiscence as devitalized and insignificant.

Of course, people of all ages review their past at various times; they look back to comprehend the forces and experiences that have shaped their lives. However, the principal concern of most people is the present, and the proportion of time younger persons spend dwelling on the past is probably a fair, although by no means definite, measure of mental health. One tends to consider the past most when prompted by current problems and crises. The past also absorbs one in attempts to avoid the realities of the present. A very similar point has been made by others in connection with the sense of identity: One is apt to consider one's identity in the face of life crisis; at other times the question of "Who and what am I?" does not arise.

At present, not enough is known about the mental disorders of the aged and how they differ from the manifestly similar disorders of younger age groups. It is known, however, that late life is the period when people are most likely to develop mental disorders—specifically, organic disorders and depressions. The question arises as to whether the life review is related to the increased occurrence as well as the character and course of these disorders.

The current nosology distinguishing the so-called exogenous or reactive depressions from the endogenous depressions may be clarified and explained in part by the concept of the life review. Endogenous depressions, which operationally are those which are least easily comprehensible in terms of environmental variables, may owe their existence to the inner process of life review. The relationships of and distinctions between depression and despair need study. The role of guilt especially requires investigation. Recently, Busse suggested, in connection with "so-called normal elderly persons," that "guilt as a psychodynamic force of importance is infrequently seen in our subjects of elderly persons living in the community. It appears that old people become involved in very little guilt-producing behavior." [36] This sanguine idea seems questionable. Not only do older people appear to maintain the capacities to undertake hurtful actions and to feel guilt but also they have not lost the past, which, indeed, comes back forcibly. It is essential to accept the occurrence of reality-based as well as imagined guilt. [37]

The oft-stated impression that the aged have relatively greater impairments of recent than remote memory—an impression not substantiated by any experimental data since "remote memory" is difficult to test—may reflect the older person's avoidance of the present as a consequence of the life review.

Other writers have offered constructs pertinent to the aged which probably relate to the life review process. The atrophy of the capacity to project oneself into the future, described by Krapf, [38] may be another way of discussing the life review; here stress is upon the absence of a process rather than upon the presence of another, active, substitutive process. Balint has written of the *Torschlusspanik* (literally, the panic at the closing of the gate), [39] which may be related to the state of terror already described in the extreme unfolding of the life review and may also be germane to the "time panic" which has been described by Krapf.

Intimations of the life review are also found in the literature of psychotherapy; indeed, the dangers involved when an older person reviews his life have been cited as either a contraindication to, or a basis for modification of technique for, psychotherapy in this age group. Rechtschaffen wrote, "also to be seriously considered in this regard is the emotional price paid when a patient reviews the failures of his past. It must be exceedingly difficult for a person nearing death to look back upon the bulk of his life as having been neurotic or maladjusted." [40] It is this consideration that led Grotjahn to suggest that it was important for the aged person to integrate his past life experiences as they have been lived, not as they might have been lived. [41] It is curious, and probably reflective of psychiatrists' own countertransference concerns, that the dangers of reviewing one's life in psychotherapy should be emphasized; underlying is the implication that truth is dangerous. [42] The existence of a life review occurring irrespective of the psychotherapeutic situation suggests that the aged particularly need a participant observer, professional or otherwise, and that the alleged danger of psychotherapy should be reevaluated.

Past and current forms of, or views about, the psychotherapy of the aged might well be evaluated in terms of their relation to the life review. The "Martin Method," for example, may have been successful because of the enthusiasm, interest, and support provided in this inspirational catechismic form of therapy, but perhaps also because the client was asked to relate his life history in detail, including the seemingly irrelevant side thoughts or images, which might help in understanding "subconscious complexes."[43]

Goldfarb and his associates, on the other hand, propose a technique based upon illusion—namely, creating the illusion of mastery in the patient. Goldfarb's brief therapy is oriented neither toward insight nor toward discharge, but rather toward amelioration of disturbed behavior.[44]

One might also speculate as to whether there is any relationship between the onset of the life review and the self-prediction and occurrence of death. Another question that arises is whether the intensity of a person's preoccupation with the past might express the wish to distance himself from death by restoring the past in inner experience and fantasy. This may be related to human narcissism or sense of omnipotence, for persons and events can in this way be recreated and brought back. At the same time a constructive reevaluation of the past may facilitate a serene and dignified acceptance of death.[45]

The phenomenon of mirror-image gazing is of both practical and theoretical interest. In addition to affording one a diagnostic clue to the existence of the life-review, it may provide an unusually excellent experimental basis for the study and further elucidation of the changing concepts of self- and body-image, and the phenomenon of depersonalization, that accompany the rapid, profound, and multiple bodily and mental changes in the aged.[46]

Certain schizophrenic and neurotic patients are also known to seek out and gaze at their images in the mirror, talk to their images, and reveal many similar behavioral manifestations. The French psychiatrist Perrier has stated flatly that the schizophrenic does not recognize himself in the mirror; he considers that this symptom shows that the patient has neglected and lost his ego.[47] Schulz has described a 25-year-old female patient whose depersonalization—she felt her right arm was not connected to her body—ceased when she was reassured about her body integrity by looking in the mirror.[48] The experience of a probably paranoid schizophrenic observing himself in mirrors is also excellently described in a novel by Simenon.[49]

Schulz also reported a neurotic patient who would examine himself in the mirror while shaving and experience the recurring inner questions, "Is that me?" and "Who am I?," probably illustrating his concern about his identity.[50] In this connection, one observes that adolescents frequently spend time examining themselves in mirrors; and analysands, especially female, often report mirror-gazing in their childhood, especially during pubescence. Persons of certain narcissistic character-types describe disrobing before a mirror and deriving great pleasure in self-observation; occasionally there are reports of actual or wished-for orgastic experiences. The theme of the mirror as revealing character is ancient, ranging from the stories of Narcissus and Snow White to the use of the mirror as a chastity test in the *Arabian Nights* tales.

Memory is an ego function whose neurophysiological mechanisms remain hypothetical and inconclusively demonstrated. It serves the sense of self and its continuity; it entertains us; it shames us; it pains us. Memory can tell us our origins; it can be explanatory and it can deceive. Presumably it can lend itself toward cure. The recovery of memories, the making the unconscious conscious, is generally regarded as one of the basic ingredients of the curative process. It is a step in the occurrence of change. Psychotherapists tend to associate self-awareness with health, and lack of awareness with morbidity.

Probably at no other time in life is there as potent a force toward self-awareness operating as in old age. Yet, the capacity to change, according to prevailing stereotype, decreases with age. "Learning capacity" falters with time, and it is fair to say that the major portion of gerontological research throughout the country is concerned almost enthusiastically with measuring decline in various cognitive, perceptual, and psychomotor functions.[51] Comparable attention toward studies of the individual, of growing wisdom, of the meaning of experience, is not ordinary. It is therefore of interest to notice the positive, affirmative changes reported by the aged themselves as part of their life experience,[52] and to find constructive alterations in character, possibly as a consequence of the life review. The relationships of changed functions to aging per se and to diseases, psychosocial crises, and personality remain obscure.[53] There is at least reason to observe that personality change can occur all along the life span, and that old age is no exception. Change obviously cannot be attributed only to professional effort, and changes in behavior outside of professional effort and beyond professional understanding should not be casually categorized as either unreal or "spontaneous." It is necessary to study the changes wrought in life by experience, eventful or uneventful, by brief or enduring relationships with other human beings, or even through images evoked by hearing or reading of the experiences or efforts of others.

In the course of the life review the older person may reveal to his wife, children, and other intimates, unknown qualities of his character and unstated actions of his past; in return, they may reveal heretofore undisclosed or unknown truths. Hidden themes of great vintage may emerge, changing the quality of a lifelong relationship. Revelations of the past may forge a new intimacy, render a deceit honest; they may sever peculiar bonds and free tongues; or they may sculpture terrifying hatreds out of fluid, fitful antagonisms.

Sameness and change may both be manifestations of the active process of ego identity. Erikson writes, ". . . identity formation neither begins nor ends with adolescence: it is a lifelong development largely unconscious to the individual and to his society." [54] He also writes that "early development cannot be understood on its own terms alone, and that the earliest stages of childhood cannot be accounted for without a unified theory of the whole span of pre-adulthood." [55] Similarly, it may be argued that the entire life cycle cannot be comprehended without inclusion of the psychology of the aged.

Notes

[1] Aristotle, *Selections*, edited by W. D. Ross; New York, Scribner's, 1927; p. 324.

[2] William Cowper, *Task;* Boston, Thomas Badger, 1819; p. 113.

[3] Somerset Maugham, *Points of View;* Garden City, N.Y., Doubleday, 1959; p. 70.

[4] Robert N. Butler, "Intensive Psychotherapy for the Hospitalized Aged," *Geriatrics* (1960) 15:644-653.

[5] Robert N. Butler, "Re-awakening Interests," *Nursing Homes: J. Amer. Nursing Home Assn.* (1961) 10:8-19.

[6] Ewald W. Busse, Robert H. Barnes, and Albert J. Silverman, "Studies in the Processes of Aging: I. Behavioral Patterns in the Aged and Their Relationship to Adjustment," *Diseases Nervous System* (1954) 15:22-26. Ewald W. Busse and others, "Studies in the Process of Aging: Factors That Influence the Psyche of Elderly Persons," *Amer. J. Psychiatry* (1954) 110:897-903. Seymour Perlin and Robert N. Butler, "Psychiatric Aspects of Adaptation to the Aging Experience," in *Human Aging: Biological and Behavioral Aspects*, Natl. Inst. Mental Health; Washington, D. C., Government Printing Office, in press.

[7] Allan Rechtschaffen, "Psychotherapy with Geriatric Patients: A Review of the Literature," *J. Gerontology* (1959) 14:73-84. See also footnote 4.

[8] See, for example: Horace B. English and Ava Champney English, *A Comprehensive Dictionary of Psychological and Psychoanalytical Terms;* New York, Longmans, Green, 1958. *The Oxford English Dictionary;* Oxford, Clarendon Press, 1933. Leland E. Hinsie and Robert J. Campbell, *Psychiatric Dictionary* (3rd Ed.); New York, Oxford Univ. Press, 1960.

[9] *Felix Frankfurter Reminisces*, recorded in talks with Harlan B. Phillips; New York, Reynal, 1960.

[10] Martin Grotjahn, "Psychoanalytic Investigation of a Seventy-One-Year-Old Man with Senile Dementia," *Psychoanalytic Quart.* (1940) 9:80-97.

[11] The recent Japanese motion picture *Ikiru* describes the salvation of a man whose thirty unproductive years as a governmental bureau chief were interrupted by cancer; he undertook a new and constructive activity following acceptance of his impending death and review of his past.

[12] Walter B. Cannon. " 'Voodoo' Death," *Amer. Anthropologist* (1942) 44:169-181. Curt P. Richter, "On the Phenomenon of Sudden Death in Animals and Man," *Psychosomatic Med.* (1957) 19:191-198. Marvin L. Adland, "Review, Case Studies, Therapy and Interpretation of Acute Exhaustive Psychoses," *Psychiatric Quart.* (1947) 21:38-69. Otto Allen Will, Jr., "Human Relatedness and the Schizophrenic Reaction," PSYCHIATRY (1959) 22:205-223. Frieda Fromm-Reichmann also wrote about loneliness in her old age in "On Loneliness," pp. 325-336, in *Psychoanalysis and Psychotherapy*, edited by Dexter M. Bullard; Chicago, Univ. of Chicago Press, 1959.

[13] See Will, in footnote 12; p. 218.

[14] The term "life review" has the disadvantage of suggesting that orderliness is characteristic. The reminiscences of an older person are not necessarily more orderly than any other aspects of his life, and he may be preoccupied at various times by particular periods of his life and not the whole of it.

[15] See Perlin and Butler, in footnote 6.

[16] Various sensory processes are involved. Older people report the revival of the sounds, tastes, smells of early life, as: "I can hear the rain against the window of my boyhood room."

[17] For example, Joyce Cary's *To Be a Pilgrim* (London, Michael Joseph, 1942) concerns an insightful old man "deep in his own dream, which is chiefly of the past," (p. 7) and describes the review of his life, augmented by the memories stimulated by his return to his boyhood home.

[18] "Old Age: Part IV," *Life*, August 3, 1959, pp. 67-74; p. 67.

[19] Samuel Beckett's one-act play *Krapp's Last Tape* dramatically illustrates the life review (*Krapp's Last Tape and Other Dramatic Pieces;* New York, Grove Press, 1960).

[20] One may compare this with Durkheim's concept of anomie (Emile Durkheim, *Suicide*, translated from *Le Suicide* [1897] by John A. Spaulding and George Simpson; Glencoe, Ill., Free Press, 1951).

[21] Adah I. Menken, *Infelicia;* London, Chatto and Wincus, 1888; p. 37.

[22] See footnote 4. I am indebted to Dr. Ping-nie Pao for making available these clinical data.

[23] Henry James, "The Beast in the Jungle (1903),"

pp. 548-602, in *The Short Stories of Henry James,* edited by Clifton Fadiman; New York, Modern Library, 1945.

[24] Footnote 23; p. 596.

[25] Footnote 23; p. 556.

[26] Footnote 23; p. 572.

[27] Footnote 23; p. 573.

[28] Footnote 23; p. 574.

[29] Footnote 23; p. 575.

[30] Footnote 23; pp. 576-577.

[31] Footnote 23; p. 589.

[32] Footnote 23; p. 593.

[33] Footnote 23; pp. 595-596.

[34] Henry James, *The Ambassadors;* Garden City, N.Y., Doubleday, 1958.

[35] Van Wyck Brooks, *The Pilgrimage of Henry James;* New York, Dutton, 1925.

[36] Ewald W. Busse, "Psychopathology," pp. 364-399, in *Handbook of Aging and the Individual,* edited by James E. Birren; Chicago, Univ. of Chicago Press, 1959; p. 390.

[37] Martin Buber, "Guilt and Guilt Feelings," PSYCHIATRY (1957) 20:114-129.

[38] E. Eduardo Krapf, "On Aging," *Proc. Roy. Soc. Med.* [London] (1953) 46:957-964.

[39] Michael Balint, "The Psychological Problems of Growing Old," pp. 69-85, in *Problems in Human Pleasure and Behavior;* London, Hogarth, 1951.

[40] See footnote 7; p. 74.

[41] Martin Grotjahn, "Some Analytic Observations About the Process of Growing Old," pp. 301-312, in *Psychoanalysis and Social Science,* Vol. 3, edited by G. Roheim; New York, Internat. Univ. Press, 1951.

[42] In the atmosphere of hospital units for the mentally disturbed aged are to be found the notions that the aged "can't stand the truth," must be protected from "bad news," and need to be reassured about their "conditions," and, curiously, that therapy may prove too "disturbing." (See footnote 4.) I submit that the hospitalized aged, already disturbed, need honesty.

[43] See footnote 7.

[44] Alvin I. Goldfarb, "The Rationale for Psychotherapy with Older Persons," *Amer. J. Med. Sci.* (1956) 232:181-185.

[45] However, I do not intend to imply that a "serene and dignified acceptance of death" is necessarily appropriate, noble, or to be valued. Those who die screaming may be expressing a rage that is as fitting as dignity.

[46] Martha M. Werner, Seymour Perlin, Robert N. Butler, and William Pollin, "Self-Perceived Changes in Community-Resident Aged," *Arch. General Psychiatry* (1961) 4:501-508.

[47] F. Perrier, "The Meaning of Transference in Schizophrenia," *Acta Psychother.* [Basel] (1955) 3, Supplement:266-272. Translation by M. A. Woodbury.

[48] Clarence Schulz, personal communication.

[49] Georges Simenon, *The Man Who Watched the Trains Go By;* New York, Berkley, 1958.

[50] See footnote 48.

[51] See footnote 4.

[52] See footnote 46.

[53] Natl. Inst. Mental Health, *Human Aging: Biological and Behavioral Aspects;* Washington, D.C., Government Printing Office, in press.

[54] Erik H. Erikson, "The Problem of Ego Identity," in *Identity and the Life Cycle, Psychol. Issues* (1959) 1:101-164; p. 113.

[55] See footnote 54; p. 121.

34

The Older Woman

by Irene de Castillejo

IT WOULD SEEM easy enough for me to write on 'The Older Woman' since I am one, but perhaps it is for that reason I find it difficult. One can really only see situations clearly when one is outside them, not when one is in the middle of living them. However there is no help for it. When I have passed the stage of being an older woman I shall also be beyond writing at all.

In is obvious that there are two distinct classes of older women: the wife and the mother on the one hand, and the professional woman on the other, although today these two merge more and more. It is with the former that I am most familiar.

The fundamental truth to remember in thinking of woman, irrespective of the role she plays, is that her life's curve, unlike that of man, is not a slow rising to the zenith of power followed by a gradual decline in the later years. The curve of a woman's life span follows more nearly the pattern of the seasons. She almost literally blossoms in the spring, but the long summer which follows is a very slow ripening with nothing much in the woman herself to show for it. If she lives a traditional family pattern she will be giving all the sap which rose so abundantly earlier to nourish her offspring, materially, emotionally and spiritually.

Then suddenly her children are all grown up, gone on their separate journeys, and she finds herself bereft. The apparent purpose of her life, for which she had strained every nerve, is snatched from her with the attainment of the goal. She feels stranded on the mud flats, while the river races by bearing away each new craft as it embarks, and she no part of the flowing waters. What then? What can happen then, with another thirty or forty years still to run and no one needing her? Even her husband has centered his life on his career and other interests apart from her while she was occupied with the growing family. At the best his need of her is not absorbing enough to assuage her aching emptiness.

What then? This is the crucial moment in the life of any wife and mother. It is then that she may notice, almost by accident, that from where the early blossoms fell fruit is hanging and almost ripe. Unsuspected fruit, fruit which has swelled and grown unheeded, is now ready and waiting to be plucked. The autumn of a woman's life is far richer

than the spring if only she becomes aware in time, and harvests the ripening fruit before it falls and rots and is trampled underfoot. The winter which follows is not barren if the harvest has been stored, and the withdrawal of sap is only a prelude to a new spring elsewhere.

Conscious modern women of course know these things. They prepare for the autumn before the long dry summer is over. But far too many women still feel that life is finished at fifty and that vibrant loving ends with the menopause. This last bogie should be swept away at the outset. It is utterly untrue.

You may know some version of the famous story of the young man who asked his mother at what age women cease to be interested in sexual intercourse. 'I do not know,' she replied, 'you had better ask your grandmother.' 'How should I know?' she answered gruffly. 'Great Granny may be able to tell you.' This is perhaps not as far-fetched as would appear.

It is true enough that some men cease to be interested sexually in women when their physical fertility is ended, causing their wives, who have a recrudescence of sexual interest at this time, great distress. Such a situation is the survival of an inherent primitive pattern where sexuality was for humanity, as it is for animals, only a matter of procreation.

Since the age of chivalry and the development of romantic love, sex has become very much more than that. And with the discovery and spread of contraceptives sex has entered a new phase. The contraceptive can certainly lead to irresponsibility, licence and a devaluation of sexuality. In fact it often does so. But on the other hand it opens the door to immensely heightened emotional experience where sex ceases to be solely a biological function, and becomes an expression of love in its own right. In this context age with its absence of fertility is irrelevant.

This cultural achievement gives mankind a chance of healing the cleavage between body and spirit which has been fostered for centuries by the Church, and may enable us to weld once more the two together.

In this whole development the older woman is actually at a great advantage. She does not need the contraceptive, and I believe this is one reason why a woman's most profound and meaningful sex life often occurs after fifty when she is no longer caught in the biological net. For the first time she is able to give herself in the sex act completely free from fear of conception, a fear which in countless women does still operate beneath the surface, even when reason and science assure them that they have taken the most complete precautions.

Moreover to a great many women contraceptives, though accepted intellectually, are still unaesthetic, and to a deep basic feminine morality they are wholly unacceptable, all of which inevitably causes inhibitions so long as they have to be used. When once a woman is free to use her body as an expression of deep feeling, without its becoming the impersonal vehicle of nature's insistent demand for life and yet more life, she can transcend her earlier inhibitions and attain physical expression of an emotional relationship beyond anything of which she had ever dreamed.

Do not misunderstand me. It is a grave mistake for a woman to look for some great spiritual experience in sex at any age, or even to assume that she ought to have such a thing. All assumptions about sex are disastrous. They tend to lead to disappointment and recriminations. To my mind most modern books on sex do more harm than good for this very reason: they fill women's heads with assumptions and expectations which actually *prevent* experience at its fullest. It is one's own personal experience that counts and it should not be measured up against any generalization. The statistical so-called normal man or woman does not in fact exist, and it is foolish to weigh our actual living experience against such a mythical figure.

Sex delight is like happiness. It does not come when sought. It is not until a woman ceases to strive for her own sensual satisfaction, but allows the voice of her heart to speak to her man through the medium of her body, that she finds that heart, spirit and body are all one.

Important as the heightening fulfilment of sex may be, it is none the less only a small part of the ripe autumnal fruit to which I have alluded. A woman's liberation from the service of nature's purposes frees an enormous amount of energy for something else. A man at fifty is probably at the height of his intellectual or administrative power. A family woman at the same age may be aware of an entirely new stirring. Latent possibilities dance before her unbelieving eyes.

I recall one such woman seated on the lawn of her house one summer evening holding forth to her family. I say holding forth but she was certainly not laying down the law. It was almost as though a dam had burst and a torrent of ideas came tumbling out to which she herself seemed to be listening with the same astonished amusement as were her hearers. She simply emanated vitality and I remember her ending up with the words: 'I have no idea what is going to happen but I am quite sure something is.' And as I watched and listened so was I. She did in fact become a writer some ten years later.

The expression 'change of life' exactly fits the situation. The menopause does not spell the end of life but a change of direction, not a living death but a change of *life*.

If this were more generally understood I am convinced that women's menopause problems would rapidly diminish. Glandular changes are inevitable but it is woman's own dread of this mysterious change on the whole tenor of her life which, I am sure, brings about the neurotic state she fears. No, change of life means an enormous release of energy for some new venture in a new direction.

The direction in which the newly released energy will flow depends of course entirely on the type of person and the particular gifts with which she has been endowed. Some may develop a latent talent, painting, writing or some such thing. Voluntary societies serving social, political and cultural causes of all kinds abound with such women. But these only cater for the more conscious and extroverted type of woman. There are innumerable others who can find no outlet. They suffer deeply, for energy which finds no channel in which to flow seeps into the ground and makes a marsh where nothing can be planted, where only slime and insects breed.

Women who find they are no longer vitally needed by their families yet have no other place where they can give themselves, sink into lassitude and finally fall ill. The magnates who organize society have hardly begun to notice this happening. The autumnal energy of countless older women escapes silently down the kitchen sink along with their tears.

Not only is the nation poorer for its loss, the wastage is double, for these women who could have been healthily active and useful become a wholly unnecessary burden upon the health services, while as likely as not their frustration poisons the atmosphere of the home. Swamps breed mosquitoes. Uncanalized, wasted energy breeds gloom and nagging.

Part-time work is at least one answer to this problem, but part-time work is not easy to find. Industry seems to frown upon it and our modern passion for degrees and paper diplomas shuts many a door. It is not sufficiently recognized that running a home can afford very valuable experience in organization, and particularly in handling other people with diverse temperaments. The mother of a family is generally an adept at that very difficult accomplishment of attending to half a dozen things all at the same time, an asset by no means to be despised if diverted to other fields.

That society is gravely at fault in not providing outlets for the older woman's energy is unquestionably true. But her real problem is to discover in which direction her newly released libido wants to flow. Libido is like water, it always seeks its proper level. No amount of coercion can make it flow uphill.

So long as a woman is fulfilling her traditional role of bringing up a family, she is carried along by the stream of life. Indeed she has no alternative. She goes with the stream even though cooking and cleaning and changing diapers are not at all her ideal occupations. She has no real choice. But she herself develops as the family grows and she learns to meet the demands as they arise. Changing diapers gives way to helping with obstreperous homework and providing meals for expanding appetites in every field. But when all this is past and the river flows on without her, her own little stream of energy is dammed up. If she is fortunate the waters will rise till they are strong enough to burst out in a channel of their own.

What the channel will be depends on her concern. Even today, when education does its best to divert women's activity into every branch of industry and money-making, there are still older women who slide happily into the estate of grandmother because their children's children do in fact become the centre of their interest and their concern. Dedicated grandmothers who gladly put themselves at the service of the future generation without trying to run the show themselves are a boon to any family, but they are becoming increasingly rare. Like maiden aunts they are dying out, and the services which both maiden aunts and grandmothers used to give as a matter of course and with genuine devotion now frequently have to be bought with money. We all know what a poor substitute that is and how expensive.

The modern trend seems to be in the opposite direction. More and more mothers wait with impatience for their children to be grown and gone. Then at last they feel free to carry on with the career which family demands had forced them to abandon. These women are faced with relatively little conflict. They nearly always succeed in finding an outlet before the problem becomes acute. As the children grow they dovetail the new life into the old so that there is no traumatic moment when they feel deserted.

The ones who cannot look forward to any vibrant future or any sphere of usefulness to which they can give themselves, are those with whom I am particularly concerned here. For them especially is the surprise and delight of discovery. And for them above all is the paramount need to know what is and what is not their true concern.

. . . In the case of woman, the outstanding almost invariable object of her concern is, as we all know, the person or persons whom she loves. This is true right through her life. It is, I repeat, the essential ingredient of her nature. When she is true to herself love is her primal driving force. Love and the service of those she loves. I mean a wholly personal love, not the love of causes or of country. I believe this to be true for all the various ranks of women, and it is as true of professional women as of wives and mothers. It is not always apparent that this is so. We are all very good at covering up our mainspring. But I have yet to meet the woman who did not know in her heart that love is her main concern and that the secret of her success in any field was her personal love in the background.

Men really can give themselves to a cause, working wholeheartedly for it and inspired by it. Unless their ingredient of masculinity is very great, women cannot. If one is allowed to penetrate their secrets one finds beneath their apparent impersonal enthusiasms some very personal love, the existence of which makes them feel whole and gives them the energy which enables them to act.

The schoolgirl will work double for a teacher whom she loves. The career woman will either have a person who is the focus of her love at work who provides her dynamism, or some love outside which is her stimulus. It may be a lover in the background or children for whom she needs to earn.

Wherever I look I meet this incontrovertible fact that a woman always needs some person to do things *for*, even though to the outsider there is no apparent connection with the loved person and what she may be doing. We all know how difficult it is for a woman even to cook a meal for herself. She cannot be bothered. A bit of bread and cheese will do. But if there is someone to cook *for* she prepares quite elaborate dishes with delight.

The same prevails throughout. The work of a woman, whether factory hand or professional, will be quite different in quality if in some way she can connect it with her love. I have talked with women artists, painters, singers, actors. They all agree that art in itself is seldom quite enough. Beneath their devotion to their art is some person whom they love and for whom in some mysterious inner way they perfect their art. Even the nun, who is an extreme case of selfless devotion, is contained in and inspired by a very personal love of Christ. I suspect that men are far more singlemindedly purposeful.

The need to have someone to do things for comes out in most curious places. I recall a woman who was threatened with blindness which only an operation could prevent. Operations of any kind had always been anathema to her, and the thought of an eye operation was more than she could face. She raged internally at the meddlesomeness of doctors. Why couldn't she be allowed to go blind in peace? Then suddenly she realized what she might be doing to her children and grandchildren if she went blind. A blind old grandmother was the last thing she wanted to impose on them. Her torment ceased. She entered hospital without a further qualm. She had found someone to have her operation *for*.

This tendency only to be able to do things for someone whom one loves makes it difficult for a woman to know what she herself really wants. She is often accused naturally by men of futility or hypocrisy, because when asked what she wants to do, she replies 'Whatever you like.' But it is not hypocrisy. She really means that her desire is to do what he wants. It has not occurred to her to have any special preference. Even if she knew she wanted to dance it would give her no pleasure to do so if her lover was longing to watch a cricket match. This adaptability is not unselfishness and has no particular merit. It is the way a woman functions. Perhaps I am describing the last generation. I think it possible that the present generation of women not only know themselves better but are far more decisive than the last, thus changing their relationship with men. Whether the change is for the good, or rather a disaster, is still an open question. Perhaps it is both.

However this may be, the older woman's dilemma is precisely here. If no one whom she loves wants her services there is no one to do things for. There is in fact no reason for which to live. She is faced with an entirely new situation in which for the first time maybe she has to discover what are her *own* wishes, her *own* tastes and in which direction her energy, with no love focus to act as magnet, will consent to flow. It is fascinating to notice how a widow will sometimes reverse the habits of a married lifetime after her husband's death. The extent to which she does so is the measure of her earlier adaptability.

In the following poem I have tried to express an old woman's bewilderment. It is called 'The Last Years':

Now that my loves are dead
On what shall my action ride?

I will not make my children
Lovers nor tune my time
By footsteps of the young
To ease my solitude;

But sing of springs, forgotten
In slow summer's tedium,
And autumn ripe with fruit;
Of winter branches, bare

Beneath the storm, bowed
With weight of rain, and after,
Lifting knotted fingers
Towards a translucent sky;

And wrest from the gathered sheaf
Forgiveness, buried in the heart
Of every grain, to knead
My bread for sustenance.

My action, sharing bread,
Love becomes ability
To bless, and be, in blessing,
Blessed.

To go back and collect up one's past as this poem suggests, writing it down in poems or as good prose as one can achieve, has in itself a healing effect. I believe one has to return to one's past, not once but many times, in order to pick up all the threads one has let fall through carelessness or unobservance.

I believe above all one has to return again and again to weep the tears which are still unshed. We cannot feel all the grief of our many losses at the time we suffer them. That would be too crippling. But if we would really gather our whole lives into a single whole, no emotion that belongs to us should be left unfelt.

Moreover, the review of our lives enables us to notice the constant repetition of the same pattern of happening, met by the same pattern of behavior. Seeing this we cannot help being struck by the apparent purposefulness of every detail of our lives even though we do not like our fate. Those who do in fact gather up and write their story are enormously enriched. And women for whom nothing is worth the effort unless it is for the sake fo someone they love, can write their outer or their inner story quite deliberately for their own grandchildren (if they have any) to read when they are grown up. If there are no grandchildren, most women will need to find someone else to write it for.

What fascinating pictures of antiquated ways of living we should have if this were done more often. Every single person has the material for at least one book. It is, I think, important that publication should not be the aim. Too many books are published already. Too many mediocre pictures are put upon the market. No, the aim is creativity for its own sake. The grandchildren or some other persons are merely the excuse which the aging woman needs to enable her to make the effort.

Creativity once begun goes on. Nothing is so satisfying to the human soul as creating something new. If the old can become creative in their own right they are lost no longer. We all long to see our works in print, I know, but this is not the point. It is the act of creation which counts. Every act of creation adds to the creativity in the world, and who knows if it has not some similar effect as the ritual, breathing towards the East at dawn of those primitive tribes who believe that their breath helps the sun to rise.

Unless some outer activity claims her, the family woman may make the discovery earlier than either men or professional women that libido changes its direction as old age approaches. It is a change that all must encounter sooner or later: at some time or other outer activities lose their glamour and the inner world demands attention. So strong is this demand that the old who refuse to turn their faces inwards, clinging desperately to outer values even though they watch them daily slipping from their grasp, are frequently made ill. Forced by illness or accident to be inactive, they are given the opportunity which they had been unable to take of their own free will, to ruminate and ponder and put forth new shoots in an unaccustomed inner world.

Illnesses at any time of life should not be merely cured, but utilized for growth in a hitherto unknown field. Particularly does this apply to the aging, whether man or woman.

If the old can become creative in their own right, they are, as I have said, lost no longer, but above all it is imperative that the older person should have a positive attitude towards death. The young can forget death with impunity. The old cannot. They are fortunate indeed who have faith that they will not be extinguished when they die, and can look forward to a new beginning in some other dimension or some other realm. But faith is a gift. Like love it comes by grace. No amount of thought or striving can achieve it; which paradoxically does not mean that there is no need to strive. We get from life in the measure with which we give to it, and our fundamental attitudes demand unceasing strife. But this is only preparing the soil. The actual planting of a spiritual seed like faith is beyond our control. It comes when it will.

To those who have been denied such faith I would ask, is it not a fact that the people who accept death most readily are the ones who have lived most fully? I do not mean necessarily the people who have done the most. Outer visible achievement is no criterion of living fully. The life of a great business magnate whose industry has erected huge buildings, set innumerable wheels whizzing and employs thousands of people, may have been so narrowly focused on the gain of material wealth that the riches of the spirit, art, music, literature and the warmth of human contacts, may have escaped him altogether. This is not full living.

At the opposite extreme I recall Spanish beggars seated on the cathedral steps, idly watching the passers by, receiving as though it were their lawful due occasional gifts of alms with a dignified 'God bless you'. How well the beggar must know those oft recurrent faces, nearly as constant in their daily presence as the stone saints and gargoyles behind him, the hourly chiming of the cathedral bells and the chant from within the church. What a setting in which to dwell and ponder! Does this man live fully? I do not know, but Unamuno, one of Spain's greatest writers believed he did. Unamuno even declared that the most interesting philosopher he had ever met was a beggar, one of a long line of beggars.

I am not advocating beggary, but neither it nor visible achievement is any criterion of the quality of living. There is no yardstick for the surmounting of obstacles, the wrestling with angels and the transcending of suffering.

There is no yardstick for the measurement of others, but maybe for ourselves there is. One's yardstick is one's full capacity to *be* as complete a person as within one lies, and that includes becoming as conscious as it is possible for one to be in order to bring out and develop the buried talents with which one was born, and in order to realize one's own innate knowledge.

The more diverse the talents of any person, the more difficult may be the task. We only have a certain amount of psychic energy and throughout our lives we have to choose the road we will take, abandoning the fascinating paths in other directions. But the development of an ability to choose, and the consistent following of the path chosen, may be a large part of becoming as whole a person as one can be. So also is our flexibility a very real asset. The man or woman who has chosen the wrong path by mistake, and we all make mistakes, may need to retrace his steps and start again. This needs courage and should not be mistaken for the idle whim of the dilettante. Moreover, many people follow a vital thread towards a wholly invisible goal. We cannot possibly judge the value of their achievement.

To be conscious is not in itself a goal. It is possible to be a highly conscious person without one's character being influenced at all. Consciousness is not enough in itself. But one cannot develop a gift if one does not know that it is there, so to be conscious is indispensable. Many of us, through ignorance of our own capacities, only allow a small part of ourselves to flower. Neither can one lop off a branch that is marring the beauty of a tree if one has not noticed its presence and seen that its unbridled growth is spoiling the harmony of the whole. Or it may have to be sacrificed because it is impeding the growth of other plants.

Our individual psyche is very like a garden. The kind of garden will be determined by the nature of the soil, whether it is on a mountain slope or in a fertile valley. It will depend upon the climate. Green lawns flourish in England. In parts of Spain to sow a lawn is to make a present to the wind, for literally the seed is blown away.

Climate and geology are powers beyond our altering. They are the conditions we have been given to make the most of it, and for some the task is immensely harder than it is for others. The slopes of arid hills in Spain are a marvel of man's endeavour. Every inch is terraced with little walls of stones so that not a drop of the rare precious rain shall be lost in tumbling streams but held for the thirsty vines and olive trees. All honour to such gardeners. Some of us dwell in more temperate climes where the task is not so hard, but any gardener will know the unceasing vigilance which is needed to tend a garden, wherever it may be. Weeds are never eradicated once for all.

So, too, our psyches. They also can be invaded by pests from other gardens which have been neglected, making it harder to maintain the health of ours. Indeed, to maintain our psyche or our garden free of pests is a responsibility to our neighbours as well as to ourselves. Some gardens are more formal than others. Some have corners deliberately left wild, but a garden with no form and no order is not a garden at all but a wilderness.

The psyche which is a total wilderness ends in the asylum or burdens its family with unhealthy emanations. The well-tendered but over conventional garden, on the other hand, may have no stamp of individuality upon it. It expresses the psyche of the mass man, and suburbia is full of them. The garden which is tended with care yet is not quite like any other garden, for it conveys the atmosphere of its owner, is like the psyche of an individual who has become a mature personality from where the scent of honeysuckle and roses and wild thyme will perfume the air for all around.

But gardens cannot grow without earth, and the loveliest flowers thrive on soil that is well manured and black. Dirt has been defined as matter in the wrong place. Manure is not dirt when dug into the borders. And rich emotional living in the right places is as indispensable for the flowering of wisdom in old age as the purity of the air and the brilliant sunlight of consciousness. No flower and no wisdom was ever reared on a ground of shiny white tiles washed daily with antiseptic.

It is the older person, whether man or woman, who has the need and the obligation to tend the garden of the psyche. The young are generally too immersed in active living; study, work, careers, and bringing up a family absorb all their energies. Indeed, a too early absorption with their own psyche may be an actual poison for the young. It may deprive them of the essential spontaneity which is needed for living. Actual experience can never be replaced by thinking about life or examining inner motives. To be ever conscious of the possible hazards before us snatches away our power to leap. We can only live fully by risking our lives over and over again.

It is in the latter part of life that people need to turn attention inwards. They need to do so because if their garden is as it should be they can die content, feeling that they have fulfilled their task of becoming the person they were born to be. But it is also an obligation to society. What a man or woman is within affects all those around. The old who are frustrated and resentful because they have omitted to become in life the persons they should have been, cause all in their vicinity to suffer.

Being is not the same as doing. Most people have had to sacrifice in some direction their capacity to *do,* but none are exempt from *being* to the full. There can be no limit to one's endeavour to become more and more aware of the depths of one's own psyche, discovering its lights and its shadows, its possibilities of unexpected vision as well as its dark regions.

The old woman, like the old man, needs to turn her natural receptivity towards the inner voices and inner whisperings, pondering on the new ideas which will come to her if she is attuned to her own inner self. Mrs. Moore, in E. M. Forster's *Passage to India*, was doing precisely this in her sudden and unexpected refusal to be drawn into the whirl of outer events. But we should not expect the insights of the *very* old to be revealed to the rest of us.

There may be weeks and months or even years of slow, quiet gestation in the minds of quite old people. To speak of half-formed ideas is to destroy their growth as surely as to burn a seedling with the sun's rays shining through a magnifying glass. The very frailty of age guards its secrets.

Indeed, the insights of the very old may never quite reach the level of consciousness where they can be clothed in words. But this does not mean that they are not at work beneath the surface. The conscious mind is only a small part of our total psyche.

The very old, those who have given up all interest in the outer world even to the stage of being withdrawn from any point of contact, may still be receiving and quietly nurturing within themselves new insights which will enable them to meet the unknown future. One wonders sometimes what holds them here. Perhaps they are not ready. They cannot die till they are ready. I have often felt that modern medicine is very cruel to the old for it keeps them here when they are longing to be allowed to go.

But perhaps longing to go is not the same as being ready to meet the other side. I doubt if science could keep anyone alive if in this sense they were truly ready for their death.

It is a fallacy that the old are necessarily lonely when they are alone. Some are. But never those who are quietly pondering, preparing themselves, albeit without deliberate intention, for their coming death. They need long hours of solitude to round out their lives within, as they have earlier done without.

There is a lovely little book *All Passion Spent*, by Victoria Sackville-West. She tells of an old lady after the death of her husband with whom she has shared a long life. Her children hold a family council. What can be done with mother? They plan it all out. She shall stay with them and their growing families in turn so they can share the burden of looking after her and keeping her from feeling lonely.

The plan is unfolded to the old lady who, to the amazement of her children, thanks them politely and declines their offer of hospitality. It transpires that for years she has been longing to have a little house of her own where she could live alone and undisturbed with her thoughts. Miraculously the chance had come and nothing should cheat her of it now.

This old woman had the good fortune to know her own mind, which many of us do not. Many old men and women are cheated of their essential solitude, and kept continually focused on outer things by the mistaken kindness of the young and their own unawareness of their need to be alone. We die alone. It is well to become accustomed to being alone before that moment comes.

Old age is the time of reckoning, our achievements balanced by our needless omissions and our mistakes. Some of our mistakes are hideous, but this is no reason for not facing them. Some we would never know if our children did not tell us the awful things we had done to them without realizing the dire effect of our advice, the example of our behavior or our condemnation.

The old are generally too much shielded. The next generation fears to hurt them. I say the next generation deliberately for it is seldom the young who overshield the old. The vital calls to live of the young are more likely to make them callous, which is really far more healthy. It is those who are already advanced in middle age, often themselves already older women, who over-protect the very old. Nothing must be told to worry them. They must have every comfort and never be left. Frequently they are so pampered and humoured that they are turned into querulous children.

Indeed, it is more often than not our own dislike of feeling hard, rather than genuine affection, which makes us so falsely kind. Moreover there is no need for us to take upon ourselves the responsibility of sheltering the very old from worry. Griefs do not shatter them as they do the young. They have their own protection from those emotions which are more than they can bear. It is not our task to turn them into breathing fossils.

That is no kindness to the old. Rather it is cruelty because it deprives them of their power still to grow. It is an unpardonable belittling of the role of the aged, for it is they who, whether they can formulate it or not, are in fact the depositories of wisdom. Very often it is they who have lived more than those who shelter them. To the older woman who has the aged in her care I would say: Be careful not to spend more energy upon the very old than you can rightly afford to do. Your own life too makes claims. Deep thought and wise judgment are needed to give them libido where it is really due. If too much is given to the aged at the expense of the giver it will only breed bitterness, and that helps no one.

The care of the very old is a terribly difficult problem and every case has to be dealt with on its own merits. Many family women find an old parent a good substitute for the children who have grown and gone. Many others who have had no children turn the parent unwittingly into the child they have never had. In either case the old person is wrapped in cotton wool which he or she has not the strength to throw aside. They can very easily become victims, rather than grateful recipients, of our over-coddling.

And so they end their days either with a complacency to which they have no right, or in puzzled resentment that the young do not give them the love they thought they had deserved. There are no deserts in love. Greater outspokenness is better for everyone concerned, though the young might certainly temper their frankness with the constant remembrance that the old have done their best. Deliberate malice on the part of parents is, I believe, very rare. The vast majority of parents undoubtedly do the best they know. And as undoubtedly the next generation will have found it wrong, and rightly so. To be a parent is the most difficult task in the world. For a parent not to be understanding enough cripples. To be too understanding imprisons.

I have yet to meet the parents who have not made serious blunders with their children in one direction or the other. The childless in this are fortunate. The false steps they have taken in life are likely to have had less dire consequences on others.

I think it is important that mistakes should be brought out into the light of day, for how otherwise may they be forgiven? Forgiven by those sinned against but also forgiven by the sinner himself. This is something very different from complacency for it implies full consciousness and condemnation of the sin. To forgive oneself is a very difficult thing to do, but perhaps it is the last task demanded of us before we die. For the man or woman who can forgive him- or herself can surely harbour no vestige of rancour against any other.

Impersonal forgiveness is very like love, but love on a higher plane than the personal love which women above all find so necessary. It is Agape as distinct from personal Eros. It is the charity spoken of by St. Paul. It is only possible for those who are completely on their own thread to God. No little isolated ego can forgive itself. In the last verses of the poem quoted the old woman found forgiveness of herself as well as others to be her inspiration and her goal.

And so, in the end, if endeavour is unceasing and the fates are kind, almost without noticing how it happened an old woman may find that love is still, as it always had been, the centre and the mainspring of her being, although, along with her years, the word has grown in meaning.

35

Simone de Beauvoir

JOIE DE VIVRE

On sexuality and old age

THOSE MORALISTS WHO VINDICATE OLD AGE claim that it sets the individual free from his body. The purification of which the moralists speak consists for them essentially in the extinction of sexual desires: they are happy to think that the elderly man escapes from this slavery and thereby achieves serenity. In his well-known poem, "John Anderson My Jo," Robert Burns described the ideal old couple in whom carnal passion has died quite away. The pair has climbed the hill of life side by side; once they tasted blissful hours; now with trembling steps but still hand in hand they must go together along the road that leads to the end of the journey. This stereotype is deeply imprinted upon the hearts of young and middle-aged people because they met it countless times in the books of their childhood and because their respect for their grandparents persuades them of its truth. The idea of sexual relations or violent scenes between elderly people is deeply shocking.

Yet there also exists an entirely different tradition. The expression, "dirty old man," is a commonplace of popular speech. Through literature and even more through painting, the story of Susanna and the Elders has taken on the value of a myth. The comic theater has endlessly repeated the theme of the ancient lover. As we shall see, this satirical tradition is closer to the truth than the edifying speeches of idealists who are concerned with showing old age as it ought to be.

In childhood, sexuality is polymorphous: it is not centered upon the genital organs. "Only at the end of a complex and hazardous evolution does the sexual drive assume a preeminently genital aspect; at this point it takes on the apparent fixity and finality of an instinct."* From this we may at once draw the conclusion that a person whose genital functions have diminished or become nonexistent is

*J. Laplanche and J.-B. Pontalis, *Vocabulaire de la psychoanalyse.*

not therefore sexless: he is a sexed being—even eunuchs and impotent men remain sexed—and one who must work out his sexuality in spite of a given mutilation.

An inquiry into the sexuality of the aged amounts to asking what happens to a man's relationship with himself, with others, and with the outside world when the preeminence of the genital aspect of the sexual pattern has vanished. Obviously it would be absurd to imagine that there is a simple return to infantile sexuality. Never, on any plane, does the aged person lapse into "a second childhood," since childhood is by definition a forward, upward movement. And then again, infantile sexuality is in search of itself, whereas the aged man retains the memory of what it was in his maturity. Lastly, there is a radical difference between the social factors affecting the two ages.

The enjoyment the individual derives from his sexual activities is rich and manifold to a very high degree. It is understandable that a man or woman should be bitterly unwilling to give it up, whether the chief aim is pleasure, or the transfiguration of the world by desire, or the realization of a certain image of oneself, or all this at the same time. Those moralists who condemn old age to chastity say that one cannot long for pleasures one no longer desires. This is a very short-sighted view of the matter. It is true that normally desire does not arise as desire in itself: it is desire for a particular pleasure or a particular body. But when it no longer rises spontaneously, reflection may very well regret its disappearance. The old person retains his longing for experiences that can never be replaced and is still attached to the erotic world he built up in his youth or maturity. Desire will enable him to renew its fading colors. And again it is by means of desire that he will have an awareness of his own integrity. We wish for eternal youth, and this youth implies the survival of the libido.

> "Never, on any plane, does the aged person lapse into 'a second childhood,' since childhood is by definition a forward, upward movement."

Its presence is found only among those who have looked upon their sexuality as something of positive value. Those who, because of complexes rooted in their childhood, took part in sexual activities only with aversion eagerly seize upon the excuse of age to withdraw. I knew an old woman who got her doctor to supply her with certificates so that she could avoid her disagreeable "conjugal duties"; as she grew older, the number of her years provided her with a more convenient alibi. A man, if he is half impotent, or indifferent, or if the sexual act worries him badly, will be relieved when age allows refuge in a continence that will seem normal for that time onward.

People who have had a happy sexual life may have reasons for not wishing to prolong it. One of these is their narcissistic relationship with themselves. Disgust at one's own body takes various forms among men and women; but in either, age may provoke it, and if this happens they will refuse to make their body exist for another. Yet there exists a reciprocal influence between the image of oneself and one's sexual activity: the beloved individual feels that he is worthy of love and gives himself to it unreservedly; but very often he is loved only if he makes a conscious effort to be attractive, and an unfavorable image of himself stands in the way of his doing this. In this event a vicious circle is created, preventing sexual relations.

Another obstacle is the pressure of public opinion. The elderly person usually conforms to the conventional ideal. He is afraid of scandal or quite simply of ridicule, and inwardly accepts the watchwords of propriety and continence imposed by the community. He is ashamed of his own desires, and he denies having them; he refuses to be a lecherous old man in his own eyes, or a shameless old woman. He fights against his sexual drives to the point of thrusting them back into his unconscious mind.

As we might on the face of it suppose, seeing that there is so great a difference between them in their biological destiny and their social status, the case of men is quite unlike that of women. Biologically men are at the greater disadvantage; socially, it is the women who are worse off, because of their condition as erotic objects. In neither case is their behavior thoroughly understood. A certain number of inquiries into it have been carried out, and these have provided the basis for something in the way of statistics. The replies obtained are always of dubious value, and in this field the notion of an average has little meaning.

The fear of ridicule

As far as men are concerned, the statistics, as it so often happens, merely confirm what everybody knows —sexual intercourse diminishes in frequency with age. This fact is connected with the degeneration of the sexual organs, a degeneration that brings about a weakening of the libido. But the physiological is not the only factor that comes into play. There are considerable differences between the behavior patterns of individuals, some being impotent at sixty and others very sexually active at over eighty. We must try to see how these differences are to be explained.

The first factor, and one of perfectly obvious importance, is the subjects' marital status. Sexual intercourse is much more frequent among married men than among bachelors or widowers. Married life encourages erotic stimulus; habit and "togetherness" favor its appeasement. The "psychological barriers" are far easier to overcome. The wall of private life protects the elderly husband from public opinion, which in any case looks more favorably upon legitimate love than upon unlawful connections. He feels that his image is less endangered. The word image in this context must be thoroughly understood. Whereas the woman object identifies herself with the total image of her body from childhood on, the little boy sees his penis as an alter ego; it is in his penis that his whole life as a man finds its image, and it is here that he feels himself in peril. The narcissistic trauma that he dreads is the failure of his sex-

ual organ—the impossibility of reaching an erection, of maintaining it, and of satisfying his partner. This fear is less haunting in married life. The subject is more or less free to choose the moment for making love. A failure is easily passed over in silence. His familiarity with his partner makes him dread her opinion less. Since he is less anxious, the married man is less inhibited than another. That is why many aged couples continue sexual activities.

The loss of his wife will often cause a trauma that shuts a man off from all sexual activities, either for a long or short period or forever. Widowers and elderly bachelors obviously have much more difficulty in finding an outlet for their libido than married men. Most have lost their charm: if they try to have an affair, their attempts come to nothing. All that remains is venal love: many men have shrunk from it all their lives, and it would seem to them a kind of giving-in, an acquiescence in the decline of age. Yet some do turn to it: they either go with prostitutes or they have a liaison with a woman they help financially. Their choice, continence or activity, depends on the balance between the urgency of their drive and the strength of their resistance.

Many find an answer in masturbation. A quarter of the subjects questioned by *Sexology* magazine said they had indulged in it either for many years or since the age of sixty: the latter were therefore brought back to it by aging. Statistical cross-checks show that even among married men, many turn to this practice. No doubt many elderly men prefer their fantasies to their wife's age-worn body. Or it may happen that either because deep-rooted complexes or awareness of age turn her against physical love, the companion refuses. Masturbation is then the most convenient outlet.

The subject's sexual activities are also influenced by his social condition. They go on far longer among manual workers, among men with a low standard of living than among those who are well to do. Workers and peasants have more straightforward desires, less dominated by erotic myths, than the middle classes; their wives' bodies wear out early, but they do not stop making love to them. When a working man's wife is old, she seems to him less spoiled than would be the case with a richer husband. Then again he has less idea of himself than the white-collar worker. And he does not take so much notice of public opinion, which has less and less force as one goes down the social scale. Old men and women who live almost entirely outside convention—tramps of both sexes, and inmates of institutions—lie together without any shame, even in front of others.

Finally, the happier and richer sexual life has been, the longer it goes on. If the subject has valued it because of the narcissistic satisfaction it gives him, he will break it off as soon as he can no longer see a flattering reflection of himself in his partner's eyes. If he has intended to assert his virility, his skill, or the power of his charm, or if he has meant to triumph over rivals, then he may sometimes be glad of the excuse of age to relax. But if his sexual activities have been spontaneous and happy, he will be strongly inclined to carry them on as long as his strength lasts.

Yet the elderly man does not take so vehement a pleasure in intercourse as a youth does, and this is because the two stages of ejaculation are reduced to one: he no longer has that piercing sensation of imminence which marks the passage from the first to the second, nor yet the triumphant feeling of a jet, an explosion—this is one of the myths that gives the male sexual act its value. Even when the aged man is still capable of normal sexual activity, he often seeks indirect forms of satisfaction; even more so if he is impotent. He takes pleasure in erotic literature, licentious works of art, dirty stories, the company of young women, and furtive contacts; he indulges in fetishism, sadomasochism, various forms of perversion, and, particularly after the age of eighty, in voyeurism. These deviations are readily comprehensible. The fact is, Freud has established that there is no such thing as a "normal" sexuality: it is always "perverted" insofar as it does not break away from its origins, which required it to look for satisfaction not in any specific activity but in the "increase of pleasure" attached to functions dependent upon other drives. Infantile sexuality is polymorphically perverse. The sexual act is considered "normal" when the partial activities are merely preparatory to the genital act. But the subject has only to attach too much importance to these preliminary pleasures to slip into perversion. Normally, seeing and caressing one's partner plays an important part in sexual intercourse. It is accompanied by fantasy; sadomasochistic elements appear; and often fetishism, clothes, and ornaments evoking the presence of the body. When genital pleasure is weak or nonexistent, all these elements rise to the first place. And frequently the elderly man prizes them very highly because they are manifestations of that erotic world that is still of the greatest value to him. He continues to live in a certain climate, his body still existing in a world filled with other bodies. Here again it is often timidity, shame, or difficulties from the outside that prevent him from indulging in what are called his vices.

WE HAVE A FAIR AMOUNT OF EVIDENCE about elderly men's sexual life. It depends on their past and also upon their attitude toward their old age as a whole and toward their image in particular. Chateaubriand so loathed his aged face that he refused to sit for his portrait. In the first part of *Amour et vieillesse—chants de tristesse*, which he wrote when he was sixty-one, he rejects the amorous advances of a young woman: "If you tell me you love me as a father, you will fill me with horror; if you claim to love me as a lover, I shall not believe you. I shall see a happy rival in every young man. Your deference will make me feel my age, your caresses will give me over to the most furious jealousy. . . . Old age makes a man as ugly as can be wished. If he is unhappy, it is even worse . . ." He was cruelly sensitive to the "insult of the years," and his refusal was dictated by a kind of inverted narcissism.

Old men's loves are not always doomed to failure: far from it. Many of them have a sexual life that goes on very late. The Duc de Bouillon was sixty-six when his son Turenne was born. The famous Duc de Richelieu's father married for the third time in 1702, at the age of seventy. When his son was sixty-two and governor of Guienne, he led a life of debauchery. In his old age he seduced a great many young women. At seventy-eight, bewigged, made-up, and very thin, he was said to look like a tortoise thrusting its head out of its shell; this did not prevent him from having affairs with the actresses of the *Comédie française*. He had an acknowledged mistress, and he spent his evenings with whores; sometimes he used to bring them home —he liked listening to their confidences. He married when he was eighty-four and had recourse to aphrodisiacs: he made his wife pregnant. Furthermore, he deceived her too. He continued his sexual activities right up until his death, at the age of ninety-two.

Tolstoy is a well-known example of sexual vitality. Toward the end of his life he preached total continence both for men and for women. Nevertheless, when he was sixty-nine or seventy he would come back from a very long ride and make love to his wife. All the next day he would walk about the house looking pleased with himself.

Sexuality was of great importance in Victor Hugo's youth and during his middle years. The image of old age that he had always set up for himself allowed him to accept his sexual desires until he was very old: no doubt he thought of Boaz when a young woman offered herself to him. In his view, age was by no means a blemish, but rather an honor; it brought one nearer to God and it was in harmony with everything that is sublime, with beauty and innocence. The aged Hugo certainly suffered from no feeling of inferiority whatsoever. In his opinion he was answerable to no one but himself: at no time in his life did he ever yield to public opinion—if he had desires, he satisfied them.

There are many other examples to show that an elderly man may be importuned by the most urgent sexual desires. H. G. Wells was sixty when he fell in love with Dolores after they had corresponded; he fell passionately in love and found himself possessed of unsuspected sexual powers. "For the first time in my life it was revealed to me that I was an astonishing fellow, an extraordinary chap, an outstanding virtuoso. Casanova certainly could never have held a candle to me," he wrote with a smile. The affair turned sour; there were ugly scenes; in the end he could no longer bear Dolores and when he was sixty-six he broke with her. Having done so, he met the girl he called Brylhil; this was the most violent passion of his life—a mutual passion that lasted many years.

Among our contemporaries there are a very great many examples of elderly men married or attached to young women: Charlie Chaplin, Picasso, Casals, Henry Miller. These examples confirm the notion that if it has been rich, sexual life goes on for a long time. But it may also happen that a man who has been indifferent to women for most of his life discovers the delights of sex in his later years. Trotsky had looked upon himself as old since the age of fifty-five, but at fifty-eight he had an odd outburst of eroticism. Bernard Berenson, who died at ninety-four, wrote, "I only really became aware of sex and of women's physical, animal life at the period that might be called my old age."

Many elderly men look for younger partners. Those subjects for whom sex continues to play an important part are gifted with excellent health and lead an active life. Impotence does not exclude desire; desire is most often satisfied through deviations in which the fantasies of middle age are accentuated.

L'Après-midi d'un faune

WE HAVE ONE MOST REMARKABLE PIECE of evidence concerning an old man's relationship with his body, his image, and his sex: this is Paul Léautaud's *Journal*.* He provides us with a living synthesis of the various points of view that we have considered in this study.

Léautaud always looked at himself with a certain approval. It was from the outside that he learned he was aging, and it made him very angry. In 1923, when he was fifty-three, a railway official referred to him as "a little old gentleman." Furious, Léautaud wrote in his *Journal*, "Little old man! Old gentleman? What the devil—am I as blind as all that? I cannot see that I am either a little or an old gentleman. I see myself as a fifty-year-old, certainly,

*Léautaud was a critic and an editor of *Mercure de France*, a literary journal.

but an exceedingly well preserved fifty-year-old. I am slim and I move easily. Just let them show me an *old gentleman* in such good shape!" At fifty-nine he looked at himself with a critical eye: "Mentally and physically I am a man of forty. What a pity my face does not match! Above all my lack of teeth! I really am remarkable for my age: slim, supple, quick, active. It is my lack of teeth that spoils everything; I shall never dare to make love to a woman again."

In him we see with remarkable clarity how impossible it is for an old man to realize his age. On his birthday he wrote, "Today I begin my sixty-fourth year. In no way do I feel an old man." The old man is Another, and this Other belongs to a certain category that is objectively defined; in his inner experience Léautaud found no such person. There were moments, however, when his age weighed upon him. On April 12, 1936, he wrote, "I do not feel happy about my health nor about my state of mind; and then there is the sorrow of aging, too. Aging above all!" But at sixty-nine he wrote, "During my seventieth year I am still as lively, active, nimble and alert as a man can be."

"Impotence does not exclude desire: desire is most often satisfied through deviations in which the fantasies of middle age are accentuated."

Léautaud had every reason to be pleased with himself: he looked after his house and cared for his animals; he did all the shopping on foot, carrying heavy baskets of provisions; wrote his *Journal*; and he did not know what it was to be tired. "It is only my sight that is failing. I am exactly as I was at twenty. My memory is as good as ever and my mind as quick and sharp."

This made him all the more irritable when other people's reactions brought the truth home to him. He was seventy when a young woman lost her balance as an underground train started off with a jerk; she cried out, "I'm so sorry, Grandpa, I nearly fell on you." He wrote angrily, "Damn it all! My age must show clearly in my face. How impossible it is to see oneself as one really is!"

The paradox lies in the fact that he did not really dislike being old. He was one of those exceptional cases I have mentioned, where old age coincides with childhood fantasy: he had always been interested in old people. On March 7, 1942, when he was seventy-two, he wrote, "A kind of vanity comes over you when you reach old age— you take a pride in remaining healthy, slim, supple and alert, with an unaltered complexion, your joints in good order, no illness and no diminution in your physical and mental powers."

But his vanity demanded that his age be invisible to others: he liked to imagine that he had stayed young in spite of the burden of his years.

He only gave way to discouragement at the very end of his life, when his health failed. On February 25, 1945, he wrote, "I am very low indeed. My eye-sight. The horrible marks of age I see on my face. My *Journal* behind-hand. The mediocrity of my life. I have lost my energy and all my illusions. Pleasure, even five minutes of pleasure, is over for me." He was then seventy-five, and his sexual life had come to an end. But except in his very last years one of the reasons for his pride was that he still felt desire and was still capable of satisfying it. We can follow his sexual evolution in his *Journal*.

LÉAUTAUD ONLY BECAME FULLY AWARE of women when he was approaching his fiftieth year. At thirty-five he wrote, "I am beginning to regret that my temperament allows me to enjoy women so little." He lacked the "sacred fire." "I always think too much of other things—of myself, for example." He was afraid of impotence and his love-making was over very quickly: "I give women no pleasure since I have finished in five minutes and can never start again. . . . Shamelessness is all I really like in love. . . . There are some things not every woman can be asked to do." He had a lasting affair with a woman called Bl——. He says he loved her very much, but he also says that living with her was hell. When he was about forty, although he was still rather indifferent, since he could give his partner no pleasure, he delighted in looking at pictures of naked women. Yet a few years later he speaks sadly of the "rare love-scenes in my life which I really enjoyed." He reproaches himself for being "timid, awkward, brusque, oversensitive, always hesitant, never able to take advantage of even the best opportunities" with women. All this changed when at fifty he met "a really passionate woman, wonderfully equipped for pleasure and exactly to my taste in these matters," and he showed himself to be "almost brilliant," although up until then he had thought that he was not very good—as he had only known women who did not suit him. From this time on, sex became an obsession to him; on December 1, 1923, he wrote, "Perhaps Madame [one of the names he gave to his mistress] is right: my perpetual desire to make love may be somewhat pathological. . . . I put it down to a lifetime's moderation—it lasted until I was over forty—and also to my intense feeling for her, which makes me want to make love to her when I see so much as a square inch of her body. . . . I think it is also because I have been deprived of so many things, such as that female nakedness for which I have acquired such a liking. I am quite amazed when I think of what has happened to me in all this. . . . Never have I caressed any other woman as I caress Madame." In the summer they parted, and abstinence lay heavy upon him: he masturbated, thinking of her. "Of course I am delighted to be such an ardent lover at my age, but God knows it can be troublesome."

Madame was a little older than he: all his life he had loved only mature women. A twenty-three-year-old virgin threw herself at his head, and he agreed to have an affair with her; but it did not give him the least pleasure and he broke immediately. Except for this one fling he was faithful to Madame for years. He liked watching himself and her in a mirror during their lovemaking. From 1927—age

"Young people are still very shocked if the old, especially old women, are still sexually active."

fifty-seven—on, he was forced to take care not to make love too often; he found consolation in bawdy talk with the Panther (another name he gave to his mistress). He did not get on well with her; "we are attached to each other only by our senses—by vice—and what remains is so utterly tenuous!" But in 1938 he did recall with great satisfaction the "seventeen years of pleasure between two creatures the one as passionate and daring as the other in amorous words and deeds." When he was fifty-nine his affair with the Scourge, as he now called her, was still going on, though she was already sixty-four. He was shocked by couples where the woman was much younger than the man. "I myself at fifty-nine would never dare to make any sort of advance to a woman of thirty."

He was still very much attracted to the Scourge, and he took great pleasure in his "sessions" with her. Yet he did complain, "What a feeble ejaculation when I make love: little better than water!" Later he wrote, "I am certainly better when I do not make love at all. Not that it comes hard—far from it—but it is always a great effort, and I do not get over it as quickly as I did a few years ago. . . What I miss most is female nakedness, licentious attitudes, and playing amorous games."

"Until I was sixty-six or sixty-seven I could make love two or three times a week." Now he complained that his brain was tired for three or four days after making love, but he still went on, and he corresponded with three of his former mistresses.

When he was seventy Léautaud wrote, "I miss women and love terribly." He remembered how he used to make passionate love to the Scourge from the age of forty-seven to sixty-three, and then for two years with CN [another mistress].

"It was only three years ago that I noticed I was slowing down. I can still make love, and indeed I quite often feel sad at being deprived of it; though at the same time I tell myself that it is certainly much better for me to abstain."

At seventy-two he was still planning idylls that never came to anything, and he had erotic dreams that gave him an erection. "At night I still feel ready for anything." But that same year he observed that his sexual powers were declining. "It is no use giving yourself over to lovemaking when the physical side is dead or nearly so. Even the pleasure of seeing and fondling is soon over, and there is not the least eagerness to begin again. For a real appreciation of all these things, there must be the heat of physical passion." It is clear that Léautaud's greatest pleasure was visual. He retained it longer than any other form of sensual enjoyment, and after the age of forty he prized it very highly indeed. When he lost it he considered that his sexual life was over. It is also clear how a man's image of himself is bound up with sexual activity. He was "in the depths of sorrow" when he could no longer experience these pleasures. Still, his narcissism did survive his sexual decline at least for some time.

The feminine disadvantage

BIOLOGICALLY WOMEN'S SEXUALITY is less affected by age than men's. Brantôme bears this out in the chapter of his *Vies des dames galantes* that he dedicates to "certain old ladies who take as much pleasure in love as the young ones." Whereas a man of a certain age is no longer capable of erection, a woman "at no matter what age is endowed with as it were a furnace ... all fire and fuel within." Popular tradition bears witness to this contrast. In one of the songs in the Merry Muses of Caledonia* an old woman laments her elderly husband's impotence. She longs for "the wild embraces of their younger days" that are now no more than a ghostly memory, since he no longer thinks of doing anything in bed except sleeping, while she is eaten up with desire. Today scientific research confirms the

*Popular Scottish songs collected in the eighteenth century.

validity of this evidence. According to Kinsey, throughout their lives women are sexually more stable than men; when they are sixty their potential for pleasure and desire is the same as it was at thirty. According to Masters and Johnson, the strength of the sexual reaction diminishes with age; yet a woman can still reach orgasm, above all if she is regularly and properly stimulated. Those who do not often have physical relations sometimes find coition painful, either during the act or after, and sometimes suffer from dyspareunia or dysuria; it is not known whether these troubles are physical or psychological in origin. I may add that a woman can take great pleasure in making love even though she may not reach orgasm. The "preliminary pleasures" count even more perhaps for her than they do for a man. She is usually less sensitive to the appearance of her partner and therefore less worried by his growing old. Even though her part in lovemaking is not as passive as people sometimes make out, she has no fear of a particular failure. There is nothing to prevent her from going on with her sexual activities until the end of her life.

Still, all research shows that women have a less active sexual life than men. Kinsey says that at fifty, 97 per cent of men are still sexually active compared with 93 per cent of women. At sixty it is 94 per cent of men and only 80 per cent of women. This comes from the fact that socially men, whatever their age, are subjects, and women are objects, relative beings. When she marries, a woman's future is determined by her husband's; he is usually about four years older than she, and his desire progressively lessens. Or if it does continue to exist, he takes to younger women. An old woman, on the other hand, finds it extremely difficult to have extramarital relations. She is even less attractive to men than old men are to women. And in her case gerontophilia does not exist. A young man may desire a woman old enough to be his mother but not his grandmother. A woman of seventy is no longer regarded by anyone as an erotic object. Venal love is very difficult for her to find. It would be most exceptional for an old woman to have both the means and the opportunity of getting herself a partner; and then again shame and fear of what people might say would generally prevent her from doing so. This frustration is painful to many old women, for they are still tormented by desire. They usually find their relief in masturbation; a gynecologist told me of the case of one woman of seventy who begged him to cure her of this practice—she was indulging in it night and day.

When Andrée Martinerie was conducting an inquiry for *Elle* magazine (March 1969) she gathered some interesting confidences from elderly women. Madame F., a rich middle-class sixty-eight-year-old, a militant Catholic, mother of five and grandmother of ten, told her, "I was already sixty-four. ... Now just listen: four months after my husband's death I went down into the street just like someone who is going to commit suicide. I had made up my mind to give myself to the very first man who would have me. Nobody wanted me. So I went home again." When she was asked whether she had thought of remarrying, she answered, "That is all I ever do think of. If I dared I would put an advertisement in *Le Chasseur français*. ... I would rather have a decrepit invalid of a man than no man at all!" Talking of desire, Madame R., sixty years old and living with her sick husband, said, "It is quite true that you don't get over it." She sometimes felt like beating her head against the wall. A woman reader of this inquiry wrote to the magazine, "I must tell you that a woman remains a woman for a very long time in spite of growing older. I know what I am talking about, because I am seventy-one. I was a widow at sixty; my husband died suddenly and it took me at least two years to realize fully what had happened. Then I started to answer advertisements in the matrimonial column. I admit that I did miss having a man—or rather I should say I do miss it: this aimless existence is terrifying, without affection or any outlet for one's own feelings. I even began wondering whether I was quite normal. Your inquiry was a great relief. . . ." This correspondent speaks modestly of "affection," an "outlet for one's own feelings." But the context shows that her frustration had a sexual dimension. The reaction of a young woman who wrote to *Elle* is typical: "In our group of young people we laughed heartily about the passionate widow (the member of the Action Catholique) who cannot 'get over it.' I wish you would now hold an inquiry on love as it appears to the fourth age of women, in other words those between eighty and a hundred and twenty." Young people are very shocked if the old, especially old women, are still sexually active.

"Whereas a man of a certain age is no longer capable of erection, a woman 'at no matter what age is endowed with as it were a furnace . . . all fire and fuel within.' "

A woman, then, continues in her state as erotic object right up to the end. Chastity is not imposed upon her by a physiological destiny but by her position as a relative being. Nevertheless it may happen that women condemn themselves to chastity because of the "psychological barriers" that I have mentioned, which are even more inhibiting for them than for men. A woman is usually more narcissistic in love than a man; her narcissism is directed at her body as a whole. She has a delightful awareness of her body as something desirable, and this awareness comes to her through her partner's caresses and his gaze. If he goes on desiring her she easily puts up with her body's aging. But at the first sign of coldness she feels her ugliness in all its horror; she is disgusted with her image and cannot bear to expose her poor person to others. This lack of assurance strengthens her fear of other people's opinions: she knows how censorious they are toward old women who do not play their proper role of serene and passion-free grandmothers.

Even if her husband wants to make love with her again later, a deeply rooted feeling of shame may make her refuse him. Women make less use of diversion than men. Those who enjoyed a very active and uninhibited sexual life before do sometimes compensate for their enforced abstinence by extreme freedom in conversation and the use of obscene words. They become something very like bawds, or at least they spy upon the sexual life of their young women friends with a most unhealthy curiosity, and do all they can to make them confide their secrets. But generally speaking their language is as repressed as their lovemaking. Elderly women like to appear as restrained in their conversation as they are in their way of life. Their sexuality now shows only in their dress, their jewelry and ornaments, and in the pleasure they take in male society. They like to flirt discreetly with men younger than themselves and they are touched by attentions that show they are still women in men's eyes.

"Venal love is very difficult for her to find. It would be most exceptional for an old woman to have both the means and the opportunity of getting herself a partner; and then again shame and fear of what people might say would generally prevent her from doing so."

However, it is clear from pathology that in women, too, the sexual drive is repressed but not extinguished. Psychiatrists have observed that in asylums female patients' eroticism often increases with age. Senile dementia brings with it a state of erotic delirium arising from lack of cerebral control. Repressions are also discarded in some other forms of psychosis. Dr. Georges Mahé recorded twenty cases of extreme eroticism out of 110 sixty-year-old female patients in an institution; the symptoms included public masturbation, make-believe coition, obscene talk, and exhibitionism. Unfortunately he gives no idea of the meaning of these displays: he puts them into no context and we do not know *who* the patients were who indulged in these practices. Many of the inmates suffer from genital hallucinations such as rape and physical contact. Women of over seventy-one are convinced that they are pregnant. Madame C., seventy and a grandmother, sings barrackroom songs and walks about the hospital half-naked, looking for a man. Eroticism is the most important factor in many delirious states; it also triggers off some cases of melancholia. E. Gehu speaks of an eighty-three-year-old grandmother who was looked after in a convent. She was an exhibitionist, showing both homosexual and heterosexual tendencies. She fell upon the younger nuns who brought her meals; during these crises she was perfectly lucid. Later she became mentally confused. She ended up by regaining her mental health and behaving normally once more. Here again, we should like a more exact, detailed account of her case. All the observations that I have just quoted are most inadequate; but at least they do show that old women are no more "purified of their bodies" than old men.

Neither history nor literature has left us any worthwhile evidence on the sexuality of old women. It is an even more strictly forbidden subject than the sexuality of old men. There are many cases of the libido disappearing entirely in old people. Ought they to rejoice in it, as the moralists say? Nothing is less certain. It is a mutilation that brings other mutilations with it: sexuality, vitality, and activity are indissolubly linked. When desire is completely dead, emotional response itself may grow loose at its edge. At sixty-three Rétif de La Bretonne wrote, "My heart died at the same time as my senses, and if sometimes a tender impulse stirs me, it is as erroneous as that of a savage or a eunuch: it leaves me with a profound feeling of sorrow." It seemed to Bernard Shaw that when he lost interest in women he lost interest in living. "I am ageing very quickly. I have lost all interest in women, and the interest they have in me is greater than ever and it bores me. The time has probably come for me to die."

Even Schopenhauer admitted, "It could be said that once the sexual urge is over life's true centre is burnt out, leaving a mere shell." Or again, "life is like a play acted at first by live actors and then finished by automata wearing the same costumes." Yet at the same time he says that the sexual instinct produces a "benign dementia." The only choice left to men is that between madness and sclerosis. In fact what he calls "dementia" is the spring of life itself. When it is broken or destroyed a man is no longer truly alive.

THE LINK that exists between sexuality and creativity is striking: it is obvious in Hugo and Picasso and in many others. In order to create there must be some degree of aggression—"a certain readiness," says Flaubert—and this aggressivity has its biological source in the libido. It is also necessary to feel united with the world by an emotional warmth; this disappears at the same time as carnal desire, as Gide understood very clearly when on April 10, 1942, he wrote, "There was a time when I was cruelly tormented, indeed obsessed by desire, and I prayed, 'Oh let the moment come when my subjugated flesh will allow me to give myself entirely to . . . ' But to what? To art? To pure thought? To God? How ignorant I was! How mad! It was the same as believing that the flame would burn brighter in a lamp with no oil left. If it were abstract, my thought would go out; even today it is my carnal self that feeds the flame, and now I pray that I may retain carnal desire until I die."

It would not be truthful to state that sexual indifference necessarily brings inertia and impotence. There are many examples to prove the contrary. Let us merely say there is one dimension of life that disappears when there is no more carnal relationship with the world; those who keep this treasure to an advanced age are privileged indeed.

Aging and Family Personality: A Developmental View

by Elaine M. Brody†

The dramatic numerical and proportional increase in the elderly population has important implications for family dynamics and the family life cycle. This paper considers some of the issues of aging, death, loss, and separation, as they relate to individual and family development and to shifting roles and responsibilities of family members.

INCREASING ATTENTION is being paid to the concept that older family members play important roles in family dynamics (24). In recent years excitement has been generated by reports in the press and professional literature about the inclusion in family and network treatment of family dogs and other pets, friends, family grocers, neighbors, milkmen, teachers, and so on. Grandparents have had a few bit parts, usually as the heavies, but have not yet made it big.

The issues of aging, death, and loss, however, have become fashionable recently. Like sex, they are no longer "X-rated." This is as it should be. After all, older people are the big "diers" and "losers."[1] The inventory of their

interpersonal losses is staggering: spouse, siblings, and peers. With the entry into the category of advanced old age of an increasing proportion of people (in the decade between 1960 and 1970, the 75 and over group increased at three times the rate of the 65–74 group (7)), more experience the loss of adult children who themselves are middle-aged and even aged. Older people also have a whole set of other losses and separations. Some lose the familiar surroundings of their own homes and communities: a million older people, or about 5 per cent of the older population, are in institutions. There are losses of physical and mental function; of economic capacity; and

This is a revision of an invited paper presented at the Conference on Loss, Death, Separation, and the Family sponsored by the Family Institute of Philadelphia, Phila., Penn., October 12–13, 1972.

† Director, Dept. of Social Work, Philadelphia Geriatric Center, 5301 Old York Road, Philadelphia, Penna. 19141.

[1] People 65 and over constitute 10 per cent of the total population. Of the 1,921,990 deaths in the U.S. during 1969, 1,183,546 or 61.4 per cent were 65 or over. The over-all death rate of the population is 9.5 per 1,000. Once the first year of life is safely past (infant mortality is 21.5 per 1,000), the death rate is less than 1 per thousand for those under 15, does not reach 10 per 1,000 til age 55, and then rises to 13.6 per 1,000 for the 55–59 year old, 20.5 for the 60–64 group, 30.6 for those 65–69, 46.4 for those 70–74, 66.1 for those 75–79, 100.8 for those 80–84, and 190.8 for those 85 and over. (Data provided by Herman B. Brotman, Assistant to the Commissioner for Statistics and Analysis, Administration on Aging, U.S. Dep't. of H.E.W. based on PHS Vital Statistics Report for 1969, issued July, 1972).

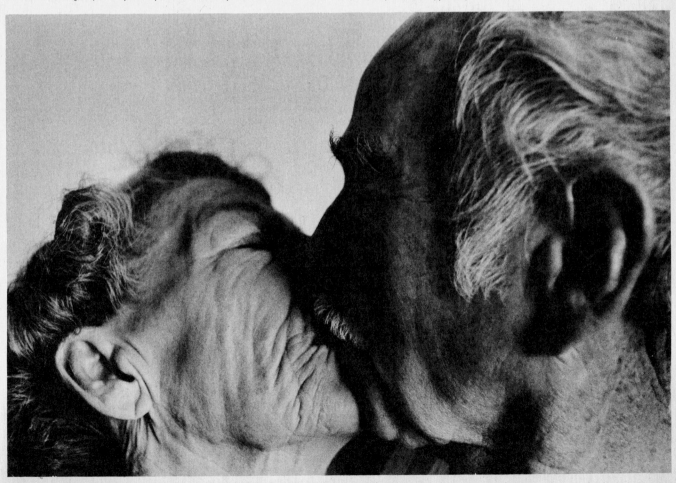

of social roles such as those of worker, parent, spouse, and friend. Each loss augurs the ultimate loss—of life itself.

These events are important to understand not only in the interests of the elderly who experience them, but because they have a direct impact on all the generations. The phrases "an untimely end" and "a timely end" recognize the qualitative differences that distinguish the premature death of a younger person from that of an elderly individual. The death of an old person can be said to be a "normal" life crisis in the family's developmental history and, thus, has a special meaning to families. The death of a grandparent or great-grandparent often is the young child's first experience with human mortality. It may place the middle-aged or aging child psychologically at the frontier of death, the buffer generation having been removed. There are renewed intimations of inevitable mortality and generational shifts occurring in the total family constellation. The management of the dying process and the reactions and adaptations of the family have implications for the psychological development of the younger generations and, in turn, for their handling of the deaths, losses, and separations that are part of the human condition.

Similarly, the functional and personal losses experienced by the oldest members of the family and their changing roles initiate shifts in the qualitative emotional balance of relationships, as well as in the instrumental activities of the entire family. Whether he is intact or impaired, the nature of the older person's relations with family at that phase of life mold those of the succeeding generations as they move inevitably toward the aging phase of the family life cycle.

If issues of death, loss, separation, and family relationships are to be illuminated, there must be exploration of what the family is like at the aging phase of the family life cycle. That is, what happens to what may be called the "family personality" as the older person and his family grow old?

The scarcity of knowledge about this subject speaks to the massive avoidance of aging and death on the part of clinicians, as well as by the public; to the concentration of attention on the younger phases of individual and family development; to the view of aging as a disease process rather than a natural process and of the elderly as dying rather than living; and to lagging recognition of the implications of the startling changes in family structure and function during this century.

The dramatic numerical and proportional increase in the elderly population, from 4 per cent (3 million people) in 1900 to 10 per cent (20 million people) at present, means that families now include many more old people. The multi-generation family is common, since 70 per cent of people 65 and over in the United States have grandchildren and 40 per cent have great grandchildren (21). These figures vastly underestimate the number of multi-generation families, since the average age at which men and women become grandparents is 57 and 54 respectively—well before old age; they become great-grandparents at 75 and 72 (26). There is, of course, wide variation, with some becoming grandparents in their late 30's, others in their 70's. Looking at the statistics another way, in the past 50 years the chances of a white

child aged ten having at least two grandparents has increased from 40 per cent to 75 per cent, and of having at least three grandparents, from 10 per cent to 38 per cent (25).

Of major psychological importance is the fact that there are now *two* significant categories: the third and fourth generations—that is, the old and the very old.

Notions based on the past must be revised in the light of these changes. For example, fewer of generation three have single children remaining at home, fewer of their children have to look after them; they have more energy to spare for grandchildren; they are often youthful, vigorous, and far from the stereotype of the grandparent of yesteryear. However, more of them have to care for the fourth generation of relatively frail, very old people. Such demographic developments have deep effects on family relations between parents and children, husbands and wives, between generations, and among households and families (26).

Are there contacts between the generations? Or do they exist in isolation from each other?

One-quarter of all old people share a household with an adult child, but only 8 per cent live in three-generation households. (Contrary to popular belief, there has not been a decline in the three- or four-generation household since the nineteenth century.) A fascinating statistic is that 5 per cent of all older people, a million individuals, live together with a very old parent (22).

Though most do not share a household, 84 per cent of those 65 and over live less than an hour away from one of their children; four out of five see an adult child as often as once a week and two-thirds as often as every day or two. Seeing adult children often means seeing grandchildren at the same time. In one study of an urban area, 58 per cent of old people saw both children and grandchildren every day, or nearly every day (23).

The large number of grandparents and great-grandparents has psychological significance, whether or not they live in common households or neighborhoods with the young. Modern means of transportation and communication are great facilitators of continuing contacts.

Of special interest is the fact that the family contacts of older people most often are with the female members of the family, who also provide most of the services needed. The younger generation, in turn, sees more of older women than men, since grandmothers and great-grandmothers are more in evidence; by age 65 women outnumber men 134 to 100, and at age 85 the ratio is 160 to 100. However, there is evidence that some retirees see more of their children and grandchildren after retirement (23).

Not only is interaction extensive between generations, but the viability of extended family ties has been documented by many studies such as those of intergenerational behavior as expressed by patterns of economic aid, exchange of services, and support in health crises.[2]

There has been some interest in relations between

---

[2] Many of the studies and literature reviews appear in Riley and Foner, *Aging and Society, Vol. One: An Inventory of Research Findings*, Russell Sage Foundation, N.Y. 1968, and in Shanas, E. and Streib, G. F., Eds., *Social Structure and the Family: Generational Relations*, Prentice Hall, Inc. Englewood Cliffs, N.J. 1965.

grandparents and grandchildren. Though scattered studies suggest a special relationship between those generations, the old adage that grandparents and grandchildren get along so well because they have a common enemy has not been put to empirical test. There are, of course, many different "styles" of grandparenting. Neugarten and Weinstein have identified some five major styles and categorized the varied significance and meaning of the grandparent role.[3]

Thus, continuing mutual intergenerational responsibility is no longer at issue. However, such descriptive and statistical material tells us little of the qualitative effects on multi-generational relations—that is, the reciprocal, psychological impact on the development and personalities of all family members. It does convey a clear message to the clinician of the need for awareness and exploration of the meaning of the shifting roles and responsibilities; of the feelings and reactions of younger family members to death and losses of the elderly; and of the reactions of the oldest members to the loss, death, and separations from the younger.

To illuminate such matters, it is first necessary to understand the nature of individual personality in old age and that of the family personality in the aging phase of the family life cycle.

Developmental Theory of Aging and Personality

A major issue in the investigation of personality in the recent years has been whether there are continuing developmental stages throughout life. That is, are changes in personality processes in part inherent, or are they simply reactive to the changing environment? As is true of biological aging, the issue is complicated by the fact that psychological problems of adjustment and adaptation *intrinsic* to the aging process (i.e. those that are built in or programmed) have not been clearly sorted out from those *associated* with old age but due to social and environmental influences.

A developmental concept of aging views aging as a *normal developmental phase of life with its own tasks that can be successfully mastered as were tasks of earlier phases of life.* It is only in recent years that psychodynamic theories of human behavior and personality development began to look beyond "maturity." The traditional psychoanalytic view, from which ego psychology evolved, emphasized early life stages of development, with the basic nature of personality and sense of identity being established finally in adolescence and remaining stable thereafter. In old age, reactive processes to changing environments were emphasized, rather than those that are inherent or developmentally controlled.

Some recent psychoanalytic theorists, notably Erikson (11) and Peck (19), move away from the view of aging as reactive toward an emphasis on development. They formulate additional stages of ego development in which a different psychological issue is the conflict or crisis at each stage; the same issue, however, is also present in preceding and later stages. Thus, for example, the problem of ego identity is predominant in adolescence but is present also in succeeding stages, though its form is qualified by the individual's life history and degree of success in meeting the earlier crises. This implies that crises of earlier stages that were not fully resolved are subsequently recapitulated and hamper successful resolution of later crises.

Erikson's formulations remind us of the continuing psychological linkages between generations and the impact of personality development in later life on the younger family members. Thus, his seventh stage, middle adulthood, is the development of *generativity vs. ego stagnation.* "Generativity is primarily the interest in establishing and guiding the next generation . . ." The concept includes productivity and creativity and is "an essential stage on the psychosexual as well as in the psychosocial schedule."

His eighth stage, "late adulthood," is the development of a sense of *ego integrity vs. despair* (fear of death). It involves in part "acceptance of one's own and only life cycle," and comes only to him "who in some way has taken care of things and people." One who successfully masters this stage, has a "new, a different love of one's parents." In Erikson's words, "The lack or loss of this accrued ego integration is signified by fear of death. . . . Despair expresses the feeling that the time is now short . . . for the attempt to start another life and to try out alternate roads to integrity. . . . it seems possible to . . . paraphrase the relation of adult integrity and infantile trust by saying that healthy children will not fear life if their elders have integrity enough not to fear death."

Peck, who further differentiated Erikson's seventh and eighth stages into seven stages, emphasizes the use of *developmental* criteria rather than *age* criteria in looking at later life stages. He points out that the study of later life is different from that of earlier life in that there is far greater variability in the chronological age at which a given psychic crisis arises. Children at the same *stage* almost all work on the same total set of developmental tasks. With adults the pattern can vary greatly, as, for example, the age of various parents at which their children leave home. Thus, at age 40, one's children may be grown, but one may not have experienced the climacteric, or menopause, and may still be working "uphill" to master one's vocational role. A 60-year-old man whose children are also grown may be nearing retirement and may have experienced death among family members and peers.

The sizable body of literature reporting empirical research on personality in later life cannot be reviewed in detail here. In the main it strongly supports a developmental view.[4] Central themes reiterated by clinicians and

---

[3] Neuggarten, B. L. and Weinstein, K. K. "The Changing American Grandparent," in Neugarten, B. L. (Ed.), *Middle Age and Aging*, University of Chicago Press, 1968, pp. 280–285. The styles identified are Formal, Fun-seeker, Surrogate Parent, Reservoir of Family Wisdom, and Distant Figure, with the quality of the relationship seemingly dependent on such factors as the ages of the generational representatives involved and the authority of the grandparent in the family structure. Grandparents over 65 are more likely to have a "formal" style and younger ones to be "fun-seeking." The significance and meaning of the grandparent role was categorized as biological revival, emotional self-fulfillment, resource person, vicarious accomplishment, and remote (little effect).

[4] For complete discussion and reviews of the literature, see Neugarten, B. L., and Associates, *Personality in Middle and Late Life*, N.Y., Atherton Press, 1964; Neugarten, B. L. "*Adult Personality:* Toward a Psychology of the Life Cycle," in Neugarten, B. L. (Ed.), *Middle Age and Aging*, Univ. of Chicago Press, Chicago, Ill., 1968, pp. 137–147;

researchers are individuality, heterogeneity, and continuity.

Older people are even more heterogeneous than younger people. Not only do they carry their own unique personalities into the aging phase of life, but they also have had longer lives and more varied experiences that produce a higher degree of differentiation. The ways in which aging individuals deal with the events and new situations related to old age—widowhood, retirement, grandparenthood, illness, process of dying—are a function of personality and reflect long-standing lifestyles. There is no sharp discontinuity of personality with age, but instead an increasing consistency. Personality is continuous over time; central characteristics become even more clearly delineated, and cherished values become even more salient.

The capacity to adapt and to cope with life stress also is continuous and is a determinant of the way in which the aging individual masters the new developmental tasks of late maturity and old age. Further, there is no one personality prescription for "successful" aging. Many different patterns of aging have been identified, and the potential for "success" is not tied to one particular pattern (17, 13, 20).

Because the disengagement theory (10) has stirred much controversy and because social interaction is of special interest to family therapists, a word is in order about it. It postulates that normal aging is a mutual withdrawal or disengagement between the aging person and others in the social system. It characterizes the process as "inevitable," as "initiated by the individual himself and by others in the system," as being intrinsic or developmental, as well as responsive, and as being desirable.

In short, the theory is both a description of a process and a theory of optimum aging. However, subsequent research, while it confirms disengagement as a process, refutes the notion that it is desirable.

Neugarten sums it up as follows:

> Psychological disengagement seems to precede social disengagement and . . . to have developmental properties. There is a positive relationship overall between *engagement* and life-satisfaction. Personality types . . . play a central role in affecting the relationships and in producing diverse patterns of aging . . . in particular, the extent to which the setting provides a wide range of colors. In short, disengagement proceeds at different rates and different patterns in different people in different places, and has different outcomes with regard to psychological well-being (18).

The theory and its thesis that the need for emotional involvement with others becomes less intense with age thus cannot be used as a rationale for ignoring the continued significance of family relationships until the end of life. Distinctions must also be drawn between family members and "others" in the interpersonal world. Studies at the Philadelphia Geriatric Center of those who might be considered the least likely candidates for emotional involvement—severely brain-damaged, institutionalized women with an average age of 83—demonstrated that their emotional involvement with others had increased in relative importance since their middle years, possibly because so many other sources of emotional gratification had become casualties of aging (14). In addition, the frequency and quality of relatedness to family is not contingent upon the older person's social skills (2), and in turn there is evidence that family members continue to have significant emotional involvement with their deteriorated, very old relatives (15).

The Family Personality

Consideration of aging and the family personality poses the same central issue as commanded attention in study of the individual, aging personality. Are there intrinsic, programmed "personality" developments stemming from the fact that the family itself and each of its members is aging while losing and gaining family members in a never-ceasing ebb and flow? Or are observed changes simply reactive to changing environment and events? Sorting out the *inherent* psychological problems of adjustment and adaptation from those *associated* with a family's aging but due to social and environmental influences is even a more complex process.

A theoretical model suggests shifts in the balance of responsibility as the family moves through various phases in its life cycle. Beginning with the total dependency of infancy, the nature of the emotional support required by the individual shifts over time, as does his need for instrumental services. As he moves through childhood and adolescence and gains competence, he assumes more and more responsibility for himself. With maturity he begins to assume a care-taking role toward others. In the aging process of life, he may once again need to be the receiver rather than the provider of help and support (3). Also, theoretically, the capacity of the family to achieve a new equilibrium in accommodating to the changing needs of its members is a mark of "health."

However, such a model must be viewed in the context of reality factors that qualify successful resolution of developmental family tasks: the larger number of older people for whom families are expected to provide emotionally, financially, and instrumentally; the lack of community services to support their efforts to do so; the older age at which generation three becomes responsible for generation four. Of particular relevance for clinicians is the need to distinguish between qualitative psychological relationships and the outmoded "etiquette" of family behavior that prescribes stereotyped behavioral responses (4).

Nevertheless, within those constraints it can be postulated that:

(*a*) intrinsic to the personality of the aging family are specific developmental tasks that can be successfully mastered;

(*b*) the basic family personality is continuous over time;

(*c*) remnants of unresolved family problems from earlier stages of the family life cycle are reactivated and

Neugarten, B. L. "Personality Changes in Later Life: a Development Perspective," in Eisdorfer, Carl and Lawton, M. Powell, (Eds.), *Psychological Processes in Aging*, Wash., D.C., American Psychological Ass'n., 1973, pp. 311–335; Riegel, K. R. "Personality Theory and Aging," in Birrin, James E. (Ed.), *Handbook of Aging and the Individual*, Chicago, Univ. of Chicago Press, 1959, pp. 797–851: Pincus, A., "Toward a Developmental View of Aging for Social Work," *Social Work*, 12(3): 33–41, July, 1967.

constrain resolution of the "normal" life crises of the aging family;

(*d*) when difficulties occur, therapeutic optimism is justified;

(*e*) successful resolution, whether spontaneous or via therapeutic intervention, can provide impetus for growth for all family members and the family as a whole.

In the main, both popular belief and therapeutic approaches have run contrary to such thinking. For example, the myth that families nowadays abandon their aged members by dumping them into institutions continues in the face of decisive empirical and clinical evidence to the contrary. At this sophisticated stage in the understanding of human psychodynamics, it is a rather peculiar premise that qualitative emotional bonds undergo radical, massive reversal with the passage of time. Clinicians often reflect the cultural ambivalence—on the one hand urging families to behave "responsibly" in caring for the aged (no matter the social, economic, or financial stress) and on the other emphasizing that the thrust for "health" and true maturation lies in separation and "independence."

In the past half-century, models of "normative" behavior have been developed for families in early phases of family life cycle. There are few, if any, "models" of behavior for aging families.

The little knowledge available is derived largely from contacts with families in crises stimulated by the increasing dependency of an elderly family member. It is necessary to distinguish between normal, healthy dependence and that which is extreme or pathological. As Goldfarb points out, "dependency" is a "critical, common, and pervasive influence in family dynamics," and psychological dependency can be, and is, a cohesive social force in family and society (12).

With respect to the relations between old people and their adult children, the increased dependencies of old people have, however, fostered such incorrect psychodynamic clichés as "role reversal" and "second childhood" —incorrect, because psychologically a child cannot become parent to his parent, nor can the parent become child to his child even though the balance of giving help and protection has shifted. In Goldfarb's words, in the older person, "a life-long maninfestation for a dependent person may emerge with greater clarity at this time . . . (and) relationships are less elaborately disguised or are displayed in socially less acceptable forms" (12). The childlike behavior of even a sick, braindamaged, old person does not make him a child; though some areas of memory and function may be eroded, there can be no consistent return in a time capsule to earlier levels of physical or psychological development.

Blenkner (1) conceptualizes a developmental phase called "filial maturity." This usually occurs when the individual is in his forties or fifties, and the "parents can no longer be looked to as a rock of support in times of emotional trouble or economic stress but may themselves need their offspring's comfort and support." Filial maturity is characterized by the adult child's capacity to be depended on by the aging parent. That is, the adult child fulfills a filial role, rather than a role-reversed "parental" role.

"Filial maturity" is, of course, a model. Ideally, the "filial crisis" should occur and be resolved as a normal developmental phase rather than in the crucible of an acute crisis. In all individuals, successful resolution of any of the normal "life crises" depends to some degree on how completely previous developmental phases were mastered. When there are gaps, or vestiges of unresolved problems, they have a direct bearing on the manner of coping with the current crisis.

This developmental phase for the individual adult child is also a developmental phase for the family, as a whole, and for each of its members. The oldest family member, in turn, must have the capacity to be dependent and, thus, to permit the adult child to become filially mature. Resolution of the developmental phase also depends on the capacity of other family members—spouse and children—to support the efforts of the individual rather than to put him or her in a bind—squeezed between the competing demands and requirements of generations one and three. Fulfillment of the filial role also may be constrained by the individual's own situation. For example, "children" in their 60's and 70's who themselves are aging and experiencing social and functional losses often must struggle to meet the needs of parents in their 90's (5).

When the losses of one or both of the generations make separation necessary via institutional placement of the oldest family members, the way in which the crisis is handled reflects the long-standing relationship patterns (6). Many families and many old people are able to mobilize and move constructively through what, by its very nature, is a disruptive experience. For others, the separation and the dying processes of the elderly may trigger extreme behavior and feelings. Intense anxiety may be stimulated in the adult child about his own aging processes; there may be massive denial of the older person's incapacities; projection of guilt may be expressed by myriads of complaints about the care given in the institution; psychological avoidance may result in infrequent visiting; the deterioration of the older person may stimulate the adult child who felt unloved all his life to beseech what the parent does not have to give and to exert frantic, time-pressured efforts to obtain that love by oversolicitous behavior or, at the other extreme, to revenge himself upon the now helpless parent. In one particularly poignant situation, an adult daughter in her late 60's, grief-stricken because of the "untimely" death of her own 42-year-old daughter, threatened to give her 90-year-old very sick mother, whose "timely" end was overdue, an overdose of sleeping pills.

In short, this phase in the family's developmental history runs the gamut from "health" to pathology. Whatever the styles of behavior, there are reverberations down through the generations.

The implications for family therapists are clear. The basic injunction, of course, is that all generations are legitimate family members. Aging families, like aging individuals, have continued adaptive capacity and potential for growth and change. Continued inter-generational involvement is healthy, desirable, and in the best interests of all family members. However, stereotyped thinking and approaches are to be avoided, since there is no one model of healthy behavior regarding the degree or quality of inter-generational involvement. The therapeutic goals depend on the ages and stages of all family members and their social and cultural context, as well as on the individuals' and families' widely diverse personalities.

In conclusion, a caveat. Even while we strive to understand the changes that have already occurred, we are confronted with additional change. As Brotman (8) points out, losses through death and promotion into the category called aging mean that in the course of every five years, 35 per cent of the individuals comprising the older population are newcomers to that category. The newcomers are different. They have lived through unique periods of history; have experienced rapid cultural, industrial, social, and economic changes; are progressively better educated and more sophisticated; have different interests and expectations; and women, in particular, will have had different roles and, therefore, different losses.

There also may in future be an even greater population explosion of the elderly. Bio-medical research may result in enabling even more people to live the maximum life-span already enjoyed by some. More radical projections include dramatic changes in life expectancy that could stretch the life-span to 130 to 140 years.

In one short story on that theme by Kurt Vonnegut, Jr., over-population has led to the establishment of thousands of government-operated suicide parlors located, naturally, adjacent to the Howard Johnson's (27). In another (28), the invention of a product called anti-gerasone has defeated illness, aging, and death altogether. By 2158 A.D., the strange new world created has exhausted natural resources and food supplies (they eat processed sawdust). The family in the story lives on the 76th floor of a 257-building development where dozens of people representing many generations share a one-bedroom apartment. The one bedroom and the TV set are monopolized by the tyrannical 172-year-old grandfather. Family tensions and conflicts are exacerbated by the over-crowding, lack of privacy, and resultant inability of young couples in their 60's to plan to have children even though they have been married for 40 years. Small wonder that some family members conspire to rid the family of grandpa by diluting his economy-size bottle of anti-gerasone.

In Vonnegut's satirical fantasy, the social and economic pressures cause the murderous impulses to surface and break through. *Age-ism* is acted out on the family level. The phenomenon of "age-ism" (9, 16)—negative or hostile attitudes between age groups that lead to socially destructive competition—is already of concern to social scientists.

When families and society act out, professionals make their contribution through objectivity and perspective. If the psychological concomitants and therapeutic implications for families of death, loss, and separation are to be explored, it is first necessary to know the real world of generational relations.

References

1. BLENKER, M., "Social Work and Family Relationships in Later Life With Some Thoughts on Filial Maturity," Chap. 3, in Shanas, E., and Streib, Gordon, (Eds.), *Social Structure and the Family: Generational Relations.* Englewood Cliffs, N.J., Prentice-Hall, 1965.
2. BRODY, E. M., KLEBAN, M. H., and Moss, M., "Family Relationships of Mentally Impaired Elderly," in preparation, 1973.
3. BRODY, E. M., "Service-Supported Living in an Urban Setting," in press, *Gerontological Society,* 1973.
4. BRODY, E. M., "The Etiquette of Filial Behavior," *Aging and Hum. Develop.,* 1: 87–94, 1970.
5. BRODY, E. M., "The Aging Family," *The Gerontologist,* 6: 201–206, 1966.
6. BRODY, E. M. and SPARK, G. M., "Institutionalization of the Aged: a Family Crises," *Fam. Proc.* 5: 76–90, 1966.
7. BROTMAN, H. B., "The Older Population Revisited," *Facts and Figures on Older Americans, No. 2,* Administration on Aging, SRS, U.S. Dept. of H.E.W.
8. BROTMAN, H. B., "Every Tenth American," Paper presented at State Conference, Iowa State Commission on the Aging, Des Moines, Iowa, Dec. 2, 1968.
9. BUTLER, R. N., "Age-ism: Another Form of Bigotry," *Gerontologist,* 9: Part I, 1969.
10. CUMMINGS, E. and HENRY, W. E., *Growing Old,* N.Y., Basic Books, 1961.
11. ERIKSON, E., *Childhood and Society,* N.Y. W. W. Norton & Co., 1950, pp. 231–233.
12. GOLDFARB, A. J., "Psychodynamics and the Three-Generation Family," in Shanas, E. and Streib, G. F. (Eds.), *Social Structure and the Family: Generational Relations,* Englewood Cliffs, N.J., Prentice-Hall, 1965, pp. 10–45.
13. HAVIGHURST, R. J., NEUGARTEN, B. L., and TOBIN, S. S. "Disengagement and Patterns of Aging," Paper presented at International Assn. of Gerontology, Copenhagen, 1963, in Neugarten, B. L. (Ed.), *op. cit.* 1968, pp. 161–172.
14. KLEBAN, M. H., BRODY, E. M., and LAWTON, M. P., "Personality Traits in the Mentally Impaired Aged and Their Relationships to Improvements in Current Functioning," *Gerontologist,* 11: Part I: 134–140, 1971.
15. MOSS, M. and KURLAND, P., "Family Visiting with Institutionalized Mentally-Impaired Aged," Paper presented at 26th annual meeting of the Gerontological Society, Miami Beach, Fla., Nov. 6, 1973.
16. NEUGARTEN, B. L., "Grow Old Along With Me! The Best is Yet To Be," *Psychol. Today,* Dec., 1971.
17. NEUGARTEN, B. L., HAVIGHURST, R. J., and TOBIN, S. S., "Personality and Patterns of Aging," in Neugarten, B. L. (Ed.), *op. cit.* 1968, pp. 173–177.
18. NEUGARTEN, B. L., "Personality Changes in Later Life: A Developmental Perspective," in Eisdorfer, C. and Lawton, M. P. (Edc.) *Psychology of Adult Developments and Aging,* American Psychological Assn., Wash., D.C. p. 330.
19. PECK, R. C., "Psychological Developments in the Second Half of Life," in Neugarten, B. L., (Ed.), *op. cit.,* 1968, pp. 88–92.
20. REICHARD, S., LIVSON, F., and PETERSEN, P. G., *Aging and Personality,* N.Y., John Wiley & Sons, 1962.
21. RILEY, M. W., and FONER, A., *Aging and Society, Volume One: An Inventory of Research Findings,* N.Y., Russell Sage Foundation, 1968, p. 160.
22. RILEY, and FONER, *op. cit.,* pp. 169–71.
23. RILEY, and FONER, *op. cit.,* pp. 541–44.
24. SPARK, G. M. & BRODY, E. M., "The Aged are Family Members," *Fam. Proc.,* 9: 195–210, 1970.
25. "This Age of Grandparents," in Statistical Bulletin, N.Y., Metro. Life Insurance Co., Sept., 1972.
26. TOWNSEND, P., "Emergence of the Four-Generation Family in Industrial Society," in Neugarten, B. L., (Ed.), *Middle Age and Aging,* Univ. of Chicago Press, 1968, pp. 255–7.
27. VONNEGUT, KURT, JR., "Welcome to the Monkey House," in *Welcome to the Monkey House,* N.Y., Dell Publishing Co., 1970.
28. VONNEGUT, KURT, JR., "Tomorrow and Tomorrow and Tomorrow," in *Welcome to the Monkey House,* N.Y., Dell Publishing Co., 1970.

Reprint requests should be addressed to Elaine M. Brody, Philadelphia Geriatric Center, 5301 Old York Road, Philadelphia, Pennsylvania 19141.

VIII. Death

C.H. ELDRIDGE '76

Human life is a finite process which begins with the union of two cells and ends with inevitable decay. Death, the end of life, is a continual reality throughout one's life, experienced in different ways, and forms as certain an end point as birth is the initial stage of life. Robert Jay Lifton and Eric Olson talk about how death fits into the life cycle, how death is a part of many ordinary developmental events in life, even though it is most often an aspect of life people prefer to deny. By old age the fact of death becomes increasingly difficult to deny, leading to adjustments in the way we regard our life and to spending more time in assessment, reflection, and introspection. Elisabeth Kübler-Ross, a psychiatrist who has dedicated her life to working with dying people, looks at how open encounter with dying people can help them find the meaning they seek in life and help them confront and face their deaths. The social denial of death, and the social isolation of dying people and lack of encounter around the death process, make it difficult for people to come to terms with their own deaths, or the deaths of their loved ones. This denial also affects the way the living deal with the deaths of loved ones, as psychiatrist Norman Paul suggests, which may lead to unresolved grief becoming an ongoing issue for a family system as they continually avoid the pain of loss.

37

Death and the Life Cycle

by Robert Jay Lifton and Eric Olson

What man shall live and not see death?
　　　　　　　—Psalms 89:49

So much of adolescence is an ill-defined dying,
An intolerable waiting,
A longing for another place and time,
Another condition.
　　　　　　　—THEODORE ROETHKE,
　　　　　　　from "I'm Here"

What can we know of death and how do we know it? Throughout history man has answered this question in many different ways. Is it true that, as Freud said, man cannot imagine his own death, or as La Rochefoucauld put it, "One cannot look directly at either the sun or death"? Erik Erikson, a psychologist well known for his studies of human development, has written that when a person tries to imagine not existing, he experiences a chill and a shudder and turns away. Many religious philosophies, on the other hand, have provided explicit images of life after death, images so attractive that people have longed for an end to earthly existence so as to experience heaven.

We want to understand what kind of knowledge people can have of death. Before proceeding to that controversial problem, we can begin by asking a more basic question about knowledge in general: How do human beings learn? Here also, there are disagreements, but two famous positions are important to consider.

One of the oldest beliefs, held by Plato in the fourth century B.C., is that all knowledge exists within one at birth. What appears to be later learning during the course of life is then really only a remembering of what was once known and then forgotten. The most one could learn before death would equal what was forgotten upon being born.

The seventeenth-century English philosopher John Locke believed the opposite. He argued that a child knows absolutely nothing prior to birth. Because we learn every-

thing from experience, said Locke, there are absolutely no limits on what a person can learn during his life provided he has the right experiences.

Modern psychological evidence now suggests that both Plato and Locke were partly correct. It appears that a child does have a kind of knowledge at birth, but that this "knowledge" is vastly extended and made concrete only by experience with the environment. We shall use the word "imagery" rather than "knowedge" when speaking of what a newborn baby knows about the world. In any case, it seems incorrect to assume, as Locke did, that a baby's mind at birth is absolutely blank.

A newborn baby expects to be fed and "knows" what to do with the mother's breast. The baby's inner imagery guides it toward the mother and helps it to become a partner with the mother in obtaining what is needed to survive. But as the inner image motivates and guides the baby, so also does experience help it to learn specific things. The image gradually begins to resemble a picture of the baby's relation to the world. After about six months, for example, the baby learns that one person is its mother. Once this happens, the baby is most content in the arms of this special person and is less easily comforted by the arms and smiles of others.

Several kinds of evidence have convinced psychologists that a baby's brain is not simply empty at birth. In watching a young baby, we become aware that it has certain innate, or inborn, expectations. Also, recent studies have given us reason to believe that infants react to images while they sleep. What it is that a baby "sees" in these states can never be fully known. But it does seem clear that the capacity to form images is present at birth.

Observations of the behavior of very young animals suggest that some kinds of knowledge are inborn. Certain young birds when they are hungry peck at a dot of color on their mothers' beaks. This is a signal for the mother to open its mouth and provide food. The young bird had to have some inner image or picture of its own relation to the world in order to begin pecking the dot.

In speaking of behavior that is directed solely from within an organism, psychologists have usually used the term "instinct." Freud thought there were two kinds of instincts: those that push the organism (animal or human) toward life and those that tend toward death. Freud saw the process of living as a kind of battle between these life and death instincts. The life instincts urge the organism to satisfy appetites and thus reduce the tension of various kinds of hunger. The death instincts pull the organism back to the inanimate state from which Freud thought all living organisms emerged. Thus, both sets of instincts lead the organism toward inactivity—the death instinct directly and the life instinct through the restful state that follows satiation. And, indeed, Freud said explicitly that "the aim of all life is death."

The problem with the word "instinct" is that it suggests a blind force that always exists in more or less the same form. The term "inner imagery" is more useful because it indicates that these inner guiding pictures are constantly changing throughout the life cycle. The baby is guided by inner imagery toward an attachment with the mother. But this imagery itself changes form and evolves as the mother-child relationship develops during the early years of life. The imagery becomes increasingly complex as the child learns to speak and acquires words with which to think about its place in the world. The term "instinct" conveys an idea of behavior more machine-like and less influenced by language and changing imagery than is appropriate to human action.

The inner imagery exists at first only on the level of physiology. At this point it is not an image at all, in the sense of being an inner picture of the world. Rather, it is simply a predisposition of the organism to move toward the nurturing it requires. Later, during early childhood, this imagery does become something of a crude picture of self and world. The child recognizes familiar faces and objects and becomes content in their presence and anxious in their absence. Later still, with the more complete learning of language, the images become concepts and forms of thought which can be communicated. During this sequence of development, the imagery takes on an ethical quality; it comes to indicate what one *should* do. Thus, inner imagery responds to changes in one's age and life situation; it evolves.

Though we will be speaking here of death *imagery* rather than death *instinct*, there is something important to be learned from what Freud said about the death instinct. He had the idea that death is somehow present in a unified way from the beginning of life. For this reason, death plays a central part in his view of life. But because he spoke of death only in terms of instinct, he underestimated the importance of imagery and language in shaping a person's evolving vision of self and world.

Man's task is to develop concepts, imagery, and symbols adequate to give a sense of significance to his experience. In saying that "the aim of life is death," Freud asserted that there is an instinctual drive toward an inanimate state. Though we now find this instinctual language misleading, we would agree with what we take to be the basic idea behind this assumption: that death is psychologically present from the beginning of life.

A child requires several years to acquire a *concept* of death. This concept is built gradually on the basis of inner imagery that the child apparently has at birth and that is developed and made concrete in relation to the child's experiences. The particular nature of those experiences can profoundly affect the "feel" that the idea of death comes to have for the child. Over the course of the life cycle, the imagery and ideas associated with death continue to evolve, reflecting both individual experiences and development of intellectual capacities.

We can understand the child's earliest imagery of life and death as organized around three sets of opposites:

connection—separation

movement—stasis (lack of movement)

integrity—disintegration

In describing the imagery surrounding the child's relationship to the mother, we spoke of the expectation of food and care. The child seeks attachment to the mother and has an inner image which guides it in this way. The baby cries, sucks, clings, follows, and smiles—trying always to get the care it needs. We can say that life for the baby means being *connected* to the source of care and support. Powerful fears and anxiety appear when the child is left alone, separated from the source of nurture. This image of *separation* is related to an image of death.

Anyone who has watched healthy babies and young children has seen their energetic motion. Muscles and muscle coordination develop with exercise. This is precisely what children seem determined to get by engaging in various kinds of play. *Movement* is life. *Stasis*—the opposite of movement—is associated with imagery of death. When a young child is held still against his will, he becomes nervous and upset. Inability to move is equated with death.

Young children are, of course, least in motion when they are asleep. And it is interesting that the most widely known of all nighttime prayers begins:

> Now I lay me down to sleep
> I pray the Lord my soul to keep.
> If I should die before I wake,
> I pray the Lord my soul to take.

The popularity of this old prayer reveals its closeness to the psychological equation made by children of sleep and death, and the need for an image of continuity. We would stress the importance of such imagery in the child's life. Later psychological disturbance can often be traced to an early impairment in this imagery of life-continuity.

In some situations this association of sleep with death can make death less frightening. This possibility is shown in an example from the life of a little girl just over three years old, reported by Sylvia Anthony in *The Discovery of Death in Childhood and After*:

Marlene was brought to school by her father, who had found her lying beside her dead mother on the floor by a half-made bed. The mother had apparently suffered a heart attack. On arrival at school, Marlene said quite happily to the teacher, "Mother lay down on the floor and went to sleep, so I went to sleep too."

Only over time does the child come to be able to

differentiate death from sleep and appreciate the finality of death. The preschool child, for example, often thinks that death is reversible, as a "coming back." Later it is recognized that death is not only final, but also inevitable, and that it happens to everyone, including oneself. The age at which children begin to understand all this varies tremendously, but in most cases it occurs between five and nine. It is important, however, to emphasize that children begin to become aware of death much earlier than this, even though their ideas may be vague and confused.

The phrase "getting it together" suggests something of what is meant by the third pair of opposites. The *integrity* of life means staying in one piece, keeping oneself intact. The opposite image is that of *disintegration* —of falling apart and going to pieces. From the earliest days of life, the fear of bodily annihilation and disintegration is strong. This fear is related to fears of separation and stasis, since all death imagery is bound closely together. But we can speak of early fears of disintegration as a threat to one's image of one's body, and of its boundaries as inviolable. Cuts, injuries, the sight of blood —these can generate extraordinary anxiety because of their closeness to the death imagery of disintegration.

Situations that relate to imagery of separation, stasis, and disintegration cause extreme anxiety even when the experiences themselves are not actually dangerous. Imagine a young child wailing and screaming when his father leaves him alone for a moment in a strange place, or the great fears which a small cut and oozing of blood can bring. These exaggerated fears become more understandable if we see them in the context of the more ultimate image of extinction to which they relate.

Otto Rank, an early psychoanalyst, believed that all anxiety in life resulted from life's first great shock: the trauma of being born. At the moment of birth the complete security of the womb is exchanged for the unpredictable stimulation of the world. In this view, birth is such a frightening experience that it creates fears which never again completely vanish.

Instead of saying that birth creates all anxiety, we prefer to say that birth is the first experience to activate the child's innate potential for death imagery. The baby is suddenly separated from its mother, must now move on its own, and is all at once vulnerable to pain and the fear of disintegration. As a baby becomes a young child, then a youth, and passes through maturity to old age, the same process will be experienced again and again. Each new step (each new "birth") on the way to becoming a fully developed person will rekindle the death anxieties associated with the innate imagery of separation, stasis, and disintegration.

This life-death imagery endures and evolves throughout life. The imagery becomes more concrete and specific as the child has experiences of seeing dead animals, severely injured people, or anything that suggests separation, stasis, or disintegration. Certain kinds of extreme experiences can heavily weight the death imagery, as opposed to the life imagery, in a young child's mind and can create lasting problems of anxiety. The death of a young brother or sister may be such an experience. This can convince a child that death happens because you're small.

Sometime around the age of three or four, a child becomes conscious of the concept of death. When death becomes a distinct idea, the imagery of separation, stasis, and disintegration becomes bound together in a unified notion of what it means to be dead. Typically, children think of the dead person as having "gone away" or having been the victim of violence such as biting, shooting, stabbing, bombing, burning, automobile crash, being flushed down the toilet, or having the body burst open so all the blood comes out. The way in which each child understands death will be strongly affected by the kinds of death he has seen or heard discussed. Middle-class children are more likely to think of death as caused by old age or disease, while poor children in inner cities often associate death with violence, accidents, or suicide.

A child's concept of death is likely to be charged with fear when earlier death imagery has overwhelmed imagery of life and continuity. Experiences that reinforce imagery of life's connection, movement, and integrity will encourage an attitude of trust and hope. A child seeks to grasp the idea of death while having the idea of continuity affirmed. This is very different from having the reality of death kept from him.

Such children's games as "hide-and-seek" reflect an early concern with disappearance and return. There is evidence that this concern is present from the first months of life, and that playing "peek-a-boo" is an earlier version of the same game. What seems most important is that the child's early curiosity in this area not be denied or ignored. A parent can use the occasion of a child's finding a dead animal to explain something about death. Or the death of a pet can be mourned, and even a grave marker erected, so as to help convey the idea of death and ongoing life. If ideas about death are not developed gradually in this way and talked about at appropriate moments, the death of a child's friend, brother, sister, or parent can be a trauma from which there will never be full recovery.

A child's early response to death affects the whole of personality development. Relaxed conversations with older people about death can make a vast difference in the way a child absorbs experiences with death. A child may develop guilt and feel responsible for the death of someone close, or think that, because a person he loves dies, it is not safe to love. Being able to discuss such matters openly may help avoid the development of harmful conflict.

Freud tended to see fear of death as secondary to fear of castration, in keeping with his sexual emphasis and his idea that death has no psychic representation. There is no doubt that fear of castration can arouse strong anxiety in young boys. But we would see the fear of death as the more fundamental anxiety, and castration epitomizing this anxiety in a particular body part. There is a further problem with Freud's theory when applied to women, because there is no precise analogy in women to castration fear in men. (Surgical excision of the breast can arouse somewhat similar anxieties in women later in life.) We are critical of the male bias in Freud's theory and of Freud's view of fear of death as subordinate to fear of castration. We should recognize, however, the ways in which—in both sexes—death anxiety can become localized in a specific part of the body.

If the conditions of a person's life suddenly change, death imagery may intensify. At a number of times in the life cycle, there are "critical points"—major transitions that occasion a flare-up of death imagery. When the changes have to do simultaneously with one's own body and with the social world in which one lives, then one may easily lose confidence in the belief that anything is definite or reliable. It's like Bob Dylan's line "How does it feel to be on your own, a complete unknown, like a rolling stone?"* There seems to be neither a comfortable world nor a known self.

The transition from childhood to adulthood is such a time. This period is known as adolescence and usually begins between the ages of twelve and fifteen, with the commencement of puberty. For girls becoming women, the transition is marked by menarche, the beginning of monthly periods of vaginal bleeding. For boys becoming men, the erect and stimulated penis is now capable of discharging semen. Both sexes may experience this new capacity to discharge bodily fluids as fearful and emotionally upsetting. The body that one has lived in for years suddenly appears to be acting unpredictably.

A girl who has not been told in advance about menstrual bleeding can become extremely frightened upon seeing blood on her clothes. If this happens at a social gathering or at school, she may feel embarrassment as well as fear. Not surprisingly, the experience of unexpected bleeding activates imagery of disintegration and thus becomes especially fearful. Girs beginning to menstruate sometimes think they are dying. The idea that one is now ready for sexual intercourse, which for a women means being penetrated by a male, may also arouse fear.

For boys, too, at adolescence, the body feels out of control. The first ejaculation often occurs at night during a dream, a "wet dream." These dreams are likely to include sexual images which can themselves cause anxiety.

One's body—suddenly growing rapidly, making one awkward, and behaving unexpectedly—seems not quite one's familiar home. But no new safe place appears to replace the lost one. Adolescence has been called a time of storm and siege. Strong sexual fantasies urge intimacy with another person, which is both fearful in itself and socially taboo. New and tougher demands are being made at school, and questions about plans for the future become more pressing. Friends suddenly seem more competitive and are often harsh in their judgments and rejections. In all of this, the search for forms of connection becomes intense and sometimes desperate.

For the first time in life, one consciously confronts the void: It suddenly seems possible that one could be nothing. One appears to rely on a past that seems lost and a future that feels unimaginable.

Where to retreat from all these assaults? It is tempting to play, in fantasy and reality, with the image of oneself as still a child. But it is precisely childhood that has been so suddenly and irredeemably taken away. When one acts like a child, one is laughed at by friends and chided by parents. The past offers no escape. Adolescence itself

is a death and rebirth experience; one dies as a child and is reborn as an adult.

All of the threats to the adolescent's self and world increase the anxiety coming from death imagery and intensify the search for new ways of affirming the imagery of life. This imagery now assumes a metaphoric and ethical quality. *Connection* comes to signify not only physical attachments, but also a sense of relation to meaningful philosophies and purposes. *Movement* for the teenager implies more than bodily activity: It includes emotional and intellectual development and a dread of stagnation. The image of *integrity* takes on the connotation of ethical intactness ("getting your head together") as well as soundness of body. Imagery of life must now be affirmed in a way that seems personally "right"—and an adolescent's judgments of his own ethical evasions can be every bit as severe as those he pronounces on others.

Adolescents frequently become extremely critical of their parents and families. This criticism is usually perceived by parents as hostility and rejection—and in a way it is. The hostility does not come entirely from hate, but also from an intense struggle to be independent of one's family and from inner doubts about one's capacity to do so. Above all, adolescence is a state of vulnerability. The emerging adult self feels impossibly frail; parents must often be attacked for the self to assert its vitality and power. Nor has it been sufficiently realized how much an adolescent's devaluing of his family can raise inner questions for himself about his own biologically mediated sense of connection.

There must always be an element of tension in the relationship between generations. But the nature of this relationship is also influenced, like everything else in psychological development, by history and historical change. In a period of rapid change, the wisdom of age has to compete on more even terms with the wisdom of youth. In such a time, the young *do* know more about certain crucial matters than their parents and teachers. Parents and teachers themselves are not so convinced of the adequacy of their own past experience as a basis on which to give advice, and often have real misgivings about their capacity to make judgments about the lives of the young.

All of this puts an element of uncertainty and fluidity into cross-generational relations. Age alone is not sufficient to make one an authority on all issues. The young become teachers of the older generation, and at certain moments of mutual trust, the rigid forms break down. The young still seek the authority of older people, but an authority based on lived experience and knowledge rather than on age alone or hierarchy—an authority which confirms rather than stifles their own emerging perceptions and critical spirit.

The fact that the parents of adolescents are usually in their forties intensifies the problems. Middle age brings its own crisis and another flare-up of the death anxiety which accompanies imagery of separation, stasis, and disintegration. (We will say more later about this mid-life transition.) But it is necessary to understand that the fires of family strife are fueled by crises of continuity and death imagery in the lives of both generations.

Adolescents are frequently described in such contradictory terms as brooding, frantic, lazy, energetic, creative, dull, friendly, spiteful, and so forth. They can be all of these at one time or another, for they find themselves subject to rapid and seemingly unpredictable swings in mood. The stress is on experimentation both in thought and action as the young person now tirelessly tries on new beliefs and stances to determine which, if any, will fit. Our historical period leaves more options open and makes this experimentation both urgent and exciting, and yet terribly difficult. It is precisely because our society needs new images of adulthood so desperately that it is not easy now to become an adult.

Adolescents struggle most to avoid deadness and to seek life. This pursuit can mean an emphasis on energetic creativity, tireless action, or the contemplation of grand visions. The foibles and failings of adult society appear inexcusable. There is much greater awareness of potential than of constraint and limitation; virtually anything seems possible. The young person restlessly seeks modes of continuity and activity that seem justifiable—goals that are worth working or even dying for. Often the beginning plans for a life's work are laid in this time of questioning and search.

One way to view the adolescent period is to see it as a time when a young person enters history. Suddenly that which is most personal—one's sexual feelings and consciousness of mortality—leads one to make connections that are more than personal. Sexual desires impel one toward intimacy with other persons and ultimately make one part of the cycle of generations. Awareness of death leads to questions about the meaning of life, and to a search for ways to relate oneself to the larger human historical project.

Sexuality and death make possible evolutionary change in the species, and in that sense they serve the impersonal natural process. The moment of exhaustion and relaxation after sexual orgasm which the French call *la petit mort* ("the little death") has been interpreted by some to suggest an experiential connection between sex and death. But we would stress the ways in which both sexuality and awareness of mortality lead to the enlargement of the boundaries of the self.

The Catholic theologian John Dunne calls this self-enlargement the making of one's "life story." There are, Dunne says, not only the given biological "events" of one's life, such as sexual maturation and death; there is also an element of leeway in how one chooses to relate oneself to these events. This process of forming meaning around biological universals enables one to have a life story rather than merely a life chronology.

A meditative youth may begin during adolescence to record his activities and feelings in a diary or journal, writing down his own history partly out of the desire to make certain he has one. Adolescent brooding may give rise to a philosophy of life, an idealistic statement of how things might be if adults didn't interfere. From political speculation and the quest for moral authenticity may emerge determined political activity both in school and in the larger community. In view of what we have said about life imagery, it is interesting that the radical politics of youth in the 1960's came to be known as "the Movement."

Not all societies have offered their young what we think of as adolescence. Puberty is biologically universal, but in some cultures this physical change also marks the beginning of adult responsibilities and privileges. In our society, many years intervene between puberty and the entry into full adulthood. This is the long period of schooling which societies with complex technologies require for access to most jobs. Moreover, this in-between time of more-than-child but less-than-adult seems to be growing longer, and the limbo status it creates can make for difficult psychological tensions.

Adolescents sense the precariousness of their own mental state. It is obvious that few things in the young person's life are stable or settled. Disappointments and hurt feelings are both frequent and extremely painful. The question that young people ask with greatest urgency is not "How can one feel?" but rather "How can one keep from feeling so deeply—how can one defend oneself from hurts that are too deep? Can one love while keeping in oneself a secret place that is safe?" There are many approaches to this problem, but no final answers; it is a problem that remains long after adolescence.

To open oneself to love and growth is to become vulnerable also to loss and disillusionment. The problem of attachment is as profound for psychology as it is for religion. Even where there is a quest for total freedom from attachments, as in some forms of Buddhism, one forms an attachment or connection with a great spiritual tradition. Whatever one's choice of attachments, they place one in a position of risk. Freud once said, "Life is impoverished, it loses in interest, when the highest stake in the game of living, life itself, may not be risked," though he did not incorporate this insight into his theory. One can, however, cultivate areas of the self that take on fierce autonomy from attachments to people around one. Such areas of commitment inevitably connect with larger traditions and enduring principles, but even these are not invulnerable.

We would emphasize the need for a sense of connectedness to currents and processes beyond the self if vitality and psychic energy are to be maintained . . .

Young people sometimes adopt special ways of *appearing*—to themselves and others—to be growing and evolving without exposing themselves to the anxiety of actually facing loss, which is a form of death imagery. One such technique is to become extremely intellectual, to explore new alternatives only in thought or in conversation. In this way one's life may seem to have connection, movement, and integrity, while actual changes and commitments are avoided. Or an adolescent can develop an ascetic style in which he denies his own strong appetites and fantasies and regulates his life with extreme control and discipline. In this way, too, life appears to have movement, while the real risks are avoided.

A third common approach is the retreat to conformity —to being like everyone else. This enables one to feel a sense of connection and shared participation, again without confronting one's own fears and doubts. A teenager in a strong group can appear to be rebelling against adult society while safe with friends who believe exactly as he does. Such youthful cliques gain a sense of power by harshly excluding those who are not "good enough," those who do not fit with themselves. The language which adolescent cliques use, their own forms of slang which change rapidly, is an effective way of defining the boundaries of one's in-group. Adolescent prejudice, stemming as it does from the anxieties aroused by unconfronted death imagery, can be cruel and inflict wounds not soon forgotten.

The quest for continuity *can* arise from a need to compensate for the overwhelming degree of death anxiety the adolescent feels. And the techniques that are used to cope with this anxiety *may* be evasive rather than honest. But the quest is also an affirmative one in which a young person attempts to stake out with integrity his own boundaries in relation to an acceptable world. Defensive and authentically exploratory approaches can be so similar as to be indistinguishable from each other. In any case, the projects of protecting and extending the self go on simultaneously. Overintellectualizing and real play with important ideas, ascetic evasion and the search for honest simplicity and purity, mindless conformity and the painful struggle to find other people worth belonging to—these are the tensions that an adolescent feels as he seeks to define himself as a person.

The struggle to achieve a sense of continuity and significance—to affirm the connection, movement, and integrity of life—becomes intense during adolescence but does not end there. Just as the adolescent searches for an authentic form of adulthood, so adulthood itself is marked by a need to feel that one's life has not stopped and become futile. But while the adolescent son or daughter reels with the dizzy freedom of having all possibilities open to him, his parents in middle age are more likely to be feeling nagging doubts about choices already made and lived with for twenty years. The approaching departure of children in whom so much has been invested means a beginning of separation from an important source of meaning. By mid-life too it may appear that one's occupational commitment, for better or worse, is final. Does one's life still have any movement and integrity left?

Children reawaken in their parents memories of their own youthful struggles. For most adults, the teenage years are remembered as a time of tension, but at least a time of some freedom and open choices. Thus, when parents see their own children reaching this time of infinite possibility—endless decisions about education, marriage, style of life—they may feel an intensification of regret about their own "roads not taken."

A parent may critically and insistently push his son or daughter toward his own lost chances. In so intruding, he is likely to succeed only in convincing his children that he has no respect for *their* integrity. Certainly, at this time of personal doubt, the last thing a parent wants to hear is endless criticism from adolescent offspring. But as we have seen, this is precisely what adolescents—for their own reasons—are likely to give. In this desire to avoid criticism while dispensing it freely (and in their separate confrontations with death imagery), the two generations closely resemble each other.

The whole issue of the generations becomes even more tense and difficult in a time of psychohistorical dislocation like our own. No institution now seems fully acceptable, no form of work or commitment goes uncriticized, no life-style completely justifiable. What it means now to be an adult in this situation is perplexingly un-

clear. If adulthood means to be somewhat settled, then one must become numb to constant criticism of whatever settlement one makes. But such numbing is itself a form of deadness, as the young are so capable of pointing out.

Does attaining adulthood require partial deadening? Our answer would be that adulthood does require certain forms of selective numbing. But that numbing need not characterize adult experience itself—and there are widespread experiments in our culture that challenge stereotyped images of adulthood and stress not only openness to feeling, but also a capacity for self-mockery and absurdity so often expressed by the young.

On the life watershed of middle age, one becomes aware that life is not unbounded at the far end. The boundary of one's death is suddenly no more distant than the boundary marked on the other end by one's birth. One is in the middle. Of course, one has always "known" that one would die, but now this knowledge becomes a compelling individual reality. One's life is suddenly felt to be limited, finite. It also becomes apparent that one cannot finish everything; there will not be time for all one's projects.

The apprehension that one's life may not only be finite but also *incomplete* sparks the fears that always accompany thoughts of premature death. For some people, this apprehension leads to a number of negative consequences: resignation and despair, retrenchment around seemingly irrevocable commitments, damning criticism of "hippies" and "bums" who live their lives more playfully. But for others, middle age brings a new birth of energy, a renewal of effort and experimentation.

Certainly, creativity and energy are not properties belonging exclusively to adolescents. However, as one psychoanalyst, Elliot Jacques, has argued, creative energy may express itself somewhat differently by the time one reaches the age of forty. Jacques points to many artists and musicians, for example, whose careers have changed dramatically around middle age. Their mode of work at this stage becomes slower, more careful and painstaking; it assumes a quality Jacques calls "sculpted"—as opposed to the more intense, spontaneous, ready-made quality of work done earlier in life. This change may have to do with a sharper awareness of personal mortality and finitude that comes with middle age.

Adults need movement and experimentation, too, and when they are unable or unwilling to acknowledge this, their lives become constricted. This very constriction of personality can be a way of evading real challenges which cause too much anxiety when confronted. But it is true as well that the burdens of adult responsibility and commitment mean that dramatic change at this time of life is more difficult and fearful. The uncertain gains of trying something new at this stage have to be balanced against the security of known patterns and achievements which one desires to protect.

Perhaps one of the most fortunate consequences of our restless culture is that more adults are making changes in ideas, work, and other life patterns when they feel themselves caught in dead ends. Ironically, the same confusion and openness of our present historical moment that increase the anxiety of life transitions for some people make experimentation possible for others.

Because our times are characterized by rapid change and scant confidence in the institutions of family, work, and church, personal quest is made both more possible and more problematic. But, however one deals with middle age, the need for a sense of life's continuity becomes more intense. One looks to family ties, commitment to work, the experience of nature or art, or the solace of religion for symbols of enduring and significant life.

A final critical point in the life cycle is that of old age. Death is near, and the aged person has ample time—usually too much time—to ponder what his life has added up to. Though the basic contours of life are set, the struggle for continuity it still very real. The tendency of the old to reminisce represents their need to reassure themselves that their lives have contained integrity, movement, and connection—a pattern which psychiatrists have now formalized in a therapeutic approach called the "life review."

The wisdom of age does not have a large role in the youth-centered culture of America. Far from worshipping our ancestors, as in traditional Asian societies, we shun the old and create separate "homes" in which our "senior citizens" can spend their "declining years." These euphemisms reflect our neglect. It is the old themselves who most painfully experience this culture's avoidance of age and death.

The generations need each other. Old people have not only wisdom to share, but playfulness as well. The fact that many older people are still interested in sexual love (a "discovery" that the mass media have been recently making) simply illustrates this potential for full human communication. Many an adolescent who has found his father or mother "impossible" to talk to has discovered in a grandparent a more flexible attitude. An old person, having less of an investment once more in what society thinks of as conventional, may feel more free to listen to and explore new ideas.

There can be "play" (in the sense of fun as well as leeway) in old age, but only when the old are respected and are part of ongoing communities. If age is denied a meaningful place in the flow of life, death—even for the old—can seem premature. At this time of life, as earlier, the fear of death is heightened by the negative death imagery of separation, stasis, and disintegration. Serenity in the face of death depends upon a sense that, in some symbolic way, one's life will endure.

38

ON DEATH AND DYING

by Elisabeth Kübler-Ross

I was asked this morning why this topic on death and dying has taken such a long time to come into public awareness. Dying and dignity have been with us for as long as there has been mankind. Why is it now that we have to give seminars and workshops on death and dying? Has it taken us all these decades to begin to be aware that we are finite and that we have to treat dying patients?

Psychiatric Basis

I believe I shall talk like a psychiatrist for about five minutes and try to explain what death means and what the fear of death really represents. In terms of the unconscious, we cannot conceive of our own death. This is very important to understand. I believe that it shall happen to everybody in this room, but not to me. If I am forced to conceive of my own death, then I can only conceive of it as a malignant intervention from the outside. I cannot possibly conceive of dying of old age at home in my own bed. If I have to die, in my unconscious, I can only conceive of it as being killed. I am not afraid of death per se, but rather the destructive catastrophic death that hits me from the outside when I am not prepared. Perhaps the most complicated thing to understand is that I cannot differentiate between the wish and the deed. In the Bible it says somewhere that to lust after your neighbor's wife is as bad as actually doing it. In terms of my reality, testing this is actually absurd. I can have all sorts of fantasies of what I would like to do, but as long as I don't do it, that is satisfactory. In terms of my unconscious that is not acceptable. If you understand this, then you can see what is relevant and what is important to understand, especially in the death of a parent of a young child.

Little children have a peculiar concept of death. They regard death not as a permanent happening, but as a temporary happening. Every normal 4- or 5-year-old child who is angry at mommy wishes mommy to drop dead. That is very normal behavior. Children think of it when they are angry, when they feel small and impotent

and helpless, and they wish mommy would drop dead only to make her get up again when they are hungry and they want a peanut butter-and-jelly sandwich. The trouble is that the little 4- or 5-year-old boy may really lose his mother by death, separation, or divorce. He then feels that he has actually contributed to her death. This thinking shows that he cannot yet differentiate between his wish to kill mommy and whether he has actually done it. If we understand this, then we appreciate many of the complications of dying patients who sometimes, decades later in their old age, moan and groan and cry and have a lot of somatic complaints which we cannot understand medically. When we talk to these people, we see that they have a peculiar sense of guilt; they feel that they have committed a crime and they have to be punished before they die. These patients suffer far beyond our medical understanding.

Our Death-Denying Society

Why is dying different now? People have the same kind of unconscious thoughts and fantasies that they had years ago. What has changed, I think, is our society, which has become increasingly a death-denying society. Half of our patients now die in hospitals, as compared to 50 years ago when people died at home in a familiar environment with a little bit of chicken soup instead of transfusions, with their families around them instead of interns, residents, and laboratory technicians. People who are dying in a hospital are attached to several pieces of monitoring equipment and we, as physicians, pay a lot of attention to these gadgets. Sometimes we feel very uncomfortable when a dying patient looks at us and would like to ask a question in regard to dying or to some unfinished business or to fears and fantasies. In Switzerland, where I am originally from, there is no embalming. They do not have drive-in funeral homes such as we are beginning to have in the United States where you drive up in your sports car, look through a glass window, sign a guest book, and take off. All of this is an attempt to deny that people die. We have a society where we deep freeze people and promise at high cost to defrost them in 50 or 100 years. We have had questions from widows about

Edited from a presentation made to a group of physicians.

whether they are eligible for social security, or if they are allowed to get married again. In this sense, people use denial that their next of kin are really dead.

Joseph Matthews has provided a beautiful description of the death-denying society and if you will bear with me I will read just one page to give you an even better description of what I mean by a death-denying society:

> To symbolize the dignity of the father's death the family decided to clothe the father in a pine box and rest him in the raw earth. Having been told that caskets ranged from one hundred to several thousand dollars, they asked for the one hundred-dollar coffin.
>
> "What $100.00 coffin?" replied the astonished undertaker.
>
> "Why, the one you mentioned."
>
> "Oh, no, caskets begin at $275.00."
>
> "Did you not mention a $100.00 coffin?"

The persistent wishes of the family were met and the pine box was selected. Later Matthews describes his experience after his father had been prepared by the undertaker:

> My father was 92. In his last few years he had wonderfully put chiseled wrinkles. I had helped to put them there. His cheeks were deeply sunken, his lips pale: he was an old man. There is a kind of glory in the face of an old man, but not so with the stranger lying there. They had my papa looking like he was 52. They had put cotton in his cheeks and has erased the best wrinkles. His lips were painted. He looked ready to step before the footlights of a matinee performance. I fiercely wanted to pluck out the cotton, but was afraid. At least the make-up could come off. I called for alcohol and linens and a very reluctant mortician brought them to me. I began the restoration. As the make-up disappeared, the stranger grew older. He never recovered the looks of his 92 years, but in the end the man in the coffin became my papa.

Later he describes his experience at the cemetery:

> I say I smelled that fresh earth, but there was none to be seen. What I did see was difficult to believe. I mean that green stuff. Someone had come before us and covered that good raw earth, every part of it, with green stuff. Every scar of the grave was concealed under simulated grass just as if nothing had been disturbed here—just as if nothing was going on here, just as if nothing were happening. What an offense against nature, against history, against papa, against us, against God.

It goes on, but I shall stop here. You have to ask yourself why we have to conceal the grave, why we have to cover up that good earth with artificial greens, why we have to pretend that nothing is happening. You must understand that the fear of death is the fear of a catastrophic happening, a catastrophic destructive force that destroys us from the outside.

Then we also have to look at death in the past and death in the present. In the old days death also came as a catastrophic happening in the form of epidemics. It erased populations of whole villages, but it was not man-made. In times of war you faced your enemy face-to-face and had a chance to kill rather than to be killed. These things have changed. In the past, epidemic disease was the killer; now we have developed antibiotics, vaccines, all sorts of things that can master the old types of death. In our fear of death we have also created weapons of mass destruction. We now have weapons that you cannot defend yourself against physically. We cannot see, smell, or hear an enemy and I am thinking of chemical warfare, bacteriological warfare, and means of mass destruction, all of which are man-made. We are afraid, we are guilty, and still hope "it shall happen to thee and to thee but not to me!" I think this is the reason why this society, especially at this time, is using such a mass denial. We live in the illusion that, since we have mastered so many things, we shall be able to master death too.

Physicians' Reactions to Dying Patients

How does this affect you as physicians? How does this affect our patients? I had a glimpse of this 4½ years ago through a chance happening. Some theology students knocked at my door and asked me if I would help them to write a paper on a crisis in human life. Several had chosen dying as the biggest crisis man had to face, but they were stuck. They did not know how to do research on dying. You cannot experience it, you cannot verify it. I suggested that one way that you could really collect some data and understand it was by getting close to dying patients and asking them to be our teachers. I had a similar experience some years earlier when I tried to understand what it is like to be schizophrenic. I spent two years in the state hospital where I sat with schizophrenic patients and asked them what is it like, how did it start, what are the changes, what does it feel like, until I had the feeling that I really knew what it was like to be a schizophrenic from the patient's point of view. Because I had this good learning experience, I recommended the same kind of methods to my theology students.

I promised them that I would interview dying patients, and that as they would become more comfortable during the interviews, I would drop out and let them continue the dialogue until they had enough data. A week later, after asking numerous people, there was not a single dying patient in that 600-bed hospital! There was just nobody dying. When I pushed, I was given all sorts of rationalizations. These patients were too sick, too weak, too tired, or "they don't feel like talking." Occasionally I was told that if I talked to patients about dying they would jump out the window. It was extremely difficult during the first year. It took an average of ten hours a week to get permission to see a single terminally ill patient. In all fairness I must say that I was new at the University of Chicago, and so the physicians had no assurance that I would not cause trauma or that I would be tactful. But this same kind of resistance I have also seen in Colorado; it was not associated with the University of Chicago alone. When we finally obtained permission to see a patient, he was an old man who was ready to talk. He put his arms out and said please sit down *now*. I told him, "No, not now," because my students were not with me. My needs as a teacher prevented me from seeing his needs. I described to the students the next day his outstretched arms, his pleading eyes, how he emphasized the *now*. The next day when I came with the students he was in oxygen, he could hardly talk, and the only thing he was able to say was, "thank you for trying anyway." He died about half an hour later. This was our first and most difficult patient, because of our own feeings, which prevented us from really listening to his needs.

We decided we would meet in my office and talk to each other about what we called our "gut reaction"—how we really felt about this type of work, about seeing these kinds of patients, and about the reception we would get from the patients. One of the students, who was as white as a bed sheet, said, "Oh, I'm not afraid of death," and the other students questioned him as to why he was so pale. They wanted to know why he was the only one who denied his fear. He said that he had been the hospital student chaplain in a state hospital the year before and that he had been assigned to a ward where a patient was dying. He had walked into the ward and said (I am quoting him almost verbatim now): "I yelled at the peak of my voice, 'God is love, God is love' until the patient dropped dead." This was his proof that he was not afraid! I told him that when I was a little girl in Switzerland, I had to go down to the wine cellar to get a bottle of wine and the darker the cellar became, the louder I yodelled. That experience reminded me of him.

What I am trying to say is that after each patient interview, we tried not only to listen to the patient, but also to ourselves, to our own reactions; we tried to get to know ourselves better. In these after-interview discussions, we analyzed how we really reacted—when we had some tender thoughts, and when we had some difficulties. We also learned to become more sensitive, not only to the patients, but to ourselves and to our own needs. Dr. Wall described beautifully in his book on the dying patient how a social worker was faced for the first time with a dying patient and what her reactions were. He said every time she entered the patient's room, she felt strong feelings of guilt.

> She was going to live, while he, of her own age, was going to die. She knew he wanted to talk to her, but she always turned the talk into a little joke or into some evasive reassurance, which had to fail. The patient knew and she knew because he saw her desperate attempts to escape; he took pity on her and kept to himself what he wanted to share with another human being. So he died and did not bother her.

We have interviewed more than 400 patients during the last four years. We have seen many times that patients want to talk and that they would very much like to share their thoughts with another human being. It is very difficult sometimes to try to do that. When we come in, we tell them that we would like them to be our teacher, that we would like to know what it is like to be very sick, and sometimes we use the word dying. Many of our patients respond like we are opening flood gates. They share with us things that we were never aware of.

I think the most important thing that we have learned, and I am summarizing a bit now, is that all our patients know when they are terminally ill, whether they have been told or not. To me this is a very consoling thought. They not only know when they are seriously ill, but patients can even tell you the approximate day of their death, right up to their actual demise. They will tell you

goodbye and you know this is the last time you will see them. This is also true for children. We asked our patients the question that we are most often asked, and that is, would the patient have liked to be told. Two-fifths of our patients had never been told, although they knew it anyway after a while. Our patients usually told us that they would like to be told if it is serious, but not without hope. Hope for the healthy and the living is a very different thing. We tend to forget that sometimes. Hope for the living is always associated with cure, treatment, and, if that is not possible, a prolongation of life and perhaps relief of pain and suffering. When a patient says to you, "I hope the research laboratories work on a new drug and I am the first one to get it and by some miracle I am going to walk out of this hospital," that is hope prior to the final stage. When the same patient then, suddenly, a few days later, looks at you and says, "I hope my children are going to make it," then you know that this patient has changed to the kind of hopes that dying patients express, which are very reasonable, very appropriate, and not unrealistic. It is not wise at this point to tell them, "Oh, come on now, you are going to make it, you are going to get well." I think at this point we should support them, encourage them, and reinforce the hope that the patient expresses.

Stages Between Awareness of Serious Illness and Death

Patients go through five stages between their awareness of serious illness and their death, if they have a minimal amount of time available.

Stage 1 (Denial)

Most patients respond with shock and denial when they are told that they have a serious illness. This may last from a few seconds to a few months. Most of the patients we interviewed had dropped their denial; only three, less than 1% maintained it to the very end. Patients begin to see, when they are seriously ill, that the family comes in and does not know what to talk about and becomes estranged. Someone may come in with a red face and smile. Others may change their conversation a bit; they may talk more about a triviality because of their discomfort. Patients accept quickly that things are not at all perfect.

Stage 2 (Anger)

When the patient cannot maintain his denial anymore, he will become difficult, nasty, demanding, criticizing; that is the common stage of anger. How do you respond to one who complains and criticizes everything you do? You may tend to withdraw and not deal with him anymore. What else can you do? You can avoid him, you can stick the needle in a bit farther—not consciously—but when you are angry you touch patients differently. We can measure some of these responses. In California some investigators measured the response time between patients ringing for the nurse and the nurse actually coming into the room. They showed that patients beyond medical help, terminally ill patients, had to wait twice as long as other patients for the nurse to respond. This behavior should not be judged; it should be understood. It is very difficult to remember that members of the helping professions, who work hard all day, may have a difficult job coming into the dying patient's room. In the first place, the professional is uncomfortable; second, she is worried that the patient may ask how long he has to live or all sorts of unpleasant questions, and then, if the nurse does something for the patient, he may begin to criticize her. The nurse comes in and shakes the pillow, and the patient says, "I just wanted to take a nap, can't you leave me alone." When you don't shake the pillow, the patient remarks, "Why can't you ever straighten up my bed?" Whatever you do is criticized. Such patients are very difficult to manage and the families suffer tremendously because, when they come in and visit, they are always too early, too late, or there are not enough people, or too many people. Someone has to do something for these patients, to facilitate life for everybody concerned. It is important to understand that these patients are not angry with the nurse or the family. The more vibrant the nurse is when she comes into the patient's room, the more energetic she is, the more she is going to get through to the dying patient. In a way she should be able to accept the anger as a compliment, because what the nurse reminds the patient of is functioning health, ability to go to work, to go for a coffee break, all those things that the patient is about to lose. Because the nurse reminds the patient of all these things, and because he is desperately attempting to deny that he is dying, he becomes angry and says in effect, "Why me?" But he is also asking, "Why couldn't this happen to Joe Blow or somebody else?" If the nurse can put fuel into the fire, if she can help him to express this anger, if she can permit him to ask the question, "Why me?" without the need to answer it, then she will have a much more comfortable patient almost immediately. We interviewed a young patient who was dying. She was in my office and looked completely numb and I asked her if she felt like screaming. She looked as if she were on the verge of an explosion. She asked if we had screaming rooms in hospitals. I said no, we had chapels. "No, this is wrong," she said, "because in chapels we have to pray and be quiet and I need just to do the opposite. I was sitting out in the car yelling at God and asking him, 'Why did you let this happen to me?' " I encouraged her to express this in my office and to cry on my shoulders. They never scream as loud as they think they will.

If you can help patients express the question, "Why me?" you can help them express their rage and anger; then your patients become more comfortable and ring for the nurse less often and stop nagging and complaining. Sometimes they even quickly become much more comfortable patients and we wonder what has happened to them.

Stage 3 (Bargaining)

That is often when they reach the stage of bargaining. In the bargaining they may pray for another year to live; they would donate their kidneys or their eyes, or they may become very good people and go to church every Sunday. They usually promise something in exchange for extension of life. Some of the promises are not made to God, but to someone on the hospital staff. We had a woman who asked to be relieved of some of her tremendous pain for one day so that she would not be dependent on injections around the clock. She said she would just love to go home one more day and the reason for this was that her favorite son was getting married. We tried everything, and finally we were able to teach her self-hypnosis to relieve her pain. She left the hospital and looked like a million dollars. She attended her son's wedding. I was curious about patients who only ask for one single day; how do they react when their bargaining time is up? It must be extremely difficult. I waited for her, she saw me in the hallway and she was not happy to see me at all. Before I could ask her a question, she said, "Dr. Ross, don't forget, I have another son." This is the most typical part of bargaining. Promises are never kept; patients say, "If I could live just long enough for my children to go through high school," and then they add college, and then they add I just want a son-in-law, and then they would like to have a grandchild, and it goes on and on.

Stage 4 (Depression)

If, in the denial stage, they say "No, not me," then in the anger stage they say, "Why me," and in the bargaining stage they say, "Yes me, but." When they drop the "but," it is, "Yes me." Then the patient becomes very depressed.

There are two kinds of depression and it is important to understand the two different kinds. The first type is a reactive depression in which the patient cries when he talks about it, and mourns the losses which he has experienced. Later on he becomes quiet and depressed. When you enter his room, you see a man crying and he doesn't say what he is crying about. It is very difficult to accept such behavior over a long period of time. What does the physician do when he enters the room of a patient who is crying, especially if it is a man? This is one area in which men have a much more difficult time than women. The physician may be quiet. Many physicians go into the room and give the patient a pat on the back and say, "Come on, it is not so bad." We try to cheer them up because, as physicians, we cannot tolerate crying patients very well. The reason our tolerance is low is not because of the patient; it is rather because of our own inability to tolerate depressed patients over a long time. Sometimes we request a psychiatric consultant, which is not appreciated by most patients. It is an inappropriate request because the patient's response represents normal, not abnormal behavior.

If I were to lose one beloved person, I would be allowed to mourn and everyone here would respect that as being socially acceptable. But who has the courage to face not only the loss of one person, but the loss of everybody he has ever loved? It is a thousand times more sad, and takes much more courage to face. What we should be trying to do is to tell our patients that it takes a man to cry and that we mean it completely and willfully. We should help them express their grief, which, in fact, is a preparatory grief. It is not mourning and grieving over things lost; rather, it is a grieving and mourning over impending loss. The patient is beginning to separate himself from the people that he has to leave in the near future. This is what we call preparatory grief.

Stage 5 (Acceptance)

If the physician can help his patient through a preparatory grief, the patients will ask once more to see the relatives, then the children, and at the very end, only one beloved person, who is usually husband or wife and, in the case of children, naturally, the parents. This is what we call . . . decathexis, when the patient begins to separate; when he begins to feel no longer like talking; when he has finished all his unfinished business; when he just wants the companionship of a person who is comfortable, who can sit and hold his hand. It is much more important than words in this final stage. If the physician can help the patient express his rage and his depression and assist him sincerely through the stage of bargaining, then most patients will be able to reach the stage of acceptance. It is not resignation—there is a big difference. Resignation, I think, is a bit like giving up. It is almost a defeat. A stage of acceptance is almost beyond any affect. It is the patient who has said, "My time comes very close now and it is all right."

A woman who was always hoping for a miracle drug that would cure her suddenly looked with an almost beaming face and said, "You know, Dr. Ross, a miracle has happened." I said, "What miracle?" and she replied, "The miracle that I am ready to go now and it is not any longer frightening." This is the stage of acceptance. It is not happy; the time is rarely ever right. People almost always want to live, but they can be ready for death and they are not petrified anymore. They have been able to finish their business.

Even children, depending on age, can show these stages, but to much less of an extent than adults. Very small children are only afraid of separation. They have no real concept of death yet. When they are a bit older, the added fear is one of mutilation. Later on they see death as a man whom they run from at night—a bad man; they want the lights on at night, as they are afraid of darkness. Later on they realize that death is not a temporary but a permanent happening. They begin to see it after the age of 9 years or so as a biological force, almost like grown ups. Sometimes children talk about death and dying, too—not in words, but in pictures. A little boy tried to paint what he felt like. He drew a huge tank and in front of the barrel was a tiny, little figure with a stop sign in his hand. This to me represents the fear of death, the fear of the catastrophic, destructive force that comes upon you and you cannot do anything about it. If you can respond to him by saying it must be terrible to feel so tiny and this thing is so big, he may be able to verbally express a sense of smallness or impotence or rage. The next picture he drew was a beautiful bird flying up in the sky. A little bit of its upper wing was painted gold. When he was asked what this was, the boy said it was the peace bird flying up in the sky with a little bit of sunshine on its wing. It was the last picture he painted before he died. I think these are picture expressions of a stage of anger and the final stage of acceptance.

Comment

A PHYSICIAN: *I wonder if I could urge you to tell a story that you told yesterday afternoon concerning the reaction of the nurse in encouraging patients to achieve a state of acceptance of death.*

DR. ROSS: *Many people wonder whether all patients should die in a state of acceptance. Somebody once asked me that, and I said you try to elicit the patient's needs. One nurse in the audience arose very angrily. "I have been angry and a rebel all my life and I hope I can die that way." My answer to her was, "I hope they let you die that way and not sedated to keep you 'nice, quiet, and peaceful.'" It is very important to remember that the patients who have used denial all their lives may want denial and may die in a stage of denial. We should not project our own values onto the patient. The "stages of dying" affect not only terminally ill patients. You can apply these lessons to everyday living.*

If a man loses a girlfriend, he may deny it at first; then he becomes angry at the other suitor. Then he sends her some flowers to bargain, and if he cannot get what he wants, he becomes depressed. Eventually, he reaches the stage of acceptance, when he finds another girlfriend.

A PHYSICIAN: *Were there any differences between the patients who were told by their physicians about their fatal illnesses as opposed to those who were not? What guidelines would you recommend to physicians in determining whether the patient should be told or not?*

DR. ROSS: *I could tell after a while whose physician the patient was by the degree of comfort experienced by the patient. I did not even have to ask anymore. I do not believe the variable is whether or not they have been told. The variable is how comfortable the physician is in facing the dying patient. We had, at our institution, one surgeon who was particularly effective in this area. I think that he conveyed to them verbally or nonverbally the belief that he would stay with them until the end. The patients were able to pick this up. It is something that is more important than anything else. It is a conviction that the doctor is going to stick it out no matter what. He always did that. The patients knew that, even though there was no more possible surgery or medical treatment, he would still come to see them and care for them. Those patients had it much easier. In fact, we hardly ever got referrals. We sometimes went to see them because we needed some "good patients" who were not troubled all the time. I am in favor of telling patients that they have a serious illness because patients accept that almost without exception, as long as you always allow for some hope.*

A PHYSICIAN: *What advice do you have for the families of patients who are dying?*

DR. ROSS: *That is only difficult if the patient or family lags behind in the stages. We have patients who have already separated themselves from their relatives. In fact, we have a patient now at the hospital who is waiting to die. His family has stopped visiting him. The nurses are terribly upset because the wife called up and said that if her husband died, they should not bother calling during the night. She would call in the morning to check. This family has already separated itself and yet the husband is still alive and very lonely. When I went to see him, he expressed a lot of grief and asked if I would pray that it* would soon be over. There is nothing much that he wants to do. It is more often true that the patient has reached a stage of acceptance and the family has not. That is the time when the family begins to run around and beg you for life-prolonging procedures. We have had one difficult case where a woman was ready to die. She had accepted it and was only concerned that her husband could not accept it. The husband was busy arranging for additional surgery, which was scheduled for the following Monday. The patient could not tolerate the thought of an additional procedure. She became very anxious and uncomfortable prior to surgery. She demanded twice as much medication for pain and finally, in the room outside of the operating room where she was prepared, she had an acute psychotic episode and became paranoid and screamed, "They are going to kill me, they are going to kill me." In her psychotic state she kept saying, "Talk to that man, talk to that man." When I talked with her husband and tried to explain what had happened, he said that he would rather have as a last memory his beautiful, dignified, wonderful wife than know that she was dying a psychotic woman. When he was able to convey to her that he had accepted and acknowledged the fact that she was terminally ill and the surgery was permanently cancelled, she soon became nonpsychotic. She lived for about one week and she even went home one more time to help her husband turn the clock back a little bit.

We have had three instances so far where patients used psychotic defenses against artificial and extraordinary life-prolonging procedures. We have had some very traumatic cases where husband and wife could not reach the same stage at the same time. I think a golden rule for us as physicians is to know enough to stop the extraordinary measures when a patient has reached the stage of acceptance. When the patient has come that far, then I think many of us know that such interference is no longer therapeutic, and may only gratify our own needs.

A PHYSICIAN: *Do you ever tell a patient he is dying?*

DR. ROSS: *You never tell a patient he is dying; never. You don't have to—you just tell him that he has a serious illness. You say, "It looks pretty grim," or "It looks pretty bad." Then you wait for and answer his next questions. He may ask you, "Is it going to be painful?" "Am I going to be alone?" "How long is this going to last?" You say you don't know, because the worst thing that we have experienced is people who tell time, for example, people who figure on six months, which is not correct anyway.*

A PHYSICIAN: *Have you noticed whether or not the*

patient's religious orientation has affected his view toward resignation in the end?

DR. ROSS: *Not resignation but acceptance! I have a peculiar patient population, or at least I tend to think so. I have very few really religious people. The few I have— and I mean those with a deep intrinsic faith—have it much easier, but they are extremely few. I have an even smaller number of real atheists who believe nothing, and they have it rather easy too. About 95% are somewhere in between. They are struggling at the end very desperately, but they would like to have the rock of Gibraltar and they only have a straw; they would like to enlarge that and get more faith, but it is somewhat too late. Many patients become more religious in the end, but it is not really effective.*

Summary

Psychiatrically it is extremely important to appreciate that, in terms of the unconscious, we cannot conceive of our own death and that, in addition, we cannot differentiate between the wish and the deed. Although people today have the same kind of unconscious thoughts and fantasies about death that other persons had years ago, our society has changed and has become increasingly a death-denying society. We live today in the illusion that, since we have mastered so many things, we shall be able to master death too.

Certain generalizations based on interviewing more than 400 dying patients in the past four years can be stated. All patients know when they are terminally ill, whether they have been told or not. Patients usually state that they would like to be told if it is serious, but not without hope.

Most, but not all, patients pass through five stages (denial, anger, bargaining, depression, and acceptance) between their awareness of serious illness and their death, when they are faced with a potentially fatal illness. The knowledgeable physician, particularly one who is himself comfortable in facing the dying patient, can help these patients pass through one or all of these stages by appropriate verbal and nonverbal support—particularly the support engendered by the patient's realization that his physician will stay with him until the end.

Reference

KÜBLER-ROSS, E. *On Death and Dying*. New York: The Macmillan Company, 1969.

39

The Uses of Empathy in the Resolution of Grief

by Norman L. Paul, M.D.†

Rage, terror, profound sadness, helplessness, acute loneliness, and despondency are among those feelings that both children and adults find most difficult to bear; all are associated with the state of grief. Through the expression of grief and empathic responses among family members, each member can be freed from these painful feelings for the pursuit of more constructive and satisfying activities. This paper explains the crucial role of empathy in the resolution of grief.

One difficulty in describing empathy, its sources, and induction lies in the limitations of language. George Engel, in his attempts to develop an adequate classification of the phenomenology of affects, or raw feelings, readily acknowledged the inadequacy of language: "We still recognize not only that in nature affects do not exist in pure, unalloyed form but also that to deal with affects in written, verbal, or conceptual terms is fundamentally inconsistent with their nature and can succeed only at the expense of their oversimplification and impoverishment" [1]. Despite the constrictions with which language hems us in, we must persist in the exploration and assessment of empathy because of its importance in human experience.

Empathy

Empathy is an interpersonal phenomenon that occurs when the empathizer, or subject, recognizes that he shares kindred feelings with another person, the object. When empathy is reciprocated, it may be regarded as love. Olden defines empathy as "the capacity of the subject instinctively and intuitively to feel as the object does. It is a process of the ego, more specifically, an emotional ego expression . . . the subject temporarily gives up his own ego for that of the object" [2].

It is imperative to make a clear distinction between empathy and sympathy. Although these terms are often used interchangeably, they describe different and mutually exclusive kinds of interpersonal experience. The two words share a common measure of meaning; both express a preoccupation with the assumed affinity between a subject's own feelings and

Presented as part of the Edward A. Strecker Award in Philadelphia, October 21, 1966.

† Assistant Clinical Professor of Psychiatry, Tufts Medical School, Boston, Mass.

the feelings of the other person. ("Object" and "other" are both used in this paper to designate the recipient of sympathy or empathy.) In sympathy, however, the subject is principally absorbed in his own feelings as projected into the object and has little concern for the reality and validity of the object's special experience. Sympathy, then, bypasses real understanding of the other person; he becomes the subject's mirror image and is thus denied his own sense of being.

Empathy, on the other hand, presupposes the existence of the other as a separate individual, entitled to his own feelings, ideas, and emotional history. The empathizer makes no judgments about what the other should feel but solicits the expression of whatever feelings may exist and, for brief periods, feels them as his own. The empathizer oscillates between such subjective involvement and a detached recognition of the shared feelings. The periods of his objective detachment do not seem to the other to be spells of indifference, as they would in sympathy; instead, they are evidence that the subject respects himself and the object as separate people. The empathizer, secure in his sense of self and his own emotional boundaries, attempts to nourish a similar security in the other. The empathic relationship is generous; the empathizer does not use the object as a means for gratifying his own sense of importance but is himself principally concerned with encouraging the other to sustain and express his feelings and fantasies as being appropriate to himself. The empathizer thus makes clear the other's individuality and his right to this individuality without apology, thereby avoiding the induction of guilt in the object, a common ingredient of sympathetic interactions. Such guilt induction is associated with the development of a hostile-dependent relationship that binds the object to the sympathizer and vice versa.

There are two kinds of empathy, intellectual and affective, both of which may exist simultaneously in the same person. Intellectual empathy describes a reciprocal process where each of two (or more) persons identifies with the other in terms of the other's verbalized thoughts, incorporating them as his own for the moment. This process seeks to understand the other's thoughts, as spoken, and the sources of those thoughts, in short, to meet the intellectual needs of the other. Two types of intellectual empathy, cognitive and associative, have been delineated. Cognitive empathy describes a structured situation in which a teacher, parent, clergyman, or other authority attempts to impart a clear body of knowledge to the other. The imparter understands both the motivations and resistances to learning that exist in the other and selects those techniques that minimize resistance. Associative empathy, by contrast, has no structured or specified goal beyond the sharing of verbalized thoughts in an effort to broaden an area of knowledge. There is a peer relationship between participants, each of whom can oscillate between the roles of empathizer and object. "Brainstorming" is one use of associative empathy. Another is that psychological treatment of neurotic patients where patient and therapist alternately respond to each other in terms of the verbalized thoughts of the moment.

This paper is concerned with affective empathy, the principal focus of my interest and work. Affective empathy seeks to meet emotional rather than intellectual needs and involves all feelings, not only those that are verbalized. Affective empathy presupposes the existence of honest, direct communication without value judgments and includes the empathizer's accepting, for a brief period, the other's total emotional individuality. In other words, the empathizer accepts the existence within himself of not only the simple emotions of the other but the other's whole state of being —the history of the other's desires, feelings, and thoughts as well as other forces and experiences that are expressed in his behavior and have produced his current adaptation to his own situation and to those around him. The empathizer is not only aware of the other's various experiences but finds himself sharing the reliving of those experiences. The object senses the empathizer's response and realizes that, for a brief point in time, they two have fused. If he then takes the initiative by communicating more of his experience, he provides a basic stimulus for what can become an affective empathic process.

Often it is difficult for an outside observer to identify the existence of empathy. It is difficult even for the participants to recognize when empathy is being induced, when it exists, when it has existed. The difficulty of recognizing the state within a therapeutic situation is further compounded by the need for the therapist's empathy to be effectively communicated and then substantiated by a response in the patient. The situation is analogous to that between a mother and infant. The mother's love, or affective empathy, may be real, but it must be communicated in some way, usually through physical contact and tone of voice, to reach the infant before its effect can be observed. The larger process of which observed communication may be merely a surface signal is expressed by Pinter when he says: "So often, below the words spoken, is a thing known and unspoken" [3]. Difficult as it is to define and describe, affective empathy, because of its importance for the growth and development of the human being, warrants more attention and research. Eventually, experiments using such psychophysiological techniques as polygraph measurements may succeed in identifying those physiological reactions associated with the beginning of empathy between two persons—that point at which their feelings become synchronized—and those reactions that mark the duration of empathy.

The material of this paper may be used to illustrate the three kinds of empathy just described: intellectual (including cognitive and associative) and affective empathy. The reader should, if the paper fulfils my intentions, experience cognitive empathy in following its development. I have organized the material so as to facilitate the transfer of information, shifting back and forth between the roles of writer and reader in order to make the presentation effective. Only through feedback from the reader can I learn whether this effort has been successful. If the reader were to follow not this paper but the tapescript of excerpted materials from a series of family therapy sessions I have conducted, he would be experiencing associative empathy induced by the dialogues as written down. To take the material back one step farther toward its origins, if the reader were to become, instead, a listener and follow the actual recordings of those sessions, he would have the opportunity to share in reliving of experiences by family members, to experience affective empathy. Each reader, while listening to those emotionally charged recordings, would observe points at which he could easily empathize and other points where he would have an aversion to doing so. There seems to be a direct relationship between a listener's ability to tune in empathically on such experiences and his own acceptance of comparable feelings in himself.

Affective empathy, referred to hereafter as empathy, is important to every person because it allows him to feel that he is not alone in his passage through life. Children often admit the existence of empathy more freely than adults; sometimes they speak of their feeling that one or the other parent is "with them inside." A large part of our cultural heritage, however, as presented both at home and at school, acts to inhibit rather than to nurture the empathic potential. Adults frequently resist empathy. Pinter expresses his insight into this resistance in saying: "To enter into someone else's life is too frightening. To disclose to others the poverty within us is too fearsome a possibility" [4]. He emphasizes a double aversion—to empathizing with someone else and to becoming the object of empathy. Apparently, the aversion is especially strong against empathizing with such uncomfortable feelings as guilt, terror, and helplessness. Before a person can empathize with an object who has these feelings, he must have been able to accept their existence within himself. But one may be unable to do this because of a natural human tendency to avoid pain and distress. Consider, for example, the reactions among the audience to certain empathic experiences on a theater stage or screen; expressions like "schmaltzy," "corny," or "childish" suggest that the dramatic portrayal of feeling has been recognized by the viewer as one of his own feelings, but that he wishes to cancel out this recognition with verbal reactions that minimize and negate his feeling.

The dearth of studies of empathy, or even of allusions to it, in scientific literature, can, perhaps, be explained both by the difficulties of coping with an essentially non-intellectual experience and by the general aversion to empathy which the scientist shares with the rest of society. Sullivan reflects on this aversion:

> I have had a good deal of trouble at times with people of a certain type of educational history; since they cannot refer empathy to vision, hearing, or some other special sense receptor, and since they do not know whether it is transmitted by the ether waves or air waves or what not, they find it hard to accept the idea of empathy. . . . So although empathy may sound mysterious, remember that there is much that sounds mysterious in the universe, only you have got used to it; and perhaps you will get used to empathy [5].

The artist, poet, or playwright is perhaps better suited than the scientist to discourse upon experiences of empathy and their relationship to frustration, loss, love, and tenderness. One can feel some of the discomforts associated with empathy in viewing the three-dimensional art forms of Edward Kienholz. Kienholz wants to jolt the viewer out of his apathy by enveloping him in some of life's most unpleasant realities. In "The Wait," for example, a very old woman, made of cow bones and wearing a necklace of Mason jars containing figurines that represent her memories of different periods in her life, sits wasting away and waiting to die among her moldering living-room furniture. On the wall and on an adjacent table are photographs of people who once filled her life. Her cow's-skull head is fronted with an oval picture of her face as she must have appeared fifty years earlier, the image of herself that she still maintains.

One is immediately aware of the pull to empathize with this sad creature whose deluded self-image is of one still young and vibrant. Yet it is repulsive to empathize with her because the scene is so thoroughly unpleasant. Kienholz seems to be demonstrating that each of us is living with a deliberately ignored anticipation of his own death and the deaths of those he loves. "The Wait" is repulsive because it reminds us of this mortality and thereby forces us to deny the truth of death even more vigorously. It may be that Kienholz is asking the viewer to face resolutely the ugly realities of existence and to use those energies customarily spent in avoidance in the pursuit of a fuller life.

Grief

Why do we feel such strong aversion to this confrontation with death? Although we are not always aware of it, each of us presumably has the deep conviction of his own God-like uniqueness. Each believes that he is immortal, omnipotent and, in fact, that he is the only real acting force in the world. These fantasies thrive because the content of our own consciousness is the only thing with which we have direct experience; they are reinforced by the continuity of our daily experiences, in which people and situations appear predictably and recurrently. Such narcissistic fantasies are threatened not only by death but by all kinds of changes that affect us.

Searles [6] believes that one of the critical sources of anxiety against which the schizophrenic patient unconsciously defends himself is the idea of mortality. This anxiety is so intense that the schizophrenic frequently imagines himself as not alive and thus beyond the reach of death. Furthermore, his behavior often suggests that he cannot discriminate between a minor change or loss and the major loss incurred in the death of a near person.

The total configuration of responses to a major loss, or death, is called "mourning." Mourning includes physical behavior, both formal and spontaneous, and psychological processes, both observable and covert, which are set in motion by loss. "Grief" is a more restricted term applied to the subjective state of mourning and excluding all the ritualistic and behavioral elements of mourning. Grief usually consists of such feelings as helplessness, anger, despair, and bewilderment, which overlap and vary in intensity from person to person as well as within any one person during the mourning process. I am primarily concerned with grief rather than with all of mourning because grief is entirely subjective and personal and so directly accessible to empathic intervention in grief work.

In their broadest uses, "grief" and "mourning" can be applied to the loss of anything valuable—the fantasy of being loved, a job, a part of the body, status, even symptoms. Here, however, the terms are restricted to situations involving the loss of a loved person through death. Grief and mourning may precede the actual loss in cases where the latent fear of death is activated by circumstances which might involve fatality. The news that a loved person has been in an automobile accident or is suffering from a serious illness may bring about the onset of grief and mourning. The wish for someone's death may be so strong as to make the death seem real for a moment and touch off a momentary reaction of grief to replace the anger that caused the wish. Anxiety about separation or the dread of being abandoned are feelings that may induce anticipatory grief and mourning.

The psychological treatment of grief has, up to now, generally been undertaken in the individual therapy setting. Such treatment has included the patient's cathartic reliving of his relationship with the lost object and his more cerebral and reflective view of this relationship. The form of treatment derives from the clinical insights of Freud [7], Abraham [8], Klein [9], and Deutsch [10], among others. Each of these has emphasized the importance of the patient's anger toward the lost object. The bereaved is angry because he feels helpless in finding that his fantasy of object constancy has been shattered; the environment that he supposed was inviolable has been suddenly and terribly changed by the disappearance of a loved person. His helplessness and anger become intensified whenever he becomes aware of the loss; one of the ways in which he tries to diminish these feelings is to imbue others with characteristics of the deceased.

In their studies of large numbers of persons suffering from grief, Parkes [11] and Lindemann [12] collected data that reveal the close relationship between unresolved grief and various degrees of disability. Parkes concluded: "Grief may prove to be as important to psychopathology as inflammation is to pathology" [13]. The clinical mandate for treatment of the condition was provided by Deutsch: "The process of mourning as reaction to the real loss of a loved person must be carried to completion" [14].

Anthropologists have been active in studying the role of ceremony and ritual in promoting the resolution of grief in other cultures. Psychiatric literature, however, generally neglects this area; those discussions of grief that it does include concern individuals whose grief has taken such a form that treatment seems advisable. In most other societies, children and adults are prepared for death through elaborate rounds of ceremony and ritual accompanied by mythical explanations of the meaning of life and death. Whereas our approach to grief is individualistic, these cultures have traditional forms of mourning that require the active participation of all bereaved family members together with the whole community. Such ceremonies have been lost to us through secularization, urbanization, and a smug reliance on rationality, and we have discovered no viable substitute. Our abbreviated and restrained mourning observances are often carefully hidden from children, who grow up without experiencing empathic understanding or catharsis. All of this tends to foster a dehumanization of the individual, who finds himself increasingly alienated not only from others in his life but from himself. Mourning is a way of emphasizing the difference between life and death, the separation of the dead from the living. When this difference is minimized and glossed over, it is not surprising that the young seem void of feeling for others or flirt casually with the idea of suicide. We have obviously neglected the broad implications of Freud's thesis, "If you want to endure life, prepare yourself for death" [15].

Implications for Treatment

What can therapy do to meet this painful human need? Foreshadowing later uses of empathy for resolving grief in the context of the family, Melanie Klein wrote, "If the mourner has people whom he loves and who share his grief, and if he can accept their sympathy, the restoration of the harmony in his inner world is promoted, and his fears and stress are more quickly reduced" [16]. The provision of these conditions, aimed at empathy rather than sympathy, is one major purpose of family therapy.

My work with a family is conducted on an out-patient basis. I use a variety of settings—interviews with individual family members; conjoint interviews with husband and wife; meetings which involve the couple, their children, and other members of the household; and larger gatherings where several nuclear families come together. The choice and sequence of settings is dictated by attempts to provide opportunities for the expression of feelings which have been suppressed in the family's own pattern of interpersonal relations.

My underlying hypothesis is that there is a direct relationship between the maladaptive response to the death of a loved person and the fixity of symbiotic relationships within the family. A husband (or wife) may have suffered the loss of a parent or sibling many years ago, before his current family came into existence. The response to that loss may have been incomplete or unsatisfying. If there was little empathy within the bereaved family, his grief may never have been resolved. In such a situation, his feelings toward the deceased may remain unchanged through the years, lingering with him to influence his adaptation to his new family. A family's inability to cope with an original loss may produce a family style that is variably unresponsive to a wide range of changes, including new losses and disappointments. Such unresponsiveness is expressed in attempts to deny the passage of time; these often bring about the family's unwittingly keeping one of its members in an inappropriately dependent position. That member, struggling in vain to free himself from the role imposed upon him, acts in ways which annoy or alarm the others. Sometimes they decide that he must be mentally ill. Such family systems, it seems, often need a scapegoat in their midst to preserve the family's equilibrium.

My studies, some in conjunction with George Grosser [17–20], have disclosed that families containing either neurotic or psychotic patients manifest a set of family relationships variably resistant to change; this resistance is especially obvious in attitudes toward the patient. These attitudes and the resulting behavior, including the patient's reactions to his family, have been regarded as expressions of a "pathologically stable equilibrium," a relatively fixed state to which the family tends to return when it is disturbed; this state often relies upon the scapegoat or patient as a point of familiar stability. The fixation is symbiotic insofar as the family needs to keep the patient and, perhaps, its other members in a kind of dependency that prevents their emancipation, which is viewed as a threat to the family unit. The patient is a symbol of the family's defense against their recognition of grief. The difference between families with neurotic patients and those with psychotic patients is that the state is maintained with greater rigidity in the latter.

Family systems, like all other social systems, tend to maintain equilibrium. In the normal family, however, this equilibrium gradually evolves and alters in response to aging and the changes in roles that life demands of its members. It appears that the way to dislodge the pathologically fixed family is to expose and set in motion toward their appropriate objects those feelings that have been distorted for the maintenance of equilibrium. Once such feelings are released, they can be neutralized and resolved in the therapeutic setting through empathic intervention. Those affects or feelings most tenaciously withheld from sharing, even from exposure, are the ones associated with grief.

Bowlby's analysis of the mourning process helps to explain the reactions of the bereaved. He has indicated that mourning, in both its observable and hidden reactions, occurs in three overlapping phases: (1) the urge to recover the lost object, (2) disorganization, and (3) reorganization, the last two being adaptive processes. The first phase is triggered by the shock of numbness when one learns of the death, and it expresses the survivor's attempt to deny that the loss has really occurred. The second phase is the disorganization of the personality associated with the reluctant acceptance of the death as fact. The third phase, the reorganization of the personality, includes a revised perspective of the loss associated with both a detachment from the loss and the integration of the mourning experience. Bowlby has suggested that an individual can become fixated anywhere in this process [21, 22]. I think it is also possible for a survivor to be fixated in a pseudo-reorganization phase that masks the fact that the first two stages have, to a degree, been avoided. Controlled hypomanic states suggest this pseudo-reorganization. Furthermore, it seems that the smaller the amount of empathy the bereaved receives from those about him for coping with his grief the greater the possibility that he will become fixated in the mourning process.

Since such fixation within the mourning process seems to be at the root of both individual psychopathology and a family's pathologically stable equilibrium, a corrective grief experience, even though belated, seems to be the means for overcoming the fixation. A specific therapeutic technique has been developed that deliberately introduces a belated grief experience and emphasizes the elements of the mourning process. This technique focuses on the reactions induced by direct inquiry about responses to actual past losses sustained by specific family members. The therapist, in assuming an empathic stance toward both the resistance to review and, ultimately, the poignant review of the loss, presents himself as an empathic model. In accepting the reality of the belated mourner's resistance and grief, the therapist encourages him and the other family members to experience empathy. The therapist's role also includes empathizing with the others in their resistance to sharing the grief experience.

The therapist does this by imagining himself to be alternately the belated mourner and the other family members. He can thus feel within himself everyone's disinclination to review a painful experience. As the therapist acknowledges the depth of this resistance, the mourner begins to expose his distress.

At this point, other family members often deny the importance of the loss and attempt to prevent further exposure of grief with such sympathetic responses as, "You can pull yourself together," "I don't know why you're worried about it now," or "Don't listen to Dr. X. He doesn't know what he's talking about." It is obvious that family members, including the mourner himself, unwittingly conspire to deprive the mourner of his right to grieve. The therapist must empathize with these expressions and explain them as difficulties family members have in sharing the pain of grief. At this stage, the therapist should emphasize the long-range influence of the loss by pointing to the mourner's present behavior. The bereaved is, by this time, downcast, possibly beginning to weep.

The therapist also feels saddened as he shares the distress of the bereaved; empathy is furthered when the therapist feels that he is living through the mourner's experience at the time of the loss. He encourages and supports the mourner in his expression of intense emotions, while remaining alert to the emergence of sympathetic resistance to the progress of the cathartic review. Frequently, this process or parts of it need repeating in later interviews because of recurring resistance within the family unit. Families with a schizophrenic member show the strongest aversion to admitting the existence of grief and require the most skilful application of empathy in repeated attempts to induce a belated experience of grief.

The therapist, after a detailed review of the loss experience as it was lived, encourages expression of the belated mourner's inner feelings. Other family members are then invited to reveal both empathic responses and other feelings generated by observing the reactions of grief. Reciprocating expressions of empathy lead to a lessening of family tensions, a sense of relief, and expressions of goodwill and love toward one another. The procedure permits children, often for the first time, to observe their parents expressing intense feelings and provides a forceful lesson in empathy. Children and parents can acquire a sense of emotional continuity between generations.

It is essential that the therapist assure every family member that these exposed feelings are natural. Because of social taboos, there is one emotion that family members may have particular trouble in regarding as normal— hostility toward the deceased. The bereaved often feels angry toward a loved person who has died, who has taken away his presence, shattered the environment, and abandoned the survivor to shift for himself. But in our culture it seems ungenerous to speak or think ill of the dead, so such hostility is often deflected from the deceased toward some other, living member(s) of the family. Once the hostility and its real object are identified, the family can understand the situation more clearly. At this stage, the person who bears the brunt of the displaced hostility may exhibit separation anxiety or threaten to remove himself from the family or both. Such responses tend to diminish and disappear as the experience of grief is worked through.

The ability of the therapist to empathize with grief and other painful states seems related to his capacity for reflective review of feelings generated by comparable situations in his own life. Loewald described tendencies on the part of analysts to resist this affective regression required for empathy because of an underlying fear "lest we may not find the way back to higher organization" [23]. To empathize with the other's grief, however, the therapist must be able to empathize with himself as he once was.

The foregoing observations support Bowlby's thesis that "three types of response—separation anxiety, grief and mourning, and defense—are phases of a single process and that when treated as such each illumines the other two" [24]. The family coming to treatment presents a problem which, I submit, masks either separation anxiety or a defensive reaction to this or both. The family sees the problem as residing either in one of its members or in a disturbed relationship. The presenting complaint, after being initially acknowledged, is set aside while historical background is explored. Such exploration, which includes scanning the lives of senior family members, usually converges on unresolved grief. It is curious to observe that, while this grief is being resolved through empathy, the symptoms that brought the family to treatment seem to fade away.

At the same time, the family equilibrium shifts from its dependency on the original scapegoat, that is, the labeled patient or disturbed relationship, to a fluid situation; as the therapist underscores the responsibility of each family member in perpetuating the original equilibrium, that member takes a turn as scapegoat. In this stage, individual disorganization and heightened intra-family frictions appear. This disorganization is equivalent to Bowlby's second phase of the mourning process. Family members need empathic help in coping with the beginnings of dissolution of their symbiotic patterns. The original scapegoat finds himself newly free, but he and other family members are ambivalent about the changing intra-family relationships that this freedom activates.

The therapist must be alert to a variety of psychological and psychosomatic disturbances that usually emerge at this stage—anxiety states, temporary paranoid reactions, depression, mood swings, and gastrointestinal disorders that simulate organic disease. To escape the intensity of feelings related to the grief work, family members may often start to search frantically for the counsel of other physicians, lawyers, and clergymen; they may become immersed in a variety of "busy-work" activities. These actions are attempts to block the recognition and expression of regrets that the family has wasted so many years in senseless discord. Empathy toward the resistance to sharing such regret leads to genuine declarations of remorse. This phase is most difficult to achieve in both parents and grandparents of schizophrenics. Such senior family members often threaten to withdraw from treatment and sometimes actually terminate their visits. Once regret is fully expressed and reviewed, the family settles into a more harmonious equilibrium where each member is able to assume his proper responsibility for the presenting complaint and the related family dissonance.

The family unit is unwittingly prepared for the experience of losing the therapist through the corrective grief experience. It seems that the belated completion of mourning for the original loss enables them to cope adequately with new losses. Another technique that encourages successful termination (the main goal of treatment whether for individuals, couples, or families) is a self-confrontation procedure where, at home, they listen to and discuss audio-tapes of their own therapy sessions. Each member is confronted with real evidence of how he functions with the others in mutual and spiraling provocations. By assessing a disturbance and his own part in it, he can begin to avoid being provoked on future occasions. The therapist must empathize with the resistance family members feel toward hearing how they actually sound. Often an individual has the greatest difficulty in empathizing with the self revealed on tape, a feeling comparable to the disgust or embarrassment some people feel when reading letters they wrote long ago. Once resistance is overcome, however, and family members achieve increasing self-control, they are freed to explore the relevance of the past to the present under circumstances where the effect can be most enduring, that is, at home in the absence of the therapist.

My work with a family unit includes the induction of the belated grief experience as part of the general focus on the critical life experiences of each family member. My approach is distilled from psychoanalytic theory as adapted for both individual and group psychotherapy, and includes dream interpretation and free association. It relies on more direct inquiry and topical focus than is usual in individual psychotherapy. After family diagnostic studies, groups are assembled for therapy, and this group work is integrated with individual psychotherapy for selected family members; I usually conduct the individual as well as the group sessions. Each family requires its own pattern of meetings. The therapist acts as a group leader whose catalytic role is gradually incorporated into intra-family patterns of action. He remains, however, sufficiently an outsider to represent both social reality and an object on whom unresolved conflicts can be projected and displaced. In contrast to individual psychotherapy, he is not the sole focus of transference, since other family members are also objects of fluctuating transference phenomena. Because the transference is scattered rather than concentrated, the therapist is in a favorable position to clarify not only the ambivalence expressed toward him but also similar expressions between family members.

My work is directed toward certain goals for each family member: an increased empathic understanding of himself and others; a greater tendency to validate against reality his impressions about the attitudes of those around him; and an ability to tolerate and accept differences, frustrations, and failure. Above all, this form of treatment aims at developing firmer individual identities through the establishment of each member's sense of self, while simultaneously reinforcing the viability of the family.

Broader Implications

There is probably a need to consider empathy as important in general as well as in therapeutic situations. Each of us appears to have a basic hunger for empathy, a wish for the intimacy that can erase, if only for a moment, the individual's sense of emptiness and aloneness. Paradoxically, we want to satisfy this hunger, but, at the same time, we erect façades and barriers to prevent our being touched by real people. This conflict can be imperfectly resolved for brief periods through the vicarious satisfactions provided by novels and the theater. In *A Long Day's Journey into Night*, for example, we can empathize with the characters without risk because we know that our engagement will be confined within the limits of the play. We know too that our empathy as spectators will involve little pain, for we are not asked to expose our own distress. And we know that the actors will not be hurt by their revelations of emotion because they are merely assuming their roles. Empathy is so vital a nutrient that human beings deliberately seek it in fiction. Would it not be desirable that they be encouraged to satisfy their hunger for empathy in real life?

In our society, the nuclear family is that social unit most responsible for the development and maintenance of personality. Each member's level of self-esteem depends upon the emotional climate of the whole family. If parents can share with each other and their children their innermost joys and sorrows, each member can observe and accept the existence of helplessness, sadness, and aloneness underneath the façades we all erect to conceal them. Parents are the most enduring models for their children's behavior and attitudes; so it is appropriate that from them each child learn the value and reality of empathic understanding. Sympathy, by precluding this sharing, promotes only frustration and isolation among those who should be closest and most real to each other. Whereas sympathy triggers mutual regression, empathy fosters mutual growth.

These considerations have generated a recent series of radio broadcasts called *A Chance to Grow*. The eleven programs in the series demonstrate the value of empathic review among "normal" people living through significant changes in the life cycle, such as graduation from school, marriage, and retirement. The listener can hear family members as they talk among themselves and with me and can share their feelings about events and their interactions with each other. The series is designed to encourage listeners to consider the important part empathy might play in their own lives.

Of all the changes in the life cycle, one of the most difficult seems to be the death of a loved person. Throughout this paper, I have tried to show the persistent and damaging consequences of unresolved grief. Such unresolved grief is probably widespread among us. Geoffrey Gorer, following his survey of reactions to bereavement in his own country, concluded: "I think that the material presented has adequately demonstrated that the majority of British people are today without adequate guidance as to how to treat death and bereavement and without social help in living through and coming to terms with the grief and mourning which are the inevitable responses in human beings to the death of someone whom they have loved" [25].

What social patterns can we devise to meet this widespread need? I am unable to go far in answering this question, but I believe that it may finally be found that, just as grief is at the root of psychopathological blight, so empathy may be the principal element of the healing process. Modern man needs a situation that provides the climate for empathy to resolve grief, a situation analogous to the primitive mourning rituals of his ancestors.

If a man does away with his traditional way of living and throws away his good customs, he had better first make certain that he has something of value to replace them.—BASUTO PROVERB.

REFERENCES

1. G. L. ENGEL. *In:* P. H. KNAPP (ed.). Expressions of the emotions in man, p. 267. New York: International Universities Press, 1963.
2. C. OLDEN. Psychoanal. Study Child, 8:111, 1953.
3. H. PINTER. Evergreen Rev., p. 81, Winter 1964.
4. ———. *Ibid.*, p. 82.
5. H. S. SULLIVAN. The interpersonal theory of psychiatry, pp. 41–42. New York: W. W. Norton, 1953.
6. H. F. SEARLES. Psychiat. Quart., 35:631, 1961.
7. S. FREUD. *In:* J. STRACHEY (ed.). The standard edition of the complete works of Sigmund Freud, vol. 14, p. 137. London: Hogarth Press, 1957.
8. K. ABRAHAM. Selected papers in psychoanalysis, p. 137. London: Hogarth Press, 1949.
9. M. KLEIN. Int. J. Psychoanal., 21:125, 1940.
10. H. DEUTSCH. Psychoanal. Quart., 6:12, 1937.
11. M. C. PARKES. Brit. J. Med. Psychol., 38:1, 1965.
12. E. LINDEMANN. Amer. J. Psychiat., 101:141, 1944.
13. M. C. PARKES. Brit. J. Med. Psychol., 38:25–26, 1965.
14. H. DEUTSCH. Psychoanal. Quart., 6:22, 1937.
15. S. FREUD. *In:* J. STRACHEY (ed.). The standard edition of the complete works of Sigmund Freud, vol. 14, p. 300. London: Hogarth Press, 1957.
16. M. KLEIN. Int. J. Psychoanal., 21:145, 1940.
17. N. L. PAUL and G. H. GROSSER. Family Processes, 3:377, 1964.
18. ———. Amer. J. Orthopsychiat., 24:875, 1964.
19. ———. Community Ment. Health J., 1:339, 1965.
20. N. L. PAUL. Psychiatric Research Report No. 20, p. 175. American Psychiatric Association, 1966.
21. J. BOWLBY. Int. J. Psychoanal., 42:317, 1961.
22. ———. *Ibid.*, 41:89, 1960.
23. H. W. LOEWALD. Int. J. Psychoanal., 41:26, 1960.
24. J. BOWLBY. Int. J. Psychoanal., 41:91, 1960.
25. G. GORER. Death, grief, and mourning, p. 126. Garden City, N.Y.: Doubleday, 1965.

We need your advice

Because this book will be revised every two years, we would like to know what you think of it. Please fill in the brief questionnaire on the reverse of this card and mail it to us.

Business Reply Mail

No postage stamp necessary if mailed in the United States

First Class
Permit No. 247
New York, N.Y.

Postage will be paid by

George A. Middendorf
Executive Editor
Harper & Row Publishers Inc.
College Dept.
10 East 53rd St.
New York, NY 10022

Adult Psychology

ADULT PSYCHOLOGY: CONTEMPORARY PERSPECTIVES

I am a ____ student ____ instructor

Term used _____ 19____

Name_____School_____

Address_____

_____

City_____ State_____ Zip_____

How do you rate this book?

1. Please list (by number) the articles you liked best.

_____   _____   _____   _____   _____

Why? _____

_____

2. Please list (by number) the articles you liked least.

_____   _____   _____   _____   _____

Why? _____

_____

3. Please evaluate the following:

	Excell.	Good	Fair	Poor	Comments
Organization of the book	____	____	____	____	_____
Section introductions	____	____	____	____	_____
Overall Evaluation	____	____	____	____	_____

4. Do you have any suggestions for improving the next edition?

_____

_____

_____

5. Can you suggest any new articles to include in the next edition?

_____

_____

_____

_____

_____

_____

_____

_____

Thank you very much

Business Reply Mail

No postage stamp necessary if mailed in the United States

First Class
Permit No. 247
New York, N.Y.

Postage will be paid by

Harper & Row Publishers Inc.

Attention: George A. Middendorf

10 East 53rd St.

New York, NY 10022

ATTENTION

Now you may order individual copies of the books in the CONTEMPORARY PERSPECTIVES READER SERIES directly from the publisher.

The following titles are now available:

Readings in ABNORMAL PSYCHOLOGY, Edited by Lawrence R. Allman and Dennis T. Jaffe (ISBN 0-06-043259-4) ($5.95)

Readings in ADOLESCENT PSYCHOLOGY, Edited by Thomas J. Cottle (ISBN 0-06-047057-7) ($7.25)

Readings in ADULT PSYCHOLOGY, Edited by Lawrence R. Allman and Dennis T. Jaffe (ISBN 0-06-047054-2) ($7.95)

Readings in AGING AND DEATH, Edited by Steven H. Zarit (ISBN 0-06-047056-9) ($5.95)

Readings in ECOLOGY, ENERGY AND HUMAN SOCIETY, Edited by William R. Burch, Jr. (ISBN 0-06-047058-5) ($5.95)

Readings in EDUCATIONAL PSYCHOLOGY, Edited by Robert A. Dentler and Bernard J. Shapiro (ISBN 0-06-047083-6) ($5.95)

Readings in HUMAN DEVELOPMENT, Edited by David Elkind and Donna C. Hetzel (ISBN 0-06-047055-0) ($6.95)

Readings in HUMAN SEXUALITY, Edited by Chad Gordon and Gayle Johnson (ISBN 0-06-047084-4) ($5.95)

Readings in SOCIAL PROBLEMS, Edited by Peter M. Wickman (ISBN 0-06-047053-4) ($5.95)

Readings in SOCIAL PSYCHOLOGY, Edited by Dennis Krebs (ISBN 0-06-043772-3) ($5.95)

Readings in SOCIOLOGY, Edited by Ian Robertson (ISBN 0-06-045502-0) ($5.95)

Paperback

Order your copies of any of the above titles by filling in the coupon below.

Please send me:

_____copies of_____ (ISBN)

_____copies of_____ (ISBN)

_____copies of_____ (ISBN)

_____copies of_____ (ISBN)

My check or money order in the amount of $_____ is enclosed. (Harper & Row will pay the postage and handling.)

_____
Name

_____
Address

_____
City

_____
State   Zip

DATE DUE

MAR 1995			
GAYLORD			PRINTED IN U.S.A.